Cortina d'Ampezzo

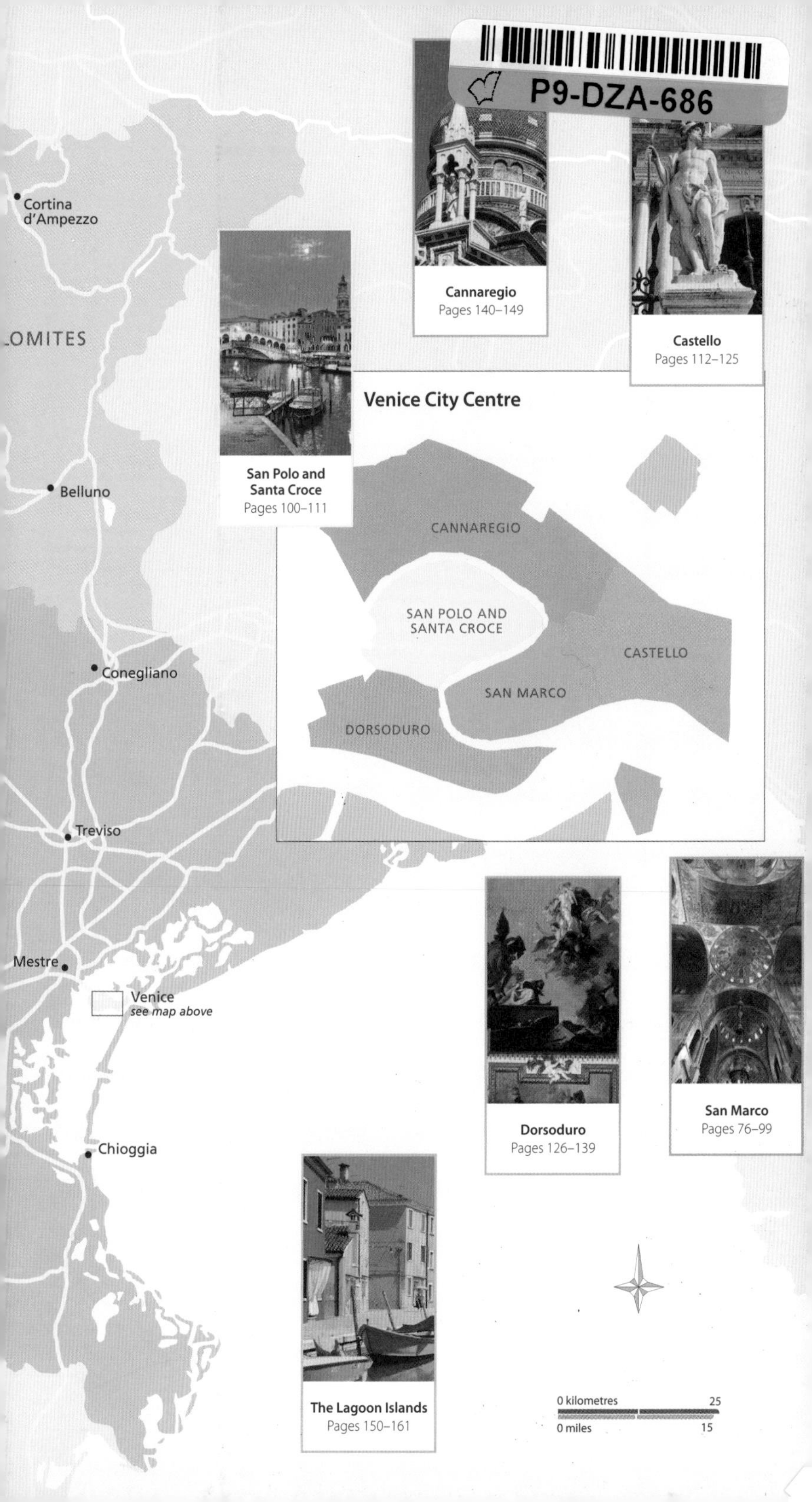

DOLOMITES

Belluno

Conegliano

Treviso

Mestre

Venice
see map above

Chioggia

Cannaregio

Castello

San Polo and Santa Croce

Venice City Centre

CANNAREGIO

SAN POLO AND SANTA CROCE

CASTELLO

SAN MARCO

DORSODURO

Dorsoduro

San Marco

The Lagoon Islands

0 kilometres 25

0 miles 15

EYEWITNESS TRAVEL

VENICE
& THE VENETO

EYEWITNESS TRAVEL

VENICE & THE VENETO

Main Contributors: **Susie Boulton, Christopher Catling**

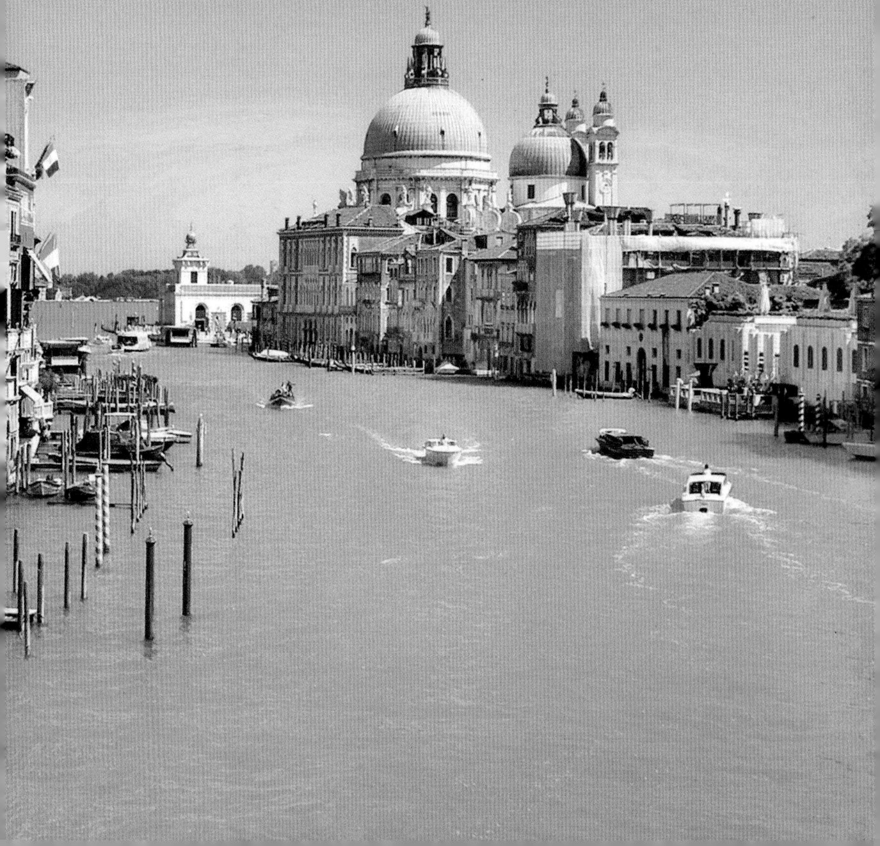

LONDON, NEW YORK,
MELBOURNE, MUNICH AND DELHI
www.dk.com

Produced by Pardoe Blacker Publishing Limited, Lingfield, Surrey

Project Editor Caroline Ball

Art Editor Simon Blacker

Editors Jo Bourne, Molly Perham, Linda Williams

Designers Kelvin Barratt, Dawn Brend, Jon Eland, Nick Raven, Steve Rowling

Map Co-Ordinators Simon Farbrother, David Pugh

Picture Research Jill De Cet

Contributor (Travellers' Needs) Sally Roy

Maps Phil Rose, Jennifer Skelley, Jane Hanson (Lovell Johns Ltd, Oxford UK)
Street Finder maps based upon digital data, adapted with permission from L.A.C. (Italy)

Photographers
John Heseltine (Venice), Roger Moss (Veneto)

Illustrators
Arcana Studios, Donati Giudici Associati Srl, Robbie Polley, Simon Roulstone

Printed and bound in China

First Amerian Edition, 1995

15 16 17 18 10 9 8 7 6 5 4 3 2 1

Published in the United States by
DK Publishing, 345 Hudson Street,
New York, New York 10014

Reprinted with revisions 1995, 1997 (twice), 1998, 1999, 2000, 2001, 2002, 2003, 2004, 2006, 2008, 2010, 2012, 2014, 2016

A catalog record for this book is available from the Library of Congress.

ISSN 1542-1554

ISBN 978 1 46543 836 2

Floors are referred to throughout in accordance with British usage, i.e. the "first floor" is the floor above ground level.

MIX
Paper from responsible sources
FSC™ C018179
www.fsc.org

The information in this DK Eyewitness Travel Guide is checked regularly.

Every effort has been made to ensure that this book is as up-to-date as possible at the time of going to press. Some details, however, such as telephone numbers, opening hours, prices, gallery hanging arrangements and travel information, are liable to change. The publishers cannot accept responsibility for any consequences arising from the use of this book, nor for any material on third party websites, and cannot guarantee that any website address in this book will be a suitable source of travel information. We value the views and suggestions of our readers very highly. Please write to: Publisher, DK Eyewitness Travel Guides, Dorling Kindersley, 80 Strand, London, WC2R 0RL, UK, or email: travelguides@dk.com.

Front cover main image: A *vaporetto* on the Venice Grand Canal

◀ View of the Grand Canal with the Basilica Santa Maria della Salute in the background

Contents

The Venetian explorer Marco Polo

Introducing Venice and the Veneto

Palazzo Pisani Moretta on the Grand Canal

Venice Area by Area

The Rialto Bridge, on the Grand Canal

Veronese's *Passion and Virtue* in the Villa Barbaro at Masèr

The Veneto Area by Area

The medieval Palio dei Dieci Comuni at Montagnana

Travellers' Needs

Survival Guide

Asparagus stalks

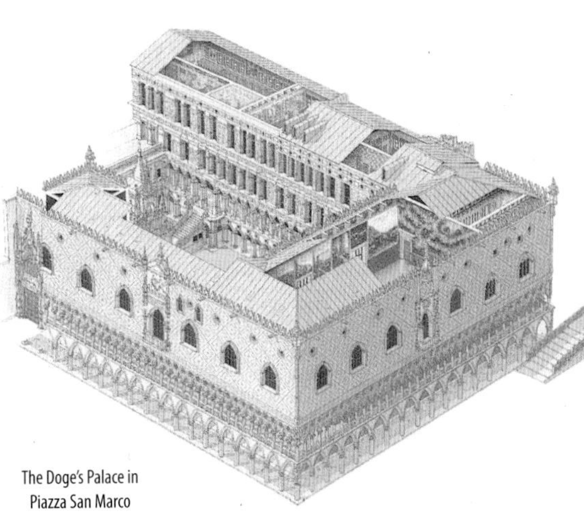
The Doge's Palace in Piazza San Marco

HOW TO USE THIS GUIDE

This guide helps you get the most from your stay in Venice and the Veneto. It provides both expert recommendations and detailed practical information. *Introducing Venice and the Veneto* maps the region and sets it in its historical and cultural context. *Venice Area by Area* and *The Veneto Area by Area* describe the important sights, with maps, pictures and detailed illustrations. Suggestions for food, drink, accommodation, shopping and entertainment are in *Travellers' Needs*, and the *Survival Guide* has tips on everything from the Italian telephone system to travelling around Venice by *vaporetto*.

Venice Area by Area

The city has been divided into five sightseeing areas. The lagoon islands make up a sixth area. Each area has its own chapter, which opens with a list of the sights described. All the sights are numbered and plotted on an *Area Map*. The detailed information for each sight is presented in numerical order, making it easy to locate within the chapter.

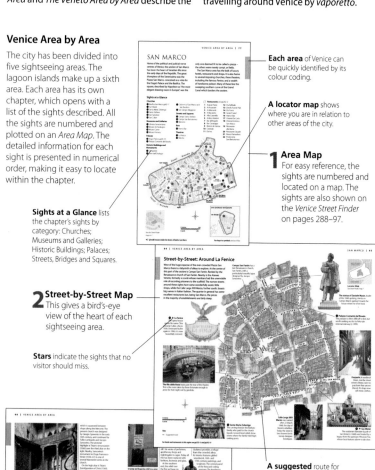

Each area of Venice can be quickly identified by its colour coding.

A locator map shows where you are in relation to other areas of the city.

1 Area Map
For easy reference, the sights are numbered and located on a map. The sights are also shown on the *Venice Street Finder* on pages 288–97.

Sights at a Glance lists the chapter's sights by category: Churches; Museums and Galleries; Historic Buildings; Palaces; Streets, Bridges and Squares.

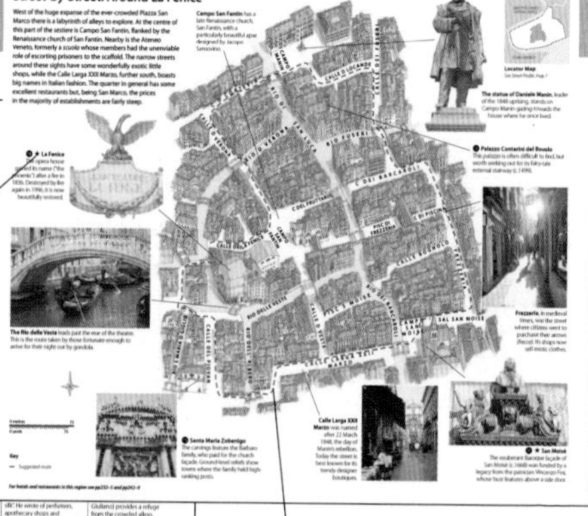

2 Street-by-Street Map
This gives a bird's-eye view of the heart of each sightseeing area.

Stars indicate the sights that no visitor should miss.

A suggested route for a walk covers the more interesting streets in the area.

3 Detailed information on each sight
All the sights in Venice are described individually. Addresses, telephone numbers, nearest *vaporetto* stop, opening hours and information on admission charges are also provided.

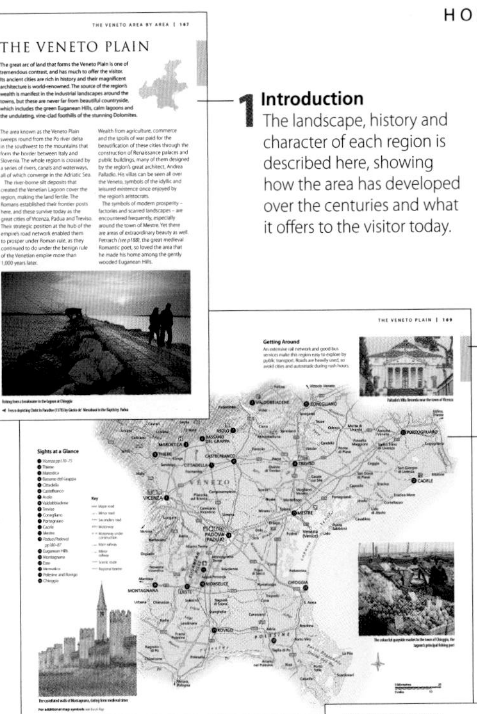

1 Introduction
The landscape, history and character of each region is described here, showing how the area has developed over the centuries and what it offers to the visitor today.

The Veneto Area by Area

In this book, the Veneto has been divided into three regions, each of which has a separate chapter. The most interesting sights to visit have been numbered on a *Regional Map*.

Each area of the Veneto can be quickly identified by its colour coding.

2 Regional Map
This shows the road network and gives an illustrated overview of the whole region. All the sights are numbered and there are also useful tips on getting around the region by car, bus and train.

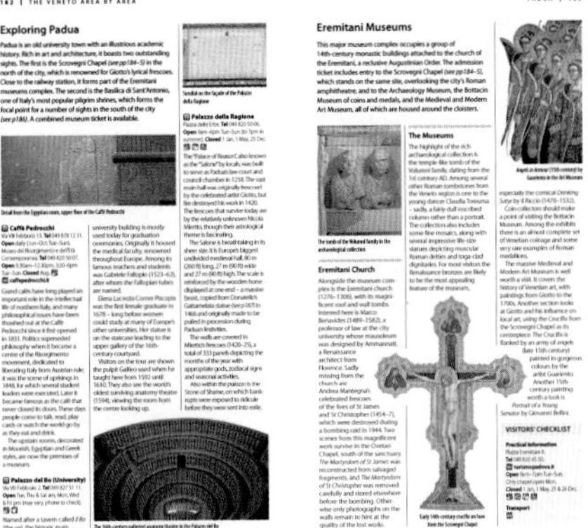

3 Detailed information on each sight
All the important towns and other places to visit are described individually. They are listed in order, following the numbering on the *Regional Map*. Within each town or city, there is detailed information on important buildings and other sights.

Stars indicate the sights that no visitor should miss.

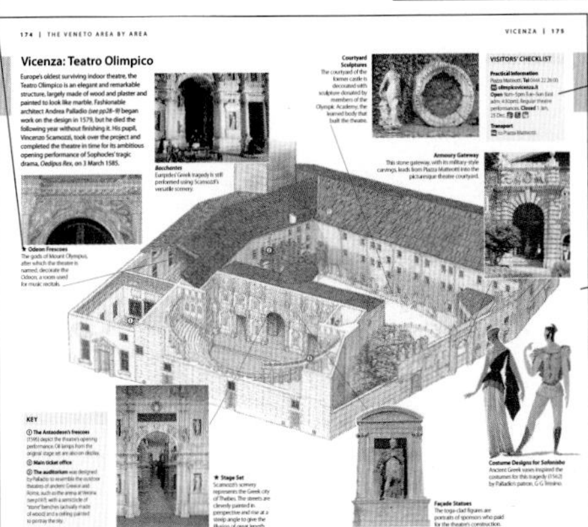

For all the top sights, a Visitors' Checklist provides the practical information you will need to plan your visit.

4 The top sights
These are given two or more full pages. Historic buildings are dissected to reveal their interiors; museums and galleries have colour-coded floorplans to help you locate the most interesting exhibits.

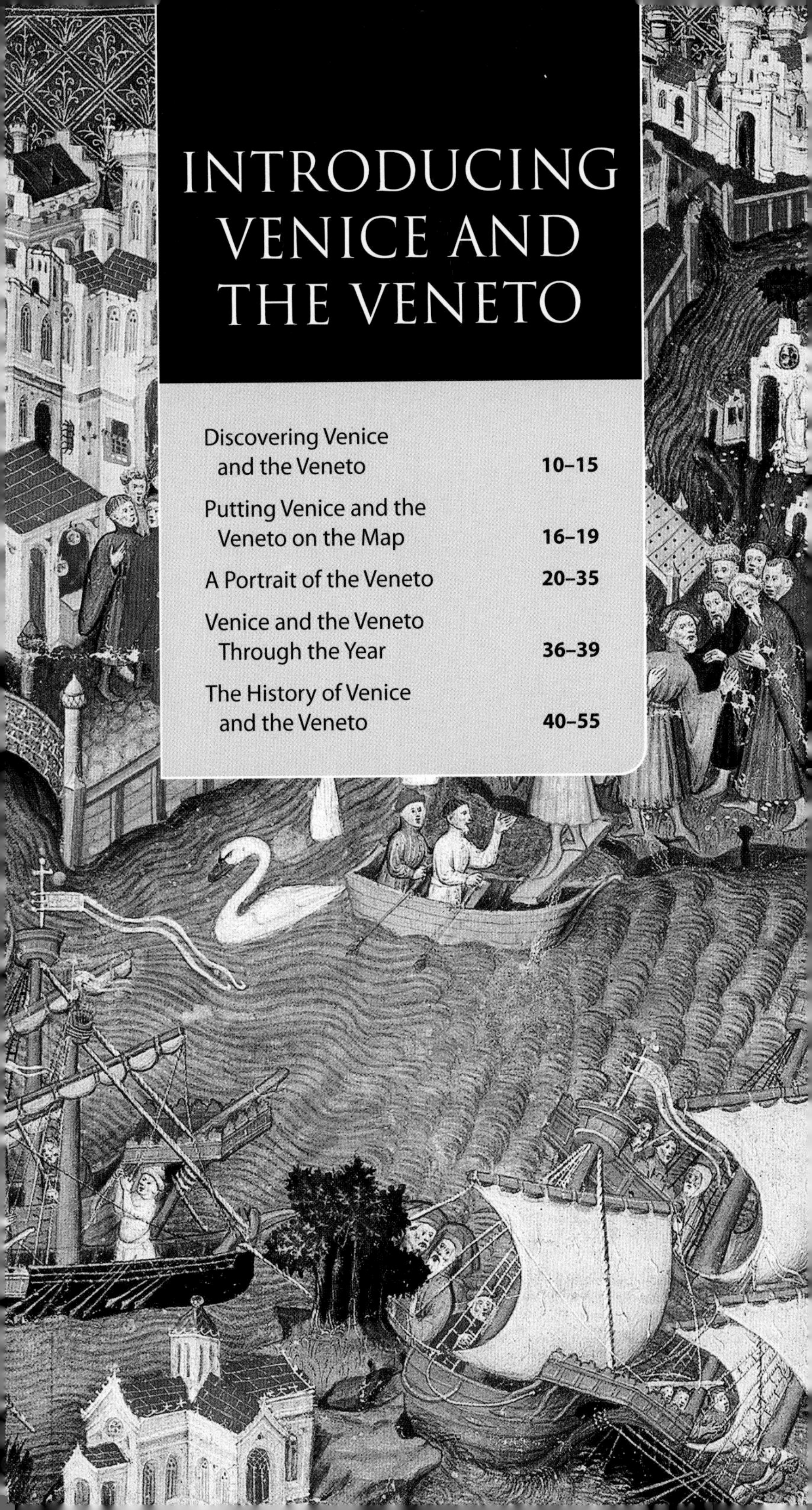

INTRODUCING VENICE AND THE VENETO

DISCOVERING VENICE AND THE VENETO

The following tours have been designed for visitors to experience Venice and the Veneto to the full. First are suggestions of how to make the most of Venice in either two or three days. These are then combined with a seven-day tour of the historic cities of Padua, Verona, Vicenza and Belluno, which can either be done by a circular journey, or by making day trips from Venice, all by train or bus. Extra suggestions are provided for those who want to extend their trip to 10 days. Finally, the 14-day itinerary includes four days in Venice and an extensive 10-day driving tour, taking in the beautiful countryside of the Veneto.

Pick one tour, combine suggestions from the different tours, or simply dip in and out to create your own itinerary.

Basilica San Marco
Regarded as one of the best examples of Byzantine architecture in the world, the Basilica San Marco has a magnificent façade and interior.

One Week in Venice and the Veneto

- Board a *vaporetto* to travel Venice's entrancing waterway, the **Grand Canal**, lined with a host of stunning *palazzi*.
- While enjoing a coffee in Venice's **Piazza San Marco**, marvel at the **Basilica San Marco** and **Doge's Palace** before climbing the **Campanile** for views to the Alps.
- Take a ferry from Venice to the islands to see intricate lace on **Burano**, handblown glass on **Murano** and ornate mosaics in the cathedral at **Torcello**.
- Wonder at the powerful frescoes by Giotto, lining the walls of the Scrovegni chapel in the lively city of **Padua**.
- See the famous Juliet's Balcony, then be amazed by the vast Roman arena in beautiful **Verona**.
- Stroll the streets of Palladio's city, **Vicenza**, and visit the oldest theatre in Europe, the Teatro Olimpico.
- In picturesque **Belluno** head to the bell tower of the Duomo for spectacular views of the Dolomite peaks.

◀ *Marco Polo sailing from Venice in 1271*, from a late 15th-century illuminated manuscript

Two Weeks in Venice and the Veneto

- Admire the magnificent art treasures of **Venice's** churches and stupendous world-class galleries.
- Cross the **Grand Canal** the Venetian way, standing up in a *traghetto* (foot ferry).
- Sip coffee in Caffè Pedrocchi in **Padua**, frequented in the 19th century by famous intellectuals. Enjoy live jazz here in the evening, too.
- Experience opera in the open air at the massive Roman arena in **Verona**.
- Take a leisurely boat trip on **Lake Garda**, soaking up the dramatic natural scenery and admiring the shoreline villas and gardens.
- Sip *grappa* on the bridge in the pretty town of **Bassano del Grappa**, with the mountains as your backdrop.
- Visit **Arquà Petrarca** in the gentle Euganean Hills and the romantic village of **Asolo**.
- Marvel at the mountain landscape on the **Dolomite Road**, then relax in the chic resort of **Cortina d'Ampezzo**.

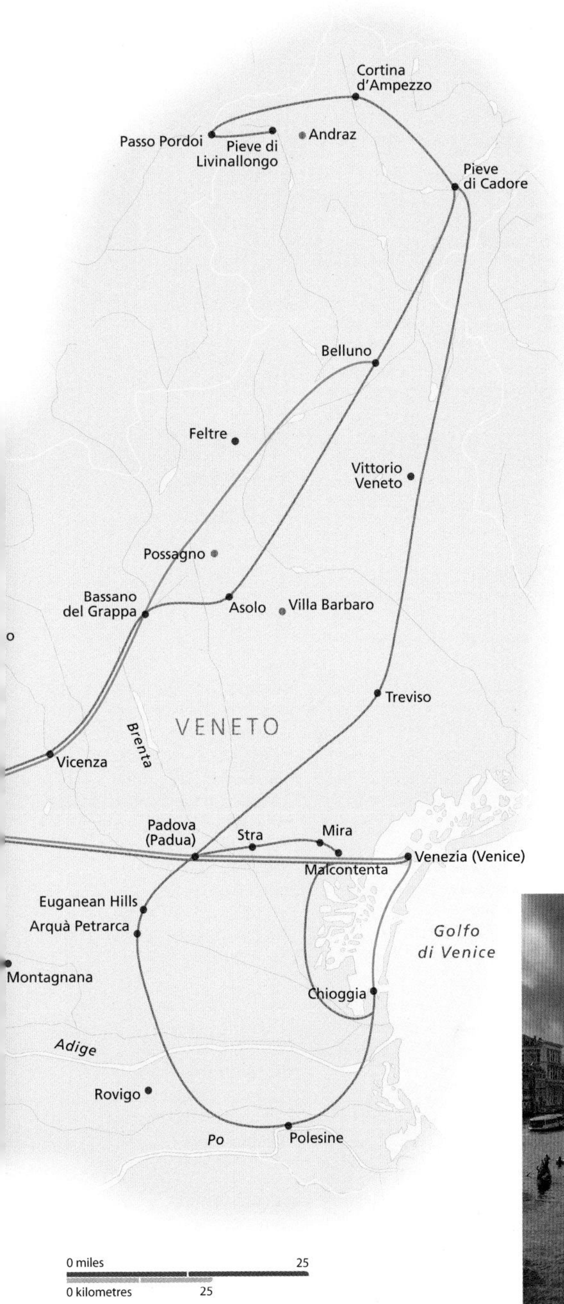

Cortina d'Ampezzo
Passo Pordoi
Pieve di Livinallongo
Andraz
Pieve di Cadore
Belluno
Feltre
Vittorio Veneto
Possagno
Bassano del Grappa
Asolo
Villa Barbaro
o
Treviso
VENETO
Brenta
Vicenza
Padova (Padua)
Stra
Mira
Malcontenta
Venezia (Venice)
Euganean Hills
Arquà Petrarca
Golfo di Venice
Montagnana
Chioggia
Adige
Rovigo
Po
Polesine

0 miles 25
0 kilometres 25

Grand Canal
The banks of Venice's busy main watercourse are filled with beautiful buildings, best viewed from a *vaporetto* or a gondola.

Two Days in Venice

You can see the major sights of Venice in two days. Use the vaporetti (water buses) and stroll the calle (alleyways) to get around.

- **Arriving** Marco Polo Airport is 13 km (8 miles) from the city centre. The Aliguna public boat takes 45 minutes to reach San Marco; the No. 5 bus takes around 25 minutes to Piazzale Roma.
- **Booking ahead** Basilica San Marco; Doge's Palace, for Secret Itineraries Tour.

Day 1

Morning Beat the queues by arriving early in **Piazza San Marco** *(pp78–9)* for the **Basilica San Marco** *(pp82–7)*, encrusted within and without with glittering mosaics. For more magnificence, head for the Gothic **Doge's Palace** *(pp88–93)*. The Secret Itineraries Tour will lead you to the prisons as well as the huge Sala del Maggior Consiglio with its marvellous Tintorettos. Put the city into context by riding to the top of the **Campanile** *(p80)* for views to the Alps. The former stables under the Doge's Palace make a handy spot for lunch.

Afternoon Venice is the ideal city for strolling, so head westwards past the Baroque church of **San Moisè** *(p96)* and the city's opera house, **La Fenice** *(p97)*, until you reach the Sant'Angelo *vaporetto* stop. Take a *vaporetto* ride to the splendid **Ca' Rezzonico** *(p130)*, a museum to 18th-century Venice. Dine out in the nearby **Campo Santa Margherita** *(p131)* before taking an evening *vaporetto* ride along the **Grand Canal** *(pp60–75)*.

The white marble façade of Ca' Rezzonico

Day 2

Morning Get your fill of art, both ancient at the **Accademia** *(pp134–7)* and modern at the **Peggy Guggenheim Collection** *(p138)*. Lunch by the waterside and watch canal boats go by.

Afternoon Leave early by ferry for three very different islands: **Murano** *(pp156–7)*, where the Museo del Vetro showcases marvellous examples of glass; **Burano** *(p156)*, whose Museo del Merletto has traditional lace; and **Torcello** *(pp154–5)*, for a cathedral full of decorative mosaics. Shuttle back to Burano for the excellent fish restaurants, then round off your stay with an evening gondola ride or with a promenade and an ice cream.

Red and ochre buildings lining a canal in Murano

Three Days in Venice

Three days in Venice allows a more leisurely pace for exploring the city.

- **Arriving** Marco Polo Airport.
- **Booking ahead** Same as for *Two Days in Venice*

Day 1

Morning Start early and orient yourself with a trip by *vaporetto* on the Grand Canal. Stop off at **Piazza San Marco** *(pp78–9)* and indulge in a coffee to the strains of an orchestra before taking a tour of the **Doge's Palace** *(pp88–93)*, where you can climb the Giants' Staircase and cross the Bridge of Sighs to see Casanova's prison cell. Take a look at the gondolas moored at the water's edge, then head away from the main piazza for lunch.

Afternoon Book an early afternoon slot to view the splendours of the **Basilica San Marco** *(pp82–7)*. Don't miss the Treasury or the balcony for a close-up view of the four horses and the façade mosaics. Walk along the famous shopping street, the Mercerie, to the busy **Rialto Bridge** *(p104)* and admire the Grand Canal in action. Seek out an *enoteca* (wine bar) to enjoy *cichetti* (snacks) and aperitifs before a leisurely dinner.

Day 2

Morning Head for the Castello district and the **Museo Storico Navale** *(p122)*, where the Doge's ceremonial barge, the golden *Bucintoro*, holds pride of place. Stroll to the **Scuola di San Giorgio degli Schiavoni** *(p122)* for exquisite frieze paintings by Carpaccio, and the Gothic church of **Santi Giovanni e Paolo** *(pp120–21)*, where 25 doges are commemorated with magnificent tombs. **Campo Santa Maria Formosa** *(p118)* is a lovely spot for lunch.

Afternoon Cross the lagoon for the islands of **Murano** *(pp156–7)*, **Torcello** *(pp154–5)* and **Burano** *(p156)*. Treat yourself to some glassware on Murano and admire the resplendent 13th-century mosaics in peaceful Torcello's cathedral. Then head to Burano, with its enchanting multicoloured houses and lacework shops. Having worked up an appetite, choose one of Burano's excellent fish restaurants for your supper.

Day 3

Morning Make for the San Polo district and the church of **Santa Maria Gloriosa dei Frari** *(pp106–7)* for masterpieces by Titian and Bellini. Squeeze in a cappuccino and pastry before going on to the **Scuola Grande di San Rocco** *(pp110–11)* and absorbing its remarkable cycle of Tintorettos. Lunch in the lively **Campo San Giacomo dell'Orio** *(p108)*.

Afternoon Cross into Dorsoduro and immerse yourself in the splendours of the Baroque **Ca' Rezzonico** *(p130)* before taking in the Renaissance masterpieces at the **Accademia** *(pp134–7)*, including Carpaccio's St Ursula's Cycle, and paintings by Picasso, Miró and Kandinsky at the **Peggy Guggenheim Collection** *(p138)*. Dine on the waterfront and perhaps attend an evening concert of Vivaldi at the church of **San Vidal** *(p261)* by Accademia Bridge.

One Week in Venice and the Veneto

Padua, Verona, Vicenza and Belluno are easy day trips from Venice. Suggestions to extend the tour to 10 days are included.

- **Airport** Arrive and depart from Marco Polo Airport.
- **Transport** Regular trains and buses go to Padua and Vicenza from Venice; trains serve Verona and Belluno.

Days 1–3

See Three Days in Venice.

Day 4: Padua

A day in Padua should include the Giotto frescoes of the **Cappella degli Scrovegni** *(pp184–5)* and the treasures of the **Eremitani Museums** *(p183)*. **Caffè Pedrocchi** *(p182)*, once a favourite of 19th-century intellectuals, makes a good refreshment stop and Piazza delle Erbe has a daily market for picnic supplies. Be sure to see the 16th-century wooden anatomy theatre at **Palazzo del Bo** *(p182)* and the frescoes in the **Duomo and Baptistry** *(p186)*. Stroll down via del Santo to the shrine of the **Basilica di Sant'Antonio** *(pp186–7)*, or shady **Orto Botanico** *(p187)* if you need a rest. **Piazza dei Signori** *(p180)* is a good place for dinner.

To extend your trip...
Tour the **Brenta Canal** *(pp186–7)* by bus or boat. Start from Padua or Venice.

Day 5: Verona

Start your day in Verona by visiting the ornate church of **San Zeno Maggiore** *(pp202–3)*, then wander through the *palazzi* to the **Casa di Giulietta** *(p201)* for its famous balcony. Continue to **Castelvecchio** *(p195)* for some of the best art in the Veneto. Stop at **Piazza Erbe** *(p198)* for lunch. Visit the vast **Roman Arena** *(p197)*, then cross the Adige river for a stroll in the Renaissance **Giardino Giusti** *(p205)* before dining near **Piazza dei Signori** *(p198)*.

To extend your trip...
Take the bus from Verona to **Lake Garda** *(pp210–15)*. Stay in **Sirmione** *(pp212–13)*.

Day 6: Vicenza

Vicenza belongs to the architect Palladio. Admire his many *palazzi* and the **Teatro Olimpico** *(pp174–5)*. You can't fail to miss the majestic **Basilica** in **Piazza dei Signori** *(p172)*, then seek out the shady **Monte Berico**, **Villa Valmarana** and **Villa Rotonda** *(p173)*, all within walking distance of the city centre.

Day 7: Belluno

Take a scenic train ride to **Belluno** *(p224)*, on a balcony over the whole Veneto plain, with the peaks of the Dolomites behind. Wander the grand squares and *palazzi*, then climb the bell tower of the Duomo for the best vista.

To extend your trip...
On returning to Venice, take a boat to **Chioggia** *(see p189)* for great views of the lagoon.

The splendid interior of the Teatro Olimpico, Vicenza

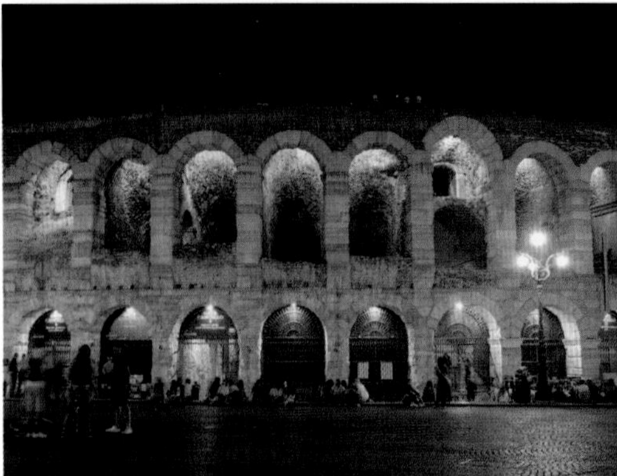

Verona's Roman amphitheatre at night

Two Weeks in Venice and the Veneto

The 14-day itinerary incorporates a day-long canal cruise, a winery tour and a spectacular road trip through the Dolomites.

- **Airport** Arrive and depart from Marco Polo Airport.
- **Transport** Arrange a hire car for pick-up in Padua on Day 7.
- **Booking ahead** Same as for *One Week in Venice and the Veneto (p13)*; Verona: Roman Arena concert tickets.

Days 1–3: Venice

See Three Days in Venice (pp12–13).

Day 4: Venice

Morning Take a short *vaporetto* hop from San Zaccaria across to Giudecca and the peaceful church of **San Giorgio Maggiore** *(p99)* and climb its campanile for a view of Venice and the lagoon. Then take a leisurely walk along the quayside, indulge in a Bellini cocktail at the famous **Hotel Cipriani** *(p265)*, or pastries, ice cream or a full lunch on the terrace of the Cipriani-owned **Harry's Dolci** *(p246)*.

Afternoon Explore the less visited **Cannaregio district** *(pp140–49)*. Walk down Fondamenta della Misericordia to the late-Gothic **Ca' d'Oro** palace *(p148)*, which fronts the Grand Canal, and see the masterpieces of art inside. Then stroll to the lovely Renaissance church of **Santa Maria dei Miracoli** *(p146)* and the Gothic **Madonna dell'Orto** *(p144)*. Explore the alleyways and find a cosy *osteria* for dinner.

Day 5: Padua

See One Week in Venice and the Veneto, Day 4: Padua (p13).

Day 6: Brenta Canal

From Padua take a leisurely day trip by boat along the **Brenta Canal** *(pp186–7)*, gliding past elegant country retreats of the Venetian gentry. Several villas – the Palladian Villa Foscari at Malcontenta and Villa Widmann-Foscari at Mira, and the late Baroque Villa Pisani at Stra – are open to the public. You can return by bus or train to Padua.

The Palladian Villa Foscari on the banks of the Brenta Canal

Day 7: Verona

After picking up your hire car, leave Padua for the lovely city of **Verona** *(pp190–207)* to soak up the Roman, the Romanesque and the romantic. Visit the **Teatro Romano** *(p204)* and the nearby **Museo Archeologico** *(p204)* for the best views, then cross by the Ponte Pietra for the vast **Roman Arena** *(p197)*, now the setting for large-scale open-air operas. From the central **Piazza dei Signori** *(p200)*, with its Renaissance arcades, you can reach the Romanesque church of **San Zeno Maggiore** *(pp202–3)*, the famous Juliet's balcony at **Casa di Giulietta** *(p201)* and the **Tombs of the Scaligeri** *(pp200–1)*, monuments honouring Verona's past rulers. Finish the day with an evening's opera in the Arena.

Day 8: Valpolicella Wine Tour and Lake Garda

In the morning wend your way to **Lake Garda** *(pp210–15)* through the vineyards of **Valpolicella** wine country *(pp214–15)*, stopping for refreshment at San Pietro in Cariano. In the afternoon head down to **Desenzano** *(p210)* on the shores of Lake Garda for a leisurely 2-hour boat trip admiring the gardens and villas of the shoreline. Take a gentle lakeside walk in the evening to the **Grotte di Catullo** *(p213)*, birthplace of the Roman poet Catullus, and spend the night in charming **Sirmione** *(pp212–13)*, where you'll find plenty of bars and shops.

Day 9: Sirmione to Vicenza

Explore the mighty 13th-century castle, the **Rocca Scaligera** in Sirmione *(pp212–13)* before driving on to **Vicenza** *(pp170–75)*, whose most famous son was the architect Palladio. Seek out his *palazzi* on the **Contrà**

The medieval Rocca Scaligera castle in Sirmione

Porti *(p172)* and his awesome **Basilica** in the **Piazza dei Signori** *(p172)*, then continue to the **Teatro Olimpico** *(pp174–75)*; the clever perspective of the stage set is the work of his pupil Scomozzi. Visit Palladio's villas, **Villa Valmarana** and **Villa Rotonda** *(p173)*, just outside the city centre, if you have time.

Day 10: Bassano del Grappa and Asolo
Head north to the Dolomites via **Bassano del Grappa** *(p176)*, where the key sight is the **Ponte degli Alpini**, another of Palladio's designs. You can sample the *grappa* that's made here, visit the **Museo degli Alpini** and the **Palazzo Sturm**, where majolica ware is on display. Then continue to the foothills of the Dolomites to the picture-perfect village of **Asolo** *(p177)*. Take in Villa Barbaro to the east of Asolo or Possagno to the north, for the family home and Gypsoteca of Canova, containg the plaster casts and models for many of his sculptures.

Day 11: Belluno to Pieve di Cadore and Cortina d'Ampezzo
Drive to **Belluno** *(p224)* and climb the campanile of the Duomo for the extensive vista over the Veneto plain. The scenic drive along the Piave river brings you to the Alpine chalets of **Pieve di Cadore** *(p221)* and the birthplace of the painter Titian, **Casa di Tiziano** *(p221)*. The scenery becomes more dramatic on the way to the resort of **Cortina d'Ampezzo** *(p220)*, full of skiers in winter, its meadows ablaze with flowers in summer. You'll find plenty of bars, restaurants and boutiques here.

Day 12: The Dolomite Road
Allow a full day for driving along the most spectacular of Alpine roads, the **Dolomite Road** *(pp220–21)*, as it twists and turns from Cortina d'Ampezzo to Passo Pordoi (4-hour return journey). Factor in plenty of time for admiring the stunning scenery, and take breaks at Pieve di Livinallongo or Andraz, which have restaurants and cafés. Stay overnight in **Pieve di Cadore** *(p221)*.

Day 13: Treviso and the Euganean Hills
Descend down to **Treviso** *(p178)*, second only to Venice for the number of its canals. Take a pleasant ramble through streets full of frescoed houses and look out for *radicchio* (red chicory) and *pasta e fagioli* (pasta and bean soup) on restaurant menus. In the afternoon explore the picturesque countryside of the **Euganean Hills** *(p188)*, where spas, mud baths and sulphur treatments abound, and where the lovely village of **Arquà Petrarca** *(p188)*, home of the poet Petrarch, is located.

Day 14: Polesine and Chioggia
Bypassing Venice, make for the waterways and mud flats of **Polesine** *(p189)* in the Po Delta, a national park and prime site for birdwatchers and nature lovers. You could take a canoe ride before continuing north to the colourful fishing port of **Chioggia** *(p189)* for a meal of freshly caught seafood, then make your way back to Venice.

The winding Dolomite Road with spectacular mountain scenery

Putting Venice and the Veneto on the Map

The Veneto lies in the northernmost sector of Italy, and stretches from the Dolomite mountains in the north to the flatlands of the Venetian lagoon in the south. One of the most prosperous regions of Italy, the Veneto covers an area of 47,562 sq km (18,364 sq miles) and has a population of 4.5 million. Rail and road links with the rest of Europe are excellent, and three international airports serve the region: Valerio Catullo in Verona, Marco Polo on the edge of the lagoon, and Treviso.

For additional map symbols *see back flap*

GERMANY
AUSTRIA
SLOVENIA
CROATIA
ITALY
SAN MARINO
Veneto
Adriatic Sea
Tyrrhenian Sea
München (Munich)
Landsberg Am Lech
Salzburg
Linz
Wels
St Pölten
Wien (Vienna)
Bregenz
Innsbruck
Steinach
Leoben
Graz
Murau
Brunico
Lienz
Villach
Maribor
St Moritz
Bolzano
Cortina d'Ampezzo
Belluno
Udine
Ljubliana
Trento
Zagreb
Novo Mesto
Treviso
Monfalcone
Trieste
Verona
Vicenza
Padova (Padua)
Venezia (Venice)
Porec
Rijeka
Pula
Parma
Bologna
Ravenna
La Spezia
Rimini
Zadar
Lucca
Firenze (Florence)
Fano
Pisa
Ancona
Arezzo
Siena
Perugia
Civitanova Marche
Ascoli Piceno
Giulianova
Viterbo
Terni
Porto S. Stéfano
L'Aquila
Pescara
Civitavecchia
Roma (Rome)
Avezzano
Termoli
Manfredonia
Cassino
Foggia
Anzio
Terracina
Cerignola
Benevento
Avellino
Napoli (Naples)
Potenza
Salerno
Lago di Garda
Inn
Po
Arno
Tevere (Tiber)
Sava
Croatia, Greece
Sicily
Sicily
Key
The Veneto
Motorway
Major road
Railway
International border
Ferry route

Central Venice

Venice is divided into six ancient administrative districts or *sestieri*. The areas described in this book mostly follow the *sestieri* boundaries, with San Polo and Santa Croce combined. Visitors usually start with the Piazza San Marco, heading for the Doge's Palace and the breathtaking Basilica, but each district has its own distinct character, and time spent exploring each will be fully rewarded.

San Polo and Santa Croce
The Rialto Bridge and markets characterize this area *(see p104)*. Pretty stone bridges, such as the one by Fondamenta del Megio, link streets unchanged for centuries.

Dorsoduro
The Baroque Santa Maria della Salute church at the mouth of the Grand Canal is a striking sight *(see p139)*. Other highlights of Dorsoduro include the Accademia and Peggy Guggenheim art galleries *(see pp134–8)*.

For additional map symbols *see back flap*

Cannaregio
The Rio Madonna dell'Orto is one of the most picturesque canals in Cannaregio *(see pp142–3)*.

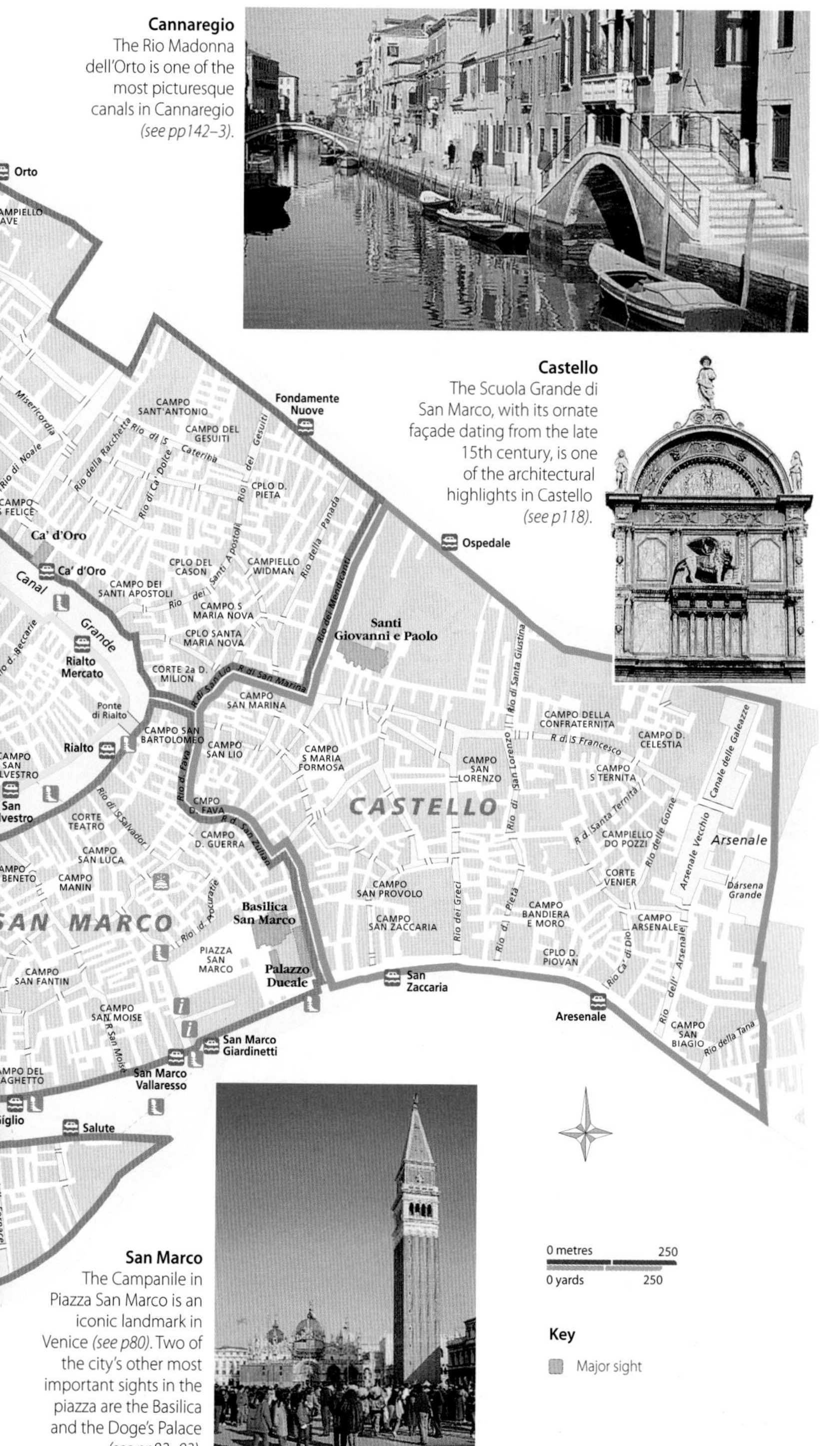

Castello
The Scuola Grande di San Marco, with its ornate façade dating from the late 15th century, is one of the architectural highlights in Castello *(see p118)*.

San Marco
The Campanile in Piazza San Marco is an iconic landmark in Venice *(see p80)*. Two of the city's other most important sights in the piazza are the Basilica and the Doge's Palace *(see pp82–93)*.

A PORTRAIT OF THE VENETO

Venice and the Veneto form, on the face of it, an unlikely partnership. Venice is a romantic tourist city frozen in time, the Veneto a forward-thinking and cosmopolitan part of modern Europe. Yet the commercial dynamism of the mainland cities is a direct legacy of the Old Lady of the Lagoon who, in her prime, ruled much of the Mediterranean.

Venice is one of the few cities in the world that can truly be described as unique. It survives against all the odds, built on a series of low mud banks amid the tidal waters of the Adriatic and regularly subject to floods. Once a powerful commercial and naval force in the Mediterranean, Venice has found a new role. Her *palazzi* have become shops, hotels and apartments, her warehouses have been transformed into museums and her convents have been turned into centres for art restoration. Yet little of the essential fabric of Venice has altered in 200 years. A prewar guide to the city is just as useful today as when it was published, a rare occurrence on a continent scarred by the aerial bombing of World War II and the demands of postwar development. More than 14 million visitors a year succumb to the magic of this improbable city where the past has more meaning than the present.

For all this, Venice has had a price to pay. So desirable is a Venetian apartment that rents are beyond the means of the Venetians themselves. Many of the city's apartments are owned by wealthy foreigners who use them perhaps for two or three weeks a year – unlit windows at night are indicative of absent owners.

Children attending their first communion at Monte Berico, outside Vicenza

◀ Elaborate costume and mask at the Venice Carnival

An elderly Venetian in an ageing Venice

In 1997 the population of the city was 68,600 (compared with 150,000 in 1950), but in 2001 the numbers rose for the first time since the 1950s. The average age of the Venetian population is nearly 50. One reason the city shuts down so early at night is that the waiters, cooks and shop assistants all have to catch the last train home across the causeway to Mestre.

Mestre, by contrast, is a bustling city of 180,000 inhabitants, with a busy oil terminal and an expanding industrial base, as well as some of the liveliest discos in Italy. Governed by the same mayor and city council, Mestre and Venice have been described as the ugliest city in the world married to the most beautiful. Yet Mestre, founded by Venetians who foresaw a day when development land would run out in the lagoon, is simply an extension of the same entrepreneurial spirit that characterized mercantile Venice in her heyday, a spirit that is now typical of the region as a whole. One move to inject new life into Venice entails reconverting former industrial sites – the abattoir and the cotton mill have become university premises, while a former flour mill has been transformed into a convention centre.

The Industrious North

The creativity and industry of the people of the Veneto contradict all the clichés about the irrationality and indolence of the Italian character. For a tiny area, with a population of 4.5 million, the Veneto is remarkably productive. Many world-renowned companies have manufacturing bases in the area, from Jacuzzi Europe and Zanussi, to Benetton, Olivetti and Iveco Ford. As a result, poverty is rare, and the region has progressed from its prewar agricultural base to a modern manufacturing and distribution economy.

Unencumbered by the rest of Italy, the three northern regions of Piedmont, Lombardy and Veneto alone would qualify for membership of the G10 group of the world's richest nations, a fact exploited by the region's politicians in separatist calls for independence from Rome. Coldshouldering the rest of the Italian peninsula, the Veneto looks east to Slovenia for an example of a small state that has achieved independence, and north to Germany as a model of political federalism and sound economic management.

Despite the ferocity of battles fought against them down the ages, the people in the north of the Veneto have a close

Visitors at a craft market in Piazza Erminio Ferretto, Mestre

Valle di Cadore in the Dolomites, close to the Austrian border

relationship with their Teutonic neighbours. Today, German signs, food and language can be easily found in the towns around Lake Garda and the Dolomites. Here, the pretty Tyrolean farmsteads and onion-domed churches are a marked contrast to the isolated fishing communities of the lagoon, where Venice's maritime heritage is still evident. Between these two extremes, however, the cities of the Veneto Plain, with their wealth of culture, provide a more typical view of Italian life.

Italian Tradition

Padua is a perfect example of the *città salotto*, a city built like a salon on a human scale, where the streets are an extension of the home and where the doorless Caffè Pedrocchi is treated like the city's main square. Here Paduans come to drink coffee or write a letter, read a newspaper or talk to friends. Just like the salons of old, the café provides a meeting place for intellectual discourse and entertainment.

Traditional Venetian rowing

It is not just the Paduans who treat their streets and squares like so many corridors and rooms in one vast communal palace. After 5pm crowds throng Verona's Via Mazzini, taking part in the evening stroll, the *passeggiata*. Against the backdrop of the Roman arena or medieval *palazzi* they argue, swap gossip, forge alliances and strike deals. Younger strollers dress to impress, while young mothers bring their babies out to be admired. For all their modernity, the people of the Veneto still understand the powerful part played by ancient rituals such as this in cementing a strong sense of community.

Wedding Ferrari decorated with typical Italian style

The Building of Venice

Venice is built on a patchwork of more than 100 low-lying islands in the middle of a swampy lagoon. To overcome these extremely challenging conditions, early Venetian builders evolved construction techniques unique to the city, building with impermeable stone supported by larchwood rafts and timber piles. This method proved effective and most Venetian buildings are remarkably robust, many having stood for at least 400 years. By 1500 the city had taken on much of its present shape and only since the 20th century has further building begun to alter the outline.

Campo Santa Maria Mater Domini is a typical medieval square, with its central wellhead and its businesslike landward façades – decoration on buildings was usually reserved for the canal façades.

Campaniles often lean because of compaction of the underlying subsoil.

Pinewood piles were driven 7.5 m (25 ft) into the ground before building work could begin. They rest on the solid *caranto* (compressed clay) layer at the bottom of the lagoon.

Istrian stone, a type of marble, was used to create damp-proof foundations.

Closely packed piles do not rot in the waterlogged subsoil because there is no free oxygen, vital for microbes that cause decay.

Bricks

Water grilles

Sand acting as a filter

The well was the source of the fresh water supply. Rainwater was channelled through pavement grilles into a clay-lined cistern filled with sand to act as a filter.

Ornate wellheads, such as this one in the Doge's Palace courtyard photographed in the late 19th century, indicate the importance of a reliable water supply for the survival of the community. Strict laws protected the purity of the source, prohibiting "beasts, unwashed pots and unclean hands".

The Campanile Foundations

When the Campanile in the Piazza San Marco *(see p80)* collapsed in 1902, the ancient pilings, underpinning the 98.5-m- (323-ft-) high landmark, were found to be in excellent condition, after 1,000 years in the ground. Like the Campanile, all buildings in Venice are supported on slender oak and pine piles, harvested in the forests of the northern Veneto and floated downriver to the Venetian lagoon. Once driven through the lagoon subsoil, they create an immensely strong and flexible foundation. Even so, there is a limit to how much weight the piles can carry – the Campanile, its height having been increased several times, simply grew too tall and collapsed. When the tower was rebuilt, timber foundations were again used, but this time more than double the size.

Strengthening the Campanile foundations

***Palazzo* roofs**, built of light, glazed tiles, had gutters to channel rainwater to the well.

Façades were built of lightweight rose-coloured bricks, sometimes left bare, sometimes weatherproofed with plaster.

Bridges were often privately owned and tolls were charged for their use. Originally, none had railings, creating a night-time hazard for the unwary in the dark streets.

High water level

Low water level

Accumulated rubbish is regularly removed by dredging to prevent the canal silting up.

Sand and clay

Caranto is compacted clay and sand in alternate layers, which provides a stable base for building.

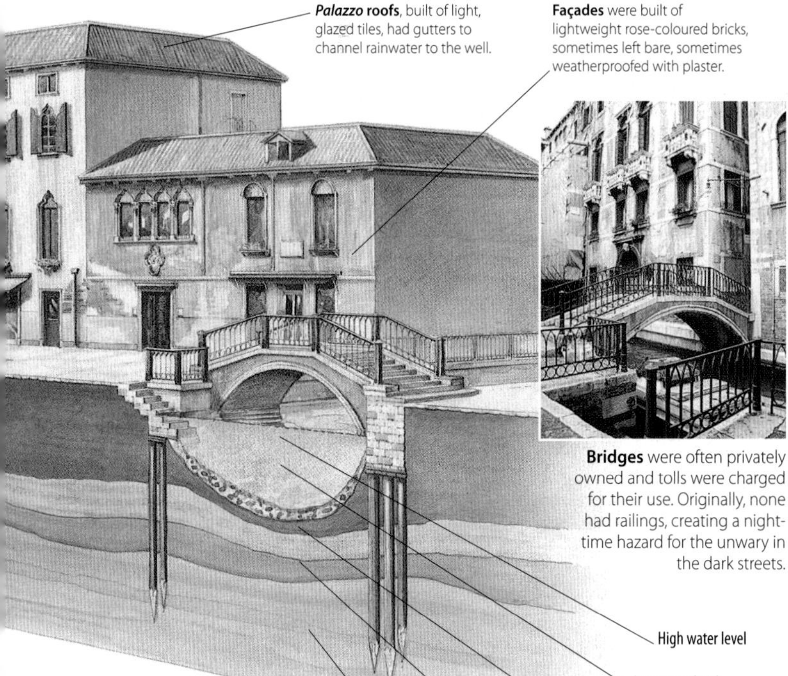

The Campo (Santa Maria Mater Domini)

The fabric of Venice is made up of scores of self-contained island communities, linked by bridges to neighbouring islands. Each has its own water supply, church and bell tower, centred on a campo *(square), once the focus of commercial life.* Palazzi, *with shops and warehouses at ground-floor level, border the* campo *which is connected to workshops and humbler houses by a maze of side alleys.*

The Venetian Palazzo

Venetian houses evolved to meet the needs of a city without roads. Visitors usually arrived by boat, so the façade facing the canal was given lavish architectural treatment, while the landward side, which was accessible from a square or alley, was rarely so ornate. Most Venetian houses were built with three storeys, with kitchens located on the ground floor for ready access to water, or in the attic to enable cooking smells to escape. Typically, a *palazzo* served as a warehouse and business premises, as well as a family home, reflecting the city's mercantile character.

Renaissance doorcase with lion

Byzantine (12th and 13th Centuries)

The earliest surviving private *palazzi* in Venice date from the 13th century and reflect the architectural influence of the Byzantine world. Façades are recognizable by their ground-floor arcades and arched open galleries which run the entire length of the first floor. Simple motifs feature leaves or palm trees.

Byzantine roundel, Fondaco dei Turchi

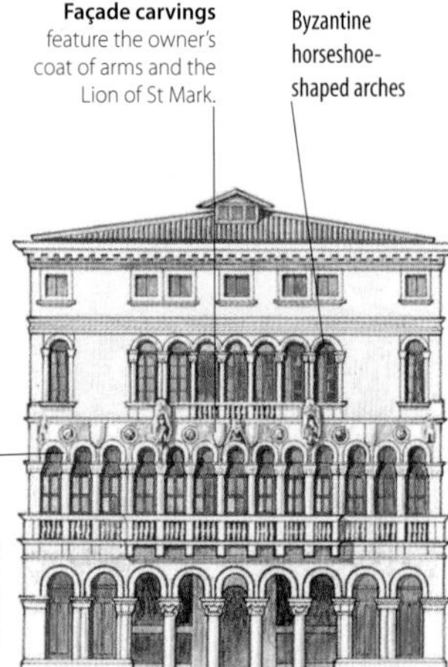

Façade carvings feature the owner's coat of arms and the Lion of St Mark.

Byzantine horseshoe-shaped arches

Cushion capitals have only simple motifs.

Palazzo Loredan *(see p68)* has an elegant ground floor arcade and first floor gallery typical of a 13th-century Byzantine palace.

The Byzantine arcades of the Fondaco dei Turchi (built 1225)

Gothic (13th to Mid-15th Centuries)

Elaborate Gothic *palazzi* are more numerous than any other style in Venice. Most famous of all is the Doge's Palace *(see pp88–93)*, with elegant arches in Istrian stone and fine tracery which give the façade a delicate, lace-like appearance. This style, emulated throughout the city, can be identified through its use of pointed arches and carved window heads.

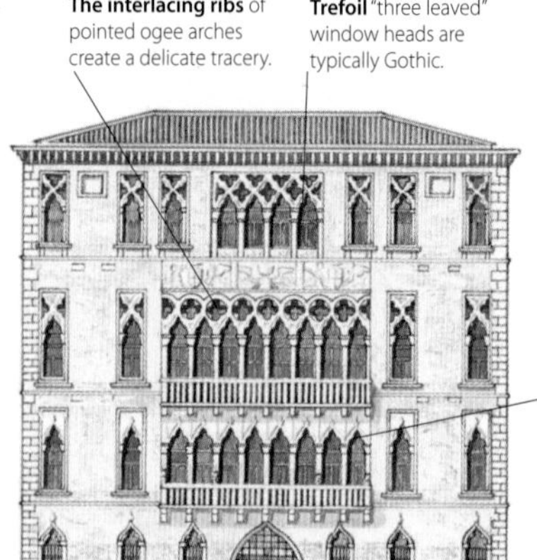

The interlacing ribs of pointed ogee arches create a delicate tracery.

Trefoil "three leaved" window heads are typically Gothic.

Gothic capitals are adorned with foliage, animals and faces.

Ca' Foscari *(see p70)* is a fine example of the 15th-century Venetian Gothic style, with its finely carved white Istrian stone façade.

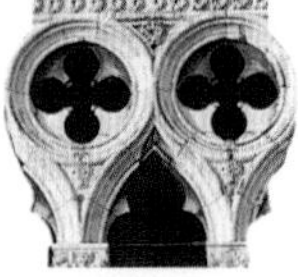

Quatrefoil patterns on elegant gallery windows

Gothic capitals (Doge's Palace)

Renaissance (15th and 16th Centuries)

Houses of the Renaissance period were often built in sandstone rather than traditional Venetian brick. The style was based on Classical architecture, with emphasis on harmonious proportions and symmetry. The decorative language, borrowing motifs from ancient Rome and Greece, typically incorporated fluted columns, Corinthian capitals and semicircular arches.

Palazzo Grimani *(see p68)* has lavish stone carving which none but the wealthy could afford; massive foundations were constructed to bear the incredible weight.

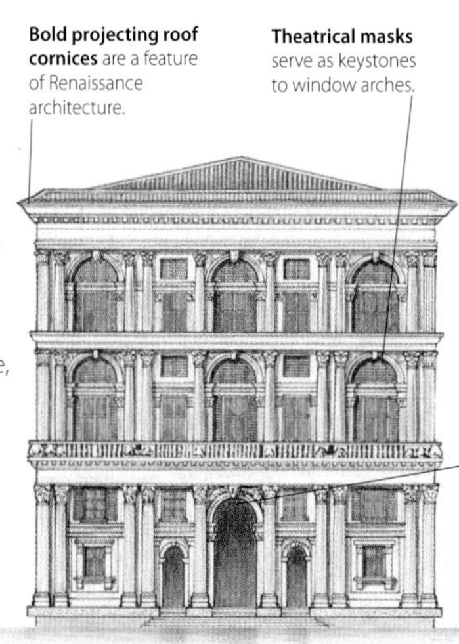

Bold projecting roof cornices are a feature of Renaissance architecture.

Theatrical masks serve as keystones to window arches.

The Venetian door, a very popular Renaissance motif, has a rounded central arch flanked by narrower side openings. This combination was also used for windows.

Corinthian pilasters on the portal to San Giovanni Evangelista

Baroque (17th Century)

Venetian Baroque has its roots in the Renaissance Classical style but is far more exuberant. Revelling in bold ornamentation that leaves no surface uncarved, garlands, swags, cherubs, grotesque masks and rosettes animate the main façades of buildings such as the 17th-century Ca' Pesaro.

Semicircular window head of Palazzo Balbi with two lights and spandrel decorated with a circle.

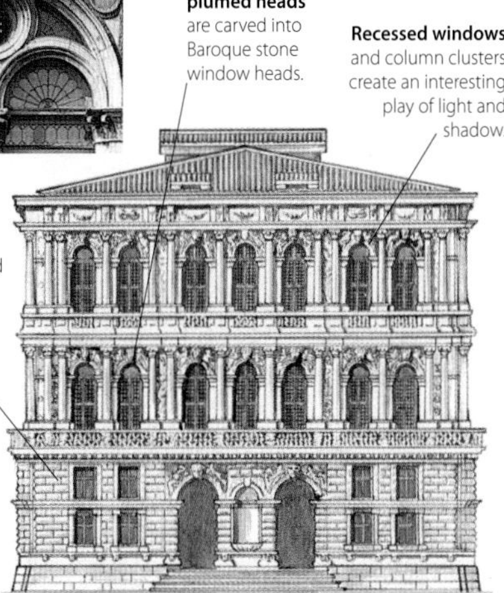

Cherubs and plumed heads are carved into Baroque stone window heads.

Recessed windows and column clusters create an interesting play of light and shadow.

Massive blocks with deep ridges give solidity to the lower walls.

Ca' Pesaro *(see p66)* is an example of Baroque experimentation, with its flat façade broken into a three-dimensional stone pattern of deep recesses and strong projections.

Baroque cartouche

The Venetian House

The layout of a typical *palazzo* (often called Ca', short for *casa*, or house) has changed little over the centuries, despite the very different styles of external decoration.

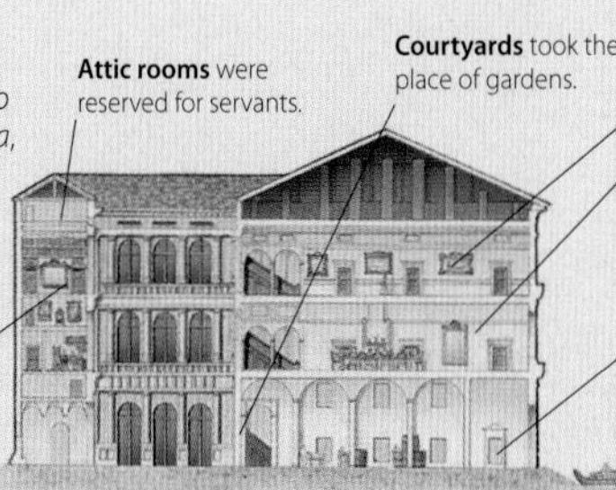

Attic rooms were reserved for servants.

Courtyards took the place of gardens.

The upper floor housed the family.

The *piano nobile* (grand floor), often lavishly decorated, was used to entertain visitors.

The ground-floor storerooms and offices were used for the transaction of business.

Offices, used for storing business records, evolved into libraries.

The Villas of Palladio

When it became fashionable in the 16th century for wealthy Venetians to acquire rural estates on the mainland, many turned to the prolific architect, Andrea Palladio (1508–80) for the design of their villas. Inspired by ancient Roman prototypes, described by authors such as Vitruvius and Virgil, Palladio provided his clients with elegant buildings in which the pursuit of pleasure could be combined with the functions of a working farm. Palladio's designs were widely imitated and continue to inspire architects to this day.

The façade is symmetrical; dovecotes and stables in the wings balance the central block.

The Room of the Little Dog is ornate and lavishly decorated with frescoes by Veronese. Look closely to see the detail of a spaniel in one of the panels.

The Nymphaeum combines utility with art; the same spring that feeds the statue-lined pool also supplies water to the villa.

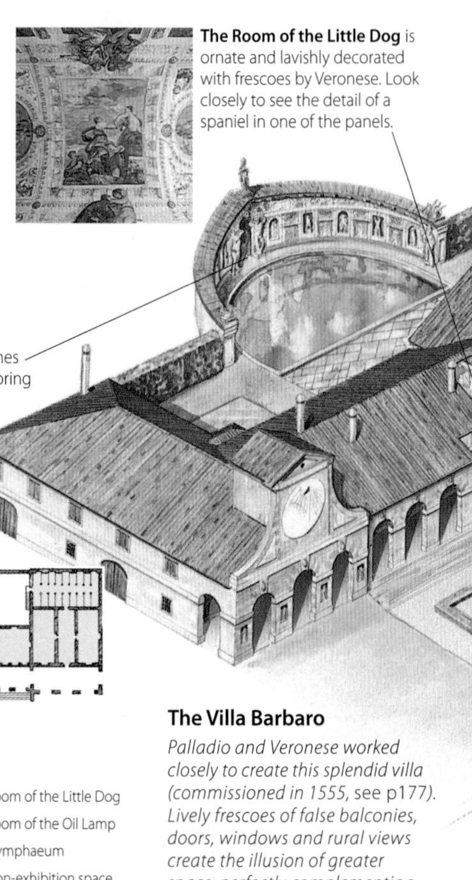

Key

- Crociera
- Bacchus Room
- Room of the Tribunal of Love
- Hall of Olympus
- Room of the Little Dog
- Room of the Oil Lamp
- Nymphaeum
- Non-exhibition space

The Villa Barbaro

Palladio and Veronese worked closely to create this splendid villa (commissioned in 1555, *see p177**). Lively frescoes of false balconies, doors, windows and rural views create the illusion of greater space, perfectly complementing Palladio's light, airy rooms.*

Development of the Villa

Palladio experimented with myriad designs, which he published in his influential Quattro Libri (Four Books) *in 1570, illustrating the astonishing fertility of his mind and his ability to create endless variations on the Classical Roman style.*

The portico statues reflect Palladio's study of ancient Roman buildings.

The pedimented pavilion is all that survives of Palladio's ambitious design; the main residence was never built.

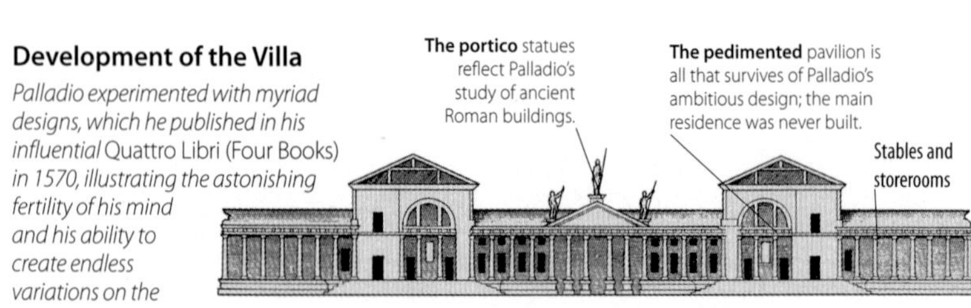

Villa Thiene (1546), now the town hall, Quinto Vicentino

The Hall of Olympus shows Giustiniana, mistress of the house and wife of Venetian ambassador Marcantonio Barbaro, with her youngest son, wetnurse and family pets.

In the Crociera, the cross-shaped central hall, servants peer round false doors, while imaginary landscapes blur the boundary between the house interior and the garden.

The Room of the Oil Lamp symbolizes virtuous behaviour; here Strength, with the club, leans on Truth, with the mirror.

The Bacchus Room, with its winemaking scenes and chimneypiece carved with the figure of Abundance, reflects the bucolic ideal of the villa as a place of good living and plenty.

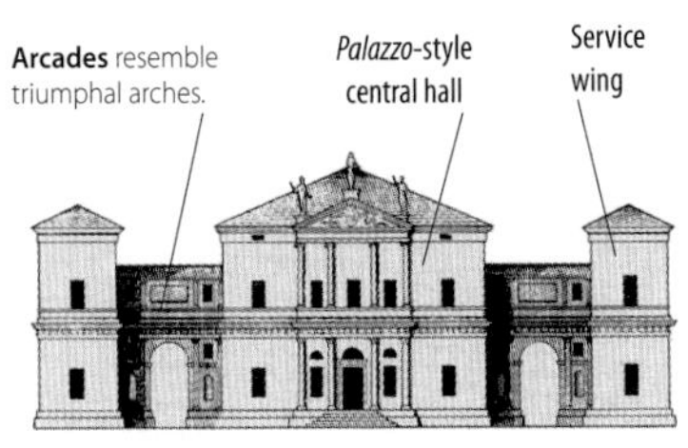

Villa Pisani (1555), Montagnana *(see p188)*

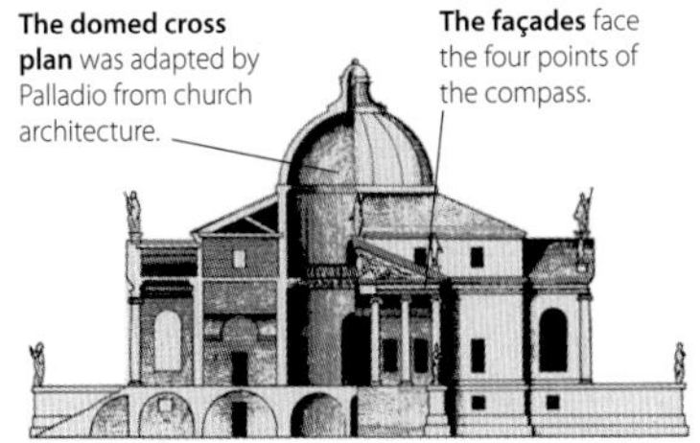

The domed cross plan was adapted by Palladio from church architecture.
The façades face the four points of the compass.

Villa Capra "La Rotonda" (1569), Vicenza *(see p173)*

Styles in Venetian Art

Venetian art grew out of the Byzantine tradition of iconographic art, designed to inspire religious awe. Because of the trade links between Venice and Constantinople, capital of Byzantium, the Eastern influence lasted longer here than elsewhere in Italy. Andrea Mantegna introduced the Renaissance style to the Veneto in the 1460s, and his brother-in-law Giovanni Bellini became Venice's leading painter. In the early 16th century Venetian artists began to develop their own style, in which soft shading and dramatic use of light distinguishes the works of Venetian masters Titian, Giorgione, Tintoretto and Veronese. The development of this characteristic Venetian style, which the prolific but lesser-known artists of the Baroque and Rococo periods continued, can be seen in the chronological arrangement of the Accademia *(see pp134–7)*.

The Last Judgment (12th century) from Torcello: in the damp climate, mosaics, not frescoes, were used to decorate Venetian churches.

Byzantine Gothic

Paolo Veneziano is credited with the move from grand-scale mosaics to more intimate altarpieces. His painting mixes idealized figures with the hairstyles, costumes and textiles familiar to 14th-century Venetians. The typically lavish use of jewel colours and gold, symbol of purity, can also be seen in the work of Veneziano's pupil (and namesake) Lorenzo, and in the gilded warrior angels of Guariento *(see p183)*.

Veneziano's entire dazzling polyptych (1325) of which this is the centrepiece, is in the Accademia *(see p136)*.

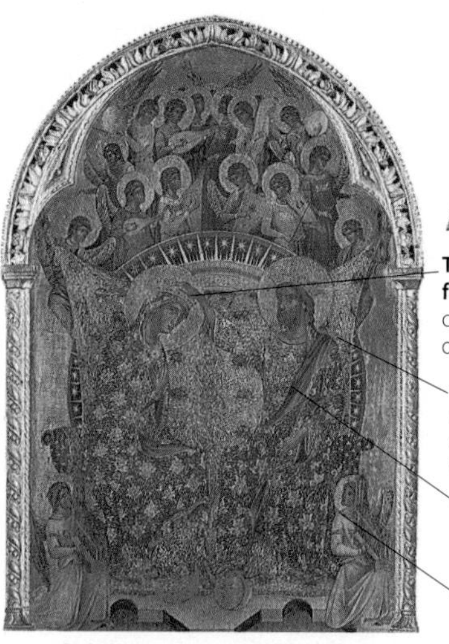

Paolo Veneziano's *Coronation of the Virgin*

The Madonna's gentle face reinforces the courtly refinement of Veneziano's work.

The composition and colours reflect the style of the early Byzantine icons which influenced the artist.

Arabesque patterns on the tunics reflect Moorish influence.

Musicians like these played at grand ceremonies in San Marco.

1356–72 (active) Lorenzo Veneziano

1338–c.1368 Guariento

1430–1516 Giovanni Bellini

1431–1506 Andrea Mantegna

1415–84 Antonio Vivarini

1483–1539 Giovanni Pordenone

1450–1526 Vittore Carpaccio

1480–1528 Palma il Vecchio

1480–1556 Lorenzo Lotto

1300 | **1350** | **1400** | **1450**

1321–62 (active) Paolo Veneziano

1395–1455 Antonio Pisanello

1400–71 Jacopo Bellini

1429–1507 Gentile Bellini

1432–99 Bartolomeo Vivarini

1441–1507 Alvise Vivarini

1467–1510 "Il Morto da Feltre"

1477–1510 Giorgione

1487–1576 Titian

Early Renaissance

Renaissance artists were fascinated by Classical sculpture and developed new techniques of perspective and shading to give their figures a three-dimensional look. Using egg-based tempera gave crisp lines and bold blocks of colour, but with little tonal gradation. The Bellini family dominated art in Renaissance Venice, and Giovanni, who studied anatomy for greater accuracy in his work, portrays the feelings of his subjects through their facial expressions.

Illusionistic details fool the eye: the real moulding copies the painted one.

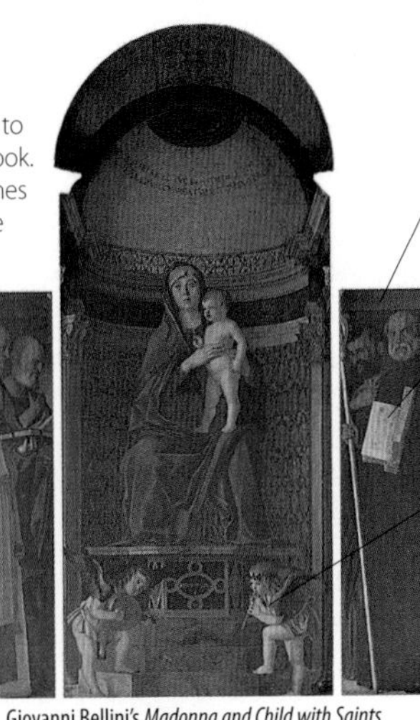

Giovanni Bellini's *Madonna and Child with Saints*

In Bellini's 1488 Frari altarpiece, the Madonna is flanked by SS Peter, Nicholas, Benedict and Mark *(see p106)*.

St Benedict carries the Benedictine book of monastic rule.

Musical cherubs playing at the feet of the Virgin are a Bellini trademark; music was a symbol of order and harmony.

High Renaissance

Oil-based paints, developed in the late 15th century, liberated artists. This medium enabled them to create more fluid effects, an advantage Titian exploited fully. The increasingly expressive use of light by Titian and contemporaries resulted in a distinctive Venetian style, leading to Tintoretto's masterly combination of light and shade *(see p110–11)*.

Titian's *Madonna di Ca' Pesaro*

Titian began this *Madonna* in 1519 for the Pesaro family altar in the great Frari church *(see p106)*, after his *Assumption* was hung above the high altar.

The Virgin is placed off-centre, contrary to a centuries-old rule, but Titian's theatrical use of light ensures that she remains the focus of attention.

St Peter looks down at Venetian nobleman Jacopo Pesaro, who kneels to give thanks to the Virgin.

Members of the Pesaro family, Titian's patrons, attend the Virgin; Lunardo Pesaro, gazing outwards, was heir to the family fortune.

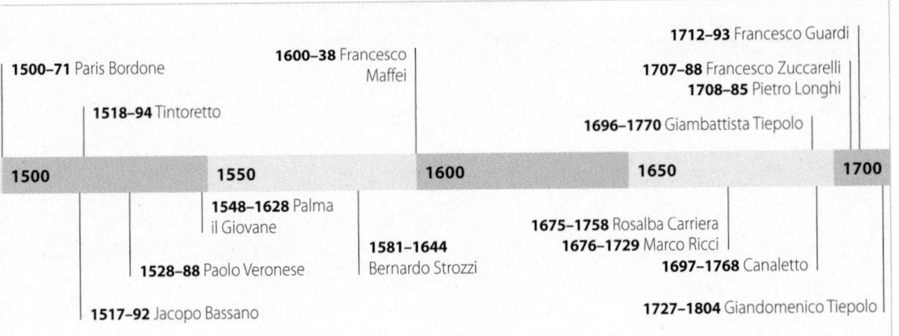

Gondolas and Gondoliers

Gondoliers are part of the symbolism and mythology of Venice. Local legend has it that they are born with webbed feet to help them walk on water. Their intimate knowledge of the city's waterways is passed down from father to son (this is still very much a male preserve). The gondola, with its slim hull and flat underside, is perfectly adapted to negotiating narrow, shallow canals. Once essential for the transport of goods from the markets to the *palazzi*, gondolas today are largely pleasure craft and a trip on one is an essential part of the Venetian experience *(see p283)*. It gives an entirely different perspective on the city, gliding past grand palatial homes, using a form of transport that dates back over 1,000 years.

Squero di San Trovaso *(see p133)* is the oldest of Venice's three surviving *squeri* (boatyards). Here, new wood is seasoned, while skilled craftsmen build new gondolas and repair some of the 400 craft in use.

Traditional dress for a gondolier is a beribboned straw hat, striped vest and black trousers.

The gondolier, unusually for an oarsman, stands upright and pushes on the oar to row the boat in the direction he is facing.

Passengers sit on upholstered cushions and low stools.

The rowlock *(forcola)* can hold the oar in eight different positions for steering the craft.

The oar has a ribbed blade.

The asymmetrical shape of the gondola counteracts the force of the oar. Without the leftward curve to the prow, 24 cm (9.5 inches) wider on the left than the right, the boat would go round in circles.

Continuing a Tradition

Gondolas are hand-crafted from nine woods – beech, cherry, elm, fir, larch, lime, mahogany, oak and walnut – using techniques established in the 1880s. A new gondola takes three months to build and costs £10,000.

Gondola Decoration

Black pitch, or tar, was originally used to make gondolas watertight. In time this sombre colour gave way to bright paintwork and rich carpets, but such displays of wealth were banned in 1562. Today all except ceremonial gondolas are black, ornamented only with their *ferro*, and a golden hippocampus on either side. For special occasions such as weddings, the *felze* (the traditional black canopy) and garlands of flowers appear, while funeral craft, now seldom seen, have gilded angels.

Ceremonial gondolas

Upper Reaches of the Grand Canal (c.1738) is one of many paintings by Canaletto to capture the everyday life of gondoliers and their craft. Since they were first recorded in 1094, gondolas have been a Venetian institution, inspiring writers, artists and musicians.

Races and parades are part of the fun during Venice regattas. Professional gondoliers race in pairs or in teams of six, using boats specially designed for competition. Many amateur gondoliers also participate in the events.

The *ferro* serves to balance the weight of the rower. Its metal teeth symbolize the six *sestieri* of Venice, beneath a doge's cap.

Seven layers of black lacquer give the gondola its gloss.

The main frame is built of oak.

More than 280 separate pieces of wood are used in constructing a gondola.

Mooring posts and channel markers feature prominently in the crowded waterways of Venice. The posts may be topped with a family crest, to indicate a private mooring.

Funeral gondola approaching San Michele *(see p157)*

Wedding gondola

Venetian Masks and the Carnival

The Venetian gift for intrigue comes into its own during the Carnival, a vibrant, playful festival preceding the abstinence of Lent *(see p36)*. Masks and costume play a key role in this anonymous world; social divisions are dissolved, participants delight in playing practical jokes, and anything goes. The tradition of Carnival in Venice began in the 11th century and reached its peak of popularity and outrageousness in the 18th century. Industrialization left little leisure time and Carnival fell into decline, but was successfully revived in 1979.

Modern Carnival Revellers
Since 1979, each year sees more lavish costumes and impromptu celebrations.

The Plague Doctor
This sinister Carnival garb is based on the medieval doctor's beaked face-protector and black gown, worn as a precaution against plague.

Laws forbidding the wearing of costly lace were suspended at Carnival.

The high spirits of Venetian women scandalized many foreign observers.

Traditional Mask Celebration
Carnival in the 18th century began with a series of balls in the Piazza San Marco, as in this fresco on the walls of Quadri's famous café in the square (see p78).

Gambling at the Ridotto
Fortunes were squandered every night of Carnival at the state-run casino depicted in Guardi's painting (c.1768).

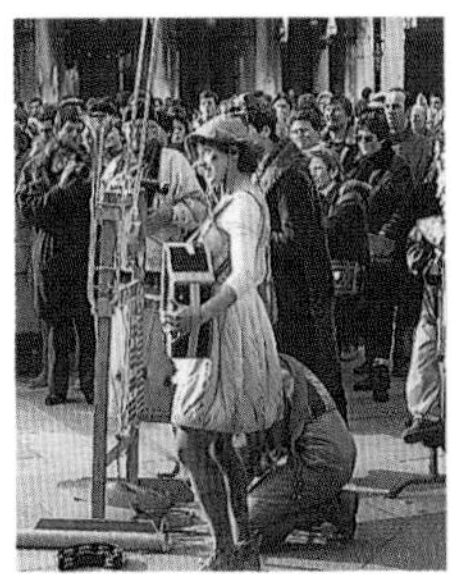

Street Entertainers Musicians and comedians attract the crowds in the piazza San Marco.

The satyr-like profile of this dancer hints that he is the devil in disguise.

Columbine A classic Carnival figure, Columbine wears lace and an apron, but no mask.

Making a Mask

Many masks, and the characters they represent, are deeply rooted in Venetian history. Though instantly recognizable by such features as the beaked nose of the Plague Doctor, each character can be interpreted in a style that is unique to its maker, making each piece a true work of art.

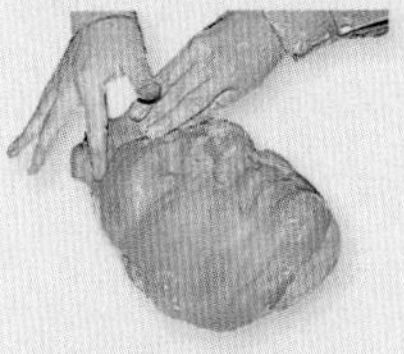

① **The form of the mask** is first modelled out of clay. Then a plaster of Paris mould is made using the fired clay sculpture as a pattern.

② **Papier mâché paste**, made from a pulpy fibrous mixture of rags and paper dipped in glue, is used to make the mask itself.

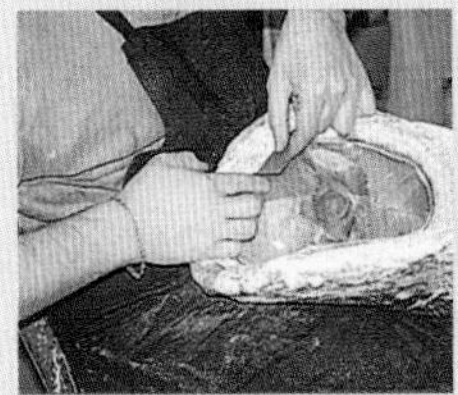

③ **To shape the mask**, papier mâché paste is pushed into the plaster mould, then put aside to set. It becomes hard yet flexible as it dries.

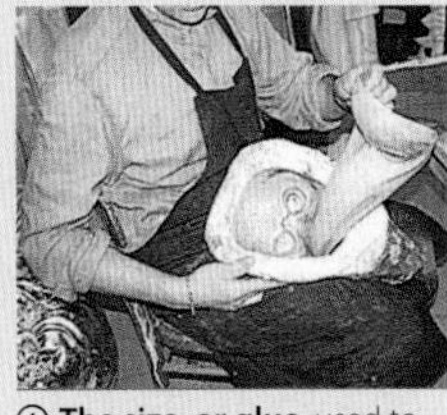

④ **The size, or glue**, used to make the papier mâché gives the mask a smooth, shiny surface, similar to porcelain, when it is extracted.

⑤ **An abrasive polish** is used to buff the surface of the mask, which is then ready to receive the white base coat.

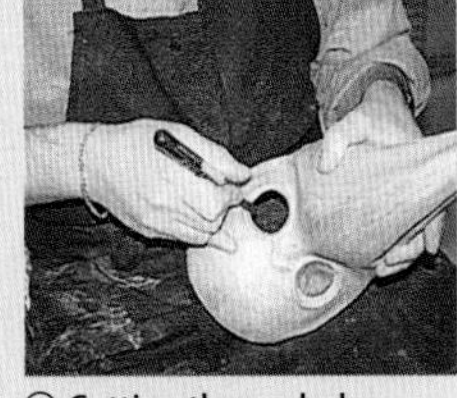

⑥ **Cutting the eyeholes** and other features requires the mask maker to have a steady hand.

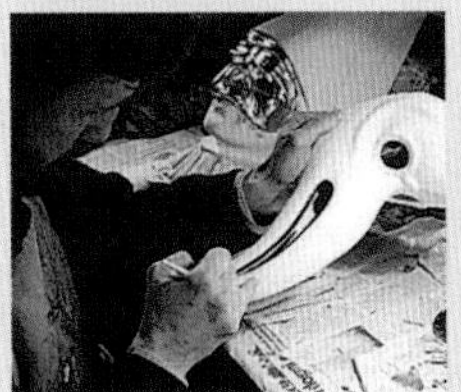

⑦ **The features** are painted on the mask and the final touches are added with a few clever brushstrokes.

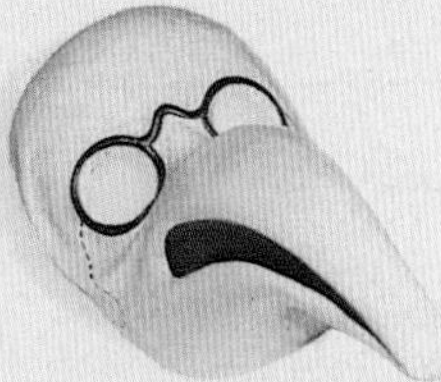

⑧ **The finished mask** is ready to wear at the Carnival or to hang on a wall – the perfect Venetian souvenir.

VENICE AND THE VENETO THROUGH THE YEAR

Venice is a city that can be enjoyed at all times of the year. Even winter's mists add to the city's romantic appeal, though clear blue skies and balmy weather make spring and autumn the best times to go. This is especially true if you combine a visit to Venice with a tour of the Veneto, where villa gardens and Alpine meadows put on a colourful display from the beginning of April. Autumn sees the beech, birch and chestnut trees of the region turn every shade of red and gold. In summer the waters of Lake Garda, fed by melted snow from the Alps, serve to moderate the heat. Winters are mild, allowing some of the crops typical of the southern Mediterranean, like lemons and oranges, to grow.

Winter in the delta of the River Po

Winter

Once a quiet time of year, winter now brings an increasing number of visitors to the city of Venice, especially over Christmas, New Year and Carnival. Many a day that begins wet and overcast ends in a blaze of colour – the kind of sunset reflected off rain-washed buildings that Canaletto liked to paint. In the resorts of the Venetian Dolomites, popular for winter sports, the conditions are perfect for skiing from early December throughout the winter months.

December

Nativity. Churches all over Venice and the Veneto mount elaborate Nativity scenes in the days leading up to Christmas. Attending Mass is a moving experience at this time, even for non-Christians.
Canto della Stella. In Desenzano, on Lake Garda *(see p210)*, Christmas is marked by the open-air procession called *Canto della Stella*, literally "singing to the stars".

January

Epiphany *(6 Jan)*. Children of the Veneto get another stocking full of presents at Epiphany, supposedly brought by the old witch Befania (also known as Befana, Refana or Berolon). She forgot about Christmas, according to the story, because she was too busy cleaning her house. Good children traditionally get sweets, but naughty children get cinders from her hearth. Images of the witch appear in cake-shop windows, along with evil-looking biscuits made to resemble charcoal.

February

Carnival *(10 days leading up to Shrove Tuesday)*. The pre-Lent festival of Carnival *(see p34)*, which means "farewell to meat", is celebrated throughout the Veneto. First held in Venice in the 11th century, it consisted of two months of revelry every year. Carnival fell into decline during the 18th century, but was revived in 1979 with such success that the causeway has to be closed at times to prevent overcrowding in the city.

Today the 10-day festival is mainly an excuse for donning a mask and costume and parading around the city. Various events are organized for which the Tourist Board will have details, but anyone can buy a mask and participate while watching the gorgeous costumes on show in the Piazza San Marco *(see pp78–9)*.
Bacanal del Gnoco *(last Fri of Carnival)*. Traditional masked procession in Verona, with groups from foreign countries and allegorical floats from the Verona area. Masked balls are held in the town's squares.

Masked revellers at the Carnival

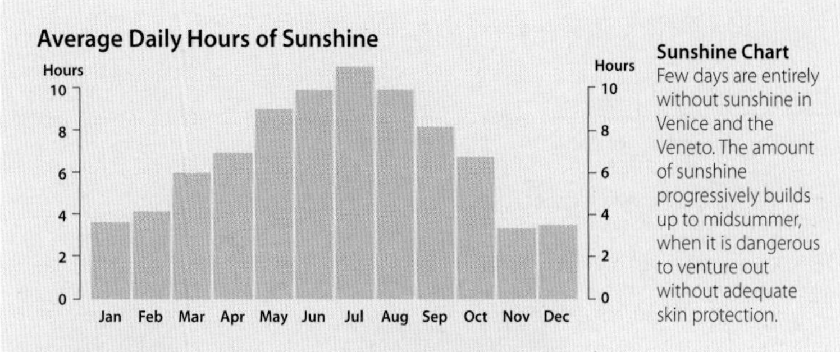

Sunshine Chart
Few days are entirely without sunshine in Venice and the Veneto. The amount of sunshine progressively builds up to midsummer, when it is dangerous to venture out without adequate skin protection.

Spring wisteria in Verona's Giardino Giusti *(see p205)*

Spring

This is the season when many fine gardens all over the Veneto and round Lake Garda come into their own. As the snow melts, there is time to catch the brief glory of the Alpine meadows and the region's nature reserves, renowned for rare orchids and gentians. Verona holds its annual cherry market and many other towns celebrate the arrival of early crops.

March

La Vecia *(mid-Lent)*. Gardone and Gargnano, villages on Lake Garda *(see p210)*, play host to festivals of great antiquity, when the effigy of an old woman is burned on a bonfire. The so-called Hag's Trials are an echo of the darker side of medieval life.

Su e Zo per i Ponti *(end Mar or early Apr)*. A marathon-style race in Venice. Participants run or walk through the city's streets *su e zo per i ponti* (up and down the bridges).

April

Festa di San Marco *(25 Apr)*. The feast of St Mark, patron saint of Venice, is marked by a gondola race across St Mark's Basin between Sant' Elena *(see p125)* and Punta della Dogana *(see p139)*. On this occasion, it is traditional for Venetian men to give their wives or lovers a red rose.

May

Festa della Sparesea *(1 May)*. A delightful festival and regatta for the new season's asparagus is held on Cavallino, in the lagoon where the crop is grown.

La Sensa *(Sun after Ascension Day)*. The ceremony of Venice's Marriage with the Sea draws huge crowds as it has every year since Doge Pietro Orseolo established the custom in AD 1000. Once marked with all the pomp that the doge and his courtiers could muster, the ceremony is not quite as magnificent today, though its symbolism remains valid: "We wed thee, O Sea, in token of true and lasting dominion" are the words spoken by a local dignitary, who then casts a laurel crown and ring into the sea.

Spring produce in the Rialto's vegetable market

Celebrating La Sensa, Venice's annual Marriage with the Sea

Vogalonga *(Sun following La Sensa)*. Hundreds of boats take part in the Vogalonga ("Long Row") from the Piazza San Marco to Burano *(see p156)* and back – some 32 km (20 miles).

Festa Medioevale del Vino Soave Bianco Soave *(16 May)*. Sumptuous medieval-style celebration of the investiture of the Castillian of Suavia. There is a procession with a historical theme, music in the town square, theatrical performances and displays of various sports.

Valpollicellore *(9 May)*. Festival of local wine, with exhibitions, in Cellore d'Illasi.

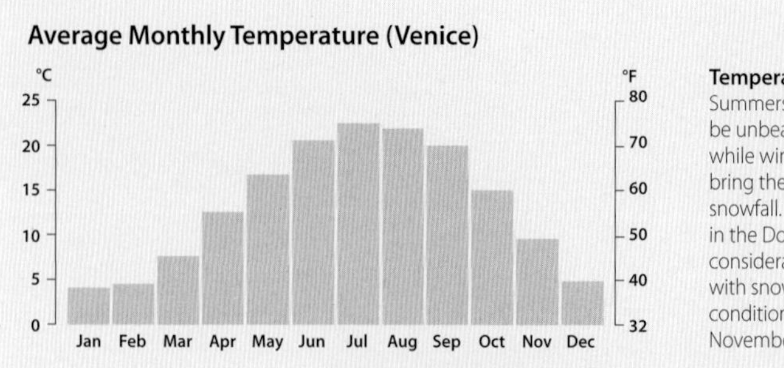

Temperature Chart
Summers in Venice can be unbearably humid, while winters can bring the occasional snowfall. Temperatures in the Dolomites are considerably lower, with snow and freezing conditions from November to March.

Summer

Summer brings the crowds to Venice. Queues for museums and popular sites are long, and hotels are frequently fully booked. Avoid visiting the city during the school holidays (mid-Jul–end Aug). Verona, too, will be full of opera lovers attending the famous festival, but elsewhere in the Veneto it is possible to escape the crowds and enjoy the spectacular countryside.

June

Sagra di Sant'Antonio *(13 Jun).* The Feast of St Anthony has been celebrated in Padua for centuries. The day is marked by a lively fair in Prato della Valle *(see p187).*

Biennale *(Jun–Oct).* The world's biggest contemporary art exhibition takes place in Venice in odd-numbered years *(see p260).*

Festa di Santi Pietro e Paolo *(end Jun).* The feast day of SS Peter and Paul is celebrated in many towns with fairs and musical festivals.

La 500 x 2 *(third Sun in Jun).* Adriatic classic sailing regatta starting from Caorle *(see p179).*

Exhibit by Japanese artist Yayoi Kusama at the Biennale

Boats for hire at Sirmione on Lake Garda

July

Opera Festival *(Jul–Sep).* Verona's renowned opera festival overlaps with the equally famous **Shakespeare Festival**, providing culture lovers with a feast of music, drama, opera and dance in the stimulating setting of the Roman Arena and the city's churches *(see pp260–61).*

Festa del Redentore *(third Sun in Jul).* The city of Venice commemorates its deliverance from the plague of 1576. An impressive bridge of boats stretches across the Giudecca Canal so that people can walk to the Redentore church to attend Mass. On the Saturday night, crowds line the Zattere or row their boats into the lagoon to watch a spectacular firework display *(see p158).*

Sardellata al Pal del Vo *(late Jul).* Moonlit sardine-fishing displays on Lake Garda at Pal del Vo. Boats are illuminated and decorated, and the catch is cooked and distributed to guests and participants.

August

Village Festivals. The official holiday month is marked by local festivals throughout the Veneto, giving visitors the chance to sample food and wines and see local costume and dance. Around Lake Garda these are often accompanied by firework displays and races in boats like large gondolas.

Palio di Feltre *(first weekend in Aug).* Medieval games, horse racing and feasts commemorate Feltre's inclusion in the Venetian empire *(see p225).*

Festa dell'Assunta *(8–16 Aug).* Spectacular nine-day celebration in Vittorio Veneto

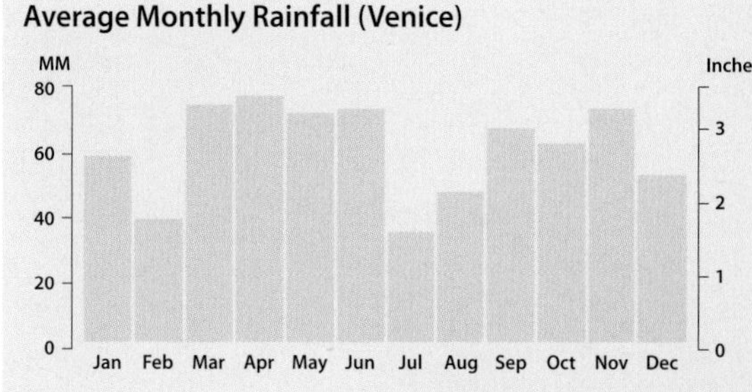

Rainfall Chart
The mountains and sea combine to give Venice and the Veneto higher rainfall than is normal in the rest of Italy, with the possibility of rain on just about any day of the year. The driest months are February and July.

(see p225). The colourful festivities feature dance, poetry, cabaret and music competitions.

Autumn

Expect to see a profusion of market stalls selling a huge range of wild fungi as soon as the climatic conditions are right for them to grow. Local people go on expeditions to harvest them, and mushroom dishes will also feature high on the restaurant menus along with game. Another feature of autumn is the grape harvest, a busy time of year in the wine-producing regions of Soave, Bardolino and Valpolicella *(see pp214–15)*.

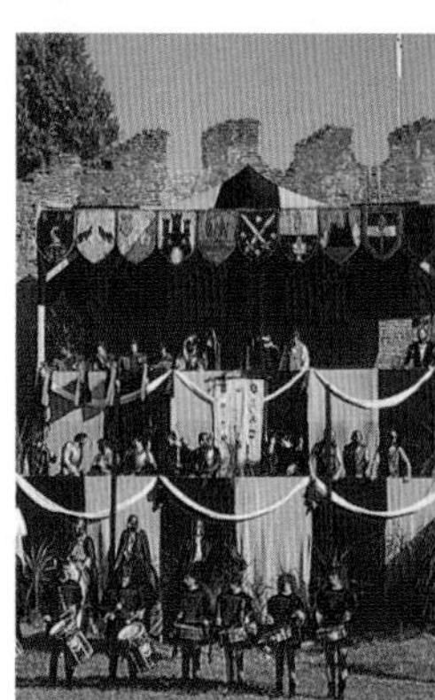

Medieval costume at Montagnana's Palio dei Dieci Comuni

September
Venice Film Festival *(early Sep)*. The International Film Festival attracts an array of film stars and paparazzi to the Lido *(see p161)*.
Regata Storica *(first Sun in Sep)*. Gondoliers and other boatsmen compete in a regatta which starts with an historic pageant down the Grand Canal.
Partita a Scacchi *(second weekend in Sep, in even-numbered years)*. Marostica's chequerboard main square hosts a human chess game in medieval costume *(see p176)*.
Palio dei Dieci Comuni *(first Sun in Sep)*. The liberation of the town of Montagnana is celebrated with a pageant and horse race *(see p188)*.

Grapes ripening in the Bardolino area

October
Bardolino Grape Festival *(first weekend in Oct)*. A festival that celebrates the completion of the harvest.
Festa del Mosto *(first weekend in Oct)*. The Feast of the Must on Sant'Erasmo, the market-garden island in the lagoon *(see p153)*.
Venice Marathon *(mid-Oct)*. This run starts on the Brenta Riviera and finishes in Venice.

November
Festa della Salute *(21 Nov)*. Deliverance from the plague is celebrated with the erection of a pontoon bridge across the Grand Canal to La Salute *(see p139)*. Venetians light candles in the church to give thanks for a year's good health.

Public Holidays

New Year (1 Jan)
Epiphany (6 Jan)
Easter Monday (variable)
Liberation Day (25 Apr)
Labour Day (1 May)
Republic Day (2 Jun)
Assumption (15 Aug)
All Saints (1 Nov)
Immaculate Conception (8 Dec)
Christmas Day (25 Dec)
Santo Stefano (26 Dec)

Rowers practising for the Regata Storica

THE HISTORY OF VENICE AND THE VENETO

The winged lion of St Mark is a familiar sight to anyone travelling in the Veneto. Mounted on top of tall columns in the central square of Vicenza, Verona, Chioggia and elsewhere, it is a sign that these cities were once part of the proud Venetian empire. The fact that the lion was never torn down as a hated symbol of oppression is a credit to the benign nature of Venetian authority.

In the 6th century AD, Venice had been no more than a collection of small villages in a swampy lagoon. By the 13th century she ruled Byzantium and, in 1508, the pope, the kings of France and Spain and the Holy Roman Emperor felt compelled to join forces to stop the advances of this powerful empire. As the League of Cambrai, their combined armies sacked the cities of the Veneto, including those such as Vicenza which had initially sided with the League. Venetian territorial expansion was halted, but she continued to dominate the eastern Mediterranean for another 200 years.

The Venetian system of government came as close to democracy as anyone was to devise until the 19th century, and it stood the city and its empire in good stead until the bumptious figure of Napoleon Bonaparte dared to intrude in 1797. But by then Venice had become a byword for decadence and decline, the essential mercantile instinct that had created and sustained the Serene Republic for so long having been extinguished. As though exhausted by 1,376 years of independent existence, the ruling doge and his Grand Council simply resigned, but their legacy lives on, to fascinate visitors with its extraordinary beauty and remarkable history.

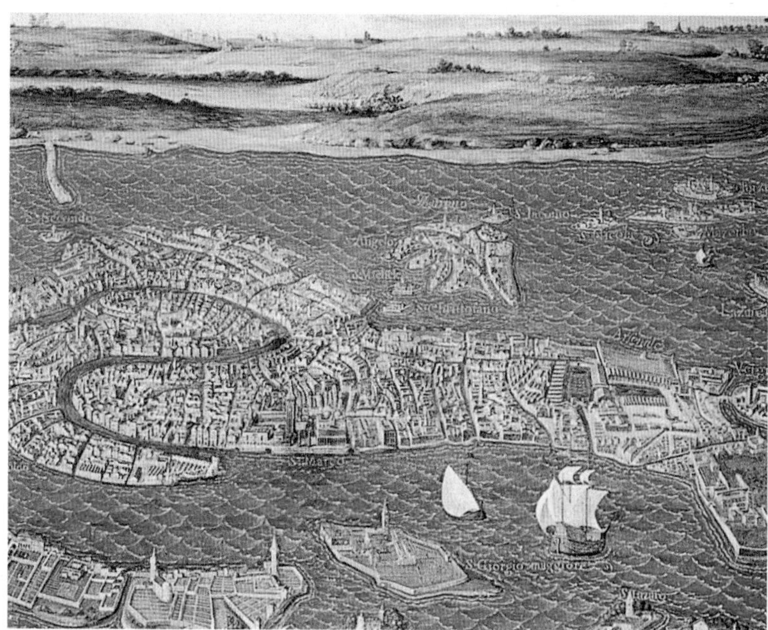

A map dated 1550, showing how little Venice has changed in nearly 500 years

◀ Tintoretto's *Triumph of Doge Nicolò da Ponte* (1580–84), Sala del Maggior Consiglio, Doge's Palace

Roman Veneto

The Veneto takes its name from the Veneti, the pre-Roman inhabitants of the region, whose territory fell to the superior military might of the Romans in the 3rd century BC. Verona was then built as a base for the thrusting and ambitious Roman army which swept northwards over the Alps to conquer much of modern France and Germany. While the Roman Empire remained intact the Veneto prospered, but the region bore the brunt of fierce and destructive barbarian attacks that began in the 4th century AD. Riddled by in-fighting and the split between Rome and Constantinople, the imperial administration began to crumble.

Horsemen in Roman Army
Goths, Huns and Vandals served as mercenaries in the Roman cavalry but later turned to plunder.

Horse-Drawn Carriage
Finds from the region show the technological skills and luxurious lifestyles of the inhabitants.

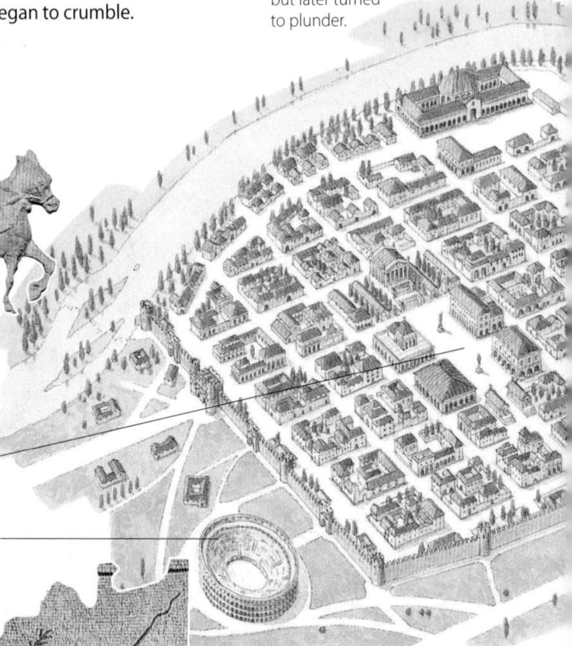

The Forum (market square)

The Arena was completed in AD 30 to entertain the troops stationed in Verona. It could hold 30,000 spectators.

Chariot Racing
A pre-Roman chariot in Adria's museum *(see p189)* suggests the Romans adopted the sport from their predecessors.

Verona

*Securely fortified and moated by the River Adige, Roman Verona was divided into square blocks (*insulae or "islands"*). The Forum has since been filled in by medieval palaces, but several landmarks are still discernible today* (see p194).

6th century BC Veneto region occupied by the Euganei and the Veneti

87 BC Catullus, Roman love poet, born in Verona

89 BC The citizens of Verona, Padua, Vicenza, Este and Treviso granted full rights of Roman citizenship

600 BC | 500 | 400 | 300 | 200 | 100

3rd century BC Veneto conquered by the Romans. The Veneti and Euganei adopt Roman culture and lose their separate identities

Catullus (87–c.54 BC)

Hunting in the Lagoon The wild lagoon, future site of Venice, attracted fishermen and huntsmen in pursuit of game and wildfowl. It also became a place of refuge during raids by Huns and Goths.

The theatre, built in the 1st century BC, is still used for open-air performances *(see p260)*.

Two arches of the Ponte Romano *(see pp204–5)* survive intact.

Gladiators Bloodthirsty citizens flocked to the gladiatorial contests in which prisoners of war, criminals and Christian martyrs were put to the sword.

Where to See Roman Veneto

Verona *(p194)* has the highest concentration of Roman sites in the region; the Archaeological Museum *(p204)* is full of fine mosaics and sculptures, and Castelvecchio *(p195)* has some very rare early Christian glass and silver. Good museums can also be found at Este *(pp188–9)*, Adria, Treviso *(p178)* and Portogruaro, situated near Concordia *(p179)*.

This fine mosaic of a nightingale in Treviso Museum is from Trevisium, the town's Roman predecessor.

Verona's Arena is an awe-inspiring home for the city's opera festival, despite the loss of its outer wall to earthquakes.

AD 100 The Arena, Verona's amphitheatre, is built. Near Eastern merchants bring Christianity to the region

360 The Roman Empire's northern borders under attack from Slavic and Teutonic tribes

401 Led by Alaric, the Goths invade northern Italy; the Veneto bears the brunt of the attack

Fierce Visigoth

AD 1 | 100 | 200 | 300 | 400

59 BC Livy, Roman historian, born in Padua

313 Constantine the Great grants official status to Christianity

331 Constantinople takes over from Rome as capital of the Roman Empire

395 Roman Empire splits into eastern and western halves

410 Alaric succeeds in sacking Rome itself, but dies the same year

The Birth of Venice

Fleeing the Goths, who were systematically looting and burning their way southwards to Rome, the people of the Veneto sought refuge among the wild and uninhabited islands of their marshy coast. There they formed villages, and from the ashes of the Roman past rose the city of Venice (founded, as tradition has it, in AD 421). Exploiting its easily defended maritime position, important trade links with Byzantium were created. Venice proclaimed its brash self-confidence by brazenly stealing the relics of St Mark the Evangelist from Alexandria, in Egypt.

Early Venetian Settlements
The Rialto Bridge (from Rivo Alto, or "high bank") marks the spot of one of many early settlements.

San Marco as it was before 14th-century rebuilding.

The First Crusade *(1095–9)*
Venice cunningly used the Crusades to her advantage, gaining valuable trading rights in captured cities such as Antioch and Tripoli.

The Bishop of Altino
The cathedral at Torcello was founded in AD 639, when Altino's bishop led a mass exodus to the lagoon island, fleeing Lombardic invaders.

The Arrival of the Relics

This 13th-century mosaic from the façade of San Marco depicts the body of St Mark being carried into the newly built basilica for reburial in AD 832. By securing the relics of such an important saint, Venice signalled its ambition to be considered one of the foremost cities in Christendom, on a par with Rome.

421 Venice founded, traditionally – and conveniently – on St Mark's Day, 25 April

452 Attila the Hun invades Italy and plunders the Veneto

570 The Lombards' first invasion of northern Italy; beginning of mass migration from the cities of the Veneto to lagoon islands

Charlemagne (742–814)

726 First documented doge, Orso Ipato

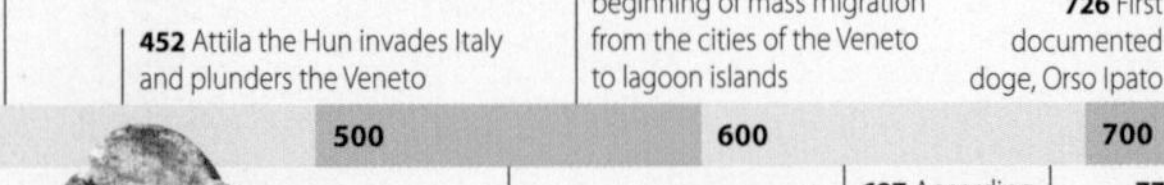

So-called "Attila's throne" in Torcello

639 Torcello cathedral founded

552 Totila the Goth invades Italy and destroys many towns in the Veneto

697 According to legend, Paoluccio Anafesta is elected first doge

774 Charlemagne invited to drive Lombards from Italy

800 Charlemagne is crowned first Holy Roman Emperor by Pope Leo III

Diplomacy
Strategically placed between the powers of Rome and Byzantium, Venice was continually exerting her powers of diplomacy. Here, Doge Ziani receives Holy Roman Emperor Frederick I, whom he reconciled with Pope Alexander III in 1177.

Looting the remains of St Mark from Alexandria was seen as an act of anti-Moslem piety.

The doge and his entourage are wearing Byzantine-style caps and robes.

St Theodore
The Byzantine emperor nominated Theodore as the patron saint of Venice. Venice chose St Mark instead, an act of defiance against Byzantine rule.

Where to See Early Venice

The cathedral at Torcello *(pp154–5)* is the oldest surviving building in Venice, and the Basilica San Marco *(pp82–7)* has many period treasures. Early Venetian coins are in the Correr Museum *(p81)*. The original statue of St Theodore is in the Doge's Palace courtyard.

Torcello cathedral's jewel-like mosaics (11th century) are masterpieces of Byzantine art, probably the work of craftsmen from Constantinople.

The Pala d'Oro, St Mark's 10th-century altarpiece, shows merchants bringing St Mark's plundered relics to Venice.

814 First Venetian coins minted; work begins on first Doge's Palace

828 Venetian merchants steal body of St Mark from Alexandria

832 First Basilica San Marco completed

900

888 King Berengar I of Italy chooses Verona as his seat

1000

1000 Doge Pietro Orseolo rids the Adriatic of pirates, commemorated by the first Marriage of Venice to the Sea ceremony

1095 First Crusade; Venice provides ships and supplies

1100

1120 Verona's San Zeno church begun

1128 First street lighting in Venice

1171 Six districts *(sestieri)* of Venice established

1173 First Rialto Bridge built

1177 Emperor Frederick I Barbarossa agrees to peace terms with Pope Alexander III

Lighting a street lamp

1200

1202 Venice diverts the Fourth Crusade to its own ends, the conquest of Byzantium

The Growth of the Empire

During the Middle Ages, Venice expanded in power and influence throughout the eastern Mediterranean, culminating in the conquest of Byzantium in 1204. At home, in contrast to the fractional strife of most of the area, Venice enjoyed a uniquely ordered administration headed by the doge, an elected leader whose powers were carefully defined by the Venetian constitution. Real power lay with the Council of Ten and the 2,000 or so members of the Grand Council, from whose number the doge and his advisers were elected.

Bocca di Leone
Such letterboxes were used to report crimes anonymously and were often abused *(p93)*.

Doge Enrico Dandolo boldly led the attack on Constantinople, despite being over 90 and completely blind.

Cangrande I
Founder of the Veronese Scaligeri dynasty *(see p213)*, Cangrande I ("Big Dog") typified the totalitarian rule of most Italian cities.

Siege of Constantinople
Facing financial difficulties, the leaders of the Fourth Crusade agreed to attack the capital of Byzantium, as payment for warships supplied by Venice. The city fell in 1204, leaving Venice ruler of Byzantium.

Marco Polo in China
Renowned Venetian merchant, Marco Polo *(see p147)* spent over 20 years at the court of Kublai Khan.

1200 – 1250 – 1300 – 1350

1204 Conquest of Constantinople; Venice's plunder includes four bronze horses

1222 University of Padua founded

1260 Scaligeri family rules Verona

1271–95 Marco Polo's journey to China

1284 Gold ducats first minted in Venice

1301 Dante, exiled from his native Florence, is welcomed to Verona by the Scaligeri rulers

1304–13 Giotto paints the Scrovegni Chapel frescoes *(pp184–5)* in Padua

1309 Present Doge's Palace begun

1310 The Venetian Constitution is passed; Council of Ten formed

1325 The names of Venice's ruling families are fixed and inscribed in the Golden Book

1348–9 Black Death plague kills half Venice's population

The Four Horses of San Marco

Decapitation
Doge Marin Falier was beheaded in 1355 for plotting to become absolute ruler of Venice. His execution was a warning to future doges.

Imperial treasures and ancient buildings were lost when the 900-year-old city was looted and burned.

Electing the Doge
This pointer was used for counting votes during dogal elections, using a convoluted system designed to prevent candidates bribing their way to power.

Troops scaled the fortifications from galleys moored against the city walls.

Queen of Cyprus
Venice shamelessly gained Cyprus in 1489 by arranging for Caterina Cornaro, from one of Venice's noblest families, to marry the island's king, and then poisoning him.

Where to See Imperial Venice

The Doge's Palace combines ceremonial splendour and the grimmer business of imprisonment and torture *(pp88–93)*. Aspects of the constitution are on display in the Correr Museum *(p81)*. A *bocca di leone* survives on the Zattere *(p133)*.

Many doges are commemorated by Renaissance-style monuments in the church of Santi Giovanni e Paolo *(pp120–21)*.

Meetings of the Grand Council, dominated by the merchant class, were held in the Sala del Maggior Consiglio *(p91)* in the Doge's Palace.

Battle of Chioggia

1489 Cyprus ceded to Venice by Queen Caterina Cornaro

1518 Titian's *Assumption* hung in Frari *(p106)*

1400 | 1450 | 1500

1380 Battle of Chioggia: Venice defeats Genoa to win undisputed maritime supremacy in the Adriatic and Mediterranean

1430 Giovanni Bellini born, greatest of the artistic family

1453 Constantinople falls to the Turks; Venice's empire reaches its zenith

Titian (1487–1576)

1508 Andrea Palladio, architect, born in Padua

The Queen of the Adriatic

By the 16th century, Venice held a monopoly on Mediterranean trade and had colonized the whole of northeastern Italy, from the Adriatic to the Alps. Keeping hold of such a vast empire meant being in a constant state of war. The League of Cambrai, dedicated to destroying Venice, was formed in 1508 by the most powerful men in Europe, Pope Julius II and the Holy Roman Emperor Maximilian. Their troops sacked the cities of the Veneto, but the region remained loyal to Venice's relatively benign rule. Far more of a threat were the Turks. They carved out the Ottoman Empire from 1522, driving Venice from the eastern Mediterranean and eventually taking Cyprus in 1570.

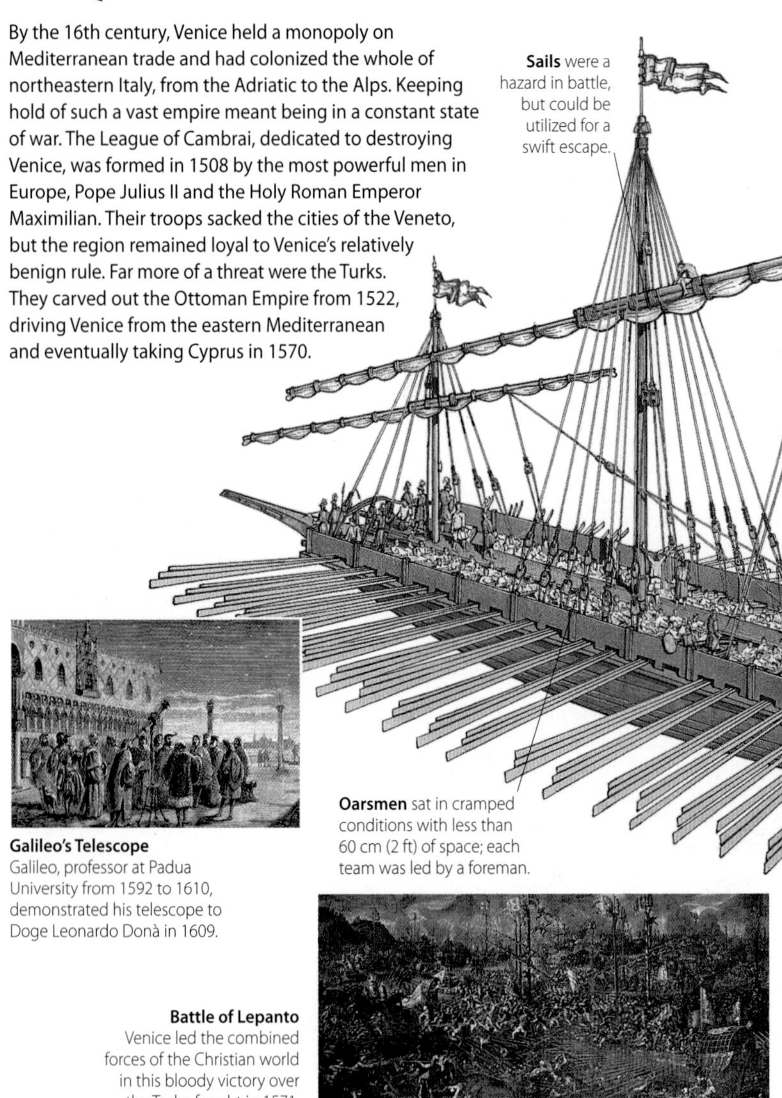

Sails were a hazard in battle, but could be utilized for a swift escape.

Oarsmen sat in cramped conditions with less than 60 cm (2 ft) of space; each team was led by a foreman.

Galileo's Telescope
Galileo, professor at Padua University from 1592 to 1610, demonstrated his telescope to Doge Leonardo Donà in 1609.

Battle of Lepanto
Venice led the combined forces of the Christian world in this bloody victory over the Turks, fought in 1571.

1500

1501 Doge Leonardo Loredan, great diplomat, begins 20-year rule

1514 Fire destroys the original timber Rialto Bridge

1516 Jews confined to the Venetian Ghetto. End of League of Cambrai wars

1518 Tintoretto born

1528 Paolo Veronese born

1529 Death of Luigi da Porto of Vicenza, author of the story of Romeo and Juliet

1550

1570 Cyprus lost to the Turks

1571 Battle of Lepanto: decisive victory for the western fleet, led by Venice, over the Turks

1577 Palladio designs the Redentore church *(p158)* to mark the end of the plague that took 51,000 lives

1585 First performance at Vicenza's Teatro Olimpico *(p174)*

1592 Galileo appointed professor of mathematics at Padua Universit

1595 Shakespeare's *Romeo and Juliet*

160

Celebrating the End of the Plague
More deadly than any opposing army, plague hit Venice in 1575 and again in 1630, carrying off Titian among its 100,000 victims.

Where to See Maritime Venice

The triumph of Venice over the sea is celebrated in the Museo Storico Navale *(p122)*. For a glimpse of the extensive and disused Arsenale shipyard in Castello, take a trip on *vaporetto* route No. 4.1, 4.2, 5.1 or 5.2 *(p284)*.

Arsenale lions, plundered from Piraeus in 1687, guard the forbidding gates of the Arsenale shipyard *(p123)*.

Santa Maria della Salute was built in thanksgiving for deliverance from the 1630 plague *(p139)*.

The Venice Arsenale
Venice was at the forefront of maritime construction. Her heavily defended shipyards were capable of turning out warships at the rate of one a day.

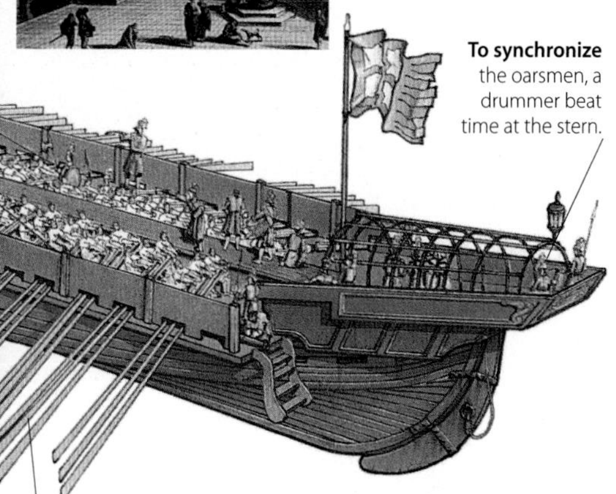

To synchronize the oarsmen, a drummer beat time at the stern.

The trireme was so named because the oars were grouped in threes. Each trireme had up to 150 oars.

Venetian Trireme

Venetian naval supremacy was based on the swift and highly manoeuvrable trireme, used to sink enemy ships by means of its pointed battering ram and its bow-mounted cannon.

Monteverdi (1567–1643)

1613 Monteverdi appointed choirmaster at Basilica San Marco

1630 Plague strikes Venice again, reducing the city's population to 102,243, its smallest for 250 years

1650

1669 Venice loses Crete to the Turks

1678 Elena Piscopia receives doctorate from Padua University, the first woman in the world ever to be awarded a degree *(p182)*

Elena Piscopia (1646–84)

1700

1703 Vivaldi joins La Pietà as musical director

1708 In a bitter winter, the lagoon freezes over and Venetians can walk to the mainland

1718 Venetian maritime empire ends with the surrender of Morea to the Turks

Glorious Decadence

No longer a major power, 18th-century Venice became a byword for decadence, as aristocratic Venetians frittered away their inherited wealth in lavish parties and gambling. All this crumbled in 1797, when the city was besieged by Napoleon, who demanded the abdication of the doge. Napoleon granted the city to his opponents, the Austrians, whose often authoritarian rule drove many people of the Veneto to join the vanguard of the revolutionary Risorgimento. This movement, led in Venice by Daniele Manin, was dedicated to creating a free and united Italy, a dream not fully realized until 1870, four years after Venice was freed from Austrian rule.

The State-Run Casino
The notorious Ridotto, open to anyone wearing a mask, closed in 1774, as many Venetians had bankrupted themselves.

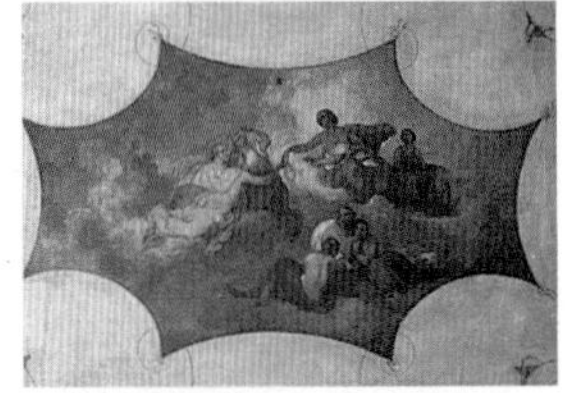

Caffè Pedrocchi
Several intellectuals who had used this lavishly decorated café *(see p182)* in Padua as their base were executed for leading a revolt against Austrian rule in 1831.

Gambling fever so gripped the city that gaming tables were set up between the columns in the Piazza.

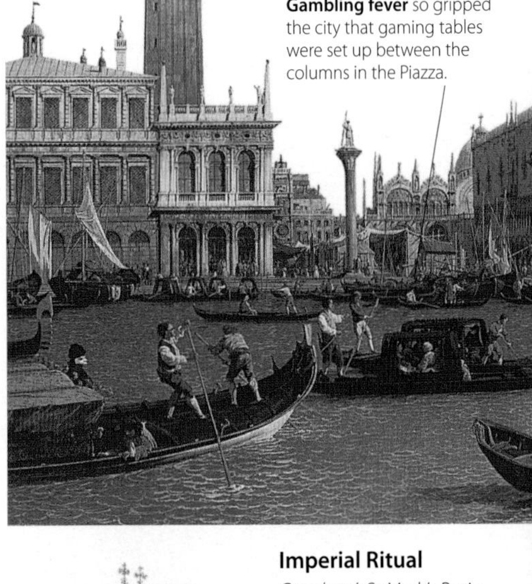

Imperial Ritual

Canaletto's St Mark's Basin on Ascension Day *(c.1733) captures the empty splendour of Venice on the eve of her demise. The doge's gold and scarlet barge has been launched for the annual ceremony of Venice's Marriage to the Sea.*

The Horses of St Mark
Among the art treasures looted by Napoleon were the Four Horses of St Mark, symbols of Venetian liberty. The horses were returned in 1815.

1720 Caffè Florian opens in Venice *(p250)*

1725 Casanova born in Venice

1752 Completion of sea walls protecting the lagoon entrances

1755 Casanova imprisoned in Doge's Palace

1775 Caffè Quadri *(p250)* opens in Venice

1789 The Dolomites named after Déodat de Dolomieu (1750–1801)

Déodat de Dolor

1720 | **1770**

Café Florian

1757 Canova, Neo-Classical sculptor, born in Venice

1790 Venetian opera house, La Fenice, opens

1797 Napoleon invades the Veneto; Doge Lodovico Manin abdicates; Venetian Republic ends

1798 Napoleon grants Venice and its territories to his Austrian allies in return for Lombardy

Antonio Vivaldi
(1678–1741)
Fashionable Venetians flocked to hear the red-haired priest's latest compositions, performed by the orphan girls of La Pietà. Vivaldi's most famous work, *The Four Seasons* (1725), was a great success throughout Europe.

Where to See 18th-Century Venice

The Museo Storico Navale *(p122)* displays a beautifully crafted model of the Bucintoro and its original banner. Vivaldi concerts are a regular feature at La Pietà church *(p116)*. Paintings by Guardi, Canaletto and Longhi capture the spirit of the age and are found in the Accademia *(pp134–7)*, Correr Museum and Ca' Rezzonico *(p130)*.

The *Bucintoro,* the doge's ceremonial barge

Sumptuary laws, passed in 1562, decreed that all Venetian gondolas must be black, to prevent lavish displays of wealth.

Fortunes were spent on opulent wigs, jewels and clothing for costume balls and the theatre. This high-heeled shoe is in the Correr Museum *(p81)*.

The comic antics of Harlequin and Pantaloon at La Fenice *(p97)* ensured the popularity of the theatre with Venetians.

No Longer an Island
Venice lost its isolation in 1846, when a causeway joined the city to the mainland and the Italian rail network.

1804 Napoleon crowned King of Italy and takes back Venice

1814–15 Austrians drive French from Venice; Congress of Vienna returns the Veneto to Austria

Daniele Manin (1804–57)

1859 Second War of Italian Independence; after Battle of Solferino, Red Cross founded

1861 Vittorio Emanuele crowned King of Italy

1820 | 1870

1818 Byron swims up the Grand Canal

Lord Byron

1846 Venetian rail causeway links the city to the mainland for the first time

1848 First Italian War of Independence; Venice revolts against Austrian rule

1849 Hunger and disease force Venetian rebels, led by Daniele Manin, to surrender

1853 Ruskin publishes *The Stones of Venice*

1866 Venice and Veneto freed from Austrian rule

Venice in Vogue

From being an introverted and unchanging city, Venice developed with remarkable speed. The opening of the Suez Canal in 1869 brought new prosperity; a new harbour was built for ocean-going ships and Venice became a favourite embarkation point for colonial administrators and rich Europeans travelling east. The fashion for sea-bathing and patronage by wealthy socialites reawakened interest in the city, and the founding of the Biennale attracted Europe's leading artists, who expressed their enthusiasm for the city in novels, paintings and music.

Peggy Guggenheim (1898–1979)
Patron of the avant garde, Peggy Guggenheim brought her outstanding art collection *(see p138)* to Venice in 1949.

Igor Stravinsky (1882–1971)
Along with Turgenev, Diaghilev and Ezra Pound, Stravinsky was one of many émigrés enchanted by the magic of Venice.

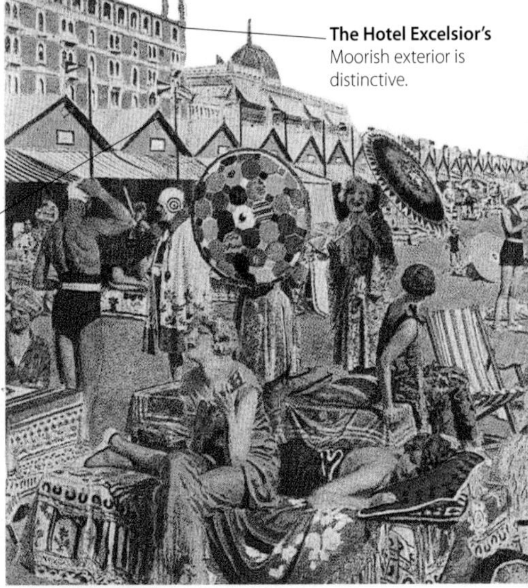

The Hotel Excelsior's Moorish exterior is distinctive.

Bathing huts, designed for modesty in the 1920s, are still a feature of the Lido.

The Lido

From the turn of the century, grand hotel developments along the sandy Adriatic shore turned the Lido into Europe's most stylish seaside resort. The island has since given its name to bathing establishments the world over.

Hotel Excelsior
When it was built in 1907, the Hotel Excelsior *(see p234)* was the world's largest hotel.

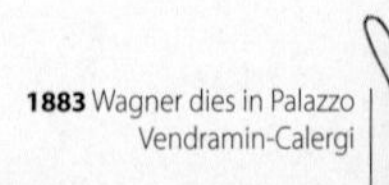

Richard Wagner (1813–83)

1870

1881 Venice becomes second-largest port in Italy after Genoa

1883 Wagner dies in Palazzo Vendramin-Calergi

1880

1889 Poet Robert Browning dies in Ca' Rezzonico

1890

1895 First Biennale art exhibition

1900

1902 Collapse of campanile in Piazza San Marco

1903 Patriarch Sarto of Venice becomes Pope Pius X

1910

1912 Opening of rebuilt campanile; Thomas Mann writes *Death in Venice*

The International Exhibition of Modern Art
Venice became a showcase for all that was new in world art and architecture when the Biennale was launched. The first exhibition, in 1895, showed work by Renoir and Monet.

Where to See Turn-of-the-Century Venice

Regular *vaporetto* services link Venice to the Lido *(p160)*, with its deluxe hotels, sports facilities and beaches. The pavilions of the Biennale *(p125)* are usually only open during the exhibition. A lift carries visitors to the top of the rebuilt Campanile *(p80)* for panoramic views of Venice.

San Michele, the cemetery isle *(p157)*, is the last resting place of eminent foreigners, such as Serge Diaghilev, Igor Stravinsky and Ezra Pound.

Residenze des Bains on the Lido *(p160)*, was formerly an exclusive hotel built in 1900 and frequented by famous people. It has been converted into private apartments, but retains its Art Deco features.

The manicured beaches of the Lido became a catwalk for style-conscious holidaymakers.

The Campanile
After the appearance of ominous warning cracks, the 1,000-year-old bell tower crashed to the ground in 1902. It was rebuilt within a decade *(see p80)*.

1917 Work starts on constructing the port of Marghera

1918 Fierce fighting in mountain passes of the Veneto in the last weeks of World War I

1920

1926 Mestre is formally granted town status

1930

1931 Venice is linked to the mainland by a road causeway

1932 First Venice Film Festival

German travel poster from 1936

1940

1943–5 Mussolini rules a puppet state, the Salò Republic

1950

1951 Stravinsky's *The Rake's Progress* premièred in Venice

1954 Britten's *Turn of the Screw* premièred in Venice

1956 Cortina d'Ampezzo hosts Winter Olympics

Olympic torch runner

1959 Patriarch Roncalli elected Pope John XXIII

1960

1960 Venice airport opens

Venice Preserved

In November 1966 Venice was hit by the worst floods in its history, sparking worldwide concern for the future of the city's delicate and decaying fabric. Major steps have since been taken to protect Venice and its unique heritage, though some difficult issues remain, including the erosion and wave damage caused by public and private waterborne craft, and pollution from the mainland. However, the allure of Venice, set in its watery lagoon, is as compelling as ever.

Pink Floyd in Venice
Pink Floyd's 1989 rock concert threatened the city's equilibrium.

Venice as Film Set
Venice has served as the backdrop to countless films, including Fellini's *Casanova* (1976) and *Indiana Jones and the Last Crusade* (1989).

The Regata Storica, held in September, is an annual trial of strength and skill for gondoliers.

Tourism
Venetian regattas are part of a rich tradition that enhances the city's attraction to tourists, providing employment for many on the mainland as well as in Venice itself. Even so, some complain that tourism has turned Venice from a living city into one vast museum.

After the Flood
During the 1966 floods, the waters rose nearly 2 m (6 ft). Great damage was done by fuel oil, washed out of broken tanks. It is now banned from the city in favour of gas.

1960

1966 Floods cause devastation in Venice. UNESCO launches its Save Venice appeal

1968 Protestors prevent part of the lagoon being drained to extend Marghera's industrial zone

1970 Luchino Visconti's film *Death in Venice*

1973 Laws passed to reduce pollution, subsidence and flooding

1975

1978 Patriarch Luciani of Venice elected Pope John Paul I, but dies 33 days later

1979 Venetian Carnival is revived

Carnival reveller

Visconti and Dirk Bogarde on the set of Death in Venice

1983 Venice officially stops sinking after extraction of underground water prohibited

1988 First experimental stage of MOSE, the lagoon flood barrier, is completed

1990

1992 Venice Film Festival celebrates 60 years

1992 Venice rocked by corruption scandals. Metro network beneath lagoon proposed

Benetton
The famous clothing firm, originating in Treviso, represents the modern face of Veneto industry.

Venice plays host to over 14 million visitors every year.

Glass Blowing
This age-old tradition still contributes to the economy.

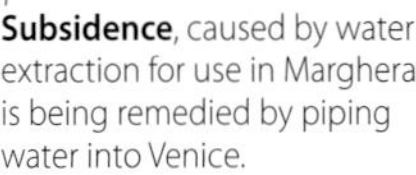

Subsidence, caused by water extraction for use in Marghera, is being remedied by piping water into Venice.

The Acqua Alta
High tides can cause floods and paralyze the city. Plans for a flood barrier across the lagoon are subject to controversy.

Restoration in Venice

One positive result of the 1966 floods was a major international appeal for funds to pay for the cleaning of historic buildings, statues and paintings. Funds raised are coordinated under the auspices of UNESCO, with offices in Venice.

Restorers learn how to repair and conserve fragile works of art at a European centre for conservation on San Servolo *(pp158–9)*.

Madonna dell'Orto *(p144)* was restored by the Italian Art and Archives Rescue Fund (later renamed Venice in Peril).

994 Voters decide against a divorce etween Venice and Mestre, which hare a mayor and city council

1995 Centenary of Biennale Exhibition

2006 Romano Prodi approves construction of the lagoon flood barrier

2010 Floods in Vicenza and Paduan plains in November cause terrible damage; half of Vicenza was under water

The fourth bridge over the Grand Canal

2005

2020

2002 Construction begins on the fourth bridge over the Grand Canal

2008 The fourth bridge over the Grand Canal opens

2013 Venice pulls out of European Capital of Culture 2019 bid, the mayor stating that it already is a capital of culture

1932–1992 Venice Film Festival poster

View over Venice rooftops ▶

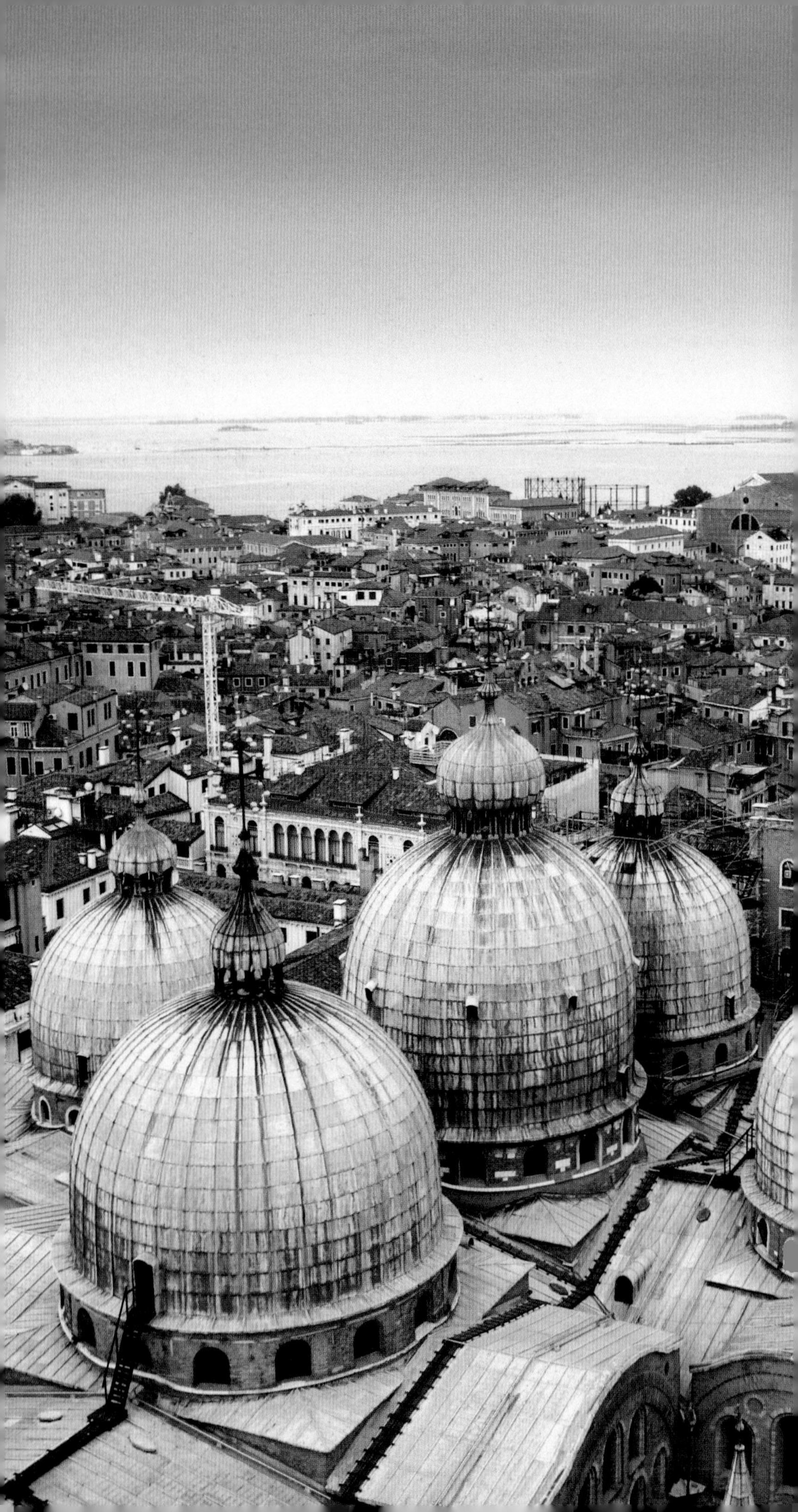

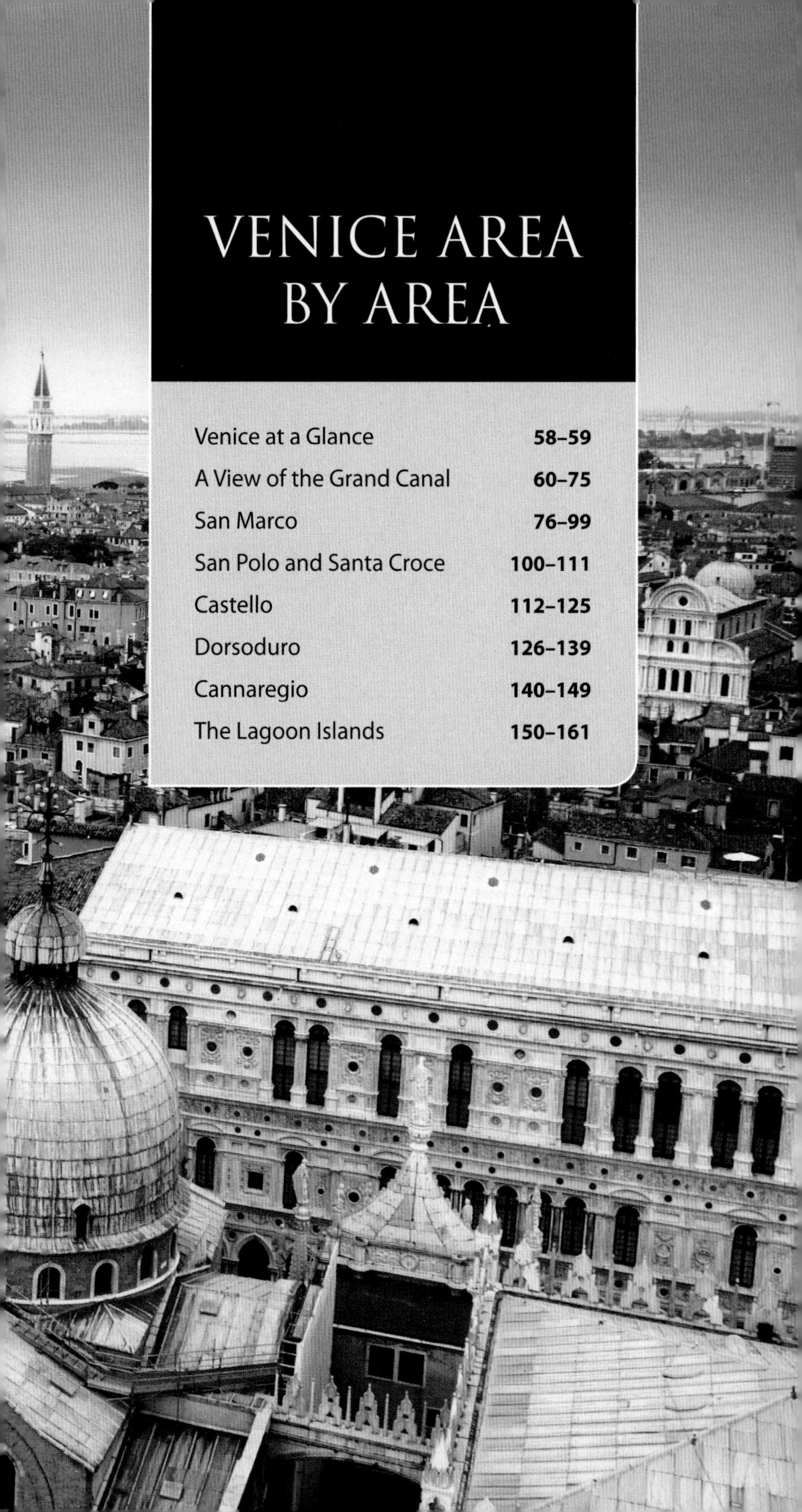

VENICE AREA BY AREA

Venice at a Glance

Venice is small and most of the sights can be comfortably visited on foot. The heart of the city is the Piazza San Marco, which is overlooked by the great Basilica and the Doge's Palace. For many, these are attractions enough, but there are delights worth exploring beyond the Piazza, such as the galleries of the Accademia, Ca' Rezzonico and the imposing Frari church. Unique to Venice are the naval Arsenale to the east and the Ghetto in the north.

Ghetto
Established in the early 16th century, this fascinating quarter was the world's first ghetto *(see p149)*.

0 metres 500
0 yards 500

CANNAREGI
(See pp140–49)

Canal Grande

SAN POLO A
SANTA CRO
(See pp100–11

Car

DORSODURO
(See pp126–39)

Santa Maria Gloriosa dei Frari
This soaring Gothic edifice, founded by the Franciscans in 1340, is a rich repository of Venetian painting and sculpture *(see pp106–7)*.

Ca' Rezzonico
The splendid rooms of this palace, overlooking the Grand Canal, are decorated with 18th-century furniture and paintings *(see p130)*.

Accademia
Carpaccio's *St Ursula* cycle (1490–95) is one of the treasures of the Accademia, which has a comprehensive collection of Venetian art *(see pp134–7)*.

Ca' d'Oro
This ornate palace is the finest example of Venetian Gothic style *(see p148)*.

Rialto Bridge
The bustling Rialto Bridge *(see p104)* was named after the ancient commercial seat of Venice, where the first inhabitants settled.

Basilica San Marco
Magnificent mosaics sheathe the domes, walls and floor of the Byzantine Basilica *(see pp82–7)*.

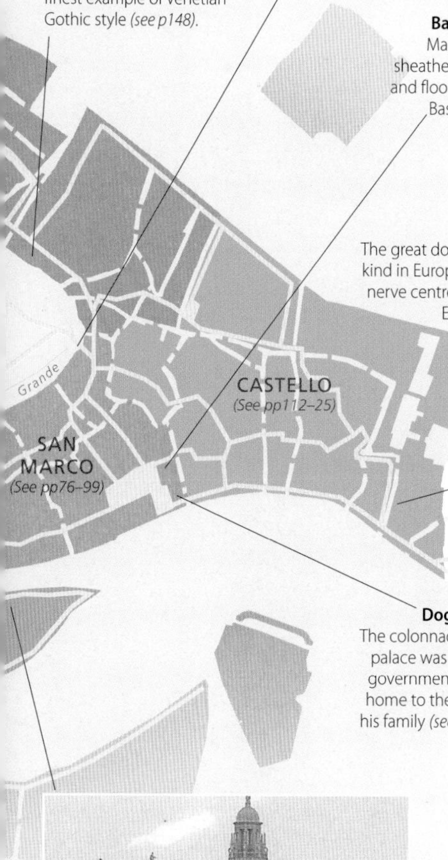

Arsenale
The great dockyard, first of its kind in Europe, was the naval nerve centre of the Venetian Empire *(see p123)*.

Grande

CASTELLO
(See pp112–25)

SAN MARCO
(See pp76–99)

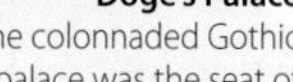

Doge's Palace
The colonnaded Gothic palace was the seat of government as well as home to the doge and his family *(see pp88–93)*.

Santa Maria della Salute
Marking the southern end of the Grand Canal, this great Baroque church is one of the city's landmarks *(see p139)*.

A VIEW OF THE GRAND CANAL

Known to the Venetians as the *Canalazzo*, the Grand Canal sweeps through the heart of Venice, following the course of an ancient riverbed. Since the founding days of the empire it has served as the city's main thoroughfare. Once used by great galleys or trading vessels making their stately way to the Rialto, it is nowadays teeming with *vaporetti*, launches, barges and gondolas. Glimpses of its glorious past, however, are never far away. The annual re-enactment of historic pageants, preserving the traditions of the Venetian Republic, brings a blaze of colour to the canal. The most spectacular is the Regata Storica held in September *(see p39)*, a huge procession of historic craft packed with crews in traditional costumes, followed by boat and gondola races down the Grand Canal.

The parade of palaces bordering the winding waterway, built over a span of around 500 years, presents some of the finest architecture of the Republic. Historically it is like a rollcall of the old Venetian aristocracy, with almost every *palazzo* bearing the name of a once-grand family. Bright frescoes may have faded, precious marbles worn, and foundations frayed with the tides, but the Grand Canal is still, to quote Charles VIII of France's ambassador in 1495, "the most beautiful street in the world".

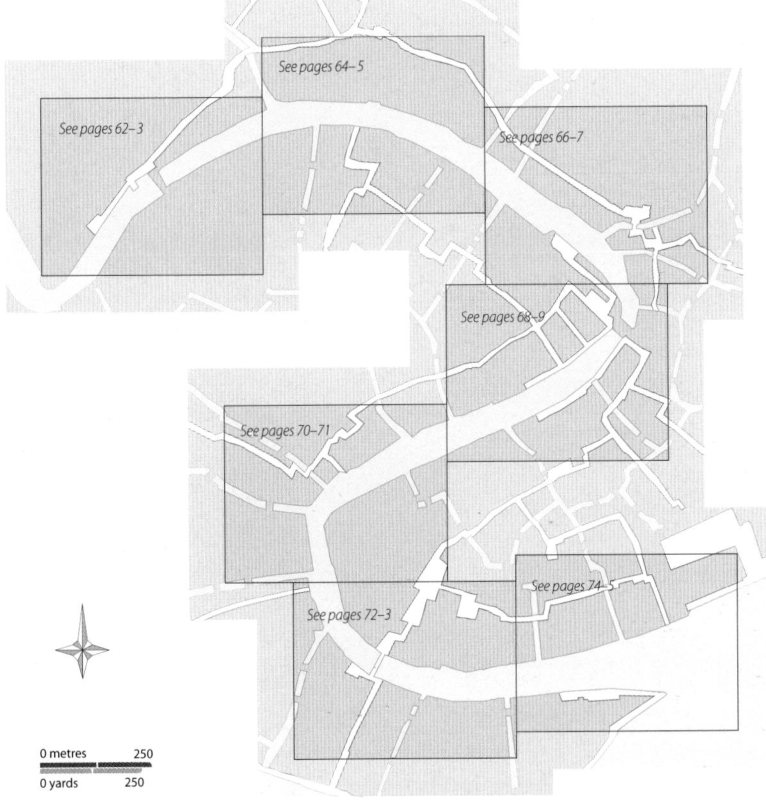

◀ The Grand Canal at its most colourful, during the Regata Storica

Santa Lucia to Palazzo Flangini

The Grand Canal is best admired from a gondola or a *vaporetto*. Several lines travel the length of the canal *(see p284)* but only the No. 1 goes slowly enough for you to take in any of the palaces. The journey from the station to San Zaccaria takes about 40 minutes. Nearly 4 km (2 miles) long, the canal varies in width from 30 to 70 m (98 to 230 ft) and is spanned by four bridges, the Scalzi, the Rialto, the Accademia and the Constituzione. The modern Constituzione bridge links Piazzale Roma and Santa Lucia station.

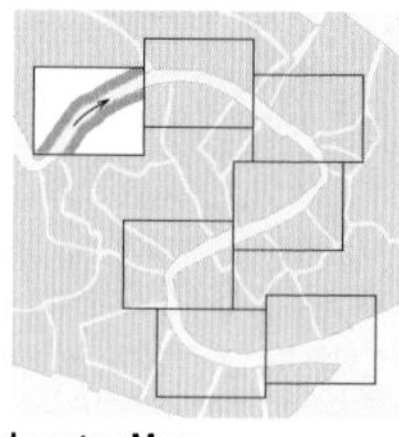

Locator Map

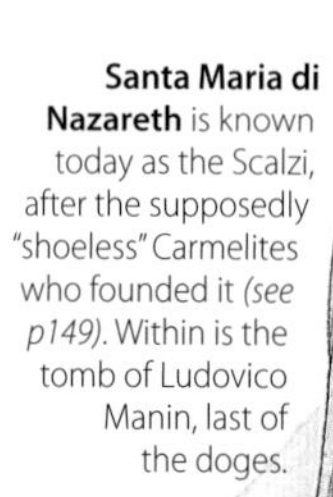

Santa Maria di Nazareth is known today as the Scalzi, after the supposedly "shoeless" Carmelites who founded it *(see p149)*. Within is the tomb of Ludovico Manin, last of the doges.

Santa Lucia railway station *(see p280)*, built in the mid-19th century and remodelled in the 1950s, links the city with the mainland.

La Direzione Compartimentale, the administration offices for the railway, was built at the same time as the station, on the site of the church of Santa Lucia and other ancient buildings.

Palazzo Diedo, also known as Palazzo Emo, is a Neo-Classical palace of the late 18th century. It is believed to be the birthplace of Angelo Emo (1731–92), the last admiral of the Venetian fleet. The palace was built by Andrea Tirali, an engineer who worked on the restoration of San Marco.

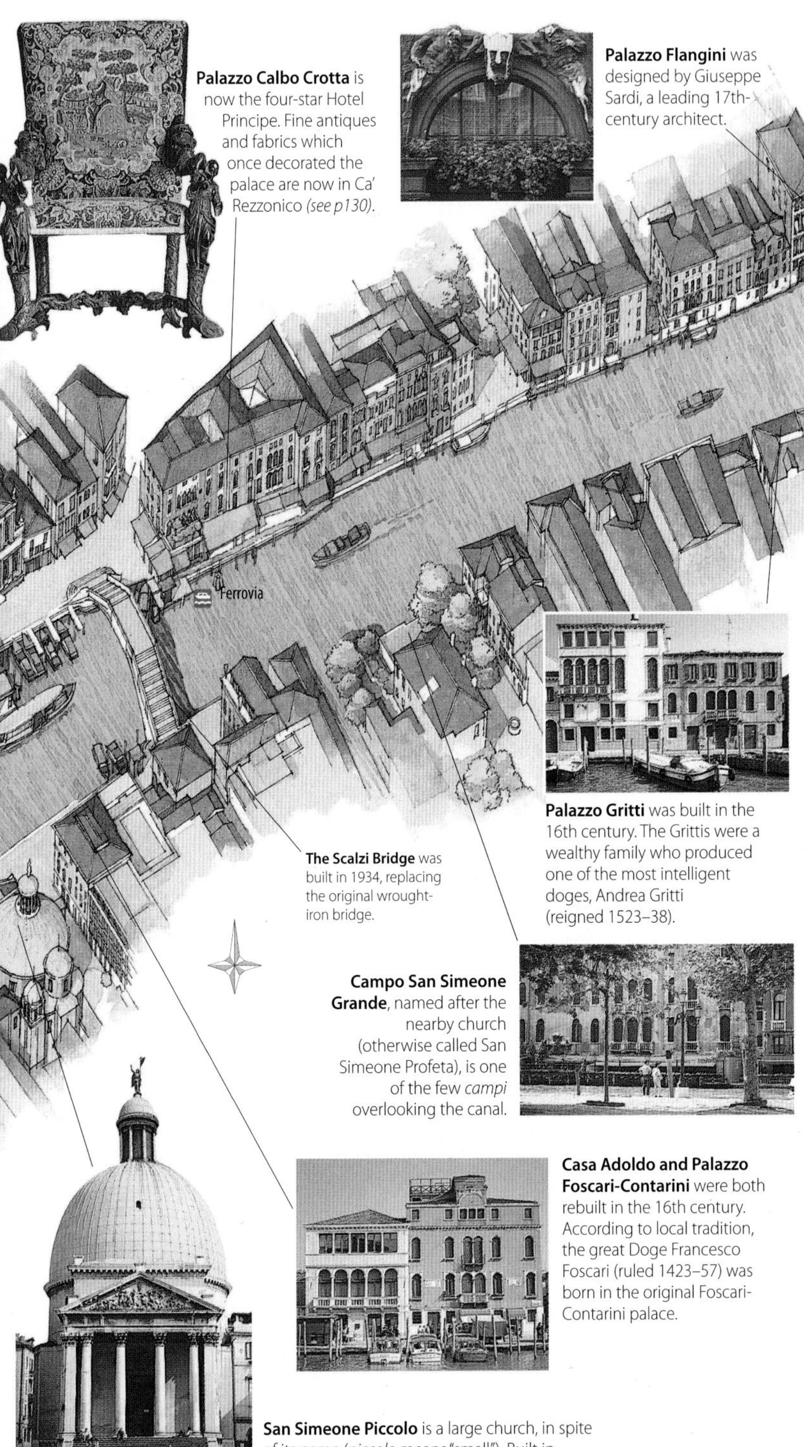

Palazzo Calbo Crotta is now the four-star Hotel Principe. Fine antiques and fabrics which once decorated the palace are now in Ca' Rezzonico *(see p130)*.

Palazzo Flangini was designed by Giuseppe Sardi, a leading 17th-century architect.

Palazzo Gritti was built in the 16th century. The Grittis were a wealthy family who produced one of the most intelligent doges, Andrea Gritti (reigned 1523–38).

The Scalzi Bridge was built in 1934, replacing the original wrought-iron bridge.

Campo San Simeone Grande, named after the nearby church (otherwise called San Simeone Profeta), is one of the few *campi* overlooking the canal.

Casa Adoldo and Palazzo Foscari-Contarini were both rebuilt in the 16th century. According to local tradition, the great Doge Francesco Foscari (ruled 1423–57) was born in the original Foscari-Contarini palace.

San Simeone Piccolo is a large church, in spite of its name (*piccolo* means "small"). Built in 1738, its design was based partly on the Pantheon in Rome. It is open for worship only.

San Geremia to San Stae

This stretch sees the start of the great palaces. The most remarkable is the Vendramin Calergi, which became a model for other Venetian palaces.

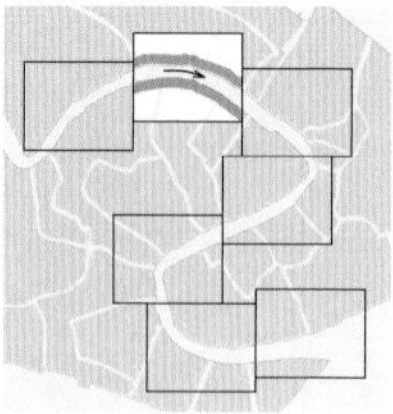

Locator Map

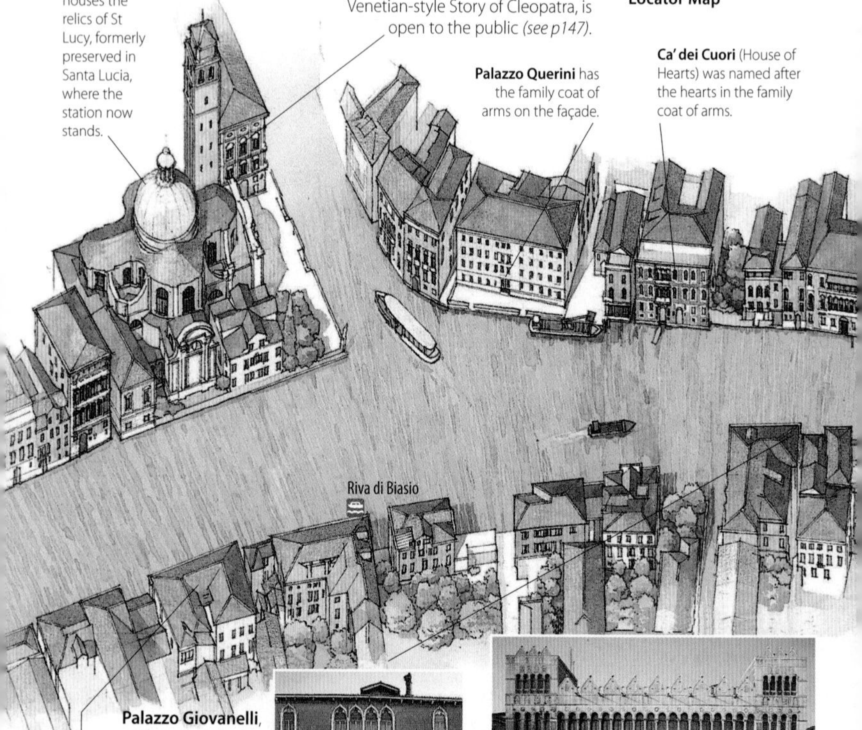

San Geremia houses the relics of St Lucy, formerly preserved in Santa Lucia, where the station now stands.

Palazzo Labia, frescoed with Tiepolo's Venetian-style Story of Cleopatra, is open to the public *(see p147)*.

Palazzo Querini has the family coat of arms on the façade.

Ca' dei Cuori (House of Hearts) was named after the hearts in the family coat of arms.

Riva di Biasio

Palazzo Giovanelli, a restored Gothic palace, was acquired by the Giovanellis in 1755. This titled non-Venetian family had been admitted into the Great Council in 1668 for a fee of 100,000 ducats.

Fondaco dei Turchi was a splendid Veneto-Byzantine building before last century's brutal restoration. Today it houses the Natural History Museum *(see p109)*.

Palazzo Donà Balbi, built in the 17th century, is named after two great Venetian families who intermarried. The Donà family produced four doges.

Deposito del Megio, a crenellated building with a reconstructed Lion of St Mark, was a granary in the 15th century.

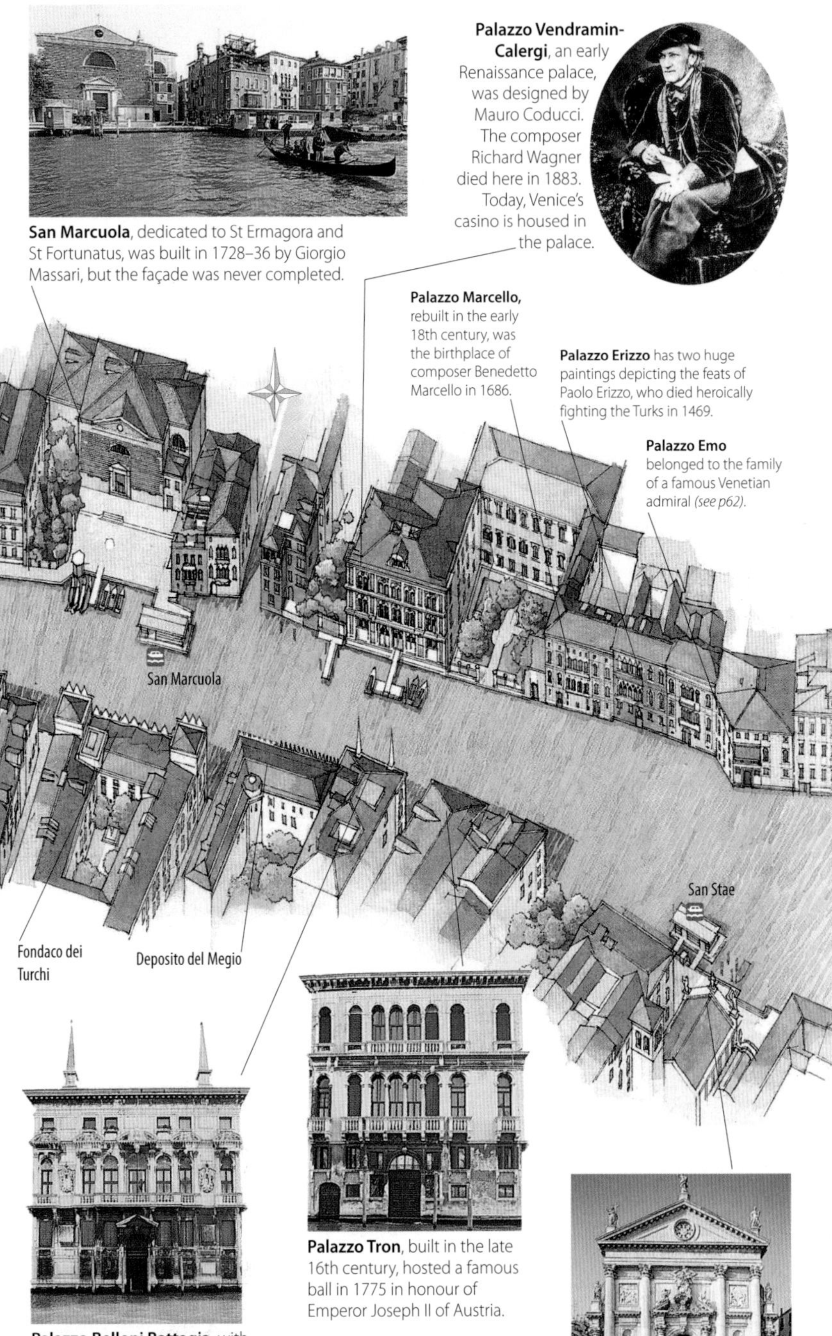

San Marcuola, dedicated to St Ermagora and St Fortunatus, was built in 1728–36 by Giorgio Massari, but the façade was never completed.

Palazzo Vendramin-Calergi, an early Renaissance palace, was designed by Mauro Coducci. The composer Richard Wagner died here in 1883. Today, Venice's casino is housed in the palace.

Palazzo Marcello, rebuilt in the early 18th century, was the birthplace of composer Benedetto Marcello in 1686.

Palazzo Erizzo has two huge paintings depicting the feats of Paolo Erizzo, who died heroically fighting the Turks in 1469.

Palazzo Emo belonged to the family of a famous Venetian admiral *(see p62)*.

Palazzo Belloni Battagia, with its distinctive pinnacles, was built by Longhena in the mid-17th century for the Belloni family, who had bought their way into Venetian aristocracy.

Palazzo Tron, built in the late 16th century, hosted a famous ball in 1775 in honour of Emperor Joseph II of Austria.

San Stae is striking for its Baroque façade, graced by marble statues. It was funded by a legacy left by Doge Alvise Mocenigo in 1709 *(see p109)*.

Palazzo Barbarigo to the Markets

Here the canal is flanked by stately palaces, built over a period of five centuries. The most spectacular is the Gothic Ca' d'Oro, whose façade once glittered with gold.

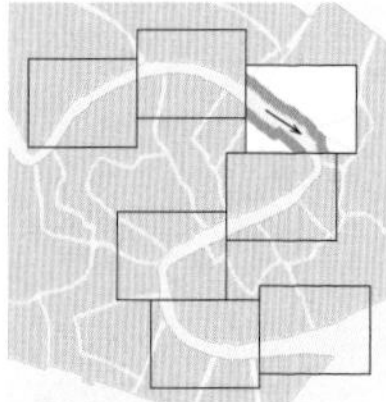

Locator Map

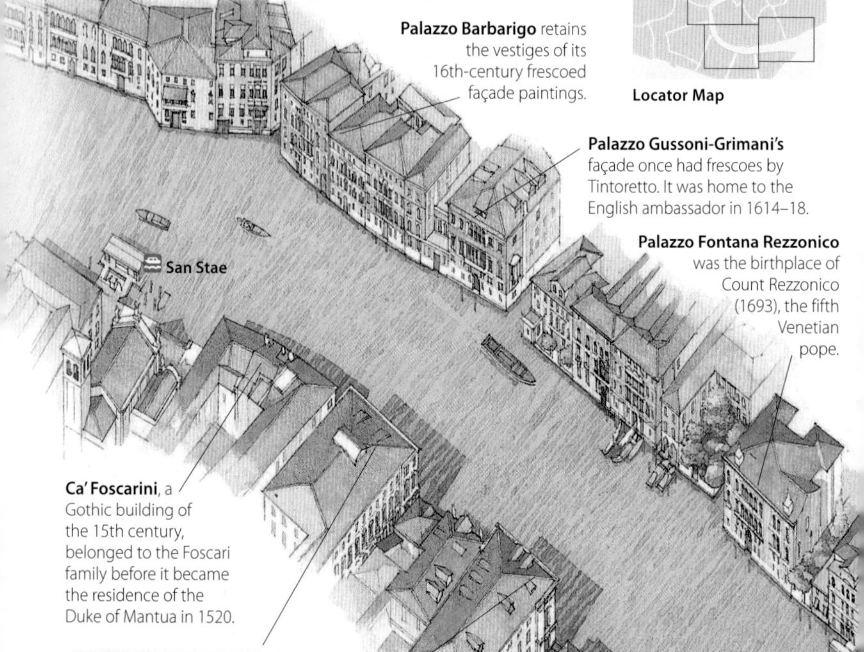

Palazzo Barbarigo retains the vestiges of its 16th-century frescoed façade paintings.

Palazzo Gussoni-Grimani's façade once had frescoes by Tintoretto. It was home to the English ambassador in 1614–18.

Palazzo Fontana Rezzonico was the birthplace of Count Rezzonico (1693), the fifth Venetian pope.

San Stae

Ca' Foscarini, a Gothic building of the 15th century, belonged to the Foscari family before it became the residence of the Duke of Mantua in 1520.

Ca' Pesaro, a huge and stately Baroque palace designed by Longhena *(see p27)*, today houses the Gallery of Modern Art and the Oriental Museum *(see p109)*. It was built for Leonardo Pesaro, a Procurator of San Marco.

Casa Favretto (Hotel San Cassiano) was the home of the painter Giacomo Favretto (1849–87).

Palazzo Morosini Brandolin belonged to the Morosini family, one of the *Case Vecchie* families, deemed to be noble before the 9th century.

Ca' Corner della Regina (1724–8) is owned by the Fondazione Prada. It houses the Prada contemporary art collection and is open during exhibitions.

The Pescheria has been the site of a busy fish market for six centuries. Today it takes place in the striking mock-Gothic market hall, built in 1907.

Ca' d'Oro, the most famous of Venetian Gothic palaces *(see p148)*, houses paintings, frescoes and sculpture from the collection of Baron Giorgio Franchetti, who bequeathed the palace and all its contents to the State.

Canaletto

Antonio Canale (Canaletto) (1697–1768) is best known for his *vedute* or views of Venice. He studied in Rome, but lived here for most of his life. One of his patrons was Joseph Smith *(see below)*. Sadly there are very few of his paintings left on view in the city.

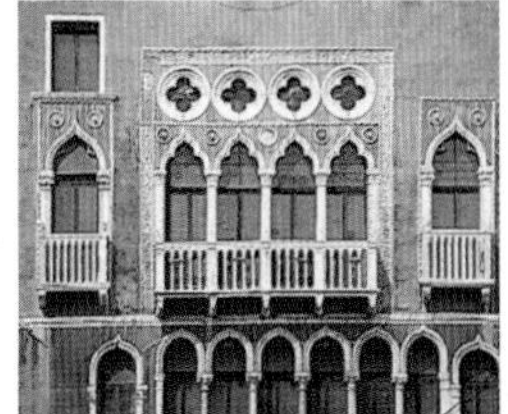

Palazzo Sagredo passed from the Morosini to the Sagredo family in the early18th century. The façade shows characteristics of both Veneto-Byzantine and Gothic styles.

Palazzo Foscarini was the home of Marco Foscarini, a diplomat, orator and scholar who rose to the position of doge in 1762.

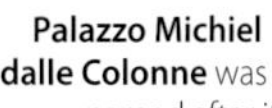

Palazzo Michiel dalle Colonne was named after its distinctive colonnade.

Palazzo Mangili Valmarana was designed by Antonio Visentini (above) in Classical style for Joseph Smith, who became the English consul in Venice. Smith (1682–1770) was a patron of both Visentini and Canaletto.

Palazzo Michiel del Brusà was rebuilt and named after the great fire *(brusà)* that swept the city in 1774.

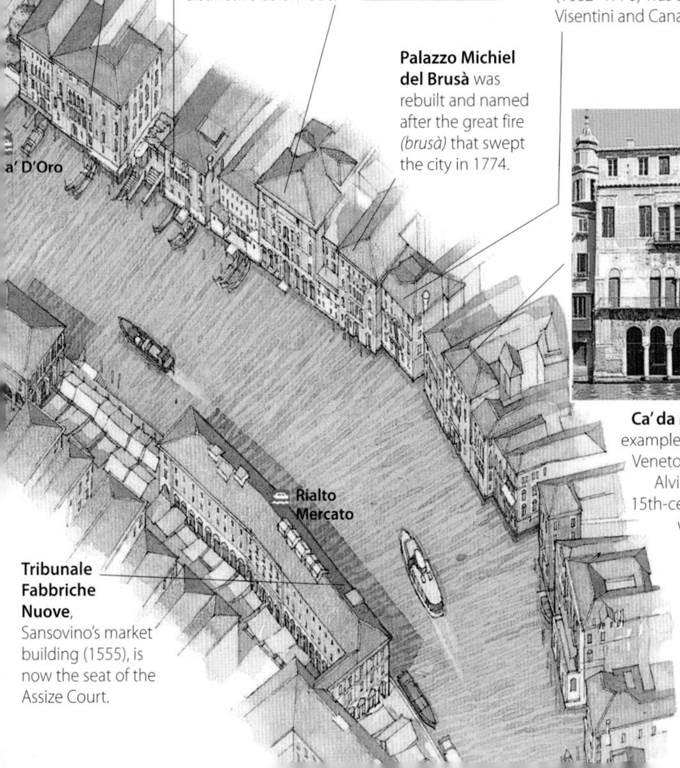

Ca' da Mosto is a good example of 13th-century Veneto-Byzantine style. Alvise da Mosto, the 15th-century navigator, was born here in 1432.

a' D'Oro

Rialto Mercato

Tribunale Fabbriche Nuove, Sansovino's market building (1555), is now the seat of the Assize Court.

The Rialto Quarter

The area around the Rialto Bridge is the oldest and busiest quarter of the city. Traditionally a centre of trade, crowded quaysides and colourful food markets still border the canal south of the bridge.

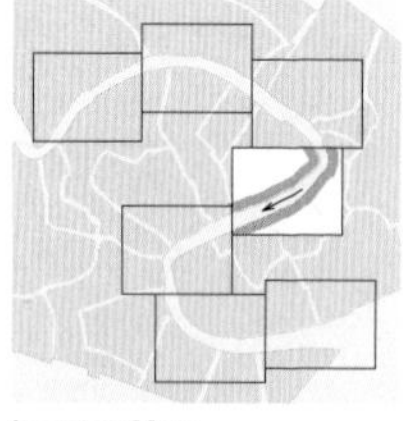

Locator Map

Palazzo Papadopoli, formerly known as Coccina-Tiepolo, was built in 1560. Although now a luxury hotel, Aman Canal Grande Venice, its splendid hall of mirrors has been preserved.

Riva del Vin is one of the few spots where you can sit and relax on the banks of the Grand Canal *(see p102)*.

Ca' Corner-Martinengo-Ravà became the Leon Bianco Hotel in the 19th century. The American writer James Fenimore Cooper stayed here in 1838.

Palazzo Barzizza, rebuilt in the 17th century, still preserves its early 13th-century façade.

Casetta Dandolo's predecessor is said to have been the birthplace of Doge Enrico Dandolo (ruled 1192–1205).

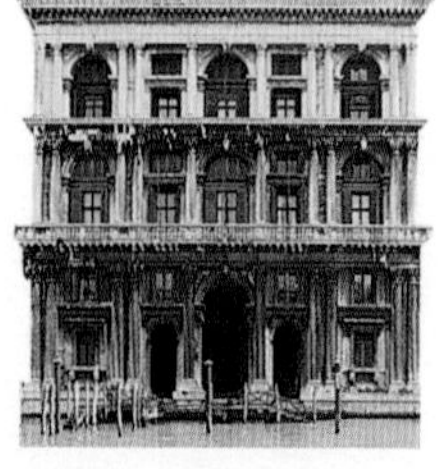

Palazzo Grimani, a fine, if somewhat austere-looking, Renaissance palace *(see p27)*, was built in 1556 by Michele Sanmicheli for the Procurator, Girolamo Grimani. The State purchased the palace in 1807 and it is now occupied by the city's Court of Appeal.

Palazzo Farsetti and Palazzo Loredan, both occupied by the City Council, were built around 1200 and finally merged in 1868. Palazzo Farsetti became an academy for young artists, one of whom was Canova.

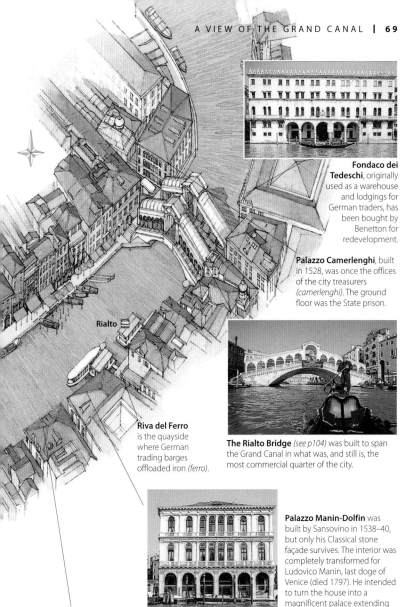

Fondaco dei Tedeschi, originally used as a warehouse and lodgings for German traders, has been bought by Benetton for redevelopment.

Palazzo Camerlenghi, built in 1528, was once the offices of the city treasurers *(camerlenghi)*. The ground floor was the State prison.

Rialto

Riva del Ferro is the quayside where German trading barges offloaded iron *(ferro)*.

The Rialto Bridge *(see p104)* was built to span the Grand Canal in what was, and still is, the most commercial quarter of the city.

Palazzo Manin-Dolfin was built by Sansovino in 1538–40, but only his Classical stone façade survives. The interior was completely transformed for Ludovico Manin, last doge of Venice (died 1797). He intended to turn the house into a magnificent palace extending as far as Campo San Salvatore.

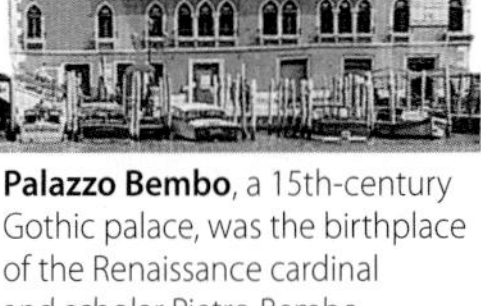

Palazzo Bembo, a 15th-century Gothic palace, was the birthplace of the Renaissance cardinal and scholar Pietro Bembo, who wrote one of the earliest Italian grammars.

The Dandolo Family

The illustrious Dandolo family produced four doges, 12 procurators of San Marco, a patriarch of Grado and a queen of Serbia. The first of the doges was Enrico, who, despite being old and blind, was the principal driving force in the Crusaders' plan to take Constantinople in 1204 *(see p46)*. The other remarkable doge in the family was the humanist and historian Andrea Dandolo (d.1354).

Doge Enrico Dandolo

La Volta del Canal

The point where the canal doubles back sharply on itself is known as La Volta – the bend. This splendid curve was long ago established as the finishing stretch for the annual Regata Storica *(see p39)*.

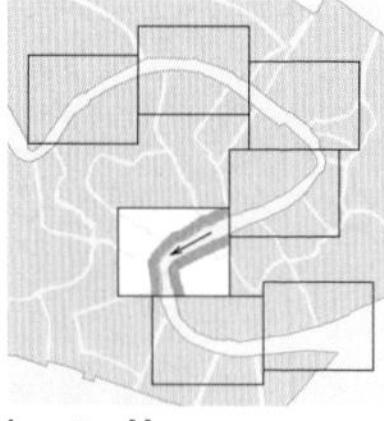
Locator Map

Palazzo Marcello, which belonged to an old Venetian family, is also called "dei Leoni" because of the lions either side of the doorway.

Palazzo Persico, on the corner of Rio San Polo, is a 16th-century house in Lombardesque style.

Palazzo Civran-Grimani is a Classical building of the early 17th century.

Palazzo Balbi, seat of the regional government, was built for Nicolò Balbi, who is said to have died of a chill surveying its construction. From here, Napoleon viewed the 1807 regatta, held in his honour.

Ca' Foscari was built for Doge Francesco Foscari in 1437 *(see p26)*. It is now part of the University of Venice.

Palazzo Giustinian was the residence of Wagner in 1858–9, when he was composing the second act of *Tristan and Isolde*.

Ca' Rezzonico, now the museum of 18th-century Venice *(see p130)*, became the home of the poet Robert Browning and his son, Pen, in 1888.

Palazzo Barbarigo della Terrazza, built in the 1560s, was known for its roof terrace. It now houses the German Institute.

Palazzo Capello-Layard was the home of Sir Austen Henry Layard, excavator of Nineveh.

Sant' Angelo

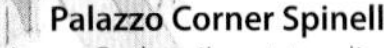

Palazzo Corner Spinelli, Mauro Coducci's outstanding Renaissance palace, built in 1490–1510, became a prototype for other mansions in Venice.

Palazzo Garzoni, a renovated Gothic palace, is now part of the university. The *traghetto* service, which links the neighbouring Calle Garzoni to San Tomà on the other side of the canal, is one of the oldest in Venice.

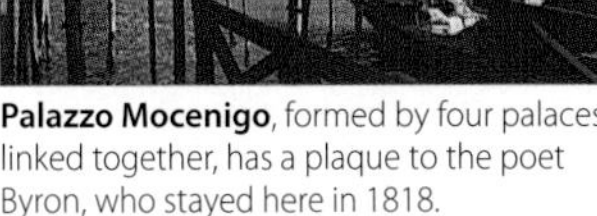

Palazzo Mocenigo, formed by four palaces linked together, has a plaque to the poet Byron, who stayed here in 1818.

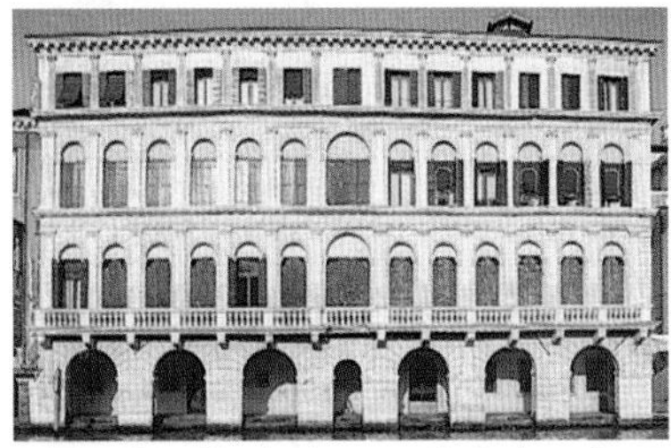

Palazzo Moro Lin, also known as the "palace of the 13 windows", was created in the 17th century for the painter Pietro Liberi by merging two Gothic houses.

Palazzo Grassi, built in the 1730s and bought by François-Henri Pinault in 2005, exhibits contemporary art.

Palazzo Capello Malipiero, a Gothic palace, was reconstructed in 1622. Beside it, in Campo di San Samuele, stands the church of San Samuele, which has a 12th-century Veneto-Byzantine campanile.

Ca' Rezzonico to the Guggenheim

This southern stretch of the canal, widening after the Accademia, is lined by a rich and varied parade of palaces.

Palazzo del Duca, planned in the 15th century as a sumptuous palace but never finished, houses a collection of porcelain.

Palazzo Falier was said to have been home to Doge Mari Falier, who was beheaded for treason in 1355 *(see p47)*.

Palazzo degli Scrigni, built in 1609, acquired its name from the coffers *(scrigni)* inherited by the Contarini in 1418.

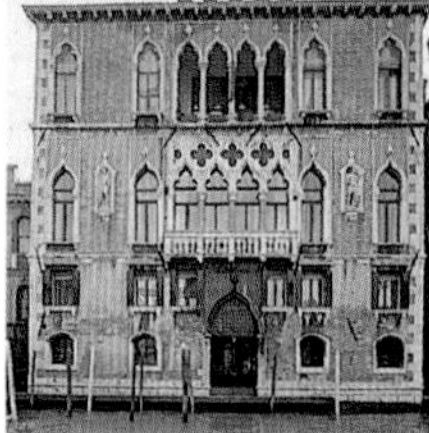

Palazzo Loredan, home of Doge Francesco Loredan (1752–62), is one of many belonging to that family.

The wooden Accademia Bridge was built in 1932 as a temporary structure to replace a 19th-century iron bridge. By popular demand it has been retained.

The Accademia galleries, within the former church, monastery and Scuola della Carità, house the world's greatest collection of Venetian paintings *(see pp134–7)*.

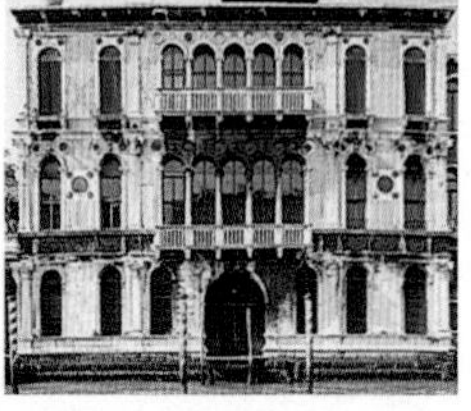

Palazzo Contarini del Zaffo, a magnificent Renaissance palace of the late 1400s, was built for a branch of the ubiquitous Contarini family. It is now owned by the Polignac family.

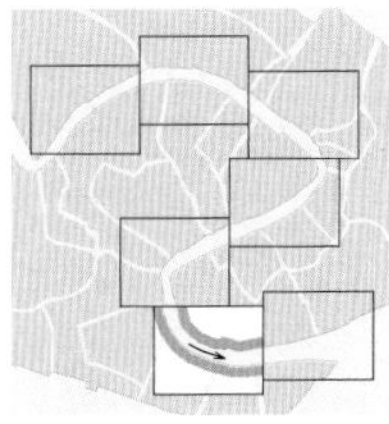

Locator Map

Ca' Grande, a huge Classical palace, was designed in 1545 by Sansovino for Giacomo Cornaro, nephew of the Queen of Cyprus. The family was one of the richest in Venice and spared no expense in the palace's decoration. This family tree illustrates the extent of the Cornaro's wealth and influence in Venice.

Palazzo Franchetti Cavalli belonged to Archduke Frederick of Austria, who died here in 1836.

Palazzo Barbaro comprises two palaces, one of which was bought by the Curtis family in 1885. Monet and Whistler painted here and Henry James (right) wrote *The Aspern Papers.*

Casetta delle Rose, one of the smallest houses on the canal, was the home of Italian poet Gabriele d'Annunzio during World War I. Canova (above) had his studio here in 1770.

Palazzo Barbarigo, beside the Campo San Vio, stands out for the harsh mosaics, added in 1887.

Peggy Guggenheim established her collection of modern art in Venice in 1951 *(see p138)*. She chose as her venue the Palazzo Venier dei Leoni, which had been built in 1749 and never finished.

Ca' Dario, built in 1487, is a charming but strangely ill-fated palace *(see pp138–9)*.

To La Salute and San Marco

The view along the final stretch of the canal is one of the finest – and most familiar – in Venice. Near the mouth rises the magnificent church of La Salute with busy St Mark's Basin beyond.

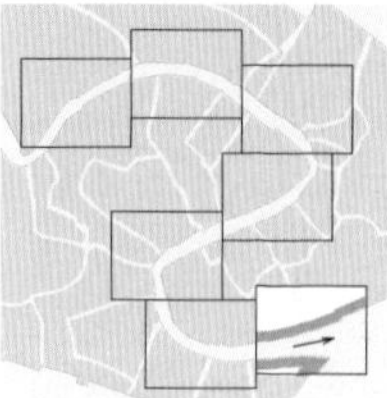

Locator Map

The Palazzo Gritti-Pisani, where Ruskin stayed in 1851, is better known today as the luxurious five-star Hotel Gritti Palace.

Palazzo Contarini Fasan, a tiny 15th-century palace with an elegant façade, is popularly known as the House of Desdemona from Shakespeare's *Othello*.

Santa Maria del Giglio

Salute

The mock-Gothic mansion, Ca' Genovese, was built in 1892 in the place of the second Gothic cloister of the San Gregorio monastery.

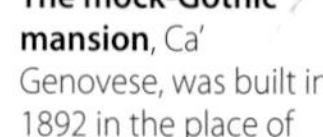

Palazzo Salviati was the headquarters of the Salviati glass-producing company, hence the glass mosaics on the façade.

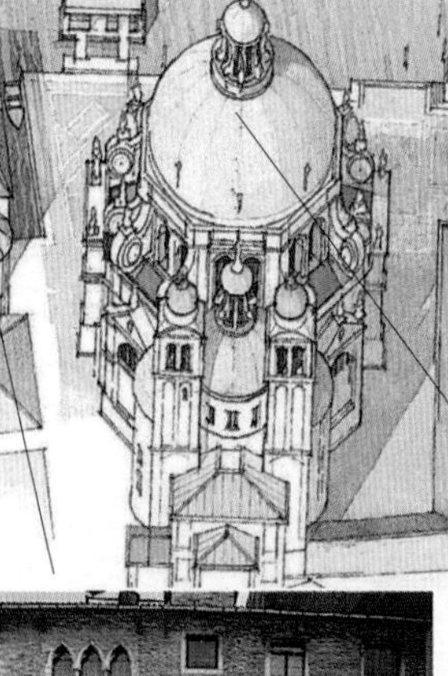

The deconsecrated Gothic brick church of Abbazia San Gregorio and a little cloister are all that survive of what was for centuries a powerful monastic centre. The church is now used as a laboratory for the renovation of large-scale paintings.

Palazzo Tiepolo, the Hotel Europa and Regina, was formerly owned by the Tiepolo family, associated with an unsuccessful uprising in 1310.

Harry's Bar *(see p96)* was popular with Hemingway and other writers. This was the very first Harry's Bar in the world.

Palazzo Giustinian, headquarters of the Biennale, used to be a hotel, where Turner, Verdi and Proust stayed.

San Marco Vallaressa

Giardinetti Reali, the Royal Gardens, were created by Napoleon to improve his view from the Procuratie Nuove.

Palazzo Treves Bonfili, a Classical building of the 17th century, is decorated with Neo-Classical frescoes, paintings and statuary.

The view from the Dogana, taking in the Doge's Palace, the Campanile of San Marco and the Zecca, is one of the most memorable in Venice.

Santa Maria della Salute, a Baroque church of monumental proportions, is supported by over a million timber piles. Built to commemorate the end of the 1630 plague, it was the work of Baldassare Longhena *(see p139)*.

The Punta della Dogana, housing an art gallery, is topped by a weathervane figure of Fortune *(see p139)*.

SAN MARCO

Home of the political and judicial nerve centres of Venice, the *sestiere* of San Marco has been the heart of Venetian life since the early days of the Republic. The great showpiece of the Serenissima was the Piazza San Marco, conceived as a vista for the Doge's Palace and the Basilica. The square, described by Napoleon as "the most elegant drawing room in Europe", was the only one deemed fit to be called a piazza – the others were merely *campi*, or fields.

The San Marco area has the bulk of luxury hotels, restaurants and shops. It is also home to several imposing churches, three theatres, including the famous Fenice, and a wealth of handsome *palazzi*. Many of these line the sweeping southern curve of the Grand Canal, which borders the *sestiere*.

Sights at a Glance

Churches

3 *Basilica San Marco pp82–7*
11 San Moisè
13 Santa Maria Zobenigo
16 Santo Stefano
18 San Salvatore
21 San Zulian

Museums and Galleries

5 Libreria Sansoviniana
6 Museo Archeologico
8 Museo Correr
17 Museo Fortuny

Palaces

4 *Doge's Palace pp88–93*
12 Palazzo Contarini del Bovolo

Historic Buildings and Monuments

1 Campanile
2 Torre dell'Orologio
7 Columns of San Marco and San Teodoro
22 San Giorgio Maggiore

Streets and Squares

15 Campo Santo Stefano
19 Campo San Bartolomeo
20 Mercerie

Bars

9 Harry's Bar

Theatres

10 Ridotto
14 La Fenice

Restaurants *see pp242–3*

1 Acqua Pazza
2 Ai Assassini
3 Ai Mercanti
4 Al Bacareto
5 Alla Caravella
6 Antico Martini
7 Bar all'Angolo
8 Bar Cavatappi
9 Bistrot de Venise
10 Centrale
11 Da Ivo
12 Da Raffaele
13 Devil's Forest Pub
14 Do Forni
15 Grand Canal
16 Harry's Bar
17 Osteria Da Carla
18 Osteria Enoteca San Marco
19 Ristorante alla Borsa
20 Ristorante Quadri
21 Rosso Pomodoro
22 Rosticceria San Bartolomeo

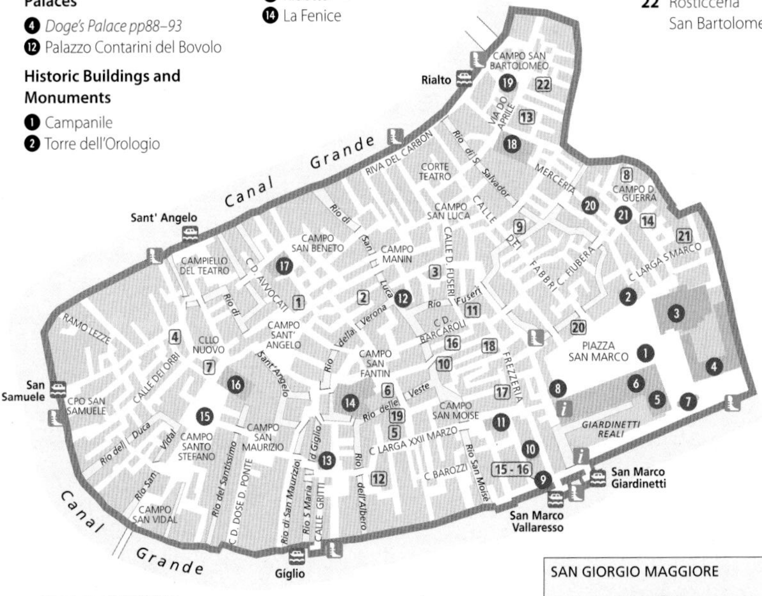

Canal Grande
Sant' Angelo
San Samuele
Giglio
0 metres 250
0 yards 250

See also Street Finder maps 6, 7

◀ Splendid mosaics inside the domes of Basilica San Marco

Street-by-Street: Piazza San Marco

Throughout its long history the Piazza San Marco has witnessed pageants, processions, political activities and countless Carnival festivities. Tourists flock here in their thousands, for the Piazza's eastern end is dominated by two of the city's most important historical sights – the Basilica and the Doge's Palace. In addition to these magnificent buildings there is plenty to entertain, with elegant cafés, open-air orchestras and smart boutiques beneath the arcades of the Procuratie. So close to the waters of the lagoon, the Piazza is one of the first points in the city to suffer at *acqua alta* (high tide). Tourists and Venetians alike can then be seen picking their way across the duckboards which are set up to crisscross the flooded square.

Gondolas Traditionally gondolas have moored in the Bacino Orseolo, named after Doge Orseolo.

Quadri's café was the favourite haunt of Austrian troops during the Occupation *(see p250)*.

8 Museo Correr
Giovanni Bellini's *Pietà* (1455–60) is one of many Renaissance masterpieces hanging in the picture galleries of the Correr.

PROCURATIE VECCHIE

PIAZZA SAN MARCO

PROCURATIE NUOVE

The Ala Napoleonica is the most recent wing enclosing the square, built by Napoleon to create a new ballroom.

Caffè Florian *(see p250)* was the favourite haunt of 19th-century literary figures such as Byron, Dickens and Proust.

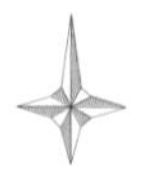

The Giardinetti Reali (royal gardens) were laid out in the early 19th century.

San Marco Vallaresso

0 metres 75

0 yards 75

2 Torre dell'Orologio
The Madonna on the clock tower is greeted each Epiphany and Ascension by clockwork figures of the Magi.

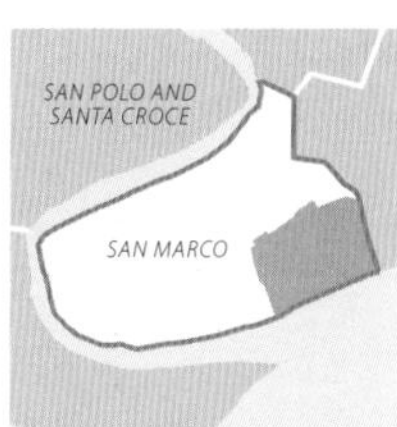

Locator Map
See Street Finder, map 7

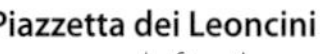

Piazzetta dei Leoncini was named after the pair of porphyry lions which stand in the square.

3 ★ Basilica San Marco
The remarkable Basilica of St Mark is a glorious reflection of the city's Byzantine connection.

4 ★ Doge's Palace
Once the Republic's seat of power and home to its rulers, the Doge's Palace, beside the Basilica, is a triumph of Gothic architecture.

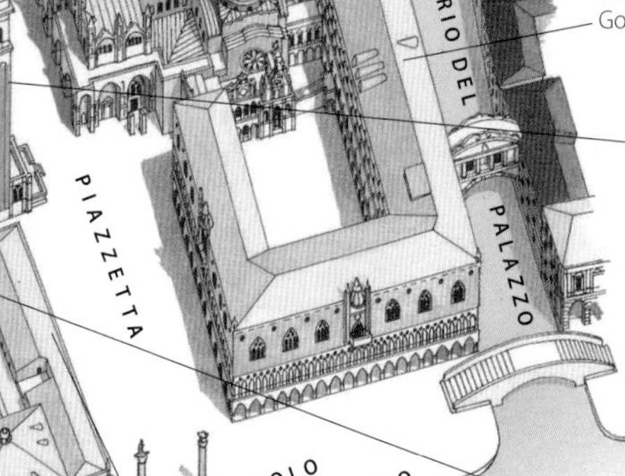

1 ★ Campanile
Today's tower replaced the one that collapsed in 1902. The top provides spectacular views of the city.

7 Columns of San Marco and San Teodoro
The columns marked the main entrance to Venice when the city could be reached only by sea.

San Marco Giardinetti

6 Museo Archeologico
The museum sculptures had a marked influence on Venetian Renaissance artists.

The Zecca, designed by Sansovino, was the city mint until 1870, and gave its name to the *zecchino* or Venetian ducat. It houses the Biblioteca Marciana.

5 Libreria Sansoviniana
The ornate vaulting of the magnificent library stairway is decorated with frescoes and gilded stucco.

❶ Campanile

Piazza San Marco. **Map** 7 B2. **Tel** 041 270 83 11. San Marco. **Open** daily. Nov–Easter: 9:30am–3:45pm (to 4:45pm Sat & Sun); Easter–Oct: 9am–7pm (Jul–Sep: to 9pm).
basilicasanmarco.it

From the top of St Mark's campanile, high above the Piazza, visitors can enjoy sublime views of the city, the lagoon and, visibility permitting, the peaks of the Alps. It was from this viewpoint that Galileo demonstrated his telescope to Doge Leonardo Donà in 1609. To do so, he would have climbed the internal ramp. Access today is via a lift for which there is usually a queue. Visitors at the top of the tower on the hour should note that the five bells ring quite loudly.

The first tower, completed in 1173, was built as a lighthouse to assist navigators in the lagoon. In the Middle Ages, it took on a less benevolent role as the support for a torture cage where offenders were imprisoned and in some cases left to die. The tower's present appearance dates from the early 16th century, when it was restored by Bartolomeo Bon after an earthquake.

The tower survived the vicissitudes of time until 14 July 1902, when its foundations gave way and it collapsed. The only casualties were the Loggetta at the foot of the tower and the custodian's cat. The following year, with the help of many donations, the foundation stone was laid for a campanile *"dov'era e com'era"* ("where it was and how it was"). The new tower was opened on 25 April (St Mark's Day) 1912. Due to small structural shifts, work has begun to reinforce the foundations. There is no known end date for the work.

The spire, 98.5 m (323 ft) high, is topped with a golden weathervane designed by Bartolomeo Bon.

The five bells in the tower each had their role during the Republic. The *marangona* tolled the start and end of the working day; the *malefico* warned of an execution; the *nona* rang at noon; the *mezza terza* summoned senators to the Doge's Palace; and the *trottiera* announced a session of the Great Council.

An internal lift, installed in 1962, provides visitors with access to one of the most spectacular views across Venice.

The Loggetta was built in the 16th century by Jacopo Sansovino. Its Classical sculptures celebrate the glory of the Republic.

The allegorical reliefs from Verona depict Justice representing Venice, Jupiter as Crete and Venus as Cyprus. All were carefully rebuilt after the Campanile's collapse in 1902.

The highly ornamented clock face of the Torre dell'Orologio

❷ Torre dell'Orologio

Piazza San Marco. **Map** 7 B2. **Tel** 848 082 000. San Marco. **Open** 10 & 11am Mon–Wed, 2 & 3pm Thu–Sun for prebooked tours in English. **Closed** 1 Jan, 25 Dec.
torreorologio.visitmuve.it

The richly decorated Renaissance clock tower stands on the north side of the Piazza, over the archway leading to the Mercerie *(see p99)*. It was built in the late 15th century, and the central section is thought to have been designed by Mauro Coducci. Displaying the phases of the moon and the zodiac, the gilt and blue enamel clock was originally designed with seafarers in mind. A story was spread by scandalmongers that, once the clock was complete, the two inventors of the complex clock mechanism had their eyes gouged out to prevent them from ever creating a replica.

During Ascension week and Epiphany, the clock draws large crowds, who watch the figures of the Magi emerge from side doors to pay their respects to the Virgin and Child, whose figures are set above the clock. At the very top are two huge bronze figures, known as the *Mori*, or Moors, which strike the bell on the hour.

❸ Basilica San Marco

See pp82–7.

❹ Doge's Palace

See pp88–93.

❺ Libreria Sansoviniana

Piazzetta (entrance Ala Napoleonica). **Map** 7 B3. **Tel** 041 240 72 11 (Biblioteca Marciana). San Marco. **Open** 10am–5pm daily. **Closed** public hols.

Praised by Andrea Palladio as the finest building since antiquity, the library was designed in the Classical style by the architect Jacopo Sansovino. During construction (1537–88) the vaulting collapsed; Sansovino was blamed and imprisoned. He was freed after appeals from eminent acquaintances, but had to reconstruct the building at his own expense.

At the top of the monumental stairway *(see p79)*, behind a booth, is a rare example of Jacopo de' Barbari's bird's-eye map of Venice dating to 1500.

The salon is sumptuously decorated and features two fine ceiling paintings by Paolo Veronese, *Arithmetic and Geometry* and *Music*.

❻ Museo Archeologico

Piazzetta (9am–7pm: entrance Ala Napoleonica). **Map** 7 B3. **Tel** 041 296 76 63. San Marco. **Open** 10am–7pm daily (Nov–Mar: to 5pm). **Closed** 1 Jan, 25 Dec.

Housed in rooms in both the Libreria Sansoviniana and the Procuratie Nuove, the museum provides a quiet retreat from the bustle of San Marco. The collection owes its existence to the generosity of Domenico Grimani, son of Doge Antonio Grimani, who bequeathed all of his Greek, Roman and earlier sculpture, together with his library, to the State in 1523.

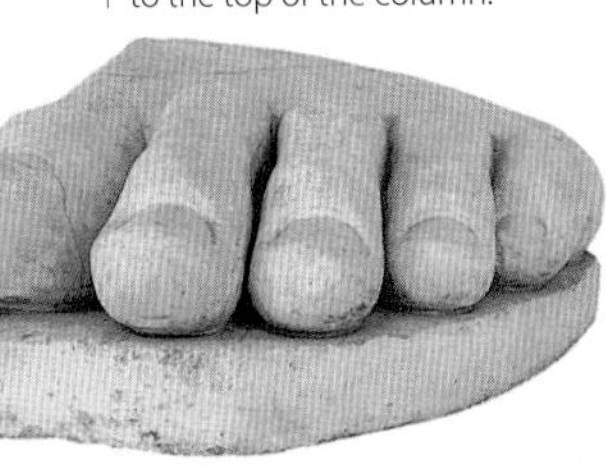

Fragment from a monumental statue, in the Museo Archeologico

❼ Columns of San Marco and San Teodoro

Piazzetta. **Map** 7 C3. San Marco.

Along with all the bounty from Constantinople came the two huge granite columns which now tower above the Piazzetta. These were said to have been erected in 1172 by the engineer Nicolò Barattieri, architect of the very first Rialto Bridge. For his efforts he was granted the right to set up gambling tables between the columns. A more gruesome spectacle on the same spot was the execution of criminals, which took place here until the mid-18th century. Even today, superstitious Venetians will not be seen walking between the columns.

Columns of San Marco and San Teodoro

The western column is crowned by a marble statue of St Theodore, who was the patron saint of Venice before St Mark's relics were smuggled from Alexandria in AD 828. The statue is a modern copy – the original is kept for safety in the Doge's Palace *(see p92)*.

The second column is surmounted by a huge bronze of the Lion of St Mark. Its origin remains a mystery, though it is thought to be a Chinese chimera with wings added to make it look like a Venetian lion. In September 1990 the 3,000-kg (3-ton) beast went to the British Museum in London for extensive restoration, and was returned with great ceremony and skill to the top of the column.

A Portrait of a Young Man in a Red Hat by Carpaccio (c.1490)

❽ Museo Correr

Procuratie Nuove (entrance Ala Napoleonica). **Map** 7 B2. **Tel** 041 240 52 11. San Marco. **Open** 10am–7pm daily (Nov–Mar: to 5pm). **Closed** 1 Jan, 25 Dec. allows access to Libreria Sansoviniana & Museo Archeologico. **correr.visitmuve.it**

The wealthy Abbot Teodoro Correr's collection of works of art and documents forms the nucleus of the civic museum.

The first rooms form a suitably Neo-Classical backdrop for early statues by Antonio Canova (1757–1822). The rest of the floor covers the history of the Venetian Republic, with maps, coins, armour and a host of doge-related exhibits.

On the second floor, the Museo del Risorgimento is devoted to the history of the city, until Venice became part of unified Italy in 1866. Also here is the Quadreria, or picture gallery. The paintings are hung chronologically and the rooms have the bonus of explanations in English. The collection enables you to trace the evolution of Venetian painting, and to see the influence that Ferrarese, Paduan and Flemish artists had on the Venetian school. The most famous works in the gallery are the Carpaccios: *A Portrait of a Young Man in a Red Hat* (c.1490) and *Two Venetian Ladies* (c.1507). The latter is traditionally, but probably incorrectly, known as *The Courtesans* because of the ladies' décolleté dresses.

❸ Basilica San Marco

This awesome Basilica, built on a Greek cross plan and crowned with five huge domes, is the third church to stand on this site. The first, built to enshrine the body of St Mark in the 9th century, was destroyed by fire. The second was pulled down in the 11th century in order to make way for a more spectacular edifice designed by an unknown architect (1063–94), reflecting the escalating power of the Republic. The basilica continued to be remodelled over the following centuries, and in 1807 it succeeded San Pietro in the *sestiere* of Castello *(see p124)* as the cathedral of Venice; it had until then served as the doge's private chapel for State ceremonies.

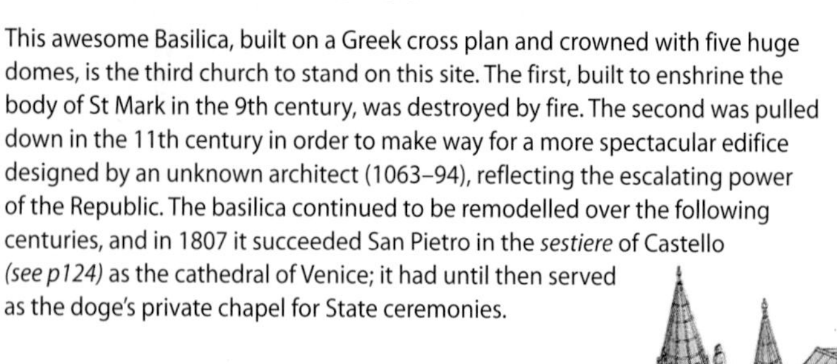

★ Horses of St Mark
The four horses are replicas of the gilded bronze originals *(see p86)*, now protected inside the Basilica.

★ Central Doorway Carvings
The central arch features 13th-century carvings of the Labours of the Month. The grape harvester represents September.

★ Façade Mosaics
A 17th-century mosaic shows the smuggling out of Alexandria of St Mark's body, reputedly under slices of pork to deter prying Muslims.

KEY

① **The Pentecost Dome**, showing the Descent of the Holy Ghost as a dove, was probably the first dome to be decorated with mosaics.

② **The Ascension Dome** features a magnificent 13th-century mosaic of Christ surrounded by angels, the 12 Apostles and the Virgin Mary.

③ **St Mark's body**, believed lost in the fire of AD 976, supposedly reappeared when the new church was consecrated in 1094. The remains are housed in the altar.

④ **Allegorical mosaics**

⑤ **St Mark's Treasury**

⑥ **The so-called Pilasters of Acre** in fact came from a 6th-century church in Constantinople.

⑦ **Baptistry**

St Mark and Angels
The statues crowning the central arch are additions from the early 15th century.

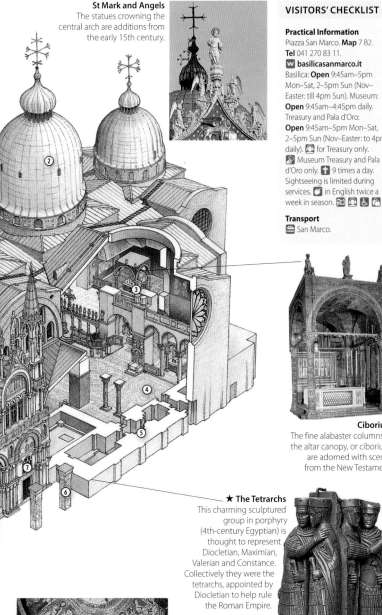

VISITORS' CHECKLIST

Practical Information
Piazza San Marco. **Map** 7 B2.
Tel 041 270 83 11.
basilicasanmarco.it
Basilica: **Open** 9:45am–5pm Mon–Sat, 2–5pm Sun (Nov–Easter: till 4pm Sun). Museum: **Open** 9:45am–4:45pm daily. Treasury and Pala d'Oro: **Open** 9:45am–5pm Mon–Sat, 2–5pm Sun (Nov–Easter: to 4pm daily). for Treasury only. Museum Treasury and Pala d'Oro only. 9 times a day. Sightseeing is limited during services. in English twice a week in season.

Transport
San Marco.

Ciborium
The fine alabaster columns of the altar canopy, or ciborium, are adorned with scenes from the New Testament.

★ The Tetrarchs
This charming sculptured group in porphyry (4th-century Egyptian) is thought to represent Diocletian, Maximian, Valerian and Constance. Collectively they were the tetrarchs, appointed by Diocletian to help rule the Roman Empire.

Baptistry Mosaics
Herod's Banquet (1343–54) is one of the mosaics in a cycle of scenes from the life of St John the Baptist.

Inside the Basilica

Dark, mysterious and enriched with the spoils of conquest, the Basilica is a unique blend of Eastern and Western influences. This Oriental extravaganza, embellished over a period of six centuries with fabulous mosaics, marble and carvings, made a fitting location for the ceremonies of the Serene Republic. It was here that the doge was presented to the city following his election, that heads of state, popes, princes and ambassadors were received, and where sea captains came to pray for protection before embarking on epic voyages.

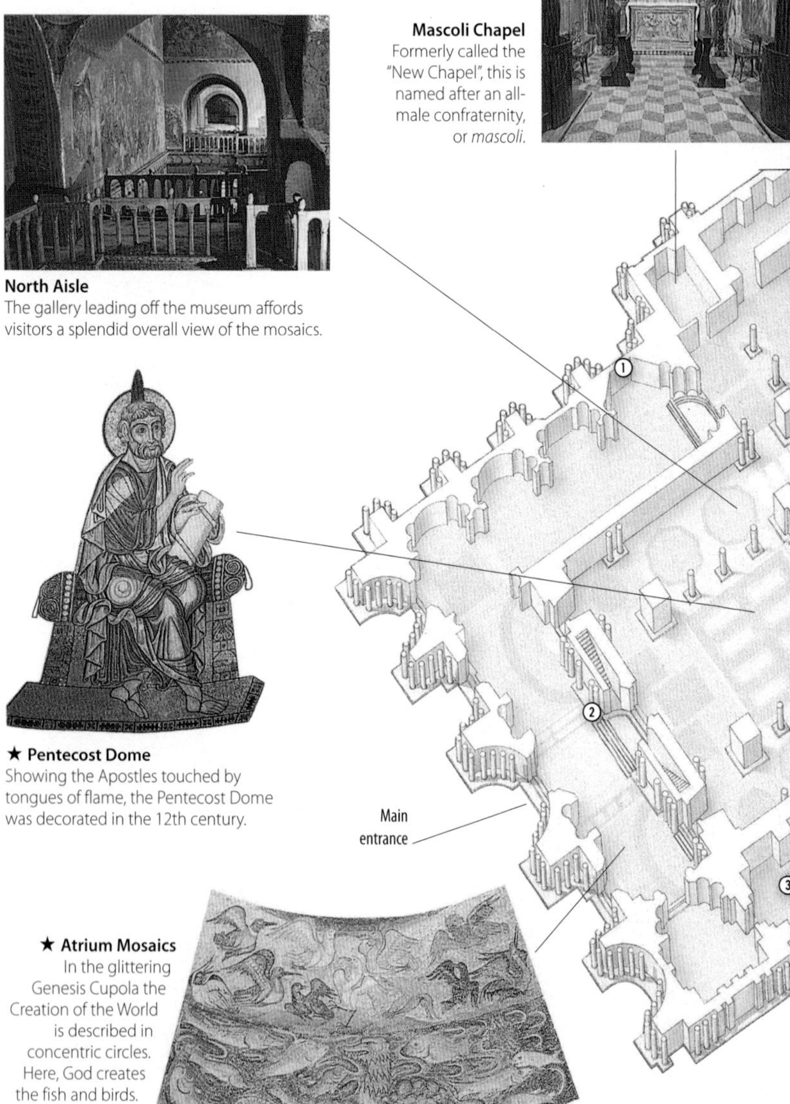

Mascoli Chapel
Formerly called the "New Chapel", this is named after an all-male confraternity, or *mascoli*.

North Aisle
The gallery leading off the museum affords visitors a splendid overall view of the mosaics.

★ Pentecost Dome
Showing the Apostles touched by tongues of flame, the Pentecost Dome was decorated in the 12th century.

★ Atrium Mosaics
In the glittering Genesis Cupola the Creation of the World is described in concentric circles. Here, God creates the fish and birds.

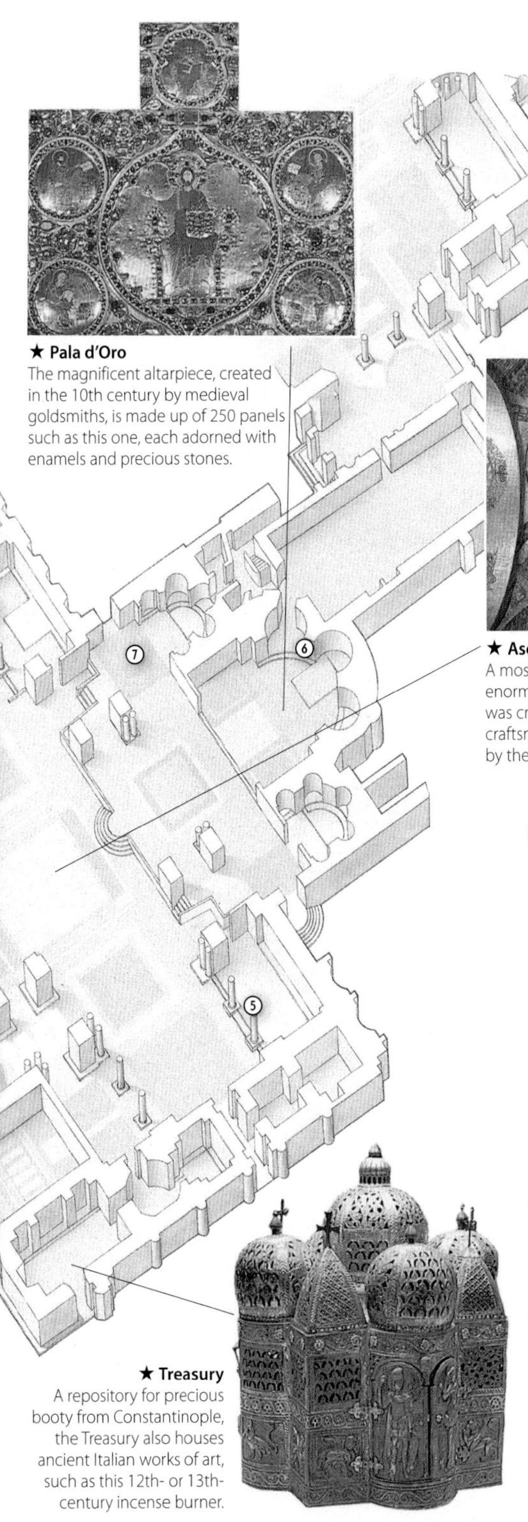

★ Pala d'Oro
The magnificent altarpiece, created in the 10th century by medieval goldsmiths, is made up of 250 panels such as this one, each adorned with enamels and precious stones.

★ Ascension Dome
A mosaic of Christ in Glory decorates the enormous central dome. This masterpiece was created by 13th-century Venetian craftsmen, who were strongly influenced by the art and architecture of Byzantium.

★ Treasury
A repository for precious booty from Constantinople, the Treasury also houses ancient Italian works of art, such as this 12th- or 13th-century incense burner.

KEY

① **The Porta dei Fiori**, or Gate of Flowers, is decorated with 13th-century reliefs.

② **The columns** of the inner façade are thought to be fragments of the first basilica.

③ **The Baptistry** is also called Chiesa dei Putti (Church of the Cherubs).

④ **South aisle**

⑤ **The Altar of the Sacrament** is surrounded by mosaics of the parables and miracles of Christ dating from the late 12th or early 13th century.

⑥ **The sacristy door** (always locked) has fine bronze panels by Sansovino, including portraits of himself with Titian and Aretino.

⑦ **The Chapel of St Peter** has a 14th-century altar screen relief of St Peter worshipped by two Procurators.

⑧ **The Altar of the Virgin** has a 10th-century icon of the Madonna of Nicopeia, which came with the spoils of war in 1204 *(see p46)*.

Exploring the Basilica

The Basilica cannot comfortably be covered in one visit. The mosaics, the rich store of eastern bounty, the mysterious lighting and the sheer size of the place create a feeling of confusion for first-time visitors. Make several visits, ideally at different times of the day. The mosaics look especially splendid when the church is fully illuminated (11:30am–12:30pm Mon–Fri, 11:30am–4pm Sat, 2–4pm Sun). Visitors with organized tours are often led towards the Pala d'Oro and Treasury and miss out on other sections of the church. Avoid the crowds by visiting early in the morning or in the evening. If a Mass is in progress, visitors are expected to be silent and will only be able to visit certain areas.

The Genesis Cupola of the atrium

Mosaics

Clothing the domes, walls and floor of the basilica are over 4,000 sq m (40,000 sq ft) of gleaming golden mosaics. The earliest, dating from the 12th century, were the work of mosaicists from the east. Their techniques were adopted by Venetian craftsmen who gradually took over the decoration, combining Byzantine inspiration with Western influences. During the 16th century, sketches and cartoons by Tintoretto, Titian, Veronese and other leading artists were reproduced in mosaic. The original iconographical scheme, depicting stories from the Testaments, has more or less been preserved by careful restoration.

Among the finest mosaics in the basilica are those decorating the 13th-century central Dome of the Ascension and the 12th-century Dome of the Pentecost over the nave.

The *pavimento*, or basilica floor, spreads out like an undulating Turkish carpet. Mosaics, made of marble, porphyry and glass, are used to create complex and colourful geometric patterns and beautiful scenes of beasts and birds. Some of these scenes are allegorical. The one in the left transept of two cocks carrying a fox on a stick was designed to symbolize cunning vanquished by vigilance.

Atrium (Vestibule)

The 13th-century mosaics decorating the cupolas, vaults and lunettes of the atrium are among the finest in the Basilica. The scenes depict Old Testament stories, starting at the southern end with the Genesis Cupola (showing 26 detailed episodes of the Creation), to the Stories of Joseph and of Moses in the domes at the north end. The figures of saints on either side of the main doorway date from the 11th century and are among the earliest mosaics in the church. Just in front of the central doorway there is a lozenge of porphyry to mark the spot where the Emperor Frederick Barbarossa was obliged to make peace with Pope Alexander III in 1177 *(see p45)*.

Museo Marciano

A precarious stairway from the atrium, marked *"Loggia dei Cavalli"*, takes you up to the church museum. The gallery gives a splendid view into the Basilica, while from the exterior loggia visitors can survey the Piazza San Marco and take a closer look at the replica horses on the church façade. It was from this panoramic balcony that doges and dignitaries once looked down on ceremonies taking place in the square. The original gilded bronze horses, housed in a room at the far end of the museum, were stolen from the top of the Hippodrome (ancient racecourse) in Constantinople in 1204, but their origin, either Roman or Hellenistic, remains a mystery. In the same room is Paolo Veneziano's 14th-century *pala feriale*, painted with stories of St Mark, which once covered the Pala d'Oro. Also on show are medieval illuminated manuscripts, fragments of ancient mosaics and antique tapestries.

The Quadriga, the original gilded bronze horses in the museum

Noah and the Flood – atrium mosaics from the 13th century

Sanctuary and Pala d'Oro

Beyond the Chapel of St Clement, tickets are sold to view the most valuable treasure of San Marco: the Pala d'Oro. This jewel-spangled altarpiece situated behind the high altar consists of 250 enamel paintings on gold foil, enclosed within a gilded silver Gothic frame. Originally commissioned in Byzantium in AD 976, the altarpiece was embellished over the centuries. Following the fall of the Republic, Napoleon helped himself to some of the precious stones, but the screen still gleams with pearls, rubies, sapphires and amethysts.

Statue of St Mark on the iconostasis

The iconostasis, the screen dividing nave from chancel, is adorned with marble Gothic statues of the Virgin and Apostles, and was carved in 1394 by the Dalle Masegne brothers. Above the high altar the imposing green marble baldacchino is supported by finely carved alabaster columns featuring scenes from the New Testament.

Baptistry and Chapels

The Baptistry (closed to the public) was added in the 14th century by Doge Andrea Dandolo (1343–54) who is buried here. Under his direction the Baptistry was decorated with outstanding mosaics depicting scenes from the lives of Christ and John the Baptist. Sansovino, who designed the font, is buried by the altar.

The adjoining Zen Chapel (currently closed to the public) originally formed part of the atrium. It became a funeral chapel for Cardinal Zen in 1504 in return for his bequest to the State.

In the left transept of the Basilica the Chapel of St Isidore, normally accessible only for worship, was also built by Dandolo. Mosaics in the barrel-vault ceiling tell the tale of the saint, whose body was stolen from the island of Chios and transported to Venice in 1125. To its left the Mascoli Chapel, used in the early 17th century by the confraternity of Mascoli (men), is decorated with scenes from the life of the Virgin Mary. The altarpiece has statues depicting the Virgin and Child between St Mark and St John.

The third chapel in the left transept is home to the icon of the Madonna of Nicopeia. Looted in 1204, she was formerly carried into battle at the head of the Byzantine army.

The revered icon of the Nicopeia Madonna, once a war insignia

Treasury

Although plundered after the fall of the Republic and much depleted by the fund-raising sale of jewels in the early 19th century, the treasury nevertheless has a precious collection of Byzantine silver, gold and glasswork. Today, most of the treasures are housed in a room whose remarkably thick walls are believed to have been a 9th-century tower of the Doge's Palace. Exhibits include chalices, goblets, reliquaries, two intricate icons of the archangel Michael and an 11th-century silver-gilt reliquary made in the form of a five-domed basilica *(see p85)*. The sanctuary, with over 100 reliquaries, is normally open to the public.

The archangel Michael, a Byzantine icon from the 11th century in the Treasury

❹ Doge's Palace

The Palazzo Ducale started life in the 9th century as a fortified castle, but this and several subsequent buildings were destroyed by a series of fires. The existing palace owes its external appearance to the building work of the 14th and early 15th centuries. The designers broke with tradition by perching the bulk of the pink Verona marble palace on lace-like Istrian stone arcades, with a portico supported by columns below. The result is a light and airy masterpiece of Gothic architecture.

Arco Foscari
The Adam and Eve figures on this triumphal arch in the courtyard are copies of the 15th-century originals by Antonio Rizzo.

★ Porta della Carta
This 15th-century Gothic gate was the principal entrance to the palace. From it, a vaulted passageway leads to the Arco Foscari and the internal courtyard.

Exit

①

KEY

① **The balcony** on the west façade was added in 1536 to mirror the early 15th-century balcony looking on to the quay.

② **Sala dei Tre Capi** (Chamber of the Three Heads of the Council of Ten)

③ **Sala della Bussola** (Compass Room)

④ **Ponte della Paglia** *(see p117)*

⑤ **Adam and Eve** with the serpent are depicted in stone on the corner of the Piazzetta.

★ Giants' Staircase
This late 15th-century staircase by Antonio Rizzo was used for ceremonial purposes. It was on the landing at the top that the doges were crowned with the glittering *zogia*.

Torture Chamber
"The court of the room of the Cord" recalls the practice of interrogating suspects as they hung by their wrists.

Bridge of Sighs
The famous bridge was crossed by offenders on their way to the State interrogators.

VISITORS' CHECKLIST

Practical Information
Piazzetta. **Map** 7 C2.
Tel 041 271 59 11.
W **palazzoducale.visitmuve.it**
Open 8:30am–7pm daily (Nov–Mar: to 5:30pm). Last adm: 1 hr before closing. Secret Itineraries (in English, 9:55am, 10:45am & 11:35am daily): book in advance at the palace or on the phone.
Closed 1 Jan, 25 Dec.  partial.

Transport
San Marco.

Drunkenness of Noah
This early 15th-century sculpture, symbolic of the frailty of man, is set on the corner of the palace.

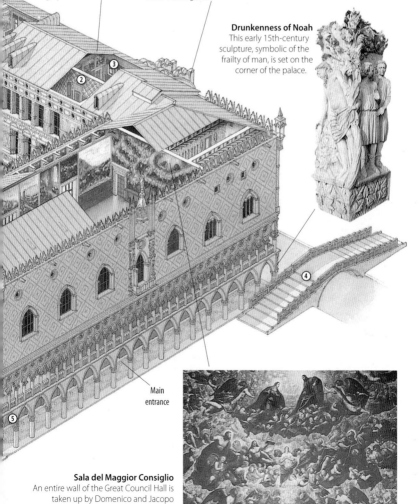

Main entrance

Sala del Maggior Consiglio
An entire wall of the Great Council Hall is taken up by Domenico and Jacopo Tintoretto's *Paradise* (1588–92).

Inside the Doge's Palace

From the early days of the Republic, the Doge's Palace was the seat of the government, the Palace of Justice and the home of the doge. For centuries this was the only building in Venice entitled to the name palazzo (the others were merely called Ca', short for Casa). The power of the Serenissima is ever present in the large and allegorical historical paintings which embellish the walls and ceilings of the splendid halls and chambers. These ornate rooms are testament to the glory of the Venetian Republic, and were designed to impress and overawe visiting ambassadors and dignitaries.

Colonnade
Sunlight streams through the arches of the Loggia on the first floor of the palace.

Mars
The Giants' Staircase is named after Sansovino's monumental figures, statues of Mars and Neptune, sculpted in 1567.

Key to Floorplan

- State Apartments
- Collegium and Senate Rooms
- Council of Ten and Armoury
- Great Council Rooms
- Prisons
- Non-exhibition space

Scala d'Oro
Sansovino's lavish staircase was built between 1554 and 1558. The arched ceiling is embellished with gilded stucco by Alessandro Vittoria.

Ground floor

Exit through Porta della Carta

Wellhead
The two 16th-century bronze wellheads in the courtyard are considered to be the finest in Venice.

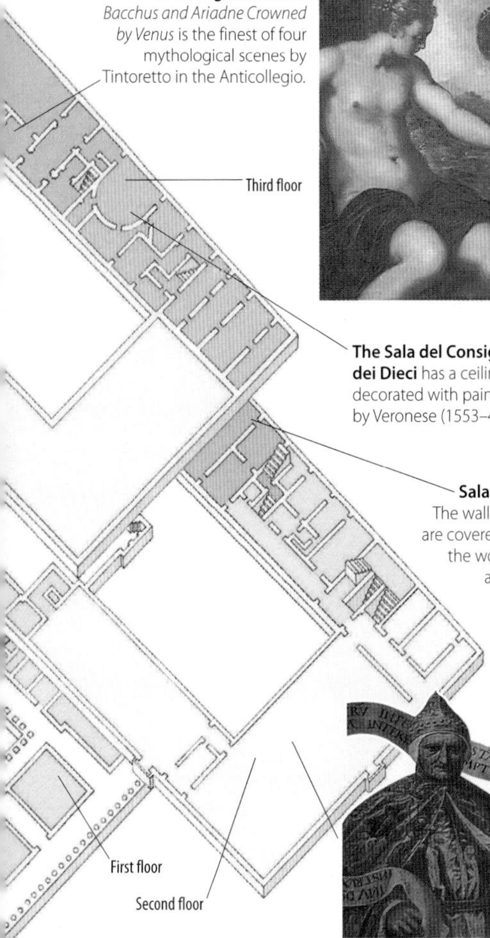

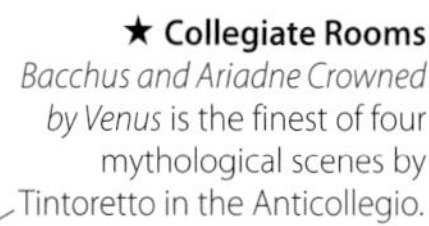

★ Collegiate Rooms
Bacchus and Ariadne Crowned by Venus is the finest of four mythological scenes by Tintoretto in the Anticollegio.

Third floor

The Sala del Consiglio dei Dieci has a ceiling decorated with paintings by Veronese (1553–4).

Sala dello Scudo
The walls of this room are covered with maps of the world. In the centre are two huge 18th-century globes.

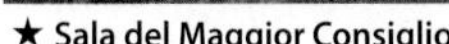

First floor

Second floor

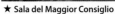

★ Sala del Maggior Consiglio
The first 76 doges, with the exception of the traitor Marin Falier, are portrayed on a frieze around the upper walls of the room.

trance

★ Prisons
These 16th-century cells were mainly used for petty offenders. Serious criminals were lodged in the dank *pozzi* (wells).

The Secret Itinerary

The fascinating, though poorly publicized, Secret Itinerary (Itinerari Segreti) tour *(see* Visitors' Checklist *p89)* takes visitors behind the scenes in the palace to the offices and Hall of the Chancellery, the State Inquisitors' room, the Torture Chamber and the prisons. It was from these cells that Casanova made his spectacular escape in 1755. Tours are available in Italian, English and French. Each is limited to 25 people and lasts for 75 minutes.

Casanova's cell door

Exploring the Doge's Palace

A tour of the palace takes visitors through a succession of richly decorated chambers and halls. The rooms are on four levels, and they all have name boards carrying an explanation of their function in Italian and English. The latest equipment available is an up-to-date infrared audioguide, which can be hired for a commentary on the whole palace or just the areas that are of particular interest.

Allow plenty of time for the visit, and try to take a break at the coffee shop. Located at water level, it affords evocative views of gondolas gliding past in the canal.

St Theodore in the palace courtyard

Courtyard

The courtyard is reached via a vaulted passage from the Porta del Frumento. At the top of the Giants' Staircase, on the opposite side of the courtyard, new doges were crowned with the *zogia* or dogal cap.

Scala d'Oro and State Apartments

The sumptuous Scala d'Oro ("golden staircase"), built between 1538 and 1559, was designed by Jacopo Sansovino. It takes its name, however, from the elaborate gilt stucco vault, which was added by Alessandro Vittoria (1554–8). The doge's private apartments on the second floor were built after the fire of 1483 and later looted on the orders of Napoleon. They are bare of furnishings, but the lavish ceilings and colossal carved chimneypieces in some of the rooms give an idea of the doges' lifestyle. The most ornate is the Sala degli Scarlatti, with a richly carved gilt ceiling, a fireplace (c.1501) designed by Antonio and Tullio Lombardo and a relief (1501–21) by Pietro Lombardo of Doge Leonardo Loredan at the feet of the Virgin.

The Sala dello Scudo, or map room, contains maps and charts. The picture gallery further on features works by Vittore Carpaccio and Giovanni Bellini, and some incongruous wooden demoniac panels by Hieronymus Bosch.

Veronese's *Dialectic* (c.1577), Sala del Collegio

Sala delle Quattro Porte to Sala del Senato

The second flight of the Scala d'Oro leads to the third floor and its council chambers. The first room, the Sala delle Quattro Porte, was completely rebuilt after the 1574 fire, its ceiling designed by Andrea Palladio and frescoed by Tintoretto.

The next room, the Anticollegio, was the waiting room. The end walls are decorated with mythological scenes by Tintoretto: *Vulcan's Forge, Mercury and the Graces, Bacchus and Ariadne* and *Minerva Dismissing Mars*, all painted in 1578. Veronese's masterly *Rape of Europa* (1580), opposite the window, is one of the most eyecatching works in the palace.

A *bocca di leone* used for denouncing tax evaders

Off the Anticollegio, the Sala del Collegio was the hall where the doge and his councillors met to receive ambassadors and discuss matters of State. Embellishing the magnificent ceiling are 11 paintings by Veronese (c.1577), of which the most notable – in the centre, far end – is *Justice and Peace Offering Sword, Scales and Olive Branch to Venice.*

It was in the next room, the Sala del Senato, that the doge would sit with some 200 senators to discuss matters such as foreign affairs or nominations of ambassadors. The wall and ceiling paintings, by pupils of Tintoretto or the master himself, are further propaganda for the Republic.

Sala del Consiglio dei Dieci to the Armeria

The route returns through the Sala delle Quattro Porte to the Sala del Consiglio dei Dieci. This was the meeting room of the awesomely powerful Council of Ten, founded in 1310 to investigate and prosecute crimes concerning the security of the State. Napoleon pilfered some of the Veroneses from the ceiling but two of the finest found their way back here in 1920: *Age and Youth* and *Juno Offering the Ducal Crown to Venice* (both 1553–4).

In the next room, the Sala della Bussola, offenders awaited their fate in front of the Council of Ten. The room's *bocca di leone* (lion's mouth), used to post secret denunciations, was just one of several within the palace. The wooden door here leads to the rooms of the Heads of the Ten, the State Inquisitors' Room and thence to the torture chamber and prisons. This is the route taken by those on the Secret Itinerary.

Age and Youth (1553–54) by Veronese

Others follow the flow to the Armoury – one of the finest collections in Europe, thanks in part to bequests by European monarchs.

Sala del Maggior Consiglio

Another staircase, the Scala dei Censori, leads down to the second floor, along the hallway and past the Sala del Guariento with fresco fragments of *The Coronation of the Virgin* by Guariento (1365–7). From the *liagò*, or veranda, where Antonio Rizzo's marble statues of Adam and Eve (1480s) are displayed, visitors pass into the magnificent Sala del Maggior Consiglio or Hall of the Great Council. A chamber of monumental proportions, it was here that the Great Council convened to vote on constitutional questions, to pass laws and elect the top officials of the Serene Republic. The hall was also used for State banquets. When Henry III of France paid a royal visit, 3,000 guests were entertained in this spectacular room.

By the mid-16th century the Great Council had around 2,000 members. Any Venetian of high birth over 25 was entitled to a seat – with the exception of those married to a commoner. From 1646, by which time the Turkish wars had depleted State coffers, nobility from the *terra firma* or those from merchant or professional classes with 100,000 ducats to spare could purchase their way in.

Tintoretto's huge, highly restored work called *Paradise* (1587–90) occupies the eastern wall. Measuring 7.45 by 24.65 m (25 by 81 ft), it is one of the largest paintings in the world. For a man in his late seventies, albeit assisted by his son, it is a remarkably vigorous composition.

The ceiling of the hall is decorated with panels glorifying the Republic. One of the finest is Veronese's *Apotheosis of Venice* (1583). A frieze along the walls illustrates 76 doges by Tintoretto's pupils. The portrait covered by a curtain is Marin Falier, beheaded for treason in 1355. The other 42 doges are portrayed in the Sala dello Scrutinio, where new doges were nominated.

The splendid Sala del Maggior Consiglio, the hall of the Great Council

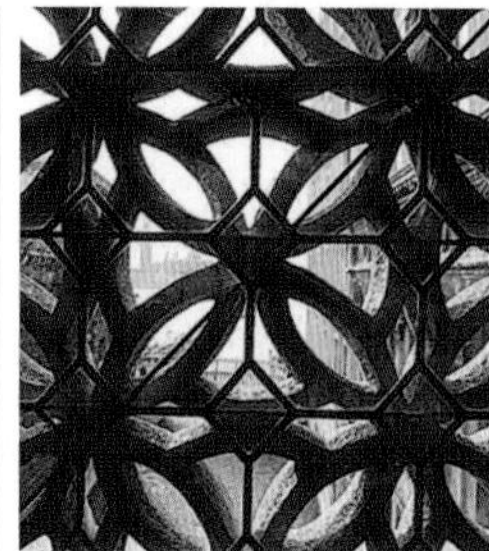

View of the lagoon through a grille on the Bridge of Sighs

Prisons

From the Sala del Maggior Consiglio a series of passageways and stairways leads to the Bridge of Sighs *(see p117)*, which links the palace to what were known as the New Prisons, built between 1556 and 1595.

Situated at the top of the palace, just below the leaded roof, are the *piombi* cells (*piombo* means "lead"). These cells are hardly inviting, but prisoners here were far more comfortable than the criminals who were left to fester in the *pozzi* – the dark dank dungeons at ground level. The windowless cells of these ancient prisons are still covered with the graffiti of the convicts. Visitors on the Secret Itinerary tour are shown Casanova's cell in the *piombi* and told of how he made his daring escape from the palace through a hole in the roof.

Visits end with the offices of the Avogaria, where the state prosecutors *(avogadori)* prepared the trials.

Street-by-Street: Around La Fenice

West of the huge expanse of the ever-crowded Piazza San Marco there is a labyrinth of alleys to explore. At the centre of this part of the *sestiere* is Campo San Fantin, flanked by the Renaissance church of San Fantin. Nearby is the Ateneo Veneto, formerly a *scuola* whose members had the unenviable role of escorting prisoners to the scaffold. The narrow streets around these sights have some wonderfully exotic little shops, while the Calle Larga XXII Marzo, further south, boasts big names in Italian fashion. The quarter in general has some excellent restaurants but, being San Marco, the prices in the majority of establishments are fairly steep.

Campo San Fantin has a late Renaissance church, San Fantin, with a particularly beautiful apse designed by Jacopo Sansovino.

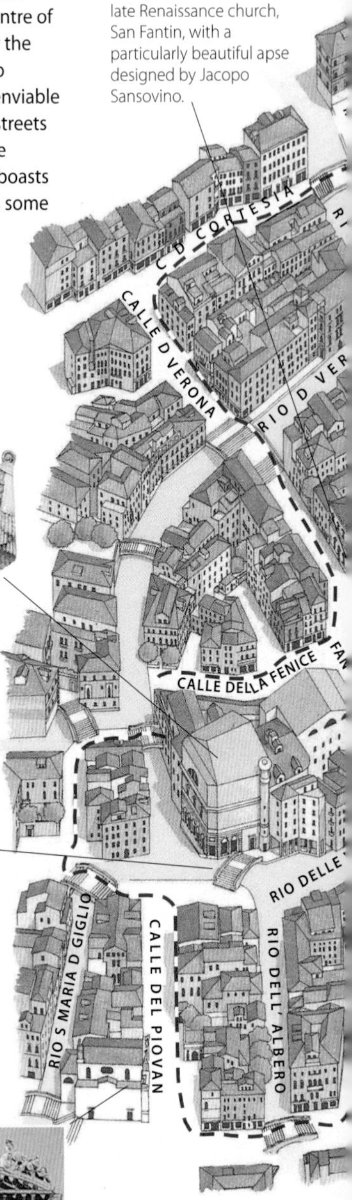

⑭ ★ La Fenice
The opera house gained its name ("the phoenix") after a fire in 1836. Destroyed by fire again in 1996, it is now beautifully restored.

The Rio delle Veste leads past the rear of the theatre. This is the route taken by those fortunate enough to arrive for their night out by gondola.

0 metres 75
0 yards 75

Key

— Suggested route

⑬ Santa Maria Zobenigo
The carvings feature the Barbaro family, who paid for the church façade. Ground-level reliefs show towns where the family held high-ranking posts.

For hotels and restaurants in this region see pp232–5 and pp242–9

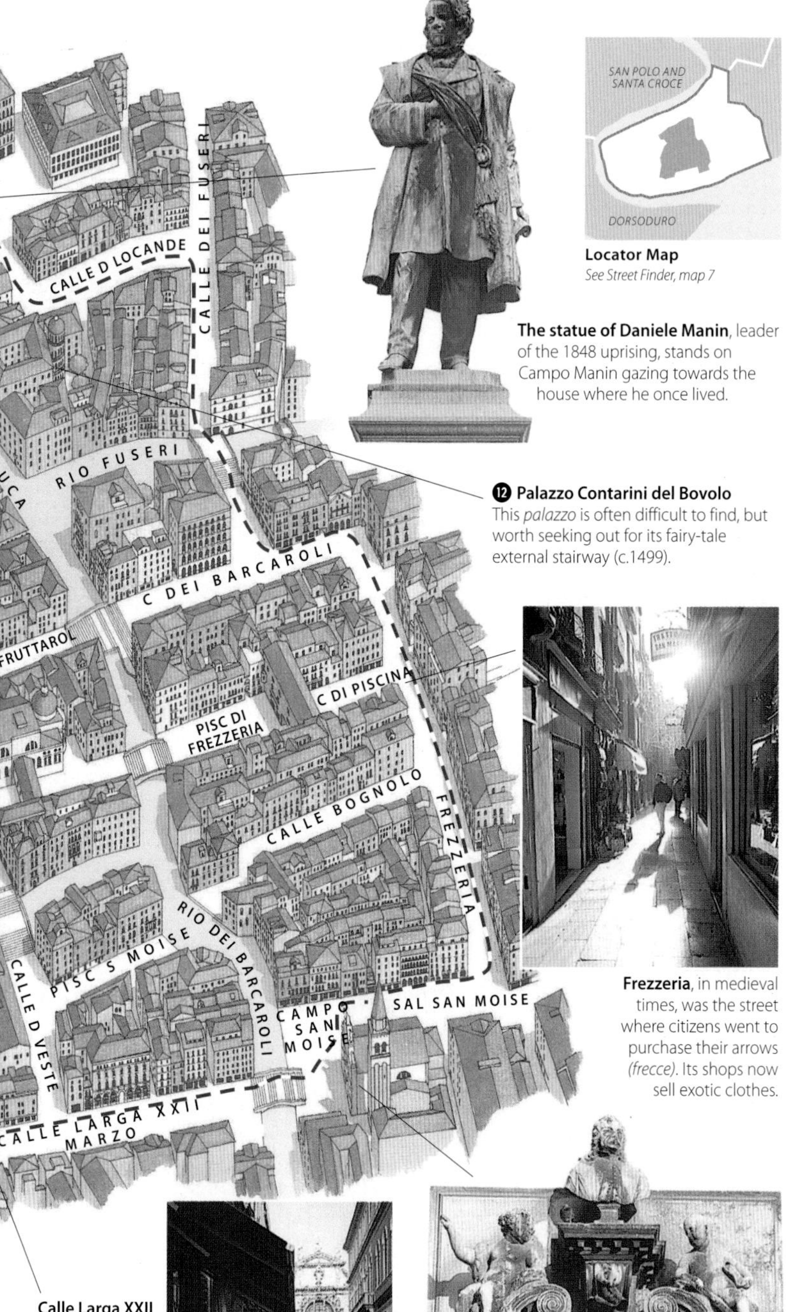

Locator Map
See Street Finder, map 7

The statue of Daniele Manin, leader of the 1848 uprising, stands on Campo Manin gazing towards the house where he once lived.

⓬ Palazzo Contarini del Bovolo
This *palazzo* is often difficult to find, but worth seeking out for its fairy-tale external stairway (c.1499).

Frezzeria, in medieval times, was the street where citizens went to purchase their arrows *(frecce)*. Its shops now sell exotic clothes.

Calle Larga XXII Marzo was named after 22 March 1848, the day of Manin's rebellion. Today the street is best known for its trendy designer boutiques.

⓫ ★ San Moisè
The exuberant Baroque façade of San Moisè (c.1668) was funded by a legacy from the patrician Vincenzo Fini, whose bust features above a side door.

❾ Harry's Bar

Calle Vallaresso 1323. **Map** 7 B3. San Marco. *See also Restaurants p243, Bars and Cafés pp250–51.*

Celebrated for cocktails, *carpaccio* and American clientele, Harry's Bar is famous throughout Venice. Founded in 1931 by the late Giuseppe Cipriani, it was financed by a Bostonian called Harry who thought Venice had a dearth of decent bars. They chose a storeroom at the Grand Canal end of the Calle Vallaresso as their location, conveniently close to the Piazza San Marco. Since then, the bar has seen a steady stream of American visitors, among them Ernest Hemingway, who used to come here after shooting in the lagoon. The bar became the most popular venue in Venice, patronized by royalty, film stars and heads of state.

These days there are far more American tourists than famous figures, often there to sample the Bellini cocktail that Cipriani invented *(see p243)*. Aesthetically, the place is unremarkable and there is no terrace for meals alfresco.

Ernest Hemingway, a regular at Harry's Bar

❿ Ridotto

Calle del Ridotto, 1332 San Marco. **Map** 7 B3. **Tel** 041 520 02 11. San Marco. **Open** to hotel guests and on request. **hotelmonaco.it**

In an effort to control the gambling mania that swept Venice in the 1600s, the State allowed Marco Dandolo to use his palace as the first public gaming house in Europe. In 1638 the Ridotto was opened, with the proviso that players came disguised in a mask. In 1774 the Great Council closed the casino's doors on account of the number of Venetians ruined at its tables.

In 1947, the old Palazzo Dandolo was converted into a theatre. Now restored, it is part of the Monaco and Grand Canal hotel *(see p232)*.

⓫ San Moisè

Campo San Moisè. **Map** 7 A3. **Tel** 041 296 06 30. San Marco. **Open** 9:30am–12:30pm & 3:30–7:30pm Mon–Sat, 9:30am–12:30pm & 2:30–6:30pm Sun.

A church that people love to hate, San Moisè displays a ponderous Baroque façade. Completed in 1668, it is covered in grimy statues, swags and busts. John Ruskin, in a characteristic anti-Baroque outrage, described it as the clumsiest church in Venice. The interior has a mixed collection of paintings and sculpture from the 17th and 18th centuries. In the nave is the tombstone of John Law, a Scottish financier who founded the Compagnie d'Occident to develop the Mississippi Valley. His shares collapsed in 1770 in the notorious South Sea Bubble, and he fled to Venice, surviving on his winnings at the Ridotto.

Façade of San Moisè, encrusted with Baroque ornamentation

⓬ Palazzo Contarini del Bovolo

Corte Contarini del Bovolo, 4299 San Marco. **Map** 7 A2. **Tel** 041 260 19 74. Rialto or Sant'Angelo. **Closed** for restoration. Call ahead for up-to-date information.

Tucked away in a maze of alleys (follow signs from Campo Manin), this *palazzo* is best known for its graceful external stairway, which is currently closed for renovation. In Venetian dialect *bovolo* means "snail shell", appropriate to the spiral shape of the stairway. The Contarini, a learned family who had the 15th-century palace built, were known as "the philosophers". There is also a collection of Byzantine wellheads.

The external stairway of the Palazzo Contarini del Bovolo

⓭ Santa Maria Zobenigo

Campo Santa Maria del Giglio. **Map** 6 F3. **Tel** 041 275 04 62. Santa Maria del Giglio. **Open** 10am–5pm Mon–Sat. **Closed** 1 Jan, Easter, 15 Aug, 25 Dec. **chorusvenezia.org**

Named after the Jubanico family, who are said to have founded it in the 9th century, this church is also referred to as "del Giglio" ("of the lily"). The exuberant Baroque façade was financed by the affluent Barbaro family and was used to glorify their naval and diplomatic achievements.

Inside is a tiny museum of church ornaments and paintings including *The Sacred Family* attributed to Rubens and two works by Tintoretto.

⓮ La Fenice

Campo San Fantin. **Map** 7 A3. Box office **Tel** 041 24 24. San Marco. **teatrolafenice.it**

Theatre houses were enormously popular in the 18th century and La Fenice, the city's oldest theatre, was no exception. Built in 1792 in Classical style, it was one of several privately owned theatres showing plays and operas to audiences from all strata of society. In December 1836, a fire destroyed the interior but a year later it was resurrected, just like the mythical bird, the phoenix *(fenice)* which is said to have arisen from its ashes.

Another fire in early 1996 again destroyed the theatre, except for its façade. Now beautifully rebuilt, La Fenice shares the concert and opera season with the Malibran Theatre near Rialto.

Throughout the 19th century the name of La Fenice was linked with great Italian composers. The many operatic premieres that took place here include Verdi's *La Traviata* (1853) and Rossini's *Tancredi* (1813) and *Semiramide* (1823). During the Austrian Occupation *(see p51)* red, white and green flowers, symbolizing the Italian flag, were thrown on stage, to shouts of "Viva Verdi" – the letters of the composer's name standing for "Vittorio Emanuele Re d'Italia". More recently, the theatre saw premieres of Stravinsky's *The Rake's Progress* (1951) and Britten's *Turn of the Screw* (1954).

Shop in Campo Santo Stefano selling antiques and masks

⓯ Campo Santo Stefano

Map 6 F3. Accademia or Sant'Angelo.

Also known as Campo Francesco Morosini after the 17th-century doge who once lived here, this *campo* is one of the most spacious in the city. Bullfights were staged until 1802, when a stand fell and killed some of the spectators. It was also a venue for balls and Carnival festivities. Today it is a pleasantly informal square where children play and visitors drink coffee in open-air cafés.

The central statue is Nicolò Tommaseo (1802–74), a Dalmatian scholar who was a central figure in the 1848 rebellion against the Austrians.

At the southern end of the square the austere-looking Palazzo Pisani, overlooking the Campiello Pisani, has been the Conservatory of Music since the end of the 19th century. Music wafts from its open windows all through the year. On the opposite side of the square, No. 2945, Palazzo Loredan, is the home of the Venetian Institute of Sciences, Letters and Arts.

The ceiling of Santo Stefano, in the form of a ship's keel

⓰ Santo Stefano

Campo Santo Stefano. **Map** 6 F2. **Tel** 041 275 04 62. Accademia or Sant'Angelo. **Open** 10am–5pm Mon–Sat. **Closed** 1 Jan, Easter, 15 Aug, 25 Dec. Sacristy only. **chorusvenezia.org**

Deconsecrated six times on account of the violence that took place within its walls, Santo Stefano today is remarkably serene. Built in the 14th century and radically altered in the 15th, the church has a notable carved portal by Bartolomeo Bon and a campanile with a typical Venetian tilt. The interior has a splendid ship's-keel ceiling, carved tie-beams and tall pillars of Veronese marble. The most notable works of art, including some paintings by Tintoretto, are housed in the damp sacristy.

La Fenice, rebuilt after it was destroyed by fire in 1996

Courtyard of the Palazzo Pesaro, where Fortuny lived

⓱ Museo Fortuny

Palazzo Pesaro degli Orfei, Campo San Beneto, San Marco 3958. **Map** 6 F2. **Tel** 041 520 09 95. Sant'Angelo. **Open** during exhibitions only. **fortuny.visitmuve.it**

Known principally for his fantastic pleated silk dresses, Fortuny was also a painter, sculptor, set designer, photographer and scientist. One of his inventions was the Fortuny Dome, which is used in theatre performances to create the illusion of sky.

Mariano Fortuny y Madrazo, or Don Mariano as he liked to be called, was born in 1871 in Granada and moved to Venice in 1889. In the early 20th century he purchased the Palazzo Pesaro, a late Gothic *palazzo* that had originally been owned by the fabulously rich and influential Pesaro family. Fortuny spent the remainder of his life here and both the house and its contents were bequeathed to the city by his wife in 1956.

The large rooms and *portego* make a splendid and appropriate setting for the precious Fortuny fabrics. Woven with gold and silver threads, these were created by Fortuny's reintroduction of Renaissance techniques and use of ancient dyes. The collection also includes paintings by Fortuny (less impressive than the fabrics), decorative panels and a few of the finely pleated, clinging silk dresses regarded as a milestone in early 20th-century women's fashion.

⓲ San Salvatore

Campo San Salvatore. **Map** 7 B1. **Tel** 041 523 67 17. Rialto. **Open** 9am–noon, 4–6:30pm Mon–Sat. **chiesasansalvador.it**

The interior of this church is an excellent example of Venetian Renaissance architecture. If the main door is closed visitors can enter by the side entrance, which is squeezed between shops along the Mercerie. The present church was designed by Giorgio Spavento in the early 16th century, and continued by Tullio Lombardo and Jacopo Sansovino. The pictorial highlight is Titian's *Annunciation* (1566) over the third altar on the right. Nearby, Sansovino's monument to Doge Francesco Venier (1556–61) is one of several Mannerist tombs in the church.

On the high altar is Titian's *Transfiguration of Christ* (1560). The end of the right transept is dominated by a vast monument to Caterina Cornaro, Queen of Cyprus *(see p47)*. Executed by the sculptor Bernardino Contino in c.1580–84, the tomb shows the queen handing over her kingdom to the doge.

⓳ Campo San Bartolomeo

Map 7 B1. Rialto.

Close to the Rialto, the square of San Bartolomeo bustles with life, particularly in the early evening, when young Venetians rendezvous here. They meet at cafés, bars or by the statue of Carlo Goldoni (1707–93), Venice's prolific and most celebrated playwright. His statue, in a fitting spot for a writer who drew his inspiration from daily social intercourse, is by Antonio del Zotto (1883).

The beautiful Renaissance interior of the church of San Salvatore

St George and Dragon bas-relief on a corner of the Mercerie

⑳ Mercerie

Map 7 B2. San Marco or Rialto.

Divided into the Merceria dell'Orologio, Merceria di San Zulian and Merceria di San Salvatore, this is, and always has been, a principal shopping thoroughfare. Linking Piazza San Marco with the Rialto, it is made from a string of narrow, bustling alleys, lined by small shops and boutiques. The 17th-century English author John Evelyn described it as "the most delicious streete in the World for the sweetnesse of it … tapisstry'd as it were, with Cloth of Gold, rich Damasks & other silk". He wrote of perfumers, apothecary shops and nightingales in cages. Today all this has been replaced with fashions, footwear and glass.

At the southern end, the relief over the first archway on the left portrays the woman who in 1310 accidentally stopped a revolt. She dropped her pestle out of the window, killing the standard-bearer of a rebel army. They retreated, and the woman was given a guarantee that her rent would never be raised.

Bronze statue of Tommaso Rangone

㉑ San Zulian

Campo San Zulian. **Map** 7 B2. **Tel** 041 523 53 83. San Marco. **Open** 8:30am–7pm daily. in English: 10:30am Sun.

On the busy Mercerie, the church of San Zulian (or Giuliano) provides a refuge from the crowded alleys. Its interior features gilded woodwork, 16th- and 17th-century paintings, and sculpture. The central panel of the frescoed ceiling portrays *The Apotheosis of St Julian*, painted in 1585 by Palma il Giovane. The 16th-century church façade was designed by Sansovino and paid for by the rich and immodest physician Tommaso Rangone. His bronze statue stands out against the white Istrian stone walls.

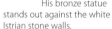

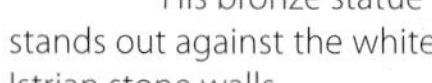

㉒ San Giorgio Maggiore

Map 8 D4. **Tel** 041 522 78 27. San Giorgio. **Open** 9:30am–12:30pm, 2:30–4:30pm (later in summer). Foundation: **Tel** 041 524 01 19. **Open** 10am–5pm Sat & Sun (Oct–Mar: to 4pm). in English: 11am, 1pm & 3pm (also 5pm in summer). **cini.it**

Appearing like a stage set across the water from the Piazzetta, the little island of San Giorgio Maggiore has been captured on canvas countless times.

The church and monastery, built between 1559 and 1580, are among Andrea Palladio's greatest architectural achievements. The church's temple front and the spacious, serene interior with its perfect proportions and cool beauty are typically Palladian in that they are modelled on the Classical style of ancient Rome. Within the church, the major works of art are the two late Tintorettos on the chancel walls: *The Last Supper* and *Gathering of the Manna* (both 1594). In the Chapel of the Dead is his last work, *The Deposition* (1592–4), finished by his son Domenico.

The top of the tall campanile, reached by a lift, affords a superb panorama of the city and lagoon.

Centuries ago Benedictine monks occupied the original monastery, which was rebuilt in the 13th century following an earthquake. It later became a centre of learning and a residence for eminent foreign visitors. Following the Fall of the Republic in 1797 (*see p50*) the monastery was suppressed and its treasures plundered.

Palladio's church of San Giorgio Maggiore on the island of the same name

Cloisters designed by Palladio in the monastery of San Giorgio Maggiore

In 1829 the island became a free port, and in 1851 the head-quarters of the artillery. By this time it had changed out of recognition. The complex regained its role as an active cultural centre when the monastery, embracing Palladio's cloisters, refectory and library, was purchased in 1951 by Count Vittorio Cini. Today it is a thriving centre of Venetian culture, with international events and exhibitions.

In the middle of the park on the island is an evocative open-air amphitheatre, or Teatro Verde, of white Vicenza stone.

L'AVVENTURA DEL VETRO
Self Service

SAN POLO AND SANTA CROCE

The *sestieri* of San Polo and Santa Croce, bordered by the upper sweep of the Grand Canal, were both named after churches which stood within their boundaries. The first inhabitants are said to have settled on the cluster of small islands called *Rivus Altus* (high bank) or Rialto. When markets were established in the 11th century, the quarter became the commercial hub of Venice. San Polo is still one of the liveliest *sestieri* of the city, with its market stalls, small shops and local bars. The bustle of the market gives way to a maze of narrow alleys opening on to squares. Focal points are the spacious Campo San Polo, the Frari church and the neighbouring Scuola di San Rocco. Santa Croce for the most part is a *sestiere* of very narrow, tightly packed streets and squares where you will see the humbler side of Venetian life. Its grandest *palazzi* line the Grand Canal. Less alluring is the Piazzale Roma, the city's giant car park, lying to the west.

Sights at a Glance

Churches

2 San Giacomo di Rialto
4 San Cassiano
6 San Polo
8 *Santa Maria Gloriosa dei Frari pp106–7*
10 San Rocco
11 San Pantalon
12 San Nicolò da Tolentino
13 San Giovanni Evangelista
14 San Giacomo dell'Orio
16 San Stae

Museums and Galleries

7 Casa di Goldoni
9 *Scuola Grande di San Rocco pp110–11*
15 Fondaco dei Turchi (Natural History Museum)
17 Palazzo Mocenigo
18 Ca' Pesaro

Streets and Squares

5 Campo San Polo

Bridges

1 Rialto Bridge

Markets

3 Rialto Markets

Restaurants *see pp243–4*

1 Al Nono Risorto
2 Al Prosecco
3 Antica Bessetta
4 Antiche Carampane
5 Da Fiore
6 Dona Onesta
7 Impronta Café
8 Osteria alla Patatina
9 Poste Vecie
10 Il Rèfolo
11 Trattoria alla Madonna
12 La Zucca

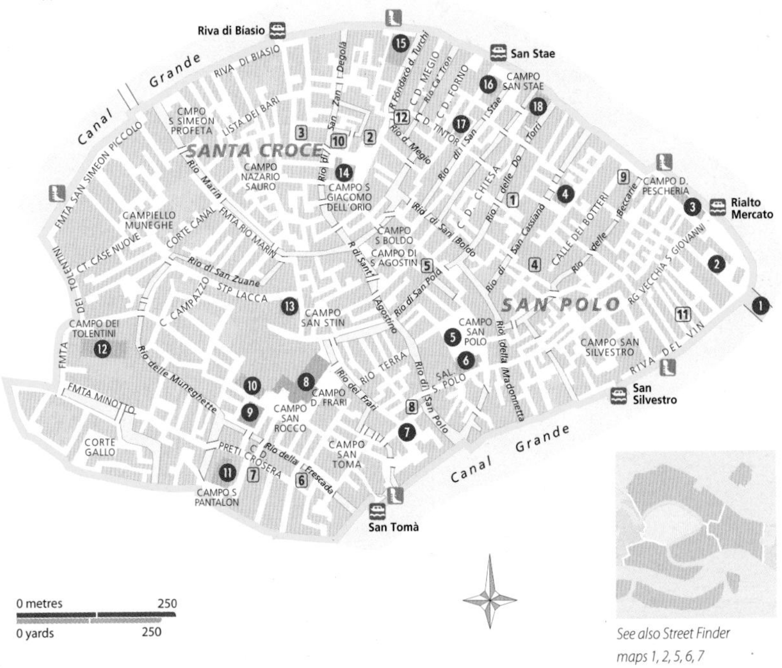

See also Street Finder maps 1, 2, 5, 6, 7

◀ The landmark Rialto Bridge spanning the Grand Canal in the heart of Venice

For keys to symbols *see back flap*

Street-by-Street: San Polo

The Rialto Bridge and markets make this a magnet for tourists. Traditionally the city's commercial quarter, it was here that bankers, brokers and merchants conducted their affairs. Streets are no longer lined with stalls selling spices and fine fabrics, but the food markets and pasta shops are a colourful sight. The old-fashioned standing-only bars called *bacari* are packed with locals. In contrast, Riva del Vin to the south, by the Grand Canal, is strictly tourist territory.

4 San Cassiano
Inside this church is a carved altar (1696) and a *Crucifixion* by Tintoretto (1568).

SAN CASSIANO
CALLE DEL CAMPANILE
CAMPO SAN CASSIANO
C D CRISTI
CALLE DEI BOTTER
RIO DI
R T D CARAMPANE
BECCARIE
RIO DELLE
CAMPIELLO ALBRIZZI
C SALVIATI
CAMPO SANT APONAL
C DELL OLIO
RUGA RAVA
C DEI LUGANEGHER
CAMPO SAN SILVESTRO

Ponte Storto is crooked, like many bridges in the city. It leads under a portico to Calle Stretta, a narrow alley that is only 1 m (3 ft) wide in places.

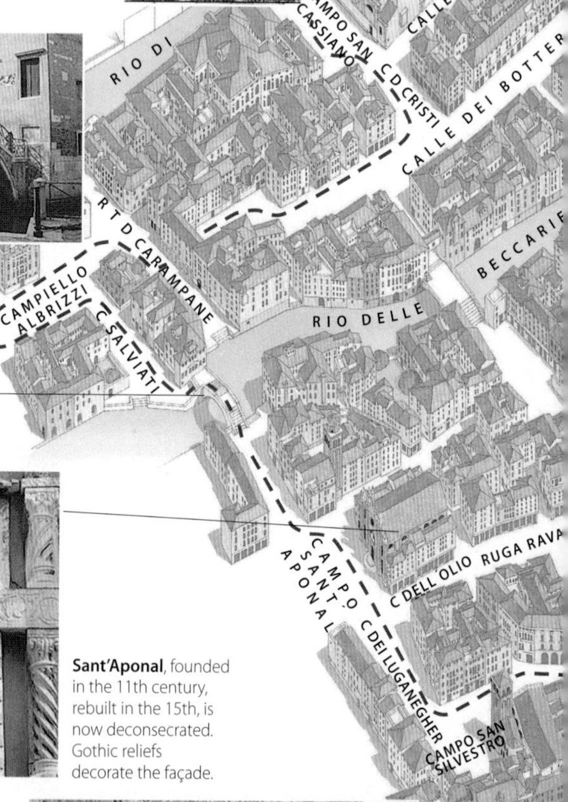

Sant'Aponal, founded in the 11th century, rebuilt in the 15th, is now deconsecrated. Gothic reliefs decorate the façade.

Key

 Suggested route

Riva del Vin, where wine was offloaded from boats, is one of the few accessible quaysides along the Grand Canal.

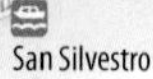

San Silvestro

3 ★ Rialto Markets
The Rialto markets have been in operation for centuries. The Pescheria (above) sells fresh fish and seafood, and the Erberia sells fruit and vegetables.

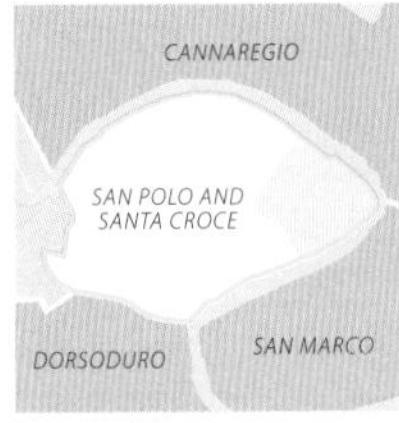

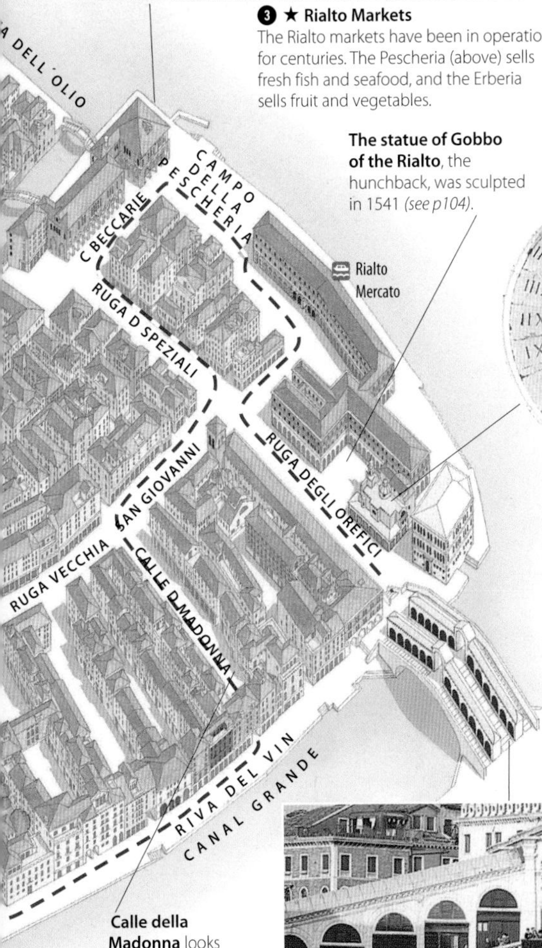

Locator Map
See Street Finder, maps 2, 3, 7

The statue of Gobbo of the Rialto, the hunchback, was sculpted in 1541 *(see p104)*.

Rialto Mercato

2 San Giacomo di Rialto
Since its installation in 1410, the clock on this church has been a notoriously poor timekeeper.

0 metres 75
0 yards 75

Calle della Madonna looks distinctly medieval with its overhanging first floors.

1 ★ Rialto Bridge
A beloved landmark of the Grand Canal, the bridge marks the geographical centre of the city. The balustrades afford fine views of the canal.

❶ Rialto Bridge

Ponte di Rialto. **Map** 7 A1. Rialto.

The Rialto Bridge has been a busy part of the city for centuries. At any time of day, you will find crowds jostling on the bridge, browsing for souvenirs or taking a break to watch the constant swirl of activity on the Grand Canal from the bridge's balustrades.

Stone bridges were built in Venice as early as the 12th century, but it was not until 1588, after the collapse, decay or sabotage of earlier wooden structures, that a solid stone bridge was designed for the Rialto. One of the early wood crossings collapsed in 1444 under the weight of spectators at the wedding ceremony of the Marchese di Ferrara.

Vittore Carpaccio's painting *Healing of the Madman* (C.1496, *see p137*) in the Accademia shows the fourth bridge – a rickety-looking structure with a drawbridge for the tall-masted galleys. By the 16th century this was in a sad state of decay and a competition was held for the design of a new bridge to be built in stone. Michelangelo, Andrea Palladio and Jacopo Sansovino were among the eminent contenders, but after months of deliberation it was the aptly named Antonio da Ponte who won the commission. The bridge was built between 1588 and 1591 and, until 1854, when the Accademia Bridge was constructed, this remained the only means of crossing the Grand Canal on foot.

Busy canalside restaurant near the Rialto Bridge

❷ San Giacomo di Rialto

Campo San Giacomo, San Polo. **Map** 3 A5. **Tel** 041 522 47 45. Rialto, Rialto Mercato, San Silvestro. **Open** 9:30am–noon, 4–5pm Mon–Sat, 11am–noon Sun. **Closed** during Mass.

The first church to stand on this site was allegedly founded in the 5th century, making it the oldest church in Venice. The present building dates from the 11th to12th centuries, with major restoration in 1601. The original Gothic portico and huge 24-hour clock are the most striking features.

The crouching stone figure on the far side of the square is the so-called Gobbo (hunchback) of the Rialto. In the 16th century this was a welcome sight for minor offenders, who were forced to run the gauntlet from Piazza San Marco to this square at the Rialto.

Traghetto ferrying passengers across to the Erberia

❸ Rialto Markets

San Polo. **Map** 3 A5. Rialto. Erberia (fruit and vegetable market) until 12:30pm Mon–Sat. Pescheria (fish market): until 12:30pm Tue–Sat.

Venetians have come to the Erberia to buy fresh produce for hundreds of years. Heavily laden barges arrive at dawn and offload their crates on to the quayside by the Grand Canal. Local produce includes red *radicchio* from Treviso, and succulent asparagus and baby artichokes from the islands of Sant'Erasmo and Le Vignole *(see p153)*. In the adjoining fish market are sole, sardines, skate, squid, crabs, clams and other species of seafood and fish. To see it all in full swing you must arrive early in the morning – by noon the vendors are starting to pack up.

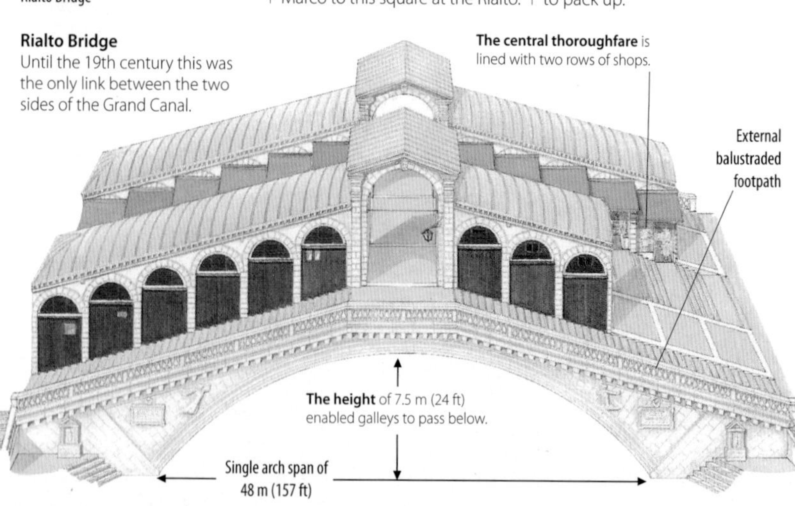
Rialto Bridge
Until the 19th century this was the only link between the two sides of the Grand Canal.
The central thoroughfare is lined with two rows of shops.
External balustraded footpath
The height of 7.5 m (24 ft) enabled galleys to pass below.
Single arch span of 48 m (157 ft)

❹ San Cassiano

Campo San Cassiano, San Polo. **Map** 2 F5. **Tel** 041 721 408. San Stae. **Open** 9am–noon, 5–7pm Tue–Sat. **Closed** during Mass.

The Medieval Church of San Cassiano is a bizarre mix of architectural styles. Of the original church, which was restored in the 19th century, only the campanile survives. The highlight of the interior is Jacopo Tintoretto's immensely powerful *Crucifixion* (1568), which is in the sacristy.

The *campo* in which the church stands was notorious for prostitutes in the 1500s.

❺ Campo San Polo

Map 6 F1. San Silvestro.

The spacious square of San Polo has traditionally been host to spectacular events. As far back as the 15th century it was the venue for festivities, masquerades, ceremonies, balls and bullbaiting.

The most dramatic event was the assassination of Lorenzino de' Medici in 1548. He had taken refuge in Venice after brutally killing his cousin Alessandro, Duke of Florence. Lorenzino was stabbed in the square by two assassins who were in the service of Cosimo de' Medici, and both were handsomely rewarded by the Florentine duke.

On the eastern side of the square is the beautiful Gothic Palazzo Soranzo. This was originally two palaces – the one on the left is the older. The building is still owned by the Soranzo family.

Palazzo Corner Mocenigo, which is situated in the northwest corner (No. 2128), was once the residence of the eccentric English writer Frederick Rolfe (1860–1913), alias Baron Corvo. He was thrown out of his lodgings when his English hostess read his manuscript of *The Desire and Pursuit of the Whole* – a cruel satirization of English society in Venice.

A detail of the Gothic façade of Palazzo Soranzo, Campo San Polo

Since 1979 the square has enjoyed a revival of Carnival festivities. This wide-open space is also a haven for local youngsters, who ride bikes, roller-skate or play football. Such activities would not have gone down well in the 17th century – a plaque on the apse of the church, dated 1611, forbids all games (or selling merchandise) on pain of prison, galley service or exile.

❻ San Polo

Campo San Polo. **Map** 6 F1. **Tel** 041 275 04 62. San Silvestro. **Open** 10am–5pm Mon–Sat. **Closed** 1 Jan, Easter, 15 Aug, 25 Dec.
W chorusvenezia.org

Founded in the 9th century, rebuilt in the 15th and revamped in the early 19th in Neo-Classical style, the church of San Polo lacks any sense of homogeneity. Yet it is worth visiting for individual features such as the lovely Gothic portal and the Romanesque lions at the foot of the 14th-century campanile – one holds a serpent between its paws, the other a human head.

Inside, follow the signs for the *Via Crucis del Tiepolo* – 14 canvases of the Stations of the Cross by Giandomenico Tiepolo. The church also has paintings by Veronese, Palma il Giovane (the Younger) and a dark and dramatic *Last Supper* by Tintoretto.

Carlo Goldoni 1707–93

❼ Casa di Goldoni

Palazzo Centani, Calle dei Nomboli, San Polo 2794. **Map** 6 E1. **Tel** 041 275 93 25. San Tomà. **Open** 10am–4pm Thu–Tue (Apr–Oct: to 5pm). **Closed** 1 Jan, 1 May, 25 Dec.
W carlogoldoni.visitmuve.it

Carlo Goldoni, one of the city's favourite sons, wrote over 250 comedies, many based on commedia dell'arte figures. Goldoni was born in the beautiful Gothic Palazzo Centani (or Zantani) in 1707. The house was left to the city in 1931 and is now a centre for theatrical studies and has a collection of theatrical memorabilia. The enchanting courtyard has a 15th-century open stairway and a magnificent wellhead, which features carved lions and a coat of arms bearing a hedgehog.

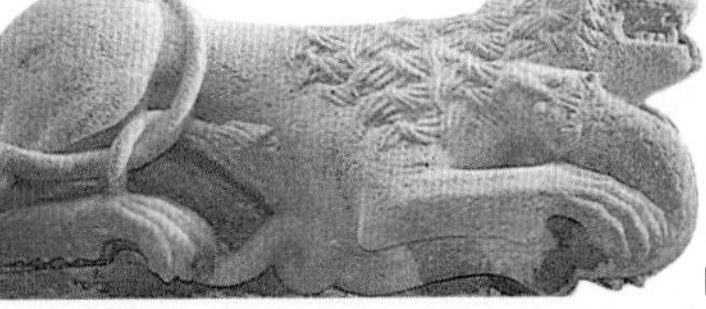

A lion at the foot of the campanile, Church of San Polo

❽ Santa Maria Gloriosa dei Frari

Known by all simply as the Frari (a corruption of *Frati*, meaning "brothers"), this huge, plain Gothic church dwarfs the eastern section of San Polo. The first church was built by Franciscan friars in 1250–1338, but was replaced by a larger building which was completed by the mid-15th century. The interior is striking for its sheer size and for the quality of its works of art. These include masterpieces by Titian and Giovanni Bellini *(see pp30–31)*, a statue by Donatello and a number of imposing monuments to famous Venetians.

Foscari Monument
Doge Foscari set a record by reigning for 34 years (1423–57).

★ ***Assumption of the Virgin***
Titian's glowing and spectacular work (1518) inevitably draws the eye through the monk's choir towards the altar.

Rood Screen (1475)
Pietro Lombardo and Bartolomeo Bon carved this and decorated it with marble figures.

★ **Monks' Choir**
This consists of three-tiered stalls (1468), carved with bas-reliefs of saints and Venetian city scenes.

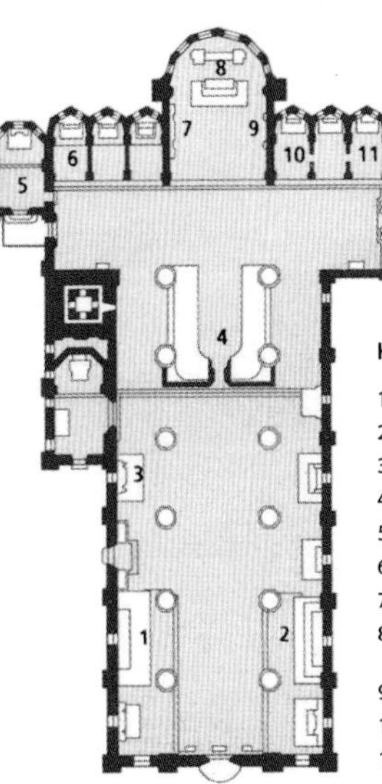

Floorplan
Exploration of the huge interior can be daunting. The floorplan pinpoints 12 highlights that should not be missed.

Key to Floorplan

1 Canova's tomb
2 Monument to Titian
3 Titian's *Madonna di Ca' Pesaro*
4 Choir stalls
5 Corner Chapel
6 Tomb of Monteverdi
7 Tomb of Doge Nicolò Tron
8 High altar with Titian's *Assumption of the Virgin*
9 Tomb of Doge Francesco Foscari
10 Donatello's *John the Baptist* (c.1450)
11 Bo Vivarini's altar painting (1474), Bernardo Chapel
12 Giovanni Bellini's *Madonna Enthroned with Saints* (1488)

VISITORS' CHECKLIST

Practical Information
Campo dei Frari. **Map** 6 D1.
Tel 041 275 04 62.
chorusvenezia.org
Open 9am–6pm Mon–Sat, 1–6pm Sun & religious hols. **Closed** 1 Jan, Easter, 15 Aug, 25 Dec. except those attending Mass. frequent.

Transport
San Tomà.

Monument to Titian (1853)
Canova's pupils Luigi and Pietro Zandomeneghi built this monument to Titian in place of the one conceived by Canova himself.

KEY

① **The campanile** is 80 m (262 ft) high, the tallest in the city after that of San Marco.

② ***Madonna di Ca' Pesaro*** (1526) shows Titian's mastery of light and colour.

③ **The former monastery**, which houses the State Archives, has two cloisters, one in the style of Sansovino, another designed by Palladio.

Canova's Tomb
Canova designed, but never actually made, a Neo-Classical marble pyramid like this as a monument for Titian. After Canova's death in 1822, his pupils used a similar design for their master's tomb.

❾ Scuola Grande di San Rocco

See pp110–11.

❿ San Rocco

Campo San Rocco, San Polo. **Map** 6 D1. **Tel** 041 523 48 64. San Tomà. **Open** 9:30am–5:30pm daily. **scuolagrandesanrocco.it**

Sharing the little square with the celebrated Scuola Grande di San Rocco is the church of the same name. Designed by Bartolomeo Bon in 1489 and largely rebuilt in 1725, the exterior is a mix of architectural styles. The façade was added in 1765–71.

Inside, the main interest lies in Tintoretto's paintings in the chancel, which depict scenes from the life of St Roch, patron saint of contagious diseases. Of these the most notable is *St Roch Curing the Plague Victims* (1549).

Fumiani's ceiling painting (1680–1704), San Pantalon

⓫ San Pantalon

Campo San Pantalon, Dorsoduro. **Map** 6 D2. **Tel** 041 523 58 93. San Tomà, Piazzale Roma. **Open** 10am–noon, 1–3pm Mon–Sat. **sanpantalon.it**

The overwhelming feature of this late 17th-century church is the painted ceiling, dark, awe-inspiring and remarkable for its illusionistic effects. The ceiling comprises a total of 40 scenes (admirers claim this makes it the world's largest work of art on canvas), depicting the martyrdom and apotheosis of the physician St Pantalon. The artist, Gian Antonio Fumiani, took 24 years (1680–1704) to achieve this masterpiece, but then he allegedly fell to his death from the scaffolding.

Paolo Veronese's emotive painting *St Pantalon Healing a Boy* (second chapel on the right) was his final work of art (1587). To see Antonio Vivarini and Giovanni d'Alemagna's *Coronation of the Virgin* (1444) and *The Annunciation* (1350), attributed to Paolo Veneziano, ask the custodian for access to the Chapel of the Holy Nail *(Cappella del Sacro Chiodo)*.

⓬ San Nicolò da Tolentino

Campo dei Tolentini, Santa Croce. **Map** 5 C1. **Tel** 041 522 21 60. Piazzale Roma. **Open** 8am–noon, 4–7pm daily. **Closed** during Mass. **tolentini.it**

Close to Piazzale Roma *(see p271)* is this imposing 17th-century church with a Classical portico. The interior, decorated with 17th-century paintings, is the resting place of Francesco Morosini (d.1678), the Venetian patriarch.

A cannonball embedded in the façade is a memento of an Austrian bombardment during the siege of 1849.

⓭ San Giovanni Evangelista

Campiello de la Scuola, San Polo. **Map** 6 D1. **Tel** 041 71 82 34. San Tomà. **Open** 9:30am–5pm on days when no events are being held, check website for details. Church & Scuola. **scuolasangiovanni.it**

A confraternity of flagellants founded the Scuola of St John the Evangelist in 1261. The complex, just north of the Frari *(see pp106–7)*, has a church, *scuola*, a bookshop and courtyard. Separating the square from the street is Pietro Lombardo's elegant white and grey screen and portal (1480),

Lombardo's marble screen and portal, San Giovanni Evangelista

and in the arch crowning the portal there is a magnificent carved eagle representing St John the Evangelist.

The main hall of the Scuola is reached via a splendid 15th-century double stairway by Mauro Coducci (1498). Large, dark canvases decorate the ceiling and walls of the 18th-century hall. The Scuola's greatest art treasure, the cycle of paintings depicting *The Stories of the Cross*, is now on display in the Accademia gallery *(see p137)*. It formerly embellished the oratory (off the main hall) where the Reliquary of the True Cross is still carefully preserved.

⓮ San Giacomo dell'Orio

Campo San Giacomo dell'Orio, Santa Croce. **Map** 2 E5. **Tel** 041 275 04 62. Riva di Biasio or San Stae. **Open** 10am–5pm Mon–Sat. **Closed** 1 Jan, Easter, 15 Aug, 25 Dec.

This church is a focal point of a quiet quarter of Santa Croce. The name "dell'Orio" (locally "dall'Orio") may derive from a laurel tree *(alloro)* that once stood near the church.

Founded in the 9th century, rebuilt in 1225 and repeatedly modified, the church is a mix of architectural styles. The campanile, basilica ground plan and Byzantine columns survive from the 13th century. The ship's keel roof and the columns are from the Gothic period, and the apses are Renaissance. The sacristy ceiling was decorated by Veronese and there are some interesting altar paintings.

⓯ Fondaco dei Turchi

Canal Grande, Santa Croce 1730. **Map** 2 E4. **Tel** 041 275 02 06. San Stae. **Open** Nov–May: 9am–5pm Tue–Fri, 10am–6pm Sat & Sun; Jun–Oct: 10am–6pm Tue–Sun. **msn.visitmuve.it**

The building that now contains Venice's Natural History Museum has a chequered history. In the 13th century it was one of the largest *palazzi* on the Grand Canal. In 1381 it was bought by the state for the Dukes of Ferrara and its lavish rooms were used for banquets and state functions. In 1621 the Turks set up a warehouse *(fondaco)*, and the portico was used for loading merchandise. As commerce with the Orient declined further, the structure fell into disrepair until, roused by Ruskin's passionate interest, the Austrians began restoration work in the 1850s.

Since 1924 the Fondaco has housed the Natural History Museum (Museo di Storia Naturale). There is a collection of stuffed animals, crustacea and dinosaur fossils and a section on lagoon life. Prize exhibits include a skeleton of an Ouranosaurus nigeriensis, 7 m (23 ft) long and 3.6 m (12 ft) tall, and a fossil of a Sarcosuchus imperator – an ancestor of the crocodile.

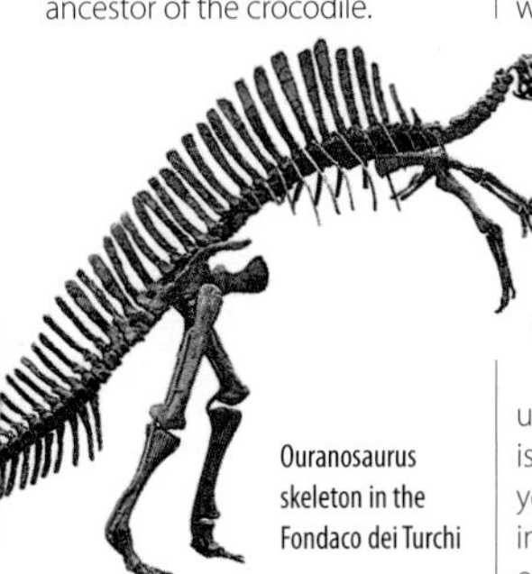

Ouranosaurus skeleton in the Fondaco dei Turchi

⓰ San Stae

Campo San Stae, Santa Croce. **Map** 2 F4. **Tel** 041 275 04 62. San Stae. **Open** 10am–5pm Mon–Sat. **Closed** 1 Jan, 25 Dec.

Restored in 1977–8 by the Pro Venezia Foundation, San Stae (or Sant'Eustachio) has a spick-and-span sculpted façade. It was built in 1709 by Domenico Rossi. Works by Piazzetta, Tiepolo and other 18th-century artists decorate the chancel. Near the second altar on the left is the bust of Antonio Foscarini, executed for treason in 1622 but pardoned the following year.

One of the finely furnished rooms of Palazzo Mocenigo

⓱ Palazzo Mocenigo

Salizzada San Stae, Santa Croce 1992. **Map** 2 F5. **Tel** 041 72 17 98. San Stae. **Open** 10am–5pm Tue–Sun (Nov–Mar: to 4pm). **Closed** 1 Jan, 1 May, 25 Dec. **mocenigo.visitmuve.it**

One of the oldest Venetian families, the Mocenigos produced seven doges. There were various branches of the family, one of which resided in this handsome 17th-century mansion. Count Alvise Nicolò Mocenigo, the last of this particular branch, died in 1954, bequeathing the palace to the Comune di Venezia (city authorities).

The entrance façade is unremarkable, but the interior is elegantly furnished and gives you a rare opportunity of seeing inside a *palazzo* preserved more or less as it was in the 18th century. The frescoed ceilings and other works of art are celebrations of the family's achievements. The illustrious Mocenigos are portrayed in a frieze around the *portego* on the first floor.

The Museo del Tessuto e del Costume inside the house contains antique fabrics and exquisitely made costumes. It also has five rooms dedicated to the history of perfumes.

⓲ Ca' Pesaro

Canal Grande, Santa Croce 2076. **Map** 2 F5. San Stae. Galleria d'Arte Moderna & Museo Orientale: **Tel** 041 72 11 27. **Open** 10am–6pm Tue–Sun (Nov–Mar: to 5pm); ticket office closes 1 hour earlier. **Closed** 1 Jan, 1 May, 25 Dec. combined ticket. **capesaro.visitmuve.it**

It took 58 years to complete this magnificent Baroque palace. Built for the Pesaro family, it was the masterpiece of Baldassare Longhena, who worked on it until his death in 1682. Antonio Gaspari then took over Longhena's design, eventually completing the structure in 1710.

In the 19th century the Duchess of Bevilacqua La Masa bequeathed the palace to the city for exhibiting the works of unestablished Venetian artists. The Galleria d'Arte Moderna was founded in 1897. Today this features a permanent exhibition of work by artists such as Bonnard, Matisse, Miró, Klee, Klimt and Kandinsky, in addition to works by Italian artists of the 19th and 20th centuries.

The Museo Orientale has an idiosyncratic collection of Chinese and Japanese artifacts collected by the Count of Bardi during his 19th-century travels.

Gustav Klimt's *Salome*, Gallery of Modern Art, Ca' Pesaro

❾ Scuola Grande di San Rocco

Founded in honour of St Roch (San Rocco), the Scuola was set up as a charitable institution for the sick. Construction began in 1515 under Bartolomeo Bon and was completed in 1549 by Scarpagnino, financed largely by donations from Venetians who believed that St Roch, the patron saint of contagious diseases, would save them from the plague. In 1564 Tintoretto *(see p144)* was commissioned to decorate the walls and ceilings of the Scuola. His remarkable cycle of paintings starts in the Sala dell'Albergo *(see Gallery Guide)*.

Restored main entrance to the Scuola di San Rocco

Sala dell'Albergo

The Crucifixion

In this panorama of Calvary, Tintoretto reached a pitch of religious feeling never hitherto achieved in Venetian art.

A self-portrait was often a feature of Tintoretto's paintings.

The subsidiary figures are full of life but do not lessen the central drama.

Figure of Christ
The crucified figure of the Redeemer is raised and leaning, accentuating His divinity and saving grace.

A competition was held in 1564 to select an artist to paint the central ceiling panel of the Sala dell'Albergo in the Scuola. To the fury of his rivals, Tintoretto pre-empted his fellow competitors by installing his painting in situ prior to judging. He won the commission and was later made a member of the Scuola. Over the next 23 years, Tintoretto decorated the entire building.

The series of paintings, completed in 1587, reveals Tintoretto's revolutionary use of light, mastery of foreshortening and visionary use of colour. The winning painting, *St Roch in Glory* ①, can be seen on the ceiling of the Sala dell'Albergo. The most moving work in the cycle is *The Crucifixion* (1565) ②. Henry James wrote: "Surely no single picture contains more of human life; there is everything in it, including the most exquisite beauty." Of the paintings on the entrance wall, portraying the Passion of Christ, the most notable is *Christ Before Pilate* (1566–7) ③.

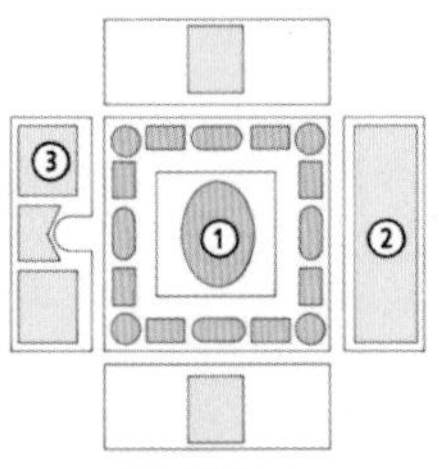

Sala dell'Albergo

Upper Hall

Scarpagnino's great staircase (1544–6), decorated with two vast paintings commemorating the plague of 1630, leads to the Upper Hall. The biblical subjects on the walls and ceiling were painted in 1575–81. The ceiling paintings (viewed most comfortably with a hired mirror) portray scenes from the Old Testament. The three large central square paintings represent *Moses Striking Water from the Rock* ④, *The Miracle of the Bronze Serpent* ⑤ and *The Gathering of the Manna* ⑥, all alluding to the Scuola's charitable aims in alleviating thirst, sickness and hunger respectively. All three paintings are crowded compositions with much violent movement. The vast wall paintings in the hall feature episodes from the New Testament. The most striking paintings are *The Temptation of Christ* ⑦, which shows a handsome young Satan offering Christ two loaves of bread, and *Adoration of the Shepherds* ⑧. Like *The Temptation of Christ*, the *Adoration* is composed in two halves, with a female figure, shepherds and ox below, and the Holy Family and onlookers above.

The beautiful carvings below the paintings were added in the 17th century by Francesco Pianta. The allegorical figures include (near the altar) a caricature of Tintoretto with his palette and brushes, which is meant to represent Painting. Near the entrance to the Sala dell'Albergo you can see Titian's *Annunciation*. The easel painting *Christ Carrying the Cross* is attributed to Giorgione, though many believe it to be a Titian.

The Temptation of Christ, 1578–81 (detail)

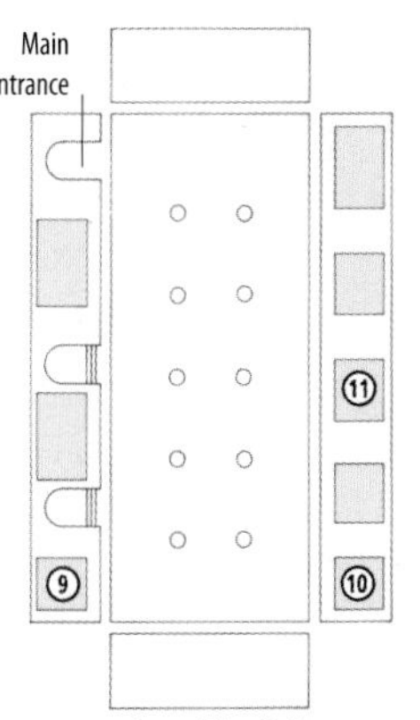

VISITORS' CHECKLIST

Practical Information
Campo San Rocco. **Map** 6 D1.
Tel 041 523 48 64. **Open** 9:30am–5:30pm daily. **Closed** 1 Jan, 25 Dec.
scuolagrandesanrocco.it

Transport
San Tomà.

The Flight into Egypt (1582–7) (detail)

Ground-Floor Hall

This final cycle, executed in 1582–7, consists of eight paintings illustrating the life of Mary. The series starts with an *Annunciation*, and ends with an *Assumption*, which was restored some years ago. The tranquil scenes of *St Mary of Egypt* ⑨, *St Mary Magdalene* ⑩ and *The Flight into Egypt* ⑪, painted when Tintoretto was in his late sixties, are remarkable for their serenity. This is portrayed most lucidly by the Virgin's isolated spiritual contemplation in the *St Mary of Egypt*. In all three paintings, the landscapes, rendered with rapid strokes, play a major role.

Gallery Guide

The paintings, which unfortunately are not well lit, have no labels, but a useful plan of the Scuola is available (in several languages) free of charge at the entrance. To see the paintings in chronological order, start in the Sala dell'Albergo (off the Upper Hall), followed by the Upper Hall and finally the Ground-Floor Hall.

Key

Wall paintings

Ceiling paintings

NAVALIS

CASTELLO

The largest *sestiere* of the city, Castello stretches from San Marco and Cannaregio in the west to the modern blocks of Sant'Elena in the east. The area takes its name from the 8th-century fortress that once stood on what is now San Pietro, the island which for centuries was the religious focus of the city. The church here was the episcopal see from the 9th century and the city's cathedral from 1451 to 1807.

The industrial hub of Castello was the Arsenale, where the great shipyards produced Venice's indomitable fleet of warships. Castello's most popular and solidly commercial area is the Riva degli Schiavoni promenade. Behind the waterfront it is comparatively quiet, characterized by narrow alleys, elegantly faded *palazzi* and fine churches, including the great Santi Giovanni e Paolo *(see pp120–21)*.

Sights at a Glance

Churches

1 San Zaccaria
2 San Giorgio dei Greci
3 La Pietà
13 *Santi Giovanni e Paolo pp120–21*
15 San Francesco della Vigna
16 San Lorenzo
18 San Giovanni in Bragora

Historic Buildings and Monuments

4 Hotel Danieli
11 Statue of Colleoni
14 Ospedaletto
20 Arsenale

Streets, Bridges and Squares

5 Riva degli Schiavoni
6 Ponte della Paglia and Bridge of Sighs
9 Campo Santa Maria Formosa

Walk

21 Exploring Eastern Castello

Museums, Galleries and Scuole

7 Museo Diocesano d'Arte Sacra
8 Fondazione Querini Stampalia
10 Palazzo Grimani
12 Scuola Grande di San Marco
17 Scuola di San Giorgio degli Schiavoni
19 Museo Storico Navale

Restaurants *see p244*

1 Aciugheta
2 Al Covo
3 Al Mascaron
4 Alla Rivetta
5 Bacarando Ai Corazzieri
6 Da Remigio
7 MET
8 L'Olandese Volante
9 Osteria Santa Marina
10 Il Ridotto
11 Trattoria Giorgione

See also Street Finder maps 3, 4, 7, 8

◀ Statue beside the gate at the entrance to Porta Magna, Arsenale

Street-by-Street: Castello

A stroll along the Riva degli Schiavoni is an integral part of a visit to Venice. Glorious views of San Giorgio Maggiore compensate for the commercialized aspects of the quayside: souvenir stalls, excursion touts and an overabundance of tourists. Associations with literary figures are legion. Petrarch lived at No. 4145, Henry James was offered "dirty" lodgings at No. 4161, and Ruskin stayed at the Hotel Danieli. Inland, the quiet, unassuming streets and squares of Castello provide a contrast to the bustling waterfront.

7 ★ Museo Diocesano d'Arte Sacra
The cloisters of the ancient Benedictine monastery of Sant'Apollonia herald the museum.

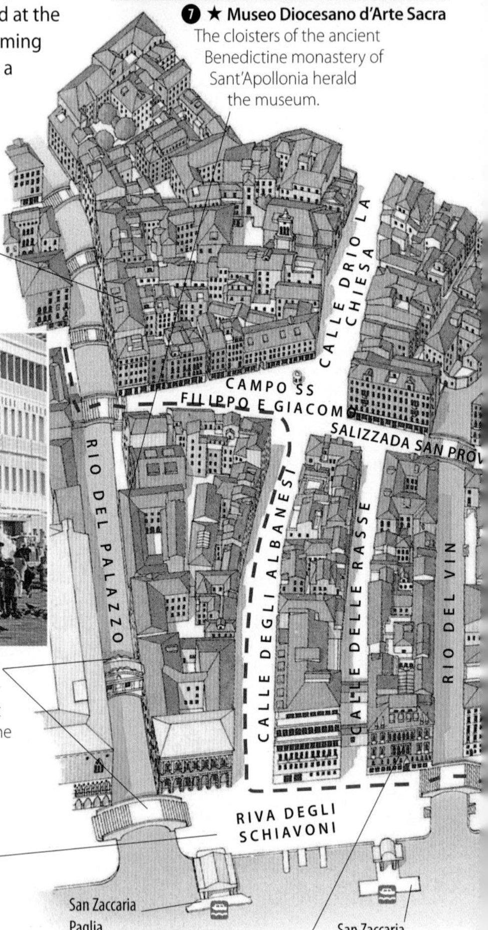

Palazzo Trevisan-Cappello, used as a showroom for Murano glass, was the home of Bianca Cappello, wife of Francesco de' Medici.

CALLE DRIO LA CHIESA
CAMPO SS FILIPPO E GIACOMO
SALIZZADA SAN PROV
RIO DEL PALAZZO
CALLE DEGLI ALBANESI
CALLE DELLE RASSE
RIO DEL VIN
RIVA DEGLI SCHIAVONI

6 Ponte della Paglia and Bridge of Sighs
Crowds throng the Istrian stone Ponte della Paglia – the "straw bridge" – for the best views of the neighbouring Bridge of Sighs, the covered bridge that links the Doge's Palace to the old prisons.

5 Riva degli Schiavoni
This paved quayside was established over 600 years ago, and widened in 1782.

San Zaccaria Paglia

San Zaccaria Danieli

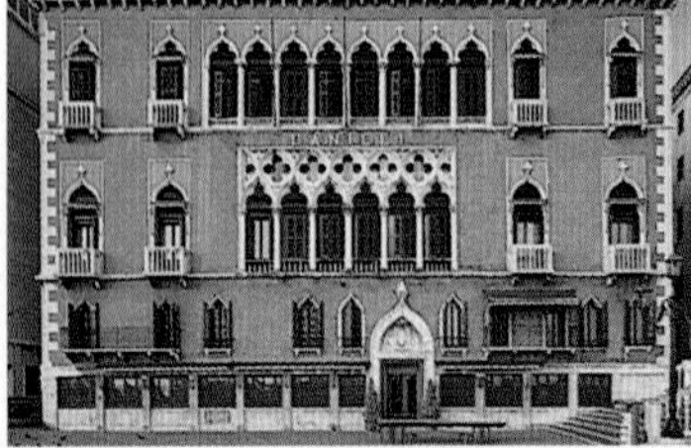

4 Hotel Danieli
Joseph da Niel, after whom this hotel was named, turned the Palazzo Dandolo into a haunt for 19th-century writers and artists.

Palazzo Priuli, overlooking the quiet Fondamenta Osmarin, is a fine Venetian Gothic palace. The corner window is particularly beautiful, but the early 16th-century façade frescoes have long since disappeared.

Locator Map
See Street Finder, maps 7, 8

❷ San Giorgio dei Greci
Subsidence is the cause of the city's tilting belltowers; San Giorgio dei Greci's looks particularly perilous.

❶ ★ San Zaccaria
Coducci added Renaissance details such as this panel to the Gothic façade.

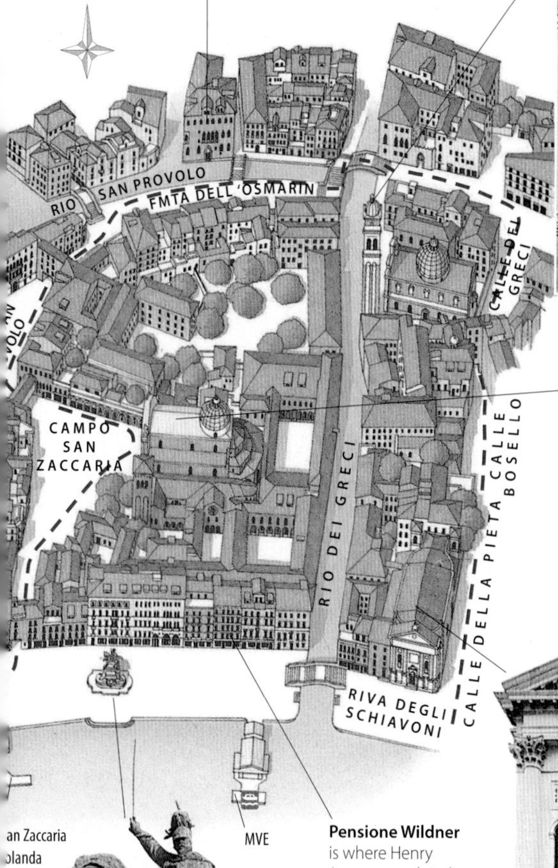

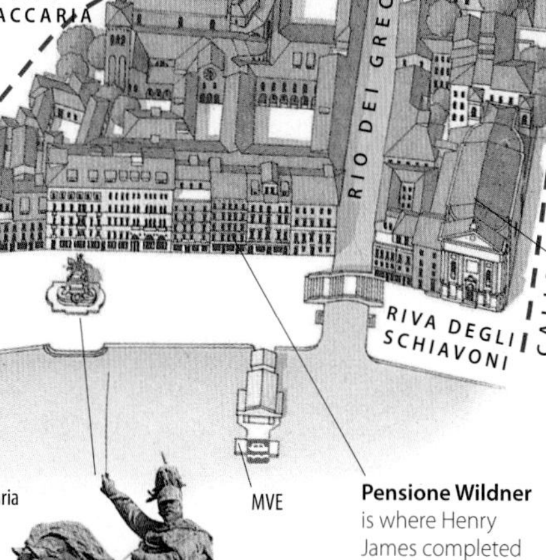

Key

▬ Suggested route

0 metres 75

0 yards 75

Pensione Wildner is where Henry James completed *Portrait of a Lady* (1881).

The Statue of Vittorio Emanuele II, the first king of a united Italy, was sculpted by Ettore Ferrari in 1887.

❸ ★ La Pietà
In Vivaldi's day, the church became famous for the superb quality of its musical performances.

For keys to symbols *see back flap*

❶ San Zaccaria

Campo San Zaccaria. **Map** 8 D2. **Tel** 041 522 12 57. San Zaccaria. **Open** 10am–noon, 4–6pm Mon–Sat, 4–6pm Sun & public hols. Chapels & Crypt.

Set in a quiet square a stone's throw from the Riva degli Schiavoni, this church blends Flamboyant Gothic and Classical Renaissance styles. Founded in the 9th century, San Zaccaria was completely rebuilt between 1444 and 1515. Antonio Gambello began the façade in Gothic style and, when Gambello died in 1481, Mauro Coducci completed the upper section, adding all the Classical detail.

The adjoining Benedictine convent, which had close links with the church, became quite notorious for the riotous behaviour of its nuns. The majority were from families of Venetian nobility, many of them sent to the convent to avoid the expense of a dowry.

Every Easter the doge came with his entourage to San Zaccaria – a custom which originated as an expression of gratitude to the nuns, who had relinquished part of their garden so that Piazza San Marco could be enlarged.

The artistic highlight of the interior (illuminate with coins in the meter) is Giovanni Bellini's sumptuously coloured and superbly serene *Madonna and Child with Saints* (1505) in the north aisle.

On the right of the church is a door to the Chapel of St Athanasius, which leads to the Chapel of San Tarasio. The chapel is decorated with vault frescoes (1442) by Andrea del Castagno of Florence, and Gothic polyptychs painted in 1443–4 by Antonio Vivarini and Giovanni d'Alemagna. The relics of eight doges lie buried in the waterlogged crypt.

Distant view of San Giorgio dei Greci's tilting campanile

❷ San Giorgio dei Greci

Map 8 D2. **Tel** 041 523 95 69. San Zaccaria. **Open** 9am–1pm, 2:30–5pm Tue–Sat, 9am–1pm Sun (for Mass only). Museo dell'Icone: **Tel** 041 522 65 81. **Open** 9am–5pm daily.

The most remarkable feature of this 16th-century Greek church is the listing campanile, which looks as if it is about to topple into the Rio dei Greci. Inside is the *matroneo* – the gallery where, in keeping with Greek Orthodox custom, the women sat apart from the men. Note also the iconostasis separating the sanctuary from the nave. The nearby Scuola di San Nicolò dei Greci, redesigned in 1678, is now the museum of icons of the Hellenic Institute.

Detail from *The Nun's Parlour at San Zaccaria* by Francesco Guardi

❸ La Pietà

Riva degli Schiavoni. **Map** 8 D2. **Tel** 041 522 21 71. San Zaccaria. **Open** 10:15am–noon & 3–5pm Tue–Fri, 10:15am–1pm & 2–5pm Sat & Sun. noon Tue–Fri. **pietavenezia.org**

The church of La Pietà (or Santa Maria della Visitazione) dates from the 15th century. It was rebuilt in 1745–60 by Giorgio Massari, and the Classical façade was added in 1906. The church has a cool, elegant interior, with an oval plan. The resplendent ceiling fresco, *Triumph of Faith* (1755), was painted by Giambattista Tiepolo.

The Pietà started its life as a foundling home for orphans. It proved so popular that a warning plaque was set up (still to be seen on the side wall), threatening damnation to parents who tried to pass off their children as orphans.

From 1703 until 1740, Antonio Vivaldi directed the musical groups and wrote numerous oratorios, cantatas and vocal pieces for the Pietà choir, and the church became famous for its performances.

It is now a popular venue for concerts, with an emphasis on Vivaldi. These are held throughout the year, usually on Mondays and Thursdays.

Bas relief on La Pietà's early 20th-century façade

❹ Hotel Danieli

Riva degli Schiavoni 4196. **Map** 7 C2. **Tel** 041 522 64 80. San Zaccaria. **danielihotelvenice.com**

One of the most celebrated hotels in Europe, the Danieli's deep-pink façade is a landmark on the Riva degli Schiavoni. Built in the 14th century, it became famous as the venue for the first opera performed in Venice, Monteverdi's *Proserpina Rapita* (1630). The palace became a hotel in 1822 and soon gained popularity with the literary and artistic set. Its famous guests included Balzac, Proust, Dickens, Cocteau, Ruskin, Debussy and Wagner. In the 1830s Room 10 witnessed an episode in the love affair between the French poet and dramatist Alfred de Musset, and novelist George Sand: when de Musset fell ill after a surfeit of orgies, Sand ran off with her Venetian doctor.

Riva degli Schiavoni – the city's most famous promenade

❺ Riva degli Schiavoni

Map 8 D2. San Zaccaria.

The sweeping promenade that forms the southern quayside of Castello was named after the traders from Dalmatia (Schiavonia) who used to moor their boats and barges here. For those who arrive in Venice by water, this long curving quayside is a spectacular introduction to the charms of the city.

At its western end, close to Piazza San Marco, the broad promenade teems during the day with tourists thronging around the souvenir stalls and people hurrying to and from the *vaporetto* stops. Nothing can detract, however, from the glorious views across the lagoon to the island of San Giorgio Maggiore *(see p99)*.

The Riva degli Schiavoni has always been busy with boats. Canaletto's drawings in the 1740s and 1750s show the Riva bustling with gondolas, sailing boats and barges. The gondolas are still here, but it is also chock-a-block with water taxis, *vaporetti*, excursion boats and tugs. Naval ships and ocean liners can also often be seen.

The modern annexe of the Hotel Danieli caused a great furore when it was built in 1948. Intruding on a waterfront graced by fine Venetian palaces and mansions, its stark outline is still something of an eyesore. The annexe marks the spot where Doge Vitale Michiel II was stabbed to death in 1172. Three centuries earlier, in 864, Doge Pietro Tradonico had suffered the same fate in nearby Campo San Zaccaria.

❻ Ponte della Paglia and Bridge of Sighs

Map 7 C2. San Zaccaria.

The name of the Ponte della Paglia may derive from the boats that once moored here to off-load their cargoes of straw *(paglia)*. Originally built in 1360, the existing structure dates from 1847.

According to legend, the Bridge of Sighs, built in 1600 to link the Doge's Palace with the New Prisons, takes its name from the lamentations of the prisoners as they made their way over to the offices of the feared State Inquisitors. Access to the bridge is available to the public via the Doge's Palace *(see p89)*.

Ponte della Paglia behind the Bridge of Sighs

❼ Museo Diocesano d'Arte Sacra

Sant'Apollonia, Ponte della Canonica, Castello 4312. **Map** 7 C2. **Tel** 041 522 91 66. San Zaccaria. **Open** 10am–5pm Thu–Tue. **Closed** public hols. includes entry to cloisters. **veneziaubc.org**

An architectural gem, the cloister of Sant'Apollonia is the only Romanesque building in the city. Only a few steps from St Mark's, it provides a quiet retreat from the Piazza.

The monastery was once the home of Benedictine monks. In 1976 its cloisters became the home of the Diocesan Museum of Sacred Art, founded to provide a haven for works of art from closed or deconsecrated churches. The collection includes paintings, statues, crucifixes and many pieces of valuable silver. There are two workshops, staffed by volunteers who restore the paintings and statues. The collection is ever-changing, but among the major permanent exhibits are works by Luca Giordano (1634–1705), which came from the Church of Sant'Aponal, and a 16th-century wood and crystal tabernacle. The museum is also home to the Salvador Dalí Universe, containing over 100 works by the artist.

❽ Fondazione Querini Stampalia

Campo Santa Maria Formosa, 5252 Castello. **Map** 7 C1. **Tel** 041 271 14 11. San Zaccaria. Palace: **Open** 10am–6pm Tue–Sun (to 10pm Fri & Sat). Library: **Open** 10am–midnight Tue–Sat, 10am–7pm Sun. **querinistampalia.org**

The large Palazzo Querini Stampalia was commissioned in the 16th century by the descendants of the old Venetian Querini family. Great art lovers, they filled the palace with fine paintings.

In 1868 the last member of the dynasty bequeathed the palace and the family collection of art to the foundation that bears his name. The paintings include works by Giovanni Bellini, Giambattista Tiepolo and some vignettes by Pietro and Alessandro Longhi. The library on the first floor, open to the public, has over 200,000 books.

❾ Campo Santa Maria Formosa

Map 7 C1. Rialto, Fondamente Nuove. Church: **Tel** 041 275 04 62. **Open** 10am–5pm Mon–Sat. **Closed** 1 Jan, Easter, 15 Aug, 25 Dec. **chorusvenezia.org**

Large, rambling and flanked by handsome palaces, this market square is one of the most characteristic *campi* of Venice. On the southern side is the church of Santa Maria Formosa, distinctive for its swelling apses. Built on ancient foundations, the church was designed by Mauro Coducci in 1492 but took over a century to assume its current form. Unusually, it has two main façades – one overlooking the *campo*, the other the canal. The campanile was added in 1688. Its most notable feature is the truly grotesque stone face that decorates its foot.

Inside, Palma il Vecchio's polyptych *St Barbara and Saints* (c.1523) ranks among the great Venetian masterpieces and looks particularly splendid since its restoration by the American Save Venice organization. Palma's portrayal of the handsome and dignified figure of St Barbara glorifies Venice's ideal female beauty. She is surrounded by saints, with a central lunette of the *pietà* above. St Barbara was the patron saint of soldiers: in wartime they prayed to her for protection; in victory they came for thanksgiving.

Palma il Vecchio's *St Barbara* in Santa Maria Formosa

❿ Palazzo Grimani

Ramo Grimani, 4858 Castello. **Map** 7 C1. San Zaccaria, Ospedale Civile. **Tel** 041 241 15 07. **Open** 8:15am–7:15pm Tue–Sun (to 2pm Mon). **Closed** 1 Jan, 25 Dec. (combined ticket with the Accademia also available). **palazzogrimani.org**

Palazzo Grimani was once a famous residence-museum. The building housed a fine collection of antiquities after the two Grimani brothers, Giovanni, Patriarch of Acquileia, and Vettore, a Procurator of St Mark's, renovated their grandfather's palace in the mid-16th century. The result is a magnificient work of architecture, which combines Tuscan and Roman elements with the original Venetian ones. The Roman courtyard and the monumental staircase are its fine examples. Although the rooms are unfurnished, the decoration is rich, with stuccoing, statues, fireplaces and stunning frescoes. Of particular note are the Tribuna and the Sala a Fogliami (Foliage Room). Temporary exhibitions are also held at the palazzo.

⓫ Statue of Colleoni

Campo Santi Giovanni e Paolo. **Map** 3 C5. Ospedale Civile.

Bartolomeo Colleoni, the famous *condottiere* or commander of mercenaries, left his fortune to the Republic on condition that his statue was placed in front of San Marco. A prominent statue in the Piazza would have broken with precedent, so the Senate cunningly had Colleoni raised before the Scuola di San Marco instead of the basilica. A touchstone of early Renaissance sculpture, the equestrian statue of the proud warrior (1481–8) is by the Florentine Andrea Verrocchio and, after his death, was cast in bronze by Alessandro Leopardi. The statue has a strong sense of power and movement which arguably ranks it alongside works of Donatello.

⓬ Scuola Grande di San Marco

Campo Santi Giovanni e Paolo. **Map** 3 C5. Ospedale Civile. Library: **Tel** 041 529 43 23. **Open** 9:30am–1pm, 2–5pm Tue–Sat. **Closed** public hols, one week in mid-Aug, 24 Dec–1 Jan. Church: **Tel** 041 522 56 62. **Open** 8am–noon Mon–Sat, 9–10am Sun. **scuolagrandesanmarco.it**

Few hospitals can boast as rich and unusual a façade as that of Venice's Ospedale Civile. It was built originally as one of the six great confraternities of the city *(see p131)*. Their first headquarters were destroyed by fire in 1485, but the Scuola was rebuilt at the end of the 15th century. The delightful asymmetrical façade, with its arcades, marble panels and trompe l'oeil effects, was the work of Pietro Lombardo working in conjunction with Giovanni Buora. The upper order was finished by Mauro Coducci in 1495. The interior was revamped in the 19th century and, since then, most of the artistic masterpieces have been dispersed.

The library, boasting a fine carved 16th-century ceiling, is now a Museum of the History of Medicine, displaying antique texts and instruments. The hospital chapel, the Church of San Lazzaro dei Mendicanti, contains an early Tintoretto, *Saint Ursula and the 11,000 Virgins*, and works by Veronese.

⓭ Santi Giovanni e Paolo

See pp120–21.

⓮ Ospedaletto

Calle Barbaria delle Tole, 6691 Castello. **Map** 4 D5. **Tel** 041 271 90 12. Ospedale Civile. **Open** on request (€60 for guided tour).

Beyond the south flank of Santi Giovanni e Paolo *(see pp120–21)* is the façade of the Ospedaletto or Santa Maria dei Derelitti. The Ospedaletto was set up by the Republic in 1527 as a charitable institution to care for the sick and aged, and to educate orphans and abandoned girls. Such an education consisted largely of the study of music. The girls performed in choirs and orchestras, bringing in funds for the 1776 *sala della musica,* which became the main performance venue and features frescoes by Jacopo Guarana.

The church, which formed part of the Ospedaletto, was built by Andrea Palladio in 1575. Its façade was added in 1674 by Baldassare Longhena. The huge, hideous heads on the façade have been described as anti-Classical abominations, likened to diseased figures and swollen fruit. The interior of the church is decorated with notable paintings from the 18th century, including *The Sacrifice of Isaac* (1720) by Giambattista Tiepolo.

Fresco by Guarana in the *sala della musica* of the Ospedaletto

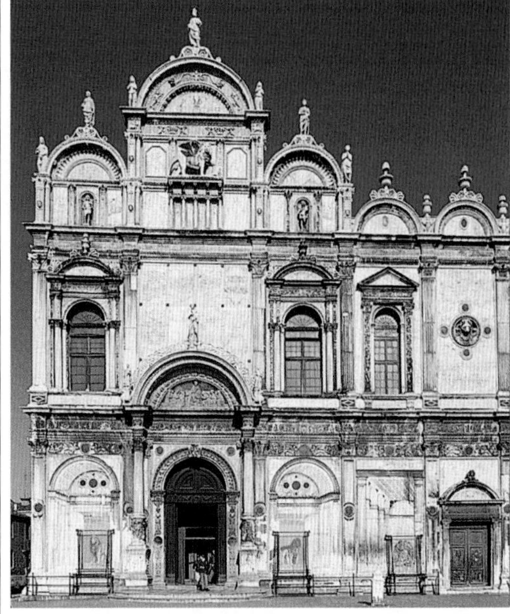

The decorative façade of the Scuola Grande di San Marco

⓯ San Francesco della Vigna

Campo della Confraternità. **Map** 8 E1. **Tel** 041 520 61 02. Celestia. **Open** 8am–12:30pm, 3–6:30pm daily.

The name "della Vigna" derives from a vineyard that was bequeathed to the Franciscans in 1253. The church which the order built here in the 13th century was rebuilt under Jacopo Sansovino in 1534, with a façade added in 1562–72 by Palladio.

The interior has a rich collection of works of art, including sculpture by Alessandro Vittoria, Paolo Veronese's *The Holy Family with Saints* (1562) and Antonio da Negroponte's *Virgin and Child* (c.1450). The *Madonna and Child with Saints* (1507) by Giovanni Bellini hangs near the cloister.

⓰ San Lorenzo

Campo San Lorenzo. **Map** 8 D1. San Zaccaria. **Closed** for restoration.

The church of San Lorenzo's only claim to fame is as the alleged burial place of Marco Polo *(see p147)*. Unfortunately, there is nothing to show for it because his sarcophagus disappeared during rebuilding in 1592.

In 1987 restorers discovered the foundations of two earlier churches, dating from AD 850 and the late 12th century. The foundations of the present medieval structure and substantial remains of the marble floor have been damaged by water seeping in from the adjacent canal. Restoration work is planned but its future use is as yet undecided.

Marco Polo

⓭ Santi Giovanni e Paolo

More familiarly known as San Zanipolo, Santi Giovanni e Paolo vies with the Frari *(see pp106–7)* as the city's greatest Gothic church. It was built in the late 13th to early 14th centuries by the Dominican friars, and is striking for its huge dimensions and architectural austerity. Known as the Pantheon of Venice, it houses monuments to no fewer than 25 doges. Many of these are outstanding works, executed by the Lombardi family and other leading sculptors of the day.

★ Cappella del Rosario
The Adoration of the Shepherds is one of many works by Paolo Veronese which decorate the Rosary Chapel.

★ Tomb of Nicolò Marcello
This magnificent Renaissance monument to Doge Nicolò Marcello (d.1474) was sculpted by Pietro Lombardo.

★ Tomb of Pietro Mocenigo
Pietro Lombardo's great masterpiece (1481) commemorates the doge's military pursuits when he was Grand Captain of the Venetian forces. This west side wall is largely devoted to Mocenigo monuments.

KEY

① **The marble columns** were taken from a former church on the island of Torcello.

② **The doorway**, which is decorated with Byzantine reliefs, is one of the earliest Renaissance architectural features in Venice. The portico carvings are attributed to Bartolomeo Bon.

③ **The sacristy** has paintings that celebrate the Dominican Order.

④ **The panel by Vivarini** shows *Christ Bearing the Cross* (1474).

⑤ **The bronze statue** is a monument to Doge Sebastiano Venier, who was Commander of the Fleet at Lepanto.

⑥ **The Baroque high altar** is attributed to Baldassare Longhena.

⑦ **St Catherine of Siena's foot** is buried here in a precious reliquary; her relics are scattered in churches throughout Italy.

VISITORS' CHECKLIST

Practical Information
Campo Santi Giovanni e Paolo (also signposted San Zanipolo).
Map 3 C5. **Tel** 041 523 59 13.
basilicasantigiovanniepaolo.it
Open 9am–6pm Mon–Sat, noon–6pm Sun. 8am & 6:30pm Mon–Sat, 9am, 11am & 6:30pm Sun.

Transport
Fondamente Nuove, Ospedale Civile.

★ Tomb of Andrea Vendramin
The nude figures of Lombardo's masterpiece (1476–8) were considered unsuitable and replaced by St Catherine and St Mary Magdalene (side statues).

★ Cappella di San Domenico
Piazzetta's *Glory of St Dominic* for this chapel – his only ceiling painting – displays a mastery of colour, perspective and foreshortening. The artist had a profound influence on the young Tiepolo.

The Nave
The vast interior is cross-vaulted, held by wooden tie-beams and supported by ten huge columns of Istrian stone blocks.

St George Slaying the Dragon by Carpaccio, in the Scuola di San Giorgio degli Schiavoni

⓱ Scuola di San Giorgio degli Schiavoni

Calle Furlani, Castello 3959A. **Map** 8 E1. **Tel** 041 522 88 28. San Zaccaria. **Open** 1:30–4:30pm Mon, 9:15am–1pm, 1:30–4:30pm Tue–Sun. **Closed** public hols & special events.

Within this surprisingly simple Scuola are some of the finest paintings of Vittore Carpaccio, which were commissioned by the Schiavoni community in Venice during the 15th century.

From the earliest days of the Republic, Venice forged trade links with the coastal region of Schiavonia (Dalmatia) across the Adriatic. By 1420 permanent Venetian rule was established there, and many of the Schiavoni came to live in Venice. By the mid-15th century the Slav colony in the city had grown considerably and the State gave permission for them to found their own confraternity *(see p131)*.

The Scuola was established in 1451. It is a delightful spot to admire Carpaccio's exceptional works of art, and has changed very little since the rebuilding of the Scuola in 1551. The exquisite frieze, executed between 1502 and 1508, shows scenes from the lives of favourite saints: St George, St Tryphon and St Jerome. Each episode of the narrative cycle is remarkable for its vivid colouring, minutely observed detail and historic record of Venetian life. Outstanding among them are *St George Slaying the Dragon*, *St Jerome Leading the Tamed Lion to the Monastery* and *The Vision of St Jerome*.

⓲ San Giovanni in Bragora

Campo Bandiera e Moro. **Map** 8 E2. **Tel** 041 520 59 06. Arsenale. **Open** 9–11am, 3:30–5pm Mon–Sat, 9:30am–noon Sun.

The foundations of this simple church date back to ancient times but the existing building is essentially Gothic (1475–9). The intimate interior has major works of art which demonstrate the transition from Gothic to early Renaissance. Bartolomeo Vivarini's altarpiece, *Madonna and Child with Saints* (1478), is clearly Gothic. Contrasting with this is Cima da Conegliano's *Baptism of Christ* (1492–5) on the main altar. This large-scale narrative scene, in a realistic landscape, set a precedent for later Renaissance painters.

Model of the *Bucintoro* in the Museo Storico Navale

⓳ Museo Storico Navale

Campo San Biagio, Arsenale, Castello 2148. **Map** 8 F3. **Tel** 041 244 13 99. Arsenale. **Open** 8:45am–1:30pm Mon–Fri (to 1pm Sat). **Closed** public hols. **marina.difesa.it/venezia**

It was the Austrians who, in 1815, first had the idea of assembling the remnants of the Venetian navy and creating a historical naval museum. They began with a series of models of vessels that had been produced in the 17th century by the Arsenale, and to these added all the naval paraphernalia they could obtain. The exhibits include friezes preserved from famous galleys of the past, a variety of maritime firearms and a replica of the Doge's ceremonial barge, the *Bucintoro*.

The collection has been housed in an ex-warehouse on the waterfront since 1958, and now traces Venetian and Italian naval history to the present day.

The first exhibits you see on entering are the World War II human torpedoes or "pigs". Torpedoes such as these helped sink HMS *Valiant* and HMS *Queen Elizabeth*: they were guided to their target by naval divers who jumped off just before impact.

The rest of the museum is divided into the Venetian navy, the Italian navy from 1860 to today, Adriatic vessels and the Swedish room. The museum is well laid out and has informative explanations in English.

⑳ Arsenale

Map 8 F1. Arsenale.
Limited public access.

Heart of the city's maritime power, the Arsenale was founded in the 12th century and enlarged in the 14th to 16th centuries to become the greatest naval shipyard in the world. The word "arsenal" derives from the Arabic *darsina'a*, house of industry – which indeed it was.

At its height in the 16th century, a workforce of 16,000, the *arsenalotti*, was employed to construct, equip and repair the great Venetian galleys *(see pp48–9)*. One of the first production lines in Europe, it was like a city within a city, with its own workshops, warehouses, factories, foundries and docks. Surrounded by crenellated walls, the site today is largely abandoned. The huge gateway and vast site are the only evidence of its former splendour. The gateway, in the form of a triumphal arch, was built in 1460 by Antonio Gambello and is often cited as Venice's first Renaissance construction.

The two lions guarding the entrance were pillaged from Piraeus (near Athens) by Admiral Francesco Morosini in 1687. A third lion, bald and sitting upright, bears runic inscriptions on his haunches, thought to have been carved by Scandinavian mercenaries who in 1040 fought for the Byzantine emperor against some Greek rebels.

Entrance to the Arsenale, guarded by 16th-century towers

By the 17th century, when the seeds of Venetian decline were well and truly sown, the number of *arsenalotti* plummeted to 1,000. Following the Fall of the Republic in 1797, Napoleon destroyed the docks and stripped the *Bucintoro* (the Doge's ceremonial ship) of its precious ornament. Cannons and bronzes were melted down to contribute to victory monuments celebrating the French Revolution.

Today the area is under military administration and for the most part closed to the public. The bridge by the arched gateway affords partial views of the shipyard, or try taking a scenic trip on a *vaporetto* (either route 4.1 or 4.2), which follows the perimeter of the Arsenal.

Some parts of the Arsenale, such as the Corderie, the old rope factory, are now being used as performance spaces or exhibition centres, mostly for the Biennale *(see p260)*. A research consortium developing marine and coastal technologies also operates from the Arsenale.

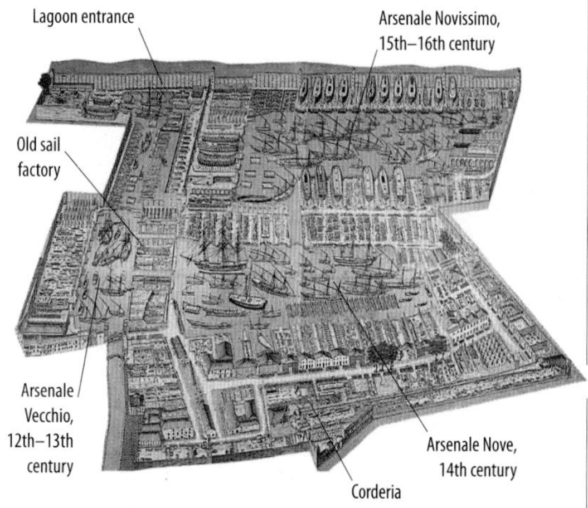

Late 18th-century engraving of the Arsenale

The Assembly-Line System

The *arsenalotti*, master shipbuilders of the 16th century

During the Arsenale's heyday, a Venetian galley could be constructed and fully equipped with remarkable speed and efficiency. From the early 16th century the hulls, which were built in the New Arsenal, were towed past a series of buildings in the Old Arsenal to be equipped in turn with rigging, ammunition and food supplies. By 1570, when Venice was faced with the Turkish threat to take Cyprus, the Arsenale was so fast it was capable of turning out an entire galley in 24 hours. Henry III of France witnessed the system's efficiency in 1574 when the *arsenalotti* completed a galley in the time it took for him to partake in a State feast.

㉑ Exploring Eastern Castello

This peaceful stroll takes you from the animated Castello quayside to the quieter eastern limits of the city. The focal point of the tour is the solitary island of San Pietro di Castello, site of the former cathedral of Venice. From here you head south to the island of Sant'Elena with its historic church and Venice's football stadium, and return via the public gardens along the scenic waterfront.

⑯ The calm and leafy Giardini Pubblici

⑱ A tribute to the women fallen in World War II

Via Garibaldi

This broad, busy street ① was created by Napoleon in 1808 by filling in a canal. The first house on the right ② was the home of John Cabot and his son Sebastian, the Italian navigators who in 1497 found what they thought to be the coast of China (but in reality was the Labrador coast of Newfoundland). Near the end of the street, through a gate on the right, a bronze monument of Garibaldi ③ by Augusto Benvenuti (1885) marks the northern end of the Viale Garibaldi, which leads to the public gardens.

Returning to Via Garibaldi, take the left-hand embankment at the end of the street, pausing on the bridge ④ for distant views of the Arsenale *(see p123)*.

Then take the first on the left, marked "Calle San Gioachin", cross a small bridge and turn left at the "crossroads". Once you are past Campo Ruga ⑤, take the second turning on the right and cross the bridge over the broad Canale di San Pietro.

The Island of San Pietro di Castello

The old church of San Pietro di Castello ⑥ and its freestanding, tilting campanile ⑦ overlook a grassy square. The island, once occupied by a fortress *(castello)*, was one of Venice's earliest settlements. The church, which was probably founded in the 7th century, became the cathedral of Venice and remained so until 1807, when San Marco took its place *(see p82)*. The existing church, built to a Palladian design in the mid-16th century, has several notable features. These include the Lando

Chapel, the Vendramin Chapel and the marble throne from an Arabic tombstone, originally said to have been the Seat of St Peter.

In the south of the square, Mauro Coducci's elegant stone campanile was built in 1482–8, and the cupola was added in 1670. Beside the church, the Palazzo Patriarcale (Bishop's Palace) ⑧ was turned into barracks by Napoleon. The old cloisters are overgrown and strung with washing and fishing nets.

From the Bishop's Palace, take the Calle drio il Campanile south from the square and turn left when you come to the canal. The first turning right takes you across the Ponte di

② The busy Via Garibaldi, with John Cabot's house on the far right

Quintavalle ⑨, a wooden bridge with good views of brightly coloured boats anchored on either side of the waterway.

San Pietro to Sant'Elena

The large and semi-derelict building at the foot of the bridge is the ex-church and monastery of Sant'Anna ⑩. Take the first left off the *fondamenta*, cross Campiello Correr and then take Calle Tiepolo and cross the Secco Marina. Continue straight ahead and over the bridge for the Church of San Giuseppe ⑪. On the rare occasions it is open you can see Vincenzo Scamozzi's monument to Doge Marino Grimani (1595–1605). Cross the square beyond the church and zigzag left, right and left again for Paludo San Antonio, an uninspiring modern street that has been reclaimed from marshland *(palude)*. At the far end cross the bridge over the Rio dei Giardini ⑫ and take the street ahead. A right turn along Viale Quattro 4 Novembre brings you down to the spacious gardens of Parco delle Rimembranze ⑬. At the southern end of the park, cut left at Calle Buccari ⑭, then right for the bridge over Rio di Sant'Elena. In front, the Church of Sant'Elena ⑮ is a pretty Gothic church founded in the 13th century. Retrace your steps over the bridge and turn left, following the waterfront back through the park.

⑦ The island of San Pietro, with its curious leaning campanile

⑮ Detail from Gothic façade of Sant'Elena

Giardini Pubblici and the Biennale Pavilions

At the far side of the park, the bridge across the Rio dei Giardini brings you to the public gardens and to the Biennale gate entrance ⑯. If it happens to be summer in an odd-numbered year, the gardens will be open with the Biennale pavilions ⑰, at which 40 to 50 nations exhibit many examples of contemporary art *(see p260)*.

Riva dei Partigiani

Outside the public gardens on Riva dei Partigiani is a large bronze statue. Lying on the steps of the embankment, the monument can only be seen at low tide. Known as La Donna Partigiana, this is a memorial to all the women who were killed fighting in World War II ⑱.

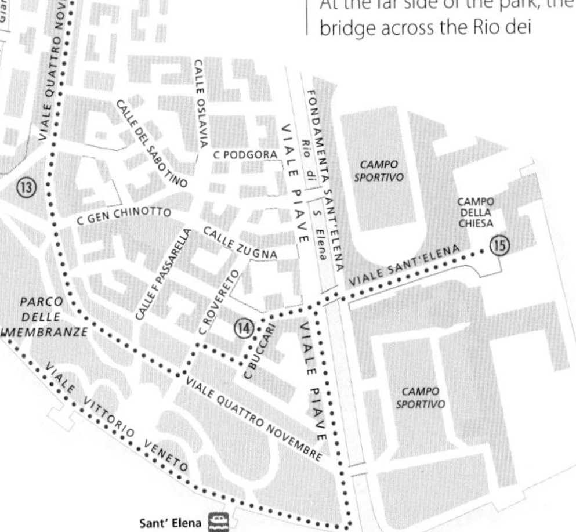

0 metres 200
0 yards 200

Key

• • • Walk route

Tips for Walkers

Starting point: The western end of Via Garibaldi.
Length: Just under 5 km (3 miles).
Getting there: *Vaporetto* No. 1, 4.1 or 4.2 to Arsenale.
Stopping-off points: There are a handful of simple cafés and trattorias along the route; most of them are found on Via Garibaldi. The waterside Caffè Paradiso at the entrance to the Giardini Pubblici has excellent views. The green shady parks are a welcome retreat from the bustle of the city, and are perfect for picnicking.

For additional map symbols *see back flap*

Sights at a Glance

Churches

- 6 Santa Maria dei Carmini
- 7 San Nicolò dei Mendicoli
- 8 Angelo Raffaele
- 9 San Sebastiano
- 12 San Trovaso
- 13 Santa Maria della Visitazione
- 14 Gesuati
- 18 Santa Maria della Salute

Museums and Galleries

- 3 Ca' Rezzonico
- 15 *Accademia see pp134–7*
- 16 Peggy Guggenheim Collection
- 19 Punta della Dogana

Historic Buildings

- 5 Scuola Grande dei Carmini
- 11 Squero di San Trovaso

Streets, Bridges and Squares

- 1 Campo San Barnaba
- 2 Ponte dei Pugni
- 4 Campo Santa Margherita
- 10 Zattere
- 17 Campiello Barbaro

Madonna del Carmelo by Tiepolo on the ceiling of the hall of the Scuola Grande dei Carmini

DORSODURO

Dorsoduro is named after the solid subsoil on which this area has been built up (the name means "hard backbone"). The western part, the island of Mendigola, was colonized centuries before the Rialto was established in AD 828 as the permanent seat of Venice. The settlement then spread eastwards, covering another six islands.

East of the Accademia, the Dorsoduro is a quiet and pretty neighbourhood with shaded squares, quiet canals and picturesque residences belonging to wealthy Venetians and foreigners. In the early 1900s the area was favoured by British expatriates who used to attend the Anglican church of St George in Campo San Vio. Among the area's attractions are the wide-embracing lagoon views, both from the eastern tip near the Salute and from the Zattere across to the island of Giudecca. West of the Accademia, the *sestiere* is more vibrant, with the busy Campo Santa Margherita as its attractive focal point. Further west, the shabbier area around the beautiful church of San Nicolò dei Mendicoli was originally the home of fishermen and sailors. The Dorsoduro plays host to several major collections of art, notably the Accademia Gallery and the Peggy Guggenheim Collection of 20th-century art. The churches are also rich repositories of paintings and sculpture: San Sebastiano has fine paintings by Paolo Veronese; the Scuola Grande dei Carmini and the church of the Gesuati have ceilings painted by Giambattista Tiepolo.

Restaurants *see p245*

1 Agli Alboretti
2 Ai Gondolieri
3 Cantinone Storico
4 Lineadombra
5 Osteria Da Codruma
6 Pizzeria ae Oche
7 Ristorante La Riviera
8 Ristoteca Oniga
9 La Rivista
10 Taverna San Trovaso

See also Street Finder maps 5, 6, 7

Street-by-Street: Dorsoduro

Between the imposing palaces on the Grand Canal and the Campo Santa Margherita lies an almost silent neighbourhood of small squares and narrow alleys. The delightful Rio San Barnaba is best appreciated from the Ponte dei Pugni, near the barge selling fruit and vegetables. The Rio Terrà, though architecturally uninspiring, has a fascinating mask shop and some cafés that are lively at nighttime. All roads seem to lead to Campo Santa Margherita, the heart of Dorsoduro. The square bustles with activity, particularly in the morning, when the market stalls are functioning.

5 ★ Scuola Grande dei Carmini
Tiepolo painted nine ceiling panels for the Scuola in 1739–44. The central panel features the Virgin and St Simeon Stock.

RIO DI SANTA MARGHERITA
C DEL
C D CAFFETT
C DEL FORNO
CAMPO S MARG
R T S
CAMPO DEI CARMINI
CALLE D PAZIENZA
R T SCOAZZERA
RIO SAN BARNABA
FONDAMENTA GHERARD
C LUNGA SAN BARNAB

Palazzo Zenobio has been an Armenian college since 1850. Occasionally visitors can see the sumptuous 18th-century ballrooom.

6 Santa Maria dei Carmini
The church's oldest feature is the Gothic side porch with fragments of decorative Byzantine reliefs.

Key

— Suggested route

0 metres 50
0 yards 50

Fondamenta Gherardini runs beside the Rio San Barnaba, one of the prettiest canals in the *sestiere*.

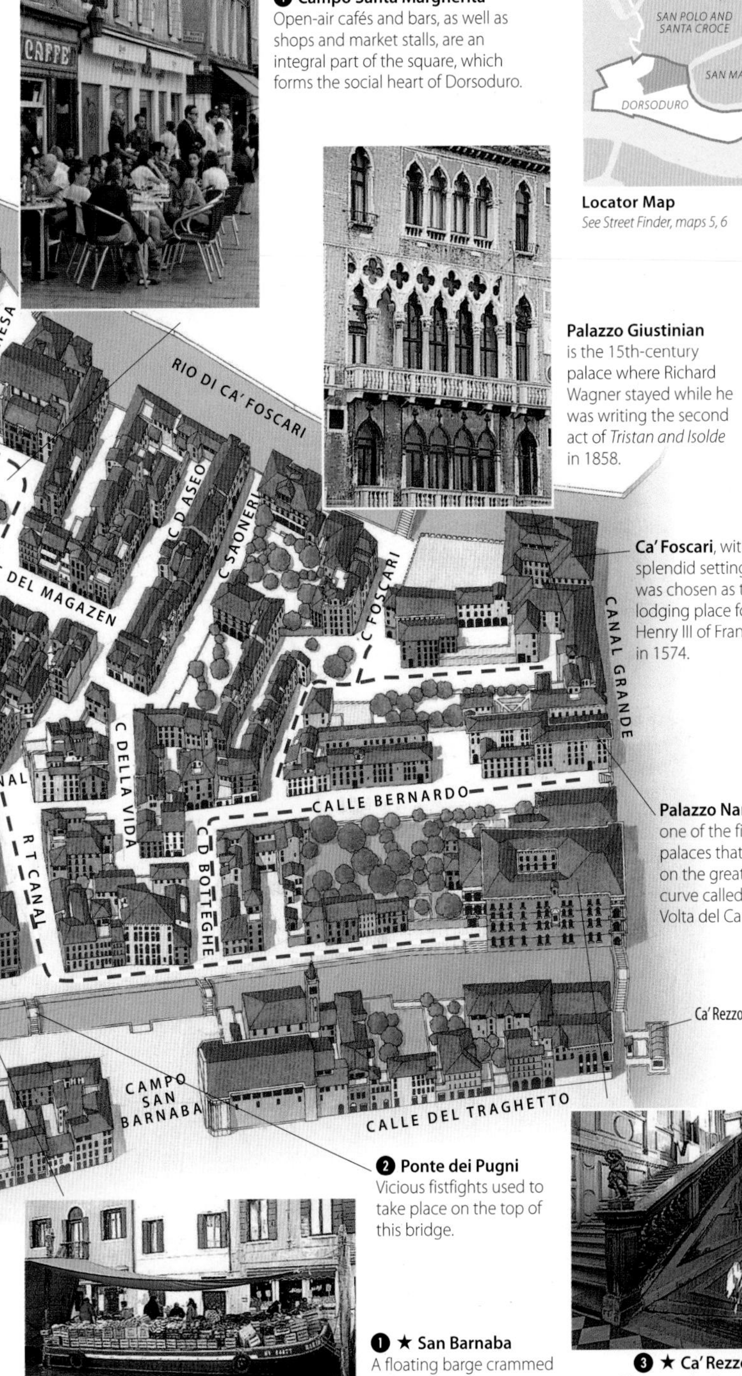

4 Campo Santa Margherita
Open-air cafés and bars, as well as shops and market stalls, are an integral part of the square, which forms the social heart of Dorsoduro.

Locator Map
See Street Finder, maps 5, 6

Palazzo Giustinian is the 15th-century palace where Richard Wagner stayed while he was writing the second act of *Tristan and Isolde* in 1858.

Ca' Foscari, with its splendid setting, was chosen as the lodging place for Henry III of France in 1574.

Palazzo Nani is one of the fine palaces that lie on the great curve called the Volta del Canal.

2 Ponte dei Pugni
Vicious fistfights used to take place on the top of this bridge.

1 ★ San Barnaba
A floating barge crammed with crates of fruit and vegetables lends a colourful note to the area.

3 ★ Ca' Rezzonico
The grand stairway has two putti, symbolizing winter and autumn.

❶ Campo San Barnaba

Map 6 D3. Ca' Rezzonico.

The Parish of San Barnaba, with its canalside square at the centre, was known in the 18th century as the home of impoverished Venetian patricians. They were attracted by the cheap rents, and while some relied on State support or begging, others worked in the State gambling house.

Today the square and canal, with its vegetable barge, are quietly appealing. The church (Tel: 041 296 06 30, open am Mon–Sat) is fairly unremarkable, apart from a Tiepolesque ceiling and a *Holy Family* attributed to Paolo Veronese.

❷ Ponte dei Pugni

Fondamenta Gherardini.
Map 6 D3. Ca' Rezzonico.

Venice has several Ponti dei Pugni ("bridges of fists"), but this is the most famous. Spanning the peaceful Rio San Barnaba, the small bridge is distinguished by two pairs of footprints set in white stone on top of the bridge. These mark the starting positions for the fights which traditionally took place between rival factions. Formerly there were no balustrades and contenders hurled each other straight into the water. The battles became so bloodthirsty that they were banned in 1705.

Boats and barges moored along the Rio San Barnaba

Tiepolo's *New World* fresco, part of a series in Ca' Rezzonico

❸ Ca' Rezzonico

Fondamenta Rezzonico 3136.
Map 6 E3. **Tel** 041 241 01 00. Ca' Rezzonico. **Open** 10am–6pm Wed–Mon (Nov–Mar: to 5pm). **Closed** 1 Jan, 1 May, 25 Dec.
carezzonico.visitmuve.it

This richly furnished Baroque palace is one of the most splendid in Venice. It is also one of the few palaces in the city, which opens its doors to the public. Since 1934 it has housed the museum of 18th-century Venice, its rooms furnished with frescoes, paintings and period pieces taken from other local palaces or museums.

The building was begun by Baldassare Longhena (architect of La Salute, *see p139*) in 1667, but the funds of the Bon family, who commissioned it, ran dry before the second floor was started. In 1712, long after Longhena's death, the unfinished palace was bought by the Rezzonicos, a family of merchants-turned-bankers from Genoa. A large portion of the Rezzonico fortune was spent on the purchase, construction and decoration of the palace. By 1758 it was in a fit state for the Rezzonicos to throw the first of the huge banquets and celebratory parties for which they later became renowned.

In 1888 the palace was bought by the poet Robert Browning and his son, Pen, who was married to an American heiress. Browning spoke of the "gaiety and comfort of the enormous rooms" but had little time to enjoy them. In 1889, he died of bronchitis.

Allegory of Strength, Andrea Brustolon

The outstanding attraction in the palace today is Giorgio Massari's ballroom, which occupies the entire breadth of the building. It has been beautifully restored and is embellished with gilded chandeliers, carved furniture by Andrea Brustolon and a ceiling with trompe l'oeil frescoes. Three rooms between the ballroom and Grand Canal side of the palace have ceilings with frescoes by Giambattista Tiepolo, including, in the Sala della Allegoria Nuziale, his lively *Nuptial Allegory* (1758).

Eighteenth-century paintings occupy the *piano nobile* (second floor). A whole room is devoted to Pietro Longhi's portrayals of everyday Venetian life. Other paintings worthy of note are Francesco Guardi's *Ridotto* (1748) and *Nuns' Parlour* (1768), and one of the few Canalettos in Venice, his *View of the Rio dei Mendicanti* (1725). Giandomenico Tiepolo's fascinating series of frescoes painted for his villa at Zianigo (1770–1800) are also to be found here. On the floor above is a reconstructed 18th-century apothecary's shop and a puppet theatre.

❹ Campo Santa Margherita

Map 6 D2. Ca' Rezzonico.

The sprawling square of Santa Margherita, lined with houses from the 14th and 15th centuries, is the lively hub of western Dorsoduro. Market stalls, offbeat shops and cafés attract many young people. The fish stalls sell live eels and lobster, the *erborista* alternative medicine, and the bakers some of the tastiest loaves in Venice.

The former church of Santa Margherita, now an auditorium owned by the university, lies to the north of the square. Visitors can see sculptural fragments from the original 18th-century church, including gargoyles, on the truncated campanile and adjacent house. The Scuola dei Varotari ("*Scuola* of the Tanners"), the isolated building in the centre of the square, has a faded relief of the Madonna della Misericordia protecting the tanners.

A 15th-century carving of Santa Margherita and the dragon

❺ Scuola Grande dei Carmini

Campo Carmini. **Map** 5 C2.
Tel 041 528 94 20. Ca' Rezzonico.
Open 11am–4pm daily.
Closed 1 Jan, 25 Dec.
W **scuolagrandecarmini.it**

The headquarters of the Carmelite confraternity was built beside their church in 1663. In the 1740s Giambattista Tiepolo was commissioned to decorate the ceiling of the *salone* (hall) on the upper floor. The nine ceiling paintings that he produced so impressed the Carmelites that Tiepolo was promptly made an honorary member of the brotherhood.

The ceiling shows *St Simeon Stock Receiving the Scapular of the Carmelite Order from the Virgin*. The Carmelites honoured St Simeon Stock because he re-established the order in Europe after its expulsion from the Holy Land in the 13th century.

The archive rooms also contain remarkable art and elaborate woodwork, with ceiling and wall paintings by Giustino Menescardi and caryatids by Giacomo Piazzetta.

Santa Maria dei Carmini

❻ Santa Maria dei Carmini

Campo Carmini. **Map** 5 C3. **Tel** 041 296 06 30. Ca' Rezzonico or San Basilio. **Open** 2:30–5pm Mon–Sat.

Known also as Santa Maria del Carmelo, this church was built in the 14th century but has since undergone extensive alterations.

The most prominent external feature is the lofty campanile, whose perilous tilt was skilfully rectified in 1688. The impressive interior is large, sombre and richly decorated. The arches of the nave are adorned with gilded wooden statues, and a series of paintings illustrating the history of the Carmelite Order.

There are two interesting paintings in the church's side altars. Cima da Conegliano's *Adoration of the Shepherds* (c.1509) is in the second altar on the right (coins in the light meter are essential). In the second altar on the left is Lorenzo Lotto's *St Nicholas of Bari with Saints Lucy and John the Baptist* (c.1529). This painting demonstrates the artist's religious devotion, personal sensitivity and his love of nature. On the right-hand side of this highly detailed, almost Dutch-style landscape, there is a tiny depiction of St George killing the dragon.

Scuole

The *scuole* were peculiarly Venetian institutions. Founded mainly in the 13th century, they were lay confraternities existing for the charitable benefit of the neediest groups of society, the professions or resident ethnic minorities (such as the Scuola degli Schiavoni, *see p122*). Some became extremely rich, spending large sums on buildings and paintings, often to the disadvantage of their declared beneficiaries.

Upper Hall of the Scuola Grande dei Carmini

Nave of San Nicolò dei Mendicoli, one of the oldest churches in Venice

7 San Nicolò dei Mendicoli

Campo San Nicolò. **Map** 5 A3.
Tel 041 275 03 82. San Basilio.
Open 10am–noon, 3–5:30pm Mon–Sat, 9am–noon Sun & public hols.

Contrasting with the remote and run-down area that surrounds it, this church remains one of the most charming and delightful in Venice. Originally constructed in the 12th century, it has been rebuilt extensively over the centuries; the little porch on the north flank dates from the 15th century.

Thanks to the Venice in Peril Fund, in the 1970s the church underwent one of the most comprehensive restoration programmes since the floods of 1966 *(see p54)*. The floor, which was 30 cm (1 ft) below the level of the canals, was rebuilt and raised slightly to prevent further damage, the roofs and lower walls were reconstructed, and paintings and statues restored. The interior is richly embellished, particularly the nave with its 16th-century gilded wood statues. On the upper walls is a series of paintings of the life of Christ by Alvise dal Friso and other pupils of Veronese.

8 Angelo Raffaele

Campo Angelo Raffaele. **Map** 5 B3.
Tel 041 522 85 48. San Basilio.
Open 10am–noon, 3–5:30pm Mon–Sat, 9am–noon Sun & public hols.

The main attraction of this 17th-century church is the series of panel paintings on the organ balustrade. These were executed in 1749 by Antonio Guardi, brother of the more famous Francesco. They tell the tale of Tobias, the blind prophet cured by the archangel Raphael, after whom the church is named.

San Sebastiano, viewed from the bridge of the same name

9 San Sebastiano

Campo San Sebastiano. **Map** 5 C3.
Tel 041 275 04 62. San Basilio.
Open 10am–5pm Mon–Sat.
Closed 1 Jan, Easter, 15 Aug, 25 Dec.
W **chorusvenezia.org**

This 16th-century church has one of the most colourful and homogeneous interiors of Venice. This is thanks to the artist Veronese, who, from 1555 to 1560 and again in the 1570s, was commissioned to decorate the sacristy ceiling, the nave ceiling, the frieze, the east end of the choir, the high altar, the doors of the organ panels and the chancel – in that order. The paintings, which are typical of Veronese, are rich and radiant, with sumptuous costumes and colours. Among the finest of his works are the three ceiling paintings that tell the story of Esther, Queen of Xerxes I of Persia, who brought about the deliverance of the Jewish people. Appropriately, the artist is buried in San Sebastiano, alongside the organ.

10 Zattere

Map 5 C4. Zattere or San Basilio.

Stretching along the southern part of the *sestiere*, the Zattere is the long quayside looking across to the island of Giudecca. The name derives from the rafts *(zattere)* made of and carrying timber from the Republic's forests. After skilful navigation along the River Piave, the rafts

Café tables laid out along the Zattere

were dismantled on arrival in Venice. On a sunny day it is a pleasure to sit at a waterside café here, looking across to the Church of the Redentore *(see p158)* or watching the waterbuses as they cross back and forth between the shores.

⓫ Squero di San Trovaso

Rio San Trovaso. **Map** 6 D4. 🚢 Zattere. No public access.

This is one of the few surviving gondola workshops in Venice *(see pp32–3)*, and the most picturesque. Its Tyrolean look dates from the days when craftsmen came down from the Cadore area of the Dolomites *(see p221)*.

It is not open to the public, but from the far side of the Rio San Trovaso it is possible to watch the upturned gondolas being given their scraping and tarring treatment. Nowadays, only around 10 boats are made each year, but there is still plenty to see.

⓬ San Trovaso

Campo San Trovaso. **Map** 6 D4. **Tel** 041 522 21 33. 🚢 Zattere or Accademia. **Open** 8–11am, 2:30–5:30pm Mon–Sat, 8–11am Sun.

The church of Santi Gervasio e Protasio, which in the eccentric Venetian dialect is slurred to "San Trovaso", was built in 1590. Unusually it has two identical façades, one overlooking a canal, the other a quiet square. The church stood on neutral ground between the parishes of the rival factions of the Castellani and Nicolotti families, and tradition has it that this necessitated a separate entrance for each party.

The interior houses some late paintings by Jacopo Tintoretto, and there are two notable works of art worth seeking out. Michele Giambono's 15th-century Gothic painting, *St Chrysogonus on Horseback*, is situated in the chapel on the right of the chancel, and exquisite marble reliefs of angels with instruments decorate the altar of the Clary chapel opposite.

⓭ Santa Maria della Visitazione

Fondamenta delle Zattere. **Map** 6 E4. **Tel** 041 522 40 77. 🚢 Zattere. **Closed** for restoration. Check ahead for details.

Situated beside the Gesuati, this Renaissance church was built between 1494 and 1524 by the Order of the Gesuati. Inside the church is a fine wooden ceiling painted by 16th-century Umbrian and Tuscan artists. The exterior *bocca di leone* to the right of the façade is one of several "lion's mouth" denunciation boxes surviving from the rule of the Council of Ten *(see p46)*; this one was used to complain about the state of the streets.

⓮ Gesuati

Fondamenta delle Zattere. **Map** 6 E4. **Tel** 041 275 04 62. 🚢 Zattere. **Open** 10am–5pm Mon–Sat. **Closed** 1 Jan, Easter, 15 Aug, 25 Dec.
W **chorusvenezia.org**

Not to be confused with the Gesuiti *(see p146)*, this church was built by the Dominicans, who took possession of the site in the 17th century, when the Gesuati Order was suppressed. Work began in 1726 and the stately façade reflects that of Palladio's Redentore church across the Giudecca. It is the most conspicuous landmark of the long Zattere quayside. The interior of the church is richly decorated.

Gesuati façade statue

Tiepolo's frescoed ceiling, *The Life of St Dominic* (1737–39), demonstrates the artist's mastery of light and colour. Equally impressive (and far easier to see) is his *Virgin with Saints* (1740), situated in the first chapel on the right. The church also boasts two altar paintings by Sebastiano Ricci and Giambattista Piazzetta.

Squero di San Trovaso, where gondolas are given a face-lift

⓯ Accademia

The largest collection of Venetian art in existence, the Gallerie dell'Accademia, is housed in three former religious buildings. The basis of the collection was the Accademia di Belle Arti, founded in 1750 by the painter Giambattista Piazzetta. In 1807 Napoleon moved the academy to these premises, and the collection was greatly enlarged by works of art from churches and monasteries he suppressed.

Ceiling Sketch
Tiepolo's *The Translation of the Holy House to Loreto* (c.1742) was a sketch for the ceiling of the Scalzi church *(see p149)*.

The Apothecary's Shop
Pietro Longhi is best known for his witty, gently satirical depictions of domestic patrician life in Venice. This detail comes from a painting dated c.1752.

Key to Floorplan

- Byzantine and International Gothic
- Early Renaissance
- High Renaissance
- Baroque, genre and landscapes
- Ceremonial paintings
- Temporary exhibitions
- Non-exhibition space

★ Cycle of St Ursula
(1495–1500) (detail)
The Arrival of the English Ambassadors is one of Vittore Carpaccio's eight paintings chronicling the tragic story of St Ursula.

The former Church of Santa Maria della Carità was rebuilt by Bartolomeo Bon in the mid-15th century.

Sala dell'Albergo

Entrance

The inner courtyard was designed by Andrea Palladio.

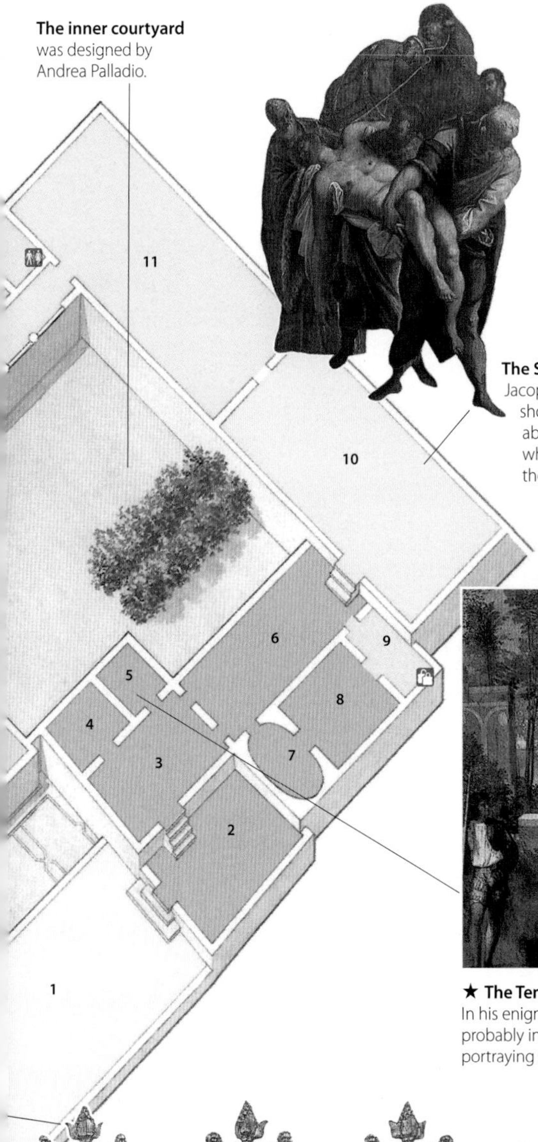

11

10

6

9

5

8

4

7

3

2

1

VISITORS' CHECKLIST

Practical Information
Campo della Carità. **Map** 6 E3.
Tel 041 520 03 45. **Open** 8:15am–7pm daily (to 2pm Mon).
Last adm: 45 mins before closing.
Closed 1 Jan, 1 May, 25 Dec.
Quadreria:
Open Fri am.
gallerieaccademia.org

Transport
Accademia.

The Stealing of St Mark
Jacopo Tintoretto's painting of 1562 shows the Christians of Alexandria abducting the body of St Mark, which was about to be burned by the pagans.

★ The Tempest (c.1507)
In his enigmatic landscape, Giorgione was probably indulging his imagination rather than portraying a specific subject.

★ Coronation of the Virgin
Paolo Veneziano's polyptych (1325) has a central image of the Virgin surrounded by a panoply of religious scenes. This detail shows episodes from the Life of St Francis.

Gallery Guide

The current programme of restoration work is ongoing; be prepared for absent paintings or whole sections closed off. It is sensible to phone ahead for more details. The paintings are dependent on natural light, so to see them at their best try to visit on a bright morning. Upstairs, a second gallery called Quadreria contains works by artists such as Bellini and Tintoretto. Guided visits are free of charge, but it is essential to book in advance.

Exploring the Accademia's Collection

Spanning five centuries, the fascinating collection of paintings in the Accademia provides a complete spectrum of the Venetian school, from the medieval Byzantine period through the Renaissance to the Baroque and Rococo *(see pp30–31)*. The order is more or less chronological, with the exception of the final rooms, which take visitors back to the Renaissance.

Portrait of a Gentleman (c.1525) by Lorenzo Lotto (detail)

Byzantine and International Gothic

Room 1 shows the influence of Byzantine art on the early Venetian painters. Paolo Veneziano, the true founder of the Venetian school, displays a blend of both Western and Eastern influences in his sumptuous *Coronation of the Virgin* (1325). The linear rhythms are quite unmistakably Gothic, yet the overall effect and the glowing gold background are distinctly Byzantine.

In the same room, *Coronation of the Virgin* (1448) by Michele Giambono shows the influence of International Gothic style, which was brought to Venice by Gentile da Fabriano and Pisanello. This particular style was characterized by delicate naturalistic detail, as typified by the birds and animals in the foreground of Giambono's painting.

Coronation of the Virgin (c.1448) by Michele Giambono

Early Renaissance

The Renaissance came late to Venice, but by the second quarter of the 15th century it had transformed the city into an art centre rivalling those of Florence and Rome. The Bellini family – Jacopo, the father, and his two sons Gentile and Giovanni – played a dominant role in the early Venetian Renaissance.

Central to Venetian art in the 15th century was the *Sacra Conversazione*, where the Madonna is portrayed in a unified composition with saints. Giovanni Bellini's altarpiece for San Giobbe (c.1487) in Room 2 is one of the finest examples. Giovanni, the younger Bellini, was profoundly influenced by the controlled rational style and mastery of perspective in the works of his brother-in-law, Andrea Mantegna, whose work *St George* (c.1460) is in Room 4. To Mantegna's rationality and harsh realism Giovanni added humanity. This is seen in his Madonna paintings (Rooms 4 and 5), which are masterpieces of warmth and harmony. Outstanding examples are *The Virgin and Child between St Catherine and St Mary Magdalene* (c.1490) in Room 4; *Madonna of the Little Trees* (c.1487) and *Virgin and Child with John the Baptist and a Saint* (c.1505) in Room 5. The inventive young artist Giorgione was influenced by Bellini, but went way beyond his master in his development of the landscape to create mood. In the famous, atmospheric *Tempest* (c.1507) in Room 5, this treatment of the landscape and the use of the figures to intensify that mood was an innovation adopted in Venetian painting of the 16th century and beyond.

Out on a limb from the main 16th-century Venetian tradition was the enigmatic Lorenzo Lotto, best known for portraits conveying moods of psychological unrest. His melancholic *Portrait of a Gentleman* (c.1525) in Room 7 is a superb example. More in the Venetian tradition, Palma il Vecchio's sumptuously coloured *Sacra Conversazione* in Room 8, painted around the same time, shows the unmistakable influence of the early work of Titian.

High Renaissance

Occupying an entire wall of Room 10, the monumental *Feast in the House of Levi* by Paolo Veronese (1573) was originally commissioned as *The Last Supper*. However, the

Paolo Veronese's *Feast in the House of Levi* (detail) (1573)

hedonistic detail in the painting, such as the drunkard and the dwarfs, was not well received and Veronese found himself before the Inquisition. Ordered to eliminate the profane content of the picture, he simply changed the title.

Jacopo Tintoretto made his reputation with *The Miracle of the Slave* (1548), which is also in Room 10. The painting shows his mastery of the dramatic effects of light and movement. This was the first of a series of works painted for the Scuola Grande di San Marco *(see p118)*. In the next room, Veronese's use of rich colour is best admired in the *Mystical Marriage of St Catherine* (c.1575).

The Rape of Europa (1740–50) by Francesco Zuccarelli (detail)

Baroque, Genre and Landscapes

Venice suffered from a lack of native Baroque painters, but a few non-Venetians kept the Venetian school alive in the 17th century. The most notable among these was the Genoese Bernardo Strozzi (1581–1644). The artist was a great admirer of the work of Veronese, as can be seen in his *Feast at the House of Simon* (1629) in Room 11. Also represented in this room is Giambattista Tiepolo, the greatest Venetian painter of the 18th century.

The long corridor (12) and the rooms which lead from it are largely devoted to light-hearted landscape and genre paintings from the 18th century. Among them are pastoral scenes by Francesco Zuccarelli, works by Marco Ricci, scenes of Venetian society by Pietro Longhi and a view of Venice by Canaletto (1763). This was the painter's entry for admission to the Accademia, and is a fine example of his sense of perspective.

Healing of the Madman (c.1496) by Vittore Carpaccio

Ceremonial Paintings

Rooms 20 and 21 return to the Renaissance, featuring two great cycles of paintings from the late 16th century. The detail in these large-scale anecdotal canvases provides a fascinating glimpse of the life, customs and appearance of Venice at the time. Room 20 houses *The Stories of the Cross* by Venice's leading artists, commissioned by the Scuola di San Giovanni Evangelista *(see p108)*. Each one depicts an episode of the relic of the Holy Cross, which the kingdom of Cyprus donated to the Scuola. In *The Procession in St Mark's Square* (1496) by Gentile Bellini, it is possible to compare the square with how it looks today.

Another, Vittore Carpaccio's *Healing of the Madman* (c.1496), shows the Rialto Bridge which collapsed in 1524.

The second series, minutely detailed *Scenes from the Legend of St Ursula* (1490s) by Carpaccio in Room 21, provides a brilliant kaleidoscope of life. Mixing reality and imagination, Carpaccio relates the episodes from the life of St Ursula using settings and costumes of 15th-century Venice.

Sala dell'Albergo

When the Scuola della Carità became the site of the Academy of Art in the early 19th century, the Scuola's *albergo* (where students lodged) retained its original panelling and 15th-century ceiling. The huge *Presentation of the Virgin* (1538) is one of the surprisingly few Titians in the gallery, and was painted for this very room. The walls are also adorned with a grandiose triptych (1446) by Antonio Vivarini and Giovanni d'Alemagna.

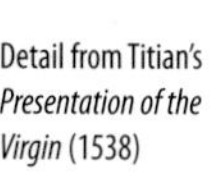

Detail from Titian's *Presentation of the Virgin* (1538)

16 Peggy Guggenheim Collection

Palazzo Venier dei Leoni, Dorsoduro 701. **Map** 6 F4. **Tel** 041 240 54 11. Accademia. **Open** 10am–6pm Wed–Mon. **Closed** 25 Dec. **guggenheim-venice.it**

Intended as a four-storey palace, the 18th-century Palazzo Venier dei Leoni in fact never rose beyond the ground floor – hence its nickname, *Il Palazzo Nonfinito* (The Unfinished Palace). In 1949 the building was bought as a home by the American millionairess Peggy Guggenheim (1898–1979), a collector, dealer and patron of the arts. A perspicacious and high-spirited woman, she befriended and furthered the careers of many innovative abstract and Surrealist artists. One was her second husband, Max Ernst. She bequeathed her vast collection of modern European and American art to her uncle Solomon R Guggenheim's foundation in 1979 with the stipulation that it remain in Venice. The museum was inaugurated in 1980.

The collection is one of Europe's leading modern art galleries. It consists of 200 paintings and sculptures, representing almost every modern art movement. The dining room has notable Cubist works of art including *The Poet* by Pablo Picasso. An entire room is devoted to Jackson Pollock, who was a Guggenheim discovery. Other artists represented are Braque, Miró, de Chirico, Magritte, Dalí, Kandinsky, Balla, Severini, Picabia, Delaunay, Duchamp, Klee, Mondrian, Malevich, Calder and Rothko.

Interno Olandese II (c.1928) by Joan Miró

Sculpture is laid out in the house and garden. One of the most elegant works is Constantin Brancusi's *Maiastra* (1912). The most provocative piece is Marino Marini's *Angelo della Città* (Angel of the City, 1948), a prominently displayed man sitting on a horse, erect in all respects. Embarrassed onlookers avert their gaze to enjoy views of the Grand Canal.

The Guggenheim is one of Venice's most visited sights. The light-filled rooms and the modern canvases provide a striking contrast to the Renaissance paintings which are the main attraction in Venetian churches and museums.

Regular events are held at the museum, including Kids' Day, for children aged 4–10. The Kids' Day project runs every Sunday in English and Italian with the aim of introducing youngsters to the world of modern and contemporary art. There are also daily presentations about Peggy Guggenheim and her collection, as well as Ask Me About Art, which actively encourages interaction between visitors and the interns working at the collection. The interns are art or art history graduates from all over the world – most speak several languages.

In 2009, a contemporary art gallery opened in the Punta della Dogana. The Guggenheim had planned to acquire the site; however, the French businessman François Pinault was granted the lease.

Maiastra by Constantin Brancusi

17 Campiello Barbaro

Map 6 F4. Salute.

An enchanting little square, Campiello Barbaro is shaded by trees and flanked on one side by the wisteria-clad walls of Ca' Dario.

Throughout the history of this Grand Canal palace, its owners have been plagued by accidents, suicides and bankruptcy, from Giovanni

Façade of the Palazzo Venier dei Leoni, the home of the Peggy Guggenheim Collection of modern art

Dario, who commissioned the building in 1479, to the industrialist Raul Gardini, who shot himself in 1993.

The ill-fated Ca' Dario, which backs on to Campiello Barbaro

⓲ Santa Maria della Salute

Campo della Salute. **Map** 7 A4. **Tel** 041 241 10 18. Salute. Church and Sacristy: **Open** 9am–noon, 3–5:30pm daily. for Sacristy.

This great Baroque Church standing at the entrance of the Grand Canal is one of the most imposing architectural landmarks of Venice. Henry James likened it to "some great lady on the threshold of her salon … with her domes and scrolls, her scalloped buttresses and statues forming a pompous crown and her wide steps disposed on the ground like the train of a robe". The church was built in thanksgiving for the deliverance of the city from the plague of 1630, hence the name *Salute*, meaning "health and salvation". Every 21 November, in celebration *(see p39)*, worshippers approach across a bridge of boats which span the mouth of the Grand Canal. Baldassare Longhena started the church in 1630. It was completed in 1687, five years after his death.

The interior consists of a large octagonal space below the cupola and six chapels radiating from the ambulatory. The altar's sculptural group by Giusto Le Corte represents the Virgin and Child protecting Venice from the plague. Some of the best works, such as Titian's ceiling paintings of *Cain and Abel, The Sacrifice of Abraham and Isaac and David and Goliath* (1540–49), are beyond the altar, where visitors are not allowed. In the sacristy is Titian's early altarpiece of *St Mark Enthroned with Saints Cosmos, Damian, Roch and Sebastian* (1511–12), while on the wall opposite the entrance is *The Wedding at Cana* (1551), a major work by Tintoretto.

Interior of the Salute showing the octagonal core of the church

The Baroque church of Santa Maria della Salute viewed from across the Grand Canal

⓳ Punta della Dogana

Campo della Salute. **Map** 7 A4. **Tel** 199 13 91 39; 044 523 03 13. Salute. **Open** 10am–7pm Wed–Mon. **Closed** 25 Dec. **palazzograssi.it**

The building housing the sea customs post was originally built in the 15th century to inspect the cargo of ships that intended to enter Venice. The customs house visitors see today was constructed in the late 17th century and replaced a tower that originally guarded the entrance to the Grand Canal. On the corner tower of the house, two bronze Atlases support a striking golden ball with a weathervane figure of Fortuna on the top.

After standing empty for many years, the building was bought by French billionaire François Pinault, who hired the Japanese architect Tadao Ando to revamp the interior. Punta della Dogana opened to the public in 2009, with an exhibition of Pinault's contemporary art collection.

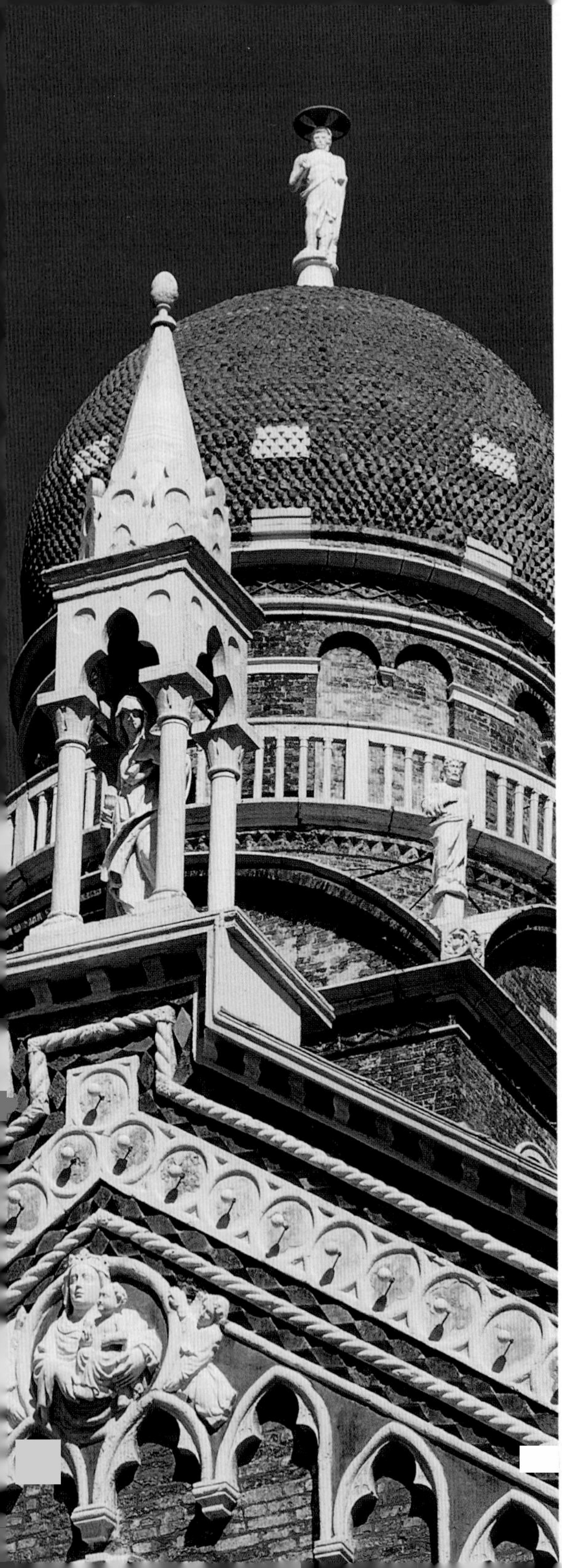

Sights at a Glance

Churches

1 Madonna dell'Orto
4 San Marziale
7 Gesuiti
8 Santa Maria dei Miracoli
9 San Giovanni Grisostomo
10 Santi Apostoli
13 Scalzi
14 San Giobbe

Streets and Squares

2 Campo dei Mori
3 Fondamenta della Sensa
5 Fondamente Nuove

Historic Buildings

6 Oratorio dei Crociferi
12 Palazzo Labia

Art Gallery

11 *Ca' d'Oro p148*

Historic Area

15 The Ghetto

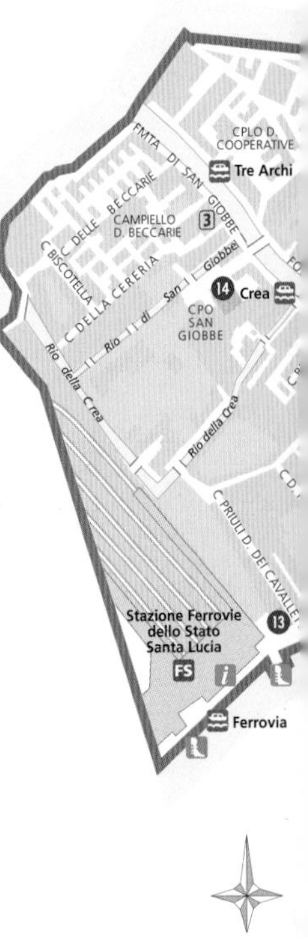

◀ Dome and richly decorated façade of the Madonna dell'Orto church

CANNAREGIO

The city's most northerly *sestiere,* Cannaregio, stretches in a large arc from the 20th-century railway station in the west to one of the oldest quarters of Venice in the east. The northern quays look out towards the islands in the lagoon, while to the south the *sestiere* is bounded by the upper sweep of the Grand Canal.

The name of the quarter derives either from the Italian *canne*, meaning "canes" or "reeds", which grew here centuries ago, or perhaps from "Canal Regio" or Royal Canal – the former name of what is now the Canale di Cannaregio. This waterway was the main entry to Venice before the advent of the rail link with the mainland. Over a third of the city's population lives in Cannaregio. For the most part it is an unspoiled area, divided by wide canals, crisscrossed by alleys and characterized by small stores, simple bars and the artisans' workshops. One of the prettiest and most remote quarters is in the north, near the church of Madonna dell'Orto and around Campo dei Mori.

Tourism is concentrated along two main thoroughfares: the Lista di Spagna and the wide Strada Nova, both on the well-worn route from the station to the Rialto. Just off this route lies the world's oldest ghetto. Though the Jewish community now lives all over the city, this is historically the most fascinating quarter of Cannaregio.

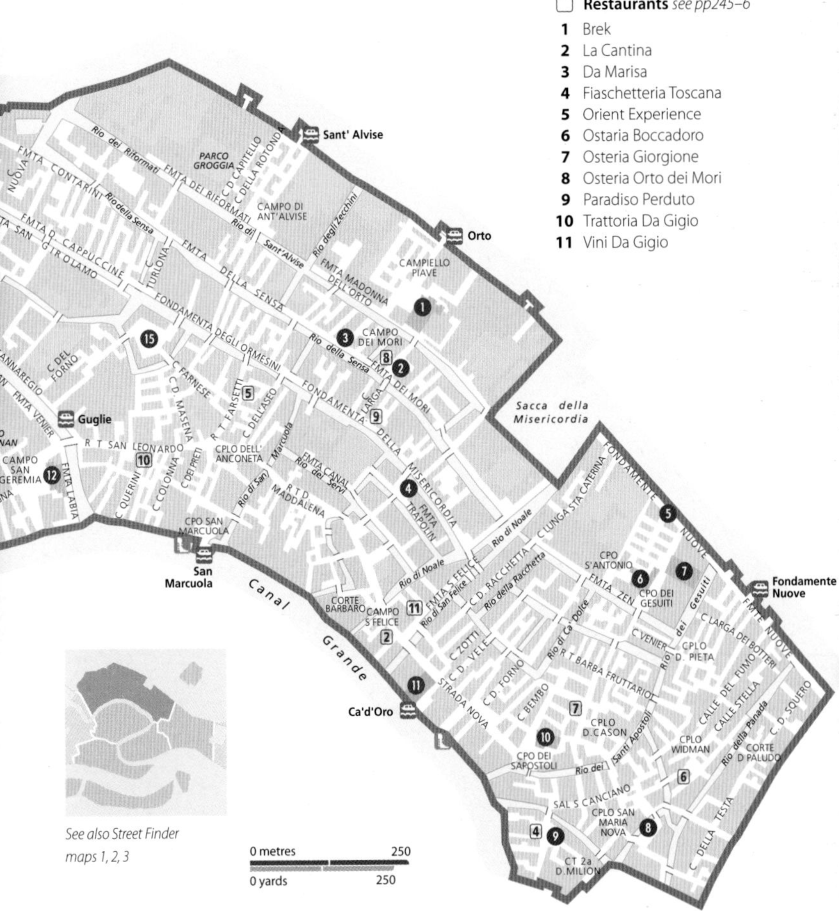

See also Street Finder maps 1, 2, 3

Street-by-Street: Cannaregio

Surprisingly few tourists find their way to this unspoiled quarter of northern Cannaregio. This is the more humble, peaceful side of Venice, where clean washing is strung over the waterways and the streets are flanked by the softly crumbling façades of shuttered houses. Along the wide *fondamente*, the little shops and stores stock basic groceries and the bars are always crowded with local Venetians. The quarter's cultural highlight is the lovely Gothic church of Madonna dell'Orto, Tintoretto's parish church.

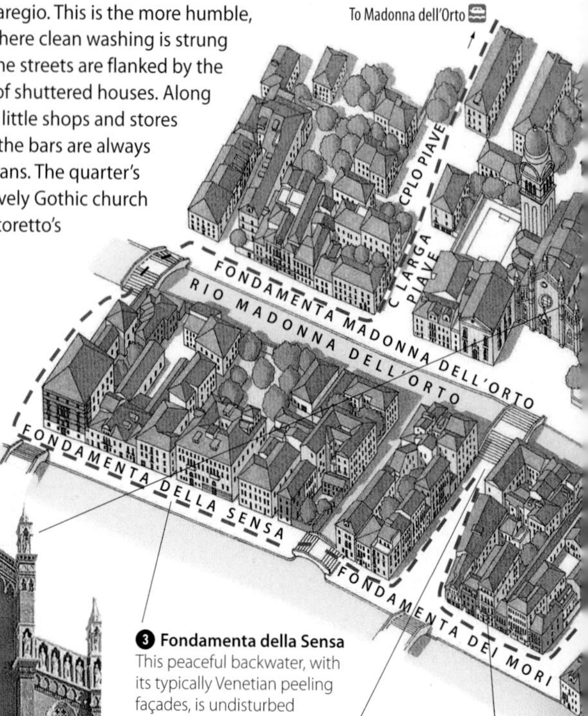

Key

Suggested route

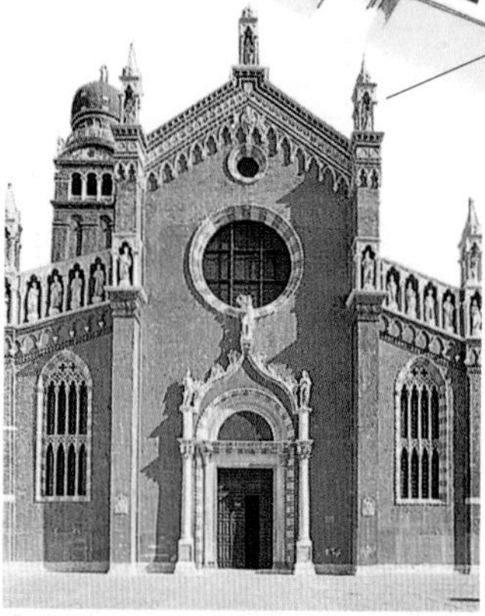

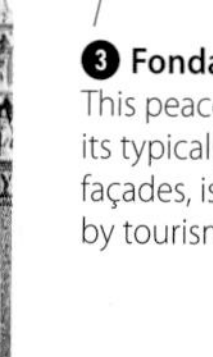

❸ Fondamenta della Sensa
This peaceful backwater, with its typically Venetian peeling façades, is undisturbed by tourism.

Tintoretto lived with his family in this house, No. 3399 Fondamenta dei Mori, from 1574 until his death in 1594.

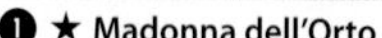

❶ ★ Madonna dell'Orto
One of the finest Gothic churches in Venice, Madonna dell'Orto has a richly decorated façade and a wealth of works by Tintoretto.

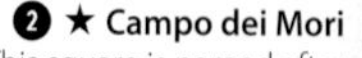

❷ ★ Campo dei Mori
This square is named after the stone statues of three Moors (*Mori*) which are carved on its walls.

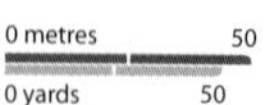

❹ San Marziale
Ceiling paintings by Sebastiano Ricci (1700–25) and a bizarre Baroque altar adorn this Baroque church.

Fondamenta Gasparo Contarini is named after the cardinal, diplomat and scholar who lived at Palazzo Contarini dal Zaffo *(see p72)* in the 16th century.

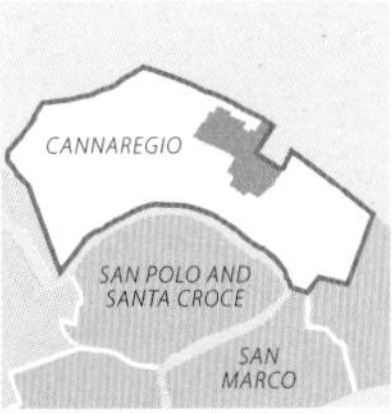

CANNAREGIO
SAN POLO AND SANTA CROCE
SAN MARCO

Locator Map
See Street Finder, maps 2, 3

Venetian oarsmen usually practise their technique on the lagoon, but they can also be seen on Cannaregio's quieter canals.

TA GASPARO CONTARINI
SACCA DELLA MISERICORDIA
RIO DEI MUTI
CORTE VECCHIA
FMTA DELL'ABBAZIA
RIO DELLA SENSA
C LARGA LEZZE
DAMENTA DELLA MISERICORDIA
DELLA MISERICORDIA
FMTA DELL'ABBAZIA
RIO DI NOALE

La Sacca della Misericordia is a large man-made basin opening out into the lagoon, with views of the islands of San Michele and Murano.

Campo dell'Abbazia, a peaceful open square with decorative herringbone floor tiles, is overlooked by the Scuola Vecchia della Misericordia and a deconsecrated church.

Fondamenta della Misericordia, named after the nearby *scuola*, was built in the Middle Ages.

For keys to symbols *see back flap*

The campanile of Madonna dell'Orto, crowned by an onion-shaped cupola

❶ Madonna dell'Orto

Campo Madonna dell'Orto. **Map** 2 F2. **Tel** 041 275 04 62. Madonna dell'Orto. **Open** 10am–5pm Mon–Sat, noon–5pm Sun & public hols. donation. on request. **madonnadellorto.org**

This lovely Gothic church is frequently referred to as the English Church in Venice, for it was British funds that helped restore the building after the 1966 floods *(see p54)*. The original church, founded in the mid-14th century, was dedicated to St Christopher, patron saint of travellers, to protect the boatmen who ferried passengers to the islands in the northern lagoon. The dedication was changed and the church reconstructed in the early 15th century following the discovery, in a nearby vegetable garden *(orto)*, of a statue of the Virgin Mary said to have miraculous powers. However, a 15th-century statue of St Christopher still stands above the portal.

The interior, faced almost entirely in brick, is large, light and uncluttered. The greatest treasures are the works of art by Tintoretto, who was a parishioner of the church. His tomb, which is marked with a plaque, lies in the chapel to the right of the chancel. The most dramatic of his works are the towering paintings in the chancel (1562–4). On the right wall is *The Last Judgment*, whose turbulent content caused John Ruskin's wife Effie to flee the church. In the painting *The Adoration of the Golden Calf* on the left wall, the figure carrying the calf, fourth from the left, is said to depict Tintoretto himself.

Inside the chapel of San Mauro visitors can see the radically restored statue of the Madonna which inspired the reconstruction of the church.

To the right of the entrance is Cima da Conegliano's magnificent painting *St John the Baptist and Other Saints* (c.1493). The vacant space opposite belongs to Giovanni Bellini's *Madonna with Child* (c.1478), which was stolen for the third time in 1993.

Tintoretto (1518–94)

Jacopo Robusti, nicknamed Tintoretto because of his father's occupation of silk dyer, was born, lived and died in Cannaregio. He left Venice only once in his life. A devout Christian, volatile and unworldly, his was a highly individual and theatrical style, conveyed by vivid exaggeration of light and movement, bold foreshortening and fiery, fluid brushstrokes. His remarkably prolific output has never been ascertained, but scores of his works survive, many still in the places for which they were painted. Examples of his canvases can be seen in the church of Madonna dell'Orto, the Accademia *(see pp134–7)*, and the Doge's Palace *(see pp88–93)*. His crowning achievement, however, was the great series of works for the Scuola Grande di San Rocco *(see pp110–11)*.

❷ Campo dei Mori

Map 2 F3. Madonna dell'Orto.

According to popular tradition, the "Mori" were the three Mastelli brothers who came from the Morea (the Peloponnese). The brothers, who were silk merchants by trade, took refuge in Venice in 1112 and built the Palazzo Mastelli, visible from Fondamenta Gasparo Contarini and recognizable by its camel bas-relief. The brothers' stone figures are embedded in the wall of the *campo* on its eastern side. The corner figure with the makeshift rusty metal nose (added in the 19th century) is "Signor Antonio Rioba", who, like the Roman Pasquino, was the focus of malicious fun and satire. A fourth Oriental merchant with a large turban faces the Rio della Sensa on the façade of Tintoretto's house *(see p142)*.

One of the stone Moors which gave the Campo dei Mori its name

The peaceful and atmospheric Fondamenta della Sensa

❸ Fondamenta della Sensa

Map 2 E2. Madonna dell'Orto.

When the marshy lands of Cannaregio were drained in the Middle Ages, three long, straight canals were created, running parallel to each other. The middle of these is the Rio della Sensa, which stretches from the Sacca di Sant'Alvise at its western end to the Canale della Misericordia in the east. The Fondamenta cuts through a quiet quarter of Cannaregio, where daily life goes on undisturbed by tourism. With its small grocery shops, and simple local bars and *trattories*, the neighbourhood feels far removed from San Marco.

This is one of the poorer areas of the city, though it is interspersed with fine (but neglected) palaces that once belonged to wealthy Venetians. Abbot Onorio Arrigoni lived at No. 3336 with his collection of antiques, and Palazzo Michiel (No. 3218) is an early Renaissance palace which became the French Embassy.

❹ San Marziale

Campo San Marziale. **Map** 2 F3. **Tel** 041 71 99 33. San Marcuola. **Open** by appointment only.

A Baroque church on medieval foundations, San Marziale was rebuilt between 1693 and 1721. The church is mainly visited for the ceiling frescoes by Sebastiano Ricci, a painter of the decorative Rococo style. Executed between 1700 and 1705, relatively early in Ricci's career, these bold, foreshortened frescoes already combine the Venetian tradition with flamboyant Rococo flourishes. Sadly, though, the vivid colours for which Ricci was known have been sullied by decades of grime. The central painting shows *The Glory of Saint Martial*, while the side paintings relate to the image of the Virgin.

❺ Fondamente Nuove

Map 3 B3. Fondamente Nuove.

The Fondamente Nuove or "New Quays" are actually over 400 years old. This chain of waterside streets borders the northern lagoon for one kilometre (over half a mile), from the solitary Sacca della Misericordia to the Rio di Santa Giustina in Castello on the eastern side.

Altar of San Marziale showing a carving of the Virgin and Child

Before the construction of the quays in the 1580s, this was a desirable residential area where the air was said to be healthy and the houses had gardens sloping down to the lagoon.

One of the residents was Titian, who lived from 1531 to his death in 1576 in a now demolished house at Calle Larga dei Botteri No. 5182–3 (a plaque marks the site).

Today the quaysides are aesthetically uninspiring but they do provide splendid views of the northern lagoon and, on a clear day, the peaks of the Dolomites. The island most visible from the quays is San Michele in Isola *(see p157)*, its dark, stately cypress trees rising high above the cemetery walls.

❻ Oratorio dei Crociferi

Campo dei Gesuiti, Cannaregio 4905. **Map** 3 B3. **Tel** 041 532 29 20, bookings 041 271 9012. Fondamente Nuove. **Open** by prior appointment for group visits only.

Founded in the 13th century as a hospital for returning Crusaders, the Oratorio dei Crociferi (built for the order of the Bearers of the Cross) was turned into a charitable institution for old people in the 15th century.

Between 1583 and 1591 the artist Palma il Giovane, commissioned by the Crociferi, decorated the chapel with a glowing cycle of paintings, depicting the crucial events in the history of this religious order. The paintings suffered terrible damage in the floods of 1966 *(see p54)*, but were successfully restored and the chapel reopened in 1984.

The inscriptions on the walls of some of the surrounding houses in the square are those of art and craft guilds, such as silk weavers and tailors, whose works formerly occupied the buildings.

The sumptuous ceiling frescoes of the Gesuiti church

❼ Gesuiti

Campo dei Gesuiti. **Map** 3 B3. **Tel** 041 528 65 79. Fondamente Nuove. **Open** 10am–noon, 4–6pm daily.

The Jesuits' close links with the papacy provoked Venetian hostility during the 17th century, and for 50 years they were refused entry to the city. However, in 1714 they were given permission to build this church in the north of Venice, on the site of a 12th-century church which had belonged to the Order of the Crociferi. Consecrated as Santa Maria Assunta, the church is always referred to simply as the Gesuiti; thus it is often confused with the Gesuati in Dorsoduro *(see p133)*.

Domenico Rossi's imposing Baroque exterior gives only a hint of the opulence of the interior. The proliferation of green and white marble, carved in parts like great folds of fabric, gives the impression that the church is clothed in damask.

Titian's *Martyrdom of St Lawrence* (c.1555), above the first altar on the left, has been described by the art historian Hugh Honour as "the first successful nocturne in the history of art".

❽ Santa Maria dei Miracoli

Campo dei Miracoli. **Map** 3 B5. **Tel** 041 275 04 62. Fondamente Nuove or Rialto. **Open** 10am–5pm Mon–Sat. **Closed** 1 Jan, Easter, 15 Aug, 25 Dec.
W **chorusvenezia.org**

An exquisite masterpiece of the early Renaissance, the Miracoli is the favourite church of many Venetians and the one where they like to get married. Tucked away in a maze of alleys and waterways in eastern Cannaregio, it is small and somewhat elusive, but well worth the effort needed to find it.

Often likened to a jewel box, the façade is decorated with various shades of marble, with fine bas-reliefs and sculpture. It was built in 1481–9 by the architect Pietro Lombardo and his sons to enshrine *The Virgin and Child* (1408), a painting believed to have miraculous powers. The picture, by Nicolò di Pietro, can still be seen above the altar. The interior of the church, which ideally should be visited when pale shafts of sunlight are streaming in through the windows, is embellished by pink, white and grey marble and crowned by a barrel-vaulted ceiling (1528) which has 50 portraits of saints and prophets. The balustrade, between the nave and the chancel, is decorated by Tullio Lombardo's carved figures of St Francis, Archangel Gabriel, the Virgin and St Clare. The screen around the high altar and the medallions of the Evangelists in the cupola spandrels are also by Lombardo. Above the main door, the choir gallery was used by the nuns from the neighbouring convent, who entered the church through an overhead gallery. The Miracoli was the subject of a major restoration programme, which was funded by the American Save Venice organization.

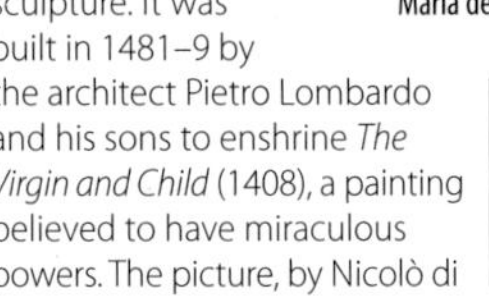

Decorative column, interior of Santa Maria dei Miracoli

Santa Maria dei Miracoli
The façade is a harmonious tapestry of decorated panels and multi-coloured polished stone.

The semicircular crowning lunette emphasizes the church's jewel-box appearance.

A false loggia is formed of Ionic arches, inset with windows. The marble used was reportedly left over from the building of San Marco.

The marble panels are fixed to the bricks by metal hooks. This method, which prevents the build-up of damp and salt water behind the panels, dates from the Renaissance.

San Giovanni Grisostomo, the last work of Mauro Coducci

❾ San Giovanni Grisostomo

Campo S Giovanni Grisostomo. **Map** 3 B5. **Tel** 041 523 52 93. Rialto. **Open** 8:15am–12:15pm, 3–7pm daily. No entry during Mass.

This pretty terracotta-coloured church is found near the Rialto. Built between 1479 and 1504, the church was the last work of Mauro Coducci.

The interior, built on a Greek-cross plan, is dark and intimate. Notable works of art include Giovanni Bellini's *St Jerome with Saints Christopher and Augustine* (1513), above the first altar on the right. Influenced by Giorgione, this was probably Bellini's last painting. Another artist inspired by Giorgione was Sebastiano del Piombo, whose *St John Chrysostom and Six Saints* (1509–11) hangs above the high altar. Some believe that the figures of St John the Baptist and St Liberal were painted by Giorgione himself.

❿ Santi Apostoli

Campo Santi Apostoli. **Map** 3 B5. **Tel** 041 523 82 97. Ca' d'Oro. **Open** 10am–noon, 3–7pm daily (may vary).

The Campo Santi Apostoli is a busy crossroads for pedestrians en route to the Rialto or the railway station. Its church is unremarkable architecturally and little remains of the 16th-century building.

Marco Polo

Born around 1254 in the quarter of Cannaregio near the Rialto, Marco Polo left Venice at the age of 18 for his four-year voyage to the court of the Emperor Kublai Khan. He impressed the Mongol emperor and stayed for some 20 years, working as a travelling diplomat.

Returning to Venice in 1295, he brought with him a fortune in jewels and a host of spellbinding stories about the Khan's court.

As a prisoner of war in Genoa in 1298 he compiled an account of his travels, with the cooperation of an inmate. Translated into French, this was to become *Le Livre des Merveilles*. Despite the fact that many Italians disbelieved his wondrous tales of the East, the book was an instant success. His nickname became Marco Il Milione (of the million lies); hence the name of the two little courtyards where the Polo family lived: Corte Prima del Milion and Corte Seconda del Milion.

Marco Polo leaving on his travels, from a manuscript c.1338

A notable exception, however, is the enchanting late 15th-century Renaissance Corner Chapel on the right of the nave, believed to have been designed by Mauro Coducci. The chapel contains *The Communion of St Lucy* by Giambattista Tiepolo (1748), the tomb of Marco Corner, probably by Tullio Lombardo (1511), and an inscription to Corner's daughter, Caterina Cornaro, Queen of Cyprus, who was buried here before she was moved to the Church of San Salvatore *(see p98)*.

Tomb of Doge Marco Corner in Santi Apostoli (Corner Chapel)

⓫ Ca' d'Oro

See p148.

⓬ Palazzo Labia

Fondamenta Labia (entrance on Campo S Geremia). **Map** 2 D4. **Tel** 041 78 11 11. Ponte Guglie. **Closed** for restoration. Call ahead for up-to-date information.

The Labias were a wealthy family of merchants from Catalonia who bought their way into the Venetian patriciate in 1646. Towards the end of the century they built their prestigious Baroque palace, with a splendid façade, on the wide Cannaregio Canal, close to its junction with the Grand Canal.

In 1745–50 the ballroom was frescoed by Giambattista Tiepolo. The wonderfully painted scenes are taken from the life of Cleopatra but the setting is Venice, and the queen's attire is that of a 16th-century noble lady.

Passed from one owner to another the palace gradually lost all trace of its former grandeur and variously served as a religious foundation, a school and a doss-house. Between 1964 and 1992 it was owned by the Italian broadcasting network, RAI, which undertook its restoration.

⓫ Ca' d'Oro

One of the great showpieces of the Grand Canal, the Ca' d'Oro (or House of Gold) is the finest example of Venetian Gothic architecture in the city. The façade, with its finely carved ogee windows, Oriental pinnacles and exotic marble tracery, has an unmistakable flavour of the east. But this once gloriously embellished *palazzo* suffered many changes of fortune and there is now little inside to remind visitors that this was once a 15th-century palace. Since 1984 it has been home to the Giorgio Franchetti Collection.

History

In 1420 the wealthy patrician Marino Contarini commissioned the building of what he was determined would be the most magnificent palace in the city. The decoration and the intricate carving were executed by a team of Venetian and Lombard craftsmen, and he had the façade adorned in ultramarine, gold leaf and vermilion.

In the course of the 16th century the house was remodelled by a succession of owners, and by the early 18th century was semi-derelict. In 1846 the Russian Prince Troubetzkoy bought it for the famous ballerina Marie Taglioni. Under her direction, the Ca' d'Oro suffered barbaric restoration. The open staircase was ripped out, the wellhead by Bartolomeo Bon (1427–8) was sold and much of the stonework removed. It was finally rescued by Baron Franchetti, a patron of the arts, who restored it to its former glory and bequeathed it to the State in 1915. A restoration programme for the façade, first put into action in the 1970s, is now finally completed, revealing the building's exotic design. The pretty paved courtyard contains Bon's beautifully carved wellhead. This was one of the pieces retrieved by Franchetti.

Tullio Lombardo's *Double Portrait*

The *Annunciation* (1504) by Vittore Carpaccio and assistants

First Floor

Pride of place is given to Andrea Mantegna's *St Sebastian* (1506), the artist's last painting and Franchetti's favourite work of art. The *portego* (gallery) opening on to the Grand Canal is a showroom of sculpture. Among the finest pieces are bronze reliefs by the Paduan sculptor Il Riccio (1470–1532), Tullio Lombardo's marble *Double Portrait* (c.1493) and Sansovino's lunette of the Virgin and Child (c.1530). Rooms to the right of the *portego* have some fine Renaissance bronzes and, among the paintings, an *Annunciation* and *Death of the Virgin* (both c.1504) by Vittore Carpaccio and assistants. A room to the left of the *portego* is devoted to non-Venetian painting, and includes Luca Signorelli's *Flagellation* (c.1480).

Second Floor

The upper floor houses paintings by Venetian masters, including a *Venus* by Titian, two Venetian views by Guardi and fresco fragments by Titian, as well as tapestries and ceramics. Explanatory cards aid visitors.

VISITORS' CHECKLIST

Practical Information
Canal Grande (Calle Ca' d'Oro).
Map 3 A4. **Tel** 041 520 03 45.
Open 8:15am–2pm Mon, 8:15am–7:15pm Tue–Sat, 10am– 6pm Sun.
Closed 1 Jan, 1 May, 25 Dec. partial. **cadoro.org**

Transport
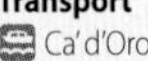
Ca' d'Oro.

⓭ Scalzi

Fondamenta Scalzi. **Map** 1 C4. **Tel** 041 71 51 15. Ferrovia. **Open** 7am–noon, 4–7pm daily.

Beside the modern railway station *(see p62)* stands the church of Santa Maria di Nazareth, known as the Scalzi. The *scalzi* were "barefooted" Carmelite friars who came to Venice during the 1670s and commissioned their church to be built on the Grand Canal. Designed by Baldassare Longhena, the huge Baroque interior is an over-elaboration of marble, gilded woodwork and sculptures. The ceiling painting, *The Council of Ephesus* by Ettore Tito (1934), replaced Giambattista Tiepolo's fresco of *The Translation of the Holy House to Loreto* (1743–5), which was destroyed by the Austrian bombardment of 24 October 1915.

⓮ San Giobbe

Campo San Giobbe. **Map** 1 C3. **Tel** 041 275 04 62. Ponte dei 3 Archi. **Open** 10am–1:15pm Mon–Sat. **Closed** 1 Jan, Easter, 15 Aug, 25 Dec. **chorusvenezia.org**

The church of San Giobbe stands in a remote *campo* full of cats. The early Gothic structure of the church was modified in the 1470s by Pietro Lombardo, who added Renaissance elements to the design, such as the saints over the portal. The Martini chapel, second on the left, is decorated with Della Robbia-style glazed terracotta. The altarpieces by Giovanni Bellini and Vittore Carpaccio were removed when Napoleon suppressed the monastery of San Giobbe, and are now in the Accademia Gallery *(pp134–7)*. The church is undergoing restoration; check the website for details.

Saint by Lombardo, San Giobbe portal

⓯ The Ghetto

Map 2 E3. **Tel** 041 71 53 59. Ponte Guglie. Museo Ebraico: Campo del Ghetto Nuovo. Ponte Guglie. **Open** 10am–7pm (Oct–May: to 5:30pm) Sun–Fri. **Closed** 1 Jan, 1 May, 25 Dec, Jewish hols. for the synagogues, in English, every hour from 10:30am. **museoebraico.it**

In 1516 the Council of Ten *(see p48)* decreed that all Jews in Venice be confined to an islet of Cannaregio. The quarter was cut off by wide canals and the two watergates were manned by Christian guards. The area was named the Ghetto after a foundry – *geto* in Venetian – that formerly occupied the site. The name was subsequently given to Jewish enclaves throughout the world. By day Jews were allowed out of the Ghetto, but at all times they were made to wear identifying badges and caps. The only trades they could pursue were in textiles, money-lending and medicine.

Campo del Ghetto Nuovo, the oldest part of the Ghetto

The wrought-iron bridge leading northwards out of the Ghetto

The rising number of Jews forced the Ghetto to expand. Buildings rose vertically and spread into the Ghetto Vecchio (1541) and the neighbouring Ghetto Novissimo (1633). By the mid-17th century the Jewish population numbered over 5,000.

In 1797 Napoleon pulled down the gates, but under the Austrians the Jews were again forced into confinement. It was not until 1866 that they were granted their freedom.

Of the 500 Jews now in Venice, only 33 live in the Ghetto. However, the quarter has not lost its ethnic character. There are kosher food shops, a Jewish baker, a Jewish library, and two synagogues where religious ceremonies still take place. There are also several shops on the large Campo del Ghetto Nuovo, which sell items such as glass rabbis and Hanukah lamps.

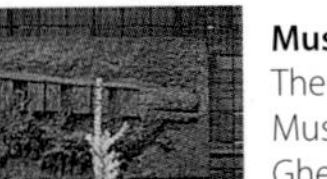

Flowers in front of the Holocaust Memorial

Museo Ebraico

The small Jewish Museum in the Ghetto Nuovo houses a collection of artifacts from the 17th–19th centuries. A guided tour of the quarter's synagogues leaves from the museum daily except Saturday, every hour from 10:30am to 5:30pm (4:30pm in winter). Led by English-speaking guides, the tours give a fascinating glimpse into the past life of the Ghetto. A short history of the quarter is followed by a visit to the lavishly decorated German, Spanish and Levantine synagogues.

DESE

THE LAGOON ISLANDS

Shrouded in myth and superstition, the lagoon was once the preserve of fishermen and hunters. But marauders in the 5th and 6th centuries AD drove mainland dwellers to the safety of the marshy lagoon *(see p44)*. Here, they conquered their watery environment, which was protected from the open sea by thin sandbanks *(lidi)*, created from silt washed down by the rivers of the Po Delta. In the 13th century the first *murazzi* were built – seawalls of angular stone which safeguard the *lidi* from erosion. Experiments with tidal barriers continue in an effort to combat the ever-present threat of flooding *(see p55)*.

The thriving communities that once lived and traded here are long gone. Many of the islands, formerly used as sites for monasteries, hospitals or powder factories, are now abandoned, but a handful of them are undergoing development – one as an international university, another as an exclusive resort.

Sights at a Glance

1 *Torcello pp154–5*
2 Burano
3 San Francesco del Deserto
4 Murano
5 San Michele
6 Giudecca
7 San Servolo
8 Santa Maria della Grazia
9 San Lazzaro degli Armeni
10 Lido
11 San Clemente
12 Lazzaretto Nuovo
13 Poveglia

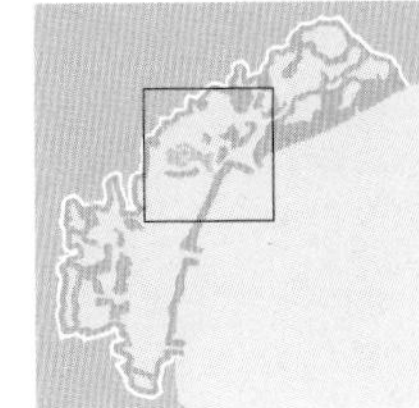

Key

Central Venice

Major road

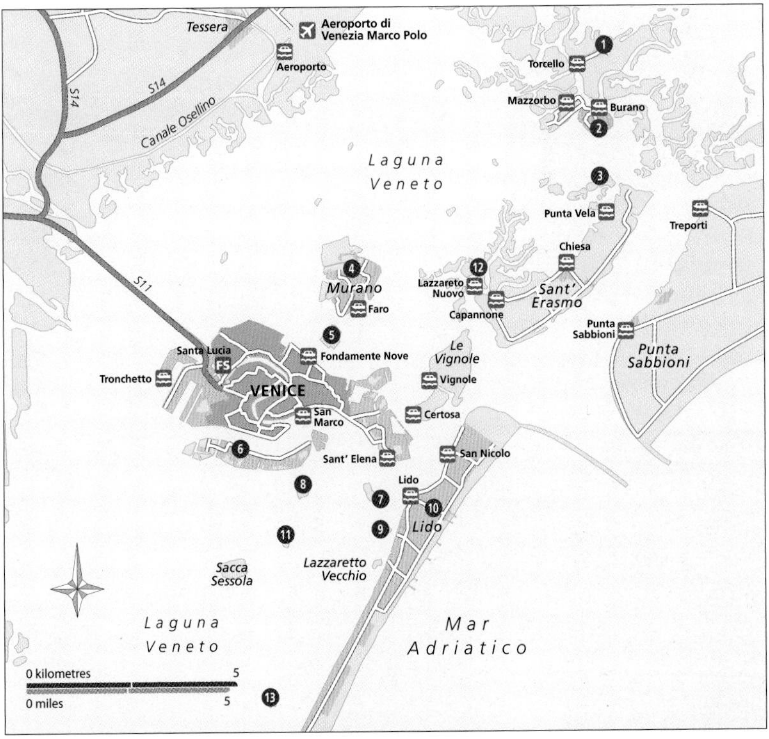

◀ Colourful houses in Burano

For keys to symbols *see back flap*

Exploring the Lagoon

A trip to the Lagoon Islands makes a welcome break from the densely packed streets of the city. Murano, celebrated for its glass, can be reached in a matter of minutes. Further north, Burano, the "lace island", and ancient Torcello are well worth the longer ride. The Lido, with its sandy beaches, is an easy journey from San Marco. Some of the lesser-known islands are worth exploring too, but access can sometimes be difficult.

❹ Murano
Some of Murano's canalside porticoes survive from medieval days.

Murano and San Michele are clearly visible from the northern quaysides of Venice.

❺ San Michele
World-famous writers and artists are buried alongside Venetians on this island.

VENEZIA

❻ Giudecca
Palladio's great church of the Redentore, on the waterfront, is the island's cultural highlight.

San Giorgio in Alga had its monastery partially destroyed by fire in 1717. It was demolished in the 19th century.

Santa Maria della Grazia ❽

⓫ San Clemente

Sant'Angelo della Polvere, recognizable by its towers, was formerly a powder factory.

San Spirito

Sacca Sessola, an artificial island, was the site of a hospital until 1980.

Poveglia ⓭

❿ Lido
Behind the crowded beaches and grand hotels, the Lido has some pleasantly peaceful waterways.

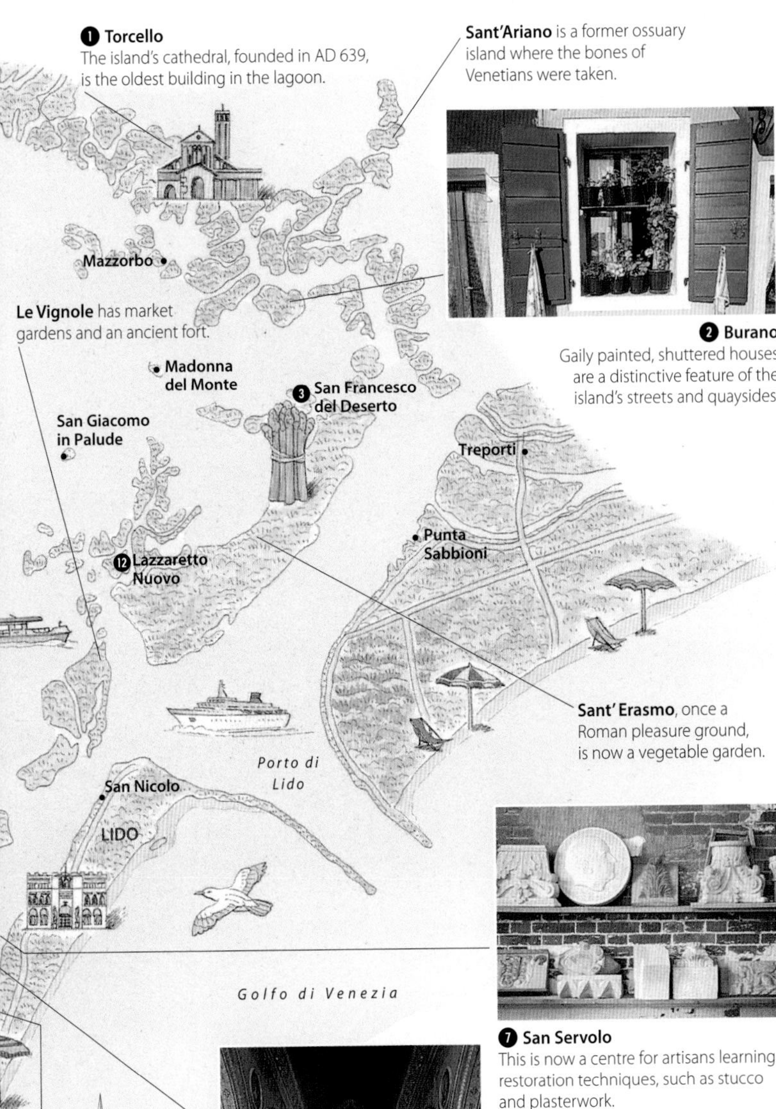

1 Torcello
The island's cathedral, founded in AD 639, is the oldest building in the lagoon.

Sant'Ariano is a former ossuary island where the bones of Venetians were taken.

Le Vignole has market gardens and an ancient fort.

2 Burano
Gaily painted, shuttered houses are a distinctive feature of the island's streets and quaysides.

Sant' Erasmo, once a Roman pleasure ground, is now a vegetable garden.

7 San Servolo
This is now a centre for artisans learning restoration techniques, such as stucco and plasterwork.

Lazzaretto Vecchio is a tiny island with a varied past. It can be seen in the distance from the boat that runs from San Marco to the Lido.

9 San Lazzaro degli Armeni
Visits to this green and pretty monastery island take in the church, library, museum and printing press.

Getting Around

The main islands of the northern lagoon are well served by the vaporetti (see pp284–5) *and the Laguna Nord boat route from Fondamente Nuove. A few of the smaller islands have a limited public service; others can only be reached by water taxi.*

Key

Major road

Minor road

0 kilometres 2

0 miles 1

❶ Torcello

Established between the 5th and 6th centuries, Torcello grew into a thriving colony *(see p44)*, with palaces, churches and a population said to have reached 20,000. But with the rise of Venice the island went into decline. Today, the population is just 60 and all that remains of this once vigorous island is the Byzantine cathedral, the church of Santa Fosca and the memory of its former glory.

★ Apse Mosaic
The 13th-century Madonna, set against a gold background, is one of the most moving mosaics in Venice.

★ Domesday Mosaics
The huge and highly decorative mosaic of the Last Judgment covers the entire west wall.

Pulpit
The present basilica dates from 1008, but includes many earlier features. The marble pulpit is made of fragments from the first, 7th-century church.

KEY

① **The Roman sarcophagus** below the altar is said to contain the relics of St Heliodorus.

② **The marble nave columns** have finely carved capitals dating from the 11th century.

③ **The central dome** and cross-sections are supported by columns of Greek marble with fine Corinthian capitals.

★ Iconostasis
The exquisite Byzantine marble panels of the rood screen are carved with peacocks, lions and flowers. This detailed relief shows two peacocks drinking from the fountain of life.

Torcello's Last Canals
Silted canals and malaria hastened Torcello's decline. One of the remaining waterways runs from the *vaporetto* stop to the basilica.

VISITORS' CHECKLIST

Practical Information
Basilica di Santa Maria dell' Assunta: **Tel** 041 296 06 30. **Open** Mar–Oct: 10:30am–6pm daily; Nov–Feb: 10am–5pm daily. Campanile: **Open** Apr–Oct: 10:30am–5:30pm daily; Nov–Mar 10am–5pm daily. Santa Fosca: **Open** Mass. Museo: **Tel** 041 73 07 61. **Open** Mar–Oct:10:30am–5:30pm Tue–Sun; Nov–Feb: 10am–5pm Tue–Sun. **Closed** public hols.

Transport
No. 12 from Fondamente Nuove to Burano, then take No. 9.

Santa Fosca
Built in the 11th and 12th centuries on a Greek-cross plan, the church has a lovely portico and a serene Byzantine interior.

Attila's Throne
It was said that the 5th-century king of the Huns used this marble seat as his throne.

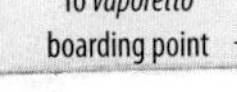

Museo dell' Estuario
Old church treasures and archaeological fragments are housed here.

A stall selling lace and linen in Burano's main street

❷ Burano

12, either from Fondamente Nuove, approx. 40–50 minutes, or from San Zaccaria via the Lido and Punta Sabbioni, approx. 1½ hours.

Burano is the most colourful of the lagoon islands. Lying in a lonely expanse of the northern lagoon, it is distinguished from a distance by the tall, dramatically tilted tower of its church. In contrast to the desolate Torcello, the island is densely populated, its waterways lined by brightly painted houses.

A tour of the island's sights will take an hour or so. The street from the ferry stop takes visitors to the main thoroughfare, Via Baldassare Galuppi, named after the Burano-born composer (1706–85). The street is lined with lace and linen stalls and open-air trattorias serving fresh fish.

Museo del Merletto

Piazza Baldassare Galuppi. **Tel** 041 730 034. **Open** 10am–6pm Tue–Sun (Nov–Mar: to 5pm). **Closed** 1 Jan, 1 May, 25 Dec. **museomerletto.visitmuve.it**

The Buranese are fishermen and lacemakers by trade. Visitors can still see the men scraping their boats or mending nets, but lacemakers are rare. In the 16th century the local lace was the most sought after in Europe. It was so delicate it became known as *punto in aria* ("points in the air"). Foreign competition, coupled with the Republic's decline, led to a slump in the 18th century in Burano's industry. However, the need for an alternative source of income led to a revival of the skill in 1872 and the founding of a lacemaking school, the Scuola dei Merletti.

Today, authentic Burano lace is hard to find. Genuine pieces take weeks of painstaking labour, and are expensive. Original pieces can be seen at the informative Museo del Merletto. Displays of household linens and clothing feature fine antique lace, much of it created at the school.

Mazzorbo

Linked to Burano by a footbridge, Mazzorbo is an island of orchards and gardens. Ferries en route to Burano and Torcello pass through its canal. The only surviving church is the Romanesque-Gothic Santa Caterina.

Brightly painted street in Burano

❸ San Francesco del Deserto

Access via water taxi from the landing stage in Burano. Visits to the island: usually 9–11am, 3–5pm Tue–Sun (see www.lagunafla.it for details). Monastery: **Tel** 041 528 68 63. Donations welcome.

This little oasis of greenery, inhabited by nine friars, lies just south of Burano. There is no *vaporetto* service and to get there you must bargain with the boatmen on Burano's quayside, who will ferry you across and await your return.

The multilingual friars who live on the island give tours of the old church and the lovely gardens, which have a tree said to have sprouted from the staff of St Francis of Assisi.

A Buranese fisherman about to haul in the day's catch

❹ Murano

No. 4.1, 4.2 or 12 from Fondamente Nuove; 3 from Piazzale Roma.

Like the city of Venice, Murano comprises a cluster of small islands, connected by bridges. It has been the centre of the glassmaking industry since 1291, when the furnaces and glass craftsmen were moved here from the city, prompted by the risk of fire to the buildings and the disagreeable effects of smoke.

Historically Murano owes its prosperity entirely to glass. From the late 13th century, when the population numbered over 30,000, Murano enjoyed self-government, minted its own coins and had its own Golden Book *(see p46)* listing members of the aristocracy. In the 15th and 16th centuries it was the principal glass-producing centre in Europe. Murano's glass artisans were granted unprecedented privileges, but for those who left the island to found businesses elsewhere there were severe penalties – even death.

Although a few of Murano's *palazzi* bear testimony to its former splendour, and its basilica still survives, most tourists visit for glass alone. Some are enticed by offers of free trips from factory touts in San Marco; others go by excursion launch or independently on the public *vaporetti*.

Some of the factories are now derelict, but glass is still produced in vast quantities. Among the plethora of kitsch (including imports from the Far East) are some wonderful pieces, and it pays to seek out the top glass factories *(see p253)*. Many furnaces, however, close at the weekend.

Museo del Vetro

Palazzo Giustinian, Fondamenta Giustinian. **Tel** 041 739 586. **Open** 10am–6pm daily (Nov–Mar: to 5pm). **Closed** 1 Jan, 1 May, 25 Dec. **museovetro.visitmuve.it**

The Museo del Vetro (glass museum) in the huge Palazzo Giustinian houses a splendid collection of antique pieces. The prize exhibit of the collection is the Barovier wedding cup (1470–80), with enamelwork decoration by Angelo Barovier. There is also a splendid section devoted to modern glass.

Basilica dei Santi Maria e Donato

Fondamenta Giustinian. **Tel** 041 73 90 56. **Open** 9am–noon, 3:30–7pm daily (Nov–Mar: to 6pm). **Closed** Sun am.

The colonnaded exterior of Murano's Basilica dei Santi Maria e Donato

The island's architectural highlight is the Basilica dei Santi Maria e Donato, whose magnificent colonnaded apse is reflected in the waters of the San Donato canal. Despite some heavy-handed restoration undertaken in the 19th century, this 12th-century church still retains much of its original beauty. Visitors should note the Veneto-Byzantine columns and Gothic ship's keel roof. An enchantingly evocative mosaic portrait of the Madonna, seen standing alone against a gold background, decorates the apse.

The church's floor, or *pavimento*, dating from 1140, is equally beautiful. With its medieval mosaics of geometric figures, exotic birds, mythical creatures and inexplicable symbols, it incorporates fragments of ancient glass from the island's foundries into its imagery.

❺ San Michele

No. 4.1 or 4.2 from Fondamente Nuove.

Studded with dark cypresses and enclosed within high terracotta walls, the cemetery island of San Michele lies just across the water from Venice's Fondamente Nuove. The bodies of Venetians were traditionally buried in church graveyards in Venice, but, for reasons of hygiene and space, San Michele and its neighbour were designated cemeteries in the 19th century.

The church of San Michele in Isola stands by the landing stage. Designed by Mauro Coducci (c.1469), it was the first church in Venice to be faced in white Istrian stone. The cemetery itself rambles over most of the island. With its carved tombstones and chapels it has a curious fascination. Some graves have suffered neglect, but most are welltended and enlivened by a riot of flowers.

Diaghilev's tombstone

The most famous graves are those of foreigners: Ezra Pound (1885–1972), in the *Evangelisti* (Protestant) section, and Sergei Diaghilev (1872–1929) and Igor Stravinsky (1882–1971) in the *Greci* or Orthodox section. These bodies have been allowed to rest in peace. Most others are dug up after about 10 years to make way for new arrivals, and the bones taken to the ossuary island of Sant'Ariano. Today, however, because of increasing lack of space on San Michele, most bodies are buried on the mainland.

Glass Blowing

A main attraction of a trip to Murano is a demonstration of the glass-blowing technique. Visitors can watch while a glass blower takes a blob of molten paste on the end of an iron rod and, by twisting, turning and blowing, miraculously transforms it into a vase, bird, lion, wine goblet or similar work of art. The display is followed by a tour of the showroom and a certain amount of pressure from the salespeople. There is no obligation to buy, however.

Glass blower at work in Murano

Boats moored along the Ponte Lungo on the Giudecca

❻ Giudecca

No. 2, 4.1 or 4.2.

In the days of the Republic, the island of Giudecca was a pleasure ground of palaces and gardens. Today it is very much a suburb of the city, its dark, narrow alleys flanked by apartments, its squares overgrown and its *palazzi* neglected. Many of its old factories have been converted into modern housing. However, the long, wide quayside skirting the city side of the island makes a very pleasant promenade and provides stunning views of Venice across the water. The island was originally named Spinalunga (long spine) on account of its shape. The name Giudecca, once thought to have referred to the Jews, or *giudei*, who lived here in the 13th century, is more likely to have originated from the word *giudicati*, meaning "the judged". This referred to troublesome aristocrats who, as early as the 9th century, were banished to the island.

Hotel Cipriani *(see p265)*, among the most luxurious places to stay in Venice, is discreetly located at the tip of the island. In contrast, at the western end of the island looms the massive Neo-Gothic ruin of the Mulino Stucky. It was built in 1895 as a flour mill by the Swiss entrepreneur Giovanni Stucky, an unpopular employer who was murdered by one of his workers in 1910. The mill ceased functioning in 1954. Following extensive renovations, it reopened in 2007 as a luxury hotel with a rooftop pool.

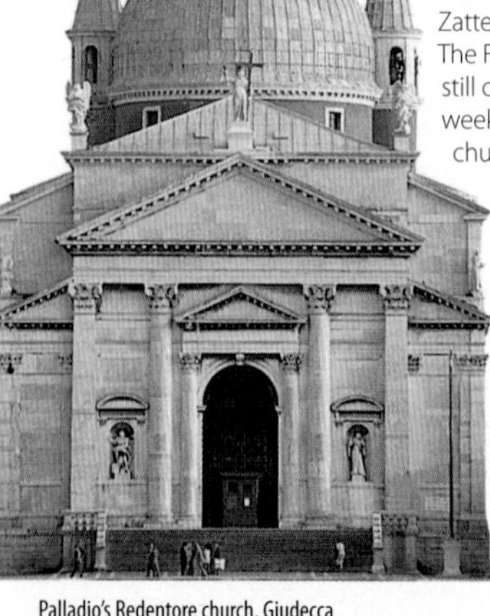

Palladio's Redentore church, Giudecca

Il Redentore

Campo Redentore. **Tel** 041 275 04 62. Redentore. **Open** 10am–5pm Mon–Sat. **Closed** 1 Jan, 25 Dec. **chorusvenezia.org**

Giudecca's principal monument is Palladio's church of Il Redentore (The Redeemer). It was built in 1577–92 in thanksgiving for the end of the 1576 plague, which wiped out a third of the city's population. Every year since its creation, the doge and his entourage would visit the church, crossing from the Zattere on a bridge of boats. The Feast of the Redeemer is still celebrated on the third weekend in July *(see p38)*. The church of Il Redentore, styled on the architecture of ancient Rome, is a masterpiece of harmony and proportion. The Classical interior presents a marked contrast to the ornate and elaborate style of most Venetian churches. The main paintings, by Paolo Veronese and Alvise Vivarini, are in the sacristy to the right of the choir. The most rewarding views of Il Redentore are from Venice across the water. For special festivities the church is often floodlit after dark, which makes a spectacular sight.

Le Zitelle

Fondamenta delle Zitelle. **Tel** 041 271 90 12. Zitelle. **Open** by appointment only.

Palladio's church is now the site of Venice's most up-to-date congress centre. The building adjoining the church used to be a hostel for spinsters *(zitelle)*, who occupied themselves by making fine lace.

An artisan at work at the San Servolo training centre

❼ San Servolo

No. 20 from San Zaccaria. Venice International University: **Tel** 041 276 50 01. **sanservolo.provincia.venezia.it**

Halfway between San Marco and the Lido is the island of San Servolo. Now a centre for teaching crafts and home to the Venice International University, it started life as one of the original monastery islands of Venice. Benedictine monks established a monastery here in the 8th century, and later added a hospital.

In 1725 the island became a lunatic asylum and a new hospital was built to house the patients. The Council of Ten *(see p46)* declared that this was to be strictly a shelter for "maniacs of noble family or comfortable circumstances". Poor maniacs were imprisoned or left to their own devices. In 1797 Napoleon scrubbed this discriminatory decree and the asylum became free to all. In 1980 this spartan island was taken over by the Venice European Centre for the Trades and Professions of Conservation, and in 1996 Venice International University opened its doors here. The historic buildings and the large park in which they are set have been extensively restored.

❽ Santa Maria della Grazia

No public access.

Originally called La Cavana or Cavanell, the island lies a short distance from San Giorgio Maggiore *(see p99)*. Formerly a shelter for pilgrims journeying to the Holy Land, it became a monastery island in the 15th century. Its name was changed when a church was constructed to enshrine a miraculous image of the Virgin, brought from Constantinople. The religious buildings, including a Gothic church with some fine paintings, were secularized under Napoleon. The island became a military zone under his rule, but the buildings were destroyed in the 1848 revolutionary uprising *(see p51)*.

Until the end of the 20th century, the island was occupied by a hospital for infectious diseases; after this department moved to the main hospital in Venice, the island was sold.

Illuminated manuscript, San Lazzaro degli Armeni

❾ San Lazzaro degli Armeni

Tel 041 526 01 04. No. 20.
Open for one visit daily. No. 20 leaves San Zaccaria at 2:45pm (Nov–Apr: 3:10pm).

Lying just off the Lido *(see p160)*, San Lazzaro degli Armeni is a small monastery island, recognizable by the onion-shaped cupola of its white campanile. The buildings are surrounded by gardens and groves of cypress trees. Since the 18th century it has been an Armenian monastery and centre of learning.

Early history

This small island served as an asylum in the 12th century and later became a hospital island for lepers, named after their patron saint, Lazarus. The lepers were then transferred to the Ospedale di San Lazzaro dei Mendicanti at Santi Giovanni e Paolo *(see pp120–21)*. In 1717 an Armenian monk, Manug di Pietro, known as Mechitar ("the consoler"), was forced to flee his homeland, the Morea, when the Turks invaded. Venetian rulers gave him the island of San Lazzaro in the southern lagoon as a place of shelter. Here, he established a religious order. The Armenians rebuilt the island, setting up a monastery, church, library, study rooms, gardens and orchards. The island became a place of study where monks taught (and still teach) young Armenians their culture.

Prince Nehmekhet's sarcophagus (c.1000 BC), San Lazzaro

The island today

Today, multilingual monks give visitors guided tours of the church, the art collection, the library and the museum, which houses Armenian, Greek, Indian and Egyptian artifacts. One of the most famous is an Egyptian sarcophagus complete with mummy, which is one of the best-preserved in the world. The most impressive exhibit is the printing hall where, over 200 years ago, a press produced works in 36 languages. A polyglot press is still in use, producing postcards, maps and prints for visitors.

Lord Byron

In 1816 the poet Byron would often row from Venice to absorb Armenian culture. Full of admiration for the monks, he wrote that the monastery "appears to unite all the advantages of the monastic institution without any of its vices … the virtues of the brethren … are well fitted to strike a man of the world with the conviction that 'there is another and a better', even in this life." The room where he studied, with mementoes, has been carefully preserved.

The garden and cloisters of San Lazzaro degli Armeni

The grand Residenze des Bains, a famous landmark on the Lido

⑩ Lido

Nos 1, 2, 5.1, 5.2 and 6 (summer) to Santa Maria Elisabetta; No. 17 from Tronchetto to San Nicolò.

The Lido is a slender sandbank 12 km (8 miles) long, which forms a natural barrier between Venice and the open sea. It is both a residential suburb of the city and – more importantly for tourists – the city's seaside resort. The only island in the lagoon with roads, it is linked to the Tronchetto island car park by car ferry. From Venice, the Lido is served by regular *vaporetti*. The fastest of these (Motonave LN) takes little more than 10 minutes to reach its destination.

The Lido's main season runs from June to September, the most crowded months being July and August. In winter most hotels are closed.

The Lido, away from the crowds and glare of the beaches

The world's first lido

In the 19th century, before the Lido was developed, the island was a favourite haunt of Shelley, Byron and other literary figures. Byron swam from the Lido to Santa Chiara via the Grand Canal in under 4 hours.

Bathing establishments were gradually opened and by the turn of the century the Lido had become one of Europe's most fashionable seaside resorts, frequented by royalty, film stars and leading lights of the literati. They stayed in the grand hotels, swam in the sea or sat in deckchairs on the sands by the striped *cabanas*. Life in the Lido's heyday was brilliantly evoked in Thomas Mann's book *Death in Venice* (1912). The Hôtel des Bains, where the melancholic Von Aschenbach stays, features in the novel and in Visconti's 1970 film, and is still a prominent landmark. It has been converted into private apartments called Residenze des Bains.

The Lido is no longer the prestigious resort it was in the 1930s. Beaches are crowded, streets busy and ferries packed with day trippers. Nevertheless the sands, sea and sporting facilities provide a welcome break from city culture. The backwaters provide a green respite from the heat of Venice.

Exploring the island

The Lido can be covered by bus but a popular form of transport is the bicycle. Visitors can hire one from the shop almost opposite the *vaporetto* stop at Santa Maria Elisabetta.

The east side of the island is fringed by sandy beaches. For passengers arriving by ferry at the main landing stage, these beaches are reached by bus, taxi or on foot along the Gran Viale Santa Maria Elisabetta. This is the main shopping street of the Lido. At the end of the Gran Viale, turn left for the beaches of San Nicolò or right along the Lungomare G Marconi, which boasts the grandest hotels and the best beaches. The hotels control the beaches in this area, and levy exorbitant charges (except to hotel residents) for the use of their beach facilities.

The long straight road parallel to the beach leads southwest to

Cabanas on the Lido beaches, hired out to holidaying Venetians

the village of Malamocco. There are some pleasant fish restaurants here, but there is little evidence that this was once the 8th-century seat of the lagoon's government.

Alberoni, at the southern end of the Lido, is the site of a golf course, a public beach and the landing stage for the ferry across to Pellestrina.

San Nicolò

The Lido's only quarter of cultural interest is San Nicolò in the north.

Across the Porto di Lido, it is possible to see the fortress of Sant'Andrea on the island of Le Vignole, built by Michele Sanmicheli between 1435 and 1449 to guard the main entrance of the lagoon.

It was to the Porto di Lido that the doge was rowed annually to cast a ring into the sea in symbolic marriage each spring *(see p37)*. After the ceremony he would visit the nearby church and monastery of San Nicolò, which was founded in 1044 and rebuilt in the 16th century.

The nearby **Jewish cemetery**, open to the public, dates from 1386. The rest of this northern area is given over to an airfield. The aeroclub located there can organize private flying lessons.

Jewish Cemetery
Tel 041 71 53 59. call in advance for a guided visit.

⓫ San Clemente

Founded in 1131 as a refuge for pilgrims and soldiers en route to the Holy Land, the crescent-shaped island of San Clemente became the site of a monastery, home to a succession of religious orders. During the Republic, doges frequently met distinguished visitors here, but from 1630, when it was hit by the plague, it served as a military depot. In the 19th century the island was turned into a lunatic asylum; most of the buildings date from that time. Today San Clemente is a peaceful island with a beautiful hotel, which is currently closed and awaiting new buyers.

International Film Festival

Film fans flock to the Lido every year in late summer for the International Film Festival. The event was inaugurated in 1932 under the auspices of the Biennale *(see p260)* and was so successful that the Palazzo del Cinema was built four years later. During its history the festival has attracted big names in the film world; it has also been plagued by bureaucracy and political in-fighting. There are signs, however, that the event is making a comeback and the famous names are now returning to the Lido.

The event takes place over two weeks in late August/early September. Films are shown day and night in numerous venues including the Palazzo del Cinema (tickets are sold outside). You can normally spot the stars (along with the paparazzi) for the price of a drink on the terrace of the Excelsior Hotel. (*See also page 259*).

Poster advertising the first Lido International Film Festival, 1932

⓬ Lazzaretto Nuovo

Tel 041 244 40 11. No. 13.
Open Apr–Oct: 9:45am & 4:30pm Sat & Sun. donation
lazzarettonuovo.com

A mere stone's throw from Sant'Erasmo, in the northern lagoon, Lazzaretto Nuovo is one of the few uninhabited visitable islands. Archaeologists continue to unearth medieval structures dating back to the late 15th century, when the island was used as a quarantine station for crews of ships hailing from distant lands where the plague was rife. Cargoes would be fumigated with rosemary and juniper. During the pestilence that afflicted Venice in 1576, the island housed 10,000 victims.

⓭ Poveglia

No public access.

Formerly called Popilia on account of all its poplar trees, the island was once a thriving community with its own government. After the 1380 war with Genoa, it fell into decline, and over the centuries became a refuge for plague victims, an isolation hospital and a home for the aged. Today the land is used for growing crops and vines.

San Clemente in the southern lagoon, seen through the evening mist

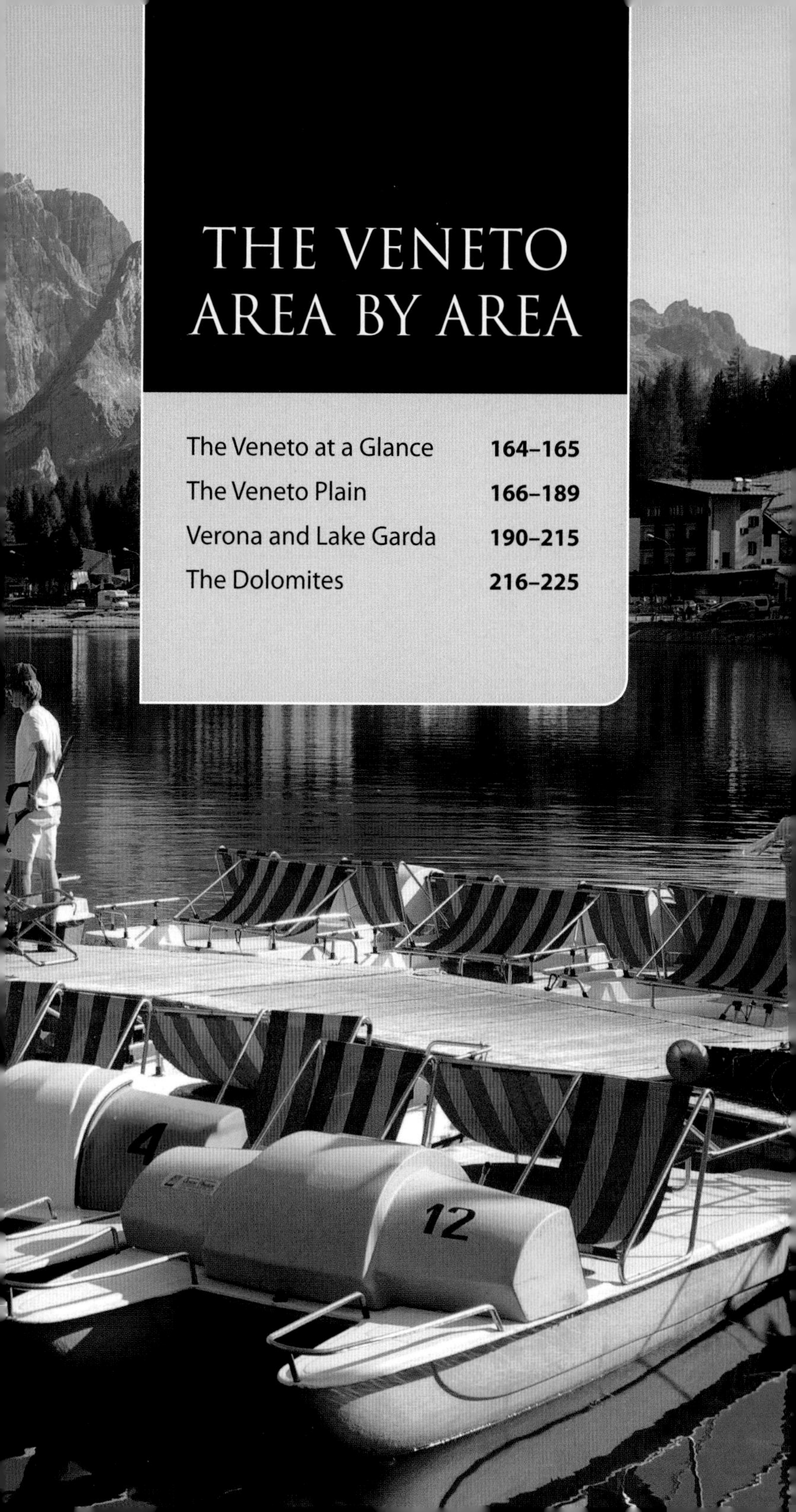

THE VENETO AREA BY AREA

The Veneto at a Glance

The Veneto's sheer variety makes it one of Italy's most fascinating regions to explore. The cities of Verona, Padua and Vicenza are all noted for outstanding architecture, churches and museums. Villas in the rural hinterland are gorgeously frescoed with scenes from ancient mythology. The lagoon has busy fishing ports and beach resorts, while Lake Garda, with its glorious mountain scenery, historic castles and watersports, makes a perfect holiday playground. Northwards lie the majestic Dolomites, Italy's premier region for skiing, which attract visitors in the summer, too, with their Alpine beauty and excellent hiking facilities.

Monti Lessini
Scores of scenic villages, such as Giazza *(see p207)*, nestle in the vineyard-clad valleys of the Lessini mountains.

Verona
An ancient Roman stronghold, famous as the home of the lovers Romeo and Juliet, Verona today is a city of opera, theatre and art *(see pp194–205)*.

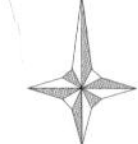

Lake Garda
Most beautiful of all the Italian lakes, Garda is surrounded by Scaligeri castles such as the magnificent Sirmione *(see p210)*.

Vicenza
Dominated by the architecture of Palladio, Vicenza *(see pp170–75)* is the model Renaissance city.

Dolomites
Erosion has sculpted the limestone peaks of the Dolomites into bizarre columns and spires, with Alpine villages hidden in steep valleys *(see p222–3)*.

Cortina d'Ampezzo

THE DOLOMITES
(pp216–25)

Belluno

Feltre

Vittorio Veneto

Conegliano

assano
el Grappa

Portogruaro

Castelfranco Veneto

Treviso

San Donà di Piave

Caorle

'HE VENETO PLAIN
(pp166–89)

Mestre

Padua

Venice

onselice

Chioggia

Rovigo

Adria

Villa Barbaro
Veronese's lavish frescoes are the perfect complement to one of Palladio's grandest rural villas, surrounded by statue-filled formal gardens, grottoes and pools *(see p28)*.

Portogruaro
Roman and early Christian finds fill the museums of this ancient town *(see p179)*.

Padua
The domes and minaret-like spires of St Anthony's basilica *(see p186)* lend an Eastern air to this historic university town.

Chioggia
Flocks of wading birds frequent the wild marshland around Chioggia *(see p189)*, the Venetian lagoon's principal fishing port.

Exploring the Veneto Plain

The landscape of the Veneto Plain is as flat as a board, but it is far from dull. Villagers in the small communities dotted throughout the region used to compete to build the tallest church tower, and these seemingly needle-thin landmarks soaring skywards draw the traveller on. Great stone castles, dating from the 14th century, rise on almost every promontory, each with a backdrop on clear days of the distant Alps.

Sights at a Glance

1. *Vicenza pp170–75*
2. Thiene
3. Marostica
4. Bassano del Grappa
5. Cittadella
6. Castelfranco
7. Asolo
8. Valdobbiadene
9. Treviso
10. Conegliano
11. Portogruaro
12. Caorle
13. Mestre
14. *Padua (Padova) pp180–87*
15. Euganean Hills
16. Montagnana
17. Este
18. Monselice
19. Polesine and Rovigo
20. Chioggia

Key

- Major road
- Minor road
- Secondary road
- Motorway
- Motorway under construction
- Main railway
- Minor railway
- Scenic route
- Regional border

The castellated walls of Montagnana, dating from medieval times

For additional map symbols *see back flap*

Getting Around

An extensive rail network and good bus services make this region easy to explore by public transport. Roads are heavily used, so avoid cities and *autostrade* during rush hours.

Palladio's Villa Rotonda near the town of Vicenza

The colourful quayside market in the town of Chioggia, the lagoon's principal fishing port

❶ Street-by-Street: Vicenza

Vicenza is known as the city of Andrea Palladio (1508–80), arguably the most influential architect of his time. Although Palladio was born in Padua, Vicenza was his adoptive home and, walking around the city, one can see the evolution of his distinctive style. In the centre is the monumental basilica he adapted to serve as the town hall, while all around are the palaces he built for Vicenza's wealthy citizens.

Loggia del Capitaniato
This covered arcade was designed by Palladio in 1571.

Contrà Porti has some of the most elegant *palazzi* in Vicenza.

Palazzo Valmarana
Palladio's impressive building of 1566 was originally intended to be three times larger. It was not completed until 1680, 100 years after the architect's death.

Duomo
Vicenza's cathedral was rebuilt after bomb damage during World War II left only the façade and choir intact.

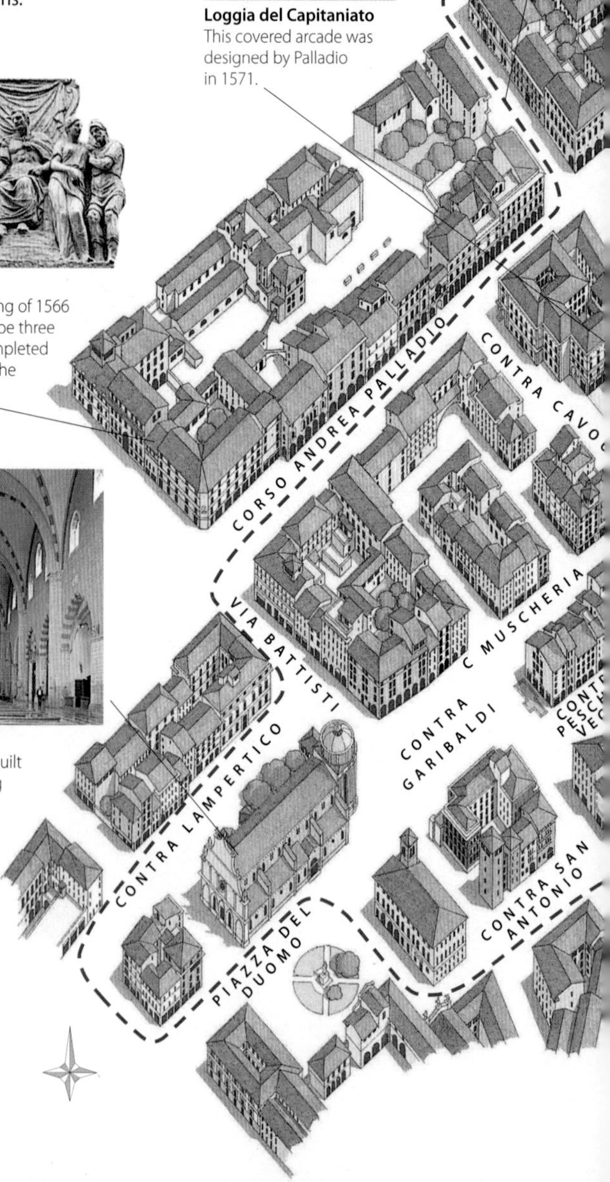

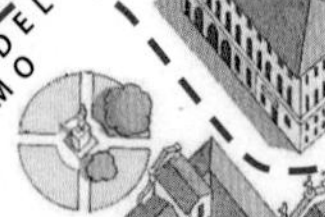

Key

— Suggested route

0 metres 150

0 yards 150

VISITORS' CHECKLIST

Practical Information
116,000. Piazza Matteotti 12 (0444 32 08 54).
vicenzae.org
Tue & Thu. Concert season (May–Jun); Classical music in villas (end Jun–early Jul); Theatre season (Sep–Oct).

Transport
FS Piazza Stazione.

★ Piazza dei Signori
Encircled by grand 15th-century buildings including the city's green-roofed basilica and slender brick tower, the piazza is a lively spot, with a colourful market and cafés.

The Torre di Piazza is 82 m (269 ft) high. Begun in the 12th century, its height was increased in 1311 and 1444.

The 15th-century basilica has a magnificent loggia built by Palladio in 1549.

Andrea Palladio
This memorial to Vicenza's most famous citizen is often surrounded by market stalls.

The Quartiere delle Barche contains numerous attractive palaces built in the 14th-century Venetian Gothic style.

Piazza delle Erbe, the city's market square, is overlooked by a 13th-century torture chamber, the Torre del Tormento.

Ponte San Michele
This elegant stone bridge, built in 1620, provides lovely views of the surrounding town.

★ Casa Pigafetta
This striking house was the birthplace of Antonio Pigafetta, who in 1519 set sail round the world with Magellan.

Exploring Vicenza

Vicenza, the great Palladian city, is celebrated all over the world for its architecture. It is also one of the wealthiest cities in the Veneto, with much to offer, from Roman and Renaissance art (a combined museum ticket is available) to elegant shops selling fine goods.

Statues gazing down from their pillars in the Piazza dei Signori

Piazza dei Signori

At the heart of Vicenza, this square is dominated by the startling bulk of the Palazzo della Ragione, often referred to as the "basilica". Open to the public, its green, copper-clad roof is shaped like an upturned boat with a balustrade bristling with the statues of Greek and Roman gods. The colonnades were designed by Palladio in 1549 to support the city's 15th-century town hall, which had begun to subside. This was his first public commission, and his solution ensured the survival of the building.

The astonishingly slender Torre di Piazza alongside has stood since the 12th century. Opposite is the elegant café Gran Caffè Garibaldi, which is next to Palladio's Loggia del Capitaniato (1571). The Loggia's upper rooms contain the city's council chamber.

Contrà Porti

Contrà (an abbreviation of *contrada*, or "district") is the local dialect word for "street". On the western side is a series of pretty Gothic buildings with painted windows and ornate balconies, including Palazzo Porto-Colleoni (No. 19). These houses reflect the architecture of Venice, a reminder that Vicenza was part of the Venetian empire.

Several fine Palladian *palazzi* stand on this street. The Palazzo Thiene (No. 12) of 1545–50, the Palazzo Porto Barbarano (No. 11) of 1570 and the Palazzo Iseppo da Porto (No. 21) of 1552 all illustrate the sheer variety of Palladio's style – Classical elements are common to all three, but each is unique. The Palazzo Thiene reveals some intriguing details of Palladio's methods: though the building appears to be of stone, close inspection reveals that it is built of cheap lightweight brick, cleverly rendered to look like masonry.

Casa Pigafetta

Contrà Pigafetta. No public access.

This Spanish Gothic building of 1481 has clover-leaf balconies, gryphon brackets and Moorish windows. The owner, Antonio Pigafetta, sailed round the world with Magellan in 1519–22, being one of only 20 men who survived the voyage.

Museo Civico

Piazza Matteotti 37–9. **Tel** 0444 22 28 11. **Open** 9am–5pm Tue–Sun. **Closed** 1 Jan, 25 Dec. **museicivicivicenza.it**

This fine museum is housed in Palladio's Palazzo Chiericati, built in 1550. Inside is a fresco by Domenico Brusazorzi of a naked charioteer, representing the Sun, who appears to fly over the ceiling of the entrance hall. In the upstairs rooms are many Gothic altarpieces from local churches, such as Hans Memling's *Crucifixion* (1468–70), the central panel of a triptych whose side panels are now in New York.

In the later rooms are works by the local artist Bartolomeo Montagna (c.1450–1523), including his remarkable *Virgin Enthroned with Child, St John the Baptist and Saints Bartholomew, Augustine and Sebastian*.

Santa Corona

Open 9am–noon, 3–6pm Tue–Sun.

This Gothic church was built in 1261 to house a thorn from Christ's Crown of Thorns, donated by Louis IX of France. In the Porto Chapel is the tomb of Luigi da Porto (d.1529), author of the novel *Giulietta e Romeo*, upon which Shakespeare based his

Brusazorzi's ceiling fresco in the large entrance hall of the Museo Civico

famous play. Notable paintings include Giovanni Bellini's *Baptism of Christ* (c.1500–5) and Paolo Veronese's *Adoration of the Magi* (1573). In the cloister the Museo Naturalistico-Archeologico exhibits natural history and archaeology.

San Lorenzo

Open 10:30am–noon, 3:30–6pm daily (from 4pm in summer), 3:30–6pm on public hols.

This church's portal is a splendid example of Gothic stone carving, decorated with figures of the Virgin and Child, and St Francis and St Clare. The frescoes inside are damaged, but there are fine tombs. The cloister, to the north, is a flower-filled haven of calm.

The beautiful cloister of the church of San Lorenzo

Palazzo Leoni Montanari

Contra' Santa Corona 25. **Tel** 800 57 88 75. **Open** 10am–6pm Tue–Sun. **gallerieditalia.com**

This Baroque building was completed around 1720, commissioned by Giovanni Leoni Montanari, who had made his fortune producing and selling cloth. Today the Palazzo houses an art gallery renowned for its collections of Venetian paintings and Russian icons.

Monte Berico

Basilica di Monte Berico. **Tel** 0444 55 94 11. **Open** 6am–12:30pm, 2:30–7:30pm (Nov–Feb: to 6pm).

Monte Berico is the green, cypress-clad hill to the south of the city to which wealthy Vicenzans once escaped in the summer to enjoy cooler air and bucolic charms. The wide avenue linking the city to the basilica on top of the hill features shady colonnades with many shrines along the route. The Baroque basilica was built in the 15th century and is dedicated to the Virgin who appeared during the 1426–8 plague to declare that Vicenza would be spared.

Many pilgrims still travel to the lovely church, where Bartolomeo Montagna's moving *Pietà* fresco (1572) makes an impact within the ornate interior. Other attractions include a fossil collection in the cloister, and Veronese's fine painting *The Supper of St Gregory the Great* (1572) in the refectory. The large canvas was cut to ribbons by bayonet-wielding soldiers during the revolutionary outbursts of 1848 and painstakingly restored.

The elegant Villa Rotonda, most famous of all Palladio's works

Villa Valmarana

Via dei Nani 2. **Tel** 0444 32 18 03. **Open** 10am–12:30pm, 3–6pm Tue–Sun (Nov–mid-Mar: 10am–noon, 2–4pm Sat & Sun). **villavalmarana.com**

The wall alongside the Villa Valmarana, built in 1688 by Antonio Muttoni, is topped by the figures of dwarfs, which give this building its alternative name – *ai Nani* (at the Dwarfs). Inside the villa, the walls are covered with frescoes by Tiepolo, in which pagan gods float on clouds watching scenes from the epics of Homer and Virgil. In the separate Foresteria (guest house), the frescoes with themes of peasant life and the seasons, painted by Tiepolo's son, Giandomenico, are equally decorative but more earthily realistic.

The villa can be reached by a 10-minute walk from the basilica on Monte Berico. Head downhill along Via M d'Azeglio to the high-walled convent on the right where the road ends, then take the Via San Bastiano. There is also a bus service from town.

The Baroque hilltop church, the Basilica di Monte Berico

Villa Rotonda

Via della Rotonda 45. **Tel** 0444 32 17 93. Villa: **Open** mid-Mar–4 Nov: Wed & Sat. Garden: **Open** 10am–noon, 3–6pm Tue–Sun (5 Nov–mid-Mar: 10am–noon, 2:30–5pm Tue–Sun). **villalarotonda.it**

With its regular, symmetrical forms, this is the epitome of Palladio's architecture and the most famous of all his villas, being the most widely copied. The design is simple yet satisfying, as is the contrast between the green lawns, white walls and terracotta roof tiles. Built between 1550 and 1552, it has inspired lookalikes in cities as far away as Delhi and St Petersburg. Fans of *Don Giovanni* will recognize locations used in Joseph Losey's 1979 film. The villa can be reached by bus from town, or on foot, following the path that passes the Villa Valmarana.

Vicenza: Teatro Olimpico

Europe's oldest surviving indoor theatre, the Teatro Olimpico is an elegant and remarkable structure, largely made of wood and plaster and painted to look like marble. Fashionable architect Andrea Palladio *(see pp28–9)* began work on the design in 1579, but he died the following year without finishing it. His pupil, Vincenzo Scamozzi, took over the project and completed the theatre in time for its ambitious opening performance of Sophocles' tragic drama, *Oedipus Rex*, on 3 March 1585.

Bacchantes
Euripides' Greek tragedy is still performed using Scamozzi's versatile scenery.

★ Odeon Frescoes
The gods of Mount Olympus, after which the theatre is named, decorate the Odeon, a room used for music recitals.

KEY

① **The Anteodeon's frescoes** (1595) depict the theatre's opening performance. Oil lamps from the original stage set are also on display.

② **Main ticket office**

③ **The auditorium** was designed by Palladio to resemble the outdoor theatres of ancient Greece and Rome, such as the arena at Verona *(see p197)*, with a semicircle of "stone" benches (actually made of wood) and a ceiling painted to portray the sky.

★ Stage Set
Scamozzi's scenery represents the Greek city of Thebes. The streets are cleverly painted in perspective and rise at a steep angle to give the illusion of great length.

Courtyard Sculptures
The courtyard of the former castle is decorated with sculpture donated by members of the Olympic Academy, the learned body that built the theatre.

VISITORS' CHECKLIST

Practical Information
Piazza Matteotti. **Tel** 0444 22 28 00.
olimpicovicenza.it
Open 9am–5pm Tue–Sun (last adm: 4:30pm). Regular theatre performances. **Closed** 1 Jan, 25 Dec.

Transport
to Piazza Matteotti.

Armoury Gateway
This stone gateway, with its military-style carvings, leads from Piazza Matteotti into the picturesque theatre courtyard.

3

Costume Designs for Sofonisba
Ancient Greek vases inspired the costumes for this tragedy (1562) by Palladio's patron, G G Trissino.

Façade Statues
The toga-clad figures are portraits of sponsors who paid for the theatre's construction.

❷ Thiene

20,000. Piazza Ferrarin 20 (0445 80 48 12). Mon am.

Thiene is one of the area's many textile towns, manufacturing jeans and sweatshirts for sale all over Europe. Two villas nearby are worth a visit. The heavily fortified towers and battlemented walls of the **Castello Porto-Colleoni** are offset by pretty Gothic windows. At the time it was built, it stood in open countryside, and the defences were a precaution against bandits and raiders. Inside, 16th-century frescoes by Giambattista Zelotti add a lighter note and many portraits of horses remind the visitor that the villa's owners, the Colleonis, were employed by the Venetian cavalry.

Zelotti also frescoed the **Villa Godi Malinverni**, the first villa designed by Palladio *(see pp28–9)*. The garden is charming and the frescoes are magnificent. Inside are works by Italian Impressionists and a lovely portrait by Pietro Annigoni (1910–88) called *La Strega* (The Sorceress).

Castello Porto-Colleoni
Corso Garibaldi 12. **Tel** 3298 54 19 62.
Open mid-Mar–mid-Nov: Sun pm & public hols; Groups by appt all year round. partial.
castellodithiene.com

Villa Godi Malinverni
Via Palladio 44. **Tel** 0445 86 05 61.
Open Mar–Nov: Tue, Sat & Sun afternoons; other times, phone ahead.

The human chess game in the town square of Marostica

❸ Marostica

12,500. Piazza Castello 1 (0424 721 27). Tue.

Marostica is an almost perfect medieval fortified town, with town walls built in 1370 by the Scaligeri *(see p213)*. The rampart walk from the **Castello Inferiore** (lower castle) to the **Castello Superiore** (upper castle) has fine views.

The lower castle exhibits costumes worn by participants in the town's human chess tournament, the Partita a Scacchi, held every other September *(see p39)*. Up to 650 people participate in this colourful re-enactment of a game first played here in 1454.

Castello Inferiore
Piazza Castello 1. **Tel** 0424 47 21 27.
Open 9am–12:30pm, 3–6:30pm daily.

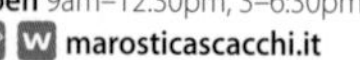

marosticascacchi.it

The Ponte degli Alpini at Bassano del Grappa

❹ Bassano del Grappa

38,770. Largo Corona d'Italia 35 (0424 52 43 51). Thu & Sat am.

This peaceful town is synonymous with Italy's favourite after-dinner drink (although *grappa* is not named after the town, but after *graspa*, the Italian term for the lees used to distil the liquor). Information on this and on the role played by Bassano during both world wars is given at the **Museo degli Alpini**, across the Ponte degli Alpini bridge. Designed in 1569 by Palladio, the current bridge dates from 1948: its timber allows it to flex when hit by spring meltwaters.

Bassano is also famous for the majolica wares *(see p256)* at **Palazzo Sturm**. The locally born artist Jacopo Bassano (1510–92) and sculptor Canova (1757–1822) are celebrated in the **Museo Civico**.

Museo degli Alpini
Via Angarano 2. **Tel** 0424 50 36 62.
Open 8am–8pm Tue–Sun.
Closed 10 days in Jan.

Palazzo Sturm
Via Schiavonetti 40. **Tel** 0424 52 49 33.
Open 9am–1pm, 3–6pm Tue–Sat (from 10:30am Sun & pub hols).

Museo Civico
Piazza Garibaldi. **Tel** 0424 52 33 36.
Open 9am–1pm, 3–6pm Tue–Sat, 10:30am–1pm, 3–6pm Sun & pub hols.
museibassano.it

❺ Cittadella

18,000. FS i Porte Bassanesi 2 (0499 40 44 85). Mon am.

This attractive town is the twin of Castelfranco. Each was fortified and Cittadella still preserves its 13th-century moated walls. These are interrupted by 4 gates and by 16 towers. The Torre di Malta near the southern gate was used as a torture chamber by Ezzelino de Romano, who ruled in the mid-13th century. Far more pleasant to contemplate is the *Supper at Emmaus* in the **Duomo**, a masterpiece by local Renaissance artist Bassano.

Fresco from the Villa Emo at Fanzolo, near Castelfranco

❻ Castelfranco

30,000. FS i Via Francesco Maria Preti 66 (0423 49 50 00). Tue & Fri am.

Fortified in 1199 by rulers of Treviso, the historic core of this town lies within the well-preserved walls. **Casa di Giorgione**, claimed to be the birthplace of artist Giorgione (1478–1511), houses a museum devoted to his life. He created such works as *The Tempest (see p134)*. His *Virgin and Child with Saints Liberal and Francis* (1504) is displayed in the **Duomo**. Tuzio Costanza commissioned it to stand above the tomb of his son, Matteo, killed in battle in 1504.

At Fanzolo, 8 km (5 miles) northeast of Castelfranco, is Palladio's **Villa Emo**, designed in 1564. Here, Zelotti's frescoes show the love lives of Greek deities.

The pretty town of Asolo in the foothills of the Dolomites

Casa di Giorgione
Piazzetta del Duomo. **Tel** 0423 72 50 22. **Open** 9:30am–12:30pm Tue–Thu, 9:30am–12:30pm, 2:30–6:30pm Fri–Sun. **Closed** Easter, 25 Dec. **W museogiorgione.com**

Villa Emo
Fanzolo di Vedelago. **Tel** 0423 47 63 34. FS Fanzolo. 5. **Open** May–Oct: 3–7pm Mon–Sat, 9:30am–12:30pm, 3–7pm Sun & pub hols; Nov–Apr: 10am–12:30pm, 2:30–5:30pm Mon–Sat, 9am–12:30pm, 2–6pm Sun & pub hols. **Closed** 1 Jan, 25 & 31 Dec. **W villaemo.org**

❼ Asolo

2,000. i Piazza Garibaldi 73 (0423 52 90 46). Sat. **W asolo.it**

Asolo is beautifully situated among the cypress-clad foothills of the Dolomites. Queen Caterina Cornaro (1454–1510) once ruled this tiny walled town *(see p47)*, and the poet Cardinal Pietro Bembo coined the verb *asolare* to describe the bittersweet life of enforced idleness she endured. Others who have fallen in love with these narrow streets include poet Robert Browning, who named a volume of poems *Asolando* (1889) after the town, and travel writer Freya Stark, who lived here until her death in 1993.

Just 10 km (6 miles) east of Asolo is the **Villa Barbaro** at Masèr *(see pp28–9)*, while 10 km (6 miles) north is the village of Passagno, birthplace of Antonio Canova. Canova's remains lie inside the huge temple-like church which he designed himself. Nearby is the family home, the **Casa di Canova**. The Gypsoteca here houses the plaster casts and clay models for many of Canova's sculptures.

Villa Barbaro
Masèr. **Tel** 0423 92 30 04. **Open** Mar–Oct: 3–6pm Tue, Sat, Sun & public hols; Nov–Feb: 2:30–5pm Sat, Sun & public hols. **Closed** 24 Dec–6 Jan, Easter. **W villadimaser.it**

Casa di Canova
Piazza Canova. **Tel** 0423 54 43 23. **Open** 9:30am–6pm Tue–Sun; ticket office closes 1 hour earlier. **Closed** 1 Jan, Easter, 25 Dec. **W museocanova.it**

❽ Valdobbiadene

10,700. i Via Piva 53 (0423 97 69 75). Mon.

Valdobbiadene, surrounded by vine-covered hills, is a centre for the sparkling white wine called Cartizze, a type of Prosecco. To the east, the Strada del Vino Bianco (white wine route) stretches 34 km (21 miles) to the town of Conegliano *(see p179)*, passing vineyards offering wine to try and to buy.

Environs
About 10 km (8 miles) northeast of Valdobbiadene is the small town of Follina, which is renowned for its wonderfully well-preserved Romanesque abbey.

Vines near Valdobbiadene

The medieval town of Treviso, built around ancient canals

❾ Treviso

81,700. FS Via Sant'Andrea 3 (0422 54 76 32). Tue & Sat am.

Full of attractive balconied houses overlooking willow-fringed canals, Treviso is a rewarding city for visitors. Comparisons are often made with Venice, but Treviso has its own distinctive character. A good place to explore the architecture is the main street, Calmaggiore, which links the cathedral with the rebuilt 13th-century town hall, the **Palazzo dei Trecento**. The tradition of painting the exterior of the houses dates back to the medieval period, and this form of decoration, applied to brick and timber, compensated for the lack of suitable building stone. The bustling **fish market** also dates back to medieval times. It is held on an island in the middle of Treviso's River Sile so that the remains of the day's trading can be flushed away instantly.

Duomo

Treviso's cathedral, founded in the 12th century, was reconstructed in the 15th, 16th and 18th centuries. Inside is Titian's *Annunciation* (1570), but it is upstaged by the striking *Adoration of the Magi* fresco (1520) of Titian's arch rival, Il Pordenone. Other memorable works are *The Adoration of the Shepherds* fresco by Paris Bordone, and the monument to Bishop Zanetti (1501) by Pietro Lombardo and his sons.

Museo Civico

Piazzetta M Botter 1. **Tel** 0422 54 48 64. **Open** 9am–12:30pm, 2:30–6pm Tue–Sun. **Closed** public hols.
museicivicitreviso.it

The Museo Civico houses an archaeology collection and a picture gallery in the restored convent of Santa Caterina dei Servi. The best works are Lorenzo Lotto's *Portrait of a Dominican* (1526), Titian's *Portrait of Sperone Speroni* (1544) and Bassano's *Crucifixion* as well as Tommaso da Modena's 14th-century frescoes of the life of St Ursula.

San Nicolò

Nestling near the 16th-century town wall is the bulky Dominican church of San Nicolò, full of tombs and frescoes, including some by Lorenzo Lotto. There is a gigantic painting of St Christopher by Antonio da Treviso and the piers of the nave bear vivid portraits of saints by Tomaso da Modena. The latter also painted the humorous pictures of monks (1352) on the walls of the chapterhouse *(Sala del Capitolo)*, which has a separate entrance through the Seminario Vescovile.

Treviso Town Centre

① Duomo and Battistero di San Giovanni
② San Nicolò
③ Palazzo dei Trecento
④ Pescheria (fish market)
⑤ Museo Civico

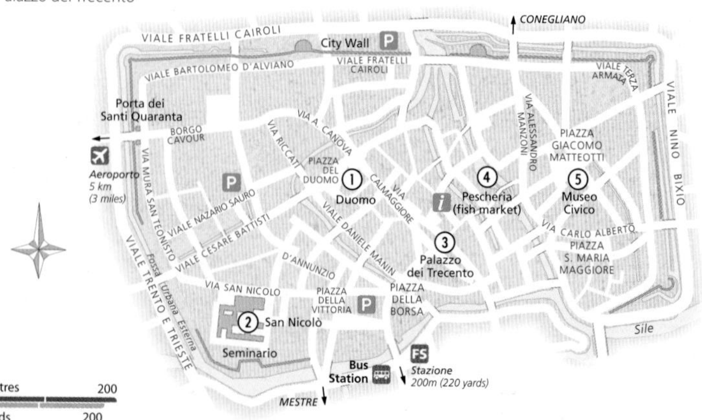

For keys to symbols *see back flap*

⑩ Conegliano

35,300. FS Via XX Settembre 61 (0438 21 230). Fri. **Shops closed** Mon am.

Conegliano lies between the Prosecco-producing vineyards and those that produce fine red wine *(see pp240–41)*. Winemakers from both areas learn their craft at Conegliano's renowned wine school. The town's winding and arcaded main street, Via XX Settembre, is lined by 15th- to 18th-century *palazzi*, some decorated with external frescoes, some in Venetian Gothic style. The **Duomo** contains a gorgeous altarpiece by Cima da Conegliano (1460–1518) showing the *Virgin and Child with Saints* (1493). This was commissioned by the religious brotherhood whose headquarters, the Scuola di Santa Maria dei Battuti *(flagellants)*, stands beside the Duomo.

Reproductions of Cima's paintings are displayed in the **Casa di Cima**, the artist's birthplace. His detailed landscapes were based on the hills around the town; they can still be seen from the gardens surrounding the **Castelvecchio** (old castle). A small museum of local history is housed in the castle.

Casa di Cima
Via Cima. **Tel** 0438 216 60. **Open** 3–6pm Sat & Sun (Apr–Sep: 4–7pm).

Castelvecchio
Piazzale Castelvecchio 8. **Tel** 0438 228 71. **Open** Museum: 8:30am–7:30pm Tue–Sun (Nov: Sat & Sun only); gardens: daily (except Nov).

A mythical statue outside the theatre in Conegliano's Via XX Settembre

The foundations of Roman buildings in Concordia, near Portogruaro

⑪ Portogruaro

26,000. FS Via Cimetta 1 (0421 735 58). Thu am. **Shops closed** Mon. **portogruaroturismo.it**

Situated on the main road linking Venice to Trieste, Portogruaro is the medieval successor to the Roman town of Concordia Sagittaria. Finds from Concordia, including statues, tomb inscriptions and mosaics, are displayed in the town's **Museo Concordiese**. These objects were unearthed in the modern village of Concordia, 2 km (1 mile) south of Portogruaro, where the footings of ruined Roman buildings can be seen all around the church and baptistry.

Museo Concordiese
Via Seminario 26. **Tel** 0421 726 74. **Open** daily. **Closed** 1 Jan, 25 Dec.

⑫ Caorle

11,700. Calle delle Liburniche 18 (0421 810 85). Sat am. **turismovenezia.it/Bibione-e-Caorle**

Like Venice, Caorle was built among the swamps of the Venetian lagoon by refugees fleeing the Goths in the 5th century. Today it is a fishing village and a busy beach resort perched on the edge of a huge expanse of purpose-built lagoons, carefully managed to encourage fish to enter and spawn. The young are then fed and farmed.

The area is also of great interest to naturalists for the abundant birdlife of the reed-fringed waters. The town's 11th-century **Duomo** is worth a visit for its Pala d'Oro, a gilded altarpiece made up of 12th- and 13th-century Byzantine panel reliefs.

Local fishermen at work in the village of Caorle

⑬ Mestre

180,000. Wed & Fri am.

Mestre, the industrial offspring of Venice, is often favoured by visitors as a relatively less expensive base for exploring the region than Venice or other towns. Flying into Venice's Marco Polo Airport *(see pp278–9)* you cannot miss the factories and oil terminals that surround Mestre and its neighbour, Marghera, vital to the region's economy.

⓮ Street-by-Street: Padua

The city centre of Padua (Padova) is one of the liveliest in northern Italy, thanks to a large student population and to the two street markets, one specializing in fruit and the other in vegetables. These take place every day except Sunday around the vast Palazzo della Ragione, the town's medieval law court and council chamber. The colonnades round the exterior of the *palazzo* shelter numerous bars, restaurants and shops selling meat, game, cheeses and wine.

Palazzo del Capitanio
Built between 1599 and 1605 for the head of the city's militia, the tower incorporates an astronomical clock made in 1344.

Piazza dei Signori is bordered by attractive arcades which house small speciality shops, interesting cafés and old-fashioned wine bars.

Corte Capitaniato, a 14th-century arts faculty (open for concerts), contains frescoes which include a rare portrait of Petrarch.

Loggia della Gran Guardia
Now used as a conference centre, this fine Renaissance building, dating from 1523, once housed the Council of Nobles.

The Palazzo del Monte di Pietà has 16th-century arcades and statues enclosing a medieval building.

★ Duomo and Baptistry
The 12th-century baptistry of the Duomo contains one of the most complete medieval fresco cycles to survive in Italy, painted by Giusto de' Menabuoi in 1378 and now restored.

★ Caffè Pedrocchi
Built like a Classical temple, the Caffè Pedrocchi has been a famous meeting place for students and intellectuals since it opened in 1831.

VISITORS' CHECKLIST

Practical Information
220,000. Piazzale Stazione 13/a. **Tel** 049 201 00 80.
turismopadova.it
Mon–Sat (Prato della Valle).
Shops closed Mon am (clothes), Wed pm (food). concert season (Oct–Apr).

Transport
FS Piazzale della Stazione.

Palazzi Communali
This complex, which houses the city's council offices, has a 13th-century defensive tower.

PIAZZA CAVOUR
VIA GORIZIA
AZZA DEI FRUTTI
VIA OBERDAN
PTTA GARZERIA
VIA 8 FEBBRAIO
PIAZZA ELLE ERBE
VIA SAN CANZIANO

The Palazzo della Ragione, the "Palace of Reason", was, in medieval times, the city court of justice. Its interior is covered with magnificent astrological frescoes.

Padua University
Founded in 1222, this is the second-oldest university in Italy. The main building dates back to the 16th century.

0 metres 75
0 yards 75

Key

— Suggested route

★ Piazza delle Erbe
There are good views on to the marketplace from Palladio's 16th-century loggia, which runs alongside the Palazzo della Ragione.

Exploring Padua

Padua is an old university town with an illustrious academic history. Rich in art and architecture, it boasts two outstanding sights. The first is the Scrovegni Chapel *(see pp184–5)* in the north of the city, which is renowned for Giotto's lyrical frescoes. Close to the railway station, it forms part of the Eremitani museums complex. The second is the Basilica di Sant'Antonio, one of Italy's most popular pilgrim shrines, which forms the focal point for a number of sights in the south of the city *(see p186)*. A combined museum ticket is available.

Detail from the Egyptian room, upper floor of the Caffè Pedrocchi

Caffè Pedrocchi

Via VIII Febbraio 15. **Tel** 049 878 12 31. **Open** daily (Jun–Oct: Tue–Sun). Museo del Risorgimento e dell'Età Contemporanea: **Tel** 049 820 50 07. **Open** 9.30am–12.30pm, 3:30–6pm Tue–Sun. **Closed** Aug.
caffepedrocchi.it

Grand cafés have long played an important role in the intellectual life of northern Italy, and many philosophical issues have been thrashed out at the Caffè Pedrocchi since it first opened in 1831. Politics superseded philosophy when it became a centre of the Risorgimento movement, dedicated to liberating Italy from Austrian rule; it was the scene of uprisings in 1848, for which several student leaders were executed. Later it became famous as the café that never closed its doors. These days people come to talk, read, play cards or watch the world go by as they eat and drink.

The upstairs rooms, decorated in Moorish, Egyptian and Greek styles, are now the premises of a museum.

Palazzo del Bo (University)

Via VIII Febbraio 2. **Tel** 049 827 51 11. **Open** Tue, Thu & Sat am, Mon, Wed & Fri pm (may vary, phone to check).

Named after a tavern called *Il Bo* (the ox), the historic main university building is mostly used today for graduation ceremonies. Originally it housed the medical faculty, renowned throughout Europe. Among its famous teachers and students was Gabriele Fallopio (1523–62), after whom the Fallopian tubes are named.

Elena Lucrezia Corner Piscopia was the first female graduate in 1678 – long before women could study at many of Europe's other universities. Her statue is on the staircase leading to the upper gallery of the 16th-century courtyard.

Visitors on the tour are shown the pulpit Galileo used when he taught here from 1592 until 1610. They also see the world's oldest surviving anatomy theatre (1594), viewing the room from the centre looking up.

The 16th-century galleried anatomy theatre in the Palazzo del Bo

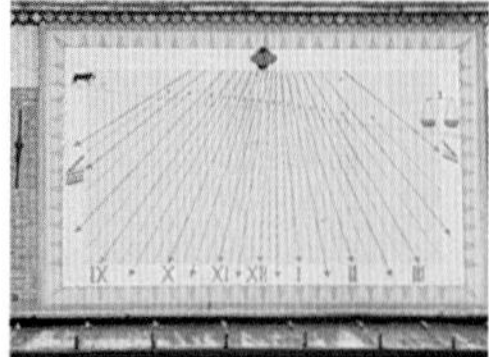

Sundial on the façade of the Palazzo della Ragione

Palazzo della Ragione

Piazza delle Erbe. **Tel** 049 820 50 06. **Open** 9am–6pm Tue–Sun (to 7pm in summer). **Closed** 1 Jan, 1 May, 25 Dec.

The "Palace of Reason", also known as the "Salone" by locals, was built to serve as Padua's law court and council chamber in 1218. The vast main hall was originally frescoed by the celebrated artist Giotto, but fire destroyed his work in 1420. The frescoes that survive today are by the relatively unknown Nicola Miretto, though their astrological theme is fascinating.

The Salone is breathtaking in its sheer size. It is Europe's biggest undivided medieval hall, 80 m (260 ft) long, 27 m (90 ft) wide and 27 m (90 ft) high. The scale is reinforced by the wooden horse displayed at one end – a massive beast, copied from Donatello's Gattamelata statue *(see p187)* in 1466 and originally made to be pulled in procession during Paduan festivities.

The walls are covered in Miretto's frescoes (1420–25), a total of 333 panels depicting the months of the year with appropriate gods, zodiacal signs and seasonal activities.

Also within the *palazzo* is the Stone of Shame, on which bankrupts were exposed to ridicule before they were sent into exile.

Eremitani Museums

This major museum complex occupies a group of 14th-century monastic buildings attached to the church of the Eremitani, a reclusive Augustinian Order. The admission ticket includes entry to the Scrovegni Chapel *(see pp184–5)*, which stands on the same site, overlooking the city's Roman amphitheatre, and to the Archaeology Museum, the Bottacin Museum of coins and medals, and the Medieval and Modern Art Museum, all of which are housed around the cloisters.

The tomb of the Volumni family in the archaeological collection

Eremitani Church

Alongside the museum complex is the Eremitani church (1276–1306), with its magnificent roof and wall tombs. Interred here is Marco Benavides (1489–1582), a professor of law at the city university whose mausoleum was designed by Ammannati, a Renaissance architect from Florence. Sadly missing from the church are Andrea Mantegna's celebrated frescoes of the lives of St James and St Christopher (1454–7), which were destroyed during a bombing raid in 1944. Two scenes from this magnificent work survive in the Ovetari Chapel, south of the sanctuary. *The Martyrdom of St James* was reconstructed from salvaged fragments, and *The Martyrdom of St Christopher* was removed carefully and stored elsewhere before the bombing. Otherwise only photographs on the walls remain to hint at the quality of the lost works.

The Museums

The highlight of the rich archaeological collection is the temple-like tomb of the Volumni family, dating from the 1st century AD. Among several other Roman tombstones from the Veneto region is one to the young dancer Claudia Toreuma – sadly, a fairly dull inscribed column rather than a portrait. The collection also includes some fine mosaics, along with several impressive life-size statues depicting muscular Roman deities and toga-clad dignitaries. For most visitors the Renaissance bronzes are likely to be the most appealing feature of the museum, especially the comical *Drinking Satyr* by Il Riccio (1470–1532).

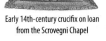

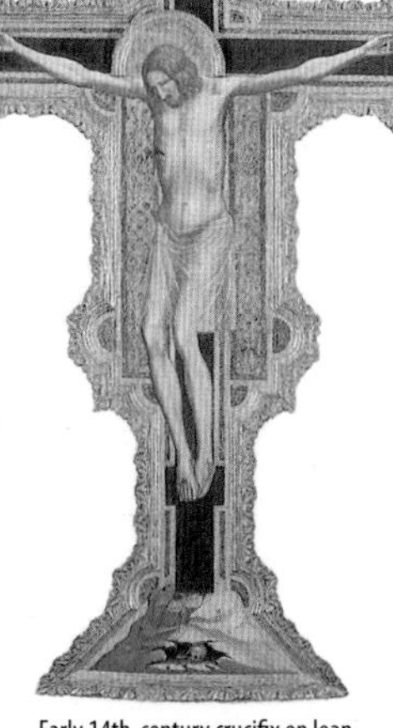
Early 14th-century crucifix on loan from the Scrovegni Chapel

Angels in Armour (15th century) by Guariento in the Art Museum

Coin collectors should make a point of visiting the Bottacin Museum. Among the exhibits there is an almost complete set of Venetian coinage and some very rare examples of Roman medallions.

The massive Medieval and Modern Art Museum is well worth a visit. It covers the history of Venetian art, with paintings from Giotto to the 1700s. Another section looks at Giotto and his influence on local art, using the Crucifix from the Scrovegni Chapel as its centrepiece. The Crucifix is flanked by an army of angels (late 15th century) painted in gorgeous colours by the artist Guariento. Another 15th-century painting worth a look is *Portrait of a Young Senator* by Giovanni Bellini.

VISITORS' CHECKLIST

Practical Information
Piazza Eremitani 8.
Tel 049 820 45 50.
W turismopadova.it
Open 9am–7pm Tue–Sun. Only chapel open Mon.
Closed 1 Jan, 1 May, 25 & 26 Dec.

Transport

Padua: Scrovegni Chapel

Enrico Scrovegni built this chapel in 1303, hoping thereby to spare his dead father, a usurer, from the eternal damnation wished upon him by the poet Dante in his *Inferno*. The chapel is filled with harmonious frescoes of scenes from the life of Christ, painted by Giotto between 1303 and 1305. As works of great narrative force, they exerted a powerful influence on the development of European art.

The Nativity
The naturalism of the Virgin's pose marks a departure from Byzantine stylization, as does the use of natural blue for the sky, in place of celestial gold.

Expulsion of the Merchants
Christ's physical rage, the cowering merchant and the child hiding his face are all typical of Giotto's style.

The Coretti
Giotto painted the two panels known as the Coretti as an exercise in perspective, creating the illusion of an arch with a room beyond.

View towards altar

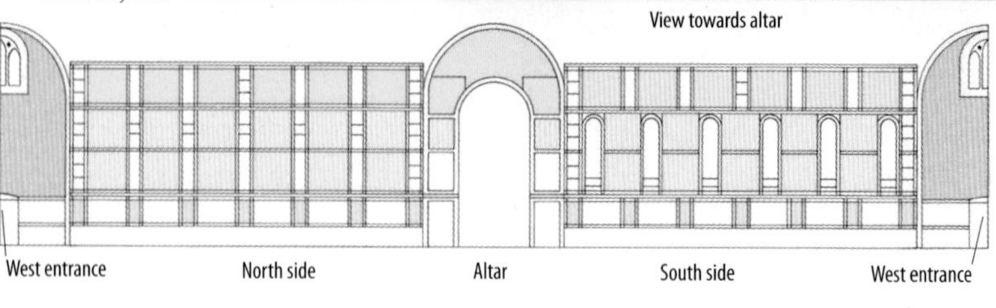

Gallery Guide

It is compulsory to book your visit to the Scrovegni Chapel in advance, since there are strict limits on the number of visitors allowed in the chapel at any one time. Prior to entry, all visitors must spend 15 minutes in a "decontamination chamber", and the duration of the visit to the chapel is also limited to 15 minutes. An explanatory film is shown while you wait in the chamber. The rest of the Eremitani complex is also worth a visit.

Key

- Episodes of Joachim and Anna
- Episodes from the Life of Mary
- Episodes from the Life and Death of Christ
- The Virtues and Vices
- The Last Judgment

The Last Judgment
This scene fills the entire west wall of the chapel. Its formal composition is closer to the Byzantine tradition than some of the other frescoes, with parts probably painted by assistants. A model of the chapel is shown, being offered to the Virgin by Scrovegni.

VISITORS' CHECKLIST

Practical Information
Giardini dell'Arena (entrance Piazza Eremitani).
Tel 049 201 00 20.
cappelladegliscrovegni.it
Open 9am–7pm daily & some late evenings. **Closed** 1 Jan, 1 May, 25 & 26 Dec. *see also Eremitani Museums p183.*
Booking compulsory.

Transport
to Piazzale Boschetti.

View towards entrance

Mary is Presented at the Temple
Giotto sets many scenes against an architectural background, using the laws of perspective to give a sense of three dimensions.

Injustice
The Virtues and Vices are painted in monochrome. Here Injustice is symbolized by scenes of war, murder and robbery.

Lament over the Dead Christ
Giotto's figures express their grief in different ways, some huddled, some gesturing wildly.

Giotto

The great Florentine artist Giotto (1266–1337) is regarded as the father of Western art. His work, with its sense of pictorial space, naturalism and narrative drama, marks a decisive break with the Byzantine tradition of the preceding 1,000 years. He is the first Italian master whose name has passed into posterity, and, although he was regarded in his lifetime as a great artist, few of the works attributed to him are fully documented. Some may have been painted by others, but his authorship of the frescoes in the Scrovegni Chapel need not be doubted.

The lofty interior of Padua's 16th-century Duomo

Duomo and Baptistry

Baptistry: **Tel** 049 65 69 14.
Open 10am–6pm daily.
Closed Easter, 25 Dec.

Padua's Duomo was commissioned from Michelangelo in 1552, but his designs were altered during the construction. Of the 4th-century cathedral which stood on the site, the domed Romanesque Baptistry still survives, with its frescoes by Giusto de' Menabuoi (c.1376). The frescoes cover biblical stories, such as the Creation, Christ's Passion, Crucifixion and Resurrection and the Last Judgment.

Basilica di Sant'Antonio

Piazza del Santo. **Tel** 049 822 56 22.
Open 7am–7:30pm daily.

This exotic church, with its minaret-like spires and Byzantine domes, is also known as Il Santo. It was begun in 1232 to house the remains of St Anthony of Padua, a preacher who modelled himself on St Francis of Assisi. Although he was a simple man who rejected worldly wealth, the citizens of Padua built one of the most lavish churches in Christendom to serve as his shrine.

The outline reflects the influence of Byzantine architecture; a cone-shaped central dome is surrounded by a further seven domes, rising above a façade that combines Gothic with Romanesque elements. The interior is more conventional, however. Visitors are kept away from the high altar, which features Donatello's magnificent reliefs (1444–5) on the miracles of St Anthony, and his statues of the Virgin, the Crucifixion and several Paduan saints. There is access to St Anthony's tomb in the north transept, hung with offerings and photographs of people who have survived serious illness or car crashes with the saint's help. The walls around the shrine are decorated with large marble reliefs depicting

The Basilica di Sant'Antonio and Donatello's statue of Gattamelata

The Brenta Canal

The River Brenta, between Padua and the Venetian Lagoon, was canalized in the 16th century. Flowing for a total of 36 km (22 miles), its potential as a transport route was quickly realized, and fine villas were built along its length. Today, these elegant buildings can still be admired. Three open their doors to the public: the Villa Foscari at Malcontenta, the Villa Widmann-Foscari at Mira and the Villa Pisani at Stra. They can be visited either on an 8- to 9-hour guided tour from Padua to Venice (or vice versa) along the river on a motor launch, or by bus, a cheaper and faster alternative.

The picturesque town of Mira on the Brenta Canal

Dolo
Fiessa d'Artico
S11
← Padova
①

Key

Tour route
Roads

0 kilometres 4
0 miles 2

① Villa Pisani
This 18th-century villa features an extravagant frescoed ceiling by Tiepolo.

For additional map symbols *see back flap*

St Anthony's life, carved in 1505–77 by various artists, including Jacopo Sansovino and Tullio Lombardo. These are rather cold by comparison with the *Crucifixion* fresco (1380s) by Altichiero da Zevio in the opposite transept. This pageant-like painting of everyday scenes from medieval life shows depictions of people, animals and plants.

One of four stone bridges spanning the canal around Prato della Valle

Statue of Gattamelata

Near the entrance to the Basilica stands one of the great Renaissance works. This gritty portrait of the mercenary soldier Gattamelata (whose name means "Honey Cat") was created in 1443–52, honouring a man who in his life did great service to the Venetian Republic. Donatello won fame for the monument, the first equestrian statue made of this size since Roman times.

Scuola del Santo and Oratorio di San Giorgio

Piazza del Santo. **Tel** 049 822 56 52. **Open** 9am–12:30pm, 2:30–7pm daily (to 5pm in winter). **Closed** 1 Jan, 25 Dec. (combined ticket).

These two linked buildings contain excellent frescoes, including the earliest documented paintings by Titian. These comprise two scenes from the life of St Anthony in the Scuola del Santo, executed in 1511. The delightful saints' lives and scenes from the life of Christ in the San Giorgio Oratory are the work of two artists, Altichiero da Zevio and Jacopo Avenzo, who painted them in 1378–84.

Orto Botanico

Via Orto Botanico 15. **Tel** 049 201 00 22. **Open** Apr, May & Oct: 9am–7pm daily; Jun–Sep: 10am–7pm Tue–Sun; Nov–Mar: 9am–5pm Tue–Sun.
W ortobotanico.unipd.it

Founded in 1545, Padua's botanical garden is the oldest in Europe, and it retains much of its original appearance; one of the palm trees dates to 1585. Originally intended for the cultivation of medicinal plants, the pathways now spill over with exotic foliage, shaded by ancient trees. The gardens were used to cultivate the first lilacs (1565), sunflowers (1568) and potatoes (1590) grown in Italy.

Prato della Valle

The Prato (field) claims to be the largest public square in Italy, and its elliptical shape reflects the form of the Roman theatre that stood on the site.

St Anthony of Padua used to preach sermons to huge crowds here, but subsequent neglect saw the area turn into a malaria-ridden swamp. The land was drained in 1767 to create the canal that now encircles the Prato. Four stone bridges cross the picturesque channel, which is lined on both sides by statues of 78 eminent citizens of Padua. On Saturdays there is a market.

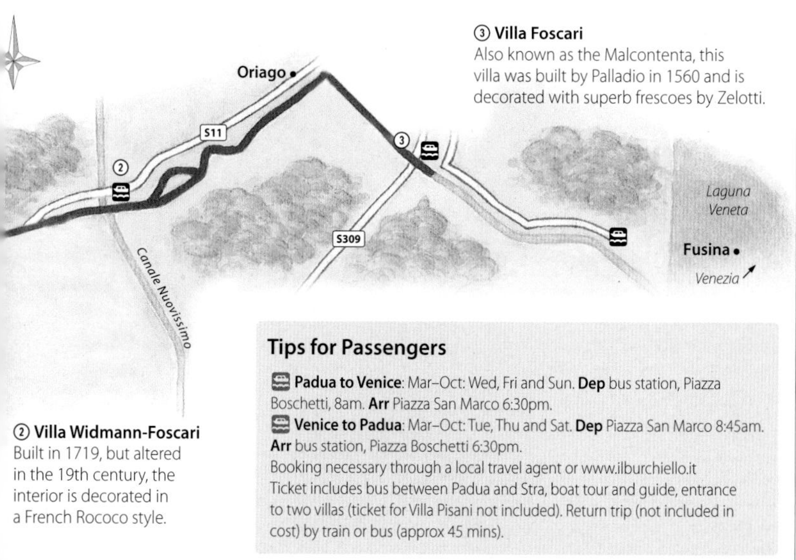

③ **Villa Foscari**
Also known as the Malcontenta, this villa was built by Palladio in 1560 and is decorated with superb frescoes by Zelotti.

② **Villa Widmann-Foscari**
Built in 1719, but altered in the 19th century, the interior is decorated in a French Rococo style.

Tips for Passengers

Padua to Venice: Mar–Oct: Wed, Fri and Sun. **Dep** bus station, Piazza Boschetti, 8am. **Arr** Piazza San Marco 6:30pm.
Venice to Padua: Mar–Oct: Tue, Thu and Sat. **Dep** Piazza San Marco 8:45am. **Arr** bus station, Piazza Boschetti 6:30pm.
Booking necessary through a local travel agent or www.ilburchiello.it
Ticket includes bus between Padua and Stra, boat tour and guide, entrance to two villas (ticket for Villa Pisani not included). Return trip (not included in cost) by train or bus (approx 45 mins).

The Euganean Hills, formed by ancient volcanic activity

⓯ Euganean Hills

10,000. Viale Stazione 60, Montegrotto Terme (049 892 83 11).

The Euganean Hills, remnants of long-extinct volcanoes, rise abruptly out of the Veneto Plain and offer plenty of walking opportunities. Hot springs bubble up out of the ground at Abano Terme and Montegrotto Terme, where scores of establishments offer thermal treatments, ranging from mudbaths to immersion in the hot sulphurated waters. Spa cures such as these date back to Roman times, and visitors can see extensive remains of the Roman baths and theatre at Montegrotto.

Abbazia di Praglia

Via Abbazia di Praglia, Bresseo di Teolo. **Tel** 049 999 93 00. **Open** Mar–Oct: 3:30–5:30pm Tue–Sun; Nov–Feb: 2:30–4:30pm Tue–Sun. Donations welcome. **praglia.it**

The Benedictine monastery at Praglia, 6 km (4 miles) west of Abano Terme, is a peaceful haven in the tree-clad hills. The monks have long been growing herbs commercially and there is a shop selling aromatic wares. They also lead guided tours of parts of the abbey and the Renaissance church (1490–1548), with its beautiful cloister.

Casa di Petrarca

Via Valleselle 4, Arquà Petrarca. **Tel** 0429 71 82 94. **Open** Tue–Sun. **Closed** most public hols.

The picturesque town of Arquà Petrarca, on the southern edge of the Euganean Hills, was once simply Arquà. Its name changed in 1868 to honour the medieval poet Francesco Petrarca, or Petrarch (1303–74), who lived here in his old age. He had often sung the praises of the well-tended landscape of olive groves and vineyards, and spent his last few years in a house frescoed with scenes from his poems. The house still contains the poet's desk and chair, his bookshelves and his mummified cat. Petrarch is buried in a sarcophagus in the piazza in front of the church.

Villa Barbarigo

Valsanzibio. **Tel** 049 913 10 65. **Open** Mar–Nov: 10am–1pm, 2pm–sunset. **valsanzibiogiardino.it**

To the north of Arquà is the Villa Barbarigo at Valsanzibio, the only one of scores of villas, built by wealthy Paduans, regularly open to the public. The villa itself is of a simple design compared with the Baroque garden. Planted from 1669, it is full of variety, with fountains, statues and lakes.

The house of the poet Petrarch in the town of Arquà Petrarca

⓰ Montagnana

12,000. FS Piazza Trieste 15 (0429 813 20). Thu am. Shops closed Mon am & Wed pm.

Medieval brick walls encircle this town, extending for 2 km (1 mile), pierced by four gateways and defended by 24 towers. Just inside the castellated Padua Gate is the town's archaeological museum. The Gothic-Renaissance **Duomo** contains Paolo Veronese's *Transfiguration* (1555). Outside the city walls is Palladio's **Villa Pisani** (c.1560). Now rather neglected, its façade features the original owner's name (Francesco Pisani) in bold letters below the pediment.

Antique market in Montagnana

⓱ Este

17,600. FS Via Guido Negri 9 (0429 600 462). Wed & Sat am. **Shops closed** Mon am (clothes) & Wed pm (food).

Excavations at Este have uncovered impressive remains of the ancient Ateste people, who flourished from the 9th century BC until they were conquered by the Romans in the 3rd century BC. The archaeological finds, including funerary urns, figurines, bronze vases and jewellery, are on display in the excellent **Museo Nazionale Atestino**, set within the walls of the town's 14th-century castle. The museum also displays examples of Roman and medieval art, and pieces of local pottery, famous since the Renaissance period, and still produced.

Museo Nazionale Atestino
Palazzo Mocenigo. **Tel** 0429 20 85. **Open** daily. **Closed** 1 Jan, 1 May, 25 Dec. **atestino.beniculturali.it**

⓲ Monselice

17,000. Via del Santuario 6 (0429 78 30 26). Mon & Fri. **Shops closed** Tue am (clothes), Wed pm (food).

The town of Monselice stands at the foot of two hills, one of which has been quarried extensively for rich deposits of crystalline minerals. The other is topped by ruined **Castle Rocca**, now a nature reserve. It is worth walking up the cobbled Via del Santuario as far as **San Giorgio**, to see its exquisite inlaid marble work.

Other features on the way up are the 13th-century cathedral and the statue-filled Baroque gardens of the Villa Nani that can be glimpsed through the villa gates. Nearby is **Castello di Monselice**, a 14th-century castle with period furnishings, suits of armour, frescoes and tapestries.

Marble inlay detail from San Giorgio

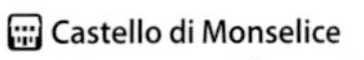

Castello di Monselice
Via del Santuario. **Tel** 0429 729 31. **Open** Apr–Nov: Tue–Sun; Dec–Mar: groups only; book in advance. on the hour 9–11am, 3–5pm. **castellodimonselice.it**

The sanctuary of San Giorgio on the hill top at Monselice

⓳ Polesine and Rovigo

Piazza Matteotti 1, Porto Viro (0426 63 30 12).

Polesine is the flat expanse of fertile agricultural land, crisscrossed by canals and subject to flooding, between the River Adige and the Po. The Po Delta is now a national park and has a wealth of fascinating birdlife, including egrets, herons and bitterns.

The most scenic areas are around Scardovari and Porto Tolle, on the south side of the Po. Companies in Porto Tolle offer canoe and bicycle hire and half-day boat cruises.

The modern city of Rovigo has one outstanding monument; the splendid octagonal church called **La Rotonda** (1594–1602), decorated with paintings and statues in niches.

Net mending in the traditional way, Chioggia

Environs
Adria, 22 km (14 miles) east of Rovigo, gave its name to the Adriatic Sea and was once a Greek and later an Etruscan port. A programme of silt deposition, undertaken to increase Adria's agricultural potential, left the city dry, apart from a 24-km (15-mile) canal. Among the exhibits on display in the **Museo Archeologico** is a complete iron chariot dating from the 4th century BC.

Museo Archeologico
Via Badini 59, Adria. **Tel** 0426 216 12. **Open** 8:30am–7:30pm daily. **Closed** 1 Jan, 1 May, 25 Dec

⓴ Chioggia

56,000. Lungomare Adriatico 101. (041 40 10 68). Thu. **chioggiaturismo.it**

Chioggia is the principal fishing port on the lagoon and the bustling, colourful **fish market** is a good reason to come here early in the day (open every morning except Monday). Many visitors enjoy the gritty character of the port area, with its smells, its vibrantly coloured boats and the tangle of nets and tackle. The town also has numerous inexpensive restaurants which serve fresh fish in almost every variety. Eel, crab and cuttlefish are the local specialities. There is a beach area at Sottomarina, on the western part of the island. Worth seeking out for a special visit is Carpaccio's *St Paul* (1520), the artist's last known work, which is permanently housed in the church of **San Domenico**.

VERONA AND LAKE GARDA

Verona is one of northern Italy's most alluring cities, its noble palaces, quiet cloisters and ancient streets every bit as romantic as you would expect of Romeo and Juliet's city. On its doorstep are the well-known vineyards of Soave, Bardolino and Valpolicella, set against the rugged slopes of the Little Dolomites. To the west lie the beautiful shores of Lake Garda, a mere 30 minutes' drive from Verona by car, but a world away in atmosphere.

Set within the curves of the Adige river, Verona has been a prosperous and cosmopolitan city since the Romans colonized it in 89 BC. It stands astride two important trade routes – the Serenissima, connecting the great port cities of Venice and Genoa, and the Brenner Pass, used by commercial travellers crossing the Alps from northern Europe. This helps to explain the Germanic influence in Verona's magnificent San Zeno church, or the realism of the paintings in the Castelvecchio museum, owing more to Dürer than to Raphael.

Verona's passion and panache, however, are purely Italian. Stylish shops and cafés sit amid the impressive remains of Roman monuments. The massive Arena amphitheatre fills with crowds of 20,000 or more, who thrill to opera beneath the stars. All over the city, art galleries and theatres testify to a crowded calendar of cultural activities.

Italy's largest lake, Lake Garda, is renowned for its beautiful scenery. The broad southern end of the lake, with its waterfront promenades, is very popular with Italian and German visitors. Those in search of peace can escape to the heights of the Monte Baldo mountain range, rising above the eastern shore. The ridge marks the western edge of the mountainous region north of Verona. Here is the great plateau of Monti Lessini, with its little river valleys that fan out southwards to join the Adige river.

Giardino Giusti in Verona, one of Italy's finest Renaissance gardens

◀ Ponte Pietra on the Adige river, with San Giorgio in Braida in the background, Verona

Exploring Verona and Lake Garda

Verona makes an excellent touring base, with lofty mountains, castles and vineyards all within easy reach of the city. Lake Garda, whose western shore is actually over the border in Lombardy, is a popular destination for excursions from Verona. The many resort towns have excellent hotels, harbourside fish restaurants and lakeside gardens, and the lake is perfect for watersports such as windsurfing or dinghy racing. Less exhausting are the steamer excursions, offering mid-lake views of entrancing beauty.

Sights at a Glance

1. *Verona pp194–205*
2. Grezzana
3. Soave
4. Montecchio Maggiore
5. Valdagno
6. Bolca
7. Giazza
8. Bosco Chiesanuova
9. Sant'Anna d'Alfaedo
10. Garda
11. Peschiera
12. Solferino
13. *Sirmione Peninsula pp212–13*
14. Salò
15. Gardone Riviera
16. Riva del Garda
17. Malcesine

Key

- Major road
- Minor road
- Secondary road
- Motorway
- Main railway
- Minor railway
- Scenic route
- Regional border
- △ Summit

Lazise harbour on the eastern shore of Lake Garda

For additional map symbols *see back flap*

Getting Around

The roads around Verona are heavily used by commercial vehicles and commuter traffic, so expect delays, especially during morning and evening rush hours. Motorways are faster, even though those in this region are among the oldest in Italy. There are good rail services linking Verona with Lake Garda to the west and with Bolzano to the north. The Brenner Pass also runs northwards from Verona. For information on ferries across Lake Garda, see p210.

The green pastures of Bolca, an area rich in fossil remains

Trento
Monte Sparavieri 1976m
Corno d'Aquilio 1546m
Monti Lessini
Staro
Recoaro Terme
Montagna Spaccata
Ongaro
Malo
Selvavecchia
7 GIAZZA
5 VALDAGNO
Priabona
SANT'ANNA D'ALFAEDO
8 BOSCO CHIESANUOVA
Selva di Progno
Vaggimàl
6 BOLCA
Castelgomberto
Cerro Veronese
Badia Calavena
Tríssino
Chiampo
Negrar
Stallavena
S. Giovanni Ilarione
Sovizzo
2 GREZZANA
Tregnano
Arzignano
Castagnè
MONTECCHIO MAGGIORE 4
Alte Ceccato
Arbizzano
Santa Maria in Stelle
Céllore
Vicenza
VENETO
Poiano
Montório
Costalunga
S. Zeno
1 VERONA
S. Martino Buon Albergo
3 SOAVE
San Bonifacio
San Giovanni Lupatoto
Adige
Zévio
S46
S246
S11
S12
S434
A4
Squaranto
Mezzane
Chiampo
Agno
Orolo
Alpone
0 kilometres 10
0 miles 5

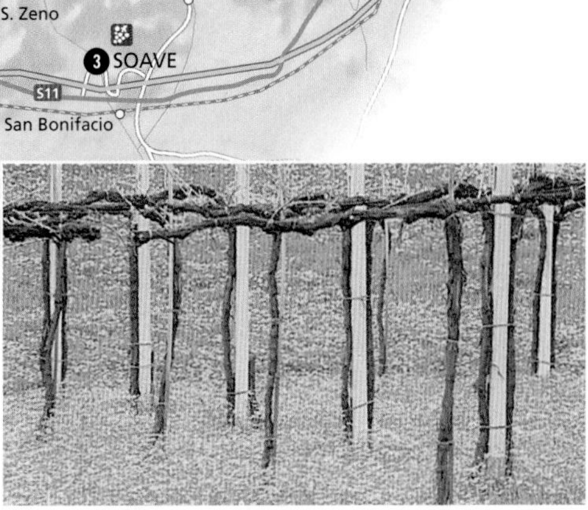

A vineyard in spring on the hillsides around Verona

❶ Verona

Verona is a vibrant city, the second biggest in the Veneto region (after Venice) and one of the most prosperous in northern Italy. A UNESCO World Heritage Site, its ancient centre boasts many magnificent Roman remains, second only to those of Rome itself, and *palazzi* built of *rosso di Verona*, the local pink-tinged limestone, by the city's medieval rulers. Verona has two main focal points: the massive 1st-century AD Arena and the Piazza Erbe with its colourful market, separated by a maze of narrow lanes lined with some of Italy's most elegant boutiques.

Verona as seen from the Museo Archeologico

Verona's rulers

In 1263 the Scaligeri began their successful 127-year rule of Verona. They used ruthless tactics in their rise to power, earning nicknames like Mastino ("Mastiff") and Cangrande ("Big Dog"), but once in power the Scaligeri family brought peace to a city racked by civil strife and inter-family rivalry. They proved to be relatively just and cultured rulers – the poet Dante was welcomed to their court in 1301–4 and dedicated his *Paradise*, the final part of the epic *Divine Comedy*, to Cangrande I.

Verona fell to the Visconti of Milan in 1387, and a succession of outsiders – Venice, France and Austria – followed before the Veneto was united with the rest of Italy in 1866.

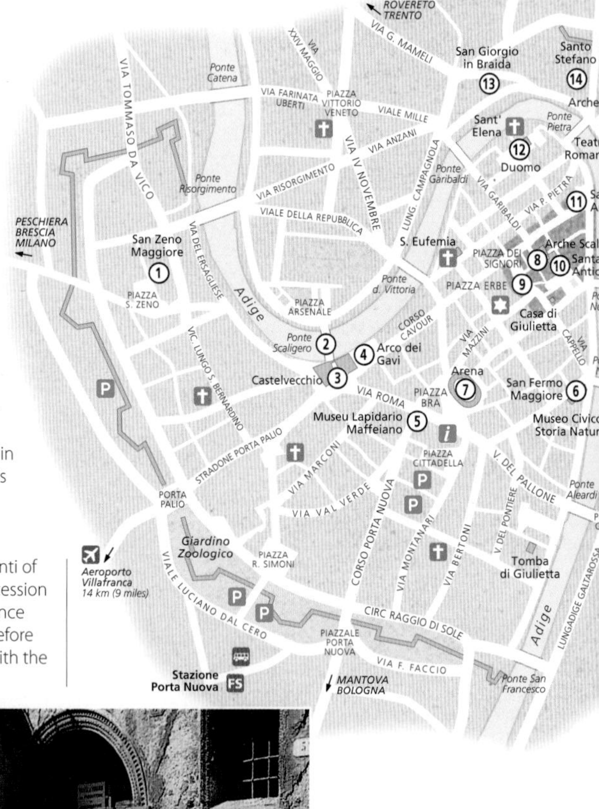

Fruit and vegetable stall in a side street of old Verona

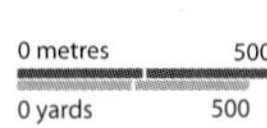

For keys to symbols *see back flap*

Castelvecchio

Corso Castelvecchio 2. **Tel** 045 806 26 11. **Open** 8:30am–7:30pm daily (from 1:30pm Mon); 9am–7pm public hols. **Closed** 1 Jan, 25 & 26 Dec. **museodicastelvecchio.comune.verona.it**

This spectacular castle, built by Cangrande II between 1355 and 1375, has been transformed into one of the Veneto's finest art galleries. Various parts of the medieval structure have been linked together using aerial walkways and corridors, designed by Carlo Scarpa to give striking views of the building itself, as well as the exhibits within, which are excellent and varied.

The first section contains a wealth of late Roman and early Christian material, including a 7th-century silver plate that shows armoured knights in combat, 5th-century brooches and glass painted with a portrait of Christ the Shepherd in gold. The martyrdom scenes depicted on the carved marble sarcophagus of SS Sergius and Bacchus (1179) are gruesomely realistic.

The following section, which is devoted to medieval and early Renaissance art, vividly demonstrates the influence of northern art on local painters, suggesting strong links with Verona's neighbours across the Alps. Here, instead of the serene saints and virgins of Tuscan art, the emphasis is on brutal realism. This is summed up in the 14th-century *Crucifixion with Saints*, which depicts the torture musculature of Christ and the racked faces of the mourners in painful detail. Far more lyrical is a beautiful 15th-century painting by Stefano da Verona called *The Madonna of the Rose Garden*. This contains many allusions to popular medieval fables, including the figure of Fortune with her wheel. In the painting the Virgin sits in a pretty garden alive with decorative birds and angels gathering rosebuds.

Other Madonnas from the 15th century, attributed to Giovanni Bellini, are displayed among the late Renaissance works upstairs. Jewellery, suits of armour, swords and shield bosses feature next, some dating back to the 6th and 7th centuries, when Verona was under attack from Teutonic invaders from beyond the Alpine range.

Cangrande I's horse in ceremonial garb

After the armour room, take the walkway that leads out along the river flank of the castle, with its dizzying views of the swirling waters of the River Adige and the Ponte Scaligero *(see p196)*. Next, turning a corner, one finds Cangrande I, his equestrian statue dramatically displayed out of doors on a plinth. This 14th-century statue once graced Cangrande's tomb *(see p200)*. It is possible to study every detail of the horse and rider draped in their ceremonial garb. Despite Cangrande's cherubic cheeks and inane grin, his face is compelling.

Beyond lie some of the museum's celebrated paintings, notably Paolo Veronese's *Deposition* (1565) and a portrait attributed by some to Titian, by others to Lorenzo Lotto.

Courtyard of Castelvecchio

VISITORS' CHECKLIST

Practical Information
261,000. Via degli Alpini 9 (045 806 86 80). **turismoverona.eu** daily. Shops: **Closed** Wed pm (food), Mon am (department & clothing stores). Vinitaly – Italy's largest wine fair (Apr); Festival della Lirica (opera festival) (end Jun–Aug); Estate Teatrale Veronese, including Shakespeare Festival (end Jun–Aug).

Transport
Villafranca 14 km (9 miles). FS Piazza Cittadella.

Sights at a Glance

1. San Zeno Maggiore
2. Ponte Scaligero
3. Castelvecchio
4. Arco dei Gavi
5. Museo Lapidario Maffeiano
6. San Fermo Maggiore
7. Arena
8. Piazza dei Signori
9. Piazza Erbe
10. Santa Maria Antica
11. Sant'Anastasia
12. Duomo
13. San Giorgio in Braida
14. Santo Stefano
15. Teatro Romano
16. Museo Archeologico
17. Santa Maria in Organo
18. Giardino Giusti
19. Museo Civico di Storia Naturale

Around the Arena

Most visitors to Verona first arrive at Piazza Brà, a large, irregularly shaped square with a public garden. On the north side is an archway known as the Portoni della Brà. Dominating the eastern side of the piazza is the Roman Arena, Verona's most important monument, still in use today for operatic performances. The piazza is ringed with 19th-century buildings resembling ancient temples and historical landmarks.

Ponte Scaligero, part of the old defence system of Castelvecchio

Ponte Scaligero

This medieval bridge was built by Cangrande II between 1354 and 1376. The people of Verona love to stroll across it to ponder the River Adige in all its moods, or to admire summer sunsets and distant views of the Alps. Such is their affection for the bridge that it was rebuilt after the retreating Germans blew it up in 1945, an operation that involved dredging the river to salvage the medieval masonry. The bridge leads from Castelvecchio *(see p195)* to the Arsenal on the north bank of the Adige, built by the Austrians between 1840 and 1861 and now fronted by public gardens. Looking back from the gardens it is possible to see how the river was used as a natural moat to defend the castle, with the bridge providing the inhabitants with an escape route.

Arco dei Gavi and Corso Cavour

Dwarfed by the massive brick walls of Castelvecchio, the monumental scale of this Roman triumphal arch is now hard to appreciate. Originally the arch straddled the main Roman road into the city, today's Corso Cavour. But French troops who were occupying Castelvecchio in 1805 damaged the monument so much that a decision was made to move it to its present, less conspicuous position just off the Corso in 1933.

Continuing up Corso Cavour, there are some fine medieval and Renaissance palaces to see (especially Nos. 10, 11 and 19) before the Roman town gate, the **Porta dei Borsari**, is reached. The gate dates from the 1st century BC, but looking at the pedimented windows and niches it is easy to see what influenced the city's Renaissance architects.

The Roman Arco dei Gavi, 1st century AD

Museo Lapidario Maffeiano

Piazza Brà 28. **Tel** 045 590 087. **Open** 8:30am–2pm Tue–Sun. **Closed** 1 Jan, 25 & 26 Dec.

This "museum of stone" displays all kinds of architectural fragments hinting at the last splendour of the Roman city. There are many carved funerary monuments, and a large part of the collection consists of Greek inscriptions collected by the museum's 18th-century founder, Scipione Maffei.

San Fermo Maggiore

Stradone San Fermo. **Tel** 045 59 28 13. **Open** Mar–Oct: 10am–6pm Mon–Sat, 1–6pm Sun; Nov–Feb: 10am–5pm Mon–Sat, 1–5pm Sun.

chieseverona.it

San Fermo Maggiore consists of not one but two churches. This can best be appreciated from the outside, where the eastern end is a jumble of rounded Romanesque arches below with pointed Gothic arches rising above. The lower church, now rather dank due to frequent flooding, dates from 1065, but the upper church (1313) is more impressive. It has a splendid ship's-keel roof and lots of medieval fresco work. Frescoes from the 14th century, just inside the main door, are by Stefano de Zevico. They show the fate of four Franciscan missionaries who journeyed to India in the mid-14th century. Nearby is the Brenzoni mausoleum (1439) by Giovanni di Bartolo, with Pisanello's *Annunciation* fresco (1426). In the south aisle is an ornate pulpit of 1396 with saints in canopied niches above, surrounded by frescoes of the Evangelists and Doctors of the Church.

The apse of the lower church of San Fermo Maggiore

The Arena

Verona's amphitheatre, completed around AD 30, is the third largest in the world, after Rome's Colosseum and the amphitheatre at Capua, near Naples. Originally, the Arena could hold almost the entire population of Roman Verona, and visitors came from across the Veneto to watch mock battles and gladiatorial combats. Since then, the Arena has been used for public executions, fairs, theatre performances, bullfighting and opera.

VISITORS' CHECKLIST

Practical Information
Piazza Brà. **Tel** 045 800 51 51.
arena.it
Open 8:30am–7:30pm daily (from 1:30pm Mon; last adm 6:30pm). Closes earlier on performance days. **Closed** 1 Jan, 25 Dec. partial. Operas & concerts *(see pp260–61).*

Interior
The interior has survived virtually intact, maintained by the Arena Conservators since 1580.

The façade of the Arena seen from Piazza Brà

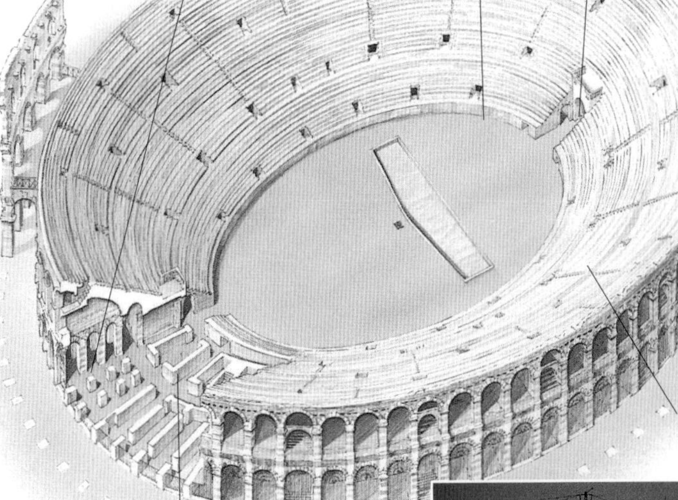

The elliptical amphitheatre is 139 m (456 ft) long and 110 m (361 ft) wide.

Gladiators and wild beasts entered the arena from both sides.

Stone seats in 44 tiers

Below ground were cages for lions, tigers and other wild beasts, and a maze of passages.

Blood Sports
Prisoners of war, criminals and Christians died in their thousands in the name of entertainment.

Opera in the Arena
Today, performances of Verdi's *Aida* and other popular operas can attract a capacity crowd of 25,000.

Street-by-Street: Verona

Since the days of the Roman Empire, the Piazza Erbe has been the centre of Verona's commercial and administrative life. Built on the site of the ancient Roman forum, it is an enjoyably chaotic square, bustling with life. Shoppers browse in the colourful market at stalls sheltered from the sun by wide-brimmed umbrellas. The massive towers and *palazzi* of the Scaligeri rulers of Verona have retained their medieval feel, even though they have been altered and adapted many times.

★ Piazza dei Signori
This square is bordered by individual Scaligeri *palazzi* linked by Renaissance arcades and carved stone archways.

Statue of Dante
Dante, the medieval poet, stayed in Verona as a guest of the Scaligeri during his period in exile from his native Florence. His statue (1865) looks down on Piazza dei Signori.

The 17th-century Palazzo Maffei is surmounted by a balustrade supporting statues of gods and goddesses.

Colonna di San Marco (1528) is surmounted by St Mark's Lion, the symbol of Venetian rule.

Piazza Erbe
Verona's medieval herb market is now lined with art galleries, upmarket boutiques and inviting pavement cafés.

The fountain of 1368 is topped by a figure known as the Madonna of Verona; in fact, the statue is Roman and probably symbolizes Commerce.

Torre dei Lamberti, 84 m (275 ft) high

Palazzo della Ragione
The medieval Palace of Reason features an elegant Renaissance staircase. It leads from the exterior courtyard into the magistrates' rooms on the upper floor.

Via Sottoriva is lined with arcaded medieval houses and typifies the heart of the old city.

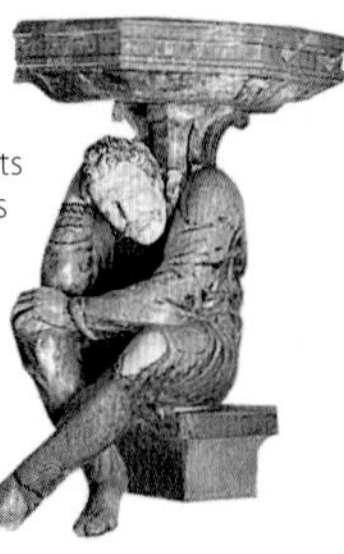

Sant'Anastasia
Carved hunchbacks *(gobbi)*, crafted in 1495, form the unusual supports for the holy water stoups in this church.

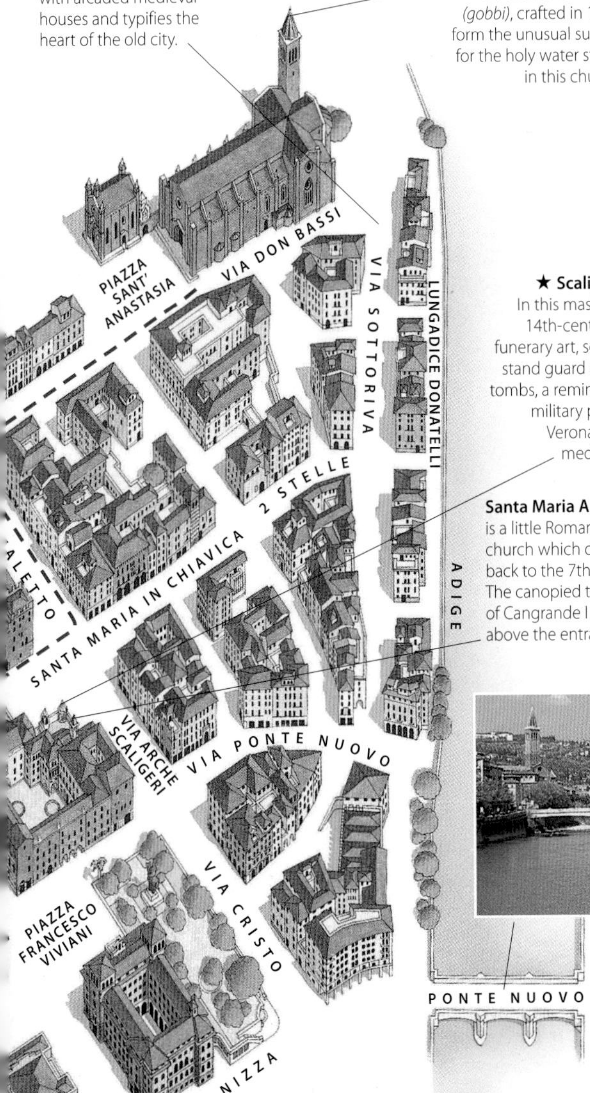

★ Scaligeri Tombs
In this masterpiece of 14th-century Gothic funerary art, soldier saints stand guard around the tombs, a reminder of the military prowess of Verona's powerful medieval rulers.

Santa Maria Antica is a little Romanesque church which dates back to the 7th century. The canopied tomb of Cangrande I rises above the entrance.

Ponte Nuovo
The "new bridge" (1540) spans the Adige river, linking the hills on the east bank of the city with Verona's historic centre.

Casa di Giulietta
The House of Juliet looks the part, with its marble balcony and romantic setting, although there is no evidence linking this house with the romantic legend.

Key

▬ Suggested route

0 metres 100

0 yards 100

Central Verona

The streets of this ancient city centre owe their grid-like layout to the order and precision of the Romans. At the heart is the lively Piazza Erbe, where crowds shop in the ancient marketplace. The fine *palazzi*, churches and monuments date mostly from the medieval period.

An elegant café in the spacious Piazza dei Signori

Piazza Erbe

Piazza Erbe is named after the city's old herb market. Today's stalls, shaded by huge umbrellas, sell everything from lunchtime snacks of herb-flavoured roast suckling pig in bread rolls to fresh-picked fruit or delicious wild mushrooms.

The **Venetian lion** that stands on top of a column to the north of the square marks Verona's absorption in 1405 into the Venetian empire. The statue-topped building that completes the north end of Piazza Erbe is the Baroque **Palazzo Maffei** (1668), now converted to shops and luxury apartments. An assortment of boutiques and cafés lines the edge of the square.

The **fountain** that splashes away quietly in the middle of the piazza is often overlooked amid the competing attractions of the market's colourful stalls. Yet the statue at the fountain's centre dates from Roman times, a reminder that this long piazza has been in almost continuous use as a marketplace for some 2,000 years.

Piazza dei Signori

Torre dei Lamberti: **Tel** 045 927 30 27. **Open** 8:30am–7:30pm daily.

In the centre of Piazza dei Signori is a 19th-century **statue of Dante**, who surveys the surrounding buildings with an appraising eye. His gaze is fixed on the grim **Palazzo del Capitano**, home of Verona's military commander, and the equally intimidating **Palazzo della Ragione**, the Palace of Reason, or law court, both built in the 14th century. The Palazzo della Ragione is not quite so grim within. The courtyard has a handsome external stone staircase, added in 1446–50. Fine views of the Alps can be had by climbing the 84-m (275-ft) **Torre dei Lamberti**, which rises from the western side of the courtyard.

Stonework detail, Piazza dei Signori

Behind the statue of Dante is the pretty Renaissance **Loggia del Consiglio**, or council chamber, with its frescoed upper façade (1493) and statues of Roman worthies born in Verona. These include Catullus the poet, Pliny the natural historian and Vitruvius the architectural theorist.

The piazza is linked to Piazza Erbe by the Arco della Costa, or the arch of the rib, whose name refers to the whale rib hung beneath it, put up here as a curiosity in the distant past.

Santa Maria Antica

This tiny Romanesque church is almost swamped by the bizarre Scaligeri tombs built up against its entrance wall. Because Santa Maria Antica was their parish church, the Scaligeri rulers of Verona chose to be buried here, and their tombs speak of their military prowess *(see p213)*.

Over the entrance to the church is the impressive tomb of Cangrande I, or Big Dog (d.1329), topped by his equestrian statue. This statue is a copy; the original is now in the Castelvecchio *(see p195)*. The other Scaligeri tombs are next to the church, surrounded by an intricate wrought-iron fence featuring the ladder motif of the family's original name (*della Scala*, meaning "of the steps"). Towering above the fence are the spire-topped

The fountain in Piazza Erbe, erected in the 14th century

tombs of Mastino II, or Mastiff (d.1351) and Cansignorio, meaning Noble Dog (d.1375). These two tombs are splendidly decorated with Gothic pinnacles. In their craftsmanship and design there is nothing else in European funerary architecture quite like these spiky, thrusting monuments.

Plainer tombs nearer the church wall mark the resting place of other members of the Scaligeri family – Mastino (d.1277) who founded the Scaligeri dynasty, having been elected mayor of Verona in 1260, and two who did not have dog-based names: Bartolomeo (d.1304) and Giovanni (d. 1359).

Sant'Anastasia

Tel 045 59 28 13. **Open** Mar–Oct: 9am–6pm Mon–Sat, 1–6pm Sun; Nov–Feb: 10am–5pm Mon–Sat, 1–5pm Sun. **chieseverona.it**

A huge church, Sant'Anastasia was begun in 1290 and built to hold the massive congregations who came to listen to the rousing sermons preached by members of the fundamentalist Dominican order. Most interesting is the Gothic portal, with its faded 15th-century frescoes and carved scenes from the life of St Peter Martyr. Inside, the two holy water stoups are supported on realistic figures of beggars, known as *i gobbi*, the hunchbacks (the one on the left carved in 1495, the other a century later).

Off the north aisle is the sacristy, home to Antonio Pisanello's fresco, *St George and the Princess* (1433–8). Despite being badly damaged, the fresco still conveys something of the aristocratic grace of the Princess of Trebizond, with her noble brow and her ermine-fringed cloak, as St George prepares to mount his horse in pursuit of the dragon.

The lofty, Romanesque interior of Sant'Anastasia

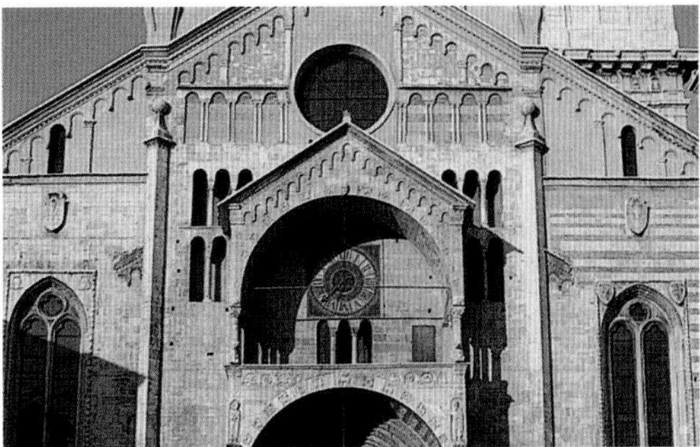

The façade of the Duomo, Santa Maria Matricolare

Duomo

Tel 045 59 56 27. **Open** Mar–Oct: 10am–5:30pm Mon–Sat, 1:30–5:30pm Sun; Nov–Feb: 10am–5pm Mon–Sat, 1:30–5pm Sun. **chieseverona.it**

Visitors to Verona's cathedral pass through a magnificent Romanesque portal carved by Nicolò, one of the master masons who carved the façade of San Zeno *(see pp202–3)*. Here he sculpted the sword-bearing figures of Oliver and Roland, knights whose exploits in the service of Charlemagne were celebrated in medieval poetry. Nearby stand saints and evangelists with bold staring eyes and flowing beards. To the south there is a second Romanesque portal carved with Jonah and the Whale (removed for restoration) and comically grotesque caryatids (load-bearing figures).

The highlight is Titian's *Assumption* (1535–40) in the first chapel on the left. Further down is the entrance to the Romanesque cloister with excavated remains of earlier churches on the site. It leads to the baptistry, known as San Giovanni in Fonte (St John of the Spring). This 8th-century church features a huge marble font carved in 1200.

Romeo and Juliet

The tragic story of Romeo and Juliet, written by Luigi da Porto of Vicenza in the 1520s, inspired countless poems, films, ballets and dramas. At the **Casa di Giulietta** (Juliet's house), Via Cappello 27, (tel: 045 803 43 03), Romeo is said to have climbed to Juliet's balcony. In reality this is a restored 13th-century inn. The run-down **Casa di Romeo** is in Via delle Arche Scaligere, while the so-called **Tomba di Giulietta**, Piazza del Pontiere 35, (tel: 045 800 03 61), is in a crypt below the cloister of San Francesco al Corso on Via del Pontiere. The stone sarcophagus is empty and rather plain, but the setting is atmospheric. Juliet's house and tomb are open 8:30am–7:30pm daily (from 1:30pm Mon).

The lovers Romeo and Juliet from a 19th-century illustration

Verona: San Zeno Maggiore

Built between 1120 and 1138 to house the shrine of Verona's patron saint, San Zeno is northern Italy's most ornate Romanesque church. The façade is embellished with marble reliefs of biblical scenes, matched in vitality by bronze door panels showing the miracles of San Zeno. Beneath an impressive rose window, a graceful porch canopy rests on two slim columns. A brick campanile soars to the south, while a squat tower to the north is said to cover the tomb of King Pepin of Italy (777–810).

Nave Ceiling
The nave has a magnificent example of a ship's-keel ceiling, so called because it resembles the inside of an upturned boat. This ceiling was constructed in 1386, when the apse was rebuilt.

Altarpiece
Andrea Mantegna's three-part altarpiece (1457–59) depicts the Virgin and Child with various saints. The painting served as an inspiration to local artists.

KEY

① **Striped brickwork** is typical of Romanesque buildings in Verona. Courses of local pink brick are alternated with ivory-coloured tufa.

② **The campanile**, started in 1045, reached its present height of 72 m (236 ft) in 1173.

③ **The sanctuary rood screen** has marble statues of Christ and the Apostles, dating from 1250, ranged along it.

④ **The rose window** symbolizes the Wheel of Fortune: figures around the rim show the rise and fall of human fortunes.

⑤ **Marble side panels**, carved in 1140, depict events from the life of Christ to the left of the doors, and scenes from the Book of Genesis to the right.

★ Cloister
North of the church the fine, airy cloister (1293–1313) has rounded Romanesque arches on one side and pointed Gothic arches on the other.

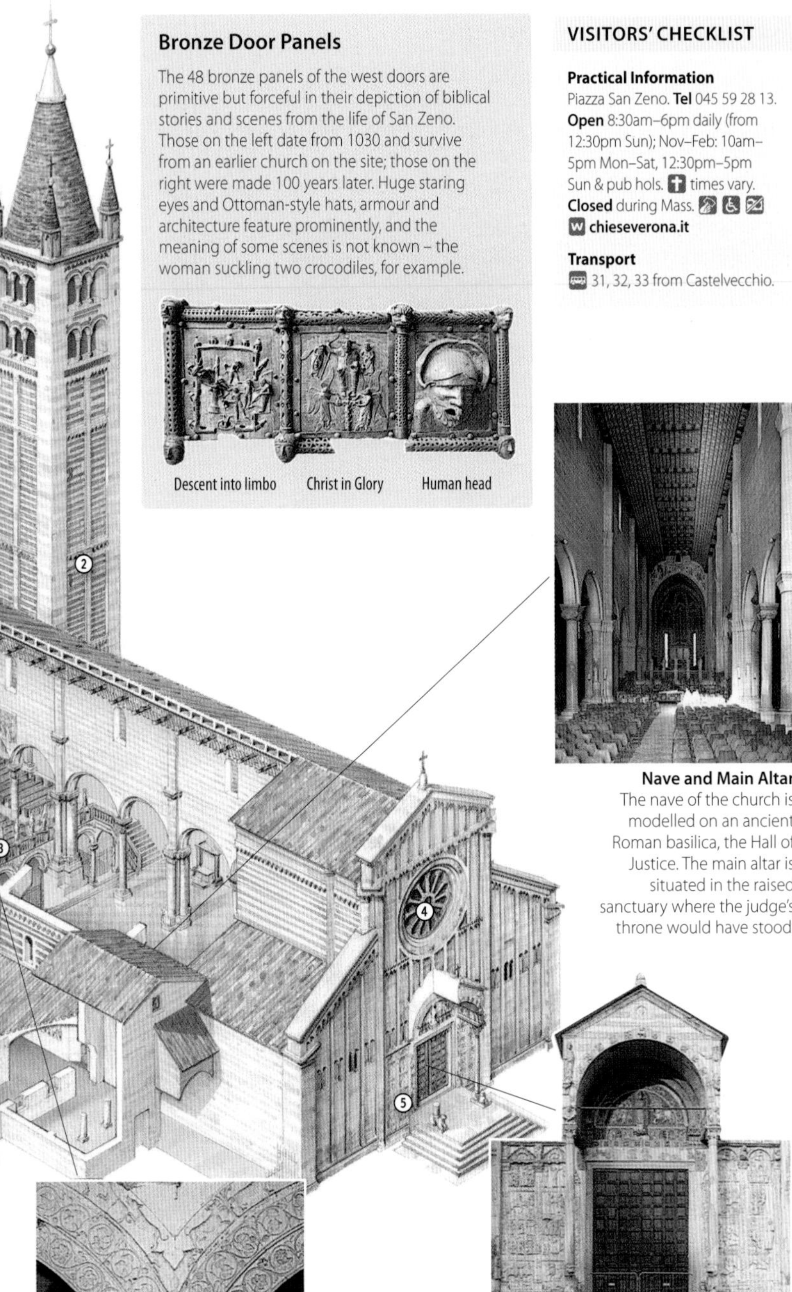

Bronze Door Panels

The 48 bronze panels of the west doors are primitive but forceful in their depiction of biblical stories and scenes from the life of San Zeno. Those on the left date from 1030 and survive from an earlier church on the site; those on the right were made 100 years later. Huge staring eyes and Ottoman-style hats, armour and architecture feature prominently, and the meaning of some scenes is not known – the woman suckling two crocodiles, for example.

Descent into limbo   Christ in Glory   Human head

VISITORS' CHECKLIST

Practical Information
Piazza San Zeno. **Tel** 045 59 28 13.
Open 8:30am–6pm daily (from 12:30pm Sun); Nov–Feb: 10am–5pm Mon–Sat, 12:30pm–5pm Sun & pub hols. times vary.
Closed during Mass.
chieseverona.it

Transport
31, 32, 33 from Castelvecchio.

Nave and Main Altar
The nave of the church is modelled on an ancient Roman basilica, the Hall of Justice. The main altar is situated in the raised sanctuary where the judge's throne would have stood.

★ Crypt
The vaulted crypt contains the tomb of San Zeno, appointed eighth bishop of Verona in AD 362, who died in AD 380.

★ West Doors
Each of the wooden doors has 24 bronze plates joined by bronze masks, nailed on to the wood to look like solid metal. A bas-relief above the doors depicts San Zeno vanquishing the devil.

Across the Ponte Romano

The Ponte Romano, or Roman Bridge, links Verona's city centre to the eastern bank of the Adige river. This upmarket residential district is dotted with fine palaces, gardens and churches, and offers good views back on to the towers and domes of the medieval city.

View from the Teatro Romano across the Adige river

Teatro Romano

Rigaste Redentore 2. **Tel** 045 800 03 60. **Open** 8:30am–7:30pm daily (from 1:30pm Mon; also open Mon am on public hols).

When this theatre was built, in the 1st century BC, the plays performed would have included satirical dramas by such writers as Terence and Plautus. The tradition continues with open-air performances at the annual Shakespeare festival.

The theatre is built into a bank above the Adige river. The views over the city must have been as entrancing to Roman theatre-goers as the events on stage. Certainly it is for the views that the theatre is best visited today, since little is left of the original stage area, though the semicircular seating area remains largely intact.

In the foreground of the view is one of three Roman bridges that brought traffic into the city. The only one to have survived, this had to be painstakingly reconstructed after being blown up in 1945 by retreating German soldiers who were attempting to delay the advance of Allied troops. Of the five arches, the two nearest to the theatre are least altered.

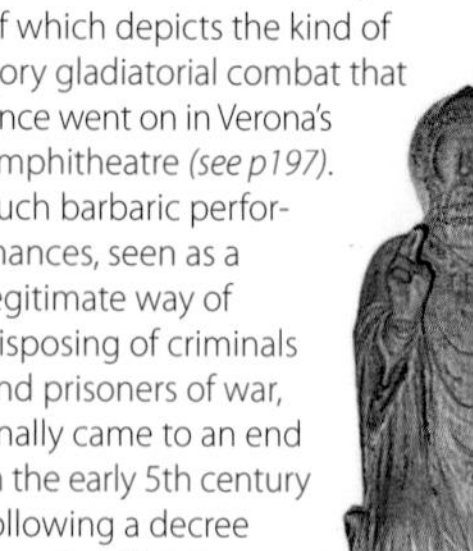

Augustus Caesar, Museo Archeologico

Museo Archeologico

Rigaste Redentore 2. **Tel** 045 800 03 60. **Open** 8:30am–7:30pm daily (from 1:30pm Mon; also open Mon am on public hols).

A lift carries visitors from the Teatro Romano up through the cliffs to the monastery above. This is now converted into an archaeological museum in which panoramic city views vie for attention with the range of exhibits.

The first part of the museum displays well-restored mosaics, one of which depicts the kind of gory gladiatorial combat that once went on in Verona's amphitheatre *(see p197)*. Such barbaric performances, seen as a legitimate way of disposing of criminals and prisoners of war, finally came to an end in the early 5th century following a decree from the Christian Emperor Honorius.

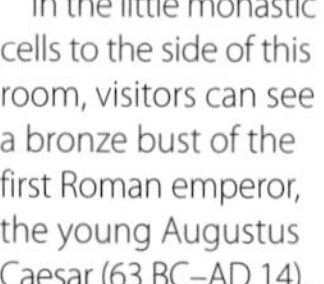

In the little monastic cells to the side of this room, visitors can see a bronze bust of the first Roman emperor, the young Augustus Caesar (63 BC–AD 14), who succeeded in overcoming his opponents, including Mark Antony and Cleopatra, to become the sole ruler of the Roman world in 31 BC. The subject of the female bust in the adjoining cell is unknown. Next comes the tiny cloister, littered with mosaics and ancient masonry fragments, and a warren of ancient rooms used to display pottery, glass, inscriptions and tombstones. Labelling stops after a while, leaving visitors to puzzle out the nature and age of exhibits for themselves.

Santo Stefano

Via Santo Stefano. **Tel** 045 834 85 29. **Open** during Mass and religious ceremonies.

This is one of the city's oldest churches; the original, long-demolished building was built in the 6th century. It served as Verona's cathedral until the 12th century when the Duomo was built *(see p201)* on the opposite bank of the Adige. Visitors are afforded a striking view of the Duomo across the river, taking in the Romanesque apse and the bishop's palace alongside. Santo Stefano itself was rebuilt at the same time by Lombard architects and given its octagonal red brick campanile, but the original apse survives.

Inside the church there is a Byzantine-influenced arrangement of a stone bishop's seat and bench, and a gallery with 8th-century carved capitals. The apse (often locked) is even older, dating back to the original 6th-century building. In the crypt there are fragments of 13th-century frescoes and a 14th-century statue of St Peter.

Figure of St Peter, Santo Stefano

Towering above the church to the east is Castel San Pietro, fronted by flame-shaped cypress trees. The present castle was built in 1854 under Austrian rule, but it stands on the ruins of an earlier castle which was built by the Visconti of Milan when they captured Verona in 1387.

San Giorgio in Braida

San Giorgio is a rare example in Verona of a domed Renaissance church. It was begun in 1477 by Michele Sanmicheli, an architect best known for his military works. Sanmicheli also designed the classically inspired altar, which is topped by Paolo Veronese's *Martyrdom of St George* (1566). This celebrated painting is outshone by the calm and serene *Virgin Enthroned between St Zeno and St Lawrence* (1526) by Girolamo dai Libri. This work has a beautifully detailed background landscape and a lemon tree growing behind the Virgin's throne.

Marquetry cockerel in Santa Maria in Organo

Santa Maria in Organo

Some of the finest inlaid woodwork to be seen in Italy is in this church. The artist was Fra Giovanni da Verona, an architect and craftsman who worked for nearly 25 years, from 1477 to 1501, on these stunning examples of illusionistic marquetry. The seat backs in the choir and cupboard fronts in the sacristy are full of entertaining detail. By clever interpretation of perspective, Fra Giovanni gave depth to flat landscapes, depicted city views glimpsed through an open window, and created "cupboard interiors" stacked with books, musical instruments or bowls of fruit. Most charming of all are the little animal pictures – look out for the rabbit on the lectern and the owl and the cockerel in the sacristy.

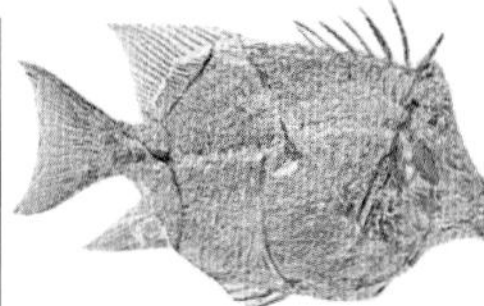

Fossilized fish from Verona's natural history museum

Museo Civico di Storia Naturale

Lungadige Porta Vittoria 9. **Tel** 045 807 94 00. **Open** 9am–5pm Mon–Thu, 2–6pm Sat, Sun & public hols. **Closed** 1 Jan, Easter, 1 May, 25 Dec.

Verona's natural history museum contains an outstanding collection of fossils, which can be enjoyed by experts and newcomers alike. Whole fish, trees, fern leaves and dragonflies are captured in extraordinary detail. The fossils were found in rock in the foothills of the Little Dolomites north of the city during quarrying for building stone (*see* Bolca, *p207*).

Human prehistory is represented by finds from ancient settlements around Lake Garda, and there are reconstructions of original lake villages. On the upper floor, cases full of stuffed birds, animals and fish provide an extensive account of today's living world, making this a good museum for visiting with children.

Giardino Giusti

Via Giardino Giusti 2. **Tel** 045 803 40 29. **Open** Apr–Sep: 9am–8pm; Oct–Mar: 9am–7pm. **Closed** 25 Dec.

Hidden among the dusty façades of the Via Giardino Giusti is the entrance to one of Italy's finest Renaissance gardens. They were laid out in 1580 and, as with other gardens of the period, artifice and nature are deliberately juxtaposed. The lower garden of clipped box hedges, gravel walks and potted plants is contrasted with an upper area of wilder woodland, the two parts linked by stone terracing.

Past visitors have included the English traveller Thomas Coryate, who, writing in 1611, called this garden "a second paradise". The diarist John Evelyn, visiting 50 years later, thought it the finest garden in Europe. Today the garden makes an excellent, picturesque spot for a quiet picnic.

Italianate topiary and statuary in the Giardino Giusti

The 14th-century Castello Romeo, on a hill overlooking Montecchio

❷ Grezzana

9,680. 1st Wed & 3rd Fri each month.

In Grezzana itself, seek out the 13th-century church of Santa Maria, which (though frequently rebuilt) retains its robustly carved Romanesque font and its beautiful campanile of gold, white and pink limestone.

Environs
Grezzana is in the foothills of the scenic Piccole Dolomiti or Little Dolomites. Close to the town, at nearby Cuzzano, is the 17th-century Baroque **Villa Allegri-Arvedi**, which is decorated with beautiful frescoes by Ludovico Dorigny. To the south, in Santa Maria in Stelle, is a Roman nymphaeum (a shrine to the nymphs who guard the freshwater spring) next to the church (known as the Pantheon).

Villa Allegri-Arvedi
Cuzzano di Grezzana.
Tel 045 90 70 45. **Open** for groups only (book by phone).
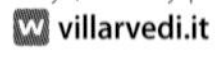
W **villarvedi.it**

❸ Soave

6,200. Foro Boario 1 (045 619 07 73). Tue am.

Soave is a heavily fortified town ringed by 14th-century walls, known all over Europe because of the light and dry white wine that is produced and exported from here in great quantity. Visitors will see few vineyards around the town, since they are mainly located in the hills to the north, but evidence of the industry can be seen in the gleaming factories on the outskirts, where the Garganega grapes are crushed and the fermented wine bottled. Cafés and wine cellars in the town centre provide plenty of opportunity for sampling the excellent local wine.

The city walls rise up the hill to the dramatically sited **Rocca Scaligera**, an ancient castle enlarged by the Scaligeri rulers of Verona in the 14th century. It has been furnished in period style.

Rocca Scaligera
Via Castello Scaligero. **Tel** 045 768 00 36. **Open** Mar–Sep: 9am–noon, 3–6:30pm daily; Oct–mid-Feb: 9am–noon, 2–4pm daily (Jan–mid-Feb: Sat & Sun only).

Rocca Scaligera, the ancient castle in Soave

❹ Montecchio Maggiore

20,000. Via Pietro Ceccato 88, Alta di Montecchio (0444 69 65 46). Fri am.

Visitors to industrialized Montecchio Maggiore come principally to see the two 14th-century castles on the hill above the town. Although these are known as the **Castello di Romeo** and the **Castello di Giulietta** (which includes a restaurant), there is no evidence that they belonged to Verona's rival Capulet and Montague families *(see p201)*, but they look romantic and provide lovely views over the vineyard-clad hills to the north.

Castello di Romeo
Via Castelli 4. **Open** Sat & Sun.

Castello di Giulietta
Via Castelli 4. **Tel** 0444 69 61 72. **Open** Wed–Sun.

The dramatic gorge of Montagna Spaccata, north of Valdagno

❺ Valdagno

28,000. Viale Trento 4–6 (0445 40 11 90). Tue & Fri am.

A scenic drive of 20 km (12 miles) from Montecchio Maggiore leads to Valdagno, a town of woollen mills and 18th-century houses. Just northwest is the Montagna Spaccata, its rocky bulk split by a dramatic 100-m- (330-ft-) deep gorge and waterfall.

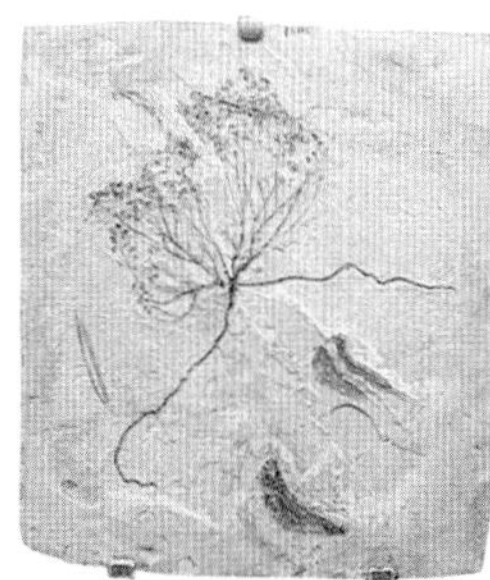

Fossilized plant remains found in the rocks near Bolca

6 Bolca

500. Via Villa Bolca (045 656 00 13). **Shops closed** Mon am (clothes), Wed pm (food).

Pretty Bolca sits at the centre of the Monti Lessini plateau, looking down the valley of the River Alpone and encircled by fossil-bearing hills. The most spectacular finds have been transferred to Verona's Museo Civico di Storia Naturale *(see p205)*, but the local **Museo di Fossili** still has an impressive collection of fish, plants and reptiles preserved in the local basalt stone. A circular walk of 3 km (2 miles) from the town (details available from the museum) takes in the quarries where the fossils were found.

Museo di Fossili
Via San Giovanni Battista. **Tel** 045 656 50 88. **Open** 9am–noon, 2–6:30pm daily (Mar–Oct: booking required).
museodeifossili.it

7 Giazza

150. **Shops closed** Wed pm (food).

The small town of Giazza has an almost Alpine appearance. Its **Museo dei Cimbri** covers the history of the Tredici Comuni (Thirteen Communes). In reality there are far more than 13 little hamlets dotted about the plateau, many of them settled by Bavarian farmers who migrated from the German side of the Alps in the 13th century. Cimbro, their German-influenced dialect, has now almost completely disappeared, but other traditions survive. For example, their huge mountain horns, *tromboni*, are still part of local festivities.

Museo dei Cimbri
Via dei Boschi, 62. **Tel** 045 784 70 50. **Open** 3–6pm Sat & Sun.
cimbri.it

8 Bosco Chiesanuova

3,000. Piazza della Chiesa 34 (045 705 00 88). Sat am.

One of the principal ski resorts of the region, Bosco Chiesanuova is well supplied with hotels, ski lifts and cross-country routes. To the east, near Camposilvano, is the picturesque **Valle delle Sfingi** (Valley of the Sphinxes), so called because of its landscape of large and impressive rock formations.

9 Sant'Anna d'Alfaedo

2,500. in Bosco Chiesanuova. Wed am.

Distinctively Alpine in character, Sant'Anna d'Alfaedo is noted for the stone tiles used to roof local houses. The hamlet of Fosse, immediately to the north, is a popular base for walking excursions up the **Corno d'Aquilio** (1,546 m/5,070 ft), a mountain which boasts one of the world's deepest potholes, the **Spluga della Preta**, 850 m (2,790 ft) deep.

More accessible is another natural wonder, the **Ponte di Veia**, just south of Sant'Anna, a great stone arch bridging the valley. Prehistoric finds have been excavated from the caves at either end. This spectacular natural bridge is one of the largest of its kind in the world.

The town of Giazza, spectacularly situated on the Monti Lessini plateau

Around Lake Garda

Garda, the largest and easternmost of the Italian lakes, is a favourite summer playground for sports lovers. Strong winds make ideal conditions for windsurfing and sailing, there are numerous yacht harbours and artificial beaches, and luxury hotels offer tennis and horse-riding facilities. The less energetic can explore the lake and shore by steamer, while the magnificent scenery of snow-capped peaks and spectacular sunsets will appeal to every visitor.

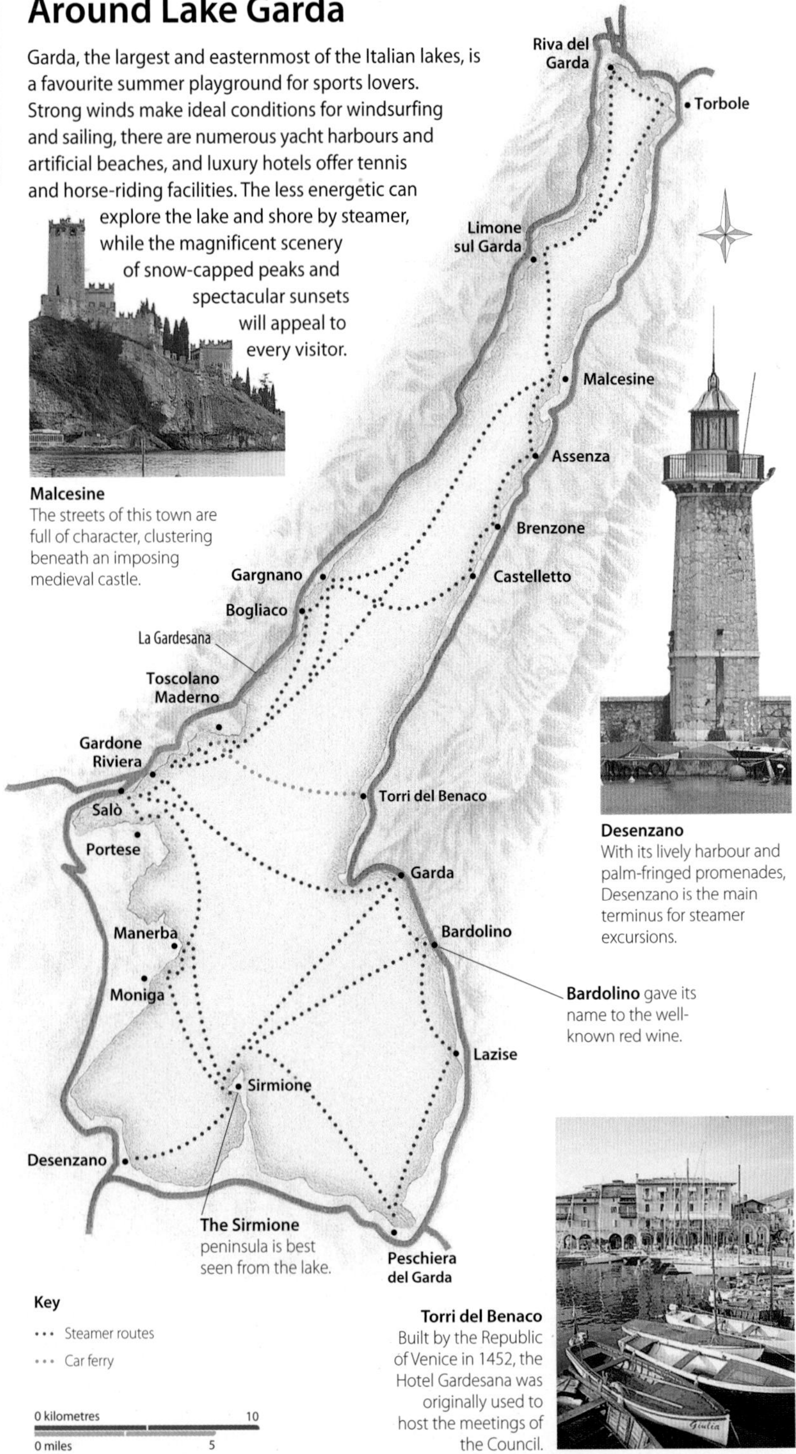

Malcesine
The streets of this town are full of character, clustering beneath an imposing medieval castle.

Desenzano
With its lively harbour and palm-fringed promenades, Desenzano is the main terminus for steamer excursions.

Bardolino gave its name to the well-known red wine.

The Sirmione peninsula is best seen from the lake.

Torri del Benaco
Built by the Republic of Venice in 1452, the Hotel Gardesana was originally used to host the meetings of the Council.

◀ Malcesine on the shore of Lake Garda, surrounded by dramatic cliffs

La Gardesana

This is the name given to the 143-km (89-mile) perimeter road that hugs the lakeshore. For much of its route the road is cut through solid rock, sometimes following a narrow ledge in the cliff face, sometimes passing through tunnels (around 80 in total). The switchback route offers spectacular views at every turn, particularly at Gargnano, and there are numerous viewing points. Places of interest along La Gardesana include the splendid 18th-century gardens of Palazzo Bettoni at Bogliaco and the castle at Riva del Garda.

The scenic road to Limone

Lake Trips

Lake Garda's ferries are still called steamers, even though they are diesel-powered today. The major towns around the southern rim of the lake all have jetties where visitors can buy a ticket and board the boat for a leisurely cruise. Gardens and villas that are otherwise hidden from view can be seen from the water. A trip from one end of the lake to the other takes approximately 2 hours 20 minutes by hydrofoil, and 4 hours by steamer. Catamarans also operate around the southern end of the lake.

The hydrofoil operating out of Desenzano harbour

Lake Garda steamer at dusk near Peschiera

⑩ Garda

3,400. Piazzetta Donatori di Sangue 1 (045 627 03 84). Fri am. **Shops closed** Wed pm (food). **turismoverona.eu**

Numerous pavement cafés brighten the streets around the central Palazzo dei Capitani, built in the 15th century for the use of the Venetian militia. Prehistoric rock engravings feature along the Strada dei Castei, an old route above the town.

⑪ Peschiera

8,900. FS Piazzale Bettelone 15. (045 755 16 73). Mon am. **Shops closed** Wed in winter. **turismoverona.eu**

At Peschiera the Mincio river flows out of Lake Garda to join the Po river. The main site of interest is a fortress built in the 19th century. Named Fortezza del Quadrilatero because of its square shape, it replaced a 15th-century stronghold.

Environs

Just outside town are **Parco Natura Viva**, a zoo with a safari park and model dinosaurs, and **Gardaland® Resort**, a theme park with a superb SEA LIFE aquarium (free bus from Peschiera station) .

Parco Natura Viva

Nr. Bussolengo. **Tel** 045 717 01 13. **Open** mid-Mar–Nov: 9am–5:30pm Mon–Sat (to 6pm Sun). **Closed** Wed in Nov. **parconaturaviva.it**

Gardaland® Resort

Loc. Ronchi, 37014 Castelnuovo del Garda. **Tel** 045 644 97 77. **Open** end Mar–Sep: daily; Oct & Christmas period: Sat & Sun. **gardaland.it**

⑫ Solferino

2,118. Sat pm. Shops closed Mon pm.

The allied armies of France and Sardinia under Napoleon III met the Austrian army at the small village of Solferino in 1859, as part of what was the wider battle for the unification of the Italian peninsula. The Battle of Solferino left more than 6,000 dead and 40,000 wounded, abandoned without medical care or burial. Shocked by such neglect, a Swiss man named Henri Dunant began a campaign for better treatment. The result was the first Geneva Convention, signed in 1863, and the establishment of the International Red Cross. In the town of Solferino there is a war museum and an ossuary chapel, lined with bones from the battlefield. There is also a memorial to Dunant built by the Red Cross with donations from member nations.

The ossuary chapel at Solferino, lined with skulls

⓭ Sirmione Peninsula

Charming Sirmione is a finger of land extending into the southern end of Lake Garda, connected to the mainland by a bridge. The Roman poet Catullus (born in 84 BC) owned a villa here: the ruins of the Grotte di Catullo lie among ancient olive trees at the northern tip. The Rocca Scaligera castle stands guard at the base of the peninsula, and beyond, the narrow stone-paved streets of the village give way to peaceful lakeside walks and elegant spa hotels.

View Towards the Grotto
The high central tower commands views over the castle and the whole of the Sirmione peninsula.

★ Rocca Scaligera
The castle was built in the 13th century by the Scaligeri of Verona. It is cleverly designed to trap shipborne invaders, leaving them vulnerable to missiles dropped from the castle walls.

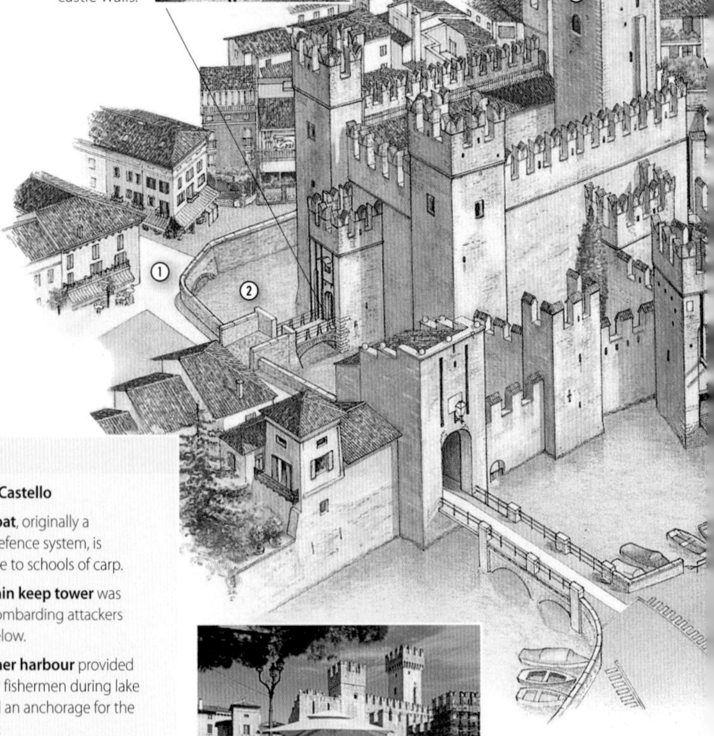

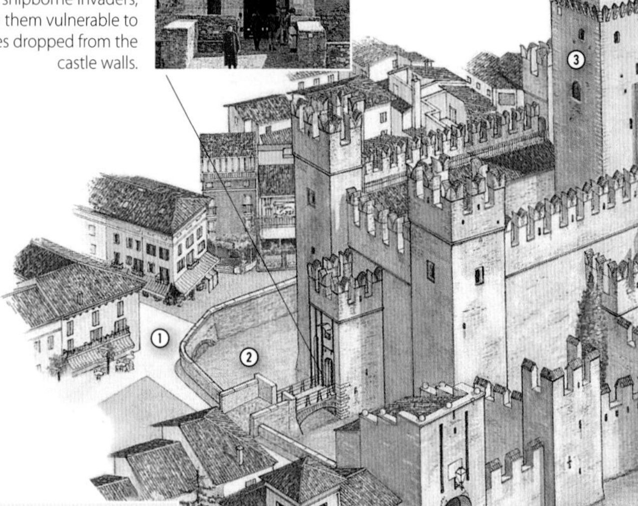

KEY

① **Piazza Castello**

② **The moat**, originally a complex defence system, is today home to schools of carp.

③ **The main keep tower** was used for bombarding attackers trapped below.

④ **The inner harbour** provided a haven for fishermen during lake storms and an anchorage for the castle fleet.

⑤ **The drawbridge** is heavily fortified, linking the castle to the mainland and offering an escape route to the castle's inhabitants.

Visiting the Peninsula
Cars must be parked before entering Sirmione, leaving the medieval streets for pedestrians.

Lakeside Walk
Following the eastern shores of the peninsula, this pretty walk links the village to the Grotte di Catullo.

VISITORS' CHECKLIST

Practical Information
Viale Marconi 8 (030 91 61 14).
sirmionebs.it
Rocca Scaligera: **Tel** 030 91 64 68. **Open** 8:30am–7:30pm Tue–Sat, 8:30am–1pm Sun. **Closed** 1 Jan, 1 May, 25 Dec. Grotte di Catullo: **Tel** 030 91 61 57. **Open** 8:30am–7:30pm Tue–Sat (Nov–Feb: to 5:30pm), 9:30am– 6:30pm Sun & pub hols (Nov–Feb: 8:30am–2pm). **Closed** 1 Jan, 1 May, 25 Dec.

Transport

San Pietro
Founded in AD 765, on Sirmione's highest point, this church contains a 12th-century fresco of Christ in Majesty.

★ Grotte di Catullo
This complex of villas, baths and shops, built as a resort for wealthy Romans from the 1st century BC, lies ruined here. Finds are displayed in the Antiquarium building.

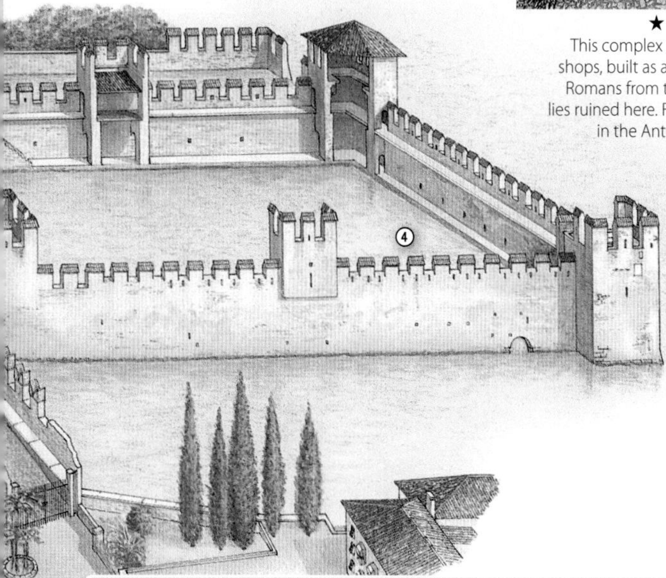

The Scaligeri

The Rocca Scaligera is one of many castles built throughout the Verona and Lake Garda region by the Scaligeri family *(see p194)*. During the turbulent 13th and 14th centuries, powerful military rulers fought each other incessantly in pursuit of riches and power. Despite the autocratic nature of their rule, the Scaligeri brought a period of peace and prosperity to the region, fending off attacks by the predatory Visconti family who ruled neighbouring Lombardy.

The Scaligeri ruler, Cangrande I

⓮ Salò

10,000. Sat am.

Locals prefer to associate this elegant town with Gaspare da Salò (1540–1609), the inventor of the violin, rather than with Mussolini, the World War II dictator. Mussolini set up the so-called Salò Republic in 1943 and ruled northern Italy from here until 1945, when he was shot by the Italian resistance.

Happier memories are evoked by Salò's buildings, including the cathedral with its unusual wooden altarpiece (1510) by Paolo Veneziano. The main appeal of the town derives from its pastel-coloured waterfront buildings, picturesque squares and alleyways, and a long pedestrian promenade with beautiful views of the lake. Salò marks the beginning of the Riviera Bresciana, where the shore is lined with lovely villas and grand hotels set in semi-tropical gardens.

⓯ Gardone Riviera

2,500. Via Repubblica 8. (0365 203 47).

Gardone's most appealing feature is the terraced public park that cascades down the hillside, planted with noble and exotic trees. Equally exotic are the Mediterranean and African plants in the **Hruska Botanical Gardens**, founded in 1910, which benefit from the town's mild winters. Gardone has long been a popular resort – the magnificent 19th-century **Villa Alba** (now a congress centre) was built for the Austrian emperor to escape the bitter winters of his own country. The Art Deco **Grand Hotel** on the waterfront was built for lesser beings.

The Art Deco Grand Hotel in Gardone Riviera

High above the town is the **Villa il Vittoriale**, built for the poet Gabriele d'Annunzio. His Art Deco villa has blacked-out windows (he professed to loathe the world) and is full of curiosities, including a coffin-shaped bed. The garden has a landlocked warship, the prow raised high over Lake Garda.

Hruska Botanical Gardens
Via Roma. **Tel** 0336 41 08 77.
Open Mar–Oct: 9am-7pm daily.
hellergarden.com

Villa il Vittoriale
Via Vittoriale 12. **Tel** 0365 29 65 11.
Open Apr–Sep: 8:30am–8pm daily; Oct–Mar: 9am–5pm daily; ticket office closes 1 hour earlier. **Closed** 1 Jan, 24 & 25 Dec. **vittoriale.it**

Valpolicella Wine Tour

This circular tour takes in the beautiful, remarkably varied scenery of the wine district that lies between Verona and Lake Garda. On the shores of Lake Garda itself, deep and fertile glacial soils provide sustenance for the grapes that are used to make Bardolino, a wine that is meant to be drunk young *(see p240)*. Inland, the rolling foothills of the Lessini mountains shelter hamlets where lives and working rhythms are tuned to the needs of the vines. These particular vines are grown to produce the equally famed Valpolicella, a red wine that varies from light and fruity to full-bodied.

④ Affi
This wine-producing village is surrounded by vineyards planted in the sheltered basin of the Adige Valley.

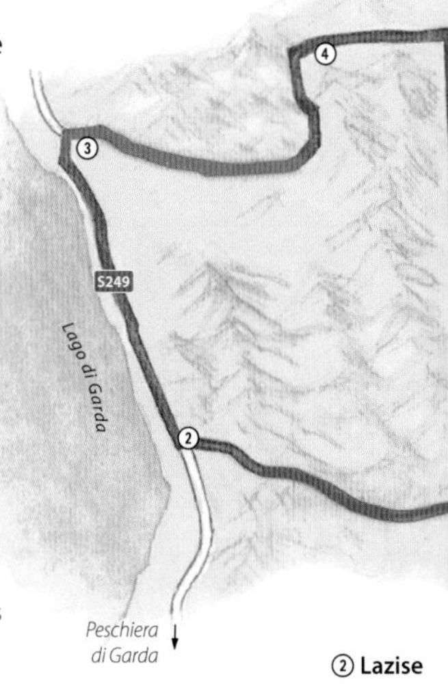

③ Bardolino
Famous for its light red wine, Bardolino hosts a grape festival in September and has numerous cellars offering tastings.

② Lazise
Lazise has long been the chief port of Garda's eastern shore, its picturesque harbour and medieval church guarded by a 14th-century castle.

Tips for Drivers

Starting point: Verona.
Length: 45 km (28 miles).
Approximate driving time: 3 hours.
Stopping-off points: The main village of the Valpolicella region, San Pietro in Cariano, has cafés and restaurants.

Key

Tour route
Other roads

Looking across Lake Garda from Riva del Garda

⑯ Riva del Garda

16,000. Largo Medaglie d'Oro (0464 55 44 44). 2nd Wed (& 4th Wed in summer). Shops: **closed** Mon (non-food) in winter. **gardatrentino.it**

Riva's waterfront is overlooked by the moated **Rocca di Riva**, a former Scaligeri fortress. Inside is a museum with exhibits from the region's prehistoric lake villages, built by driving huge piles into the lake bed to support platforms. The lake is popular with windsurfers.

Rocca di Riva
Piazza Cesare Battisti 3/a. **Tel** 0464 57 38 69. **Open** mid-Mar–Oct: Tue–Sun (daily in Jul–Sep). **museoaltogarda.it**

⑰ Malcesine

3,500. Sat.

German visitors who come to Malcesine trace the journey taken by the poet Goethe in 1788. His travels were full of mishaps, and at Malcesine he was accused of spying and was locked up.

From Malcesine, visitors can take the rotating **cable car** up to the broad ridge of Monte Baldo (1,745 m/ 5,725 ft). The journey takes 15 minutes, and on a clear day it is possible to see the distant peaks of the Dolomites, including the Brenta range. Footpaths for walkers are signposted at the top. The lower slopes are designated nature reserves; a good place to see the local flora is the **Riserva Naturale Gardesana Orientale**, just to the north of Malcesine, on the western side of Monte Baldo.

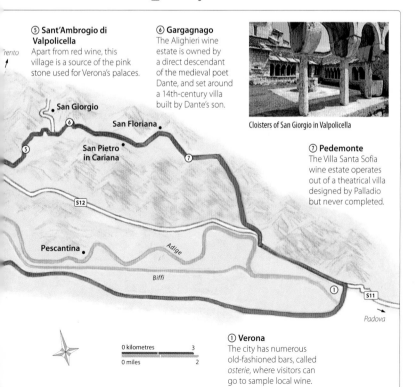

⑤ Sant'Ambrogio di Valpolicella
Apart from red wine, this village is a source of the pink stone used for Verona's palaces.

⑥ Gargagnago
The Alighieri wine estate is owned by a direct descendant of the medieval poet Dante, and set around a 14th-century villa built by Dante's son.

Cloisters of San Giorgio in Valpolicella

⑦ Pedemonte
The Villa Santa Sofia wine estate operates out of a theatrical villa designed by Palladio but never completed.

Trento
San Giorgio
San Floriana
San Pietro in Cariana
S12
Pescantina
Adige
Biffi
S11
Padova

0 kilometres 3
0 miles 2

① Verona
The city has numerous old-fashioned bars, called *osterie*, where visitors can go to sample local wine.

THE DOLOMITES

The name of the Dolomites conjures up a vision of spectacular mountains, as noble and awe-inspiring as the Alps. To the south of the region lie the cities of Feltre, Belluno and Vittorio Veneto. To the north is the renowned ski resort of Cortina d'Ampezzo. In between, travellers will encounter no more cities – just ravishing panoramas unfolding endlessly before them, and pretty hamlets tucked into remarkably lush and sunny south-facing valleys.

The Dolomites cover a substantial portion of the Veneto's landmass, and it is easy to forget, when visiting the cities of the flat Veneto Plain, that behind them lies this range of mountains rising to heights of 2,000 m (6,500 ft) and more. Catering for an urban population hungry for fresh air and freedom, the towns and villages of the Dolomites have striven to balance the needs of tourism and nature.

Italian is the region's principal language, but in the northwest a German influence can sometimes be heard, reflecting the region's strong historic links with the Austrian Tyrol. Once ruled by the Habsburgs, certain areas of the region only became part of Italy in 1918, after the breakup of the Austro-Hungarian empire at the end of World War I. Some of that war's fiercest fighting took place in the Dolomites, as both sides tried to wrest control of the strategic valley passes linking Italy and Austria-Hungary. Striking war memorials in many villages and towns provide a sad reminder of that time.

Today the region is renowned for its winter sports facilities. International cross-country ski competitions were held in Cortina d'Ampezzo as early as 1902, and in 1956 the town hosted the Winter Olympics. Today, Cortina is considered to be Italy's most exclusive resort, the winter playground of film stars and royalty.

Outdoor café in the old town of Feltre

◀ Dito di Dio (God's Finger) mountain reflected in Lake Sorapiss at sunrise

Exploring the Dolomites

The environment of the Dolomites is completely different from the industrialized Veneto Plain. Huge areas are designated nature reserves, while others, accessible by chair lifts, allow visitors to enjoy the views and appetite-sharpening treks in the mountain meadows. Refuges, dotted along the high trails, offer dormitory accommodation and refreshments, while hamlets have comfortable hotels. Snow covers the peaks from October to May, and it is possible to ski all year round on Marmolada; at 3,343 m (10,970 ft), the highest peak in the Dolomites.

Mountain chalet near the stadium at Cortina d'Ampezzo

Sights at a Glance

1. Cortina d'Ampezzo
2. Misurina
3. Pieve di Cadore
4. *The Dolomites (Dolomiti) pp222–3*
5. Belluno
6. Valzoldana
7. Feltre
8. Vittorio Veneto

Key

- Major road
- Minor road
- Motorway
- Main railway
- Minor railway
- Scenic route
- Regional border
- International border
- △ Summit

For additional map symbols *see back flap*

CORTINA D'AMPEZZO 1
S51
S48
Falzarego
Cinque Torri 2366m
Bolzano
S48
Arabba
Pieve di Livinallongo
THE DOLOMITES
Selva di Cadore
4
VALZOLDANA
S251
Marmolada 3343m
S641
Rocco Piétore
S203
Alleghe
Zoldo Alto
Monte Civetta 3220m
6
S346
Falcade
Celàt
Cencenighe Agordino
Dont
S203
Listolde
Cordevole
S347
Monte S. Lucano 2409m
Monte Agner 2872m
Agordo
VENETO
Gosaldo
Parco Nazionale delle Dolomiti Bellunesi
S203
Vignole
Gron
Sédico
Bolzano
Monte Pavione 2334m
S. Giustina
Trichiana
Áune
Piave
Lamòn
Pedavena
Busche
Mel
S50
7 FELTRE
Cismon
Fonzaso
S50
S348
Giaroni
Brenta
Primolano
Carpèn
Casere
Cismon
Stizzon
S141
S47
Bassano del Grappa
Duero
Treviso

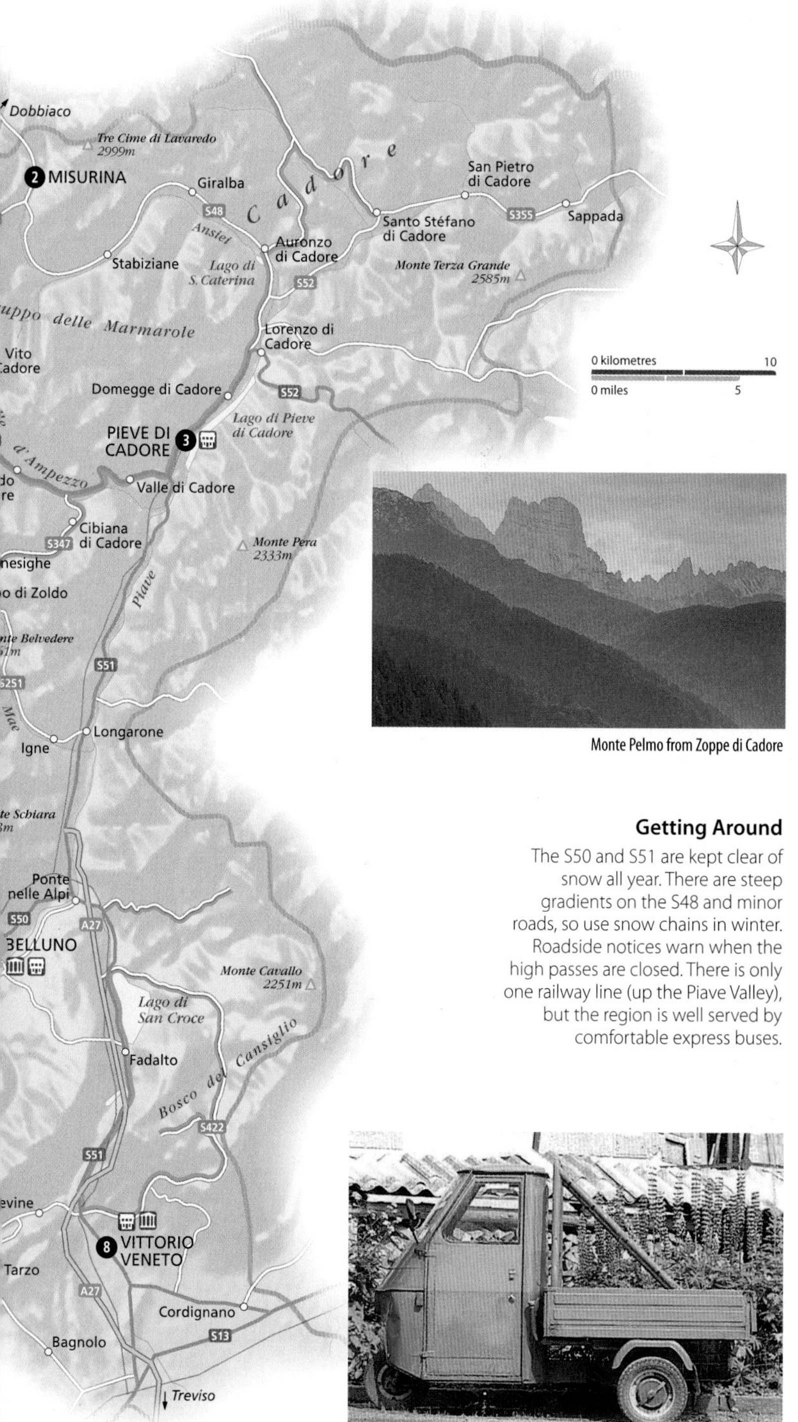

Monte Pelmo from Zoppe di Cadore

Getting Around

The S50 and S51 are kept clear of snow all year. There are steep gradients on the S48 and minor roads, so use snow chains in winter. Roadside notices warn when the high passes are closed. There is only one railway line (up the Piave Valley), but the region is well served by comfortable express buses.

Piaggio Vespa truck, a common sight in the Dolomites

❶ Cortina d'Ampezzo

6,800. Corso Italia 81 (0436 86 90 86). Tue & Fri am.
infodolomiti.it

Italy's top ski resort, much favoured by the smart set from Turin and Milan, is well supplied with restaurants and bars. The reason for its popularity is the dramatic scenery, which adds an extra dimension to the pleasure of speeding down the slopes. Guests are surrounded by crags and spires, which rise skyward, thrusting their weather-sculpted shapes above the trees.

Skiers at Cortina

Strolling along the Corso Italia in Cortina d'Ampezzo

As a consequence of hosting the 1956 Winter Olympics, Cortina has better-than-normal sports facilities. There is a ski jump and a bobsleigh run, the Olympic ice stadium holds skating discotheques, and there are several swimming pools as well as tennis courts and riding facilities.

During the summer months, Cortina becomes an excellent base for walkers. Information on the many trails and guided walks is available from the tourist office or, during the summer, from the Guides' office opposite.

Visitors can also take the cable car *Freccia nel Cielo* (Arrow in the Sky), which goes to a height of 3,243 m (10,639 ft) above sea level.

The Dolomite Road

The Strada delle Dolomiti, or Dolomite Road, is one of the most beautiful routes anywhere in the Alps and is a magnificent feat of highway construction. It starts in the Trentino-Alto Adige region at Bolzano and enters the Veneto region at Passo Pordoi, at 2,239 m (7,346 ft) the most scenic of all the Dolomite passes. From here the route follows the winding S48 for another 35 km (22 miles) east to the resort of Cortina d'Ampezzo.

There are plenty of stopping places along the route where it is possible to stop and enjoy the spectacular views. In many of the ski resorts, cable cars will carry visitors up to Alpine refuges (some with cafés attached) that are open from mid-June to mid-September. These refuges mark the start of a series of signposted walks.

Tips for Drivers

Starting point: Passo Pordoi.
Length (within the Veneto): 35 km (22 miles).
Approximate driving time: Two hours, but allow a full day to include the return journey and time to stop and enjoy the stunning scenery.
Stopping-off points: The small towns of Pieve di Livinallongo and Andraz have good cafés and restaurants.

S48
Bolzano

Key

Tour route

Other roads

① Passo Pordoi
To the north of Passo Pordoi, the Gruppo di Sella rises to 3,152 m (10,340 ft).

② Arabba
Arabba is a pleasant resort with a cable car to Porta Vescovo (2,478 m/ 8,129 ft) to the south.

❷ Misurina

82. Via Misurina (0435 390 16). **Open** Jul–Aug; late Dec–early Jan. **infodolomiti.it**

Smaller and quieter than Cortina, Misurina nestles by the exquisite Lake Misurina. The lake's mirror-like surface reflects the peaks of Monte Sorapiss and the Cadini group.

One of the creeks flowing into Lake Misurina

Take the toll road that climbs northeast for 8 km (5 miles) to the Auronzo mountain refuge and to the base of the Tre Cime di Lavaredo peaks (2,999 m/9,840 ft).

Titian's house at Pieve di Cadore

❸ Pieve di Cadore

4,000. Piazza Tiziano 3 (0435 325 56). Wed am (at Tai). **infodolomiti.it**

For centuries the Cadore forests supplied Venice with its timber. The main town of this vast mountainous region is Pieve di Cadore, primarily known as the birthplace of Titian. The humble **Casa di Tiziano** can be visited, and the nearby **Museo Archeologico** has exhibits of finds from the pre-Roman era.

Principally, though, this is a base for touring the scenic delights of the region. North of Pieve the valley narrows to a dramatic ravine, and the road north to Comelica and Sesto is noted for its Alpine scenery and its traditional balconied houses. Continuing northeast, the Piave river can be followed to its source, 8 km (5 miles) north of Sappada.

Casa di Tiziano
Via Arsenale 4. **Tel** 0435 322 62. **Open** 10am–noon, 4–6:30pm daily.

Museo Archeologico Romano e Preromano
Palazzo della Magnifica Comunità Cadorina, Piazza Tiziano 2. **Tel** 0435 322 62. **Open** Jun–Sep: Tue–Sun (Aug: daily); Oct–May: by appt.

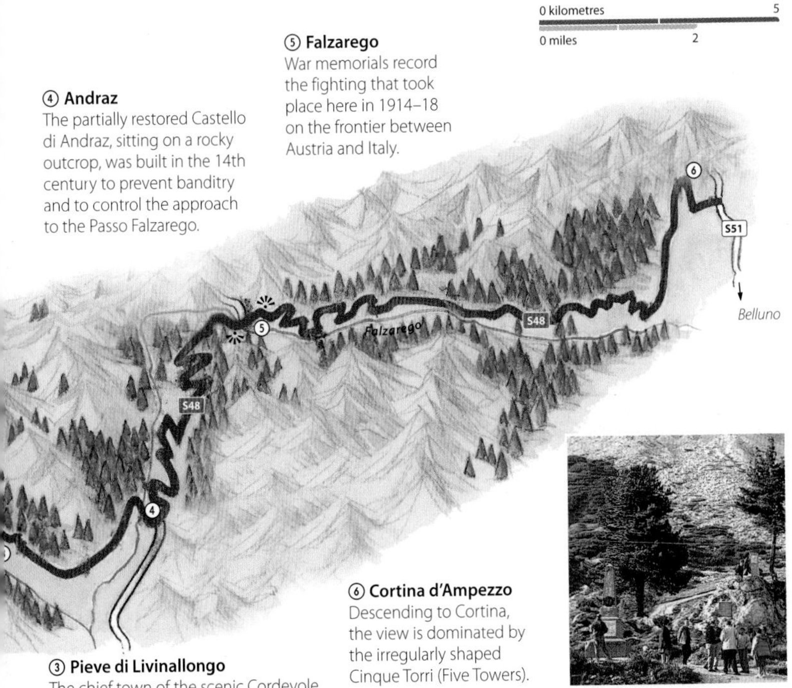

0 kilometres 5
0 miles 2

⑤ **Falzarego**
War memorials record the fighting that took place here in 1914–18 on the frontier between Austria and Italy.

④ **Andraz**
The partially restored Castello di Andraz, sitting on a rocky outcrop, was built in the 14th century to prevent banditry and to control the approach to the Passo Falzarego.

S51
Belluno
S48
Falzarego
S48

⑥ **Cortina d'Ampezzo**
Descending to Cortina, the view is dominated by the irregularly shaped Cinque Torri (Five Towers).

Visitors at Passo Falzarego, by the war memorials

③ **Pieve di Livinallongo**
The chief town of the scenic Cordevole Valley, Pieve offers spectacular views of dolomitic peaks and cliffs.

❹ The Dolomites

The Dolomites are the most distinctive and beautiful mountains in Italy. They were formed of mineralized coral which was laid down beneath the sea during the Triassic era, and uplifted when the European and African continental plates dramatically collided 60 million years ago. Unlike the glacier-eroded saddles and ridges of the main body of the Alps, the pale rocks here have been carved by the corrosive effects of ice, sun and rain, sculpting the cliffs, spires and "organ pipes" that we see today. The eastern and western ranges of the Dolomites have slightly different characteristics. The eastern section is the more awe-inspiring, especially the Catinaccio (or Rosengarten) range, which is particularly beautiful, turning rose pink at sunset.

Onion dome, a common local feature

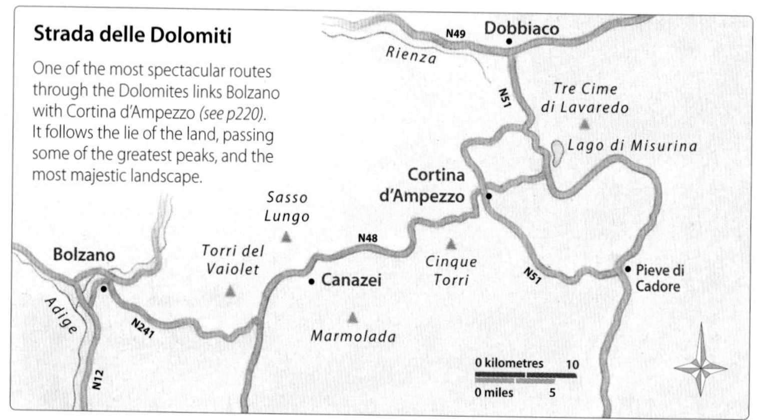

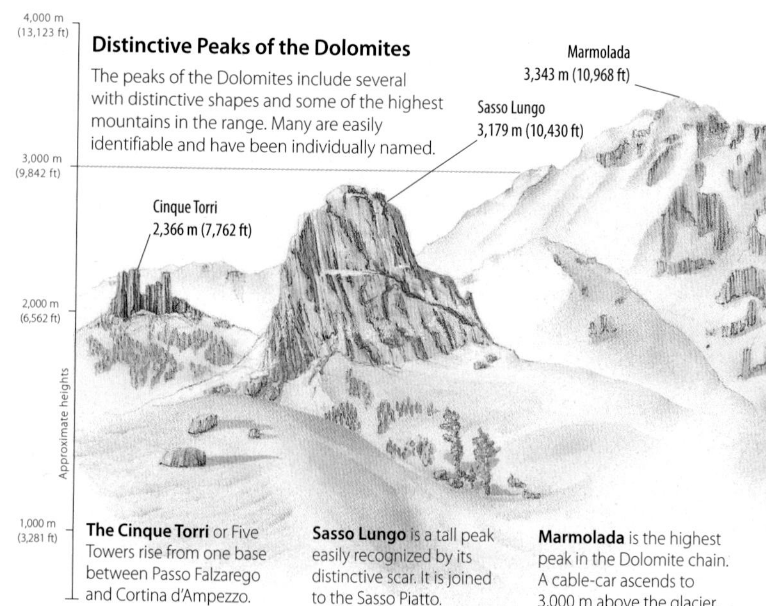

Distinctive Peaks of the Dolomites

The peaks of the Dolomites include several with distinctive shapes and some of the highest mountains in the range. Many are easily identifiable and have been individually named.

The Cinque Torri or Five Towers rise from one base between Passo Falzarego and Cortina d'Ampezzo.

Sasso Lungo is a tall peak easily recognized by its distinctive scar. It is joined to the Sasso Piatto.

Marmolada is the highest peak in the Dolomite chain. A cable-car ascends to 3,000 m above the glacier.

Lago di Misurina is a large and beautiful lake lying beside the resort of Misurina. The crystal-clear waters reflect the surrounding mountains, mirroring various peaks such as the distinctive and dramatic Sorapiss, in shimmering colours.

Outdoor activities in this area of dramatic landscapes include skiing in winter, and walking and rambling along the footpaths, and to picnic sites, in summer. Chairlifts from the main resorts provide easy access up into the mountains themselves, transporting you into some breathtaking scenery.

Torri del Vaiolet
2,243 m (7,375 ft)

Tre Cime di Lavaredo
2,999 m (9,839 ft)

The Torri del Vaiolet is part of the beautiful Catinaccio range, known for its colour.

Tre Cime di Lavaredo or Drei Zinnen dominate the valleys north of the Lago di Misurina.

Nature in the Dolomites

Forests and meadows support a breathtaking richness of wildlife in the region. Alpine plants, which flower between June and September, have evolved their miniature form to survive the harsh winds.

The Flora

Gentian roots are used to make a bitter local liqueur.

The orange mountain lily thrives on sun-baked slopes.

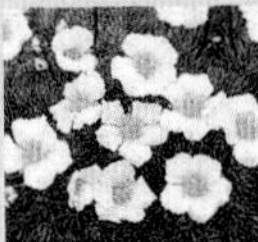

The pretty burser's saxifrage grows in clusters on rocks.

Devil's claw has distinctive pink flower heads.

The Fauna

The ptarmigan changes its plumage from mottled brown in summer to snow white in winter for effective camouflage. It feeds on mountain berries and young plant shoots.

The chamois, a shy mountain antelope prized for its soft skin, is protected in the national parks, where hunting is forbidden.

Roe deer are very common, as their natural predators – wolves and lynx – have now died out. Their keen appetite for tree saplings causes problems for foresters.

❺ Belluno

35,800. FS Sat am.
Shops closed Mon am (clothes) & Wed pm (food). **infodolomiti.it**

Picturesque Belluno, capital of Belluno province, serves as a bridge between the two very different parts of the Veneto, with the flat plains to the south and the Dolomite peaks to the north. Both are encapsulated in the picture-postcard views to be seen from the 12th-century **Porta Rugo** at the southern end of Via Mezzaterra, the main street of the old town. Even more spectacular are the views from the campanile of the 16th-century **Duomo**, which was designed by Tullio Lombardo, but rebuilt twice after damage by earthquakes.

The nearby baptistry contains a font cover with the figure of John the Baptist carved by Andrea Brustolon (1662–1732), whose elaborate furnishings decorate Ca' Rezzonico in Venice *(see p130)*. Brustolon's works also grace the churches of **San Pietro** (two altarpieces) and **Santo Stefano** (crucifix and angels). Close by is the 12th-century **Torre Civica**, all that survives of the Bishop's Palace, and the city's most elegant building, the Renaissance **Palazzo dei Rettori** (1491), once home to Belluno's Venetian rulers.

Façade and entrance to Palazzo dei Rettori in Belluno

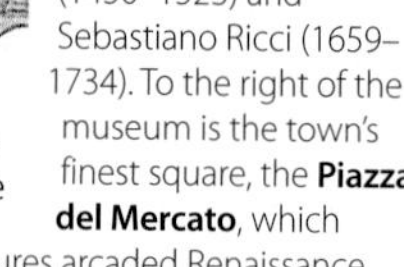

Exterior fresco, Zoppe di Cadore

The **Museo Civico** is worth visiting for the archaeological exhibits, and the paintings by Bartolomeo Montagna (1450–1523) and Sebastiano Ricci (1659–1734). To the right of the museum is the town's finest square, the **Piazza del Mercato**, which features arcaded Renaissance palaces and a fountain built in 1410.

South of the town are the ski resorts of the Alpe del Nevegal. It is worth taking the chair lift in the summer to the Rifugio Brigata Alpina Cadore (1,600 m/5,250 ft), which has superb views and a botanical garden specializing in Alpine plants.

Museo Civico
Piazza Duomo 16. **Tel** 0437 94 48 36.
Open May–Sep: Tue–Sun; Oct–Apr: daily.
museo.comune.belluno.it

❻ Valzoldana

from Longarone. Viale Dolomiti 4, Loc Mareson (0437 78 91 45).

The wooded Zoldo Valley is a popular destination for walking holidays. Its main resort town is Forno di Zoldo and the surrounding villages are noted for their Tyrolean-style Alpine chalets and haylofts. Examples built in wood on

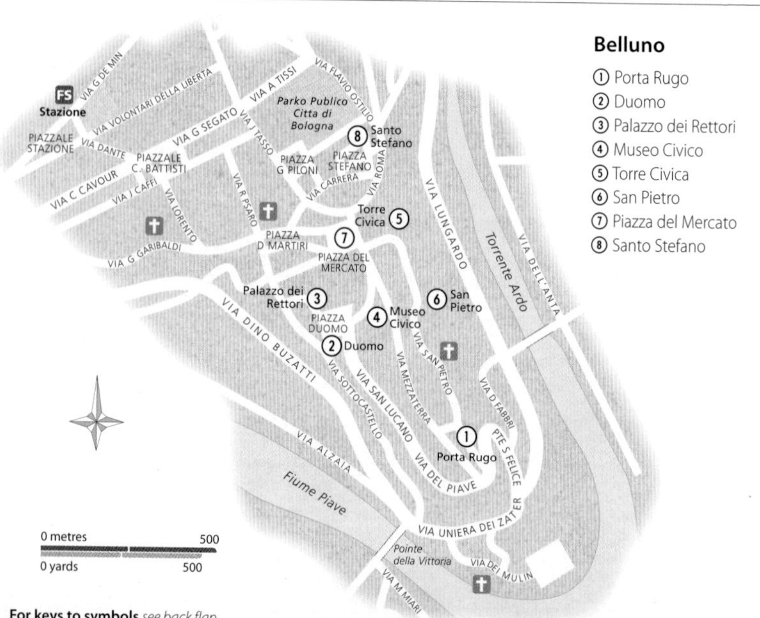

stone foundations can be seen at Fornesighe, 2 km (1 mile) northeast of Forno di Zoldo, and on the slopes of Monte Penna at Zoppe di Cadore, 8 km (5 miles) north.

If there is time, a circular tour is a good way to explore the area. Drive north on the S251, via Zoldo Alto to Selva di Cadore, then west via Colle di Santa Lucia (a favourite viewpoint for photographers). From here take the S203 south through the lakeside resort of Alleghe. The route passes through wonderful scenery with woodland, flower-filled meadows and pretty mountain hamlets which complement the splendour of the rocky crags.

The southernmost town of the area is Agordo, nestling in the Cordevole Valley. From here, a spectacularly scenic route follows the S347 northeast to the Passo Duran (1,605 m/5,270 ft), descending to Dont, close to the starting point of the tour. Wayside shrines mark the route and it is worth stopping on the way down to visit village shops selling local woodcarving. Take care when driving along this narrow and winding road.

Selva di Cadore from Colle di Santa Lucia, northwest of Valzoldana

Palazzo Guarnieri, one of the Renaissance palaces in Feltre

❼ Feltre

19,600. FS Tue & Fri am. **Shops closed** Mon am (clothes), Wed pm (food). **infodolomiti.it**

Feltre owes its venerable good looks to the vengeful Holy Roman Emperor Maximilian I. He sacked the town twice, in 1509 and in 1510, at the outbreak of the war against Venice waged by the League of Cambrai *(see p48)*. Despite the destruction of its buildings and the murder of most of its citizens, Feltre remained stoutly loyal to Venice, and Venice repaid the debt by rebuilding the town after the war. Thus the main street of the old town, Via Mezzaterra, is lined with arcaded early 16th-century houses, most with steeply pitched roofs to keep snow from settling.

Follow the steep main street to the striking Piazza Maggiore, where it is possible to see the remains of Feltre's medieval castle, the church of **San Rocco** and a fountain by Tullio Lombardo (1520).

On the eastern side of the square is Via L Luzzo, a beautiful street lined with Renaissance palaces, one of which houses the **Museo Civico**. The museum displays a fresco by the local artist Lorenzo Luzzo, who was known as Il Morto da Feltre (The Dead Man of Feltre), a nickname given to him by his contemporaries because of the deathly pallor of his skin.

Museo Civico
Palazzo Villabruna, Via Luzzo 23. **Tel** 0439 88 52 41. **Open** Thu–Sun. **Closed** pub hols.
comune.feltre.bl.it

❽ Vittorio Veneto

30,000. FS Viale della Vittoria 110 (0438 572 43). **Shops closed** Tue (clothes), Wed pm (food). Mon. **visittreviso.it**

Two separate towns, Ceneda and Serravalle, were merged and renamed Vittorio Veneto in 1866 to honour the unification of Italy under King Vittorio Emanuele II. The town later gave its name to the last decisive battle fought in Italy in World War I. The **Museo della Battaglia** in the Ceneda quarter commemorates this. Serravalle is more picturesque, with many fine 15th-century *palazzi* and pretty arcaded streets. Franco Zeffirelli shot scenes for his film *Romeo and Juliet* in this town that sits at the base of the rocky Meschio gorge. To the east, via Anzano, the S422 climbs up to the Bosco del Cansiglio, a wooded plateau.

Museo della Battaglia
Piazza Giovanni Paolo I. **Tel** 0438 576 95. **Open** 9:30am–12:30pm Tue–Fri, 10am–1pm, 3–6pm Sat & Sun.
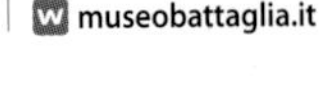
book in advance.
museobattaglia.it

Vittorio Veneto old town and river

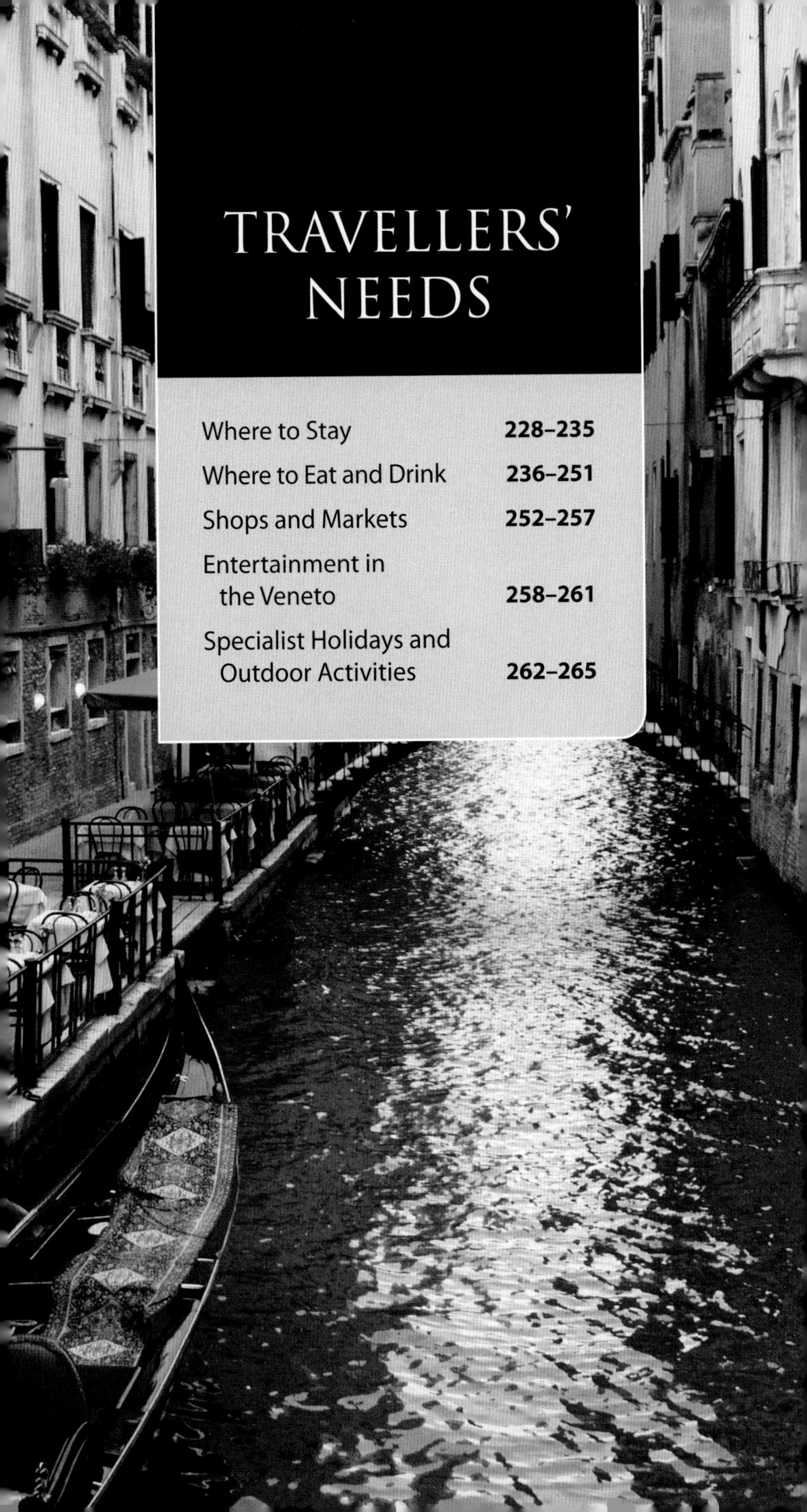

TRAVELLERS' NEEDS

WHERE TO STAY

Venice's enduring appeal to romantics and art lovers means that it has an astonishing number of hotels for its size, many of them in former *palazzi*. On the mainland, hotels and *pensioni* abound, frequently housed in magnificent old buildings. Those in the smaller towns of the region are often run by families who take great pride in their hospitality.

Lake Garda is a long-established resort area with many hotels to choose from, while the mountainous north of the Veneto is a year-round holiday destination with accommodation of all types. These include self-catering farmhouses, idyllically situated and well-equipped campsites and even simple refuges for walkers. Budget options in the cities include self-catering flats, hostels and dormitory-style accommodation. For more information on hotels in Venice and the Veneto, see the hotel listings *(pp232–5)*.

Where to Look

Unlike most other cities, Venice has hardly any "undesirable" areas. Hotel prices are sometimes higher in the immediate vicinity of the Piazza San Marco, but in such a compact city areas such as Santa Croce or Cannaregio are never far from places of interest. Addresses in Venice can be immensely confusing *(see p282)*, but a map reference for each hotel on the main islands is given in the listings. These Street Finder maps can be found on *pp290–97*.

Remember, if you are travelling by car, you will have to pay stiff parking charges at the Piazzale Roma car park or one of its satellite operations for the duration of your stay in Venice *(see p280)*.

Many of the hotels in minor inland towns of the Veneto cater primarily to business travellers, but visitors planning to explore the region will find lovely villa and farm hotels dotted around the countryside. Padua and Verona have a number of hotels, but Verona's are fully booked for months ahead in the summer opera season and during the Vinitaly trade fair in early April, so it is essential to plan ahead. Further north there is more choice. The hotels are geared to holidaymakers, with lovely gardens, swimming pools and sports facilities. Bear in mind that Italians as well as foreign tourists holiday in the lakes and mountains, so it is always advisable to book in advance.

The picturesque Villa Cipriani in Asolo *(see p234)*

The grandiose Moorish-style Hotel Excelsior on the Venice Lido *(see p234)*

Hotel Prices

Venice is an expensive place to stay and can hardly be said to have a "low season" with the benefits of lower or negotiable prices. It is difficult – but not impossible – to find a basic double room for less than €100. Occasionally you can find cheaper rooms from November to February, when the weather is often superbly sunny but chilly. But remember that some hotels close out of season for maintenance or staff holidays. All reopen for Carnival and raise their prices accordingly.

July and August are the most expensive months at the resorts along Lake Garda, and the majority of hotels here close over winter. In the Dolomites, however, both winter and mid-summer are high seasons, with skiers and outdoor enthusiasts flocking to the area; hotels close inbetween those peak times.

Single room rates are higher than individual rates for two people sharing a double room. Prices include tax.

By law all hotel rooms have a card on the back of the door showing current rates. Booking on the Internet is the best bet to securing the cheapest rates.

Hidden Extras

Accommodation across the board in Italian cities is subject to an additional tourist tax

◀ Pavement cafés lining the Riva del Vin by the Grand Canal in Venice

levied by the City Council, purportedly as a contribution to maintaining the city's splendour. The amount varies depending on the type of lodging, number of people and time of year, but usually amounts to a couple of euros per person per day.

If travelling on a budget, avoid hotels with inclusive breakfast (rarely good value for money). Tipping is a personal choice, though at least €1 for room service and bellboys is suggested, even if service is included in the price of the room. Laundry services are usually expensive, as are drinks from the minibar and telephone calls made from the rooms. Wi-Fi may be charged extra.

Hotel Gradings and Facilities

Italian hotels are classified by a rating system from one to five stars. However, each province sets its own level for grading, so standards for each category vary from one area to another. Some hotels may not have a restaurant, but those that do sometimes welcome non-residents who wish to eat.

Old buildings will rarely have airconditioning but the thick stone walls provide good insulation against the summer heat. If you cannot tolerate high temperatures, it is well worth choosing air-conditioned accommodation during the hottest months. Central heating is usually turned on at the beginning of November.

Travelling with Children

Children are welcome everywhere, but smaller hotels and guesthouses can occasionally have limited facilities. However, amenities such as cots, high chairs and a babysitting service will still be available.

Many of the hotels around the lakes and in the mountains region offer a range of activities for children, from a swimming pool to riding lessons or skiing with ski instructors.

Families with young children should note that many Venetian hotels are converted palaces, so some rooms can be cramped. In addition, most hotels do not have gardens. An alternative for travellers with young children is to stay in the Lido, with its long stretches of sandy beaches and a range of hotels with gardens.

What to Expect

Hotels are obliged by law to register guests with the police, so they will ask for your passport when you arrive. They may need to keep it for a few hours, but make sure you take it back; you will need identification to change money.

Simple elegant room at Via Paradiso 32, a boutique hotel in Feltre *(see p235)*

Hotel staff tend to be friendly and helpful, and the standard of cleanliness is very high. Rooms without a bathroom usually have a washbasin.

Continental breakfast is usually very light – a cup of coffee and a pastry or bread rolls and jam, though hotels increasingly include a buffet. It is cheaper to have breakfast at a bar. On the other hand, *mezza pensione*, or half board, can be a good deal as it includes accommodation, full dinner and breakfast.

Italian towns can be noisy. Light sleepers should ask for a room that is away from the street, or come equipped with earplugs to deaden the sounds of traffic and church bells.

Check-out time is usually between 10am and noon. If you linger longer, you will be asked to pay for an extra day. However, some hotels will hold your luggage for a few hours after you have checked out.

A plush room in the five-star Hotel Metropole *(see p233)*

Booking and Paying

It is advisable to book at least 2 months in advance in the high season; some people book as far as 6 months or a year ahead for hotels in Venice. Hotels above the €100 price bracket usually take credit cards and generally accept them for paying the deposit.

Under Italian law, a booking is valid as soon as a confirmation of the deposit made has been received. As in restaurants, visitors are required by law to retain hotel receipts until they have left the country.

Disabled Travellers

Facilities for the disabled are limited throughout Italy, and Venice poses its own particular problems, with many stepped bridges across the canals.

A list of tour operators that specialize in holidays for the disabled can be obtained from ENIT, the Italian State Tourist Board *(see p271)*. For more information, *see p269*.

Hotels in Historic Buildings

Many of Venice's hotels are housed in buildings of historical or artistic interest, for example in Gothic *palazzi*. Architectural highlights can range from wonderful early Renaissance windows to 18th-century frescoes, and antique bare beams or bricks. Even relatively humble B&Bs often hold architectural treasures. Converted palaces abound in Venice, but further afield former abbeys, farm-houses and taverns are also open to paying guests. There are also numerous attractive villa hotels in the Veneto. The **Villa Venete** website lists places individually.

The elegant drawing room of La Residenza in Venice *(see p233)*

Boutique Hotels

Venice has seen a rise in hotels offering a stay in luxurious or unusual settings. Most Venecian Boutique hotels are small and independent, where particular attention is given to style and design. Special focus is on details such as the quality of fabrics and furnishings. Whether it is stark contemporary design or sumptuous opulence, a rural idyll or a swish metropolitan feel, all boutique hotels strive to offer a different experience from the average hotel.

Self-Catering

Self-catering flats in Venice proper are very easy to find. Many local Venetian agents can arrange self-catering stays

DIRECTORY

Hotels in Historic Buildings

Ville Venete
W **villevenete.net**

Self-Catering

Luxrest
Ponte del Pistor, Castello 5990.
Map 7 B1.
Tel 377 708 60 73.
W **luxrest-venice.com**

Immobiliare Rio Alto
Campo San Tomà, San Polo 2863.
Map 6 E2.
Tel 041 244 00 23.
W **immobiliare rioalto.com**

Mitwohnzentrale Venice
Calle Vitturi, San Marco 2923. **Map** 6 E3.
Tel 041 523 16 72.
W **mwz-online.com**

Budget Accommodation

Associazione Italiana Alberghi per la Gioventù
Via Nicotera 1, 00195 Rome. **Tel** 06 487 11 52.
W **aighostels.com**

Foresteria Valdese
Campo Santa Maria Formosa, Castello 5170.
Map 7 C1.
Tel 041 528 67 97.
W **foresteriavenezia.it**

Ostello Venezia
Fondamenta delle Zitelle, Giudecca 86.
Map 7 B5.
Tel 041 523 82 11.
W **ostellovenezia.it**

Santa Fosca
Fmta Diedo, Cannaregio 2372. **Map** 2 F3.
Tel 041 71 57 75.
W **ostellosantafosca.it**

Campsites and Mountain Refuges

Club Alpino Italiano
Via Petrella 19, 20124 Milan.
Tel 02 205 72 31.
W **cai.it**

Marina di Venezia
Via Montello 6, Punta Sabbioni.
Tel 041 530 25 11.
W **marinadivenezia.it**

San Nicolò
Via dei Sanmicheli 14, Lido.
Tel 041 526 74 15.
W **campingsannicolo. com**

Touring Club Italiano
W **touringclub.it**

Floating Accommodation

Venice Houseboats
Via Tiro 2, Lido di Venezia.
Tel 345 986 67 24.
W **houseboats venice.com**

ranging from small apartments on the Lido to a palatial home on the Grand Canal. Another option on the mainland might be a luxurious and spacious villa with a swimming pool. Prices reflect the options, and they also fluctuate according to the time of year. Low-season prices for four people start at about €850 per week. **Luxrest** has a tantalizing choice of locations across the city, and offers both short- and long-term rentals. Other city agencies include **Immobiliare Rio Alto** and the well-established **Mitwohnzentrale Venice.**

Budget Accommodation

Those looking for cheaper accommodation can find one- or two-star budget hotels charging around €40 per person per night. These are generally small, modest, family-run places that rarely offer breakfast and usually have shared bathrooms.

Hostel or dormitory rooms are often available at convents and religious institutions, such as the **Foresteria Valdese** and **Santa Fosca**. It is often possible to book these rooms through the local tourist offices. The main youth hostel in Venice is the beautifully situated **Ostello Venezia** on the Giudecca island. The **Associazione Italiana Alberghi per la Gioventù** (Italian Youth Hostel Association) has lists of youth hostels throughout the country. It is essential to book well ahead if you want to stay in July or August. All these establishments can be contacted directly through their websites.

Campsites and Mountain Refuges

There are good campsites throughout the region, concentrated on the mainland to the north of Venice, on the shores of Lake Garda and in the northern mountains. Among the best are **Marina di Venezia** and **San Nicolò**.

Handy high-altitude refuges offer packages for walkers and climbers in the Dolomites during the summer months. Most are owned by the **Club Alpino Italiano** and offer dormitory accommodation as well as meals and drinks. A list of campsites can be obtained from ENIT *(see p271)* or local tourist offices, which also list refuges. The **Touring Club Italiano** annually publishes a list of campsites, the *Campeggi e Villaggi Turistici in Italia*.

Floating Accommodation

For a city that is based on water Venice has surprisingly little in the way of buoyant lodgings. The options that are available often represent good value for money and a more exciting alternative to a standard hotel room.

Comfortable, modern watercraft are available for hire from the Certosa port in the Castello district. They provide rooms and kitchen facilities for up to six passengers, with prices starting at €1300 a week. **Venice Houseboats** has several kinds of boats for weekly rentals, some requiring little to no navigation experience.

Recommended Hotels

The hotels listed on pages 232–5 cover the best B&B, boutique, historic, family and luxury accommdation types in Venice and the Veneto. They are listed by price within each area. Each has earned a good reputation for hospitality and charm and is representative of its setting, be that of magical Venice, the fascinating regions in the Veneto Plain, beautiful Lake Garda or the mountainous Dolomites. Establishments range from simple farmhouses to Alpine chalets and from family-run B&Bs to superb luxury palaces.

Throughout the listings certain hotels have been marked as DK Choice. These offer a particularly special experience – for their beautiful surroundings, historic setting, romantic atmosphere, artistic decor, excellent service, outstanding rooms, superb spa or wellness facilities, spectacular views or a combination of these.

The Lady Anne Yacht, a Venice houseboat moored on the Canale di San Marco

A room at the opulent Ca' Sagredo in Cannaregio, Venice *(see p234)*

Where to Stay

Venice

San Marco

Antico Panada €
Historic **Map** 7 A2
Calle Specchieri 646, 30124
Tel *041 520 90 88*
W hotelpanada.com
This converted 17th-century mansion with a cosy bar is decorated with antique mirrors. A breakfast buffet is provided.

Locanda ai Bareteri €
B&B **Map** 7 B1
Calle di Mezzo 4966, 30124
Tel *041 523 22 33*
W bareteri.it
Located close to the main sights this quiet and friendly B&B has spacious, simply furnished rooms.

Locanda Fiorita €
Boutique **Map** 6 F2
Campiello Novo, San Marco 3457/a, 30124
Tel *041 523 47 54*
W locandafiorita.com
The bright, airy rooms at this delightful hotel have stylish 18th-century furniture.

La Fenice & Des Artistes €€
Historic **Map** 7 A2
Campiello Fenice 1936, 30124
Tel *041 523 23 33*
W fenicehotels.com
Antiques and period-style furniture characterize this pretty hotel in a superb central location.

Hotel Flora €€
Boutique **Map** 7 A3
Via XXII Marzo–Calle Bergaschi 2283/a, 30124
Tel *041 520 58 44*
W hotelflora.it
This small but fully equipped hotel is in the heart of the city's upmarket shopping district.

One of the six rooms at La Villeggiatura, a B&B of understated elegance

Hotel Santo Stefano €€
Historic **Map** 6 F3
Campo Santo Stefano 2957, 30124
Tel *041 520 01 66*
W hotelsantostefanovenezia.com
Housed in a 15th-century watch-tower, this charming hotel in a bustling square has elegant rooms.

Novecento €€
Boutique **Map** 6 F3
Calle del Dose 2683–4, 30124
Tel *041 241 37 65*
W novecento.biz
A relaxing atmosphere and rooms with Oriental-style furnishing are offered at this hotel.

Palace Bonvecchiati €€
Luxury **Map** 7 B2
Calle dei Fabbri 4680, 30124
Tel *041 296 31 11*
W palacebonvecchiati.it
This friendly hotel has bright rooms with modern decor, plus a rooftop gym and a designer lobby.

Rialto €€
Family **Map** 7 A1
Riva di Ferro 5149, 30124
Tel *041 520 91 66*
W rialtohotel.com
The Rialto, situated next to the Rialto Bridge, has large family rooms with fantastic views.

DK Choice

Bauer il Palazzo €€€
Luxury **Map** 7 A3
Campo San Moisè 1459, 30124
Tel *041 520 70 22*
W ilpalazzovenezia.com
Enjoy breathtaking views over the Grand Canal from this 18th-century palace, which features lavishly furnished rooms and suites with Murano glass chandeliers. There is a rooftop terrace bar, a restaurant and a spa.

Luna Hotel Baglioni €€€
Luxury **Map** 7 B3
Calle Larga dell'Ascension 1243, 30124
Tel *041 528 98 40*
W baglionihotels.com
The spacious Luna hotel has sumptuous suites and a breakfast room decorated with frescoes.

Monaco and Grand Canal €€€
Historic **Map** 7 B3
Calle Vallaresso 1332, 30124
Tel *041 520 02 11*
W hotelmonaco.it
Formally a palace theatre, this hotel is near the Grand Canal and has attractive rooms and a fine dining restaurant.

Price Guide
Prices are based on one night's stay in high season for a standard double room, inclusive of service charges and taxes.

€	up to €150
€€	€150–€300
€€€	over €300

Palazzina Grassi €€€
Luxury **Map** 6 F3
Calle Grassi 3247, 30124
Tel *041 528 46 44*
W palazzinag.com
At this stylish establishment, maximum comfort is combined with great Grand Canal views and contemporary design furnishings.

San Polo

Al Campaniel €
B&B **Map** 6 E2
Calle del Campaniel 2889, 30125
Tel *041 275 07 49*
W alcampaniel.com
This family guesthouse, with cosy rooms, is run by a Spanish-Italian couple. Located on a quiet street.

Locanda Sturion €€
Historic **Map** 7 A1
Calle del Sturion 679, 30125
Tel *041 523 62 43*
W locandasturion.com
Dating back to the 13th century, this charming hotel has rooms decorated with red damasks and Venetian furniture.

DK Choice

Oltre il Giardino €€
Boutique **Map** 6 E1
Fondamenta San Stin 2542, 30125
Tel *041 275 00 15*
W oltreilgiardino-venezia.com
This attractive house, with six rooms that overlook the garden, offers tranquillity away from the bustle of the city. Enjoy a drink in the garden or relish the owner's home-made cakes and pies for breakfast.

DK Choice

La Villeggiatura €€
B&B **Map** 2 F5
Calle dei Botteri 1569 , 30125
Tel *041 524 46 73*
W lavilleggiatura.it
Run by a Venetian lady, this home-away-from-home is a charming place to come back to after a day's sightseeing. It has six light-filled, individually styled rooms with king-size beds and elegant modern bathrooms.

The warm decor of the opulent Hotel Metropole

Palazzo Barbarigo €€€
Luxury **Map** 6 E1
Calle Corner 2765, 30125
Tel *041 74 01 72*
W palazzobarbarigo.it
Contemporary design, Art Deco furnishings and four-poster beds feature at this stylish hotel.

Santa Croce

Bed & Breakfast "al Gallion" €
B&B **Map** 2 D5
Calle Gallion 1126, 30135
Tel *041 524 47 43*
W algallion.com
A former Gothic palace converted into a guesthouse, this place is located in a quiet neighbourhood and has lovely rooms.

DK Choice

Hotel Al Sole €
Historic **Map** 5 C1
Fondamenta Minotta 134–136, 30135
Tel *041 244 03 28*
W alsolehotels.com
Housed in Palazzo Marcello, this 15th-century palace, with a beautiful façade, offers well-appointed rooms with period furniture. Enjoy the rich breakfast spread served in a patio garden.

Ai Due Fanali €€
Historic **Map** 2 D5
Campo San Simeon Grande 946, 30135
Tel *041 71 84 90*
W aiduefanali.com
This converted monastery offers a peaceful atmosphere. Some rooms have old timber rafters.

Hotel Falier €€
Family **Map** 5 C1
Salizzada San Pantalon 130, 30135
Tel *041 71 08 82*
W hotelfalier.com
Large well-equipped rooms are provided at this hotel. There is also a pretty garden with wisteria and a rooftop terrace.

Castello

Bed & Breakfast San Marco €
B&B **Map** 8 D1
Fondamenta San Giorgio dei Schiavoni 3385L, 30122
Tel *041 522 75 89*
W realvenice.it
This cosy B&B has a lovely view of the city's canals. All rooms have kitchen facilities.

Casa per Ferie La Pietà €
Family **Map** 8 D2
Calle della Pietà 3701, 30122
Tel *041 244 36 39*
W bedandvenice.it
Featuring large rooms with shared bathrooms, this hotel also boasts breakfast rooms that have panoramic views of the city.

Foresteria Valdese €
Family **Map** 7 C1
Calle Lunga Santa Maria Formosa 5170, 30122
Tel *041 528 67 97*
W foresteriavenezia.it
This welcoming guesthouse in an 18th-century palace is run by the Waldensian and Methodist church. Choose between cosy rooms with en suites or dormitory accommodation.

Ai Reali €€
Historic **Map** 7 B1
Campo della Fava 5527, 30122
Tel *041 241 02 53*
W hotelaireali.com
This sumptuous palace has beautiful furnishings. The wellness facilities are housed in the attic rooms.

Locanda La Corte €€
Historic **Map** 3 C5
Calle Bressana 6317, 30122
Tel *041 241 13 00*
W locandalacorte.it
Housed in a converted 16th-century palace, with a lovely courtyard, the delightful rooms at this hotel feature the original floors and wooden beams.

Londra Palace €€
Luxury **Map** 8 D2
Riva degli Schiavoni 4171, 30122
Tel *041 520 05 33*
W londrapalace.com
Elegant rooms with lagoon views are offered at the Londra Palace. Head to the bar for a cocktail or an espresso. Excellent service.

La Residenza €€
Historic **Map** 8 E2
Campo Bandiera e Moro 3608, 30122
Tel *041 528 53 15*
W venicelaresidenza.com
La Residenza is a Gothic-style palace. The comfortable rooms have frescoes, and some overlook the *campo* or the church of La Pietà.

Aqua Palace €€€
Luxury **Map** 7 B1
Calle della Malvasia 5492, 30122
Tel *041 296 04 42*
W aquapalace.it
This boutique palace hotel is situated on a quiet canal. The rooms are large and modern, and some boast canal views.

Hotel Metropole €€€
Luxury **Map** 8 E2
Riva degli Schiavoni 4149, 30122
Tel *041 520 50 44*
W hotelmetropole.com
This hotel offers magnificent rooms with antiques. Its restaurant is famous *(see p244)* and the garden is an oasis of green in the heart of the city.

Dorsoduro

Locanda San Barnaba €
Family **Map** 6 D3
Calle del Traghetto 2785–6, 30123
Tel *041 241 12 33*
W locanda-sanbarnaba.com
A converted palace with a spacious foyer and a pretty garden, this hotel offers spotless rooms that are named after plays by Carlo Goldoni.

Avogaria €€
B&B **Map** 5 C3
Fondamenta dell' Avogaria 1629, 30123
Tel *041 296 04 91*
W avogaria.com
Avogaria has five lavishly furnished rooms with luxurious bathrooms. Three rooms have their own private courtyard. Closed Jan.

Ca' Pisani €€
Boutique **Map** 6 E4
Rio Terrà Foscarini 979/a, 30123
Tel *041 240 14 11*
W capisanihotel.it
Located in a quiet street, Ca' Pisani provides sleek modern decor and comfort. There is also a Turkish bath and a roof terrace.

Charming House DD724 €€
Boutique **Map** 6 F4
Ramo da Mula 724, 30123
Tel *041 277 02 62*
W thecharminghouse.com
The cosy, elegant rooms in this hotel, located in Venice's art district, are decorated with works by contemporary Italian artists.

Locanda Ca' Zose €€
B&B **Map** 6 F4
Calle del Bastion 193B, 30123
Tel *041 522 66 35*
W hotelcazose.com
This friendly, small hotel has tastefully furnished rooms, many with charming canal views.

DK Choice

Pensione Accademia Villa Maravegie €€
Historic **Map** 6 E3
Fondamenta Bollani 1058, 30123
Tel *041 521 01 88*
pensioneaccademia.it
Once the Russian embassy, this beautiful 17th-century villa is a tranquil haven away from the bustle of the city. Rooms are decorated in Venetian style and have views over the canal or the garden. Alfresco buffet breakfast.

Ca' Maria Adele €€€
Luxury **Map** 7 A4
Rio Terà Catecumeni 111, 30123
Tel *041 520 30 78*
camariaadele.it
A lavish hotel with exotic decor and a romantic atmosphere. The rooms offer great views of the adjacent Santa Maria della Salute church and the Grand Canal.

Cannaregio

Al Saor €
B&B **Map** 3 A4
Calle Zotti 3904/a, 30125
Tel *041 296 06 54*
alsaor.com
This friendly guesthouse is run by a local family. Some rooms have their own kitchen.

Carnival Palace €
Boutique **Map** 1 C3
Fondamenta di Cannaregio 929, 30121
Tel *041 244 03 20*
carnivalpalace.com
Many of the rooms at the Carnival Palace overlook the canals. Breakfast is served in a lovely garden.

DK Choice

Ca' Sagredo €€
Historic **Map** 3 A5
Campo Santa Sofia 4198, 30121
Tel *041 241 31 11*
casagredohotel.com
A grandiose 15th-century palace houses this luxurious hotel. The individually decorated rooms are spacious and have period furnishings. Paintings by 17th- and 18th-century Venetian artists and frescoes adorn the walls. There is a magnificent marble stairway.

Palazzo Abadessa €€
Historic **Map** 3 A4
Calle Priuli 4011, 30131
Tel *041 241 37 84*
abadessa.com
This charming 16th-century palace has frescoed ceilings, antique furniture and chandeliers, plus a splendid private garden. Closed 3 weeks Jan.

The Lagoon Islands

Ca' del Borgo €
Historic
Piazza delle Erbe 8, Malamocco, 30126
Tel *041 77 07 49*
cadelborgo.com
Located in an old fishing village, this villa has a garden for relaxing in summer and an open fireplace in winter. Closed Nov–Mar.

Il Lato Azzurro €
Family
Via Forti 13, Sant'Erasmo, 30141
Tel *041 523 06 42*
latoazzurro.it
This place offers simple country-style accommodation and a lovely garden. Bicycles are available for hire.

Villa Mabapa €
Boutique
Riviera San Nicolò 16, Lido, 30126
Tel *041 526 05 90*
villamabapa.com
This 1930s villa has been converted into a guesthouse, with tastefully decorated rooms. The restaurant serves meals in the lush garden. Closed Nov–mid-Mar.

Locanda Cipriani €€
Historic
Piazza Santa Fosca 29, Torcello, 30142
Tel *041 73 01 50*
locandacipriani.com
Housed in an old-style inn, this hotel has five rooms that feature high-vaulted ceilings and Venetian mosaics in the bathrooms. Closed Jan–mid-Feb.

Bauer Palladio Hotel €€€
Luxury **Map** 7 5B
Fondamenta delle Zitelle, Giudecca 33, 30133
Tel *041 520 70 22*
palladiohotelspa.com
A peaceful hotel in an old monastery, boasting beautiful rooms, four gardens and a luxurious spa. Open Mar–Nov.

DK Choice

Hotel Excelsior €€€
Luxury
Lungomare Marconi 41, Lido, 30126
Tel *041 526 02 01*
hotelexcelsiorvenezia.com
This flamboyant Moorish-style beachfront hotel, constructed in the early 1900s, has a swimming pool and *cabanas* in the shape of Arab tents. It is popular with stars during the Film Festival. Closed Nov–mid-Mar.

The Veneto Plain

ASOLO: Albergo Al Sole €€
Boutique
Via Collegio 33, 31011
Tel *042 395 13 32*
albergoalsoleasolo.com
Old-fashioned luxury and contemporary amenities are combined at this hotel. Rooms are spacious and well-furnished. There is a Lovely terrace for breakfast. Closed Jan.

ASOLO: Villa Cipriani €€
Luxury
Via Canova 298, 31011
Tel *042 352 34 11*
villacipriani.it
This picturesque 16th-century villa has an infinity pool with great views of the countryside.

BASSANO DEL GRAPPA: Ca' Sette €€
Historic
Via Cunizza da Romano 4, 36061
Tel *042 438 33 50*
ca-sette.it
Set in a converted 1700s villa with a formal garden, this stylish hotel has individually decorated rooms.

CHIOGGIA: Grande Italia €€
Historic
Rione S Andrea 597, 30015
Tel *041 40 05 15*
hotelgrandeitalia.com
The elegant rooms in this hotel overlook the lagoon and canals. There is also an attic gym.

Hotel Excelsior pool by night

For key to price guide *see p232*

CONEGLIANO: Il Faè €
B&B
Via Faè 1, San Pietro di Feletto, 31020
Tel *043 878 71 17*
W ilfae.com
This family-run B&B is in a converted farmhouse. Cooking classes are offered. Closed Nov–Easter.

DK Choice

FOLLINA: Villa Abbazia €€€
Luxury
Piazza IV Novembre 3, 31051
Tel *043 897 12 77*
W hotelabbazia.it
This delightful 17th-century villa with a pretty garden has been tastefully restored. The spacious rooms are individually decorated in English country-house style and have modern amenities and hydromassage baths.

MONTEGROTTO TERME: Hotel Augustus €
Family
Viale Stazione 150, 35036
Tel *049 79 32 00*
W hotelaugustus.com
Hotel Augustus is modern and comfortable. There are spa facilities and hot thermal springs. Closed mid-Jan–mid-Feb.

PADUA: Al Santo €
Family
Via del Santo 147, 35139
Tel *049 875 21 31*
W alsanto.it
In a great location for exploring the city, this hotel has charming rooms. Closed 6 Jan–end Jan.

TREVISO: Relais Monaco €€
Historic
Via Postumia 63, Ponzano Veneto, 31050
Tel *042 296 41*
W relaismonaco.it
This beautifully converted villa with elegant decor lies in spacious parkland. Spa and pool facilities.

VICENZA: Campo Marzio €€
Boutique
Viale Roma 21–27, 36100
Tel *044 454 57 00*
W hotelcampomarzio.com
Campo Marzio is a stylish design hotel with bright, attractive rooms. Situated just outside the city gate.

VITTORIO VENETO: Hotel Ristorante Le Macine €
Historic
Via Boni 34, 31029
Tel *043 894 02 91*
W hotelristorantelemacine.it
This hotel is housed in an ancient building in the city centre and provides contemporary rooms.

Rustic chic bathroom at Via Paradiso 32, where the modern blends with the old

Verona and Lake Garda

GARDA: Locanda San Vigilio €€€
Luxury
Punta San Vigilio, 37016
Tel *045 725 66 88*
W locanda-sanvigilio.it
In a lakeside villa, this hotel provides great service and comfort. Private beach. Closed mid-Nov–Mar.

MALCESINE: Hotel Castello €€€
Boutique
Via Paina 21, 37018
Tel *045 740 02 33*
W h-c.it
Situated at the foot of Scaligeri Castle, this pleasant hotel offers beach facilities. Closed Nov–Mar.

SIRMIONE: Villa Paradiso €
B&B
Via Arici 7, 25019
Tel *030 91 61 49*
W villaparadisosirmione.it
Rustic rooms, most of which have views of Lake Garda, are offered at this hotel. There is a peaceful private garden. Closed Oct–Mar.

DK Choice

TORRI DEL BENACO: Hotel Gardesana €€
Historic
Piazza Calderini 5, 37010
Tel *045 722 54 11*
W gardesana.eu
This charming 15th-century former harbour master's house overlooking Lake Garda has been converted into a lovely hotel. The rooms are furnished in 19th-century Venetian style. Live music in summer. Closed Nov–Mar.

VERONA: Hotel Aurora €€
Historic
Piazza delle Erbe 2, 37121
Tel *045 59 47 17*
W hotelaurora.biz
At the Aurora the rooms (some with balconies) overlook the bustling Piazza delle Erbe. There is a good buffet breakfast.

VERONA: Il Torcolo €€
B&B
Vicolo Listone 3, 37121
Tel *045 800 75 12*
W hoteltorcolo.it
Housed in a former tavern, this is now a popular family-run hotel with pretty rooms and a breakfast terrace. Closed 1 week Christmas and 2 weeks Jan.

The Dolomites

BELLUNO: Albergo delle Alpi €
Family
Via Jacopo Tasso 13, 32100
Tel *043 794 05 45*
W dellealpi.it
This comfortable hotel has basic rooms and modern amenities. Good on-site restaurant.

DK Choice

CORTINA: Grand Hotel Savoia €€€
Luxury
Via Roma 62, 32043
Tel *043 63 201*
W grandhotelsavoiacortina.it
This splendid hotel, dating to the early 1900s, stands in the centre of the bustling Alpine resort town. Rooms have contemporary decor with modern comforts. It offers a pool, relaxing massages and Turkish baths. Closed Apr–Jun.

FELTRE: Via Paradiso 32 €
Boutique
Via Paradiso 32, 32032
Tel *348 870 96 22*
W viaparadiso32.it
The tastefully restored rooms at this delightful hotel have marble fittings.

SANTA FOSCA: Ca' del Bosco €
Family
Via Monte Cernera 10, 32020
Tel *043 752 12 58*
W hotelcadelbosco.it
Located in a pretty Alpine village, this family-run guesthouse offers rooms with mountain views. Closed Oct–Nov and Apr–May.

ZOLDO ALTO: Hotel Maè €
Family
Via Masarei 4, 32010
Tel *043 778 87 07*
W residence-panorama.net
This pleasant hotel, with a garden and playground, has basic rooms and self-catering apartments. Closed Oct–Nov and Apr–May.

For more information on types of hotels *see pp228–31*

WHERE TO EAT AND DRINK

Restaurants in Venice and the Veneto serve predominantly Italian food from the region, with a special emphasis on fish in Venice. Wherever visitors go, they will find the cooking simple, with dishes that make full use of traditional, locally grown ingredients.

Most Venetians eat *pranzo* (lunch) at around 12:30pm and *cena* (dinner) from 8pm, though restaurants start serving dinner earlier to cater for the many foreign visitors. Restaurants may be closed for a week or so for staff holidays, but these vary from year to year. Ask your hotel to first call and confirm that the restaurant is open to avoid disappointment. Finding restaurants can be confusing in Venice, so use the map references provided. The restaurants listed in the following pages are some of the best across all price ranges.

Lunching alfresco at a pizzeria in Venice

Types of Restaurants

Eating places in Italy have a variety of names. For example, a *ristorante* is smarter and more expensive than a *trattoria*. A *birreria* and a *spaghetteria* are more downmarket eating places selling beer, pasta and snacks. There are also a large number of fast-food joints and *tavola calda* (cafeteria-style) establishments, which have no cover or service charge. A good *pizzeria* will use wood-fired ovens and normally be open only in the evenings. An *enoteca* is a wine bar that often serves meals too, while an *osteria* is a typical neighbourhood bar that often does bar snacks. Those not looking for a full meal at lunchtime can stop at a bar or café for a light snack. For more on bars and cafés, *see p250.*

Opening Times and Closing Days

Opening times are virtually the same throughout Venice and the Veneto – from noon to 2:30pm for lunch, and from 7:30pm to 10:30pm for dinner. Many restaurants close one or two days a week. Closing days for individual restaurants are given in the listings.

Fixed-Price Menus

Restaurants may have a *menu turistico* pinned up in the street. Such menus offer little opportunity to taste the local cuisine. However, they can be a good deal if service and cover charge are included.

A *menu gastronomico* or *menu degustazione* is a fixed-price menu consisting of six or seven courses, which allows you to sample the full range of the chef's offerings.

A blackboard menu displayed in front of a restaurant

How Much to Pay

Transport charges can add as much as 30 per cent to the price of basic commodities coming into Venice. In cheaper places and *pizzerie*, a two-course meal with half a litre of wine will cost around €15. Three-course meals average about €30 and could cost up to €100 or more in up-market restaurants. In the Veneto, prices are lower, except for stylish restaurants in Verona and along Lake Garda during the summer.

Nearly all restaurants apply a cover charge *(pane e coperto)* of €1–3. Many also add a 10 per cent service charge *(servizio)* to the bill *(il conto)*, so always establish whether or not this is their policy. While leaving a tip is a matter of the customer's discretion, 12 to 15 per cent is acceptable. Restaurants are obliged by law to give a proper receipt *(una ricevuta fiscale)*. The preferred form of payment is cash, but many will accept payment by major credit cards. Check which cards are accepted when booking.

Making Reservations

Whatever the price range, Venice's best restaurants are always busy, so it is best to reserve a table. If restaurants do not accept bookings, try to arrive early to avoid queuing.

Dress Code

Italians like to dress up in general, and dining out is no exception. Smart casual clothes are the general rule for both men and women.

Reading the Menu

Both lunch and dinner in a restaurant usually start with an *antipasto*, or hors d'oeuvres (seafood, olives, beef *carpaccio*, ham or salami), followed by the *primo* (soup, rice or pasta). The main course, or *secondo*, will be fish or meat, either served alone or accompanied by *contorni* (vegetables) or *insalata* (salad). These are rarely included in the price of the main course. To finish, there will probably be a choice of *frutta* (fruit), a *dolce* (pudding) or *formaggio* (cheese). Coffee is ordered and served right at the end of the meal, often with a *digestivo*. Italians drink espresso – never a cappuccino other than at breakfast. In some restaurants, the menu may be chalked up or the waiter may simply recite the day's special dishes at the table.

Vegetarian Food

Vegetarians always find a choice of seasonal vegetables and pulses in Italian eateries. Most menus include a variety of meatless dishes since many *antipasti* (starters), soups and pasta sauces are vegetable based. Most places will be happy to serve a *frittata* (omelette), salad and a selection of cheese. Coeliacs are well catered for and should ask for *senza glutine* (gluten-free).

Typical seafood *antipasto* consisting of small crabs

Rosticceria San Bartolomeo in San Marco, Venice *(see p242)*

Most restaurants, however, do not offer much choices for vegans, although many ice-cream parlours have soya and non-dairy options.

Choice of Wine

House wines are usually local *(see pp240–41)*. Cheaper restaurants will have a limited wine list, but at the top of the scale there should be a wide range of Italian wines and a selection of foreign vintages.

Children

Children are welcome in restaurants, particularly in simple, family-run establishments. Smart restaurants may be less welcoming, especially in the evenings. Facilities such as highchairs are not commonly provided. Most restaurants will prepare a half-portion *(mezza porzione)* if requested, and some charge less for these smaller helpings.

Smoking

Smoking in enclosed public spaces, including restaurants, is banned across Italy. Outdoor terraces are exempt.

Wheelchair Access

There are few restaurants in Venice that offer any special provision for wheelchair users, though a word when booking should ensure a conveniently situated table and assistance, if required, on arrival.

Eating on a Budget

Eating out all the time can become very expensive, especially in Venice, so a cheaper option is to make your own picnic. Supermarkets stock a range of fresh salads, local cheeses and tasty cold cuts. The Coop chain has several outlets in Venice and the Veneto, including a flagship store at Piazzale Roma. Billa has stores throughout the Veneto. Alternatively, many local shops will make large rolls with your choice of fillings.

There are plenty of places to stop and enjoy an alfresco meal. All the towns in the Veneto have picturesque squares and quiet parks. In Venice, the park at Sant'Elena is a shady spot even in summer, but picnicking in Piazza San Marco *(see pp78–9)* will invite a fine.

Recommended Restaurants

The restaurants listed on pages 242–9 have all earned a noteworthy reputation. The listings cover a variety of eateries, from the simple *pizzeria*, cafeteria-style *tavola calda* and family-run *trattoria* to the smarter *ristorante*, *enoteca* and neighbourhood *osteria*. The cuisine ranges from regional and traditional specialities to modern Italian fare, creative fusion dishes and Mediterranean options. The venues are listed by price category within each area of Venice or region of the Veneto.

Throughout the listings certain restaurants have been highlighted as DK Choice. These offer at least one particularly special quality, such as exceptional cuisine, a romantic setting, beautiful surroundings, a charming ambience, a historic location, excellent value, or a combination of these.

The Flavours of Venice and the Veneto

The cuisine of Venice and the Veneto reflects the region's varied landscape, from cattle-grazing and agricultural land to mountains and coastline. The most important sources of ingredients, however, are the waters – both inland and coastal – that yield a constant supply of fish and seafood. In general, the cooking is light, fresh and delicately flavoured, without heavy sauces. Fish may be simply grilled or poached with herbs, while *carpaccio* of raw beef is sliced to transparent thinness. The vibrant colours of dishes recall canvases by Tintoretto or Titian: bright yellow saffron or polenta, emerald green fresh peas, dark red *radicchio* and the blue-black stain of cuttlefish ink in *riso nero* risotto.

Saffron

Produce from the Veneto is loaded onto the Venetian canalside

Venetian Food

Food in Venice is almost always Italian, and many restaurants serve local specialities. There are very few ethnic eating places despite the city's long history as a trading port and home to foreign settlers. Foodstuffs have always been traded, starting with the local salt and fish. In the 15th and 16th centuries, when Venice was the prosperous gateway to the East, imported spices, pepper, raisins, pine nuts and sugar made their way into the diet. Recipes from the period cite ingredients such as ginger, nutmeg, saffron, cloves, cinnamon and coriander. The city's noble families liked their food to be appealing to the eye as well as the palate, and so they introduced fine, locally made glassware to enhance the table. They served extravagant fare such as peacock, roasted whole with spices and then garnished with gold leaf. A few traces of these exotic influences still appear in classic Venetian cooking, such as Asian-style sweet and sour combinations and the use of spices as well as herbs. *Baccalà* (dried salted cod) originally brought from the Baltic area, is still very popular, often cooked with milk or wine and garlic or onion. Superb vegetables are grown in market gardens on the islands of the lagoon, not least the delicious purple artichokes *(castraure)* from Sant'Erasmo.

Selection of Venetian *antipasti*, the perfect appetizer

Regional Dishes and Specialities

Antipasto di frutti di mare (a mixed seafood appetizer) is a special favourite in Venice, where the ingredients come fresh from the Adriatic. From lovely Lake Garda, *anguilla del pescatore* (stewed eel), *lavarelli al vino bianco* (lake fish in white wine) and *carpione* (a type of lake trout) are all fishy delights. Another fish speciality of the region is *baccalà alla veneziana*, made with dried salt cod. Pork and salamis feature throughout the area, but closer to Friuli, goose is often used as an alternative to pork, with succulent cured meat offerings such as *salame d'oca* (goose salami). Game is also found on the menu, together with sauerkraut and filling goulash, while desserts often have an Austrian flavour, too, such as *Apfelstrudel*. But the region is also proud of claiming as its own the voluptuous, classic Italian dessert *tiramisù*.

Asparagus

Sarde in Saor is a Venetian speciality of fried sardines in a sweet and sour onion marinade, with pine nuts.

Enjoying an apéritif in the sunshine of St Mark's Square in Venice

Food of the Veneto

The region's staples have long been polenta and rice, although pasta is also popular. Polenta, made from ground maize (corn) that was originally imported from America in the 16th century, was always a peasant food. Today, it often accompanies a main course and can appear as a thick purée or be allowed to set into in a more solid form, when it can be cut into slices and grilled. The Veneto is one of Italy's main rice-growing regions. Rice was introduced from Spain by the Arabs, and the *vialone nano* variety grown around Verona is the favourite for risotto, giving a superbly creamy finish when cooked in stock with meat, fish or vegetables in season. A huge range of vegetables is grown in the Veneto. Bassano di Grappa is noted for its asparagus, and Treviso for a long variety of *radicchio* that is eaten raw, baked *(radicchio in forno)*, grilled or in risotto. Soups are made from vegetables and beans, notably *pasta e fagiola* – a thick brown soup of highly prized borlotti beans from Lamon, near Belluno. Fish comes from the inland rivers and Lake Garda, while farms produce chicken, duck, turkey and goose. Towards the mountains there are pigs for cured hams, salami and sausages like the pork *sopressa*, as well as veal, beef and dairy cattle, and wild game in season. An Austrian legacy is tasted in the dumplings and apple strudels of the Dolomites.

Fishing on the tranquil waters of Lake Garda

VENETIAN FISH DISHES

The catch from the region's waters includes sardines, mussels, clams, sea snails, squid, cuttlefish, eel, prawns, crab and lobster. These are served as *antipasti*, made into soups *(brodo di pesce)*, and cooked in risottos or with pasta, such as the popular *spaghetti alle vongole* (with clams). Regional specialities include:

Schie alla Polenta Minuscule lagoon prawns, shelled and served up with creamy corn polenta.

Sarde in Saor Sardines in a sweet and sour sauce.

Moleche frite Soft-shelled crabs from the lagoon, coated with beaten egg and fried.

Seppie alla Veneziana Cuttlefish cooked in their own ink.

Peoci Saltai Mussels steamed with white wine, garlic and parsley.

Risotto di Pesce is a mix of rice with fish and prawns in a soft, moist risotto, usually made for a minimum of two in restaurants.

Fegato alla Venezia is calf's liver served on a bed of sautéed onions. Grilled polenta is a good side dish.

Tiramisù (the name means "pick me up") is rich pudding of mascarpone, sponge fingers, coffee and Marsala.

What to Drink in Venice and the Veneto

Italy has been making wine for over 3,000 years, and production in the Veneto reflects this, with the largest output in Italy of superior DOC wines. The area produces an abundance of different wines, which include not only well-known names such as Soave, Valpolicella and Bardolino, but many others which are also excellent value for money. Although Italians tend to drink lighter wines with their food, the area is also noted for some excellent strong wines. Italy's famous *digestivo*, *grappa*, originated in this corner of the country, and meals are often preceded by an *aperitivo* or a glass of sparkling local Prosecco.

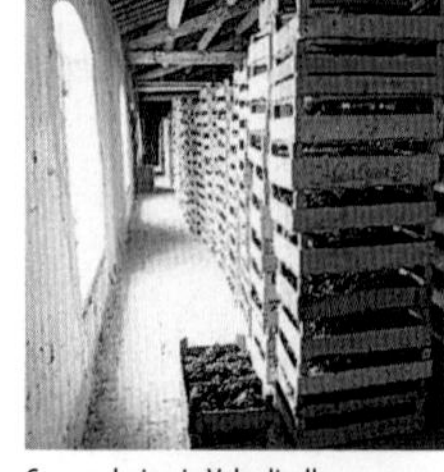

Grapes drying in Valpolicella

Red Wine

Red wines in the Veneto are produced mainly near Bardolino and Valpolicella between Verona and Lake Garda *(see pp214–15)*. Made predominantly from the Corvina grape, they are usually light and fruity, but quality can vary so, it is worth looking for reliable names.

Valpolicella comes in several forms. In addition to the normal easy-drinking wine, it is available as a *ripasso*, boosted in colour and strength by macerating the skins of the grapes before pressing. Recioto della Valpolicella is very different, a rich, sweet wine made from selected air-dried grapes. Some Reciotos undergo further fermentation to remove the sweetness, producing the strong, dry Recioto Amarone. These are some of the strongest naturally alcoholic wines in the world and are delicious but expensive.

Excellent red wines are also made by producers such as Venegazzù and Maculan from the Cabernet Sauvignon and Merlot grapes.

Red Venegazzù

Masi's *ripasso*

Bardolino wine is light, fruity and garnet-red in colour.

Amarone is full-bodied, rich, full of fruit and very alcoholic.

Reading Wine Labels

Italian wines are classified by four quality levels. Starting at the top, DOCG status *(Denominazione di Origine Controllata e Garantita)* has been awarded to a small number of Italian growing areas, none of which are in the Veneto. Most quality wines – more than 250 in the whole of Italy – are in the DOC category (as above but without the "guarantee") and these can be relied on as good-value, quality wines. The IGT *(Indicazione Geografica Tipica)* category corresponds to the popular French Vin de Pays. The final classification is *vino da tavola*, or table wine, but due to the inflexible Italian wine laws many superb wines appear in this category.

No vintage recommendations are given in the chart because almost all Veneto wines are made for young drinking.

Wine Type	Recommended Producers
White Wine	
Soave	Anselmi, Bertani, Col Baraca (Masi), Boscaini, CS di Soave, Masi, Pieropan, Scamperle, Tedeschi, Zenato, Zonin
Bianco di Custoza	Cavalchina, Le Tende, Le Vigne di San Pietro, Pezzini, San Leone, Tedeschi, Zenato
Breganze di Breganze	Maculan
Gambellara	CS di Gambellara, Zonin
Red Wine	
Bardolino	Alighieri, Bertani, Bolla, Boscaini, Guerrieri-Rizzardi, Masi, Tedeschi
Valpolicella	Alighieri, Allegrini, Bertani, Bolla, Boscaini, Guerrieri-Rizzardi, Masi, Tedeschi, Zenato
Ripasso-Valpolicella (non-DC)	Serègo Alighieri, Jago (Bolla), Le Cane (Boscaini), Le Sassine (Le Ragose), Campo Fiorin (Masi), Capitel San Rocco (Tedeschi)
Recioto and Recioto Amarone della Valpolicella	Serègo Alighieri, Allegrini, Masi, Quintarelli, La Ragose, Tedeschi

White Wine

Bianco di Custoza White Recioto

The Veneto produces more white wine than red, and most of the region's whites are from vineyards around the hilltop town of Soave *(see p206)*. These wines can be dull, but increasing numbers of producers are trying to raise Soave's image. Bianco di Custoza, a creamy, richer-tasting "super Soave" from the eastern shores of Lake Garda, is well worth trying. Breganze is a name to look out for, with Maculan a leader in making fresh, clean, inexpensive wines and world-class dessert wines. Gambellara is made mainly from Soave's Garganega grape and is seldom of poor quality. Venegazzù is another producer you can trust for good-quality white wines.

Pieropan is a top-quality producer of Soave. The single-vineyard wines from here are superb.

Venegazzù's Pinot Grigio wine is dry and goes well with Venetian seafood.

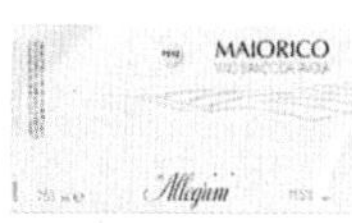

White *vino da tavola* wines range from pale and dry to sweet and golden coloured.

Puiatti's white Ribolla wine is fruity but dry. It is made in neighbouring Friuli.

Apéritifs and other Drinks

Grappa *Crodino*

Italian apéritifs tend to be wine-based, bitter, herb-flavoured drinks such as Martini and Campari. Less familiar are the herbal Punt e Mes, Cynar (made from artichokes), and the vivid orange Aperol, which is good mixed with white wine and soda. Crodino is a popular non-alcoholic choice. For settling the stomach after a good meal there are *amari* (bitters) and *digestivi*. Montenegro and Ramazzotti are well worth trying, and *grappa*, distilled from wine lees *(see Bassano del Grappa p176)*, is another favourite. A local speciality, Trevisana, is mixed with an extract of the long red *radicchio* from Treviso. Italian brandy can be rather oily, but Vecchia Romagna is a reliable name.

Prosecco

Prosecco Bellini cocktail

The Veneto's own sparkling wine, Prosecco is perfect as either a refreshing light *aperitivo* or with a meal. It originates in Conegliano *(see p179)*, the home of Italy's greatest wine school, and comes in both *secco* (dry) or *amabile* (medium-sweet) forms, and as *frizzante* or *spumante* (semi- and fully sparkling). An excellent accompaniment to both fruit and seafood, it is also the traditional base for Bellini, a delicious *aperitivo* of wine mixed with fresh white peach juice *(see p96)*. This drink has bred several variants, such as Mimosa (with orange) and Tiziano (with red grape juice).

Soft Drinks

Italian bottled fruit juices come in delicious flavours such as pear, apricot and peach. Many bars will squeeze you a *spremuta* of fresh orange *(arancia)* or grapefruit *(pompelmo)* juice on the spot. A *frullato* is an ice-cold mix of milk and fresh fruit.

Spremuta di arancia

Coffee

Coffee is an essential part of Italian life. Milky *cappuccino* with chocolate powder is drunk at breakfast time, and tiny cups of strong black *espresso* throughout the day. If you like your coffee with milk, choose a *caffè con latte*, or with just a dash of milk, *caffè macchiato*. Black coffee that is not too strong is *caffè lungo*; a *doppio* has an extra kick and a *corretto* has a good measure of alcohol.

Espresso *Cappuccino*

Where to Eat and Drink

Venice

San Marco

Bar all'Angolo €
Enoteca **Map** 6 F2
Campo Santo Stefano 3465, 30124
Tel *041 522 07 10* **Closed** *Sun*
Friendly corner bar offering sandwiches, light meals and salads. Great spot for people-watching over a glass of chilled Prosecco.

Devil's Forest Pub €
Venetian **Map** 7 B1
Calle dei Stagneri 5185, 30124
Tel *041 520 06 23*
A buzzing pub with good-value light meals such as delicious pasta with prawns and pumpkin, served till midnight.

Rosso Pomodoro €
Venetian **Map** 7 C2
Calle Larga San Marco 404, 30124
Tel *041 243 89 49*
Daily menus and set favourites from the Naples area feature mozzarella and local tomatoes. Pizzas are cooked in a wood oven.

Rosticceria San Bartolomeo €
Tavola calda **Map** 7 B1
Calle della Bissa 5424, 30124
Tel *041 522 35 69*
The crowds at Rosticceria San Bartolomeo are a reflection of the excellent food served here. The deep-fried *mozzarella in carrozza* is the house speciality.

Acqua Pazza €€
Mediterranean **Map** 6 F2
Campo Sant'Angelo 3808-10, 32014
Tel *041 277 06 88* **Closed** *Mon; 7 Jan–end Jan*
A winning blend of cuisine with fresh ingredients from the Amalfi Coast and the Campania region is on the menu. There is outdoor seating in the square in summer.

The traditional, elegant interior of Bistrot de Venise

Ai Assassini €€
Venetian **Map** 7 A2
Rio Terrà dei Assassini 3695, 30124
Tel *041 528 79 86* **Closed** *Sun*
The menu at Ai Assassini changes daily, with meat and fish dishes alternating every three days. It uses strictly seasonal produce.

Ai Mercanti €€
Italian **Map** 7 B2
Corte Coppo 4346/a, 30124
Tel *041 523 82 69* **Closed** *Sun; Mon lunch*
Creative Italian and some international dishes are served in cosy premises that expand to a quiet courtyard in the summer at this family-run establishment.

DK Choice

Al Bacareto €€
Venetian **Map** 6 F2
Calle delle Botteghe 3447, 30124
Tel *041 528 93 36* **Closed** *Sun*
This cheerful, family-run *osteria* prides itself on its local dishes such as *baccalà* (salt cod), prepared *mantecato* (creamed), *in umido* (stewed with tomato) or *alla Vicentina* (with polenta). Another traditional dish is *bigoli in salsa* (wholemeal spaghetti with anchovies and onion). An assortment of seafood *antipasti* makes a perfect start to an unforgettable dining experience.

Antico Martini €€
Italian **Map** 7 A2
Campo San Fantin 2007, 30124
Tel *041 522 41 21* **Closed** *7 Jan–end Jan*
This historic luxury restaurant alongside La Fenice theatre boasts high-quality cuisine, a vast wine list, creative dishes and impeccable service. Its terrace enjoys views over the theatre square.

Bar Cavatappi €€
Enoteca **Map** 7 B2
Campo della Guerra 525–526, 30124
Tel *041 296 02 52*
Just a few steps away from Piazza San Marco, this friendly bar serves excellent dishes, such as pumpkin ravioli or *porcini* (cep or mushroom) risotto.

Bistrot de Venise €€
Fine dining **Map** 7 B2
Calle dei Fabbri 4685, 30124
Tel *041 523 66 51*
Traditional Venetian cuisine, as well as innovative dishes based on historic recipes, are served in an elegant setting.

Price Guide
Prices are based on a three-course meal per person, with a half-bottle of house wine, including tax and service.

€	up to €30
€€	€30–€65
€€€	over €65

Extensive choice of wines on display at Osteria Enoteca San Marco

Centrale €€
Italian **Map** 7 A2
Piscina Frezzaria 1659, 30124
Tel *041 241 39 52*
Dishes at this glamourous canalside restaurant range from snacks to full meals accompanied by fine wines. The menu changes daily, but dishes such as lamb shank generally feature. A good place to party.

Da Ivo €€
Venetian **Map** 7 A2
Calle dei Fuseri 1809, 30124
Tel *041 528 50 04* **Closed** *Sun; Jan–early Feb*
Long-established exclusive restaurant located adjacent to a canal. Local seasonal specialities include *moeche* (soft shell crabs). Advance reservation is essential.

Da Raffaele €€
Venetian **Map** 7 A3
Ponte delle Ostreghe 2347, 30124
Tel *041 523 23 17* **Closed** *Thu Nov–Easter*
A well-established Venetian restaurant with romantic canalside seating. Seafood specialities include *granseola* (spider crab) and risotto with scampi and *radicchio* (chicory).

Osteria Da Carla €€
Osteria **Map** 7 B2
Corte Contarina 1535, 30124
Tel *041 523 78 55* **Closed** *Sun*
Squeeze in with the locals to enjoy typical *cicchetti* (bar snacks) or sit down for a meal with seasonal ingredients.

Osteria Enoteca San Marco €€
Enoteca **Map** 7 B2
Frezzeria 1610, 30124
Tel *041 528 52 42* **Closed** *2 weeks mid-Aug, 3 weeks Jan*
This elegant wine bar has an ambitious menu concentrating on regional produce. The wine list favours niche producers.

Ristorante alla Borsa €€
Mediterranean **Map** 7 A2
Calle delle Veste 2018, 30124
Tel *041 523 54 34*
Alla Borsa was named after the former stock exchange nearby. An extensive choice of meat and fish dishes and Italian and international wines are served in refined surroundings.

Alla Caravella €€€
Venetian **Map** 7 A2
Via XXII Marzo 2399, 30124
Tel *041 520 89 01*
Sophisticated versions of local meat and fish dishes are served at this well-reputed stylish restaurant decked out like a caravel sailing ship.

Do Forni €€€
Fine dining **Map** 7 B2
Calle Specchieri 468, 30124
Tel *041 523 21 48*
This prize winning elegant restaurant boasts a long list of celebrity guests. The menu features seasonal specialities and an extensive wine list.

Grand Canal €€€
Fine dining **Map** 7 B3
Calle Vallaresso 1332, 30124
Tel *041 520 02 11*
Part of the Hotel Monaco *(see p232)*, Grand Canal offers stylish dining year round. The extensive menu features Venetian cuisine, fresh pasta and meat and fish dishes. There is a summer terrace.

Harry's Bar €€€
Fine dining **Map** 7 B3
Calle Vallaresso 1323, 30124
Tel *041 528 57 77*
Once Hemingway's cosy watering hole, Harry's Bar is an international landmark today. Serves coffee and sandwiches, as well as the Bellini cocktail and *carpaccio*, both of which were invented here.

Ristorante Quadri €€€
Italian **Map** 7 B2
Piazza San Marco 1/f, 30124
Tel *041 522 21 05* **Closed** *Mon*
Inventive takes on traditional Venetian and regional cuisine have earned this restaurant a Michelin star. Tables look onto the square.

San Polo

Al Nono Risorto €
Pizzeria **Map** 2 F5
Sottoportego di Sior Bettina 2337, 30135
Tel *041 524 11 69* **Closed** *Wed; Thu lunch*
A lively and popular pizzeria, Al Nono Risorto has a shady courtyard for summer dining. Advance booking is recommended.

Impronta Café €
Enoteca **Map** 6 D2
Crosera San Pantalon 3814, 30123
Tel *041 275 03 86* **Closed** *Sun*
This trendy wine bar is open until late. Order a glass of wine, a coffee or a plate of pasta or salad.

Dona Onesta €€
Trattoria **Map** 6 D2
Calle Larga Foscari 3922, 30123
Tel *041 71 05 86*
This old-style canalside restaurant serves traditional Venetian fare at affordable prices. Convivial atmosphere and helpful staff.

Osteria alla Patatina €€
Osteria **Map** 6 E1
Ponte San Polo 2741/a, 30123
Tel *041 523 72 38* **Closed** *Sun*
Delicious battered vegetables and creamy *baccalà* appetizers can be eaten at the bar or as part of a full meal at one of the tables.

Poste Vecie €€
Fine dining **Map** 3 A5
Rialto Pescheria 1608, 30125
Tel *041 72 18 22* **Closed** *Tue*
Dating back to the 1500s, this claims to be the oldest restaurant in the city. Home-made pasta and fresh fish abound on the menu.

Trattoria alla Madonna €€
Trattoria **Map** 7 A1
Calle della Madonna 594, 30123
Tel *041 522 38 24* **Closed** *Wed; 3 weeks Jan*
This well-known, bustling restaurant is the perfect place for traditional seafood and fish such as delicate *granseola* (spider crab) or *seppie in nero* (squid in black ink sauce). The seafood risotto is a speciality. Diners often queue up outside.

DK Choice

Antiche Carampane €€€
Venetian **Map** 2 F5
Rio Terà Carampane 1911, 30125
Tel *041 524 01 65* **Closed** *Sun & Mon; 2 wks Jan; end Jul–mid-Aug*
This local favourite offers a memorable dining experience, with a wide variety of fresh seafood, great pasta and seasonal vegetables served simply. The seafood stir-fry is a must have. Other highlights include spaghetti with crab, seabass served with a pepper sauce and tagliatelle with duck ragut. A little difficult to locate, but worth it. Booking ahead is essential.

Centrale's stylish modern interior

Da Fiore €€€
Fine dining **Map** 2 E5
Calle del Scalater 2202, 30125
Tel *041 72 13 08* **Closed** *Sun; Mon; 2 weeks Aug*
The exclusive Da Fiore is possibly one of the best restaurants in Venice. Excellent use of seasonal produce has made this hidden gem a gourmet heaven.

Santa Croce

Al Prosecco €
Enoteca **Map** 2 E5
Campo San Giacomo dell'Orio 1503, 30135
Tel *041 524 02 22* **Closed** *Sun*
A bar serving regional cheeses and simple meals to accompany a great range of wines. Summer seating in a shady square.

Antica Bessetta €€
Venetian **Map** 2 D5
Salizzada Ca' Zusto 1395, 30135
Tel *041 72 16 87* **Closed** *Tue; Wed lunch*
Tiny, historic restaurant specializing in beautifully presented traditional dishes including *spaghetti allo scoglio* (pasta with crustaceans).

Il Rèfolo €€
Pizzeria **Map** 2 E5
Campo del Piovan 1459, 30135
Tel *041 524 00 16* **Closed** *Dec–Jan; Mon; Tue lunch*
Gourmet pizzas with innovative flavour combinations and simple pasta dishes are served in a pretty canalside square.

La Zucca €€
Italian **Map** 2 E5
Calle del Megio 1762, 30135
Tel *041 524 15 70* **Closed** *Sun; 25 Dec*
A favourite with visitors and locals alike, this restaurant specializes in a range of flavoursome vegetarian dishes. There are also meat options. Booking ahead is recommended.

Castello

L'Olandese Volante €
Osteria **Map** 7 B1
Campo San Lio 5658, 30122
Tel *041 528 93 49* **Closed** *Sun breakfast*
Tuck into a freshly made roll or a light meal, or relax with an evening drink at this casual pub in a neighbourhood square. .

Trattoria Giorgione €
Trattoria **Map** 8 F3
Via Garibaldi 1533, 30122
Tel *041 522 87 27* **Closed** *Wed*
Friendly neighbourhood *trattoria* that serves authentic flavoursome meals. The owner Lucio entertains guests with live folk music after dinner.

The façade of the cosy, family-run Da Remigio

Aciugheta €€
Osteria **Map** 7 C2
Campo SS Filippo e Giacomo 4357, 30122
Tel *041 522 42 92*
Pasta, salads or freshly baked miniature pizzas with anchovies, accompanied by an apéritif, can be enjoyed inside or outside in the pleasant square.

Al Mascaron €€
Osteria **Map** 7 C1
Calle Lunga Santa Maria Formosa 5225, 30122
Tel *041 522 59 95* **Closed** *Sun;* mid-Dec–mid-Jan
It is advisable to book well ahead for this cramped but lively old-style *osteria*. Wash down memorable pasta and fish dishes with glasses of house wine.

DK Choice

Alla Rivetta €€
Trattoria **Map** 7 C2
Ponte San Provolo 4625, 30122
Tel *041 528 73 02* **Closed** *Mon*
The tiny Alla Rivetta, located next to a bridge, serves Venetian-style, mouthwatering dishes of seasonal fish and seafood, including *canoce* (mantis shrimp) and *folpetti* (octopus and celery). It is extremely popular with locals, including gondoliers, and fills up quickly. Book ahead or be prepared to share a table.

Bacarando Ai Corazzieri €€
Venetian **Map** 8 E2
Calle dei Corazzieri 3839, 30122
Tel *041 528 98 59*
Superb meat dishes and a great selection of cheeses and wines feature on the menu here. Alfresco dining in summer, friendly service and occassional live music.

Da Remigio €€
Venetian **Map** 8 D2
Salizzada dei Greci 3416, 30122
Tel *041 523 00 89* **Closed** *Mon dinner; Tue; 20 Dec–20 Jan*
Enjoy superb seafood at this family-run *trattoria*. The *risotto di pesce* (fish risotto) is a menu highlight. Very popular with Venetians so book ahead.

Al Covo €€€
Fine dining **Map** 8 E2
Campiello della Pescaria 3968, 30122
Tel *041 522 38 12* **Closed** *Wed & Thu*
This place is a hidden gem run by a husband-and-wife team. Chef Cesare focuses on excellent fish dishes. Leave room for one of Diane's delicious desserts.

MET €€€
Fine dining **Map** 8 E2
Riva degli Schiavoni 4149, 30122
Tel *041 520 50 44* **Closed** *Mon; Tue–Fri lunch*
This sophisticated Michelin-starred restaurant belongs to the lagoon-front Hotel Metropole *(see p233)*.The menu features great meat and fish dishes.

Osteria Santa Marina €€€
Italian **Map** 3 B5
Campo Santa Marina 5911, 30122
Tel *041 528 52 39* **Closed** *Sun; Mon lunch; 2 weeks Jan*
A well-reputed friendly restaurant, Osteria Santa Marina serves creative versions of Venetian and Italian fare. Excellent home-made pasta is a highlight. Candlelit dining outside in summer.

Il Ridotto €€€
Fine dining **Map** 7 C2
Campo SS Filippo e Giacomo 4509, 30122
Tel *041 520 82 80* **Closed** *Thu lunch*
Small restaurant that serves excellent Italian fish and meat dishes. The lunchtime set menu is a bargain.

For key to prices *see p242*

Dorsoduro

Pizzeria ae Oche €
Pizzeria **Map** 6 E4
Fondamenta Zattere 1414, 30123
Tel *041 520 66 01*
This lively, friendly pizzeria offers a vast selection of pizzas as well as salads, pastas and meat dishes at reasonable prices. In summer tables are set up along the Zattere waterfront.

Agli Alboretti €€
Venetian **Map** 6 E4
Rio Terrà Foscarini 882, 30123
Tel *041 522 99 37* **Closed** *Wed dinner; Thu; 20 days Jan; 10 days Aug*
Excellent Venetian fare including fresh ravioli with *branzino* (sea bass) and pumpkin cream. The *antipasto misto* features an array of delicious seafood.

Ai Gondolieri €€
Venetian **Map** 6 F4
San Vio 366, 30123
Tel *041 528 63 96* **Closed** *Tue*
Fine Italian wines accompany a superb menu of seasonal local vegetables such as baby purple artichokes and Treviso *radicchio*. Excellent meat dishes, too.

Cantinone Storico €€
Trattoria **Map** 6 E4
Fondamenta Bragadin 660, 30123
Tel *041 523 95 77*
This *trattoria* boasts a cavernous wine cellar and a lovely canalside setting. Try the signature *gran fritto reale* (mixed fried fish) or the always excellent risotto of the day.

Ristoteca Oniga €€
Trattoria-Enoteca **Map** 6 D3
Campo San Barnaba 2852, 30123
Tel *041 522 44 10* **Closed** *Tue Jan–Feb*
A great spot for people-watching with tables in the square. Well-presented meat and fish dishes are served with a choice of more than 150 different wines.

Diners enjoying the convivial atmosphere of Paradiso Perduto

La Rivista €€
Enoteca **Map** 6 E4
Rio Terrà Foscarini 979/a, 30123
Tel *041 240 14 25* **Closed** *Mon*
This wine bar with modern sophisticated decor serves light salads and cold platters of cheeses and meats. Charming outdoor terrace as well.

Taverna San Trovaso €€
Trattoria **Map** 6 E3
Fondamenta Priuli 1016, 30123
Tel *041 520 37 03*
Popular bustling restaurant with reliable service and tasty fish, meat and pizza dishes. Booking is recommended.

Lineadombra €€€
Italian **Map** 6 F7
Ponte dell'Umiltà 19, 30123
Tel *041 241 18 81* **Closed** *End Nov–Jan; Tue Nov & Feb–Apr*
Modern twists to Venetian cuisine are served in the bright interior or on the waterfront terrace at Lineadombra. Excellent French and Italian wines.

Osteria Da Codruma €€€
Osteria **Map** 5 C3
Fondamenta Briati 2540, 30123
Tel *041 524 67 89* **Closed** *Sun & Mon*
Cosy venue serving traditional Venetian fare. The seafood platter is particularly good. Excellent wine list.

Ristorante La Riviera €€€
Italian **Map** 6 E4
Zattere al Ponte Lungo 1473, 30123
Tel *041 522 76 21* **Closed** *Mon*
Creative Italian fare such as ricotta-filled pasta with *borlotti* beans and crunchy *guanciale* bacon is on the menu here. Romantic seating on the waterfront.

Cannaregio

Brek €
Tavola calda **Map** 2 D4
Lista di Spagna 124, 30121
Tel *041 244 01 58*
This self-service restaurant offers freshly made meals all day long. Meat, pasta, rolls and desserts to eat in or take away. Excellent value.

Da Marisa €
Trattoria **Map** 1 C3
Fondamenta di San Giobbe 652, 30121
Tel *041 72 02 11* **Closed** *Sun, Mon & Wed lunch; 2 weeks Aug*
Huge servings of fried fish, seafood and meat are served in this locally renowned down-to-earth *trattoria*. The menu changes daily. Booking is essential.

Orient Experience €
Middle Eastern **Map** 2 E3
Rio Terà Farsetti 1847/b, 30121
Tel *041 822 69 19*
Take away or sit and enjoy appetizing mounds of spicy Asian and Middle Eastern food. Live music gigs take place regularly here.

La Cantina €€
Enoteca **Map** 2 F4
Strada Nuova 3689, 30121
Tel *041 522 82 58* **Closed** *Sun; first 2 weeks Aug; 2 weeks Jan*
Cosy wine bar with outdoor tables for people-watching. Mouthwatering snacks and seafood, meat and cheese dishes are prepared to order.

Ostaria Boccadoro €€
Venetian **Map** 3 C4
Campo Widmann 5405, 30121
Tel *041 5211021* **Closed** *Mon Oct–Apr; 2 weeks Jan*
Creative pasta dishes and delicate blends of seafood and seasonal vegetables are on offer here, as well as superb chocolate desserts and a good wine list. There is a vine-clad pergola for romantic outdoor dining.

Osteria Giorgione €€
Venetian **Map** 3 B4
Calle Larga dei Proverbi 4582/a, 30121
Tel *041 522 17 25* **Closed** *Mon*
Cosy refined restaurant serving seasonal fish specialities such as *seppie in nero* (cuttlefish in black sauce). Good wine list.

DK Choice

Paradiso Perduto €€
Mediterranean **Map** 2 F3
Fondamenta Misericordia 2540, 30121
Tel *041 72 05 81* **Closed** *Tue & Wed*
This atmospheric neighbourhood *osteria* and watering hole next to a canal is a Venetian institution. The affable owner-chef Maurizio brings fresh fish from the Rialto Markets every morning. Also to be enjoyed are the home-made pasta, excellent house wine and plenty of live music. Booking is essential.

Trattoria Da Gigio €€
Trattoria **Map** 2 D3
Rio Terrà San Leonardo 1594, 30121
Tel *041 71 75 74* **Closed** *Sun; Mon dinner*
Huge fillet steaks, grilled fish and an *antipasto misto*, consisting of a tempting selection of fresh seafood, feature here. Friendly service and a pleasant summer garden.

For more information on types of restaurants *see pp236–7*

Works of art adorning the walls of Da Romano

Vini Da Gigio €€
Venetian **Map** 3 A4
Fondamenta San Felice 3628/a, 30121
Tel *041 528 51 40* **Closed** *Mon & Tue; 2 weeks Jan; 2 weeks Aug*
Well-established canalside restaurant serving innovative versions of traditional dishes. Try the *tagliata di tonno* (fresh tuna with sesame) and *agnello* (lamb).

Fiaschetteria Toscana €€€
Fine dining **Map** 3 B5
Salizzada San Giovanni Grisostomo 5719, 30121
Tel *041 528 52 81* **Closed** *Tue; Wed lunch; 1 week Dec; 2 weeks Jul–Aug*
One of Venice's leading restaurants. Ask for the day's specialities, and leave room for one of Signora Mariuccia's desserts. Book ahead.

Osteria Orto dei Mori €€€
Mediterranean **Map** 2 F3
Campo dei Mori 3386, 30121
Tel *041 524 36 77* **Closed** *Tue; 1 week Jul*
Delicious meals are served in warm interiors or alfresco in one of the city's prettiest squares. The menu changes with the seasons and features exquisite desserts.

The Lagoon Islands

Ai Pescatori €€
Venetian
Via Galuppi 371, Burano, 30012
Tel *041 73 06 50* **Closed** *Tue; Jan*
Delicate seafood soup, risotto with fish and a host of grilled and baked fish dishes and seasonal vegetables are on the menu at Al Pescatori.

DK Choice

Da Romano €€
Fine dining
Via Galuppi 221, 30012, Burano
Tel *041 73 00 30* **Closed** *Sun dinner; Tue; Jan*
Burano's leading restaurant, Da Romano is especially popular with artists, and paintings by many of its patrons crowd the walls. The fresh seafood is prepared in traditional Venetian fashion under the watchful eye of the Barbaro family, who have owned this establishment since the 19th century. Top-quality wines accompany the highly memorable meals. Advance reservation is essential.

Figli delle Stelle €€
Italian
Fondamenta della Croce 70–71, Giudecca, 30133
Tel *041 523 00 04* **Closed** *Jan–Feb*
At Figli delle Stelle inventive takes on Puglian and Venetian cuisine are served in casual light-filled premises with splendid waterside seating.

La Perla Ai Bisatei €€
Trattoria
Campo San Bernardo, Murano, 30141
Tel *041 73 95 28* **Closed** *Wed; dinner daily*
This no-frills restaurant, which is hugely popular with the locals, serves delicious regional fish dishes, seafood risotto and classic meat dishes in pleasant and friendly surroundings.

Trattoria Alla Maddalena €€
Trattoria
Fondamenta di Santa Caterina 7/b, Mazzorbo, 30142
Tel *041 73 01 51* **Closed** *Thu*
Pretty canalside *trattoria* with a delightful summer garden. This traditional place specializes in fish, though meat is on the menu as well.

Trattoria Busa alla Torre da Lele €€
Venetian
Campo Santo Stefano 3, Murano, 30141
Tel *041 73 96 62* **Closed** *dinner daily (except Fri & Sat May–Sep)*
Friendly restaurant in a pretty neighbourhood square. Innovative fish and vegetable dishes, as well as memorable desserts are on the menu.

Cip's Club €€€
Fine dining
Giudecca 10, Giudecca, 30133
Tel *041 24 08 01* **Closed** *Nov–Mar; lunch daily*
Part of Hotel Cipriani *(see p234)*, Cip's Club has a canalfront terrace and elegant interiors. Seasonal produce and seafood are used to make up inventive dishes. Book ahead.

Harry's Dolci €€€
Fine dining
Fondamenta San Biagio 773, Giudecca, 30133
Tel *041 522 48 44* **Closed** *Nov–Easter; Mon dinner; Tue*
This elegant restaurant serves delicious meals, Bellini cocktails, pastries and ice cream on a charming waterfront veranda.

Locanda Cipriani €€€
Fine dining
Piazza Santa Fosca 29, Torcello, 30012
Tel *041 73 01 50* **Closed** *Tue; early Jan–mid-Feb*
Refined cuisine, featuring home-grown vegetables and creatively prepared fish and meat, is served at the exclusive Locanda Cipriani. The desserts are heavenly. There is also an attractive garden.

Venissa €€€
Italian
Fondamenta Santa Caterina 3, 30142, Mazzorbo
Tel *041 527 22 81* **Closed** *Nov–Mar; Tue*
This country-style island restaurant has been awarded a Michelin star. Locally produced wines accompany the simple, delicious dishes made with locally sourced seasonal ingredients.

For key to prices *see p242*

The Veneto Plain

ARQUÀ PETRARCA: La Montanella €€
Regional
Via dei Carraresi 9, 35032
Tel *042 971 82 00* **Closed** *Tue dinner; Wed; Jan*
Set in the Euganean Hills, La Montanella uses local olive oil and mushrooms in its recipes. Try the *pappardelle* pasta and the desserts made with chestnuts.

ASOLO: Al Sole €€
Italian
Via Collegio 33, 31011
Tel *042 395 13 32* **Closed** *Sun Nov–Easter; lunch in low season*
Enjoy creative blends of *radicchio*, beans, meat and seafood on a charming terrace at Al Sole.

ASOLO: Villa Cipriani €€€
Fine dining
Via Canova 298, 31011
Tel *042 352 34 11*
Part of a grand hotel, this restaurant looks over magnificent gardens and serves creative Italian and regional cuisine using locally sourced produce.

BASSANO DEL GRAPPA: Osteria Trinità €
Osteria
Via Contrà San Giorgio 17, 36061
Tel *042 450 37 00* **Closed** *Thu; Sat lunch*
Cosy, smart Veneto *osteria* that specializes in grilled meats and wines. Leave room for a dessert from the mouthwatering trolley display.

BASSANO DEL GRAPPA: Antico Ristorante Cardellino €€
Regional
Via Bellavitis 17, 36061
Tel *042 422 01 44* **Closed** *Thu*
This restaurant has a seasonal menu. In spring, local white asparagus is served with tagliatelle ribbon pasta, in flans or in the traditional way with hard-boiled eggs.

CAORLE: Duilio €€
Regional
Via Strada Nuova 19, 30021
Tel *042 18 10 87* **Closed** *Mon in low season*
This hotel restaurant has a vast choice of fresh seafood dishes such as exquisite grilled sole.

CASTELFRANCO: Alla Torre €
Pizzeria
Piazza XXIV Maggio 2/4, 31033
Tel *042 349 54 45*
Huge choice of pasta, grilled meat and desserts are on offer here. Pizzas are cooked in a wood-fired oven.

Patrons dining beneath the brickwork arches at El Gato

CHIOGGIA: El Gato €€
Italian
Corso del Popolo 653, 30015
Tel *041 40 02 65* **Closed** *Mon*
A bright dining room is the venue for cuisine based on fresh fish and seafood. Try the calamari stuffed with vegetables and served with creamed pumpkin.

CONEGLIANO: Al Salisa €€
Trattoria
Via XX Settembre 2/4, 31015
Tel *043 82 42 88* **Closed** *Wed & Thu lunch*
Elegant *trattoria* with a pretty veranda for alfresco dining in summer. The regional menu includes *lumache* (snails) and vegetarian sauces.

DOLO: Osteria da Caronte €€
Regional
Via Dolo 29, Paluello di Stra, 30039
Tel *041 41 20 91* **Closed** *Tue dinner; Wed; 2 weeks mid-Aug*
Friendly country *osteria* with dishes featuring seasonal produce prepared with an innovative touch. Excellent value.

DOLO: Villa Goetzen €€
Italian
Via Matteotti 2/c, 30031
Tel *041 510 23 00* **Closed** *Sun dinner; Thu; 3 weeks Aug*
Part of a boutique hotel housed in an 18th-century villa, this charming riverside restaurant specializes in fish dishes. Do not miss the home-made desserts.

DOLO: Villa Nani Mocenigo €€
Fine dining
Riviera Martiri della Libertà 113, 30031
Tel *041 560 81 39* **Closed** *Mon; Tue dinner*
Delicious risottos and seafood are served in this splendid villa setting. There is also an *enoteca* in the former stables.

GRANCONA: Da Isetta €€
Trattoria
Via Pederiva 96, 36040
Tel *044 488 95 21* **Closed** *Tue dinner; Wed*
Located in the Berici hills, this welcoming, family-run *trattoria* specializes in dishes with polenta, chestnuts, mushrooms, steaks and a long list of mouthwatering desserts, including tangy sorbets.

NOVENTA PADOVANA: Boccadoro €€
Regional
Via della Resistenza 49, 35027
Tel *049 62 50 29* **Closed** *Wed*
This well-established family-run restaurant has an excellent reputation for Paduan cuisine such as *bigoli* pasta. There is an impressive wine list and excellent service.

PADUA: Ristorante Antico Brolo €€
Osteria
Corso Milano 22, 35139
Tel *049 66 45 55* **Closed** *Mon lunch; 1 week mid-Aug*
Sample traditional *osteria* fare such as *polpette* (meatballs) and tripe, as well as creative Italian cuisine, at Brolo. Large salads and a range of pizzas are also on the menu. Vegetarians are well catered for.

PADUA: Vecchia Padova €€
Tavola calda-Pizzeria
Via Cesare Battisti 41, 35100
Tel *049 875 96 80* **Closed** *Mon; 2 weeks Aug*
Delicious pizza and a huge choice of pasta and meat dishes can be enjoyed at this bustling venue. The seafood is also excellent and there is a lunch buffet menu available. Great value for money.

Villa Ciprani's elegant dining room overlooking beautiful landscaped gardens

For more information on types of restaurants *see pp236–7*

REFRONTOLO: Antica Osteria al Forno €€
Regional
Via degli Alpini 5, 31020
Tel *043 889 44 96* **Closed** *Mon; Tue; Wed & Thu dinner; 3 weeks Jan; 3 weeks Aug*
Rustic yet homely *osteria* run by a friendly couple. Locally grown vegetables and herbs, as well as organic wines and Prosecco feature on the menu.

SARMEOLA DI RUBANO: Le Calandre €€€
Italian
Via Liguria 1, 35030
Tel *049 63 03 03* **Closed** *Sun, Mon & Tue lunch; 2 weeks Jan; 2 weeks Aug*
This renowned restaurant has been awarded three Michelin stars thanks to chef Max's creative cooking. The lavishly presented dishes are served in a contemporary setting. Reserve ahead.

TREVISO: Ristorante Beccherie €€
Regional
Piazza Ancilotto 9, 31100
Tel *042 254 08 71*
Set in an amospheric old building, Beccherie whips up traditional Treviso dishes such as guinea fowl in pepper sauce. Leave room for dessert – *tiramisù* was invented here!

DK Choice

TREVISO: Toni del Spin €€
Trattoria
Via Inferiore 7, 31100
Tel *042 254 38 29* **Closed** *Mon lunch; 2–3 weeks end Jul–Aug*
This wonderful *trattoria* is crammed with people, paintings and memorable food. A blackboard lists the seasonally changing menu. Highlights include *pasta e fagioli* (pasta and bean soup), rabbit with olives, veal with local *radicchio* and desserts galore. Book ahead.

VALDOBBIADENE: Bar Alpino €
Enoteca
Via Mazzolini 14, 31049
Tel *0423 98 21 18* **Closed** *Wed*
A range of seafood, cheeses and meats are served here to accompany choice wines from the surrounding hills, such as Prosecco.

VENEGAZZU: Trattoria Da Celeste €€€
Regional
Via Diaz 12, 31040
Tel *042 362 04 45* **Closed** *Mon dinner; Tue*
A well-loved traditional restaurant with a vast wine list. Choose from a range of grilled meats and seasonal delicacies including delicious mushrooms, asparagus and *radicchio* (chicory) Excellent service.

VICENZA: Antica Casa della Malvasia €
Enoteca
Contrà Morette 5, 36100
Tel *044 454 37 04* **Closed** *Mon; last 2 weeks Jul*
In the heart of historic Vicenza, this bustling friendly *osteria* is a favourite with the locals and has an imaginative menu with local specialities such as *bigoli all'arna* (spaghetti with duck sauce).

VICENZA: Antico Guelfo €€
Regional
Contrà Pedemuro San Biagio 92, 36100
Tel *044 454 78 97* **Closed** *Tue; Sun dinner*
This upmarket restaurant offers more than the usual fare, with both *kamut* and *quinoa* (ancient grains) on the menu. Choose from an eclectic mix of traditional Veneto and modern dishes. Very popular, so book ahead

Verona and Lake Garda

BOSCOCHIESANUOVA: Locanda Maregge €
Trattoria
Località Maregge 1, 37021
Tel *045 705 00 63* **Closed** *Thu*
This friendly roadside *trattoria* in the Lessini hills specializes in polenta with *grigliata mista* (mixed grilled meat) and gnocchi with local *malga* cheese.

GARDA: Locanda San Vigilio €€€
Fine dining
Punta San Vigilio, 37016
Tel *045 725 66 88* **Closed** *mid-Nov–Mar*
Part of the beautiful lakeside hotel *(see p235)*, this superb restaurant serves traditional cuisine. A signature dish is grilled fish seasoned with local olive oil. There is a buffet lunch in the garden courtyard in summer and candlelit dining in the evening.

ISOLA DELLA SCALA: Risotteria Melotti €
Risotteria
Piazza Martiri della Libertà, 37063
Tel *045 730 02 36* **Closed** *Tue; 3 weeks Aug*
Nestled among rice fields, this risotto heaven has over 20 varieties on offer daily, along with rice-based entrées and desserts. Advance booking recommended.

MALCESINE: Ristorante La Pace €€
Regional
Via Casella 1, 37018
Tel *045 740 00 57*
Enjoy grilled lake fish and fresh home-made pasta in a tiny waterfront square at the picturesque old harbour. Book ahead in summer.

RIVA DI GARDA: Osteria Il Gallo €
Trattoria
Piazza San Rocco 12, 38066
Tel *046 455 62 00* **Closed** *Jan; Mon–Fri lunch Nov–Feb*
Friendly, good-value *trattoria* with a huge choice of local Trentino specialities such as *carne salada con fasoi* (cured meat with beans).

The minimalist monochromatic decor of Le Calandre

Large selection of wines at Ristorante Taverna

SANT'ANNA DI ALFAEDO: Ponte di Veja €
Regional
Ponte di Veja, 37020
Tel *045 754 50 48* **Closed** *Tue except in summer*
This bustling rustic eatery serves grilled meat, *polenta con soppressa* (thick sausage) and game dishes.

SIRMIONE: Antica Trattoria La Speranzina €€€
Italian
Via Dante 16, 25019
Tel *030 990 62 92* **Closed** *Mon Nov–Mar*
Romantic terraces overlook the lake at this *trattoria*. The refined creative cuisine includes *tagliolini all'astice* (thin ribbon pasta with crayfish). The desserts are divine.

TORRI DEL BENACO: Gardesana €€€
Fine dining
Piazza Calderini 5, 37010
Tel *045 722 54 11* **Closed** *Tue*
The Gardesana serves fish and meat dishes in a romantic lakefront setting. Try the *carpaccio di tonno affumicato* (thin-sliced smoked tuna).

VALEGGIO SUL MINCIO: Antica Locanda Mincio €€
Regional
Via Michelangelo Buonarroti 12, 37067
Tel *045 795 00 59* **Closed** *Wed; Thu; 2 weeks Nov; 2 weeks Feb*
Formerly a staging post, this delightful restaurant features a frescoed dining room and shaded tables that overlook the river. The lake fish and eel are specialities.

VERONA: Arche €€
Trattoria
Via Arche Scaligere 6, 37121
Tel *045 800 74 15* **Closed** *Sun; Mon lunch; 2 weeks Jan*
Established in 1877, this is one of the best restaurants in Verona. Fish features prominently on the menu.

VERONA: Ristorante Castelvecchio €€
Regional
Corso Castelvecchio 21/a, 37121
Tel *045 803 00 97* **Closed** *Tue; Wed lunch; Aug*
A warm, well-established restaurant specializing in Verona cuisine such as Risotto all'Amarone and liver dishes. There are good vegetarian options and an impressive wine list.

DK Choice

VERONA: Ristorante Greppia €€
Regional
Vicolo Samaritana 3, 37121
Tel *045 800 45 77* **Closed** *Mon*
Run by the Guizzardi family since 1975, this warm and inviting restaurant is named after a feeding trough. Diners who go for the Verona signature dish *bollito misto* are treated to a spectacular trolley of steaming meats and attendant sauces (starting with the *pearà* – pepper sauce), served with great flourish at their table.

VERONA: Il Desco €€€
Italian
Via Dietro San Sebastiano 5-7, 37121
Tel *045 59 53 58* **Closed** *Sun & Mon (open Mon dinner July, Aug & Dec)*
This Michelin-starred restaurant run by a father-and-son team is set in a 16th-century *palazzo*. The imaginative menus change with the seasons.

The Dolomites

BELLUNO: Ristorante Taverna €
Trattoria
Via Cipro 7, 32100
Tel *0437 251 92* **Closed** *Sun; 1 week Jan; 2 weeks Jun–Jul*
Popular restaurant that specializes in grilled meat, game and *schiz*, a local cheese baked in the oven.

BELLUNO: Terracotta €€
Italian
Borgo Garibaldi 61, 32100
Tel *0437 29 16 92* **Closed** *Tue; Wed lunch*
Friendly family-run restaurant serving seasonal specialities, which include venison, snails and pumpkin-filled ravioli. Excellent wine list.

CORTINA D'AMPEZZO: Pizzeria Ristorante Croda Cafè €
Pizzeria
Piazza Pittori Fratelli Ghedina 28, 32043
Tel *0436 86 65 89* **Closed** *Tue*
Choose from pizzas, good-value pasta and local dishes such as *polenta con funghi* (mushrooms) at this restaurant. The *frutti di bosco* (summer berries) with ice cream is a perfect dessert.

CORTINA D'AMPEZZO: Baita Fraina €€
Regional
Fraina 1, 32043
Tel *0436 36 34* **Closed** *Mon in low season; mid-Apr–mid–Jun; Oct; Nov*
Enjoy traditional *casunzièi* (home-made pasta with beetroot), hearty soups and flavoursome roast meats at this Alpine chalet with a convivial, family atmosphere and fabulous views of the Dolomites.

DK Choice

CORTINA D'AMPEZZO: El Zoco €€
Regional
Località Cademai 18, 32043
Tel *0436 86 00 41* **Closed** *Lunch daily & Mon in low season*
This romantic restaurant lined with old wood panelling is run by an attentive wine expert who is always at hand to present the menu and suggest suitable wines. The chef serves up generous portions of hearty Italian mountain fare such as *canederli* (dumplings), *ciaspes* (pasta au gratin), delicate paté and game. Excellent value for money.

NEVEGAL: Ristorante La Casera €
Regional
Via Faverghera 752, 32100
Tel *0437 90 81 80* **Closed** *Mon*
Perched high on Col Visentin, this rustic mountain restaurant offers sweeping panoramic views and a traditional menu that focuses on delicious grilled meats and polenta. Advance reservation is recommended.

For more information on types of restaurants *see pp236–7*

Bars and Cafés in Venice

Many bars in Venice draw their trade from tourists and are busy throughout the day, as visitors ease their aching feet and consult their guidebooks. Custom is swelled mid-morning and around lunchtime as the Venetians drop in for a drink or snack. Cafés range from basic one-room bars patronized by local workmen, to opulent coffeehouses in old-world style, such as Caffè Quadri and Caffè Florian. Even the humblest establishment provides a continuous range of refreshments and you can enjoy anything from a morning coffee or lunchtime beer, to an apéritif or a final brandy before bed. Bars also serve snacks throughout their opening hours: freshly baked morning pastries and lunchtime sandwiches, rolls, cakes, biscuits and sometimes home-made ice cream. Wine bars often have a wide range of traditional Venetian snacks, and so make good places to stop for lunch.

Bars

Italians will often stop for breakfast in a bar on their way to work.This normally consists of a *cappuccino* (milky coffee) and a *brioche* (a plain, jam- or cream-filled pastry). **Pasticceria Dal Mas**, on the main route from the station to the Rialto, is much favoured by early-morning commuters.

A wide range of alcoholic drinks is on offer, and you can ask for a glass of wine or beer on tap. Beer from the keg is called *birra alla spina* and comes in three different sizes: *piccola, media* and *grande*. Italian and imported bottled beers are also available, though the latter can be expensive. All bars serve glasses of mineral water and it is acceptable to request a glass of tap water *(acqua del rubinetto)*, which will be free. Most bars also serve delicious freshly squeezed fruit juices *(una spremuta)* and milkshakes made with fruit *(un frullato)*. Italian bottled juices are good and are available in unusual flavours such as apricot and pear.

All bars serve a range of sandwiches *(tramezzini)* and filled rolls *(panini)*, and often have toasted sandwiches and pizzas as well. Some double as cake shops *(pasticceria)*, and these have a tempting range of calorie-filled delights on display to eat in or take away. If you are near the Accademia, seek out the tiny **Bar Pasticceria Vio** for wonderful cakes, or for an expensive treat, go to **Harry's Dolci** on the Giudecca *(see p246)*.

Bear in mind that sitting down to drink in a bar or café can cost a lot more than standing at the bar, as there is a table charge, which can be high. This rises proportionally as you draw nearer San Marco. Some bars, particularly in the less tourist-frequented areas, have a stand-up counter only. All have a lavatory *(il bagno* or *il gabinetto)*, though you may have to ask at the desk for the key. It is also worth noting that bars and cafés tend to shut earlier here than in other parts of Italy, particularly in winter.

The normal procedure is to choose what you want to eat or drink, then ask for it and pay at the cash desk. You will be given a receipt *(lo scontrino)* which you present at the bar. If they are busy, a small tip will usually speed things up. If you decide to sit down, either inside or at an outside table, your order will be taken by a waiter who will bring the bill when he delivers the drinks. You should expect to pay double or more for this, but you can stretch your drink out for as long as you like.

Wine Bars

There is an old tradition in Venice called *cichetti e l'ombra*, meaning "a little bite and the shade". The little bite ranges from a slice of bread and *prosciutto crudo* (raw cured ham), meatballs or fried vegetables, to sardines and *baccalà* (salt cod). The shade is a glass of wine, so called because the gondoliers used to snatch a glass in the shade away from the glare of the sun on the water. Wine bars serving these snacks and a range of wines are numerous and heavily populated by locals. Many, such as **Do Mori**, are in the crowded alleys off the Rialto, but one of the nicest is the **Cantina del Vino già Schiavi** near the Ponte San Trovaso.

Cafés and Ice-Cream Parlours

Coffeehouses have played their part in the history of the Veneto – notably Padua's Caffè Pedrocchi *(see p182)* – and a visit to Venice would not be complete without a drink at the historic **Caffè Florian** or **Caffè Quadri**. It is a hard decision whether to take a table outside and watch the crowds or to experience the elegant charm of the interior rooms, with their atmosphere of past eras. The prices are sky-high, but you can take your time and be entertained by the resident orchestras.

Harry's Bar *(see p96)*, is another world-famous bar and café. In summer it is crammed with foreigners and the prices are always high, but for a treat, sip a Bellini, a mixture of Prosecco and fresh white peach juice, in the place where it was invented.

The cafés along the Zattere, with their lovely views across the Giudecca Canal, make good places to pause, and the prices are much lower. Many Venetian squares have cafés with tables outside. There are several in the Campo Santo Stefano, or try **Bar Colleoni** in Campo Santi Giovanni e Paolo (San Zanipolo). **Il Caffè** is the nicest in Campo Santa Margherita.

Venetian ice cream is definitely among the best in

Italy, with ice-cream shops *(gelaterie)* serving a wide selection of seasonal flavours, some unique to Venice. The Venetians eat ice cream all year round, often instead of pudding or as the finale to the evening stroll, or *passeggiata*. It comes as either a cone *(un cono)* or a cup *(una coppa)* and it is normal to have at least two flavours. **Paolin** on Campo Santo Stefano is one of the best ice-cream shops. You could also try **Il Doge**, which is in Campo Santa Margherita, and **Nico** on the Zattere, where you will find *gianduiotto*, a rich chocolate-based Turin speciality. Make certain you buy ice cream made on the premises, *artigianato* or *produzione propria*, and experiment with what is clearly seasonal; the high-summer fruit ices such as melon, peach and apricot are delightfully refreshing.

DIRECTORY

San Marco

Bar Gelateria Paolin
Campo Santo Stefano, San Marco 2962a.
Map 6 F3.

Caffè Florian
Piazza San Marco, San Marco 56/59.
Map 7 B2.

Caffè Quadri
Piazza San Marco, San Marco 120–24.
Map 7 B2.

Harry's Bar
Calle Vallaresso, San Marco 1323.
Map 7 B3.

Hostaria ai Rusteghi
Campiello del Tentor, San Marco 5513.
Map 7 B1.

Osteria Terrà Assassini
Rio Terrà degli Assassini, San Marco 3695.
Map 7 A2.

Rosa Salva
Calle Fiubera, San Marco 951. **Map** 7 B1.

Vino Vino
Ponte delle Veste, San Marco 2007.
Map 7 A3.

San Polo and Santa Croce

Al Prosecco
C. San Giacomo dell'Orio, S Croce 1503. **Map** 2 E5.

Bottega del Caffè Dersut
Campo dei Frari, San Polo 3015.
Map 6 E1.

Do Mori
Calle Do Mori, San Polo 429.
Map 3 A5.

Gelateria Alaska
Calle Larga dei Bari, Santa Croce 1159.
Map 2 D5.

Castello

Bar Colleoni
Campo Santi Giovanni e Paolo, Castello 6811.
Map 3 C5.

Bar Gelateria Riviera
Ponte de la Pietà, Riva degli Schiavoni 4153.
Map 8 D2.

Bar Mio
Via Garibaldi, Castello 1820.
Map 8 F3.

Bar Orologio
Campo Santa Maria Formosa, Castello 6130.
Map 7 C1.

La Boutique del Gelato
Campo San Lio, Castello 5727.
Map 7 B1.

Caffè al Cavallo
Campo Santi Giovanni e Paolo, Castello 6823.
Map 3 C5.

Snack & Sweet
Salizzada San Lio, Castello 5689.
Map 7 B1.

Dorsoduro

Accademia Foscarini
Rio Terra A Foscarini, Dorsoduro 878/c. 0.
Map 6 E4.

Ai do Draghi
Calle della Chiesa, Dorsoduro 3665.
Map 6 F4.

Al Chioschetto Zattere
Dorsoduro 1406a.
Map 6 D4.

Bar Gelateria Il Doge
Campo Santa Margherita, Dorsoduro 3058a.
Map 6 D2.

Bar Gelateria Nico
Zattere ai Gesuati, Dorsoduro 922.
Map 6 D4.

Bar Pasticceria Vio
Rio Terrà della Toletta, Dorsoduro 1192.
Map 6 D3.

Cantina del Vino già Schiavi
Ponte San Trovaso, Dorsoduro 992.
Map 6 E4.

Il Caffè
Campo Santa Margherita, Dorsoduro 2963.
Map 6 D3.

El Sbarlefo
Calle San Pantalon, Dorsoduro 3757.
Map 6 D2.

Cannaregio

Alla Bomba
Calle dell'Oca, Cannaregio 4297.
Map 3 A5.

Bar Algiubagio
Fondamente Nuove, Cannaregio 5039.
Map 3 C4.

Bar Gelateria Solda
Campo Santi Apostoli, Cannaregio 4440.
Map 3 B5.

Caffè Pasqualigo
Salizzada Santa Fosca, Cannaregio 2288.
Map 2 F4.

Enoteca Boldrin
San Canciano, Cannaregio 5550.
Map 3 B5.

Il Gelatone
Rio Terrà Maddalena, Cannaregio 2063.
Map 2 F3.

Osteria da Alberto
Calle Larga Giacinto Gallina, Cannaregio 5401.
Map 3 C5.

Pasticceria Dal Mas
Lista di Spagna, Cannaregio 150/a.
Map 2 D4.

The Lagoon Islands

Al Bar Trono di Attila
Via Borgognoni 7/a, Torcello.

Bar della Maddalena
Via Mazzorbo 7/b, Mazzorbo – Burano.

Bar Ice
Campo San Donato, Murano.
Map 4 F2.

Bar La Palanca
Fondamenta Santa Eufemia, Giudecca 448.
Map 6 D5.

Bar Palmisano
Via Baldassare Galuppi 351, Burano.

Harry's Dolci
Fondamenta San Biagio, Giudecca 773.
Map 6 D5.

Lo Spuntino
Via Baldassare Galuppi, Burano.

SHOPS AND MARKETS

The narrow streets of Venice are lined with beautifully arranged windows that cannot fail to tempt shoppers, and the city has the additional bonus of being truly pedestrianized. Few cities of similar size have such a wide variety of goods to browse through as you explore the fascinating and diverse neighbourhoods. There is still a strong artisan tradition in Venice, and alongside papier-mâché carnival masks, glass and lace, you will find high-quality fashion and leather goods, antiques and jewellery, as well as fine food. In the Veneto, which is one of Italy's most prosperous regions, every town boasts a wide range of shops, and many have seasonal speciality markets. In country areas you can buy wine and olive oil direct from the producers.

Display of jewellery in a shop window in the Frezzeria

When to Shop

Generally, shops open around 9 or 9:30am and close for lunch at 12:30 or 1pm, with the exception of food shops and markets, which are in business from 8am. In the afternoon stores are open from 3:30pm to 7:30pm in winter, and 4pm to 8pm in summer. In Venice, many stores aimed directly at tourists are open all day and even on Sundays, as are big out-of-town supermarkets and hyper-markets – useful if you are self-catering in the region.

Monday is usually the traditional closing day in northern Italy, though again this does not apply to all shops in Venice itself. The smaller towns in the Veneto often have very variable opening hours, with perhaps food shops closing on Mondays but ironmongers and clothes shops closing on Wednesdays. Shops and markets in the Veneto are often closed for two or three weeks during the national holiday time in August.

The best time for finding bargains is during the January and July sales: look out for window signs with the words *saldi* or *sconti*.

Where to Shop in Venice

The glittering Mercerie *(see p99)*, which runs from Piazza San Marco to the Rialto, has been the main shopping street since the Middle Ages and, together with the parallel Calle dei Fabbri, is still a honey pot for the crowds. West of San Marco, the zigzagging Frezzeria is full of interesting and unusual shops. The main route from the Piazza to the Accademia Bridge is lined with upmarket speciality stores, while the streets north of Campo Santo Stefano *(see p97)* are another excellent trawling ground for quality souvenirs and gifts.

Across the Grand Canal, the narrow streets from the Rialto southwest towards Campo San Polo *(see p105)* are lined with a wide variety of less expensive stores, while near the station the bustling Lista di Spagna and the route along the Strada Nova towards the Rialto cater for the everyday needs of ordinary Venetians.

A colourful display of T-shirts with the "Venezia" logo

The islands of Murano and Burano *(see pp156–7)* are *the* places to buy traditional glass and lace.

How to Pay

Major credit cards are usually accepted in the main stores for larger purchases, but cash is preferred for small items, and smaller shops will want cash. Travellers' cheques are also accepted, though the rate that you will get is less favourable than at a bank.

By law, shopkeepers should give you a receipt *(ricevuta fiscale)*, which you should keep until you are some distance away from the store (legally this is 600 m/660 yards). If a purchased item is defective, most shops will change the article or give you a credit note, as long as you show the till receipt. Cash refunds are not usually given.

VAT Exemption

Visitors from non-European Union countries can reclaim about 12 per cent of the sales tax (IVA) on goods exceeding €154 from the same shop. Ask for an invoice when you buy the goods and inform the shop that you intend to reclaim the tax. The invoice must be stamped at customs as you leave Italy. The shop will reimburse the tax in euros once they have received the stamped invoice.

Designer clothes shop in Treviso

Fashion and Accessories

In Venice, the big names in fashion are all found near San Marco. **Armani**, **Gucci**, **Missoni** and **Roberto Cavalli** all have stylish shops just off the Piazza. For really innovative and outrageous designs visit **Fiorella** in Campo Santo Stefano. The stalls at the foot of the **Ponte delle Guglie** on Strada Nuova sell a range of good value leather shoes and a wide variety of traditional Venetian slippers in a stunning range of colourful velours. For a genuine gondolier's shirt, take a look in **Emilio Ceccato**.

Fabrics and Interior Design

Venice has long been famed for sumptuous brocades, fine silks and figured velvets. **Trois** sells silks by the metre, including the gossamer-fine pleated silks invented by Fortuny for his Delphos dresses *(see p98)*, and **Il Canapè** has wonderful designer silks and other fabrics in its shop near Campo San Pantalon. The famous house of **Rubelli** has its headquarters at Palazzo Corner Spinelli near Campo Sant'Angelo. Here you will find a variety of rich brocades and velvets. **Color Casa**, in San Polo, has equally lovely textiles at slightly lower prices. **Luigi Bevilacqua**, at Ponte della Canonica, sells beautiful brocades, velvets, damasks and other luxury fabrics, all woven on 17th- century hand-operated looms.

Masks and Costumes

You can buy cheap, mass-produced masks all over the city, but a genuine one is a good souvenir, and you will be spoiled for choice. **Papier Maché** in Castello specializes in traditional mask making and their designs are absolutely stunning. Near Campo San Polo **Tragicomica** sells costumes and masks, as well as commedia dell'arte figures. You will find these at **Leon d'Oro** on the Frezzeria too, where they also make string puppets. Dorsoduro has several workshops; **Il Pirata**, near the Santa Maria dei Miracoli church, has a marvellous selection of papier-mâché masks. In the weeks leading up to Carnival, mask makers are, of course, extremely busy, but at other times of the year many workshops welcome visitors and are pleased to show you their craft *(see p35)*.

A typical Venetian mask

Glass

The best place to buy glass is on the island of Murano, where it has been made since the 13th century *(see p157)*. All the main manufacturers have their furnaces and showrooms here, catering to mainstream taste. Some manufacturers also have showrooms in Venice itself.

On Murano, **Seguso** and **Barovier e Toso** make glass to traditional designs with good simple lines. Another option is **Totem-il Canale**, which has an excellent selection of both traditional and contemporary designs. **Venini** has shops near San Marco; it represents the top end of the market and some of its designs are very pleasing. For other important glass designware, go to **Ma.Re** in Frezzeria.

Jewellery

Venice's smartest jewellers are **Missiaglia** and **Nardi**, both in the arcades of Piazza San Marco. Shops on the Rialto Bridge sell cheaper designs, and this is a good place to find bracelets and chains, whose price is determined by the weight of the gold. For inexpensive, pretty Venetian glass earrings, necklaces and bracelets try **FGB** in Campo Santa Maria Zobenigo.

Wide range of fruit and vegetables for sale in the Rialto market

A typical general food store in the San Marco area

Department Stores

Department stores are not as common in Italy as in many other countries. The main chain store in Venice is Coin, which sells everything from umbrellas to tableware. Oviesse and Upim are cheaper supermarket-style options. You will find branches of these in other towns in the Veneto.

Treasure trove in one of the art shops on Murano

Books and Gifts

Filippi Editori Venezia stocks facsimile editions of old books and books about Venice. **Fantoni** is a specialist art bookshop, and English-language books are sold at **Cafoscarina 3**, **Libreria Marco Polo** and **Libreria Emiliana**.

Handmade marbled and dragged paper are typically Venetian, and used as book covers and made up into writing desk equipment. **Paolo Olbi** has a wide range of papers, while **Alberto Valese-Ebru** uses a distinctive marbling technique on fabrics as well as paper. For watercolour views of Venice, try the stalls in Campo dei Santi Apostoli.

The San Barnaba area has several art and craft shops where you can buy unusual gifts and souvenirs. **Signor Blum** on the Campo San Barnaba has charming carved and painted wooden objects and toys. Another carver, **Livio de Marchi**, makes large whimsical wooden ornaments. **Gilberto Penzo** offers boat models – you can even buy a kit to make your own. **Lanterna Magica** sells interesting children's games and toys. For unusual trinkets and ornaments, browse in **Officina Veneziana**.

Markets and Food Shops

One of the delights of Venice is a morning spent exploring the food markets and shops around the Rialto. Fruit and vegetable stalls sprawl to the west of the bridge and the Pescheria, or fish market, lies right beside the Grand Canal *(see p104)*. The neighbouring streets are full of unusual and excellent food shops. Olive oil, vinegar and dried pasta, which comes in many colours, shapes and flavours, are all good choices if you are looking for food to take home. **Aliani (Casa del Parmigiano)** is a superlative cheese shop right by the vegetable market, where you can also buy a selection of fresh pasta, salamis and ready-made dishes for a picnic.

On Ruga Rialto, the **Drogheria Mascari** has a fine range of coffees, teas, dried fruits and nuts. **Pasticceria Tonolo** is one of Venice's best *pasticcerie*, selling traditional sweetmeats, as well as cakes and biscuits. **Vizio Virtù** makes wonderful chocolates, some in the shape of Venetian masks.

Viale Santa Maria Elisabetta, the main shopping street of the Lido

DIRECTORY

Fashion and Accessories

Armani
Calle Goldoni, San Marco 4412. **Map** 7 A2. **Tel** 041 523 47 58.

Emilio Ceccato
Sottoportico di Rialto, San Polo 16/17. **Map** 7 A1. **Tel** 041 522 27 00.

Fiorella Gallery
Campo Santo Stefano, San Marco 2806. **Map** 6 F3. **Tel** 041 520 92 28.

Gucci
Calle Larga XXII Marzo, San Marco 2102. **Map** 7 A3. **Tel** 041 277 73 01.

Missoni
Calle Vallaresso, San Marco 1312. **Map** 7 B3. **Tel** 041 520 57 33.

Roberto Cavalli
Calle Vallaresso, San Marco 1314. **Map** 7 B3. **Tel** 041 520 57 33.

Stalls at the foot of Ponte delle Guglie
Strada Nuova, Cannaregio. **Map** 2 D3.

Fabrics and Interior Design

Color Casa
Calle della Madonneta, San Polo 1990. **Map** 6 F1. **Tel** 041 523 60 71.

Il Canapè
Calle San Pantalon, Dorsoduro 3736. **Map** 6 D2. **Tel** 041 714 264.

Luigi Bevilacqua
Ponte della Canonica, San Marco 337/b. **Map** 7 C2. **Tel** 041 528 75 81.

Rubelli
Campiello del Teatro, San Marco 3877. **Map** 7 B2. **Tel** 041 523 61 10.

Trois
Campo San Maurizio, San Marco 2666. **Map** 6 F3. **Tel** 041 522 29 05.

Masks and Costumes

Il Pirata
Salizzada San Canciano, Cannaregio 5559. **Map** 3 B5. **Tel** 041 520 65 29.

Leon d'Oro
Frezzeria, San Marco 1770. **Map** 7 A2. **Tel** 041 520 33 75.

Papier Maché
Calle Lunga Santa Maria Formosa, Castello 5175. **Map** 7 C1. **Tel** 041 522 99 95.

Tragicomica
Calle dei Nomboli, San Polo 2800. **Map** 6 F1. **Tel** 041 72 11 02.

Glass

Barovier e Toso
Fondamenta Vetrai 28, Murano. **Map** 4 E3. **Tel** 041 73 90 49.

Ma.Re
Frezzeria, San Marco 1586–8. **Map** 7 B3. **Tel** 041 241 26 87.

Seguso
Fondamenta Vetrai 143, Murano. **Map** 4 E2. **Tel** 041 73 94 23.

Totem-il Canale
Campo Carità, Dorsoduro 8786. **Map** 6 E3. **Tel** 041 522 36 41.

Venini
Piazzetta dei Leoncini, San Marco 314. **Map** 7 B2. **Tel** 041 522 40 45.

Jewellery

FGB
Campo Santa Maria Zobenigo, San Marco 2514. **Map** 7 C1. **Tel** 041 523 65 56.

Missiaglia
Procuratie Vecchie, San Marco 125. **Map** 7 B2. **Tel** 041 522 44 64.

Nardi
Procuratie Nuove, Piazza San Marco, San Marco 69/71. **Map** 7 B2. **Tel** 041 522 57 33.

Books and Gifts

Alberto Valese-Ebru
Campiello Santo Stefano, San Marco 3471. **Map** 6 F3. **Tel** 041 523 88 30.

Cafoscarina 3
Calle Foscari, Dorsoduro 3259. **Map** 6 D2. **Tel** 041 522 18 65.

Fantoni
Salizzada San Luca, San Marco 4119. **Map** 7 A2. **Tel** 041 522 07 00.

Filippi Editori Venezia
Calle Casselleria, Castello 5284. **Map** 7 C1. **Tel** 041 523 69 16.

Gilberto Penzo
Calle dei Saoneri, San Polo 2681. **Map** 6 E1. **Tel** 041 524 61 39.

Lanterna Magica
Ponte San Barnaba, Dorsoduro 2808. **Map** 6 D3. **Tel** 041 523 83 13.

Libreria Emiliana
Calle Goldoni, San Marco 4487. **Map** 7 A2. **Tel** 041 522 07 93.

Libreria Marco Polo
Calle Teatro Malibran Cannaregio 5886/a. **Map** 3 B5. **Tel** 041 522 63 43.

Livio de Marchi
Salizzada San Samuele, San Marco 3157/a. **Map** 6 E2. **Tel** 041 528 56 94.

Officina Veneziana
Calle San Pantalon, Dorsoduro 3752/a. **Map** 6 D2. **Tel** 041 720 313.

Paolo Olbi
Calle Foscari, Dorsoduro 3253. **Map** 6 D2. **Tel** 041 523 76 55.

Signor Blum
Campo San Barnaba, Dorsoduro 2840. **Map** 6 D3. **Tel** 041 522 63 67.

Food Shops

Aliani (Casa del Parmigiano)
Erberia Rialto, San Polo 214/5. **Map** 3 A5. **Tel** 041 520 65 25.

Drogheria Mascari
Ruga Rialto, Calle dei Spezieri San Polo 381. **Map** 3 A5. **Tel** 041 522 97 62.

Pasticceria Tonolo
Calle San Pantalon, Dorsoduro 3764. **Map** 6 D2. **Tel** 041 523 72 09.

Vizio Virtù
Calle del Campaniel, San Polo 2898/A. **Map** 6 E2. **Tel** 041 275 01 49.

What to Buy in the Veneto

Glass is the most popular Venetian souvenir, but there are many other possibilities, ranging from Carnival masks and ceramics to fabrics and lace. For food lovers there is a wide selection of local olive oils, honey, wines and preserves. In the Veneto many food producers sell direct to the public, while different craft and food specialities are found in individual towns and islands.

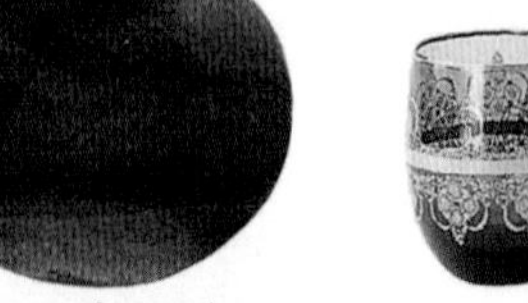

Modern vase of opaque glass

Traditional glass with gold overlay

Two-coloured goblet

Venetian Glass
In traditional rich colours of blue and claret, or in striking modern designs, you will find anything from scent bottles to chandeliers.

Gift box covered in marbled paper

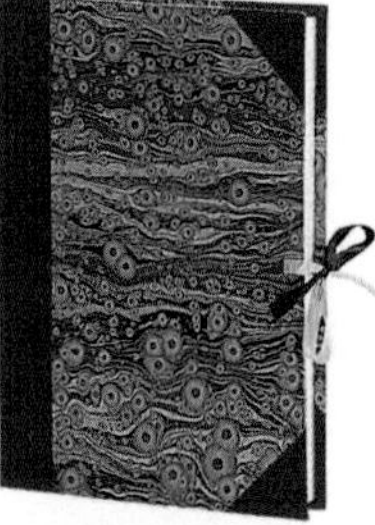

Address book

Venetian Marbled Paper
Marbled paper is a Venetian speciality. The sheets of paper are dipped into liquid gum before adding the paint. You can buy a large range of stationery items covered in the paper, as well as paper by the individual sheet. Each sheet of marbled paper is unique.

Pretty trinket box

Sheets of marbled paper

Decorated ceramic vase from Bassano

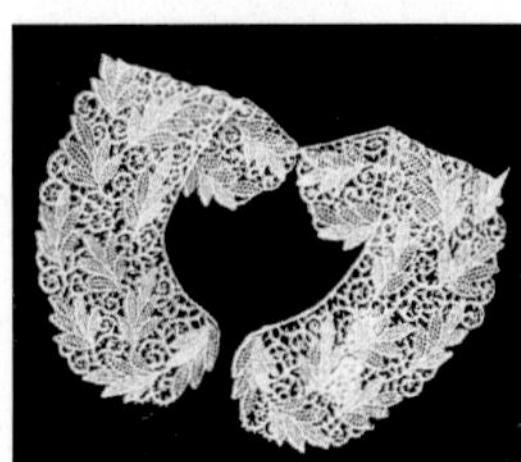

Delicate lace collar from Burano

Crafts from the Veneto
The ancient patterns of Burano lace are used to great advantage on table linen and to trim exquisite lingerie. Hand-painted vases, plates and bowls are produced in the picturesque old town of Bassano del Grappa.

Silver spoon with Venetian lion finial

Red and gold mask

Masks *(see pp34–5)*
Mask designs range from Commedia dell'Arte motifs to modern abstracts from young designers, and many are intricate and colourful. They are available all year, but at Carnival time you can buy them from street stalls.

Carnival mask

Colourful child's sweater

Velvet slippers

Clothing
As everywhere in Italy, stylish designer shops abound. Clothes for children are particularly bright and inventive. Velvet slippers, which are made in rich jewel-like colours, are worn at home as well as to dress up in at Carnival time.

Pasta
Attractively packaged dried pasta comes in many colours, shapes and flavours. Tomato, herb and spinach are the most popular varieties, but beetroot, garlic, artichoke, salmon, squid, and even chocolate can also be found in many shops.

Artichoke

Beetroot

Squid

Pasta shapes

Balsamic vinegar and extra virgin olive oil

Panettone

Amaretto biscuits

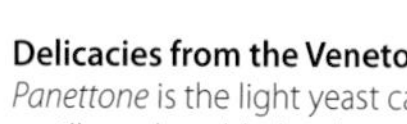

Delicacies from the Veneto
Panettone is the light yeast cake, flavoured with vanilla and studded with currants and candied peel, that is traditionally eaten at Christmas. Other local delicacies include olive oil from the shores of Lake Garda, vinegars, mountain honey from Belluno, fruit-flavoured liqueurs, *grappa* from Bassano *(see p176)*, and after-dinner Amaretto biscuits.

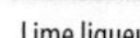

Orange liqueur Lime liqueur Pear liqueur

ENTERTAINMENT IN THE VENETO

Venice was once one of Europe's liveliest night-time cities, and today it still has an impressive range of special events throughout the year. At every season there are some splendid festivals unique to Venice, and in late summer the normal city diet of opera, theatre and concerts is augmented by the International Film Festival and the Biennale, which rank among the best world-class cultural events. The day-to-day evening entertainment in Venice itself now tends to be far less frenetic than in the heyday of the Republic *(see pp50–51)*, but there are a few clubs and discos, and many more across the causeway in Mestre. Or you could have a little flutter at the casino.

Whatever you choose, your enjoyment will be enhanced by the idyllic backdrop of Venice itself. The ultimate and quintessential Venetian romantic experience is, of course, a gondola ride by moonlight *(see p283)*. However, an evening's entertainment could more usually comprise the traditional stroll, or *passeggiata*, followed by a drink at a bar or café in one of the squares or amid the floodlit splendours of the Piazza San Marco.

Practical Information

Information about what's on in Venice can be found in *Leo Bussola*, a free bilingual Italian and English booklet published quarterly by the Tourist Board. *2Night* is a free fortnightly publication with listings of concerts and events. Another publication, *Un Ospite di Venezia* (A Guest in Venice), comes out fortnightly during the summer and monthly in the winter, and is available from most hotels. The Venetian newspaper *Il Gazzettino* also lists cinema performances, rock concerts and discos under *Spettacoli*. Posters advertising forthcoming cultural events are displayed all over town.

For details of events and festivities in the other towns and cities in the Veneto, ask at the local tourist offices. Regional newspapers also often have listings of what is on in their area.

The historic Caffè Florian on Piazza San Marco *(see p251)*

Booking Tickets

Booking in advance is not part of the Italian lifestyle, where decisions are made on the spur of the moment. If you want to be certain of a seat you will have to visit the box office in person, as they usually do not take bookings over the telephone. You may also have to pay an advance booking supplement, or *prevendita*, which is usually about 10 per cent of the price of the seat.

The price of a theatre ticket starts at about €16, though prices are likely to be five times as much for star-name performances. Tickets for popular music concerts are normally sold through record and music shops whose names are displayed on the publicity posters.

Whereas tickets for classical concerts are sold on the spot for that day's performance, opera tickets are booked months ahead. There are very few ticket touts, so it is almost impossible to obtain tickets when the box office has sold out. The **Teatro Goldoni** box office is open 10am–1pm and 3–7pm.

The lavish interior of La Fenice opera house *(see p97)*

Cinema and the Film Festival

There are several cinemas in Venice, mainly showing dubbed versions of international films. These are known as *prima visione* (first run). The **Giorgione Movie d'Essai** and **Cinema Rossini** show arthouse films as well as the usual commercial fare. **Multisala Astra** screens mainly blockbusters, as well as some arthouse films. You will find these listed in *Il Gazzettino*.

The annual Film Festival, which takes place in August and September, is one of the major world cinema showcases and has been running since 1932. Screenings are held in the **Palazzo del Cinema** on the Lido, the Giorgione and the **Arena di Campo San Polo**, an open-air cinema. Tickets are sold to the public direct from the cinema on the day of screening. Programmes can be obtained in advance from the tourist office.

Outdoor entertainment in the courtyard of the Doge's Palace

Teatro Goldoni, Venice's main theatre

Music and Theatre

Like many Italian cities, Venice makes good use of the most magnificent churches as concert halls. La Pietà *(see p116)* was Vivaldi's own church and is still used for concerts, as are the churches of the Frari *(see pp106–7)* and **San Vidal**. Other concerts are held from time to time in Scuola di San Giovanni Evangelista *(see p108)* and the Palazzo Prigioni Vecchie, the old prison attached to the Doge's Palace *(see pp88–93)*. In the summer, the garden of Ca' Rezzonico *(see p130)* is also used as an outdoor concert hall, as is the Doge's Palace's courtyard, albeit occasionally.

La Fenice *(see p97)*, one of Italy's most charming opera houses and the main local venue for major operas, suffered a disastrous fire in early 1996. It reopened in November 2004 and now shares the opera, classical music and ballet programme with **Teatro Malibran**.

Venice's principal theatre is **Teatro Goldoni** where, not surprisingly, the repertoire is mainly drawn from the 250 or more comic works written by the Venetian dramatist Carlo Goldoni (1707–93). Most performances are staged in Italian and run from November to June.

At Carnival time in February *(see pp34–5)*, the whole city takes on a party atmosphere as it is invaded by merry-makers in fancy dress. Many theatrical and musical events take place, both in theatres and in the streets and *campi*.

Facilities for the Disabled

Access for disabled people is difficult everywhere in Venice, and theatres are no exception, although concerts are often held in easily accessible churches. PalaFenice and Teatro Malibran guarantee obstacle-free entrance for the disabled if contacted one week in advance (fax: 041 786 50). For more advice, see page 269.

Masked reveller at Carnival time *(see pp34–5)*

The Biennale and other Exhibitions

Venice is without doubt one of the leading art exhibition centres in Europe, offering shows on themes ranging from art history to photography, and frequently playing host to the world's major travelling exhibitions. There are excellent facilities for such exhibitions, and these include the Doge's Palace, the Museo Correr, the Palazzo Grassi, the Querini-Stampalia, the Peggy Guggenheim and the Fondazione Cini. *Un Ospite di Venezia* will give details, as will the tourist office and posters around the city.

One of the best and largest exhibitions is the Biennale, an international display of contemporary and avant-garde art which was first begun in 1895. It is held from June to September in odd-numbered years. The main site is the Giardini Pubblici *(see p125)*, where the specially built pavilions represent about 40 different countries. Another branch of the exhibition showing the work of less established artists, takes place around the city in venues such as the old rope factory in the Arsenale *(see p123)*. The Biennale also organizes architecture, theatre, dance and music festivals.

Casinos, Clubs and Discos

If you want to gamble or play roulette during your visit to Venice, there is a magnificent casino housed in the **Palazzo Vendramin-Calergi** on the Grand Canal *(see p65)* and you can sweep up to the stately entrance by gondola. **Bacaro Jazz** is popular with both tourists and locals. Open until 2am, it serves cocktails and a selection of food. A few other bars also feature live bands, including **Paradiso Perduto** in Cannaregio. Discos are few and far between in Venice. You could try **Piccolo Mondo**, near the Accademia; **Café Blue**, near Piazzale Roma; or alternatively go to the mainland, where Mestre has a few discos to choose from. You will find these clubs advertised in the *Spettacoli* listings in *Il Gazzettino*.

Palazzo Vendramin-Calergi on the Grand Canal in Venice, housing a casino

Sport and Children

Venetians are very keen on rowing and sailing. There are several clubs in the city, and the tourist office will be able to give you information. Most of the other sporting facilities are on the Lido, where you can ride, swim, cycle and play golf or tennis.

In the city itself, there are few attractions for young children, but the mainland is more promising. Around Lake Garda there are plenty of watersports and a theme park, Gardaland® Resort *(see p211)*.

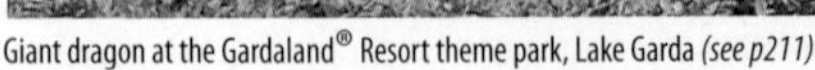

Giant dragon at the Gardaland® Resort theme park, Lake Garda *(see p211)*

Music and Theatre in Verona

Verona has two exceptional venues for theatre and music: the superb Arena *(see p197)*, and the 1st-century Teatro Romano *(see p204)* on the far side of the River Adige. Both stage open-air performances during the summer months.

The Arena is a popular site for rock concerts and is internationally renowned for its summer opera season. The Teatro Romano stages a succession of ballets and drama, including a Shakespeare Festival, in Italian translation. Tickets for the Teatro can be ordered by post; they are also sold at the box office at the Arena. Tickets to some events are free. Information about all the entertainment is given in the Verona newspaper *L'Arena*.

Placido Domingo singing at the Verona Festival

Opera at the Arena

Almost everyone will enjoy the experience of hearing opera in the magnificent open-air setting of the Arena. Real opera buffs should be aware, however, that Verona performances are very much "opera for all". You should be prepared for less-than-perfect acoustics, noisy audiences and even small children running about. The opera season runs from the first week in July until the beginning of September, and every year features a lavish production of Verdi's *Aida*. Performances start at 9pm, as dusk is falling, and it is customary to buy one of the little candles that are on sale. Ten minutes before the "curtain goes up", the whole Arena becomes a breathtaking sight, with a sea of flickering lights.

Aida, performed annually in Verona's Roman Arena

During the intervals, most people eat the picnics they have brought with them, or buy *panini* and ice creams. Glass bottles are not allowed in the Arena, so if you are taking a drink make sure it is in a plastic bottle. Be warned that toilets are few and far between and are most likely to have lengthy queues during the intervals. Ticket prices are high, though there are some concessions. An unreserved, un-numbered, backless seat in the *gradinata*, or tiers, is €21, while the *poltrone*, literally "armchairs", either on the steps or in the stalls, range from €85 to €160. If you decide to get a cheap seat, arrive at least 2 hours before the performance and sit halfway down the tiers, where the acoustics are better. You can hire an air cushion for about €3. Numbered seats are more comfortable, but seats lower in the Arena can be very hot and airless and the view of the stage can be restricted. You may well prefer to sacrifice comfort for fresh air and a bird's-eye view. Unless you have a seat in the best stalls with the glitterati, there is no need to dress up.

Visitors flock to Verona to attend the opera season, so you need to book accommodation well in advance.

DIRECTORY

Music and Theatre

San Vidal
Campo San Vidal, San Marco 2862/b. **Map** 6 E3. **Tel** 041 277 05 61. **W interpretiveneziani.com**

Teatro La Fenice
Campo San Fantin, San Marco 1965. **Tel** 041 24 24. **W teatrolafenice.it**

Teatro Goldoni
Calle Goldoni, San Marco 4650/b. **Map** 7 A2. **Tel** 041 240 20 11. **W teatrostabileveneto.it**

Teatro Malibran
Corte del Milion, Cannaregio 5873. **Map** 7 B1. **Tel** 041 24 24. **W teatrolafenice.it**

Cinemas

Arena di Campo San Polo
Campo San Polo, San Polo. **Map** 6 F1. **Tel** 041 524 13 20.

Cinema Rossini
Salizzada del Teatro, San Marco 3997/a. **Map** 6 F2. **Tel** 041 241 72 74.

Giorgione Movie d'Essai
Rio Terra dei Franceschi, Cannaregio 4612. **Map** 7 A2. **Tel** 041 522 62 98.

Multisala Astra
Via Corfù 9, Lido. **Tel** 041 526 57 36.

Palazzo del Cinema
Lungomare G Marconi, Lido. **Tel** 041 272 65 01.

Casinos, Clubs and Discos

Bacaro Jazz
Campo San Bartolomeo, San Marco 5546. **Map** 7 B1. **Tel** 041 528 5249. **W bacarojazz.com**

Café Blue
Calle della Scuola, Dorsoduro 3778. **Map** 5 C1. **Tel** 041 522 76 13.

Palazzo Vendramin-Calergi
Strada Nuova, Cannaregio 2040. **Tel** 041 529 71 11. **W casinovenezia.it**

Paradiso Perduto
Fondamenta della Misericordia, Cannaregio 2540. **Map** 1 C4. **Tel** 041 72 05 81. **W ilparadisoperduto.com**

Piccolo Mondo
Calle Corfù, Dorsoduro 1056/a. **Map** 6 E3. **Tel** 041 520 03 71. **W piccolomondo.biz**

Sports

Cycling
Bruno Lazzari
21/b Gran Viale, Lido. **Tel** 041 526 80 19.

Golf
Alberoni
Strada Vecchia 1, Lido. **Tel** 041 73 13 33. **W circologolfvenezia.it**

Rowing
Canottieri Bucintoro
Punta Dogana, Dorsoduro 15. **Map** 7 B4. **Tel** 041 520 56 30. **W bucintoro.org**

Tennis
Tennis Club Venezia
Lungomare G Marconi 41/d, Lido. **Tel** 041 526 03 35. **W tennisclubvenezia.com**

Verona Opera

Main Box Office
Tel 045 800 51 51. **W arena.it**

Ticket Agent
Vertours, Galleria Pellicciai 13, 37121 Verona. **Tel** 045 929 82 00. **W vertours.com**

SPECIALIST HOLIDAYS AND OUTDOOR ACTIVITIES

The Veneto's rich cultural heritage and wide range of natural landscapes makes it a perfect location for numerous specialist holidays and outdoor excursions. The city of Venice hosts a dazzling array of study courses and craft workshops, including traditional mask making and glass blowing. It is also an unforgettable location in which to learn Italian. Outside of the city, the region's coastal and inland waterways provide space for many types of boating as well as more active watersports and birdwatching. The towering mountains in the Alpine hinterland are challenging walking and climbing country, while in the winter there is skiing, facilitated by an excellent network of cable cars and lifts. Between mountain and sea are gentle hills, perfect for horse-riding enthusiasts and home to various relaxing local spas.

Cookery courses at Tasting Places

Cookery Courses and Wine Tasting

Visitors wishing to discover the secrets of the local cusine should try one of the cookery courses on offer in Venice. Most include a shopping visit to the fish and fresh produce market at Rialto followed by the preparation of a meal using seasonal ingredients. The enthusiastic young chefs at **Venice & Veneto Gourmet** cater to groups. Alternatively, longer intensive classes are held, often by Michelin-starred chefs, at the exclusive **Hotel Cipriani**. In the hills outside Verona a magnificent country estate hosts tempting cooking classes run by **Tasting Places**. The Rome-based organization **Delicious Italy** can arrange for residential cooking lessons around the Veneto that focus specifically on regional specialities.

Lessons on wine appreciation are organized by **Millevini**, a well-stocked winery at the foot of the Rialto Bridge.

Arts and Crafts

Each summer the **Venice in Peril Fund** organizes a series of lectures on the precious heritage of the city, aimed at history of art enthusiasts.

More practical courses are given by expert local crafts-people to anyone wishing to discover the intricacies of a range of crafts. Following a centuries-old tradition of glass-making, the **Scuola del Vetro Abate Zanetti** prides itself on teaching traditional and contemporary methods and styles at its premises on the island of Murano, the heart of the city's glass trade. Glass-making is also on offer through the craft organization Confartigianato, as are lessons in furniture restoration. Techniques for repairing stucco and marble work can be learned at the well-established **European School for Heritage Crafts and Professions** set in the grounds of Villa Fabris near Vicenza.

IED Venezia offers a range of workshops and courses in fields such as photography and art throughout the summer. Lessons in crafting papier-mâché Carnival masks are given at the dynamic **Ca' Macana** workshop and can be followed in several different European languages.

Year-round courses in oil and watercolour painting, as well as printmaking, are run by the friendly atelier **Bottega del Tintoretto**. A larger institution, with a vast range of open-air painting and graphics classes, is the **Scuola Internazionale di Grafica**. Courses on old textiles are occasionally held at **Palazzo Mocenigo**, home to the Centro Studi di Storia del Tessuto e del Costume. Even the ancient intricate art of lacemaking is still demonstrated, by its few remaining expert practitioners, at the **Museo del Merletto** on the distant and colourful island of Burano.

Students gaining practical experience in restoration techniques

Climbing in the spectacular Dolomites

Walking and Climbing

During the summer and autumn months, keen walkers and trekkers should head straight up to the imposing Dolomites, where hundreds of kilometres of clearly marked pathways wind their way through brightly flowered meadows and spectacular rocky landscapes. Easy access combined with a network of high-altitude refuge huts make this a very accessible activity. For walkers who require extra assistance, **Cortina Guides** can provide specialist help with their team of friendly experts. **Club Alpino Italiano** offers qualified Alpine guides for such climbs as the *via ferrata* routes, as well as for more general walking tours. The club has branches in all major towns, so it is not difficult to find help when needed. UK-based **Colletts Mountain Holidays** also offers a good range of walking and climbing trips.

Watersports

A quick glance at a map reveals the many coastal and inland waterways along the Veneto's Adriatic coast. It is unsurprising that watersports are a speciality here. It is possible to explore the region at your own pace by hiring a motor boat from **Cristiano Brussa**. (Customers will need to demonstrate some experience in handling craft.) Another truly unique holiday can be experienced on a houseboat in the lagoon, exploring its myriad islands and waterways. **Italiabella** have a fleet anchored at Chioggia, while **Houseboat Holidays Italia** are based at Porto Levante in the Po Delta. For those who have never sailed before, or would like a more relaxed trip, **Il Bragozzo** arrange day trips on the Venice Lagoon, with an experienced sailor at the helm.

In Venice there are many opportunities to take advantage of the waterways. A good sense of balance and plenty of energy are required for rowing in the traditional standing-up style. Clubs such as the **Bucintoro** on the Zattere, active since 1882, welcome visitors and provide lessons for novices. Sailing enthusiasts, on the other hand, can contact one of the city's clubs: those keen on old-style wooden craft with colourful sails should contact the **Associazione Vela al Terzo**, or for sleek modern yachts there is the prestigious **Compagnia della Vela**, which is based on the island of San Giorgio.

Further afield Lake Garda is the place for windsurfers. Schools such as **Surfsegnana**, at Torbole in the northern reaches of the lake, offer a good range of courses and holidays. The lake also guarantees superb swimming, especially off Sirmione in the south, where the bleached rocks and crystal clear water are reminiscent of the Caribbean. A string of yellow-sand beaches lines the Adriatic coast of the Veneto. Well frequented in summer by the locals, the Veneto seaside resorts also cater to the needs of overseas visitors. Caorle and Jesolo, close to Venice, are very popular, as is Rosolina Mare and Albarella, which is near the Po Delta. The Venice Lido is also a very pleasant place to swim, although a fee is charged to use the beach huts. For a free public beach, head along to the Alberoni.

Lastly, for those in search of a more challenging experience, there is white-water rafting and canoeing at Valstagna on the Brenta River. The experienced crew at **Ivan Team** can arrange a craft, with all the necessary equipment, and transport.

Windsurfing near Torbole Lago di Garda Veneto

Language Courses

One of the best and most beautiful places to learn the Italian language is in Venice. Visitors who are keen to take part in a course should enrol in Italian for Foreigners at the **Centro Linguistico Ateneo** of the Ca' Foscari University. Classes are in an atmospheric modernized *palazzo* and are supplemented by access to well-stocked multimedia labs with all manner of support material. Another centrally located school is the **Istituto Venezia**, which offers a good range of lessons, including a cookery course in Italian, as well as arranging for concerts, cultural initiatives and excursions. Accommodation is either homestays or self-catering flats.

Winter Sports

A winter holiday in the breathtaking Dolomite mountains can include an extraordinary range of activities. Wrapped up warm and plastered with high-factor sun protection cream, visitors in need of relaxation can laze on the sun decks in the ski resorts. Those in search of exciting downhill skiing can head for Arabba, which has a superb series of cable cars to whisk skiers up to the snow fields, including the Marmolada glacier. Val Zoldana, dominated by the magnificent Civetta and Pelmo mountains, is another excellent location. If a chic ambience is important, you must stay at Cortina d'Ampezzo, which hosted the Winter Olympics in 1956 and now boasts excellent modern ski facilities and lifts, including the Tofana cable car. All the resorts are managed by **Dolomiti Superski**, which includes 12 ski areas and an amazing 1,200 km (750 miles) of pistes all covered by a single pass. Slopes for intrepid snowboarders are also included.

Toddlers to adults, beginners to more advanced skiers, and anyone in between can attend the ski school run by the qualified ski instructors of the **Scuola Sci**, which is found at all the main centres.

Cortina d'Ampezzo, Alleghe and Val Zoldana also have indoor ice rinks, which make a refreshing change to the high energy of the slopes.

Experienced skiers wishing to get away from the pistes can join a group accompanied by a local Alpine guide to explore the more secluded slopes. Snowshoeing is also undergoing a revival. Guides and modern equipment can be found at all the major resorts. There is superb cross-country skiing in the Veneto. The vast undulating Asiago plateau north of Vicenza has hundreds of kilometres of prepared tracks for both classical and skating techniques. Contact the **Consorzio Turistico** for information about the main centres, such as Campolongo and Enego, which all have top-level facilities. Further west is the Monti Lessini above Verona, where pistes fan out from Bosco Chiesanuova; the best source of information is the **Lessinia Turistsport**.

Spa Holidays

As the ancient Romans discovered to their delight, naturally occurring spas are dotted across the Veneto, and visitors can pamper body and mind with a soak in a thermal pool or with a relaxing massage. Abano-Montegrotto Terme in the Euganean Hills has numerous hotels with steaming outdoor and indoor pools, catering to both long-term and day visitors. The **Consorzio Terme Euganee** can help organize your holiday.

Further afield, on the southern shore of Lake Garda, is the state-of-the-art spa facilities at **Terme di Sirmione**, which continue a tradition going back to the 1500s.

Cable car and downhill slopes in the Dolomite mountains

Birdwatching

Pink flamingoes flock in spectacular numbers to the sprawling **Po Delta Park** in the winter months, though the local waterfowl are worth visiting at any time of year. Also, on the western edge of the Venice Lagoon, located on the Romea road that links Mestre with Chioggia, is the wetland reserve **Oasi Valle Averto**, run by the World Wide Fund for Nature. This reserve is accessible by bus.

Horse riding at Salten Jenesien

Horse Riding and Golf

The rolling Euganean Hills east of Venice together with the foothills of the Dolomites have plenty of quiet roads and lanes suitable for horse riding. Several agriturismo establishments, such as **Il Faè** near Conegliano and **Le Frassanelle** beyond Padua, keep stables and all the facilities needed for riding holidays. Le Frassanelle also has access to a golf course.

Many of the other notable golfing facilities in the Veneto are to be found in the hinterland. These include a course in the lovely garden premises of **Golf Club Villa Condulmer** at Mogliano. However, for a game with a difference, visitors can play a few rounds at the **Circolo Golf Venezia** at Alberoni, situated on the Venice Lido.

DIRECTORY

Cookery Courses and Wine Tasting

Delicious Italy
Via Angelo Piliziano 58, Rome. **Tel** 064 547 61 23.
W deliciousitaly.com

Hotel Cipriani
Giudecca 10, 30133, Venice. **Map** 7 C5.
Tel 041 24 08 01.
W hotelcipriani.com

Millevini
San Marco 5362, Venice. **Map** 7 B1. **Tel** 041 520 60 90. **W** millevini.com

Tasting Places London
Tel +44 (0)20 8964 5333.
W tastingplaces.com

Venice & Veneto Gourmet
San Polo 2308, Venice. **Map** 6 E2. **Tel** 041 275 06 87. **W** veniceveneto gourmet.com

Arts and Crafts

Bottega del Tintoretto
Fondamenta dei Mori, Cannaregio 3400, Venice. **Map** 2 F3.
Tel 041 72 20 81.
W tintorettovenezia.it

Ca' Macana
Calle delle Botteghe, Dorsoduro 3172, Venice. **Map** 6 D3.
Tel 041 277 61 42.
W camacana.com

European School for Heritage Crafts and Professions
Villa Fabris, Via Trieste 43, Thiene. **Tel** 044 537 23 29.
W villafabris.eu

IED Venezia
Palazzo Franchetti, Campo San Vidal, San Marco 2842, Venice. **Map** 6 F3.
Tel 041 277 11 64.
W ied.it

Museo del Merletto
Piazza Galuppi 187, Burano, Venice.
Tel 041 73 00 34.
W museomerletto. visitmuve.it

Palazzo Mocenigo
Santa Croce 1992, Venice. **Map** 2 F5. **Tel** 041 72 17 98. **W** mocenigo. visitmuve.it

Scuola del Vetro Abate Zanetti
Calle Briati 8/b, Murano, Venice. **Map** 4 F2.
Tel 041 273 77 11.
W abatezanetti.it

Scuola Internazionale di Grafica
Calle del Cristo, Cannaregio 1798, Venice. **Map** 2 E4.
Tel 041 72 19 50.
W scuolagrafica.it

Venice in Peril Fund
Unit 4, Hurlingham Studios, Ranelagh Gardens, London, UK.
Tel (44) 020 7736 6891.
W veniceinperil.org

Walking and Climbing

Club Alpino Italiano
Via Petrella 19, Milan.
Tel 02 205 7231. **W** cai.it

Colletts Mountain Holidays
3A Market Hill, Saffron Walden, Essex, UK.
Tel (44) 01799 513 331.
W colletts.co.uk

Cortina Guides Office
Corso Italia 69/a, Cortina d'Ampezzo.
Tel 043 686 85 05.
W guidecortina.com

Watersports

Associazione Vela al Terzo
Giardinetti Reali, San Marco 556, Venice.
W velaalterzo.it

Bucintoro Rowing Club
Zattere, Dorsoduro 263, Venice. **Map** 7 A4.
Tel 041 520 56 30.
W bucintoro.org

Compagnia della Vela
S Marco 2, Venice. **Map** 7 A3. **Tel** 041 522 25 93.
W compvela.com

Cristiano Brussa
Ponte delle Guglie, Cannaregio 1030, Venice. **Map** 2 D3.
Tel 041 275 01 96.
W cristianobrussa.com

Houseboat Holidays Italia
Via C. Colombo 36/a, Porto Levante, Porto Viro.
Tel 042 666 60 25.
W houseboat.it

Il Bragozzo
Tel 388 182 60 09.
W ilbragozzo.it

Italiabella
Viale delle Terme 163, Abano Terme.
Tel 049 66 72 01.

Ivan Team
Via Oliero di Sotto 85, Valstagna. **Tel** 042 455 82 50. **W** ivanteam.com

Surfsegnana
Foci del Sarca, Torbole.
Tel 046 450 59 63.
W surfsegnana.it

Language Courses

Centro Linguistico Ateneo
Campiello San Sebastiano, Dorsoduro 1686, Venice. **Map** 5 C3. **Tel** 041 234 97 13. **W** unive.it/cli

Istituto Venezia
Campo S Margherita, Dorsoduro 3116/a, Venice. **Map** 6 D2.
Tel 041 522 43 31.
W istitutovenezia.com

Winter Sports

Consorzio Turistico Asiago 7 Comuni
Viale Trento Trieste 19, Asiago. **Tel** 042 446 41 37.
W asiago7comuni.it

Dolomiti Superski
W dolomitisuperski.com

Lessinia Turistsport
W leturispo.it

Scuola Sci Alleghe Civetta
Corso Italia 1, Alleghe.
Tel 043 772 37 16.
W scuolascialleghe civetta.it

Scuola Sci Arabba
Via Boè 14, Livinallongo.
Tel 043 67 91 60.
W scuolasciarabba.com

Scuola Sci Cortina d'Ampezzo
Corso Italia 67, Cortina d'Ampezzo.
Tel 043 629 11.
W scuolascicortina.com

Spa Holidays

Consorzio Terme Euganee
Largo Marconi 8, Abano Terme.
Tel 049 866 62 62.
W abanomonte grottosi.it

Terme di Sirmione
Piazza Virgillo 1, Sirmione. **Tel** 030 916 81.
W termedisirmione. com

Birdwatching

Oasi Valle Averto
Lugo di Campagnalupia.
Tel 041 518 53 77.
W wwf.it/oasi

Po Delta Park
Via Marconi 6, Ariano nel Polesine. **Tel** 042 637 22 02. **W** parcodeltapo.org

Horse Riding and Golf

Circolo Golf Venezia
Strada Vecchia 1, Alberoni, Lido di Venezia.
Tel 041 73 13 33.
W circologolfvenezia.it

Golf Club Villa Condulmer
Via della Croce 3, Zerman di Mogliano, Veneto.
Tel 041 45 70 62.
W golfvillacondulmer. com

Il Faè
Via Faè 1, S Pietro di Feletto.
Tel 043 878 71 17.
W ilfae.com

Le Frassanelle
35030 Rovolon.
Tel 049 990 00 54.
W frassanelle.it

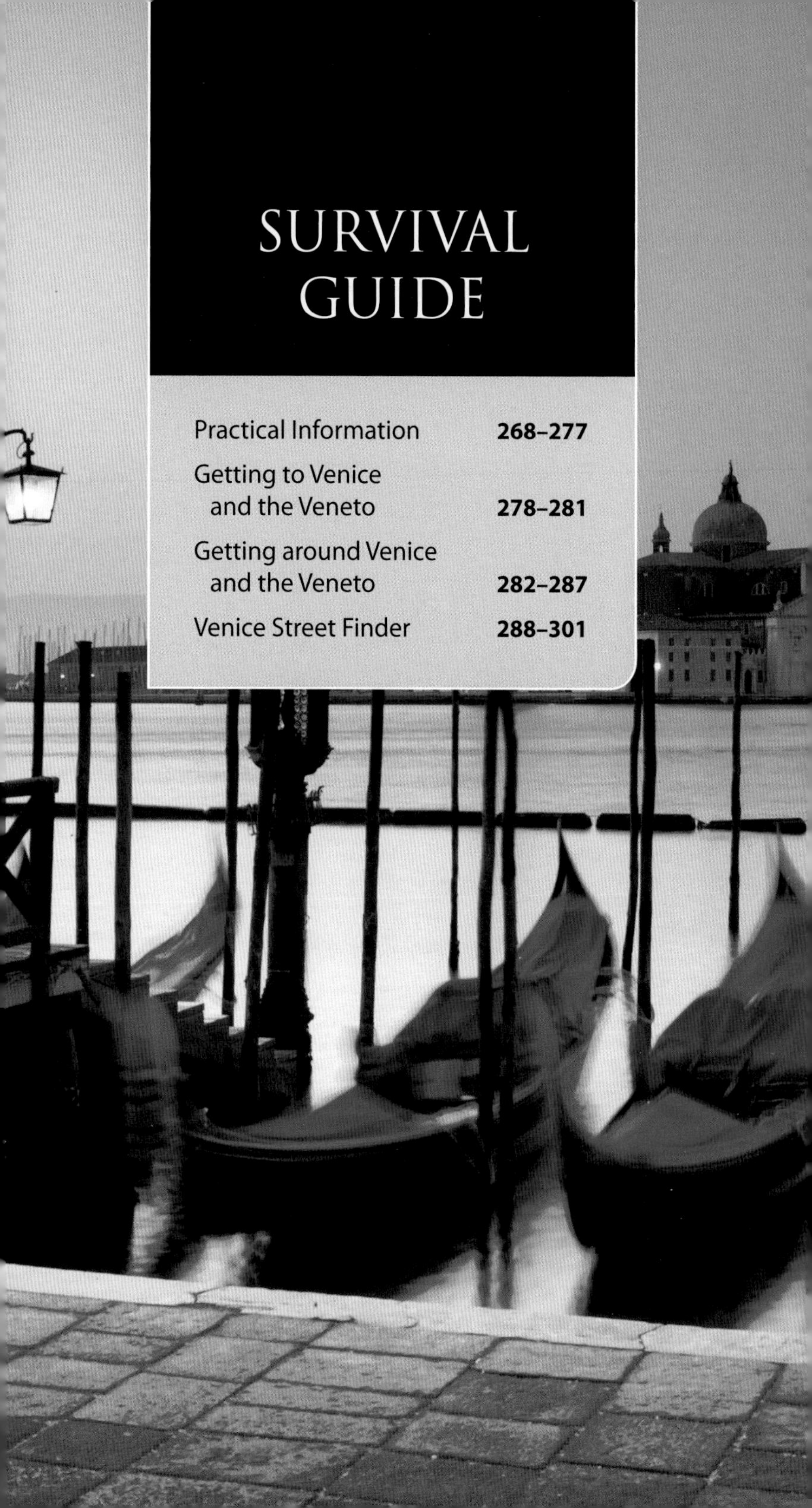

SURVIVAL GUIDE

PRACTICAL INFORMATION

The wealth of art and architecture found in Venice and the cities of Padua, Verona and Vicenza can dazzle and overwhelm. Avoid cultural overload by sightseeing in the morning, relaxing over lunch as the Italians do and shopping or visiting churches in the late afternoon. In the Veneto, restoration of buildings and artworks is an ongoing process, and you may often see the sign *chiuso per restauro* (closed for restoration). Always check opening hours in advance with individual museums or the tourist office. Italians also enjoy visiting their art cities, so public holidays and weekends often mean larger crowds. To make the most of your stay, take a tour by bus or on foot with a qualified guide who can explain the key sights and history. For lovers of outdoor pursuits, the Veneto also has areas of outstanding natural beauty along its coast and inland, in the hills and mountains.

Tourists shopping and sightseeing on Venice's Rialto Bridge

When to Go

July and August can get very hot and sticky in Venice and the Veneto towns. For a cooler, quieter time, visit in winter, spring and autumn. However, be aware that Venice is often subject to *acqua alta* (tidal flooding) in autumn (*see Walking, p282*), and the whole of the Veneto experiences thick fog in winter.

Most places around Lake Garda close during winter, while the Dolomites have two distinct seasons: December–March for skiing and snow-related activities, and June–September for hiking. Hotels, guesthouses and restaurants tend to cease trade between these times.

Visas and Passports

All visitors need a valid passport. European Union (EU) residents and visitors from the United States, Canada, Australia and New Zealand do not need visas for stays of up to three months. However, a visa may be needed for longer stays – check with your embassy – and is required for business or study related trips.

By law, all visitors to Italy must register with the police within three days of arrival; all hotels will request your passport on checking in for such purpose.

The **Ministero degli Affari Esteri** (Foreign Office) or any *questura* (police station) can provide information on any visa requirements (*see p273*).

Customs Information

Duty free are as follows: non-EU residents can bring in either 200 cigarettes, 50 cigars, 100 cigarillos or 250 grams of tobacco; 1 litre of alcohol above 22 per cent volume; 4 litres of wine; 50 grams of perfume. Allowances for EU residents are almost unlimited, providing that the goods are for personal use only.

The tax refund system *(Imposta sul Valore Aggiunto)* for non-EU residents is complicated; it is worth reclaiming only if you have spent at least €154 in one establishment. Ask the cashier to fill out the form for you, and when leaving the country take the goods in your carry-on luggage for approval at the airport tax refund office. The website of the **Agenzia delle Dogane** (Italian customs) provides further information.

Tourist Information

All major towns in the Veneto have excellent tourist offices. In high season, Venice, Verona and Padua also have several information points at railway stations and key sights. The offices in smaller towns may be of limited help. Tourist offices in Venice have city maps, *vaporetto* maps, lists of accommodation options and other literature. Travel agents and hotels are also good sources for information on the city, tours and local events (*see pp36–9*). In Venice, *Eventi e Manifestazioni* is a useful free booklet with listings information; its equivalent in Verona is *Carnet Verona*. Both are available from tourist information offices.

A Tourist Information sign

To obtain information prior to travelling, contact **ENIT** (Italian State Tourist Board) in

◀ San Giorgio Maggiore church and gondolas at dawn, Venice

your home country. An array of publications and maps can also be downloaded from each city's tourist board website.

Admission Prices

Most museums, art galleries and archaeological sites charge an entry fee, but there are usually concessions for children, students and senior citizens over 65. Venice's civic museums pass, valid for six months, is available from any of the sights included in the deal or online at **Venice Connected**. You can also purchase a VENICEcard online from **Hello Venezia**. This pass includes entry to museums and churches, and savings on other admission fees, *vaporetto* tickets and car parking. However, you must buy the card at least 15 days in advance for discounted rates to apply.

Verona has the Verona Card (€15 for 2 days or €20 for 5 days), which covers entry to the main churches, museums and monuments, as well as travel on the city buses. The card is available from Verona's tourist office and any of the participating sights.

Some churches in smaller towns may not charge an admission fee.

Opening Hours

Due to ongoing restoration of many ageing palaces, museums and galleries, opening hours are subject to change. The tourist office can supply a list of opening times or, if you are in Venice, you can also consult the booklets *Eventi e Manifestazioni* or ***Un Ospite di Venezia***, which are available from most hotels. Museums are often shut on Mondays.

Churches are usually open mid-morning and late afternoon. Most Venetian churches are managed by **Chorus**, which sells a useful pass for multiple church entries.

Most food shops open at 8am, while other stores open at 9 or 10am. Many close for a long lunch break from 12:30pm to around 4pm, then stay open until about 7:30pm. However,

Basilica di Sant'Antonio in Padua

in tourist areas, no lunch break is observed. Many supermarkets in the larger towns stay open all day, seven days a week.

Etiquette

Any attempt by foreign visitors to speak Italian is always appreciated by the locals. Few people speak English in the Veneto, but hotel receptionists are usually helpful and will readily make any enquiries and reservations on your behalf.

To avoid offence, always dress decently, particularly if visiting churches, where bare shoulders and shorts are considered unsuitable. Photography is forbidden in most churches. Being drunk in a public place is frowned upon, and smoking is banned in all public buildings, including restaurants and bars, as well as on *vaporetti*. Feeding the pigeons in Piazza San Marco is illegal, and if caught you may be fined.

Public Conveniences

There are few public toilets in the Veneto, although Venice is better served. Public conveniences in Venice are usually signed and cost €1. You can also use the toilets at railway stations and in cafés and bars. Ask for *il bagno* (the bathroom) or *il gabinetto* (the toilet). Public toilets are always short of paper, so it is a good idea to carry tissues with you.

Taxes and Tipping

Like other EU countries, Italy has a form of Value Added Tax (VAT), which is called *Imposta sul Valore Aggiunto (IVA); see Customs Information*. The standard rate of IVA on goods and services is 21 per cent. Hotels generally include the tax in the room rate.

Always keep a few euros close to hand for hotel staff such as porters and chambermaids. In restaurants you may like to round up the bill, though a service charge is often already added. Italian taxi drivers do not expect a tip, and there is no need to tip a gondolier.

Travellers with Special Needs

Venice's many stepped bridges make it difficult for the wheelchair-bound to get around the city; in addition, many bridge lifts are being removed, further limiting disabled access.

Normal *vaporetti* (such as line 1) are accessible to wheelchairs since the deck is on the same level as the landing stages, and there is reserved space on board. Water taxis *(see p283)*, however, are hazardous for wheelchair users and should be avoided.

The Venezia Accessibile information pack details a wide range of barrier-free itineraries, with maps and route instructions. It also shows places of interest that can be visited by or have special facilities for the disabled, and how to reach them by *vaporetto* or by land. Venezia Accessibile is available at tourist offices or downloadable from the **Informahandicap** website.

A mechanically operated wheelchair ramp across a bridge

Travelling with Children

Italians love children, and while hotels and restaurants may not always be equipped for young visitors, they will be happy to accommodate them. Most restaurants have highchairs and will serve children simple meals such as pasta with olive oil or tomato sauce. It is best to request a cot at your hotel in advance of your visit. A holiday-let apartment *(see pp230–31)* is an excellent solution if you need kitchen access and play space. A useful website, **Italy Family Hotels** allows you to search and book accommodation for specifically child-friendly hotels throughout the Veneto and the country.

Venice is a wonderland for children, but it can also be very tiring for both kids and parents. It is best to invest in family passes or boat travel, so you can hop on and off at will. Limit the number of art galleries and museums you visit, and opt instead for more hands-on activities, such as glass-blowing demonstrations. Seek out the city's parks and playgrounds – such as Sant'Elena and Cannaregio, near the Ponte delle Guglie. In the summer, your kids can play with the local children on the Lido beaches; at other times of year, they can run around and let off steam in the neighbourhood squares. Most sights throughout the Veneto offer discounted admission for families.

Students relaxing in the sun in Verona

Student Travellers

Full-time students who are in possession of a valid **International Student Identity Card (ISIC)** will usually get reductions on museum entry fees and other charges across the Veneto. However, occasionally this is restricted to students residing in the EU. The Rolling VENICEcard, available to 14- to 29-year-olds for a small fee, provides a package of useful information on the city. This includes alternative itineraries, fashionable haunts and lists of shops, hotels, theatres and restaurants offering card-holder discounts. The pass also offers a reduced-price travelcard for the *vaporetti*. The Rolling VENICEcard is available online at Hello Venezia *(see p269)*, or at any *vaporetto* boarding point in Venice.

Senior Travellers

Travellers over 65 years of age are entitled to free entry to State-run museums and archaeological sites. In addition, discounted entry fees are available at many locally managed museums and historical sites throughout the Veneto. Photographic identification, such as a passport or driver's licence, needs to be shown upon entry as proof of age.

Like its younger "Rolling" version, the VENICEcard is a good pass to purchase, as it offers information on Venice's sights and transport savings as well as free entry to the Casino di Venezia *(see p260)*. It is available from Hello Venezia, and the main *vaporetto* stops.

If you are planning to do a fair amount of train travel while in the Veneto, you might want to consider purchasing a **Carta d'Argento**. This card entitles people over 60 to discounts of 15 per cent on first- and second-class train tickets. Yearly membership to the Carta d'Argento costs €30 for those over 60 years of age and is free to seniors who are over 75 years old. This can be applied for at the main train stations and travel agencies.

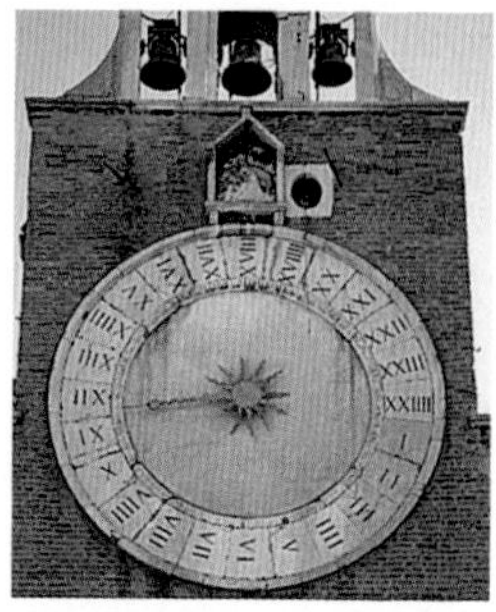

The clock of San Giacomo di Rialto in San Polo, Venice

Time

Italy is 1 hour ahead of Greenwich Mean Time (GMT). Daylight saving time is between April and October. For all official purposes, the Italians use the 24-hour clock.

Electricity

Electrical current in Italy is 220V AC, with two-pin, round-pronged plugs. Most hotels graded above three stars have electrical points for shavers (check the voltage first) and hairdryers in all bedrooms.

Conversion Chart

Imperial to Metric

1 inch = 2.54 centimetres
1 foot = 30 centimetres
1 mile = 1.6 kilometres
1 ounce = 28 grams
1 pound = 454 grams
1 pint = 0.6 litres
1 gallon = 4.6 litres

Metric to Imperial

1 centimetre = 0.4 inches
1 metre = 3 feet, 3 inches
1 kilometre = 0.6 miles
1 gram = 0.04 ounces
1 kilogram = 2.2 pounds
1 litre = 1.8 pints

Responsible Tourism

Italy is very aware of ethical and environmental issues. There are many projects to help its citizens live more sustainably and there are also steps visitors can take to enjoy the Veneto responsibly.

It should be easy to recycle as every town operates a *raccolta differenziata* (separate waste collection), with individual containers for glass, paper and plastic.

Organic, Fairtrade and local food is widely accessible in the Veneto. A range of organic products are available at the many **Coop** supermarkets dotted around the region; they stock Fairtrade items too. Venice also has the **Rialto Biocenter** supermarket. Located in the vicinity of the Rialto Bridge in San Polo, the Biocenter is a modestly sized health-food shop that stocks everything from tofu and wholewheat pasta to incense and natural cosmetics. In addition to the famous Rialto markets *(see p104)*, where you can buy fruit, vegetables and fish, farmers' markets and organic fairs are held regularly at Piazzale Roma. Some resident groups buy direct from growers on the island of **Sant'Erasmo**, who deliver by boat.

Buy your souvenirs at local artisan workshops, which help the community maintain the skills needed to make these regional products. Venice is known in particular for hand-blown glass.

Fruit and vegetables stalls at Rialto market

DIRECTORY

Embassies and Consulates

Australia
Via Antonio Bosio 5, Rome 00198. **Tel** 06 852 721. **W italy.embassy.gov.au**

Canada
Piazza Cavour 3, Milan 20121. **Tel** 02 626 942 38. **W canadainternational.gc.ca/italy**

New Zealand
Via Clitunno 44, Rome 00198. **Tel** 06 853 7501. **W nzembassy.com/italy**

United Kingdom
Via San Paolo 7, Milan 20121. **Tel** 06 422 024 31. **W gov.uk/government/world/italy**

United States
Via Principe Amedeo 2/10, Milan 20121. **Tel** 02 290 351. **W italy.usembassy.gov**

Visas and Passports

Ministero degli Affari Esteri
W esteri.it/visti

Customs Information

Agenzia delle Dogane
W agenziadogane.it

Tourist Information

ENIT UK
1 Princes St, London W1B 2AY. **Tel** 020 7408 1254. **W enit.it**

ENIT USA
Tel 212 245 48 22. **W italiantourism.com**

Padua Tourist Board
Railway station. **Tel** 049 201 00 80. **W turismopadova.it**

Venice Tourist Board
Piazza San Marco 1. **Map** 7 B2. Piazzale Roma. **Map** 1 B5. Ferrovia Santa Lucia. **Map** 1 B4. **Tel** 041 529 87 11 (for all offices). **W turismovenezia.it**

Verona Tourist Board
Via degli Alpini 9. **Tel** 045 806 86 80. **W turismoverona.eu**

Vicenza Tourist Board
Piazza dei Signori 8. **Tel** 044 454 41 22. **W vicenzae.org**

Admission Prices

Hello Venezia
Tel 041 24 24. **W hellovenezia.com**

Venice Connected
W veniceconnected.com

Opening Hours

Chorus
Tel 041 275 04 62. **W chorusvenezia.org**

Un Ospite di Venezia
W unospitedivenezia.it

Travelling with Children

Italy Family Hotels
W italyfamilyhotels.it/en

Travellers with Special Needs

Informahandicap
Tel 041 274 81 44. **W comune.venezia.it/informahandicap**

Student Travellers

International Student Identity Card (ISIC)
W isic.org

Senior Travellers

Carta d'Argento
W trenitalia.com

Responsible Tourism

Coop
Piazzale Roma. **Map** 1 B5. **Tel** 041 296 06 21. **W e-coop.it**

Rialto Biocenter
Calle della Regina, Santa Croce 2264. **Map** 2 F5. **Tel** 041 523 95 15. **W rialtobiocenter.it**

Sant'Erasmo Growers
Tel 041 528 29 97. **W isaporidisanterasmo.com**

Personal Security and Health

Venice is one of the safest cities in Europe, and visitors are unlikely to encounter any unpleasant situations. Violent crime is very rare, and petty crime is minimal in comparison with other main urban centres. Nevertheless, it is wise to take a few simple precautions, particularly against pickpockets, both in Venice and throughout the Veneto. Always leave valuables and important documents in the hotel safe, and carry only the minimum amount of money necessary for the day. Make sure you take out adequate travel insurance before leaving for Italy, as it is very difficult to obtain once you are in the country.

Two Venetian *polizia* on the Riva degli Schiavoni

Police

The *vigili urbani*, or municipal police, are most often seen in the streets regulating traffic and enforcing local laws. Their uniform is blue in winter and white in summer. The *carabinieri*, with red striped trousers, are the armed military police, responsible for public law and order. The *polizia*, or state police, wear blue uniforms with white belts and berets. They specialize in serious crimes. Any of these forces should be able to help you in an emergency.

In the event of theft, go to the nearest ***questura*** (police station) and make a statement. If there is a language problem, consult your nearest consulate *(see p271)*.

What to be Aware of

Always keep your valuables and personal documents in a safe place when travelling. It is also wise to keep a photocopy of all vital papers, including your passport, separately. Try not to attract the attention of pickpockets and bag-snatchers by having your bag unzipped, particularly at railway stations, markets and on public transport. In Venice, take care while waiting at the *vaporetto* landing stages, and be especially vigilant when people are jostling to get on board. On crowded boats, hold your handbag or rucksack in front of you.

Rented cars and vehicles with foreign number plates are favourite targets of car thieves. Always lock the car before you leave it, and never leave valuables on display inside.

Venice is fairly uneventful after dark, and you can generally stroll through the streets without any threat. There is no red-light quarter or any area that could be described as unsavoury, though the beaches are best avoided at night.

Women alone in Venice are unlikely to encounter anything more troublesome than the Latin roving eye; however, in the evening it is best to stick to well-trodden and well-lit routes. Elsewhere in the Veneto, particularly in the less touristy towns, unescorted females are likely to attract more attention.

Make sure you take only official taxis, which have the licence number clearly displayed *(see p287)*. Avoid unauthorized taxi drivers, who may not be insured and almost invariably overcharge. Airports are their favourite haunts.

In an Emergency

In the event of an emergency, call 112 or 113 to get hold of the **Soccorso Pubblico** (public assistance). Dialling 115 alerts the **Vigili del Fuoco** (fire brigade). If you are in need of urgent medical attention, go to the *Pronto Soccorso* (emergency) department of the nearest main hospital. There are often queues, so be prepared to wait. Doctors and hospital staff in tourist localities usually speak at least some English.

If you need an **Ambulanza** (ambulance), phone 118. In Venice, this will get you an ambulance boat; in the Dolomites, you will be connected to the *Soccorso Alpino* (mountain rescue). If necessary, a helicopter will be sent. If you do not speak Italian, use simple English to explain where you are and what the problem is.

All towns have a Guardia Medica service, with a doctor on duty for urgent problems at night-time and weekends. Ask the tourist office for the relevant phone numbers. In tourist resorts, the Guardia Medica is generally available on site and 24 hours a day in season.

Police boat

Ambulance boat

Lost and Stolen Property

If you lose anything valuable, such as your passport, contact your consulate at once *(see p271)*. Items lost on public transport in Venice and Mestre end up at the **ACTV Oggetti Rinvenuti** offices – the one in Piazzale Roma is for items left on the *vaporetti*, the one in Mestre is for items lost on buses.

There are no railway lost property offices, so if you leave anything on a train, contact the lost property office – **Oggetti Rinvenuti** – in the nearest town.

In the event of stolen property, go to the nearest *questura* (police station; *see Police*) to make a statement. Take your passport with you for identification purposes.

Pharmacy sign

Hospitals and Pharmacies

Standards of health care in Italy are on a par with those in the UK and the US. Should you need a doctor, ask your concierge or look in the Yellow Pages, under *Medici*. If you have a serious medical complaint or allergy, it might be wise to bring a letter, preferably translated, from your doctor at home. Most doctors in the region speak some English.

Pharmacies *(farmacie)* are generally open 9am–12:30pm and 4–7:30pm Monday–Friday, and 9am–noon on Saturdays. All towns offer a 24-hour pharmacy service *(farmacia di turno)*, with a night-time and Sunday rota. You will find the rota posted on the doors of all pharmacies. Opening times can also be found in the local newspapers or, if you are in Venice, in the booklet *Un Ospite di Venezia (see p271)*.

Italian pharmacists are well trained to deal with minor ailments and can sell many drugs without needing a doctor's prescription. If you are taking prescribed medication, take enough supplies or a prescription including the generic name of the medication – pharmacies can usually distribute the local equivalent. Many of the words for minor complaints and remedies are similar in Italian, for example *aspirina* (aspirin), *tranquillante* (tranquillizer), and *lassativo* (laxative).

Dentists are expensive in Italy. You can find the nearest one in the Yellow Pages, under *Dentisti medici chirurghi*, or ask your hotel receptionist to give you a recommendation.

Minor Hazards

Inoculations are not needed for the Veneto, but it is wise to take high-factor sunscreen, especially if you plan on travelling in spring or summer. Insect repellent is a must in the summer, as mosquitoes can be irksome in Venice. An electric gadget, available from pharmacies or department stores, will repel insects in your room for up to 12 hours.

Tap water is safe to drink, as is the water from fountains, unless a sign warns that it is *non potabile* (undrinkable).

Travel and Health Insurance

Visitors from the EU are entitled to reciprocal state medical care in Italy. Before you travel, obtain a European Health Insurance Card (EHIC), from the post office or online, which covers you for emergency medical treatment. You may wish to take out additional medical insurance as the EHIC does not cover repatriation costs.

Australia also has a reciprocal medical agreement with Italy, but other visitors from outside the EU should take out a comprehensive medical insurance policy. For claims, make sure you keep all receipts for medical treatment and any medicines prescribed.

Purchasing additional travel insurance before leaving home is recommended. If you intend to do any winter sports you will need extra cover.

DIRECTORY

Police

Questura
Venice: Fondamenta di S Chiara, Santa Croce 500. **Map** 1 B5. **Tel** 041 271 55 11.
Padua: Piazzetta G Palatucci 5. **Tel** 049 83 31 11.
Verona: Lungadige Galtarossa 11. **Tel** 045 809 04 11.
Vicenza: Viale Mazzini 213. **Tel** 044 433 75 11.

In an Emergency

General Emergency (Soccorso Pubblico)
Tel 112 or 113.

Fire (Vigili del Fuoco)
Tel 115.

Ambulance (Ambulanza)
Tel 118.

Lost and Stolen Property

ACTV Oggetti Rinvenuti
1st Floor, Garage Comunale, Piazzale Roma. **Map** 5 B1. **Tel** 041 272 21 79. Via Martiri della Libertà, Mestre. **Tel** 041 272 27 23.

Oggetti Rinvenuti
Venice: **Tel** 041 274 82 25.
Padua: **Tel** 049 820 49 25.
Verona: **Tel** 045 805 78 81.
Vicenza: **Tel** 044 422 10 30.

Hospitals

Venice: Campo Santi Giovanni e Paolo. **Map** 3 C5. **Tel** 041 529 43 11.

Padua: Via Giustiniani 2. **Tel** 049 821 11 11.

Verona: Piazzale Stefani 1. **Tel** 045 812 11 11.

Vicenza: Via Rodolfi 37. **Tel** 044 475 31 11.

Pharmacies

Venice: Campo San Polo. **Map** 6 F1. **Tel** 041 522 06 75.

Padua: Via Daniele Manin, 67. **Tel** 049 875 83 63.

Verona: Piazza delle Erbe 20. **Tel** 045 800 62 64.

Vicenza: Corso Santi Felice e Fortunato 117. **Tel** 044 43211 82.

Dentists

Venice: **Tel** 041 522 81 37.
Padua: **Tel** 049 872 16 38.
Verona: **Tel** 045 803 46 88.
Vicenza: **Tel** 044 456 49 80.

Banking and Local Currency

Visitors to the Veneto have a number of options available to them for changing money. Banks tend to give more favourable rates than bureaux de change, hotels and travel agents, but the paperwork is usually more time-consuming. Alternatively, you can use a credit card for purchasing goods and services. If using a debit card, check with your bank about fees for overseas withdrawals before departing from home.

The waiting area of a bank in Vicenza

Banks and Bureaux de Change

It is a good idea to acquire some euros before you arrive in Italy. Changing foreign currency at a bank can be a frustrating process because it involves endless form-filling and queuing. You must apply first at the window displaying the *cambio* sign, then move to the *cassa* to obtain your euros. If in doubt, ask a member of staff in order to avoid waiting in the wrong queue.

For security reasons, most banks have electronic double doors with metal detectors, allowing only one person in at a time. Metal objects and bags should first be deposited in lockers situated in the foyer. Press the button to open the outer door, step in and wait for it to close behind you. The inner door will then open automatically.

Banks are usually open from 8:30am–1:30pm Monday to Friday. Most also open for an hour in the afternoon. They are closed at weekends and public holidays, and they also close early the day before a major holiday. One of the main banks in Venice is the **Cassa di Risparmio di Venezia**.

Bureaux de change stay open longer and work seven days a week. The exchange offices at Venice's Stazione Venezia Santa Lucia *(see p280)*, Marco Polo Airport and Antonio Canova Airport at Treviso *(see p279)*, stay open until the evening and at weekends.

Exchange rates vary from place to place, but banks usually offer the best deal. Some hotels also offer a currency exchange service; rates tend to be poor, but the commission is modest.

If you need to have money sent to you in Italy, banks in your home country can wire money to an Italian bank, but this can take up to a week. For a swifter money-transfer service, try **Travelex**, the Italian agent for Western Union.

Credit and Debit Cards

Credit cards are widely accepted throughout Italy and can be very useful, particularly for hotel and restaurant bills, shopping, car hire, booking tickets by telephone and emergency situations. **Visa**, **MasterCard** and **American Express** are the most popular. Be aware that most credit cards levy a surcharge on overseas transactions. Some establishments require a minimum expenditure to accept credit card payment, so always make sure that you have enough cash just in case.

To avoid your card being unnecessarily blocked, notify your bank of your travel plans before you set off. If your credit card is lost or stolen, contact the relevant emergency telephone number immediately. The card will be blocked, and any unauthorized payments will then be refused. Keep a copy of your credit card number in a safe place, separate from the actual card, in case of loss. Prepaid credit cards are also a safe option.

Travellers' cheques are another safe way to carry money. They are still accepted at leading exchange offices, though these may charge hefty commissions to convert them into currency.

ATMs

Most banks have an ATM *(bancomat)* that will accept debit and major credit cards (Visa, MasterCard and American Express). Cash dispensers will be located throughout the main cities. Instructions are given in different languages. You will need to enter your personal PIN number for a cash withdrawal. Be aware that a percentage charge will usually be applied by your home bank for this service.

Always take precautions to ensure that your PIN number remains a secret, and make sure nobody is looking over your shoulder as you type it in when using an ATM.

DIRECTORY

Banks and Bureaux de Change

Cassa di Risparmio di Venezia
Campo Manin, San Marco.
Map 7 A2.
Tel 041 529 11 11.

Travelex
Riva del Ferro, Rialto, San Marco 5126. **Map** 7 A1.
Tel 041 528 73 58.
W travelex.it

Credit and Debit Cards

For lost or stolen cards:
American Express
Tel 06 7290 0347.
MasterCard
Tel 800 870 866 (freephone).
Visa
Tel 800 819 014 (freephone).

The Euro

The euro (€) is the common currency of the European Union. It came into general circulation on 1 January 2002, initially for 12 participating countries, including Italy. The previous Italian currency, the lira, was phased out by March 2002. EU members using the euro as their sole official currency are known as the Eurozone. Several EU members have opted out of joining this common currency.

Euro notes are identical throughout the Eurozone countries, each one including designs of fictional architectural structures. The coins, however, have one side identical (the value side) and one side with an image unique to each country. Notes and coins are exchangeable in each participating country.

Banknotes

Euro banknotes have seven denominations. The €5 note (grey in colour) is the smallest, followed by the €10 note (pink), €20 note (blue), €50 note (orange), €100 note (green), €200 note (yellow) and €500 note (purple). All notes show the 12 stars of the European Union.

€5 note

€10 note

€20 note

€50 note

€100 note

€200 note

€500 note

€2 coin

€1 coin

50 cents

20 cents

10 cents

Coins

The euro has eight coin denominations: €1 and €2; 50 cents, 20 cents, 10 cents, 5 cents, 2 cents and 1 cent. The €2 and €1 coins are both silver and gold in colour. The 50-, 20- and 10-cent coins are gold. The 5-, 2- and 1-cent coins are bronze.

5 cents

2 cents

1 cent

Communications and Media

Although there are still plenty of public telephones throughout the Veneto, mobile phone networks are far-reaching, efficient and relatively low priced. Most hotels offer an Internet or Wi-Fi service to their guests; if not, Internet points are easy to find in the region, even in small towns. Foreign-language newspapers and magazines are on sale in all cities and main towns, and satellite TV has a vast range of foreign-language programmes from around the world. There are post offices located in all towns and villages for buying stamps and sending letters and parcels.

Telephones in a call centre run by Venetian Navigator

International and Local Telephone Calls

A wide range of phonecards *(carte telefoniche prepagate)* are available at newsagents and tobacconists *(tabacchi)*. The latter are easily recognized thanks to the black-and-white "T" sign they display. For making local and Italian calls, the best option is a Telecom card; simply remove the dotted corner before inserting it into the phone. For overseas calls, specify the country you will be calling, so the vendor can advise you on the best card. To use these, call the toll-free number displayed on the card, enter the bar code information, then proceed with the overseas number. A recording will tell you how much credit is left before each call. These cards expire three months after the first call you make.

If you opt to use the phone in your hotel room, ask beforehand about the charges, which tend to be steep. A cheaper option is to use the privately owned call centres that are scattered around main cities.

Any Italian number must be prefixed by its full area code (including the "0"), even if it is a local number. Similarly, do not drop the "0" from in front of the area code when dialling an Italian number from abroad. The only numbers that do not require the "0" are those for the emergency services *(see p273)*, mobile phones (which start with a "3") and toll-free numbers (which begin with an "8").

Mobile Phones

Mobile phones are extremely useful when travelling abroad. If you have a tri-band/GSM phone it should work in Italy, but check with your mobile provider that this is the case before you leave. Your handset will need to have "roaming" activated in order to use it abroad and be aware that you will be charged extra for making and receiving calls while away. Reasonably priced prepaid phonecards can be used for long-distance calls from a mobile *(see International and Local Telephone Calls)*. Alternatively, you might want to consider purchasing an Italian mobile phone or a SIM card through one of the major companies such as **TIM**, **Wind** and **Vodafone**. You will need to show your passport for identification. Take note that to activate your SIM card you will need to make a short call to a landline or another mobile phone, and that the cards usually expire 12 months after the last top-up.

Public Telephones

You can find the silver-and-orange Telecom public telephones on the streets and squares of all the main towns in the Veneto, as well as at railway and bus stations. In Venice there are public telephones at most *vaporetto* landing stages and in privately owned call centres. Coin-operated phones have virtually been phased out in favour of phones that take phonecards.

Tabacchi sign

Reaching the Right Number

To ring Italy from the UK and Ireland, dial 00 39 then the number, including the full area code. From the US and Canada dial 0 11 39, and from Australia dial 00 11 39.

- Dialling code for
  - Venice 041
  - Verona 045
  - Vicenza 0444
  - Padua 049
  - Treviso 0422
- International directory enquiries 176
- International operator assistance 170
- Telegrams and cables in Italy and abroad 186
- *See also* In an Emergency, p273.

Computer terminals at an Internet café

Internet and Email

Across the Veneto, Wi-Fi or Internet points are available in most hotels although a time-related fee may be charged.

Internet cafés are found in every city and most small towns. The main ones in Venice are **Venetian Navigator** and **Teleradiofuga**. Wi-Fi is available in many outdoor spaces in Venice and Padua for a fee; **Verona WiFi** offers free internet access in some public areas of the municipality. To access these Wi-Fi services you must register with **Venice Connected**, **Padua WiFi** or, if in Verona, at **URP** or a local library.

Post Office sign

Postal Service

In summer, post sent from Venice to destinations abroad takes some time to arrive, as thousands of postcards are sent from the city every day. For important communications, use the *Posta Prioritaria* (priority mail) or ask for a *Raccomandata* (registered post), which can be traced.

Stamps *(francobolli)* are available from post offices and tobacconists. Post office hours are usually 8:30am–1:30pm Monday to Friday (but main city offices close at 6pm) and 8:30am–12:30pm on Saturdays.

Large items to be sent abroad must be in a rigid cardboard box, which can be purchased at most post offices. You will also need to fill in a customs declaration form. Small items can be sent in a padded envelope. The postal system offers a well-priced tracked courier service, Paccocelere, for sending packages both within Italy and overseas.

For a rapid worldwide delivery, consider a private courier. Both **DHL** and **UPS** have bases in Venice and the Veneto.

Newspapers and Magazines

The local daily newspapers *Il Gazzettino* and *La Nuova Venezia* have separate editions for Padua, Venice, Verona and Vicenza as well as covering national and some international news. Local event listings can be found in the dailies and also in *Eventi e Manifestazioni* (Venice) and *Carnet Verona* *(see p268)*. European and US newspapers and magazines such as the *Guardian* and *Time*, are available at large newsagents (such as those found at main railway stations) a day or two after publication.

Television and Radio

In Italy there are three state TV channels – Rai 1, Rai 2 and Rai 3 – and a myriad of private channels. Satellite and cable TV transmit foreign channels such as CNN in English and BBC World Service in many languages.

The main radio stations, also run by Rai, are Radio 1, Radio 2 and Radio 3. The frequencies vary depending on where you are in the Veneto and if you have a digital or analogue radio. Visit www.raiway.it for more details.

DIRECTORY

Mobile Phones

TIM
Rio Terà San Leonardo, Cannaregio 1412–1412/b, Venice. **Map** 2 E3. **Tel** 041 244 85 25.

Vodafone
Salizada Pio X, San Marco 5169–5171, Venice. **Map** 7 A1. **Tel** 041 523 90 16.

Wind
Salizzada San Pantalon, S Croce 48, Venice. **Map** 6 D1. **Tel** 041 524 41 74.

Internet and Email

Padua WiFi
W **padovawifi.it**

Teleradiofuga
San Pantalon, Dorsoduro 3812/a. **Map** 6 D2. **Tel** 041 71 46 66.
Calle della Mandola, San Marco 3713. **Map** 7 A2. **Tel** 523 92 63.
W **teleradiofuga.com**

URP
Via Adigetto 10, Verona 37122. **Tel** 045 807 75 00.
W **portale.comune.verona.it**

Venetian Navigator
Calle degli Stagneri, San Marco 5239. **Map** 7 B1. **Tel** 349 666 87 84. W **venetiannavigator.com**

Venice Connected
W **veniceconnected.com**

Verona WiFi
W **turismoverona.eu**

Postal Service

DHL
c/o Novotour, Garage Comunale 496/f/g, Piazzale Roma, Venice. **Map** 1 B5. **Tel** 199 19 93 45.
W **dhl.it**

Post Offices
Padua: Corso Garibaldi 25. **Tel** 049 877 22 09.

Venice: Calle San Salvador, San Marco 5016. **Map** 7 B1. **Tel** 041 240 41 49.

Verona: Piazza Isolo 13. **Tel** 045 805 03 49.

Vicenza: Contrà Garibaldi 1. **Tel** 044 454 44 49.
W **poste.it**

UPS
c/o Brusato Trasporti, Barbaria delle Tole, Castello 6366, Venice. **Map** 4 D5. **Tel** 041 528 99 82.
W **ups.com**

GETTING TO VENICE AND THE VENETO

The easiest way to reach the Veneto is by air. Direct flights link Venice to other major European cities, and there are several intercontinental flights available too, although visitors travelling from outside Europe must transfer at Milan or Rome. Venice's Marco Polo Airport, located 10 km (6.5 miles) north of the city, is supplemented by smaller airports at Treviso, 40 km (29 miles) northwest of Venice, and Verona, which is useful for Lake Garda. The Italian rail network is far-reaching, and both Venice and Verona train stations have excellent links with all the other Veneto towns and major European cities. Car drivers must bear in mind toll charges on European motorways and heavy traffic. Visitors to Venice itself will have to leave their cars in one of the large car parks on the outskirts of the city, because cars are not allowed in the centre. Parking fees are high.

View of the lagoon from Venice's Marco Polo Airport

Arriving by Air

Venice is served by two airports: **Marco Polo** at Campalto, which is the closest to the city, and **Antonio Canova** at Treviso, a short distance inland. These airports receive both low-cost and commercial flights from cities in the United Kingdom and other European countries. Direct flights from the UK to Venice are operated by **British Airways**, **easyJet** and **Jet2**, whereas the national Italian carrier **Alitalia** flies via Rome.

Few intercontinental flights operate, but it is possible to fly direct from New York to Venice with **Delta Airlines**. Visitors from outside Europe can take a flight to London, Amsterdam, Frankfurt or Paris and connect to Venice or Treviso from there. **Emirates** also flies to Marco Polo Airport from Dubai, which is the stopover of choice for many travellers from Australia and Asia on long-haul flights.

Most charter flights operate to Antonio Canova Airport, as does the low-cost airline **Ryanair**.

Valerio Catullo Airport is 12 km (7.5 miles) west of Verona. It is perfectly placed for visitors to Lake Garda and the Dolomites. Alitalia and low-cost airlines, such as Ryanair, have regularly scheduled flights to Verona.

Tickets and Fares

The best deals on tickets are usually found on the Internet. However, these offers are usually only available to those who book well in advance and avoid travelling over the peak periods: Christmas, New Year and Easter, as well as the European school holidays during July and August. Remember to have a credit card to hand when booking online. If you wish to book a flight during your stay in the Veneto, travel agents such as **Bucintoro Viaggi** offer a good service.

For visitors who prefer the convenience of a package holiday, Venice is either offered as a single destination or as part of a two- or three-city holiday alongside Florence and Rome. Taking a package holiday with a tour operator may be less costly than going independently. It is always worth comparing the costs, however, particularly if you intend to travel off-season, when charter flights are at their cheapest. Transfers from the airport are usually included in the price of the holiday.

In the Veneto, most tour operators tend to concentrate on Venice alone, though some offer packages to Verona or tours of the wider region, taking in the most popular villas, museums and art galleries.

On Arrival

Passengers on flights originating within the EU do not need to pass through customs. Intercontinental flight passengers need to have both their passports and visas ready to show staff. For visa information, *see p268*.

A *vaporetto* boarding point along the Grand Canal

Marco Polo Airport (Venice)

The facilities available at Marco Polo Airport include a tourist information kiosk, hotel reservation service, car-hire offices, post office, self-service restaurant and currency exchange office.

The most exciting entry from the airport in to Venice is by *vaporetto*. **Alilaguna** operate *vaporetti* terminal routes A, B, O and R that travel to Venice and the Lido, departing regularly from 6:10am to around midnight daily. The journey to Venice takes about an hour; tickets start at €15 per person, depending on your destination, and are available from the boarding point on the quayside, a short stroll away. The *vaporetto* stops at several *landing stages*, including San Marco, San Zaccaria and Fondamente Nuove. Water taxis operating from the airport to San Marco take about half the time but will cost around €100. There is also a €10 surcharge at night. Beware of water-taxi touts, who will charge you more than the official fare.

The less spectacular – but quicker and cheaper – alternative to the lagoon crossing is by an **ATVO** bus to Piazzale Roma. This service meets all scheduled flights and costs €7. Cheaper still (€6) is the **ACTV** public bus No. 5 to Piazzale Roma, which departs every 30 minutes and makes several stops along the way. There is also a land taxi rank in front of the airport. The journey takes 15 minutes, and the drop-off point is Piazzale Roma.

Antonio Canova Airport (Treviso)

This small but modern airport receives low-cost flights from cities in the UK and other European countries. It has a tourist information office, foreign exchange and cafés.

To reach Venice, take a shuttle service to Piazzale Roma; this costs €5 and takes about 45 minutes. Or, you can take a public bus No. 6 for €1, which runs to Treviso station, from where there is a regular rail service to Venice.

Valerio Catullo Airport (Verona)

Verona airport receives flights from cities in the UK, other European countries and Africa. The bus service to Verona town centre, which links up with scheduled flights, costs about €5. In summer there is usually a direct minibus to localities on Lake Garda.

Arriving by Sea

Minoan Lines and **Anek** run large ferries with cabins and vehicle decks from several ports in Greece most months of the year. A grand way to travel, the Istrian peninsula and the Dalmatian coast are linked to Venice through the summer by fast catamarans and ferries run by operators such as **Venezia Lines**, **Atlas** and **Commodore Cruises**.

Venice is also a key port for state-of-the-art cruise ships bound for the Mediterranean. Companies stopping here include **P&O Cruises** and **MSC Crociere**.

Both ferries and cruise ships dock at **Venezia Terminal Passeggeri**, a large terminal near Tronchetto that spreads along the lagoon and canalside from the Stazione Marittima basin to Santa Marta and San Basilio. Most of the six terminal sections have full passenger facilities, including cafés, ATMs, duty-free shops, waiting halls and information points.

An automated people mover carries passengers from the central part of the terminal to Piazzale Roma in minutes. However, for cruise passengers it is usually more convenient to travel by the shuttle buses that are provided by the individual cruise companies as they pull up at boarding points. The ACTV bus No. 6 also links the main terminal entrance with Piazzale Roma. Santa Marta and San Basilio are served by ACTV *vaporetto* line No. 6, which terminates at the Lido.

The terminal is spread over a large area, so it is important for departing passengers to be clear about which section their ferry or ship leaves from. The terminal's website is very helpful, with clear maps.

Cruise ship moored at Venezia Terminal Passeggeri

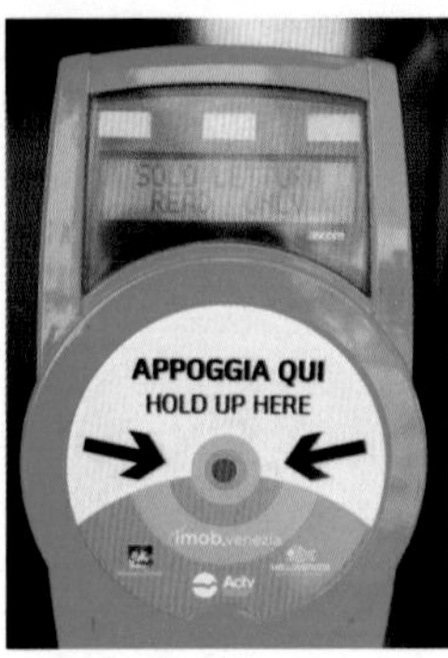

An electronic ticket machine at a *vaporetto* stop on the Grand Canal

Arriving by Coach

Long-distance regional and international coaches use Piazzale Roma as their terminus in Venice. Regular lines run by **SITA** link Venice with Padua, while services run by **Dolomiti Bus** travel to various localities in the Dolomite Mountains. For Europe-wide routes, try **Eurolines**, which offers a good-value multi-day pass and pick-ups from Piazzale Roma, or the slightly more costly **Busabout**, with similar routes but pick-ups outside Venice. Tickets can be purchased at the office in Piazzale Roma or online in advance of your travels.

Arriving by Train

The **Stazione Venezia Santa Lucia**, Venice's railway station, is a modern, well-equipped station located at the western end of the Grand Canal. Santa Lucia is the terminus for trains from Paris, Munich, Innsbruck, Vienna, Geneva, Zurich and other European cities. Passengers travelling from London will have to change in Paris or Ostend. Fast intercity trains link Venice with Verona, Bologna, Milan, Rome and other major Italian cities.

If the ticket office is closed, it is possible to purchase train tickets from the automatic machines in the station. They display instructions in six languages and accept notes, coins and some credit cards. Electronic display screens give up-to-date information on arrivals and departures, as well as notice of any delays. Facilities include a tourist information office, hotel reservation service, telephones, bank, currency exchange office, left-luggage storage, self-service restaurant and café, and a shop that sells international newspapers and magazines.

Just below the steps of the station are *vaporetti* landing stages with lines to all parts of the city. There are also water taxis, a gondola service and porters. The bus and coach terminal and the land taxi rank are located in Piazzale Roma, a short walk away.

Trenitalia offers reduced-price tickets for travel throughout Italy and Europe if you buy them in advance online. Europe-wide train passes such as **Eurail** (no age limit) and **InterRail** (for those under 26 years of age) are accepted; however, you will have to pay a supplement to travel on the fast trains.

The German **DB Bahn** and the Austrian **OEBB** also provide rail links between Venice, Verona, Munich and Innsbruck. Tickets for these services can be purchased online or on board.

Eurostar train travelling through the countryside in the Veneto

Orient-Express

Operating between March and November, the Venice Simplon **Orient-Express** travels between London and Venice, stopping at Paris, Innsbruck and Verona en route. A one-way journey with cabin from London to Venice is the ultimate romantic experience, but it can cost as much as 10 times the price of a low-cost flight. Prices are more reasonable for a return trip. Visit the website for further information.

Orient-Express logo

Arriving by Car

To drive your own car in Italy you will need an international Green Card and your vehicle registration documents. Also, check that your car insurance covers you to drive abroad. EU nationals who do not have the standard pink-coloured driving licence will need an Italian translation of their licence, available from most Italian tourist offices. UK drivers do not require a translation; however, those with an old paper licence will need to carry additional photo ID, such as a passport. Requirements for visitors from non-EU countries vary; check with your insurance company.

The toll-paying A4 *autostrada* (motorway) links Turin to Venice via Padua, Verona and Vicenza – simply take the relevant exit for your destination. The A27 from Venice leads north beyond Vittorio Veneto towards the Dolomites.

In Venice, parking is prohibitively expensive. The closest car parks to the city centre are at Piazzale Roma or on the Tronchetto, linked to Venice by *vaporetto* and bus. There are cheaper car parks at Fusina and San Giuliano, near Mestre *(see City Map)*.

For information on Italian road rules, *see p287*.

Car Hire

All the major international car-hire companies, such as **Hertz**, **Avis** and **Europcar**, have offices in the Veneto, both at airports and at the main train stations. It is worth doing an online search to find the best price or, if you fly with a low-cost carrier, check out the deals they offer. Always make sure that quoted prices include collision damage waiver, theft protection, unlimited mileage, a breakdown service and *Imposta sul Valore Aggiunto* (Value Added Tax; *see p269*).

To hire a car you must be over 25 and have held a licence for at least a year. You will also need to show your passport and a credit card. Visitors from outside the EU need an international licence, though not all hire firms insist on this. Vehicles are usually supplied with a full tank of fuel, so try to refill it before returning the car to avoid inflated costs. Child seats need to be booked in advance.

Vaporetto boarding point and water-taxi rank at Stazione Venezia Santa Lucia

Porters in Venice

Unless you are staying very close to your arrival point, you will need to take a *vaporetto* to the boarding point nearest to your hotel. Porters *(portabagagli)* are very expensive; not only do you have to pay their boat fare, you must also pay for each item of luggage, which are charged an adult fare. In addition to the *vaporetto* fares, the cost of a porter handling two suitcases could easily amount to €40.

DIRECTORY

Arriving by Air

Alitalia
Tel 06 22 22.
w alitalia.it

Antonio Canova Airport (Treviso)
Tel 042 231 51 11.
w trevisoairport.it

British Airways
Tel 199 712 266.
w britishairways.com

Delta Airlines
Tel 848 780 376.
w delta.com

easyJet
w easyjet.com

Emirates
Tel 02 9148 3383.
w emirates.com

Jet2
w jet2.com

Marco Polo Airport (Venice)
Tel 041 260 92 60.
w veniceairport.it

Ryanair
w ryanair.com

Valerio Catullo Airport (Verona)
Tel 045 809 56 66.
w aeroportoverona.it

Tickets and Fares

Bucintoro Viaggi
Campo S Luca, San Marco 4267/c, Venice. **Map** 7 A2.
Tel 041 521 06 32.
w bucintoro viaggi.com

Transport from the Airport

ACTV
Tel 041 24 24. **w actv.it**

Alilaguna
Tel 041 240 17 01.
w alilaguna.com

ATVO
Tel 042 138 36 72.
w atvo.it

Arriving by Sea

Anek
w anekitalia.com

Atlas
w atlas-croatia.com

Commodore Cruises
w commodore-cruises.hr

Minoan Lines
w minoanlines.it

MSC Crociere
w msccrociere.crocierissime.it

P&O Cruises
w pocruises.com

Venezia Lines
w venezialines.com

Venezia Terminal Passeggeri
w vtp.it

Arriving by Coach

Busabout
w busabout.com

Dolomiti Bus
w dolomitibus.it

Eurolines
w eurolines.com

SITA
w sitabus.it

Arriving by Train

DB Bahn
w bahn.de

Eurail
w eurail.com

InterRail
w interrail.eu

OEBB
w oebb.at

Orient-Express
w orient-express.com

Stazione Venezia Santa Lucia
Map 1 C5.
Tel 041 78 56 70.

Trenitalia
Tel 89 20 21. Disabled Passengers: **Tel** 199 303 060. **w trenitalia.com**

Car Hire

Venice
Avis: **Tel** 041 523 73 77.
w avisautonoleggio.it
Europcar: **Tel** 041 523 86 16. **w europcar.it**
Hertz: **Tel** 041 528 40 91.
w hertz.com

Padua
Avis: **Tel** 049 864 7661.
Europcar: **Tel** 049 65 78 77.
Hertz: **Tel** 049 875 22 02.

Verona
Avis: **Tel** 045 800 66 36.
Europcar: **Tel** 045 927 3161.
Hertz: **Tel** 045 800 08 32.

Vicenza
Avis: **Tel** 044 432 16 22.
Europcar: **Tel** 044 428 00 42.
Hertz: **Tel** 044 423 17 28.

Porters in Venice

Tel 041 720 686.

GETTING AROUND VENICE AND THE VENETO

Venice is a small city, and most of the main sights can be covered comfortably on foot. Cars are not allowed; instead pedestrians stroll the avenues and narrow passageways. To avoid getting lost in the maze of alleys and squares, use the Street Finder *(see pp288–301)*. The iconic gondola is the most romantic way to see the city from the canals and the lagoon. However, the excellent network of *vaporetti* is more affordable. The boats also travel across the lagoon to the outlying islands. For those in a hurry, a water taxi is the fastest means of travelling across Venice. Day trips to the Veneto can be made by train or bus, and most of the cities can easily be explored on foot. For longer stays, a car is more practical, as it offers complete independence to enjoy the countryside.

Green Travel

Most Venetian motorboats and ferries run on diesel; however, efforts are under way to switch to a less polluting fuel. At least one battery-operated *vaporetto* is in service, and an eco-friendly Alilaguna *vaporetto* offers trips to and from the airport *(see p279)*. This boat was designed to minimize wave damage in the canals.

Other cities in the Veneto are served by large fleets of buses powered by clean methane gas.

Car-hire companies Hertz and Europcar *(see p281)* offer some "ecological" vehicles with reduced CO_2 emissions.

There are also a number of bicycle tours that operate in the Veneto. See local tourist offices for details.

Finding Your Way around Venice

Venice's system of addresses can be very confusing. All buildings are numbered by the *sestiere* (administrative district) in which they fall rather than the street. A typical address might read, for example, "San Marco 2517" or "Cannaregio 3499". In order to locate an address, therefore, it is essential to establish the name of the actual street or square or, failing that, the nearest landmark. Do not hesitate to ask for assistance, as Venetians are very helpful. Translations of Venetian words commonly used in place names can be found on *p288*.

Walking

The absence of traffic makes exploring Venice on foot a great pleasure. Wear comfortable footwear as a day's sightseeing can be tiring. You will have to contend with the constant flow of other tourists, especially around San Marco and Rialto, where the narrow alleys become extremely congested. An unwritten Venetian rule is to keep to the right and avoid stopping on bridges and in narrow streets. However, most tourists never venture beyond San Marco, so it may be little more than a matter of minutes before you find yourself with only a few locals for company.

An ornate Venetian door knocker

You need to allow just 45 minutes to cross the city from north to south on foot – provided you do not lose your way, though that is half the fun. The Street Finder and City maps in this guide will help you find your way around.

As the city is so compact, you are never far from the yellow signs that give directions to the main sights. Venice has countless *campi* (squares) that open out from narrow alleys. Many of these are equipped with public benches, and weary tourists can enjoy a drink in an open-air café.

In July and August, when temperatures are at their highest, avoid walking in the middle of the day, unless you have a broad-rimmed sunhat. From October there is a risk of high tides *(acqua alta)*, which cause flooding across the city, starting with Piazza San Marco. Duckboards are laid out in the square, however, and along main thoroughfares. If you are not equipped with Wellington boots, you can buy cheap knee-high plastic shoe covers from local shops.

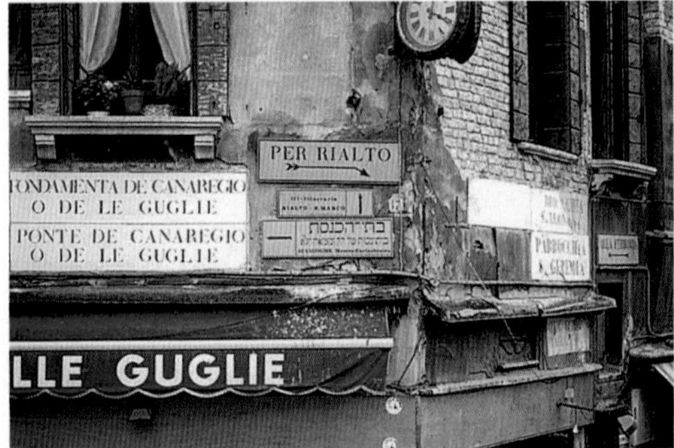

A plethora of confusing signs in Cannaregio

Guided Tours

Tours with English-speaking guides in Venice and the outlying islands can be booked through tourist offices and travel agencies such as Bucintoro Viaggi *(see p281)*. One popular water tour takes you down the Grand Canal in a sleek *vaporetto*, with running commentary about the palaces en route. Other tours are on foot, visiting the city's main monuments. Costs range from €18 to €40 and can be booked at the Venetian tourist office *(see p271)*. Tours operated by the tourist board usually start at the main office in Piazza San Marco. The boat trips begin at various boarding points, mainly around the San Marco area.

In Verona and Padua, half-day tours are organized by each town's tourist office. Boat trips along the Brenta Canal between Venice and Padua *(see pp186–7)* are available from March to late October.

Gondolas

Gondolas are a luxury form of transport used only by tourists (apart from Venetians on their wedding day). There are a number of gondola ranks throughout the city and plenty of gondoliers in striped shirts and beribboned boater hats waiting for business on bridges and squares.

Before boarding, check the official tariffs and agree a price with the gondolier. Prices are posted on the **Gondoliers' Association** website, in the booklet *Un Ospite di Venezia (see p271)* and at gondola ranks. Official costs are around €80 for 40 minutes, rising to €100 from 7pm to 8am, but gondoliers are notorious for overcharging. Try bargaining – during the low season you may be able to negotiate a fee below the official rate and a journey shorter than the minimum of 40 minutes. Another way of cutting costs is to share a gondola – six is the maximum number of passengers.

Gondoliers all speak a smattering of English and have taken basic exams in Venetian history and art. Do not expect them to burst into "O Sole Mio", however; the most you are likely to hear are low cries of *oe* (watch out), *premi* (bear left) and *stai* (bear right) – the warning calls that have been echoing down the canals of Venice for centuries. If you want to go on a serenaded tour, travel agents regularly organize evening flotillas with accompanying musicians.

The romance of an early evening gondola ride

Crossing the Grand Canal by *traghetto*

Traghetti

Traghetti are gondola ferries that cross the Grand Canal at eight different points, providing an invaluable service for pedestrians. Surprisingly few tourists make use of this constant service, which costs only 50 cents. The points where the *traghetti* cross the Grand Canal are marked on the Street Finder maps *(see pp288–301)*. Yellow street signs show the way to the *traghetti*, illustrated with a little gondola symbol. You will be expected to do as the Venetians do, and travel the short distance standing up.

Water Taxis

For those with plenty of funds, the fastest means of getting around Venice is by water taxi. These sleek motorboats, all equipped with a cabin, zip to and from the airport in only 30 minutes. There are 16 water-taxi ranks, including one at the Lido and one at Marco Polo Airport. Water-taxi companies include **Consorzio Motoscafi**, **Serenissima** and **Veneziana Motoscafi**. Tariffs are listed in the booklet *Un Ospite di Venezia (see p271)*. There are extra charges for luggage, waiting, night service and for booking a taxi.

A water taxi

DIRECTORY

Gondolas

Gondola Stands

S. Marco (Molo). **Tel** 041 520 06 85.

Rialto (Riva Carbon). **Tel** 041 522 49 04.

Railway Station (San Simeone Piccolo). **Tel** 041 71 85 43.

Gondoliers' Association

Tel 041 528 50 75.

W gondolavenezia.it

Water Taxis

Consorzio Motoscafi

Tel 041 522 23 03.

W motoscafivenezia.it

Serenissima

Tel 041 522 12 65.

W serenissimamotoscafi.it

Veneziana Motoscafi

Tel 041 716 000/124.

Getting Around Venice by Vaporetto

For visitors to Venice, the *vaporetti*, or water buses, provide an entertaining form of public transport, although most journeys within the city can usually be covered just as quickly on foot. These water buses also supply a useful service connecting outlying points on the periphery of Venice and a link with the islands in the lagoon. The main route through the city is the Grand Canal, and the most useful service from a visitor's point of view is the No. 1. This line operates from one end of the Grand Canal to the other and travels sufficiently slowly for passengers to admire the parade of palaces at the waterside *(see pp60–75)*.

Sightseeing from a *vaporetto* on the Grand Canal

The Boats

The original *vaporetti* were steam-powered motorboats (*vaporetto* means "little steamer"); today they run on diesel. Although all the boats tend to be called *vaporetti*, strictly speaking this word applies only to the large, wide boats used on the slow routes, such as the No. 1. These boats provide the best views. The *motoscafi* are the slimmer, smaller and faster boats, such as the No. 5.2. Some of them might look old and rusty, but they go at quite a pace. The two-tier *motonavi*, which look huge in comparison to the *vaporetti* or *motoscafi*, are used on routes to outlying islands and the Lido.

Tickets and Fares

Tickets for the *vaporetti* are the same price irrespective of the length of journey, making the service very straightforward to use. Moreover, a range of timed tickets and passes provides decent savings over the standard single ticket price, especially if purchased in advance online.

If you only want to cross the Grand Canal, you can buy a *traghetto* ticket for 50 cents *(see p283)*. A 60-minute *vaporetto* ticket costs €7 and allows travel for 1 hour from the time of validation. There are also 12-hour (€18), 24-hour (€20), 36-hour (€25), 48-hour (€30) and 72-hour (€35) tickets that entitle the holder to unlimited travel on most lines and offer better value. A one-week pass costs €50.

IMOB (electronic smart-card) passes are available from all ticket offices, such as the ones at Piazzale Roma, Ferrovia, Rialto and San Marco, as well as from tobacconists and newsagents displaying the **ACTV** logo. Reduced-price tickets can be purchased online through **Venice Connected**. Holders of the Rolling VENICEcard *(see p270)* can buy a *Tre Giorni Giovane*, or 3-day youth pass, for €18 *(see City Map)*.

Note that the Alilaguna (to and from Marco Polo Airport; *see p279*), Clodia (from Chioggia to San Zaccaria) and Fusina (from Le Zattere to Fusina) lines need separate tickets.

Timetables

The *vaporetti* are renowned for their punctuality, and the Venetians boast they can set their watches by them. There is just one timetable, covering both weekdays and public holidays. The only restrictions concern rowing events such as the Vogalonga *(see p37)* and the Regata Storica *(see p39)*, when services are partially suspended, and the *acqua alta* high-tide flooding, when some lines are limited due to low bridges.

The main routes run every 10 to 20 minutes until the early evening, then at slightly less frequent intervals. All services are reduced at night, particularly after 1am, but a night route operates along the Giudecca and down the Grand Canal and to Rialto every 20 minutes (every 40 minutes to the Lido) through to early morning, when normal timetables resume. All of the outlying islands have round-the-clock *vaporetto* services.

Details of all the main *vaporetto* lines are in the ACTV timetable, available at most boarding points or online.

A *vaporetto* or water bus

The smaller, sleeker *motoscafo*

DIRECTORY

Tickets and Fares

ACTV
Piazzale Roma. **Map** 5 B1.
Tel 041 24 24. **W** **actv.it** or **W** **hellovenezia.com**

Venice Connected
W **veniceconnected.com**

The Main Routes

(1) This is the slow *vaporetto* down the Grand Canal, stopping at every boarding point. The route starts at Piazzale Roma and travels the length of the Grand Canal; then, from San Marco, it heads east to the Lido.

(2) The No. 2 is the faster route down the Grand Canal. The whole route goes in a loop, starting at San Zaccaria, continuing westwards along the Giudecca Canal to Tronchetto and Piazzale Roma, then down the Grand Canal back to San Zaccaria, and from there out to the Lido (summer only).

(5.1) (5.2) The 5.1 and 5.2 lines skirt the periphery of Venice and extend to the Lido. The circular "Giracittà" route provides a scenic tour of Venice, though to do the whole circuit you have to change at Fondamente Nuove.

(4.1) (4.2) Circular "Giracittà" lines taking in Murano. The No. 4.1 travels anticlockwise, while the No. 4.2 goes clockwise.

(5) The No. 5 is a tourist route connecting San Zaccaria and Murano.

(6) This route is the fast way to reach the Lido from Piazzale Roma.

(13) The No. 13 leaves from Fondamente Nuove and travels to the "garden" islands, including Vignole and Sant'Erasmo.

(12) Departing from the Fondamente Nuove, the 12 line serves the main islands in the northern lagoon: Murano, Mazzorbo, Burano and Torcello, circling via Punta Sabbioni and the Lido, before returning to San Zaccaria.

(N) The N (night-time) line services all stops from Piazzale Roma, cruising along the Grand Canal to Lido Santa Maria Elisabetta.

Using the Vaporetti

The service is run by ACTV *(Azienda Consorzio Trasporti Veneziano)*. The water-bus system is constantly being modified, and thus, while every effort is made to keep the map on the inside back cover of this guide up-to-date, it may not reflect the most recent changes. If you are not sure which *vaporetto* to take to reach your destination, check with the boatman – the *vaporetti* crew tend to be very helpful.

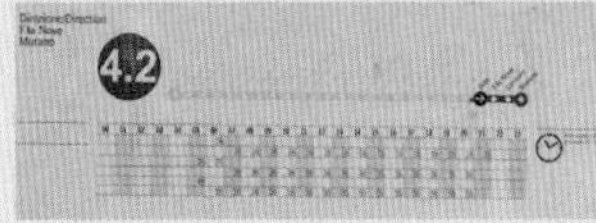

Timetable and route at a *vaporetto* boarding point

1 Tickets are available at most boarding points, some bars, shops and tobacconists displaying the ACTV sign. The price of a ticket is the same whether you are going one stop or doing the whole circuit. There are also a variety of special tickets available *(see Tickets and Fares, opposite)*.

2 Signs on the boarding point tell you which lines stop there.

3 Tickets should be swiped against the automatic machines on the boarding points before each journey. Inspectors travel on the *vaporetti*, and there are steep fines for passengers without valid tickets. There are notices in English to this effect in all the *vaporetti*.

4 An indicator board at the front of each *vaporetto* gives the line number and main stops. (Ignore the large black numbers on the side of the boat.)

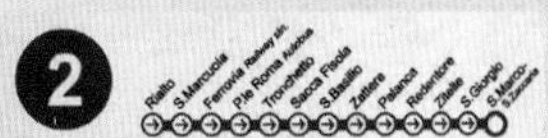

5 Each boarding point has its name clearly marked on a yellow board. Most stops have two landing stages, and it is quite easy, particularly if it is crowded and you can't see which way the *vaporetto* is facing, to board a boat travelling in the wrong direction. It is helpful to watch which direction the *vaporetto* is approaching from; if in doubt, check with the boatman on board.

Getting Around the Veneto

The Veneto has many famous and historical cities, most of which are a comfortable day trip from Venice by train or bus. The smaller towns that surround Lake Garda are accessible by local bus, while the city centres of Verona and Padua can be explored on foot. The public transport networks are excellent and reasonably priced, discouraging car travel especially as motorways can be congested and tourist traffic is banned in city centres. Nevertheless, cars are more convenient when touring the Dolomites. Travelling by taxi is very expensive.

Train Travel

Trenitalia, Italy's state railway, runs an extensive and efficient network throughout the Veneto. Trains are regular and mostly punctual, and the cost of travel is reasonable. The variety of train services range from the slow *regionale*, stopping at almost every station en route, through the various intercity trains to the high-speed Freccia and Eurostar, which link Venice with Verona and beyond. Reduced fares are available if you book in advance online; otherwise tickets are available at stations. There are facilities for disabled travellers on intercity services *(see p281)*.

Main Train Stations

For information on Venice's Santa Lucia Station, *see p280*. The nearest mainland station to Venice is Mestre, which lies at the end of the causeway leading to Venice. It is also the junction for lines to Conegliano, Treviso, Calalzo and the Friuli region.

Verona lies at the intersection of the main railway lines from Venice to Milan and from Bologna to Munich. The main station, Porta Nuova, lies a short distance south of the city centre and is connected to it by frequent buses. Facilities include a tourist office, left-luggage storage and a newsagent that sells bus tickets. The small Porta Vescovo station, serving local stations to the east of Verona, is used mainly by locals.

Padua (Padova) is only 30 minutes by train from Venice. The station is in the north of the town; buses and a tram leave from outside the station for the centre, which is only a 10-minute walk away. Padua's station houses many facilities including a tourist office, a left-luggage office and a bureau de change. The main bus terminal, with services to Venice and other towns in the Veneto, is adjacent.

Vicenza, 55 minutes from Venice, is on the main railway line between Verona and Padua. The station is a 5-minute stroll south of the city centre, and services here include left luggage, ticket offices, tourist information and currency exchange.

Tickets and Fares

Main train stations have both ticket offices and easy-to-use self-service machines, which have clear instructions in several languages and accept both cash and credit cards. Ticket offices at many small railway stations have been replaced by a simpler machine that accepts cash only. Tickets can also be purchased on board all trains, but be aware that they will then be subject to a considerable surcharge.

Remember to stamp your ticket in the yellow machines at the entrance to the platform or on the platform before boarding the train.

Booking is compulsory when travelling on all of the fast Freccia, Eurostar and Intercity trains; it is also advisable to book in advance on other trains, especially if you wish to travel at busy times. If you are travelling less than 200 km (125 miles) on a *regionale* (local) train, ask for a *biglietto a fasce chilometriche* (short-range ticket). Available from the ticket office, as well as from tobacconists and newsagents at railway stations, this ticket is stamped with the destination you require. Both outward and return portions of a ticket must be used within three days of purchase. Like all other tickets, a *biglietto a fasce chilometriche* must be validated by inserting it in one of the yellow machines at the entrance to the platforms.

All tickets can be purchased on the Trenitalia website, often with good discounts if booked well ahead of the travel date.

Bus Travel

City buses are cheap and regular. Tickets, which must be bought prior to travel, are available from newsstands, tobacconists and shops that display the bus company's logo. A flat fee is charged for rides within the city and the suburbs. The ticket becomes valid only when time-stamped in the machine on board the bus.

An ATV bus in front of the Roman arena in Verona

It is normally cheaper and quicker to travel between towns by train – in some cases, the bus can take twice as long as the train. However, there are a few towns, such as Asolo *(see p177)*, where your only choice of public transport is by bus. In most cases the bus departure point is near the train station. You can usually buy a ticket valid for 1, 2 or more hours of travel to cover longer distances.

Venice has excellent bus connections to the Veneto from the hub at Piazzale Roma, where the main ticket offices are located.

Taxis

Travelling by taxi in the Veneto is not cheap. Meters show a fixed starting charge, then clock up every kilometre. There are extra charges for luggage, trips to the airports and journeys taken between 10pm and 7am, on Sundays and on public holidays. Taxi drivers do not necessarily expect a tip – Italians give small tips or none at all.

Take taxis only from the official ranks, not from touts at railway stations and airports. In Venice the taxi rank is in Piazzale Roma; in Padua, Verona and Vicenza, taxis can be found in the main squares.

Disco orario parking disc

Driving and Parking

Many of the main roads in the region are old, with only a couple of lanes, and traffic can be heavy. What looks like a short trip on the map may take much longer than you expect. For more details on road conditions, contact the **CIS (Centro Informazione Stradale)**. Drivers must pay a toll to travel on Italian motorways *(autostrade)*. Payment can be made in cash or by prepaid magnetic cards called Viacards. These are available from the offices of the **ACI (Automobile Club d'Italia)** and tobacconists.

Motorway service stations are open 24 hours a day. Petrol stations are scarce in the countryside, and many do not accept credit cards. However, there are self-service petrol stations that accept notes.

The ACI provides an efficient 24-hour breakdown service also available to foreign visitors. The organization has reciprocal arrangements with affiliated associations in other countries, such as the AA and RAC in Britain.

Many cities in the Veneto have limited-traffic zones, and normally only residents and taxis can drive into the centre. Visitors can drive up to their hotel to unload their luggage, but they must then park on the outside of town and come in on foot or by bus. Some hotels have a limited number of parking permits, but this is no guarantee of a space. Your best bet is to telephone in advance and warn the hotel of your arrival.

Official parking areas are marked by blue lines, usually with meters. The *disco orario* (parking disc) system allows free parking for a limited period in certain areas. Car-hire companies provide the cardboard discs to place on your windscreen, indicating the time of your arrival. If your car is towed away, phone the **Polizia Municipale** (municipal police).

Rules of the Road

Drive on the right and, generally, give way to the right. Seat belts are compulsory in the front and back, and children should be properly restrained. You must also carry a warning triangle in case of breakdown. On secondary roads the speed limit is 90 km/h (55 mph), on main roads it is 110 km/h (70 mph) and on motorways 130 km/h (80 mph), though these are lower in fog or heavy rain. Penalties for speeding include spot fines and points added to your licence. There are also drink-driving laws; the blood-alcohol limit is 0.05 per cent. The use of mobile phones is forbidden, unless hands-free.

DIRECTORY

Train Travel

Trenitalia
Tel 892 021.
W trenitalia.com

Bus Travel

Belluno
Dolomiti Bus: **Tel** 043 721 71 11.
W dolomitibus.it

Padua
APS Holding: **Tel** 049 824 11 11.
W apsholding.it

Verona
ATV: **Tel** 045 805 78 11.
W atv.verona.it

Vicenza
Aziende Industriali Municipalizzate:
Tel 044 439 49 09.
W aimvicenza.it

Driving and Parking

ACI (Automobile Club d'Italia)
Emergencies:
Tel 803 116. **W aci.it**

Via Castello di Monselice 67/d, Mestre. **Tel** 041 531 03 62.

Via degli Scrovegni 19, Padua. **Tel** 049 65 48 80.

Via della Valverde 34, Verona. **Tel** 045 485 48 41.

Via Enrico Fermi 233, Vicenza. **Tel** 0444 96 60 46.

CIS (Centro Informazione Stradale)
Tel 1518 (Italian only).

Polizia Municipale
Venice: **Tel** 041 274 70 70.
Padua: **Tel** 049 820 51 00.
Verona: **Tel** 045 807 84 11.
Vicenza: **Tel** 044 439 49 09.

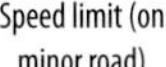
Speed limit (on minor road)

End of speed restriction

Pedestrianized street – no traffic

Give way 320 m (350 yards) ahead

VENICE STREET FINDER

All the sights, hotels, restaurants, shops and entertainment venues in Venice have map references which refer you to this section of the book. The key map below indicates the areas of the city covered by the Street Finder, and includes the colour coding specific to each area. Following the map section is a complete index of street names *(see pp298–301)*. The standard Italian spelling has been used on the maps throughout this book, but when exploring the city you will find that the street signs are often printed in Venetian dialect. Sometimes this means only a slight variation in the spelling (see the word *Sotoportico/ Sotoportego* below), but some names look completely different. For example, Santi Giovanni e Paolo *(see Map 3 C5)* is often signposted as "San Zanipolo". Major sights are labelled in Italian.

Recognizing Street Names

The signs for street *(calle)*, canal *(rio)* and square *(campo)* will soon become familiar, but the Venetians have a colourful vocabulary for the maze of alleys which makes up the city. When exploring, the following may help.

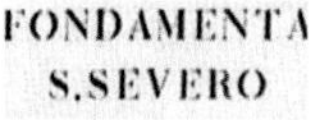

FONDAMENTA S.SEVERO

Fondamenta
A street that runs alongside a canal, often named after the canal it follows.

RIO TERRA GESUATI

Rio Terrà
A filled-in canal. Similar to a *rio terrà is a piscina*, which often forms a square.

SOTOPORTEGO E PONTE S.CRISTOFORO

Sotoportico or Sotoportego
A covered passageway.

SALIZADA PIO X

Salizzada
A main street (formerly a paved street).

RIVA DEI PARTIGIANI

Riva
A wide *fondamenta*, often facing the lagoon.

RUGAGIUFFA

Ruga
A street lined with shops.

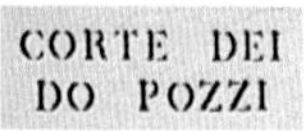

CORTE DEI DO POZZI

Corte
A courtyard.

RIO MENUO O DE LA VERONA

Many streets and canals in Venice often have more than one name: o means "or".

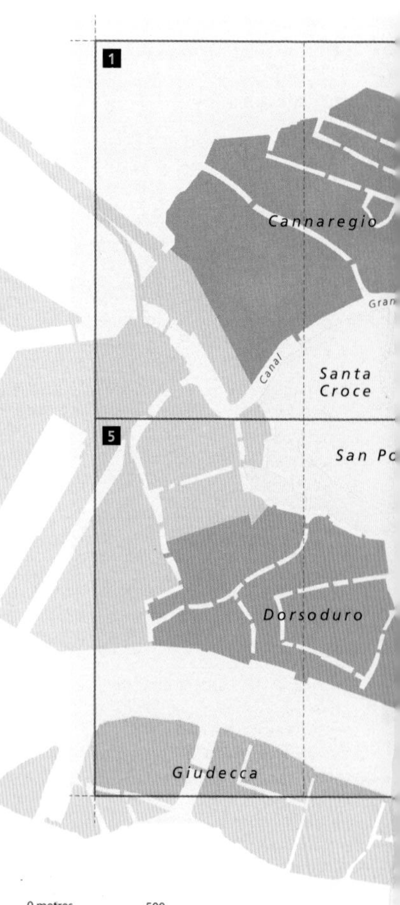

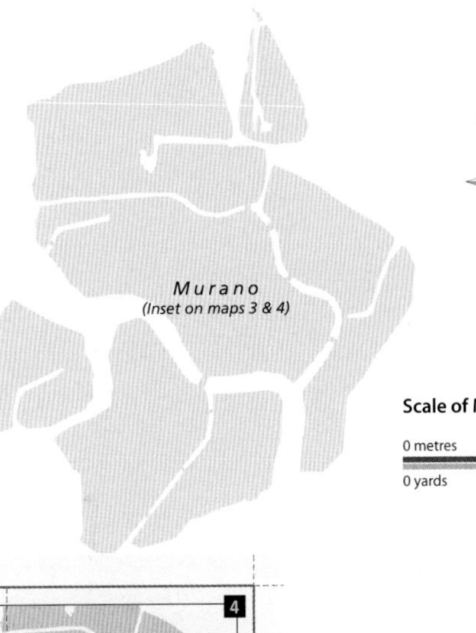

Scale of Murano Inset

0 metres 500
0 yards 500

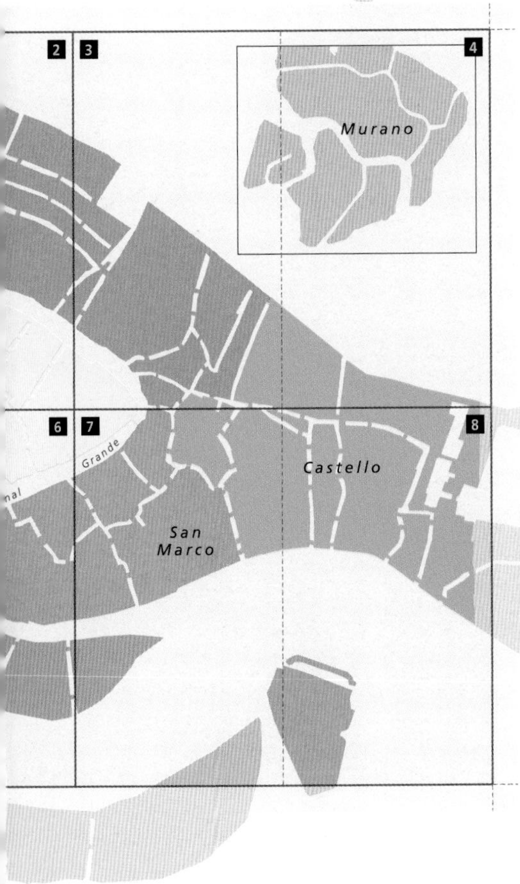

Key to Street Finder

- Major sight
- Place of interest
- Railway station
- *Vaporetto* boarding point
- *Traghetto* crossing
- Gondola mooring
- Bus terminus
- Tourist information
- Hospital with casualty unit
- Police station
- Church
- Synagogue
- Railway line

Scale of Map Pages

0 metres 200
0 yards 200

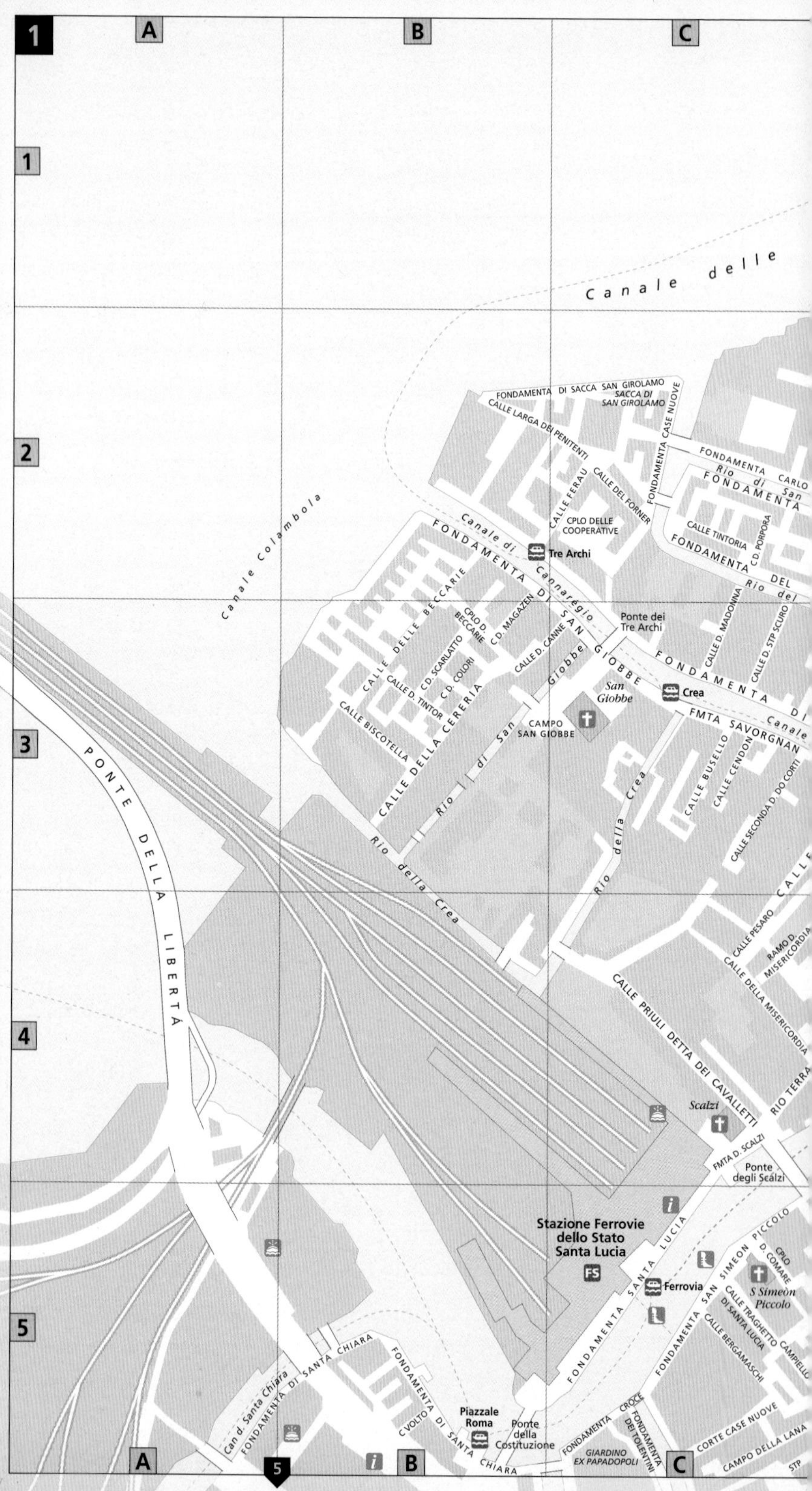
Canale delle
Canale Colambola
FONDAMENTA DI SACCA SAN GIROLAMO
SACCA DI SAN GIROLAMO
CALLE LARGA DEI PENITENTI
FONDAMENTA CASE NUOVE
FONDAMENTA CARLO
Rio di San
FONDAMENTA
CALLE FERAU
CALLE DEL FORNER
CPLO DELLE COOPERATIVE
Canale di Cannaregio
FONDAMENTA DI SAN GIOBBE
Tre Archi
CALLE TINTORIA
C.D. PORPORA
FONDAMENTA DEL
Rio del
CALLE DELLE BECCARIE
CPLO D. BECCARIE
C.D. MAGAZEN
CALLE D. CANNE
Ponte dei Tre Archi
CALLE D. MADONNA
CALLE D. STP SCURO
FONDAMENTA DI
C.D. SCARLATTO
C.D. COLORI
CALLE D. TINTOR
CALLE BISCOTELLA
CALLE DELLA CERERIA
Rio di San Giobbe
San Giobbe
CAMPO SAN GIOBBE
Crea
FMTA SAVORGNAN
Canale
CALLE BUSELLO
CALLE CENDON
CALLE SECONDA D. DO CORTI
PONTE DELLA LIBERTÁ
Rio della Crea
CALLE PESARO
RAMO D. MISERICORDIA
CALLE DELLA MISERICORDIA
CALLE PRIULI DETTA DEI CAVALLETTI
RIO TERRA
Scalzi
FMTA D. SCALZI
Ponte degli Scalzi
Stazione Ferrovie dello Stato Santa Lucia
FS
FONDAMENTA SANTA LUCIA
Ferrovia
FONDAMENTA SAN SIMEON PICCOLO
CPLO D. COMARE
S Simeon Piccolo
CALLE TRAGHETTO DI SANTA LUCIA
CALLE BERGAMASCHI
CAMPIELLO
Can d. Santa Chiara
FONDAMENTA DI SANTA CHIARA
FONDAMENTA DI SANTA CHIARA
C VOLTO
Piazzale Roma
Ponte della Costituzione
FONDAMENTA CROCE
FONDAMENTA DEI TOLENTINI
GIARDINO EX PAPADOPOLI
CORTE CASE NUOVE
CAMPO DELLA LANA
STP
A
B
C
1
2
3
4
5

D
E
F
2
1
2
3
4
5
3
3
6
Sacche
Sant'Alvise
Orto
PARCO GROGGIA
CALLE DEL CAPITELLO
CALLE DELLA ROTONDA
CALLE LARGA
DEL LEGNAME
CALLE LONGA CANOSSIANE
CAMPO DI SANT'ALVISE
Sant' Alvise
Rio dei Riformati
FONDAMENTA DEI RIFORMATI
Rio di Sant'Alvise
FONDAMENTA CONTARINI
CALLE NUOVA
CALLE RIZZO
CALLE D. CAPPUCCINE
C.DEI RIFORMATI
Palazzo Michiel
Rio della Sensa
FONDAMENTA DELLA SENSA
CALLE D. CAPITELLO
C.D. MUNEGHE
Rio degli Zecchini
CALLE GRADISCA
CAMPIELLO PIAVE
CALLE LARGA PIAVE
FONDAMENTA MADONNA DELL'ORTO
Rio Madonna dell'Orto
Madonna dell'Orto
CALLE CONTARINA
CALLE D. SQUERO
CALLE D. MAGAZEN
Rio d. Torrette
CALLE TURLONA
COLETTI
FONDAMENTA DELLE CAPPUCCINE
Girolamo
SAN GIROLAMO
CANNAREGIO
CALLE LOREDAN
CALLE ARRIGONI
CALLE BRAZZO
FONDAMENTA DELLA SENSA
Palazzo Mastelli
CAMPO DEI MORI
Casa del Tintoretto
FMTA DEI MORI
BATTELLO
Battello
FONDAMENTA DEGLI ORMESINI
Rio della Misericordia
CALLE D. MALVASIA
CALLE CALIARI
C ZUDIO
CALLE CORDELLINA
CALLE D. FORNO
R d. Lustraferri
Rio della Sensa
CALLE LARGA
CAMPO GHETTO NUOVO
Museo Ebraico
Rio del Ghetto Nuovo
C.D. PORTON
CALLE FARNESE
CALLE DEGLI ORMESINI
CALLE NUOVA
RIO TERRA FARSETTI
CALLE DELL'ASEO
FONDAMENTA DELLA MISERICORDIA
CALLE D. SAN GIOVANNI
CALLE D. CHIOVERETTE
CALLE DEL FORNO
CALLE D. GHETTO VECCHIO
Sinagoga
FMTA DI GHETTO NUOVO
R D. ZOLFO
C.D. PERLERI
C.D. TIRACANNA
C.D. CASE NUOVE
CALLE DELLA MASENA
C.D. RABBIA
C.D. ZOCCOLO
CANNAREGIO
di Cannaregio
FONDAMENTA VENIER
RIELLO
Guglie
Ponte delle Guglie
Rio di San Marcuola
CPLO DELL' ANCONETA
CALLE DELL'ANCONETA
RIO TERRA SAN LEONARDO
FONDAMENTA CANAL
Rio dei Servi
FMTA MORO
FMTA DIEDO
CALLE ZANCANI
San Marziale
CAMPO SAN LEONARDO
CALLE DEI PRETI
R T DEL CRISTO
STP D. PEGOLOTTO
C.D. CRISTO
CALLE D. FORNO
RIO TERRA DELLA MADDALENA
PARCO SAVORGNAN
CALLE VERGOLA
SALIZZADA SAN GEREMIA
FONDAMENTA LABIA
C.D. MOSTO BALBI
CALLE D. CHIESA
CALLE DELLA PAGLIA
CALLE COLONNA
CALLE DEL CRISTO
C COLOMBINA
CALLE LARGA VENDRAMIN
C VENDRAMIN
C.D. CRISTO
VIA VITTORIO EMANUELE
Rio di Sta Fosca
FMTA VENDRAMIN
C.D. PROCURATIE
Palazzo Làbia
CAMPO SAN GEREMIA
CALLE EMO
C SANT'ANTONIO
CALLE QUERINI
San Marcuola
R T DIETRO LA CHIESA
C MALVASIA
Palazzo Vendramin Calergi
C.D. FORNO
CALLE CORRER
C.DELL' OLIO
CALLE GIOCHIN
CPLO FLANGINI
CAMPO SAN MARCUOLA
San Geremia
San Marcuola
LISTA DI SPAGNA
C.D. SPEZIER
C.D. FORNO
R T DEI SABBIONI
Riva di Biasio
Palazzo Belloni Battagia
CPLO DEI FIORI
C NOEL
STRADA NOVA
CORTE BARBARO
Canal Grande
FMTA CROTTA
RIVA DI BIASIO
CALLE ZEN
RIO TERRA
Rio di San Zan Degolà
Fondaco dei Turchi
CALLE DEL MEGIO
Rio Ca' Tron
CALLE DEL FORNO
San Stae
CAMPO SAN STAE
Palazzo Donà Balbi
RAMO ZEN
C BEMBO
San Zan Degolà
FMTA DEL MEGIO
Rio Fondaco dei Turchi
C TRON
SALIZZADA SAN STAE
San Stae
Ca' Pesaro
C PESARO
Ca' Corner della Regina
SALIZZADA DELLA CHIESA
CAMPO SAN SIMEON PROFETA
CALLE PISANI
CALLE DEL PISTOR
LISTA DEI BARI
SALIZZADA ZUSTO
CORTE CAZZA
RM CAZZA
RAMO
Rio Dell'Isola
CALLE DEL TINTOR
Ca' Mocenigo
C.D. FORNER
C DEL RAVANO
CALLE CORNER
CALLE DELLA ROSA
CPO S SIMEON PROFETA
S Simeone Grande
C LUNGA CHIOVERETTE
C BERGAMI
CALLE LARGA DEI BARI
CALLE GALLION
CALLE ORSETTI
C.D. SAVIO
CALLE LARGA
Rio del Megio
CALLE COLOMBO
SALIZZADA CARMINATI
Rio di San Stae
Sta Maria Mater Domini
C TEATRO VECCHIO
C.D. CAMPANILE
C MIANI
CALLE RUGA VECCHIA
San Giàcomo dell'Orio
CALLE ZAMBELLI
FMTA D. GRUE
Rio Marin
FONDAMENTA
FMTA GRADENIGO
CALLE D. CROCE
CAMPO NAZARIO SAURO
RG BELLA
Rio San
CPO S GIACOMO DELL'ORIO
SANTA CROCE
CALLE DELLA CHIESA
Rio Do Torri
CALLE DELLA REGINA
San Cassiano
CAMPO SAN CASSIANO
C.D. CRISTI
RM CHIOVERETTE
RIO MARIN O GARZOTTI
C GRADISCA
CAMPO D. STROPE
Rio San Giàcomo dell'Orio
CALLE DELLE OCHE
CALLE DEL TINTOR
CAMPO SAN BOLDO
C.D. MODENA
Rio di San Boldo
CORTE ROTTA
CALLE FILOSI
Rio delle
C DELL'AGNELLO
Rio di San Cassiano
CALLE DEI BOTTERI
CORTE CANAL
CALLE VISCIGA
FONDAMENTA RIO MARIN
CAMPIELLO DEL CRISTO
CALLE CAPPELLO
RIO TERRA PARRUCCHETTA
RIO TERRA SECONDO
C DEL CRISTO
C.D. BOTTA
C RASPI
Beccarie
CALLE SANSONI
MUNEGHE
CALLE LARGA CONTARINA
C SAN ZUANE
CALLE DELL'OLIO
CALLE CALDARER
R di Sant'
CAMPO DI SANT'AGOSTIN
RAMO ASTORI
C BERNARDO
C.D. TEATRO
CALLE ALBRIZZI
Rio delle
C.D. SOLE
DARIO
Rio di San Zuane
C.D. LACCA

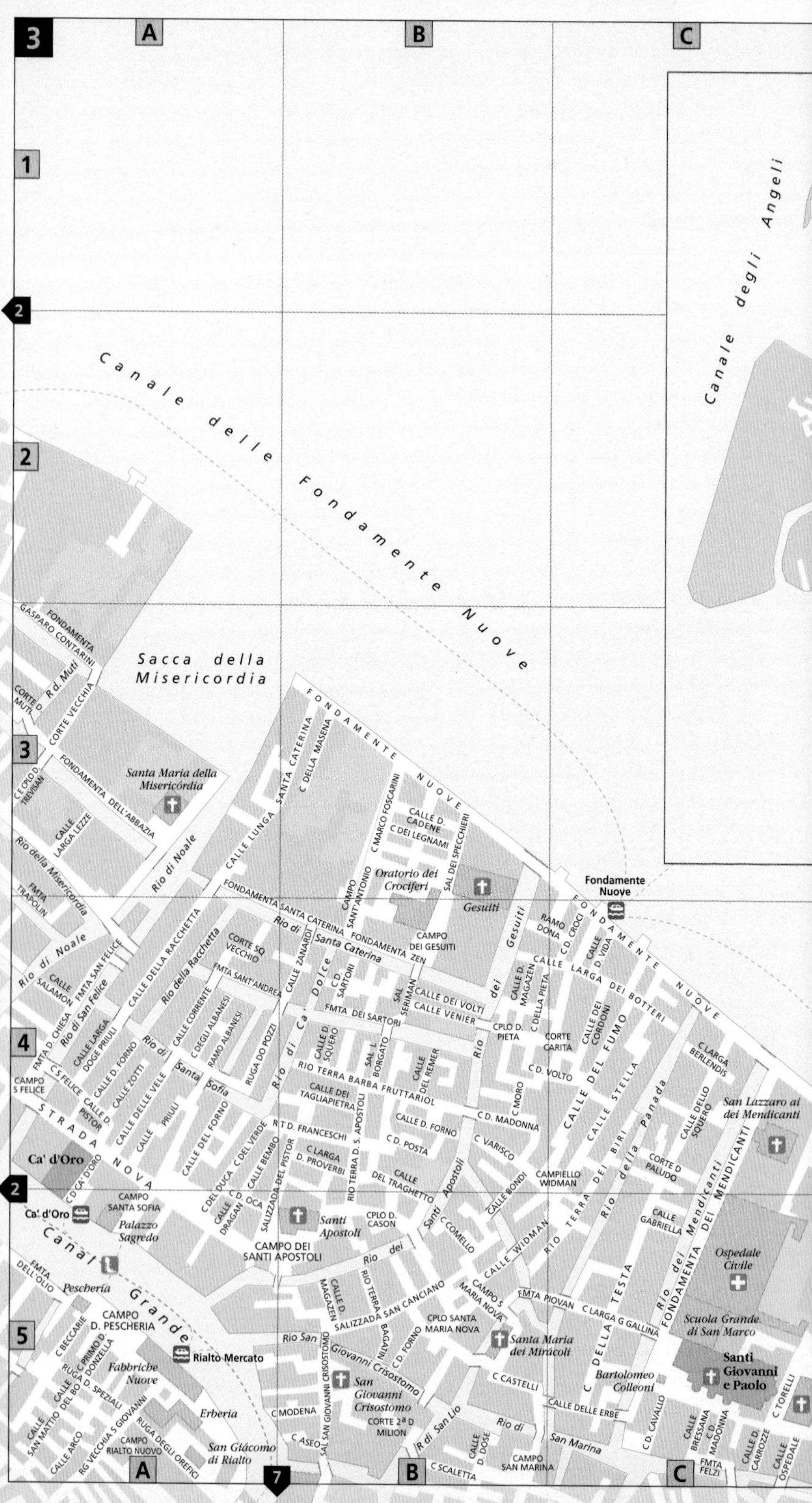

3
A
B
C
1
2
3
4
5
7
Canale delle Fondamente Nuove
Canale degli Angeli
Sacca della Misericordia
FONDAMENTA GASPARO CONTARINI
R. d. Muti
CORTE D. MUTI
CORTE VECCHIA
FONDAMENTA DELL'ABBAZIA
C.E CPLO D. TREVISAN
CALLE LARGA LEZZE
Santa Maria della Misericórdia
Rio della Misericordia
FMTA TRAPOLIN
Rio di Noale
FONDAMENTE NUOVE
CALLE LUNGA SANTA CATERINA
C. DELLA MASENA
C MARCO FOSCARINI
CALLE D. CADENE
C DEI LEGNAMI
SAL DEI SPECCHIERI
Oratorio dei Crociferi
Gesuiti
CAMPO SANT'ANTONIO
CAMPO DEI GESUITI
Fondamente Nuove
FONDAMENTA SANTA CATERINA
Rio di Santa Caterina
FONDAMENTA ZEN
RAMO DONA
C.D. CROCI
CALLE D VIDA
CALLE LARGA DEI BOTTERI
Rio dei Gesuiti
CALLE SALAMON
FMTA SAN FELICE
Rio di San Felice
CALLE DELLA RACCHETTA
Rio della Racchetta
CORTE SQ VECCHIO
FMTA SANT'ANDREA
CALLE ZANARDI
C.D. SARTORI
SAL SERIMAN
CALLE DEI VOLTI
CALLE VENIER
CALLE D. MAGAZEN
C DELLA PIETA
CALLE DEI CORDONI
FMTA D. CHIESA
CALLE LARGA DOGE PRIULI
CALLE CORRENTE
C DEGLI ALBANESI
RAMO ALBANESI
RUGA DO POZZI
Rio di Ca' Dolce
FMTA DEI SARTORI
CPLO D. PIETA
CORTE CARITA
CALLE DEL FUMO
C LARGA BERLENDIS
CAMPO S FELICE
C S FELICE
CALLE D. FORNO
CALLE ZOTTI
Rio di Santa Sofia
CALLE D. SQUERO
SAL L BORGATO
CALLE DEL REMER
RIO TERRA BARBA FRUTTARIOL
C.D. VOLTO
CALLE STELLA
San Lazzaro ai dei Mendicanti
CALLE D. PISTOR
CALLE DELLE VELE
PRIULI
CALLE DEI TAGLIAPIETRA
CALLE D. FORNO
C.D. MADONNA
C MORO
Rio della Panada
CALLE DELLO SQUERO
STRADA NOVA
CALLE DEL FORNO
C DEL VERDE
RT D. FRANCESCHI
RIO TERRA D. S. APOSTOLI
C.D. POSTA
C VARISCO
CORTE D PALUDO
FONDAMENTA DEI MENDICANTI
Rio dei Mendicanti
Ca' d'Oro
C D CA' D'ORO
CAMPO SANTA SOFIA
C DEL DUCA
CALLE C.D. DRAGAN
C.D. OCA
CALLE BEMBO
SALIZZADA DEL PISTOR
C LARGA D. PROVERBI
CALLE DEL TRAGHETTO
Rio dei Santi Apostoli
CALLE BONDI
CAMPIELLO WIDMAN
RIO TERRA DEI BIRI
CALLE GABRIELLA
Palazzo Sagredo
Santi Apostoli
CPLO D. CASON
C COMELLO
CALLE WIDMAN
Ospedale Civile
Canal Grande
FMTA DELL'OLIO
Pescheria
CAMPO DEI SANTI APOSTOLI
Rio dei
CALLE D. MAGAZEN
RIO TERRA
CAMPO S MARIA NOVA
FMTA PIOVAN
C LARGA G GALLINA
CALLE DELLA TESTA
Scuola Grande di San Marco
CAMPO D. PESCHERIA
C BECCARIE
RUGA C PRIMO D.
D. DONZELLA
SALIZZADA SAN CANCIANO
CPLO SANTA MARIA NOVA
Santa Maria dei Miracoli
Santi Giovanni e Paolo
Rialto Mercato
Rio San Giovanni Crisostomo
BAGATIN
C.D. FORNO
Fabbriche Nuove
CALLE DEL BO
RUGA D. SPEZIALI
SAL SAN GIOVANNI CRISOSTOMO
San Giovanni Crisostomo
C CASTELLI
Bartolomeo Colleoni
CALLE SAN MATTIO
CALLE ARCO
RG VECCHIA S GIOVANNI
RUGA DEGLI OREFICI
CAMPO RIALTO NUOVO
Erberia
San Giácomo di Rialto
C MODENA
C ASEO
CORTE 2ª D MILION
R di San Lio
CALLE D. DOSE
Rio di San Marina
CALLE DELLE ERBE
CAMPO SAN MARINA
C SCALETTA
C.D. CAVALLO
CALLE BRESSANA
C.D. MADONNA
CALLE D. CARROZZE
C TORELLI
CALLE OSPEDALE
FMTA FELZI

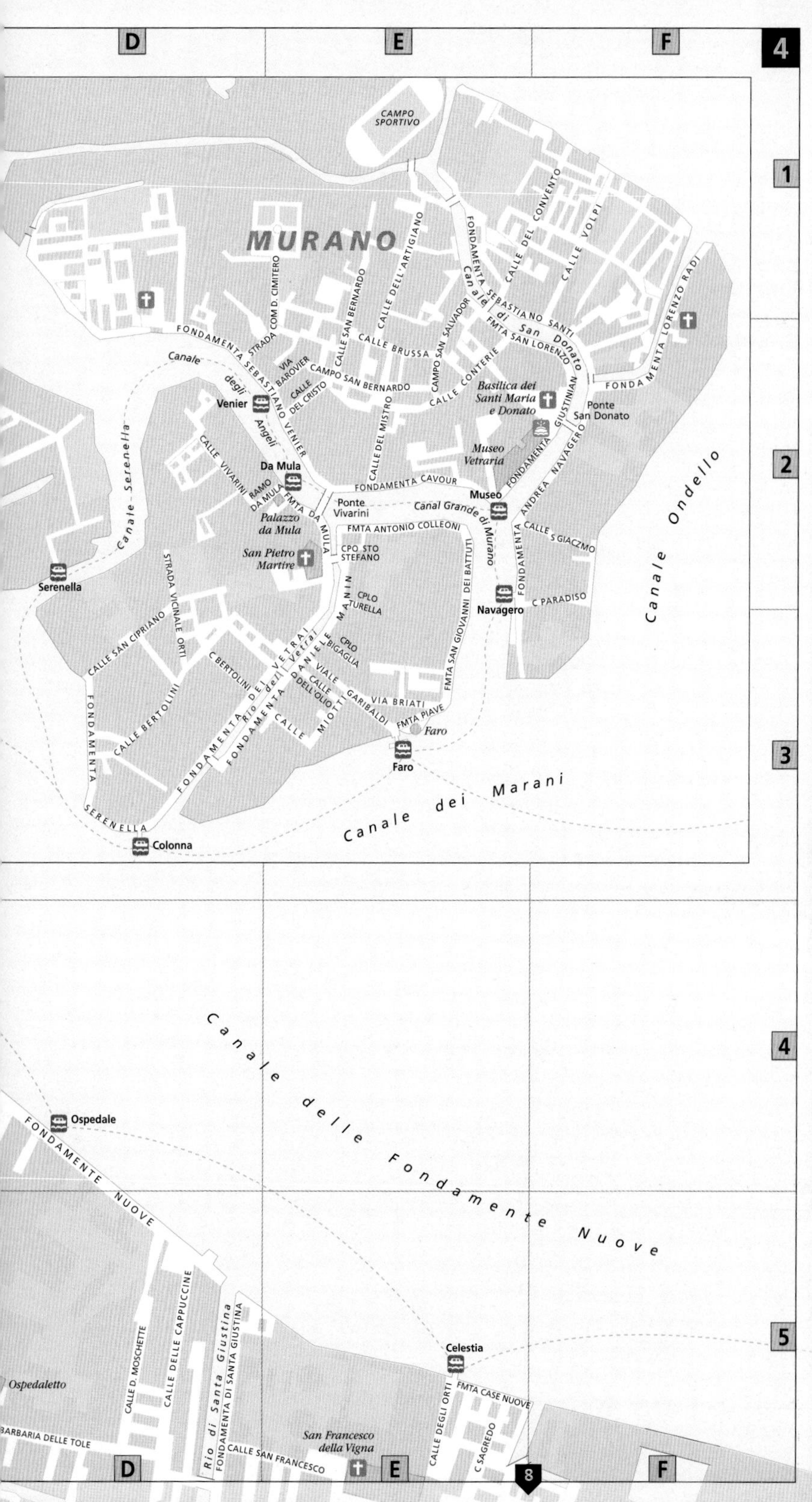

D
E
F
4
1
2
3
4
5
MURANO
CAMPO SPORTIVO
FONDAMENTA SEBASTIANO VENIER
STRADA COM D. CIMITERO
VIA BAROVIER
CALLE DEL CRISTO
CAMPO SAN BERNARDO
CALLE SAN BERNARDO
CALLE DELL'ARTIGIANO
CALLE BRUSSA
CAMPO SAN SALVADOR
CALLE CONTERIE
CALLE DEL MISTRO
FONDAMENTA SEBASTIANO SANTI
Canale di San Donato
FMTA SAN LORENZO
CALLE DEL CONVENTO
CALLE VOLPI
FONDAMENTA LORENZO RADI
Basilica dei Santi Maria e Donato
FONDAMENTA GIUSTINIAN
Ponte San Donato
Museo Vetraria
Canale degli Angeli
Venier
Da Mula
CALLE VIVARINI
RAMO DA MULA
FMTA DA MULA
Palazzo da Mula
FONDAMENTA CAVOUR
Ponte Vivarini
Museo
Canal Grande di Murano
FONDAMENTA ANDREA NAVAGERO
Canale Ondello
FMTA ANTONIO COLLEONI
CPO STO STEFANO
San Pietro Martire
CALLE S GIACZMO
Canale Serenella
Serenella
STRADA VICINALE ORTI
MANIN
CPLO TURELLA
FMTA SAN GIOVANNI DEI BATTUTI
Navagero
FONDAMENTA
C PARADISO
CALLE SAN CIPRIANO
C BERTOLINI
Rio dei Vetrai
FONDAMENTA DANIELE
CPLO BIGAGLIA
VIALE GARIBALDI
CALLE DELL'OLIO
VIA BRIATI
FMTA PIAVE
Faro
CALLE BERTOLINI
FONDAMENTA DEI VETRAI
CALLE MIOTTI
FONDAMENTA SERENELLA
Colonna
Canale dei Marani
Canale delle Fondamente Nuove
Ospedale
FONDAMENTE NUOVE
CALLE D. MOSCHETTE
CALLE DELLE CAPPUCCINE
Rio di Santa Giustina
FONDAMENTA DI SANTA GIUSTINA
Ospedaletto
BARBARIA DELLE TOLE
CALLE SAN FRANCESCO
San Francesco della Vigna
Celestia
FMTA CASE NUOVE
CALLE DEGLI ORTI
C SAGREDO
8

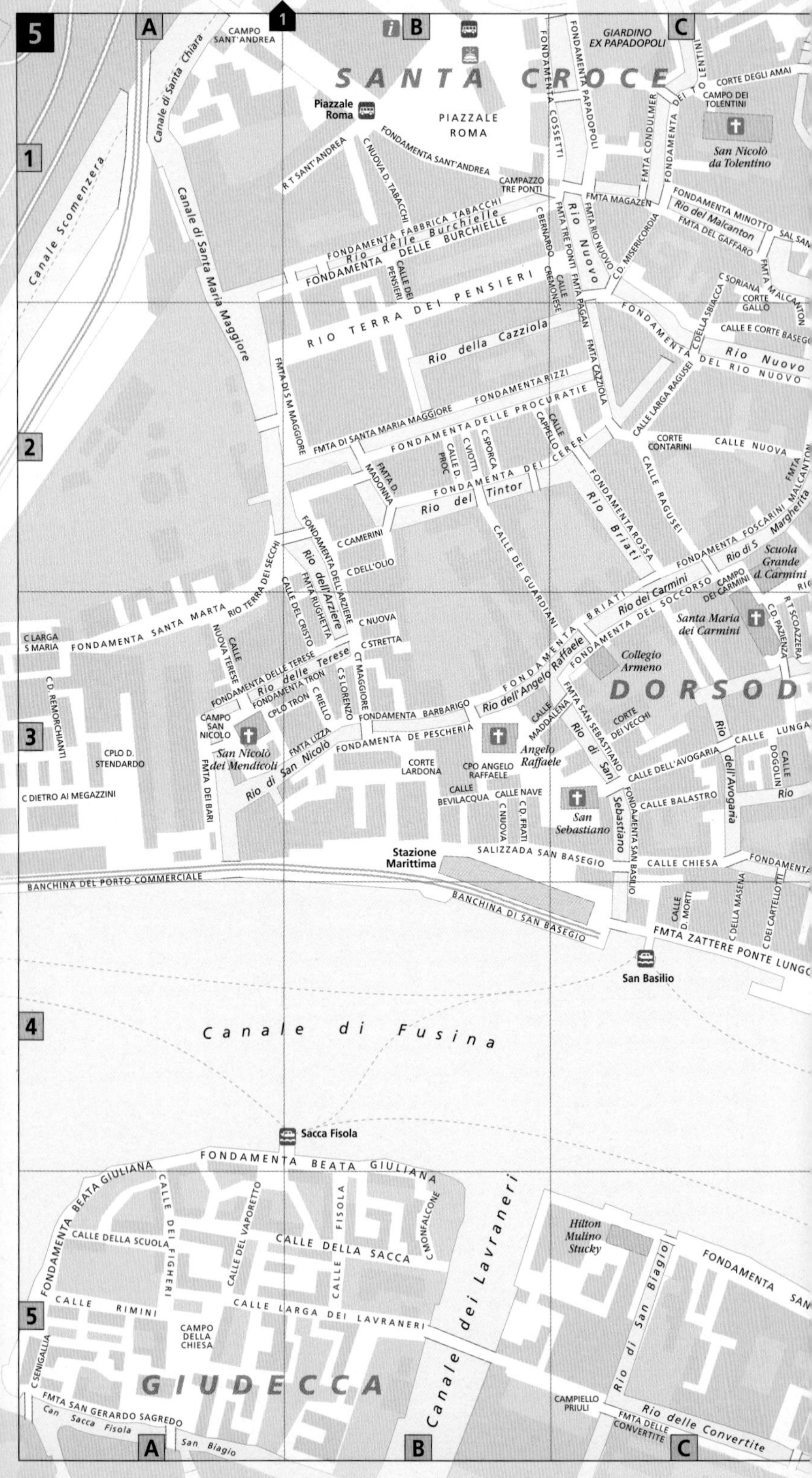

5
A
B
C
1
2
3
4
SANTA CROCE
DORSODURO
GIUDECCA
Piazzale Roma
PIAZZALE ROMA
CAMPO SANT'ANDREA
GIARDINO EX PAPADOPOLI
Canale Scomenzera
Canale di Santa Chiara
Canale di Santa Maria Maggiore
FONDAMENTA SANT'ANDREA
R T SANT'ANDREA
C NUOVA D. TABACCHI
CAMPAZZO TRE PONTI
FONDAMENTA PAPADOPOLI
FONDAMENTA COSSETTI
FMTA CONDULMER
FONDAMENTA DEI TOLENTINI
CORTE DEGLI AMAI
CAMPO DEI TOLENTINI
San Nicolò da Tolentino
FMTA MAGAZEN
FONDAMENTA MINOTTO
Rio del Malcanton
FMTA DEL GAFFARO
FMTA MALCANTON
Rio Nuovo
FONDAMENTA FABBRICA TABACCHI
Rio delle Burchielle
FONDAMENTA DELLE BURCHIELLE
CALLE DEI PENSIERI
RIO TERRA DEI PENSIERI
C BERNARDO
FMTA TRE PONTI
CALLE CREMONESE
FMTA RIO NUOVO
C.D. MISERICORDIA
FMTA PAGAN
C SORIANA
CORTE GALLO
C DELLA SBIACCA
CALLE E CORTE BASEGO
FONDAMENTA DEL RIO NUOVO
Rio della Cazziola
FMTA CAZZIOLA
FONDAMENTA RIZZI
FMTA DI S M MAGGIORE
FMTA DI SANTA MARIA MAGGIORE
FONDAMENTA DELLE PROCURATIE
CALLE LARGA RAGUSEI
CALLE CAPPELLO
C SPORCA
C VIOTTI
CALLE D. PROC
FMTA D. MADONNA
FONDAMENTA DEI CERERI
CORTE CONTARINI
CALLE NUOVA
CALLE RAGUSEI
Rio del Tintor
C CAMERINI
C DELL'OLIO
FONDAMENTA DELL'ARZIERE
Rio dell'Arziere
FMTA RUGHETTA
CALLE DEL CRISTO
CALLE DEI GUARDIANI
FONDAMENTA ROSSA
Rio Briati
FONDAMENTA FOSCARINI
Rio di S Margherita
Scuola Grande d. Carmini
CAMPO DEI CARMINI
Rio dei Carmini
FONDAMENTA DEL SOCCORSO
Santa Maria dei Carmini
R T SCOAZZERA
C.D. PAZIENZA
Collegio Armeno
RIO TERRA DEI SECCHI
FONDAMENTA SANTA MARTA
C LARGA S MARIA
CALLE NUOVA TERESE
C NUOVA
C STRETTA
FONDAMENTA DELLE TERESE
Rio delle Terese
FONDAMENTA TRON
CPLO TRON
C RIELLO
C S LORENZO
CT MAGGIORE
FONDAMENTA BARBARIGO
Rio dell'Angelo Raffaele
FMTA SAN SEBASTIANO
CALLE MADDALENA
Rio di San Sebastiano
CORTE DEI VECCHI
Rio dell'Avogaria
CALLE LUNGA
CALLE DOGOLIN
CALLE DELL'AVOGARIA
CALLE BALASTRO
C.D. REMORCHIANTI
CAMPO SAN NICOLO
San Nicolò dei Mendicoli
CPLO D. STENDARDO
C DIETRO AI MEGAZZINI
FMTA DEI BARI
FMTA LIZZA
Rio di San Nicolò
FONDAMENTA DE PESCHERIA
CORTE LARDONA
Angelo Raffaele
CPO ANGELO RAFFAELE
CALLE BEVILACQUA
CALLE NAVE
C NUOVA
C.D. FRATI
San Sebastiano
FONDAMENTA SAN BASILIO
Stazione Marittima
SALIZZADA SAN BASEGIO
CALLE CHIESA
BANCHINA DEL PORTO COMMERCIALE
BANCHINA DI SAN BASEGIO
CALLE D. MORTI
C DELLA MASENA
C DEI CARTELLOTTI
FMTA ZATTERE PONTE LUNGO
San Basilio
Canale di Fusina
Sacca Fisola
FONDAMENTA BEATA GIULIANA
CALLE DEI FIGHERI
CALLE DEL VAPORETTO
CALLE FISOLA
C MONFALCONE
CALLE DELLA SCUOLA
CALLE DELLA SACCA
CALLE RIMINI
CALLE LARGA DEI LAVRANERI
Canale dei Lavraneri
CAMPO DELLA CHIESA
C SENIGALLIA
FMTA SAN GERARDO SAGREDO
Can Sacca Fisola
San Biagio
Hilton Mulino Stucky
FONDAMENTA SAN
Rio di San Biagio
CAMPIELLO PRIULI
FMTA DELLE CONVERTITE
Rio delle Convertite

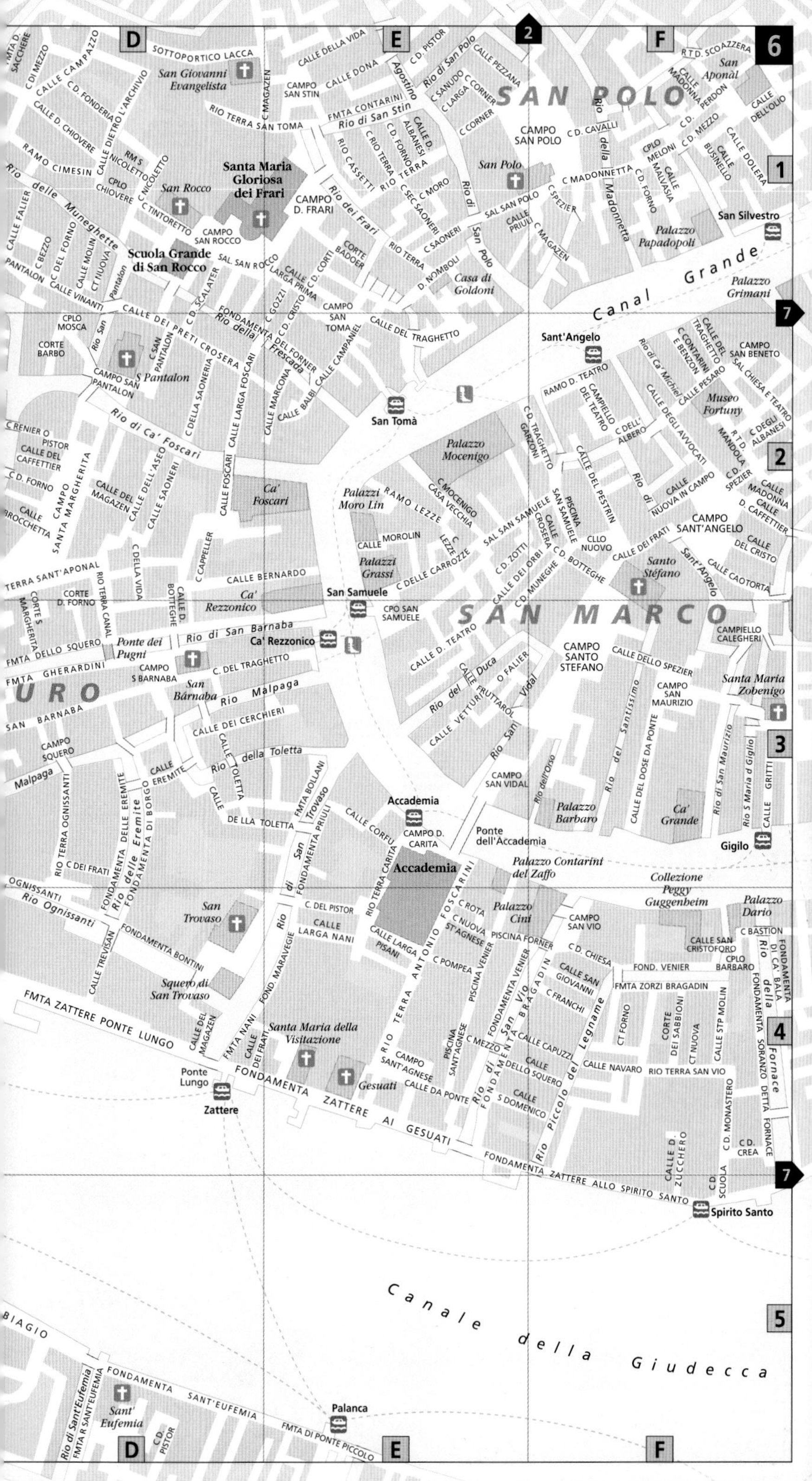

D
E
F
6
2
7
1
2
3
4
5
SAN POLO
SAN MARCO
Canal Grande
Canale della Giudecca
Santa Maria Gloriosa dei Frari
Scuola Grande di San Rocco
San Giovanni Evangelista
San Rocco
San Polo
Casa di Goldoni
Palazzo Papadopoli
Palazzo Grimani
San Silvestro
Sant'Angelo
San Tomà
Museo Fortuny
Palazzo Mocenigo
Palazzi Moro Lin
Palazzi Grassi
Ca' Foscari
Ca' Rezzonico
San Samuele
S Pantalon
Ponte dei Pugni
San Bárnaba
Santo Stéfano
Campo Santo Stefano
Santa Maria Zobenigo
Accademia
Ponte dell'Accademia
Palazzo Barbaro
Ca' Grande
Gigilo
Palazzo Contarini del Zaffo
Collezione Peggy Guggenheim
Palazzo Dario
Palazzo Cini
San Trovaso
Squero di San Trovaso
Santa Maria della Visitazione
Gesuati
Ponte Lungo
Zattere
Spirito Santo
Palanca
Sant' Eufemia
Fondamenta Zattere ai Gesuati
Fondamenta Zattere allo Spirito Santo
Fmta Zattere Ponte Lungo
Fondamenta Sant'Eufemia
Fmta di Ponte Piccolo
Campo San Polo
Campo D. Frari
Campo San Rocco
Campo San Barnaba
Campo Sant'Angelo
Campo San Vidal
Campo San Maurizio
Campo San Vio
Campo Sant'Agnese
Rio di Ca' Foscari
Rio di San Barnaba
Rio Malpaga
Rio della Toletta
Rio di San Trovaso
Rio Ognissanti
Rio del Duca
Rio San Vidal
Rio di San Vio
Rio Piccolo del Legname
Rio della Fornace

Street Finder Index

Key to Abbreviations

C	Calle	**Rm**	Ramo	**S**	San/Sant'
Can	Canale	**R**	Rio	**Sta**	Santa
Cpo	Campo	**RT**	Rio Terrà	**Sto**	Santo
Cplo	Campiello	**Rg**	Ruga/ Rughetta	**SS**	Santi/ Santissimi
Ct	Corte				
Fmta	Fondamenta	**Sal**	Salizzada	**StP**	Sottoportico

T

U

V

W

Z

General Index

Page numbers in **bold** refer to main entries

E

F

G

Acknowledgments

Dorling Kindersley would like to thank the many people whose help and assistance contributed to the preparation of this book.

Main Contributors
Susie Boulton studied Languages and History of Art at the University of Cambridge. She has been visiting Venice for over 20 years and is the author of several guide books on the city.

Christopher Catling has been visiting Italy for over 25 years since his first archaeological dig there while he was a student at Cambridge University. He is the author of several guide books on Italian cities and regions, including *The DK Travel Guide to Florence and Tuscany*.

Additional Contributors
Gillian Price was born in England in 1953 but grew up in Sydney, Australia. She moved to Venice in 1981 and has written nine books on walking in Italy. Gillian has been contributing to Dorling Kindersley's Eyewitness Travel Guide series since 1998.

Sally Roy first got to know Venice while at school in Rome and has been returning to the country ever since. She read Medieval History at St Andrew's University, Edinburgh, and has contributed to several books on Italy.

Additional Illustrations
Annabelle Brend, Dawn Brend, Neil Bulpitt, Richard Draper, Nick Gibbard, Kevin Jones Associates, John Lawrence, The Maltings Partnership, Simon Roulstone, Sue Sharples, Derrick Stone, Paul Weston, John Woodcock.

Additional Photography
James McConnachie, Anna Mockford, Ian O'Leary, Martin Richardson, Jo-Ann Titmarsh.

Design and Editorial
Deputy Editorial Director Douglas Amrine
Deputy Art Director Gaye Allen
Map Co-ordinators Simon Farbrother, David Pugh
Production Hilary Stephens
Picture Research Ellen Root

Revisions Team
Beverley Ager, Jasneet Arora, Marta Bescos Sanchez, Uma Bhattacharya, Hilary Bird, Michael Blacker, Dawn Brend, Divya Chowfin, Lucinda Cooke, Michelle Crane, Felicity Crowe, Neha Dhingra, Stephanie Driver, Michael Ellis, Gadi Farfour, Emer FitzGerald, Anna Freiberger, Camilla Gersh, Vinod Harish, Mohammad Hassan, Irena Hoare, Kate Hughes, Shobhna Iyer, Annette Jacobs, Stuart James, Bharti Karakoti, Jasneet Kaur, Sumita Khatwani, Steve Knowlden, Vincent Kurien, Erika Lang, Jude Ledger, Carly Madden, Hayley Maher, Nicola Malone, Alison McGill, Ian Midson, Deepak Mittal, Shubhi Mittal, Sonal Modha, Gillian Price, Pete Quinlan, Rada Radojicic, Erin Richards, Lucy Richards, Steve Rowling, Simon Ryder, Sands Publishing Solutions, Azeem Siddiqui, Rituraj Singh, Meredith Smith, Jo-Ann Titmarsh, Nikky Twyman, Janis Utton, Conrad Van Dyk, Deepika Verma, Lynda Warrington, Fiona Wild.

Research Assistance
Jill De Cet, Hans Erlacher, Paolo Frullini, Oscar Gates, Marinella Laini, Elizabetta Lovato, Fabiola Perer, Alan Ross, Sarah Sole.

Index
Helen Peters.

Special Assistance
Comune di Vicenza; Arch. Gianfranco Martinoni at the Assessorato Beni Culturali Comune di Padova; Ca' Macana; Cesare Battisti at the Media Tourist Office, Venice; Curia Patriarcale Venezia; D.ssa Foscarina Caletti at the Giunta Regionale di Venezia; Jane Groom, Brian Jordan; Alexandra Kennedy; Joy Parker; Frances Hawkins, Lady Frances Clarke and John Millerchip of the Venice in Peril Fund; the staff of the APT offices throughout the Veneto, in particular Anna Rita Bisaggio in Montegrotto Terme, Stephano Marchioro in Padua; Anna Maria Carlotto, Virna Scarduelli and Christina Erlacher in Verona, Anselmo Centomo in Vicenza; Heidi Wenyon.

Photography Permissions
Dorling Kindersley would like to thank the following for their kind permission to photograph at their establishments:
Venice: Amministrazione Provinciale di Venezia (Museo dell'Estuario, Torcello); Ca' Mocenigo; Ca' Pesaro; Ca' Rezzonico; Caffè Quadri; Collegio Armeni; Fondazione Europea Pro Venetia Viva, San Servolo; Fondazione Giorgio Cini (San Giorgio Maggiore); Peggy Guggenheim Museum; Hôtel des Bains; Libreria Sansoviniana; Museo Archeologico; Museo Correr; Museo Diocesano d'Arte Sacra; Museo Fortuny; Museo Storia Navale; Museo Storico Naturale; Museo Vetrario, Murano; Arch. Umberto Franzoi and staff at the Palazzo Ducale; Procuratie di San Marco (Basilica San Marco); Santi Giovanni e Paolo; San Lazzaro degli Armeni; Santa Maria Gloriosa dei Frari; Scuola Grande dei Carmini; Scuola Grande di San Rocco.
Veneto: Arena Romano, Verona; Basilica, Vicenza; Caffè Pedrocchi, Padua; Duomo, Padua; Duomo, Vicenza; Giardini Giusti, Verona; Museo Archeologico, Verona; Museo di Castelvecchio, Verona; Museo Civico, Malcésine; Museo Civico, Vicenza; Museo Concordiese, Portogruaro; Museo degli Eremitani, Padua; Museo Lapidario Maffeiano, Verona; Museo dei Storia Naturale, Verona; Ossuario di San Pietro, Solferino; Sant'Anastasia, Verona; San Fermo Maggiore, Verona; San Giorgio, Monsélice; San Giorgio in Braida, Verona; San Lorenzo, Vicenza; Santa Maria in Organo, Verona; San Pietro in Malvino, Sirmione; San Severo, Bardolino; San Stefano, Verona; San Zeno Maggiore, Verona; Santuario di Monte

Berico, Vicenza; Teatro Olimpico, Vicenza; Università di Padova; Contessa Diamante Luling-Buschette, Villa Barbaro, Masèr; Conte Marco Emo, Villa Emo, Fanzolo di Vedelago.

Picture Credits

a = above; b = below/bottom; c = centre; f = far; l = left; r = right; t = top.

Works of art have been reproduced with the permission of the following copyright holders: *Maiastra* 1912 Constantin Brancusi © ADAGP, Paris and DACS, London 2011 138cr; *Interno Olandese II* c.1928 Joan Miró © Successio Miró/ADAGP, Paris and DACS, London 2011 134c; *Matisse at Venice Biennale* 1992 Larry Rivers © DACS, London/VAGA, New York 2011 256tc.

The publishers are grateful to the following museums, companies and picture libraries for permission to reproduce their photographs:

Accademia Olimpica, Vicenza: 174tr, 175crb; **Actv S.p.A**: 279tl, 284clb; **Aeroporto di Venezia Marco Polo:** 278cl; **Alamy Images**: AA World Travel Library 140, 239cl; David Angel 10cl; Greg Balfour Evans 22b; directphoto.bz 272br; VIEW Pictures Ltd./Daniel Clements 55br; FAN travelstock/ Michael Schindel 264cr; Cris Haigh 239tl; Iconotec 60; imagebroker 15b; Jon Arnold Images/Demetrio Carrasco 263cr; Iain Masterton 280tl; JTB Media Creation, Inc. 13br; Michael Juno 238cla; Aguilar Patrice 34tr; Matthias Scholz 129tl Paul Shawcross 231tr; Kumar Sriskandan 236cl; **Ancient Art & Architecture Collection**: 42cla, 44br; **Apt Del Bresciano**: 39br; **Archiv für Kunst und Geschichte**: 30c/cr, 34bl, 47br, 48crb, 49bl, 49t, 50tr, 52cla, 53clb, 54b, 58br, 134bl, 135bl, 135cr, 136b, 137tr, 34/35c; **Archivio Veneziano**: Sarah Quill 33br, 55crb, 71cl, 110tr, 148tr; **ATV – Azienda Trasporti Verona s.r.l.:** 286br.

Biblioteca Civica di Trieste (Foto Halupca): 123br; **Bridgeman Art Library, London**: *Madonna and Child and Saints* (triptych altarpiece) by Giovanni Bellini (c.1431–1516), Santa Maria dei Frari, Venice 31tc/tr; *The Siege of Antioch* 1098 by William of Tyre. Bibliothèque Nationale, Paris 44cla; *Marco Polo with Elephants and Camels* from Livre des Merveilles, Bibliothèque Nationale, Paris, 46cb; *Family Tree of the Cornaro Family*, Italian School (18th century), Palazzo Corner Ca' Grande, Venice, 73tr; *Salome* by Gustav Klimt (1862–1918) Museo d'Arte Moderna, Venice, 109br; *The Nuns' Visiting Day* by Francesco Guardi (1712–93), Museo Ca' Rezzonico, Venice, 116bl; *St George Killing the Dragon* by Vittore Carpaccio (c.1460/5–1523/6), Scuola di San Giorgio degli Schiavoni, Venice, 122tc; *The Stealing of the Body of St Mark* by Tintoretto (1518–94), Accademia, Venice, 135tc; *The Rape of Europa* by Francesco Zuccarelli, Accademia, Venice, 137cl; *Marco Polo dressed in Tartar costume* (c.1700) Museo Correr, Venice/ Giraudon, 4tr/119br; **Osvaldo Böhm**: 24bl, 24cl, 33bl, 45crb, 67tl, 83tl, 136cl, 136tr, 148c.

Le Calandre: 248bl; **Demetrio Carrasco**: 128bc, 143br, 145tl; **Ca'Sagredo Hotel:** 231b; **Cephas Picture Library**: Mick Rock, 39cra, 238tr; **Ciga Hotels**: 74tl; **Claire Calman**: 59cr; **Stephanie Colasanti**: 197br; **Giancarlo Costa**: 51cb; **Corbis**: 150; Atlantide Phototravel 100; Jon Arnold/JAI 76; Ashley Cooper 263tl, Francis G. Mayer 14bc; Jose Fuste Raga 150; Heritage Images 8–9; **Joe Cornish**: 19bl, 215cr, 222tr.

Dolomiti Superski: Freddy Planinschek 264bl; **Chris Donaghue The Oxford Photo Library**: 5cla, 80tr, 160br; **Michael Dent**: 86br, 256tl; **Dreamstime.com:** Miroslava Arnaudova 226-7; Claudio Balducelli 261t; Giovanni Boscherino 239bl; Francesca Costanzo 12tr; Dark3y3s 260tc; Iurii Davydov 56–7; Dennis Dolkens 15tl; Andrey Emelyanenko 11br; Radu Razvan Gheorghe 259cl; Rostislav Glinsky 20; Roland Nagy 266-7; Jakob Radigruber 2–3; Tosca Weijers 14tl.

E.T. Archive: Sala dei Prior Siena, 45tl; Baroque Hall of Mirrors, Palazzo Papadopoli, Venice, 68tl; *The Apothecary's Shop* by Pietro Longhi, Accademia, Venice, 134cl; **Electa, Milan:** 184cr, 185tc/cl; **Erizzo Editrice srl**: 109clb; **The Eurail Group:** 280bl, 281tr; **Mary Evans Picture Library**: 43clb, 48bl, 51br, 51tc, 62cra, 68ca, 73ca, 147tr, 163; **Hotel Excelsior, Venice Lido:** 228bl, 234bl.

Getty Images: Alinari 126; annhfhung 12bl; Stuart Black/ Robert Harding World Imagery 190; Matteo Colombo 216; Axel Fassio 258bl; Mondadori Portfolio 166; Peter Stastny 208-9; **Jackie Gordon**: 273t; **Grazia Neri**: 5tr, 54crb, 54tr, 69br, 96tl, 161br; Marco Bruzzo, 5tr, 39clb, 176tr; Cameraphoto 44tr, 45br, 75tr, 119bl, 46/47c; Graziano Arici 104tr; **Peggy Guggenheim Museum, Venice**: 138b; **The Ronald Grant Archive**: 54cla.

Robert Harding Picture Library: 222cl; **Hotel Excelsior, Venice Lido**: 52cb; **The Hulton Deutsch Collection**: 42br, 42tr, 43br, 47cb, 50br, 52bc, 53br, 65tr, 70bl, 70ca, 73cla, 105cr, 144bl, 185br, 201br.

Image Select: Ann Ronan, 48cl.

Hugh McKnight Photography: 75tl; **Magnum Photos/ David Seymour**: 52tr; **Marka**: 41b; Enrico Cerretelli 156bl; Cristina Dogliani 262br; **Hotel Metropole:** 229b, 233tl; **Moro Roma:** 34cl, 52/53c; **Museo Civico agli Eremitani**: 183 all; **Museo Civico di Oderzo**: 43tc; **The Mansell Collection**: 50cb, 51bl.

Newimage S.R.L.: 37bc; **NHPA/Gerard Lacz**: 223br; **NHPA/Laurie Campbell**: 223cr; **NHPA/Silvestris Fotoservice**: 223crb; **The National Gallery, London**: 33tr.

OFFicina: 277tl; **Olympia/Select**: 38bl, 55cb, 55bl, 161tr, 259tr; **Orient-Express Hotels, Trains & Cruises:** 280cra.

Performing Arts Library/Gianfranco Fainello: 260c; **Polizia di Stato, Questura di Venezia:** 272cla, 272crb; **Porto di Venezia (campione/develon.com):** 279br.

Residenze Des Bains: 53crb, 160tl; **The Royal Collection** ©1994 **Her Majesty Queen Elizabeth** 11: 50/51c.

John Ferro Sims: 177tr; **Scala, Firenze**: *Madonna di Ca' Pesaro* by Titian (1477/89–157), S. Maria Gloriosa dei Frari, Venice, 31c/cr; *Ultimi Momenti del Doge Marin Faliero* by Francesco Hayez (1791–1881), Pinacoteca di Brera, Milan, 47tl; *Banquet of Antony and Cleopatra* by Giambattista Tiepolo (1692–1770), Palazzo Labia, Venice, 64t; *Ultimi Momenti del Doge Marin Faliero* by Francesco Hayez (1791–1881), Pinacoteca di Brera, Milan, 72cra; *Crocifissione* by Tintoretto (1518–94), Scuola Grande di S. Rocco, Venice, 110c/cb; *Il Trasporto della Santa Casa di Loreto* by Giambattista Tiepolo (1692–1770), Accademia, Venice, 134tc; *Presentazione al Tempio* by Titian (1477/89– 1576), Accademia, Venice,137bc; *Intérieur Hollandais II* by Joan Miró (1928), Museo Guggenheim, Venice, 138tc; *Madonna col Bambino* by Filippo Lippi (1406–69), Cini Collection, Venice 138t; *Annunciazione* by Vittore Carpaccio (1460 c.–1526), Ca' d'Oro, Venice,148bl; Pala di San Zeno by Andrea Mantegna (1431–1506), San Zeno, Verona, 202cl; **Settore Beni Culturali, Padua**: 184t/cla/clb, 185cra/crb/bl; **Spectrum Colour Library**: 32br; **Studio Pizzi**: 49cla, 51crb; **Tony Stone Images**: 220cla, 223cla, 54/55c; **Superstock**: Melvyn Longhurst 112; Frank Neil/ Robert Harding Picture Library 162–3.

Tasting Places: 262cla; **Ristorante Taverna:** 249tr.

United Colors of Benetton: Josh Olins 55tl.

Venetian Navigator: 276cla; **Via Paradiso 32:** 229tr, 235tc; **Hotel Villa Cipriani:** 228cr., 247br; **La Villeggiatura:** 232bl.

Front Endpaper – Alamy Images: AA World Travel Library rtc; **Corbis:** Jon Arnold/JAI Rf crb; Atlantide Phototravel rtl; Jose Fuste Raga rbl; **Getty Images:** Alinari rcb; Stuart Black/ Robert Harding World Imagery ltl; Matteo Colombo ltr; Mondadori Portfolio lbc.

Map Cover – Alamy Images: eye35.pix.

Front Jacket and Spine – Alamy Images: eye35.pix.

Phrase Book

In Emergency

Help!	**Aiuto!**	*eye-**yoo**-toh*
Stop!	**Fermate!**	*fair-**mah**-teh*
Call a doctor.	**Chiama un medico.**	*kee-**ah**-mah oon **meh**-dee-koh*
Call an ambulance.	**Chiama un' ambulanza.**	*kee-**ah**-mah oon am-boo-**lan**-tsa*
Call the police.	**Chiama la polizia.**	*kee-**ah**-mah lah pol-ee-**tsee**-ah*
Call the fire brigade.	**Chiama i pompieri.**	*kee-**ah**-mah ee pom-pee-**air**-ee*
Where is the telephone?	**Dov'è il telefono?**	*dov-**eh** eel teh-**leh**-foh-noh?*
The nearest hospital?	**L'ospedale più vicino?**	*loss-peh-**dah**-leh pee-**oo**vee-**chee**-noh?*

Communication Essentials

Yes/No	**Si/No**	***see/noh***
Please	**Per favore**	*pair fah-**vor**-eh*
Thank you	**Grazie**	***grah**-tsee-eh*
Excuse me	**Mi scusi**	*mee **skoo**-zee*
Hello	**Buon giorno**	*bwon **jor**-noh*
Goodbye	**Arrivederci**	*ah-ree-veh-**dair**-chee*
Good evening	**Buona sera**	***bwon**-ah **sair**-ah*
morning	**la mattina**	*lah mah-**tee**-nah*
afternoon	**il pomeriggio**	*eel poh-meh-**ree**-joh*
evening	**la sera**	*lah **sair**-ah*
yesterday	**ieri**	*ee-**air**-ee*
today	**oggi**	***oh**-jee*
tomorrow	**domani**	*doh-**mah**-nee*
here	**qui**	***kwee***
there	**la**	***lah***
What?	**Quale?**	***kwah**-leh?*
When?	**Quando?**	***kwan**-doh?*
Why?	**Perchè?**	*pair-**keh**?*
Where?	**Dove?**	***doh**-veh*

Useful Phrases

How are you?	**Come sta?**	***koh**-meh stah?*
Very well, thank you.	**Molto bene, grazie.**	***moll**-toh **beh**-neh **grah**-tsee-eh*
Pleased to meet you.	**Piacere di conoscerla.**	*pee-ah-**chair**-eh dee coh-**noh**-shair-lah*
See you soon.	**A più tardi.**	*ah pee-**oo tar**-dee*
That's fine.	**Va bene.**	*va **beh**-neh*
Where is/are …?	**Dov'è/Dove sono …?**	*dov-**eh**/doveh **soh**-noh?*
How long does it take to get to …?	**Quanto tempo ci vuole per andare a …?**	***kwan**-toh **tem**-poh chee voo-**oh**-leh pair an-**dar**-eh ah …?*
How do I get to....?	**Come faccio per arrivare a …?**	*koh-meh **fah**-choh pair arri-**var**-eh ah…?*
Do you speak English?	**Parla inglese?**	***par**-lah een-**gleh**-zeh?*
I don't understand.	**Non capisco.**	*non ka-**pee**-skoh*
Could you speak more slowly, please?	**Può parlare più lentamente, per favore?**	*pwoh par-**lah**-reh pee-**oo** len-ta-**men**-teh pair fah-**vor**-eh*
I'm sorry.	**Mi dispiace.**	*mee dee-spee-**ah**-cheh*

Useful Words

big	**grande**	***gran**-deh*
small	**piccolo**	***pee**-koh-loh*
hot	**caldo**	***kal**-doh*
cold	**freddo**	***fred**-doh*
good	**buono**	***bwoh**-noh*
bad	**cattivo**	*kat-**tee**-voh*
enough	**basta**	***bas**-tah*
well	**bene**	***beh**-neh*
open	**aperto**	*ah-**pair**-toh*
closed	**chiuso**	*kee-**oo**-zoh*
left	**a sinistra**	*ah see-**nee**-strah*
right	**a destra**	*ah **dess**-trah*
straight on	**sempre dritto**	***sem**-preh **dree**-toh*
near	**vicino**	*vee-**chee**-noh*
far	**lontano**	*lon-**tah**-noh*
up	**su**	***soo***
down	**giù**	***joo***
early	**presto**	***press**-toh*
late	**tardi**	***tar**-dee*
entrance	**entrata**	*en-**trah**-tah*
exit	**uscita**	*oo-**shee**-ta*
toilet	**il gabinetto**	*eel gah-bee-**net**-toh*
free, unoccupied	**libero**	***lee**-bair-oh*
free, no charge	**gratuito**	*grah-**too**-ee-toh*

Making a Telephone Call

I'd like to place a long-distance call.	**Vorrei fare una interurbana.**	*vor-**ray far**-eh oona in-tair-oor-**bah**-nah*
I'd like to make a reverse-charge call.	**Vorrei fare una telefonata a carico del destinatario.**	*vor-**ray far**-eh oona a teh-leh-fon-**ah**-tah ah **kar**-ee-koh dell dess-tee-nah-**tar**-ree-oh*
I'll try again later.	**Ritelefono più tardi.**	*ree-teh-**leh**-foh-noh pee-oo **tar**-dee*
Can I leave a message.	**Posso lasciare un messaggio?**	***poss**-oh lash-**ah**-reh oon mess-**sah**-joh?*
Hold on.	**Un attimo, per favore**	*oon **ah**-tee-moh, pair fah-**vor**-eh*
Could you speak up a little please?	**Può parlare più forte, per favore?**	*pwoh par-**lah**-reh up pee-**oo for**-teh, pair fah-**vor**-eh?*
local call	**la telefonata locale**	*lah teh-leh-fon-**ah**-ta loh-**kah**-leh*

Shopping

How much does this cost?	**Quant'è, per favore?**	*kwan-**teh** pair fah-**vor**-eh?*
I would like …	**Vorrei …**	*vor-**ray***
Do you have …?	**Avete …?**	*ah-**veh**-teh…?*
I'm just looking.	**Sto soltanto guardando.**	*stoh sol-**tan**-toh gwar-**dan**-doh*
Do you take credit cards?	**Accettate carte di credito?**	*ah-chet-**tah**-teh **kar**-teh dee **creh**-dee-toh?*
What time do you open/close?	**A che ora apre/ chiude?**	*ah keh **or**-ah **ah**-preh/ kee-**oo**-deh?*
this one	**questo**	***kweh** -stoh*
that one	**quello**	***kwell** -oh*
expensive	**caro**	***kar**-oh*
cheap	**a buon prezzo**	*ah bwon **pret**-soh*
size, clothes	**la taglia**	*lah **tah**-lee-ah*
size, shoes	**il numero**	*eel **noo**-mair-oh*
white	**bianco**	*bee-**ang**-koh*
black	**nero**	***neh**-roh*
red	**rosso**	***ross**-oh*
yellow	**giallo**	***jal**-loh*
green	**verde**	***vair**-deh*
blue	**blu**	*bloo*
brown	**marrone**	*mar-**roh**-neh*

Types of Shop

antique dealer	**l'antiquario**	*lan-tee-**kwah**-ree-oh*
bakery	**la panetteria**	*lah pah-net-tair-**ree**-ah*
bank	**la banca**	*lah **bang**-kah*
bookshop	**la libreria**	*lah lee-breh-**ree**-ah*
butcher's	**la macelleria**	*lah mah-chell-eh-**ree**-ah*
cake shop	**la pasticceria**	*lah pas-tee-chair-**ee**-ah*
chemist's	**la farmacia**	*lah far-mah-**chee**-ah*
delicatessen	**la salumeria**	*lah sah-loo-meh-**ree**-ah*
department store	**il grande magazzino**	*eel **gran**-deh mag-gad-**zee**-noh*
fishmonger's	**la pescheria**	*lah pess-keh-**ree**-ah*
florist	**il fioraio**	*eel fee-or-**eye**-oh*
greengrocer	**il fruttivendolo**	*eel froo-tee-**ven**-doh-loh*
grocery	**alimentari**	*ah-lee-men-**tah**-ree*
hairdresser	**il parrucchiere**	*eel par-oo-kee-**air**-eh*
ice cream parlour	**la gelateria**	*lah jel-lah-tair-**ree**-ah*
market	**il mercato**	*eel mair-**kah**-toh*
newsstand	**l'edicola**	*leh-**dee**-koh-lah*
post office	**l'ufficio postale**	*loo-**fee**-choh pos-**tah**-leh*
shoe shop	**il negozio di scarpe**	*eel neh-**goh**-tsioh dee **skar**-peh*
supermarket	**il supermercato**	*su-pair-mair-**kah**-toh*
tobacconist	**il tabaccaio**	*eel tah-bak-**eye**-oh*
travel agency	**l'agenzia di viaggi**	*lah-jen-**tsee**-ah dee vee-**ad**-jee*

Sightseeing

art gallery	**la pinacoteca**	*lah peena-koh-**teh**-kah*
bus stop	**la fermata dell'autobus**	*lah fair-**mah**-tah dell **ow**-toh-booss*
church	**la chiesa**	*lah kee-**eh**-zah*
	la basilica	*lah bah-**seel**-i-kah*
closed for the public holiday	**chiuso per la festa**	*kee-**oo**-zoh pair lah **fess**-tah*
garden	**il giardino**	*eel jar-**dee**-no*
library	**la biblioteca**	*lah beeb-lee-oh-**teh**-kah*
museum	**il museo**	*eel moo-**zeh**-oh*
railway station	**la stazione**	*lah stah-tsee-**oh**-neh*
tourist information	**l'ufficio turistico**	*loo-**fee**-choh too-**ree**-stee-koh*

Staying in a Hotel

Do you have any vacant rooms?	**Avete camere libere?**	*ah-**veh**-teh **kah**-mair-eh **lee**-bair-eh?*
double room	**una camera doppia**	*oona **kah**-mair-ah **doh**-pee-ah*
with double bed	**con letto matrimoniale**	*kon **let**-toh mah-tree-moh-nee-**ah**-leh*
twin room	**una camera con due letti**	*oona **kah**-mair-ah kon **doo**-eh **let**-tee*
single room	**una camera singola**	*oona **kah**-mair-ah **sing**-goh-lah*
room with a bath, shower	**una camera con bagno, con doccia**	*oona **kah**-mair-ah kon **ban**-yoh, kon **dot**-chah*
porter	**il facchino**	*eel fah-**kee**-noh*
key	**la chiave**	*lah kee-**ah**-veh*
I have a reservation.	**Ho fatto una prenotazione.**	*oh **fat**-toh oona preh-noh-tah-tsee-**oh**-neh*

Eating Out

Have you got a table for ...?	**Avete una tavola per ...?**	*ah-**veh**-teh oona a table **tah**-voh-lah pair ...?*
I'd like to reserve a table.	**Vorrei riservare una tavola.**	*vor-**ray** ree-sair-**vah**-reh oona **tah**-voh-lah*
breakfast	**colazione**	*koh-lah-tsee-**oh**-neh*
lunch	**pranzo**	***pran**-tsoh*
dinner	**cena**	***cheh**-nah*
The bill, please.	**Il conto, per favore.**	*eel **kon**-toh pair fah-**vor**-eh*
I am a vegetarian.	**Sono vegetariano/a.**	***soh**-noh **veh**-jeh-tar ee-**ah**-noh/nah*
waitress	**cameriera**	*kah-mair-ee-**air**-ah*
waiter	**cameriere**	*kah-mair-ee-**air**-eh*
fixed price	**il menù a prezzo fisso**	*eel meh-**noo** ah menu **pret**-soh **fee**-soh*
dish of the day	**piatto del giorno**	*pee-**ah**-toh dell **jor**-no*
starter	**antipasto**	*an-tee-**pass**-toh*
first course	**il primo**	*eel **pree**-moh*
main course	**il secondo**	*eel seh-**kon**-doh*
vegetables	**il contorno**	*eel kon-**tor**-noh*
dessert	**il dolce**	*eel **doll**-cheh*
cover charge	**il coperto**	*eel koh-**pair**-toh*
wine list	**la lista dei vini**	*lah **lee**-stah day **vee**-nee*
rare	**al sangue**	*al **sang**-gweh*
medium	**al puntino**	*al poon-**tee**-noh*
well done	**ben cotto**	*ben **kot**-toh*
glass	**il bicchiere**	*eel bee-kee-**air**-eh*
bottle	**la bottiglia**	*lah bot-**teel**-yah*
knife	**il coltello**	*eel kol-**tell**-oh*
fork	**la forchetta**	*lah for-**ket**-tah*
spoon	**il cucchiaio**	*eel koo-kee-**eye**-oh*

Menu Decoder

l'acqua minerale gasata/naturale	***lah**-kwah mee-nair-**ah**-leh gah-**zah**-tah/ nah-too-**rah**-leh*	mineral water fizzy/still
l'agnello	*lahn-**yell**-oh*	lamb
al forno	*al **for**-noh*	baked
alla griglia	*ah-lah **greel**-yah*	grilled
l'anguilla	*lahng-**gwee**-lah*	eel
l'aragosta	*lah-rah-**goss**-tah*	lobster
arrosto	*ar-**ross**-toh*	roast
il baccalà	*eel bahk-kah-**lah***	dried salted cod
la birra	*lah **beer**-rah*	beer
la bistecca	*lah bee-**stek**-kah*	steak
il brodetto	*eel-broh-**det**-toh*	fish soup
il burro	*eel **boor**-oh*	butter
il caffè	*eel kah-**feh***	coffee
i calamari	*ee kah-lah-**mah**-ree*	squid
il carciofo	*eel kar-**choff**-oh*	artichoke
la carne	*la **kar**-neh*	meat
carne di maiale	***kar**-neh dee mah-**yah**-leh*	pork
i fagioli	*ee fah-**joh**-lee*	beans
il fegato	*eel **fay**-gah-toh*	liver
il formaggio	*eel for-**mad**-joh*	cheese
le fragole	*leh frah-goh-leh*	strawberries
il fritto misto	*eel free-toh **mees**-toh*	mixed fried fish
la frutta	*la **froot**-tah*	fruit
frutti di mare	***froo**-tee dee **mah**-reh*	seafood
i funghi	*ee **foon**-ghee*	mushrooms
i gamberi	*ee **gam**-bair-ee*	prawns
il gelato	*eel jel-**lah**-toh*	ice cream
l'insalata mista	*leen-sah-lah-tah **mees**-tah*	mixed salad
l'insalata verde	*leen-sah-lah-tah **vehr**-day*	green salad
il latte	*eel **laht**-teh*	milk
i legumi/ i contorni	*ee leh-**goo**-mee/ ee kon-**tor**-nee*	vegetables
il manzo	*eel **man**-tsoh*	beef
la melanzana	*lah meh-lan-**tsah**-nah*	aubergine
la minestra	*lah mee-**ness**-trah*	soup
il pane	*eel **pah**-neh*	bread
il panino	*eel pah-**nee**-noh*	bread roll
le patate	*leh pah-**tah**-teh*	potatoes
le patatine fritte	*leh pah-tah-**teen**-eh **free**-teh*	chips
il pepe	*eel **peh**-peh*	pepper
la pesca	*lah **pess**-kah*	peach
il pesce	*eel **pesh**-eh*	fish
il pollo	*eel **poll**-oh*	chicken
il prosciutto cotto/crudo	*eel pro-**shoo**-toh **kot**-toh/**kroo**-doh*	ham cooked/cured
il riso	*eel **ree**-zoh*	rice
il sale	*eel **sah**-leh*	salt
la salsiccia	*lah sal-**see**-chah*	sausage
le seppie	*leh **sep**-pee-eh*	cuttlefish
secco	***sek**-koh*	dry
la sogliola	*lah **soll**-voh-lah*	sole
i spinaci	*ee spee-**nah**-chee*	spinach
succo d'arancia/ di limone	***soo**-koh dah-**ran**-chah/ **dee lee-moh-neh***	orange/lemon juice
il tè	*eel **teh***	tea
la tisana	*lah tee-**zah**-nah*	herbal tea
il tonno	*eel **ton**-noh*	tuna
la torta	*lah **tor**-tah*	cake/tart
la trippa	*lah **treep**-pah*	tripe
vino bianco	***vee**-noh bee-**ang**-koh*	white wine
vino rosso	***vee**-noh **ross**-oh*	red wine
il vitello	*eel vee-**tell**-oh*	veal
le vongole	*leh **von**-goh-leh*	clams
lo zucchero	*loh **zoo**-kair-oh*	sugar
gli zucchini	*lyee dzu-**kee**-nee*	courgettes
la zuppa	*lah **tsoo**-pah*	soup

Numbers

1	**uno**	***oo**-noh*
2	**due**	***doo**-eh*
3	**tre**	*treh*
4	**quattro**	***kwat**-roh*
5	**cinque**	***ching**-kweh*
6	**sei**	***say**-ee*
7	**sette**	***set**-teh*
8	**otto**	***ot**-toh*
9	**nove**	***noh**-veh*
10	**dieci**	*dee-**eh**-chee*
11	**undici**	***oon**-dee-chee*
12	**dodici**	***doh**-dee-chee*
13	**tredici**	***tray**-dee-chee*
14	**quattordici**	*kwat-**tor**-dee-chee*
15	**quindici**	***kwin**-dee-chee*
16	**sedici**	***say**-dee-chee*
17	**diciassette**	*dee-chah-**set**-teh*
18	**diciotto**	*dee-**chot**-toh*
19	**diciannove**	*dee-chah-**noh**-veh*
20	**venti**	***ven**-tee*
30	**trenta**	***tren**-tah*
40	**quaranta**	*kwah-**ran**-tah*
50	**cinquanta**	*ching-**kwan**-tah*
60	**sessanta**	*sess-**an**-tah*
70	**settanta**	*set-**tan**-tah*
80	**ottanta**	*ot-**tan**-tah*
90	**novanta**	*noh-**van**-tah*
100	**cento**	***chen**-toh*
1,000	**mille**	***mee**-leh*
2,000	**duemila**	***doo**-eh **mee**-lah*
5,000	**cinquemila**	***ching**-kweh **mee**-lah*
1,000,000	**un milione**	*oon meel- **yoh**-neh*

Time

one minute	**un minuto**	*oon mee-**noo**-toh*
one hour	**un'ora**	*oon **or**-ah*
half an hour	**mezz'ora**	*medz-**or**-ah*
a day	**un giorno**	*oon **jor**-noh*
a week	**una settimana**	*oona set-tee-**mah**-nah*
Monday	**lunedì**	*loo-neh-**dee***
Tuesday	**martedì**	*mar-teh-**dee***
Wednesday	**mercoledì**	*mair-koh-leh-**dee***
Thursday	**giovedì**	*joh-veh-**dee***
Friday	**venerdì**	*ven-air-**dee***
Saturday	**sabato**	***sah**-bah-toh*
Sunday	**domenica**	*doh-**meh**-nee-kah*

Venice Vaporetto Routes

The ACTV network runs regular services around the city and out to most of the islands. Some services are circular; others extend their routes during the high season. There are also additional lines during the summer months. More details of the different types of *vaporetti* and how to use them are given on pages 284–5.

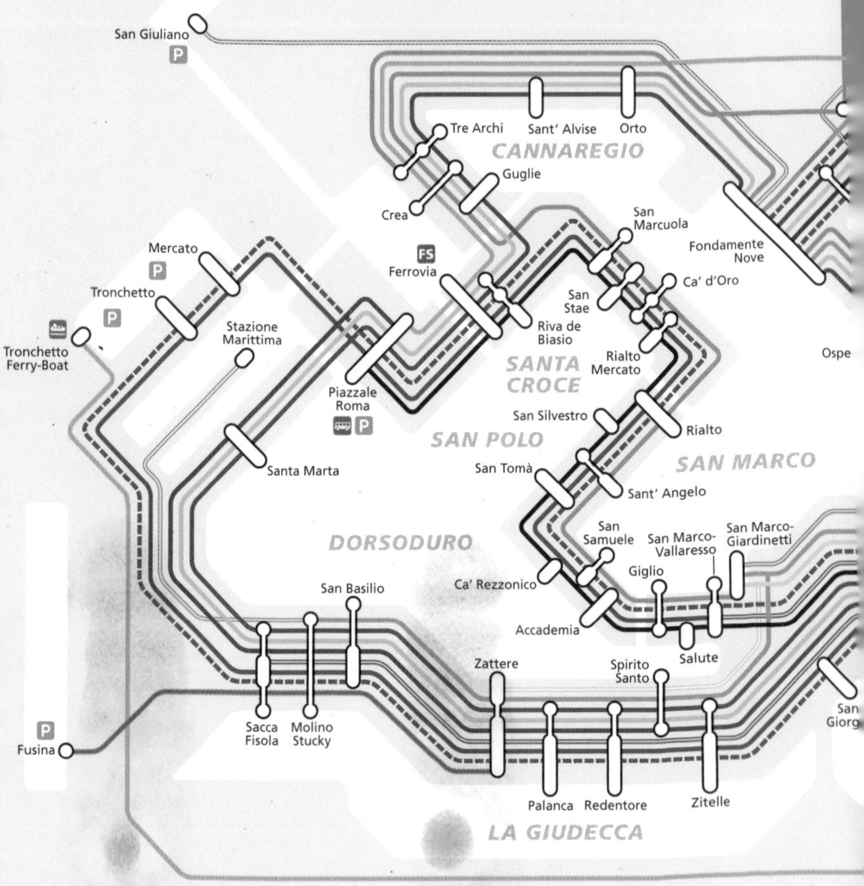

Key

Airport	City centre route 1	City centre route 5.2 (clockwise)
Railway station	City centre route 2 (part seasonal)	City centre route 6
Car ferry	City centre route 3	City centre route 7 (seasonal)
Car parking	City centre route 4.1 (anticlockwise)	City centre route 8 (seasonal)
Main bus terminal	City centre route 4.2 (clockwise)	City centre route 10 (part seasonal)
Water-bus stop	City centre route 5.1 (anticlockwise)	Night service N